THE FRAMING OF SACRED SPACE

THE FRAMING OF SACRED SPACE

The Canopy and the Byzantine Church

Jelena Bogdanović

OXFORD
UNIVERSITY PRESS

OXFORD
UNIVERSITY PRESS

Oxford University Press is a department of the University of Oxford. It furthers the University's objective of excellence in research, scholarship, and education by publishing worldwide. Oxford is a registered trade mark of Oxford University Press in the UK and certain other countries.

Published in the United States of America by Oxford University Press
198 Madison Avenue, New York, NY 10016, United States of America.

Library of Congress Cataloging-in-Publication Data
Names: Bogdanović, Jelena, 1973– author.
Title: The framing of sacred space : the canopy and the Byzantine church/
Jelena Bogdanović.
Other titles: Canopies
Description: New York : Oxford University Press, 2017. | Revised and expanded version of the author's thesis (doctoral—Princeton University, 2008) under the title: Canopies : the framing of sacred space in the Byzantine ecclesiastical tradition. | Includes bibliographical references and index.
Identifiers: LCCN 2016045073 | ISBN 9780190465186 (hardback : alk. paper)
Subjects: LCSH: Architecture, Byzantine. | Canopies, Architectural—Byzantine Empire. | Ciboria (Architecture)—Byzantine Empire. | Church architecture—Byzantine Empire—Details. | Symbolism in architecture—Byzantine Empire.
Classification: LCC NA5453 .B59 2017 | DDC 723/.2—dc23
LC record available at https://lccn.loc.gov/2016045073

1 3 5 7 9 8 6 4 2

Printed by Sheridan Books, Inc., United States of America

To Dušan
and
to my parents

Contents

List of Tables

List of Illustrations

Acknowledgments

The Framing of Sacred Space: The Canopy and the Byzantine Church is the result of more than a decade of research on canopies of Byzantine-rite churches. With this book reaching its publication, I owe a debt of gratitude to many individuals and institutions.

My first debt of gratitude belongs to my family. My grandparents, Danilo, Jelena, Stana, and Aleksandar; my parents, Selena and Vojislav; my sister, Snežana; and my husband, Dušan Danilović, each in their own and unique way, were always there for me. I extend my thanks to my sister's family, my brother-in-law Bratislav and nephew Josif Dragić, as well as to my sister-in-law Biljana and father-in-law Stevan Danilović. My family supported me, brought me happiness, and encouraged me to work with love and to love my work. Even as my mother Selena and all my grandparents, who believed in education as an endless but meaningful pursuit, left me one by one through the course of my work on this study, the warmth of their unconditional support and love have remained. The last words my mother told me just before she passed away haunted me for a while: "Things will change with your book, and do not forget to eat." At that time, the last thing I could think of was the book, and only now do I realize that she believed in this book even before I had any idea that I would ever have a chance to pursue it.

Three persons and two scholars in the field are crucial for my initial involvement in Byzantine studies and for nourishing my love towards the subject. My husband, Dušan Danilović, encouraged me first to combine my training in traditional architectural design with the joy and wonder I experience when encountering Byzantine architecture and art. Architect and architectural historian, the late Professor Svetlana Popović was the first scholar who effectively introduced me to the discipline of Byzantine architecture. Just as important to my development as a student of art and architecture was my graduate advisor at Vanderbilt University, Ljubica D. Popovich, professor *emerita*. She helped me understand my own source of inspiration and love for art and architecture. This book was initiated as a master's thesis in 2002 and expanded upon with the dissertation research completed at Princeton University in 2008.

As my work developed, a number of individuals supported my work with well-balanced advice, comments, and criticism. I am truly humbled by the generosity and long-term support I have received from so many individuals who made this project come to life. Above all, a special debt of gratitude goes to those who believed in me when I needed support the most: Richard Etlin, Alexei Lidov, Miloš R. Perović, Carol Krinsky, John Pinto, Michael

Aurbach, Lubomíra Havlíková, Dimitri Gondicas, William Caferro, Anne-Marie Bouché, Anoush Terjanian, and Tan Yuen. Cristina Carile, Nebojša Stanković, Ljubomir Milanović, Marina Mihaljević, Ida Sinkević, Mark Johnson, Daniel C. Waugh, Robin Jensen, Jelena Palić, Paul Denis, Ivan Drpić, Stavros Mamaloukos, April Eisman, Thomas Leslie, Carlton Basmajian, Kathryn Blair Moore, Čedomila Marinković, Dubravka Preradović, Athanasios Koumantos, Svetlana Smolčić Makuljević, Jadranka Prolović, Maria Evangelatou, Petre Guran, Robert Ousterhout, Nino Zchomelidse, and Maria Mavroudi were especially supportive by commenting on various aspects of the manuscript, for showering me with photographs, sometimes made especially for this project, and for pointing me to the relevant material stemming from their own work. Alexei Lidov offered me excellent advice for my research in Moscow and the Suzdal-Vladimir regions. Based on our shared interest in sacred space, Alexei Lidov was most crucial for the advancement of this study because he regularly invited me to participate at research symposia on the sacred space in Byzantium that he organized in Moscow, where I benefited from the most collegiate and rigorous feedback from my peers there. A number of scholars and supportive friends provided me with additional questions, critiques, references, and material for refining my research: Kevin Kalish, Milan Radujko, Miodrag Marković, Vladimir Božinović, Adeline Jeudy, Jelena Trkulja, Jaroslav Folda, Paul Magdalino, Ludovico Geymonat, the late Lois Drewer, David Michelson, Daniel Schwartz, Loukas Karentzos, Jeremy Thompson, Lorenzo Riccardi, Ljiljana Ševo, Irma Karaushvili, Arseniy Petrov, Olga Shashina, Evelyn Bazalgette, Ivan Krstić, Yuliana Boycheva, Elisabeth Yota, Teresa Shawcross, Alexis Belis, Suna Çağaptay, Warren Woodfin, Thomas DaCosta Kaufmann, Stephen Morris, George Baloglou, George S. Tsapanos, Lampros F. Kallenos, Jan van Ginkel, Anna Karpathakis, Greame Clarke, and Thaddeus Gutierrez. My research assistants at Iowa State University, Zhengyang Hua, Heidi Reburn, and Darin Bouska, helped me prepare architectural drawings and searched for image copyrights and bibliographical references.

My studies on archeological, visual, and textual evidence for canopies have been done in the United States and have been complemented by trips to Bulgaria, Great Britain, Greece, Russia, Serbia, and Turkey. In addition to visiting numerous archeological sites and churches, I also consulted the services and collections of various institutions: at Princeton—Marquand, Speers, and Firestone Libraries and their interlibrary loan services, the Index of Christian Art, and Princeton Theological Seminary library; in other parts of the United States—Walters Art Museum, Baltimore; the Dumbarton Oaks Research Library and Collection, Washington, D.C.; Metropolitan Museum, New York; in Bulgaria—museums in Burgas and Nessebar; in Great Britain—National Museum in London and Bodleian Museum at Oxford University; in Greece—National Archaeological Museum, Christian and Byzantine Museum, Acropolis Museum, Museum of Athens University, and Benaki Museum, all in Athens; Byzantine Museum, Thessaloniki; Museum of Byzantine Culture, Kastoria; Archaeological Museum on Paros; and Museum of the Great Meteoron Monastery; in Russia—Kremlin Museums, Museum of the New Jerusalem, Tretyakov Gallery, and Museum in Vladimir; in Serbia—Library of the Serbian Academy of Arts and Sciences, National Museum and the Institute for the Protection of Cultural Monuments; in Turkey—Archeological Museum in Istanbul.

In 2010, Paul Denis, curator of Byzantine art at the Royal Ontario Museum in Ottawa, Canada, invited me to provide professional expertise on an early Christian ciborium from the Syro-Palestinian region they had acquired for their Joey and Toby Tanenbaum Gallery of Byzantium. It was the most enriching experience to discuss this unique object based on its physical presence only, because of the evident lack of textual resources. I am particularly grateful to Paul Denis for our continual communication and for his granting me the rights to publish the material on this canopy for the first time in this book. Nicola Woods from the photo archive at the Royal Ontario Museum further granted high-quality images of this object, some of them made especially for this book. Megan Doyon from Yale Art Gallery was most supportive to grant the rights for the image of the reconstruction of the Dura Europos baptistery. Elena Ottina from the Castello Sforzesco was most helpful for obtaining the image of the ivory showing St. Menas in front of his canopy-like shrine. I am also grateful to Lidija Fekeža from the Zemaljski Muzej, the regional museum in Sarajevo, Bosnia and Herzegovina, for material on the little-known medieval canopies in their museum.

Special thanks go to Gabriela Drinovan from the interlibrary loan services at Firestone Library at Princeton, as well as to Jeff Alger and the late Carlota Gutierrez from the Parks and Architectural Libraries at Iowa State University, who went a step beyond the call of duty to ensure that I received all the books I needed for my research. John Hanson, curator of the Byzantine collection of the Dumbarton Oaks Research Facilities in Washington, D.C., helped immensely with the material in their collection. At the moments when I needed public feedback for my work, Susan Boynton, Dimitri Gondicas, Michael Aurbach, Alexei Lidov, Sabine Feist, Franz Alto Bauer, Holger Klein, Cecilia Olovsdotter, and Johanes Mårtelius granted me opportunities to present excerpts of my research to scholarly audiences at the Biblical Museum in New York, at the Hellenic Studies program at Princeton, at the Southeastern College Art Conference at Vanderbilt University, Nashville, Tennessee, at the Research Institute for the World Culture in Moscow, at the Ludwig Maximilian University in Munich, and at the Swedish Research Institute in Istanbul.

During my long-term study on canopies, I was financially supported through a number of stipends that allowed me to travel and otherwise get access to resources for my research. As a graduate student, I was supported by a two-year Honors Fellowship at Vanderbilt University and a four-year Princeton University Fellowship. At Princeton, I received several graduate school summer stipends; a one-year Lee Stipend; Spears travel and research funds from the Department of Art and Archaeology; and short-term stipends from the Group for the Study of Late Antiquity, the Center for Regional and International Studies, the Dean's Fund for Scholarly Travel, the Princeton Institute for International and Regional Studies, and the Greek Ministry of Culture. I am especially thankful for the Stanley J. Seeger Fellowship from the Princeton Program in Hellenic Studies and funding from the Center for the Study of Religion. At Princeton, I also thank Diane Schulte, Susan Lehre, and members-advisers of the fund established by architectural historian Barr Ferree. The publication of this book is made possible due to the generous subvention funds from the Barr Ferree Foundation Fund. At Iowa State University, where I now teach architectural history and theory, I received one course release during spring 2015 to work on the book manuscript. At Iowa State University, I also thank Deborah Hauptmann, Chair of the Architectural Department, and Luis Rico-Gutierrez, Dean of the College of Design.

Without continuous support and most professional guidance from my commissioning editor, Sarah Pirovitz from the Oxford University Press, this book would not have been possible. At Oxford University Press, I would also like to acknowledge the insightful guidance of the editorial board. Book reviewers provided constructive critiques, and their suggestions are reflected in the final manuscript. For book production, I thank Rajakumari Ganessin and her team. For indexing, I thank Mary Harper. For proofreading and editing my English through all stages from the book proposal project to the final preparation of the manuscript for publication, I am grateful to Erin Kalish and for final polishing of the text to Beverly Gail Cooper, copyeditor with the Oxford University Press.

Notes on Sources, Translations, and Illustrations

For textual references from Byzantine and other primary sources, I have supplied translations into English or pointed to translations to other languages. As regards precise terminology, when English terms are not entirely accurate, I have given the original term along with an English transliteration. Greek and Slavic terminology are related to the widely known and used English terminology whenever I thought it did not compromise the essential meanings. Whenever it was difficult to make a definite and adequate choice for a term or translation, several options have been offered. Selected primary sources from the bibliography are presented in Table 1 in chronological manner and in Tables 2 and 3 with more contextual details on the type and use of selected texts.

For references to the Bible, I have consulted a range of texts and translations: *The Holy Bible, Containing the Old and New Testaments, King James Version* (Nashville, 1984); *The Living World Bible Collection* CD (Waconia, Minn., 2002–2004), which has Hebrew, Greek, and Russian versions of the Holy Scriptures; the Septuagint, as printed by the *Thesaurus Lingua Graecae* (*TLG*) Online; *The New Oxford Annotated Bible; New Revised Standard Version with the Apocrypha* (Oxford, 1991); and the *Orthodox Study Bible* (Nashville, 2008).

Because of the plethora of scholarly works related to various aspects of canopies analyzed in this work, the references usually reflect either the most relevant or the most recent publications, together with older bibliography. The architectural drawings presented in this book serve predominantly as a framework for the discussion of canopies, not as archeological documentation of specific examples. I am immensely grateful to Zhengayng Hua, an architect but with limited previous knowledge of Byzantine architecture, who agreed to work on computer modeling of an "ideal," conceptual Byzantine church based on a model of a canopy. The overall design of a computer model and the issues that arose in the process of transitioning from the scale of an installation to the scale of a church building recalled numerous attested Byzantine-rite churches and their interior fittings, which largely confirms the sophisticated knowledge and practice of architectural design by the Byzantines. Heidi Reburn prepared the maps that show the geographical and chronological distribution of canopies; the numbers on the maps coincide with the numbers of archeologically attested canopies as listed in Table 5. Drawings prepared for this book are based on ones published by other scholars. I have also benefited tremendously from the image database of the Index of Christian Art while preparing my working photo-documentation. Any mistakes, both technical and factual, remain my responsibility.

List of Abbreviations

*	online database or source
AA	Archäologischer Anzieiger, supplement to Jahrbuch des Deutschen Archäologischen Instituts
AB	Analecta Bollandiana
AH	Artibus et Historiae
AJA	American Journal of Archaeology
ALw	Archiv für Liturgiewissenschaft
AMIT	Architecture and Modern Information Technologies
AnTard	Antiquité tardive
ArchM	Archéologie Médiévale
ArsM	Ars Medievale
ArtB	Art Bulletin
ArteL	Arte Lombarda
ArteM	Arte Medievale
BA	Biblical Archeologist
BABesch	Bulletin Antieke Beschaving
BASOR	Bulletin of the American Schools of Oriental Research
BCH	Bulletin de Correspondance Hellénique
BM	Burlington Magazine
BMFD	Byzantine Monastic Foundation Documents, J. P. Thomas and A. C. Hero, eds.; 5 vols. *DOS*, 35. (Washington, D.C., 2000)
BMGS	Byzantine and Modern Greek Studies
BSA	Annual of the British School at Athens
BSAC	Bulletin de la Société d'archéologie copte
BSCA	Byzantine Studies Conference Abstracts of Papers
Byz	Byzantion
ByzAus	Byzantina Australiensia
ByzELatW	Byzantine East, Latin West. Art-historical Studies in Honor of Kurt Weitzmann. D. Mouriki, S. Ćurčić, et al., eds. Princeton: Department of Art and Archeology, Princeton University Press, 1995.
ByzMetabyz	Byzantina kai Metabyzantina
BZ	Byzantinische Zeitschrift

CA	Cahiers archéologiques: fin de l'antiquité et Moyen âge
CAA	College Art Association of America
CANU	Crnogorska Akademija nauka i umetnosti
CM	Cyrillomethodianum
CMG	Corpus medicorum Graecorum
CorsiRav	Corsi di cultura sull'arte ravennate e bizantina
CSHB	Corpus scriptorium historiae byzantinae
CSMC	Cahiers de Saint-Michel de Cuxa
DACL	Dictionnaire d'archéologie chrétienne et de liturgie, eds. F. Cabrol and H. Leclercq, 15 vols. (Paris, 1920–1953)
DALA	J. S. Curl, A Dictionary of Architecture and Landscape Architecture (Oxford, 2nd edition 2006)
DArt	The Dictionary of Art, ed. J. Turner, 34 vols. (New York, 1996)
ΔXAE	Δελτίον τῆς Χριστιανικῆς Ἀρχαιολογικῆς Ἑταιρείας (Athens, 1924–)
DOP	Dumbarton Oaks Papers
DORLC	Dumbarton Oaks Research Library and Collection
DOS	Dumbarton Oaks Studies
DrevIsk	Drevnerusskoe iskusstvo
EAM	Enciclopedia dell'arte medievale, ed. A. M. Romanini, 12 vols. (Rome, 1991–c2002.)
EcclSilver	Ecclesiastical Silver Plate in Sixth-Century Byzantium: Papers of the Symposium Held May 16–18, 1986, at the Walters Art Gallery, Baltimore, and Dumbarton Oaks, Washington, D.C. S. A. Boyd and M. Mundell Mango, eds. (Washington, D.C.: DORLC, ca. 1992)
EEBS	Ἐπετηρὶς Ἑταιρείας Βυζαντινῶν Σπουδῶν
EHR	English Historical Review
EO	Échos d'Orient
EtLP	Etude sur le Liber Pontificalis, ed. L. Duchesne, 2 vols. (Paris, 1877)
Faith and Power	Byzantium: Faith and Power (1261–1557) H. C. Evans, ed. (New York and New Haven [Conn.], c2004)
FGrH	Die Fragmente der griechischen Historiker
FHG	Fragmenta historicorum Graecorum
Glory of Byz	The Glory of Byzantium, Art and Culture of the Middle Byzantine Era A.D. 843–1261, H. C. Evans and W. D. Wixom, eds. (New York, 1997)
GPMK	Godišnjak pomorskog muzeja u Kotoru
GRBS	Greek, Roman and Byzantine Studies
GZMS	Glasnik Zemaljskog muzeja u Sarajevu
HAM	Hortus artium medievalium
HUkSt	Harvard Ukrainian Studies
Iconoclasm	Iconoclasm. Papers given at the Ninth Spring Symposium of Byzantine Studies, University of Birmingham, March 1975. Eds. A. Bryer and J. Herrin (Birmingham: University of Birmingham, 1975)
Index	Index of Christian Art (Database: http://ica.princeton.edu/)
JAAC	The Journal of Aesthetics and Art Criticism
JBAA	Journal of the British Archaeological Association
JewArt	Jewish Art
JÖB	Jahrbuch der Österreichischen Byzantinistik
JQR	Jewish Quarterly Review
JRS	Journal of Roman Studies
JSAH	Journal of the Society of Architectural Historians

JWCI	Journal of the Warburg and Courtauld Institutes
ΚΣ	ΚΥΠΡΙΑΚΑΙ ΣΠΟΥΔΑΙ (Cypriot Studies)
Lampe	G. W. H. Lampe, A Patristic Greek Lexicon, 5 vols. (Oxford, 1961–1968)
Liddell	H. G. Liddell, An Intermediate Greek-English Lexicon (Oxford, 2nd edition 1997a)
LMA	Lexikon des Mittelalters
LS	Λακωνικαὶ Σπουδαί
Mansi	G. D. Mansi, Sacrorum conciliorum nova et amplissima collectio, 53 vols. (Paris and Leipzig. 1901–1927)
MünchJb	Müncher Jahrbuch der Bildenden Kunst
NEA	Near Eastern Archaeology
OC	Orientalia Christiana
OCA	Orientalia Christiana Analecta
ODA	Oxford Dictionary of Art, ed. I. Chilvers (Oxford, 3rd edition 2004)
ODB	Oxford Dictionary of Byzantium, ed. A. Kazhdan et al., 3 vols. (New York–Oxford, 1991)
ODE	Oxford Dictionary of English (revised edition), eds. C. Soanes and A. Stevenson (Oxford, 2005)
**ORO*	Oxford Reference Online. Oxford University Press. Princeton University; http://www.oxfordreference.com/
OrSyr	L'Orient syrien
PAPS	Proceedings of the American Philosophical Society
PBSR	Papers of the British School at Rome
PG	Patrologiae cursus completus, Series graeca, ed. J.-P. Migne, 161 vols. (Paris, 1857–1866)
PL	Patrologiae cursus completus, Series latina, ed. J.-P. Migne, 221 vols. (Paris, 1844–1880)
PPD	Prilozi povijesti umjetnosti u Dalmaciji
PPTS	Palestine Pilgrims Text Society
PrIz	Problemi na izkustvoto
RA	Revue Archéologique
RAC	Reallexikon für Antike und Christentum, ed. Th. Klauser, 21– vols. (Stuttgart, 1950–)
RACr	Rivista di archeologia cristiana
RArt	Revue de l'Art
RBK	Reallexikon zur Byzantinischen Kunst, ed. K. Wessel, 6– vols. (Stuttgart, 1963–)
RIPU	Radovi instituta za povijest umjetnosti
RSBN	*Rivista di studi bizantini e neoellenici*
RSBS	Rivista di studi bizantini e slavi
RussTravelers	Russian travelers to Constantinople in the fourteenth and fifteenth centuries. G. P. Majeska, Washington, D.C.: DORLC, 1984.
RZZSK	Republički zavod za zaštitu spomenika kulture
SANU	Srpska Akademija nauka i umetnosti
SC	Sources chrétiennes
SD	Art of the Byzantine Empire, 312–1453; Sources and Documents. Ed. C. Mango (Englewood Cliffs, N.J., 1972)
SH	Subsidia hagiographica
SHP	Starohrvatska prosvjeta
SJT	Scottish Journal of Theology

SKZ	Srpska književna zadruga
SR	Slavic Review
TAPA	Transactions and Proceedings of the American Philological Association (=Transactions of the American Philosophical Society)
**TLG*	Thesaurus Lingua Graecae online
TM	Travaux et mémoires
Vyz	Βυζαντινὰ (Thessalonikē, 1969–)
WA	World Archeology
ZAltW	Zeitschrift für die Alttestamentliche Wissenshaft
ZKunstg	Zeitschrift für Kunstgeschichte
ZLU	Zbornik Matice srpske za likovne umetnosti
ZRVI	Zbornik radova Vizantološkog instituta

Maps

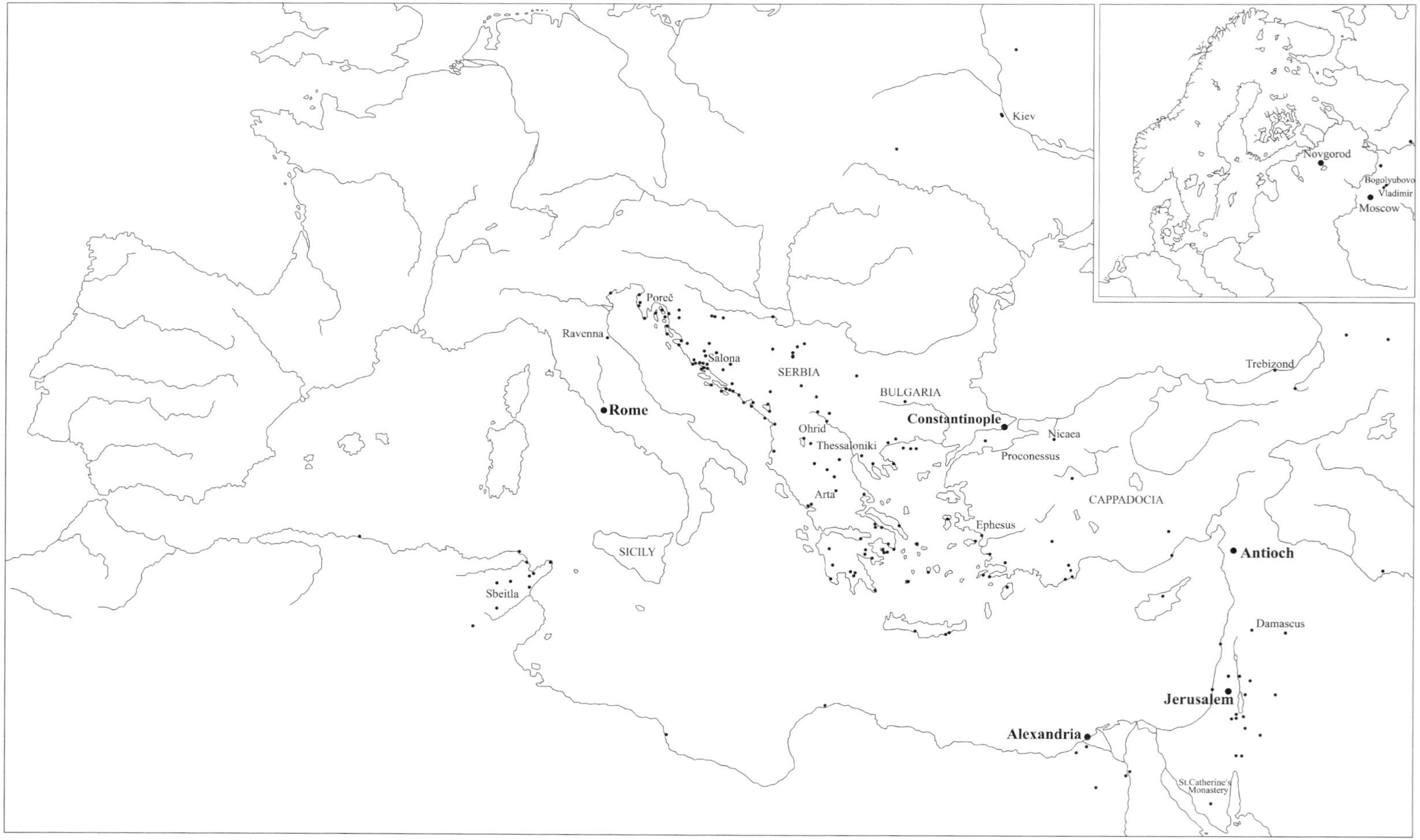

MAP 1 *Canopies in Byzantine Ecclesiastical Tradition ca. 300–1500*

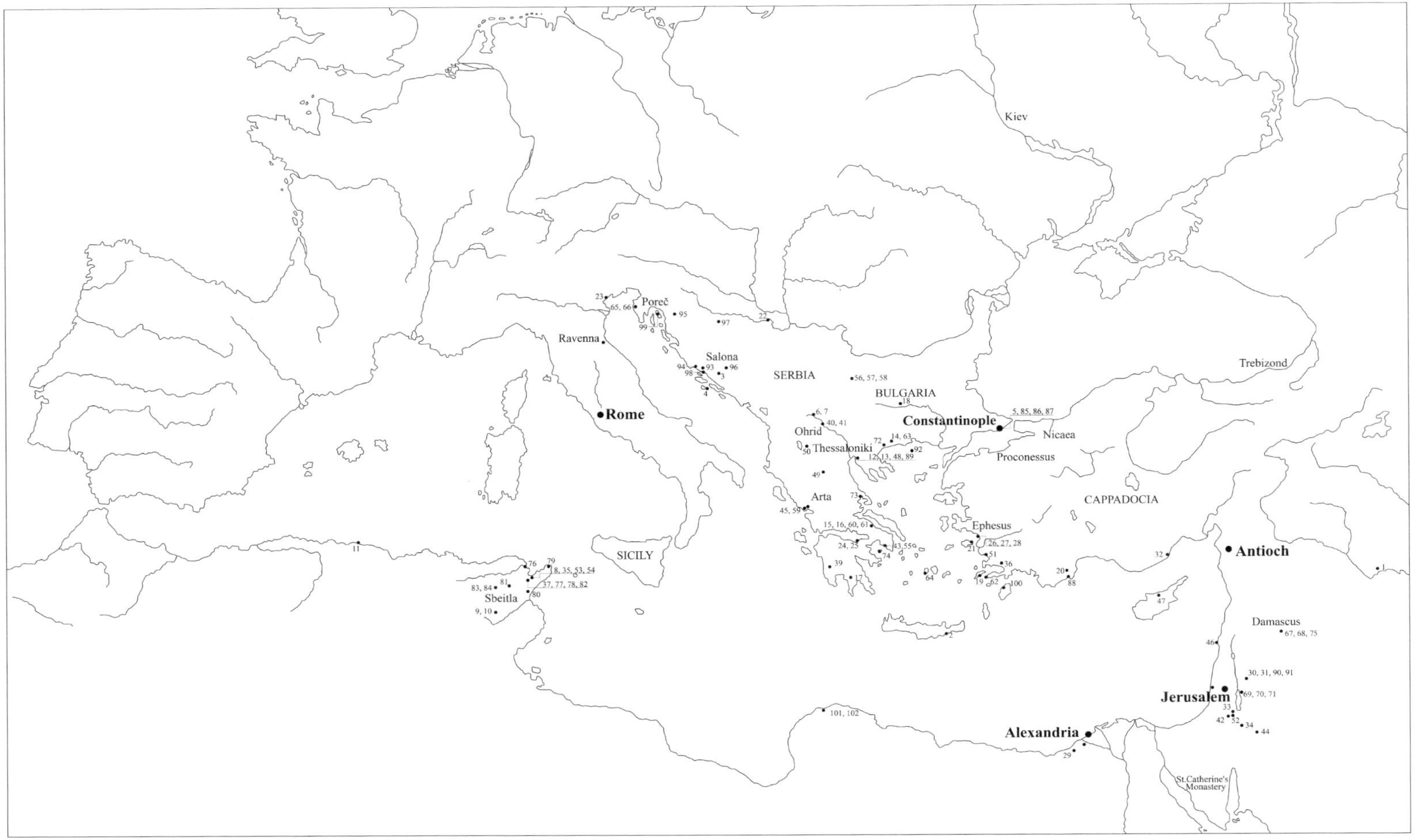

MAP 2 *Canopies in Early Christian and Early Byzantine Period ca. Fourth–Sixth Centuries*

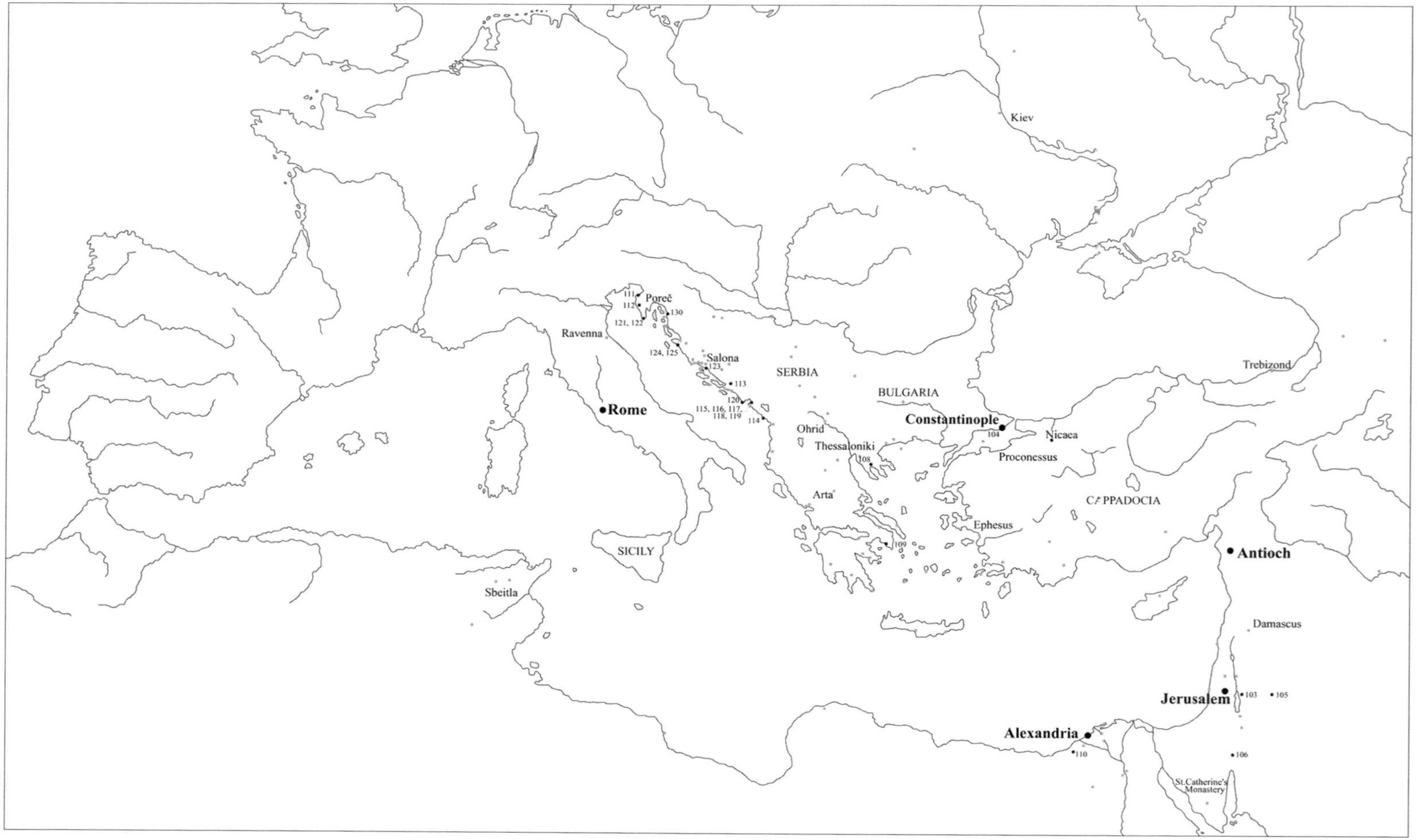

MAP 3 *Canopies in the "Transitional Period" ca. Seventh–Mid-Ninth Centuries*

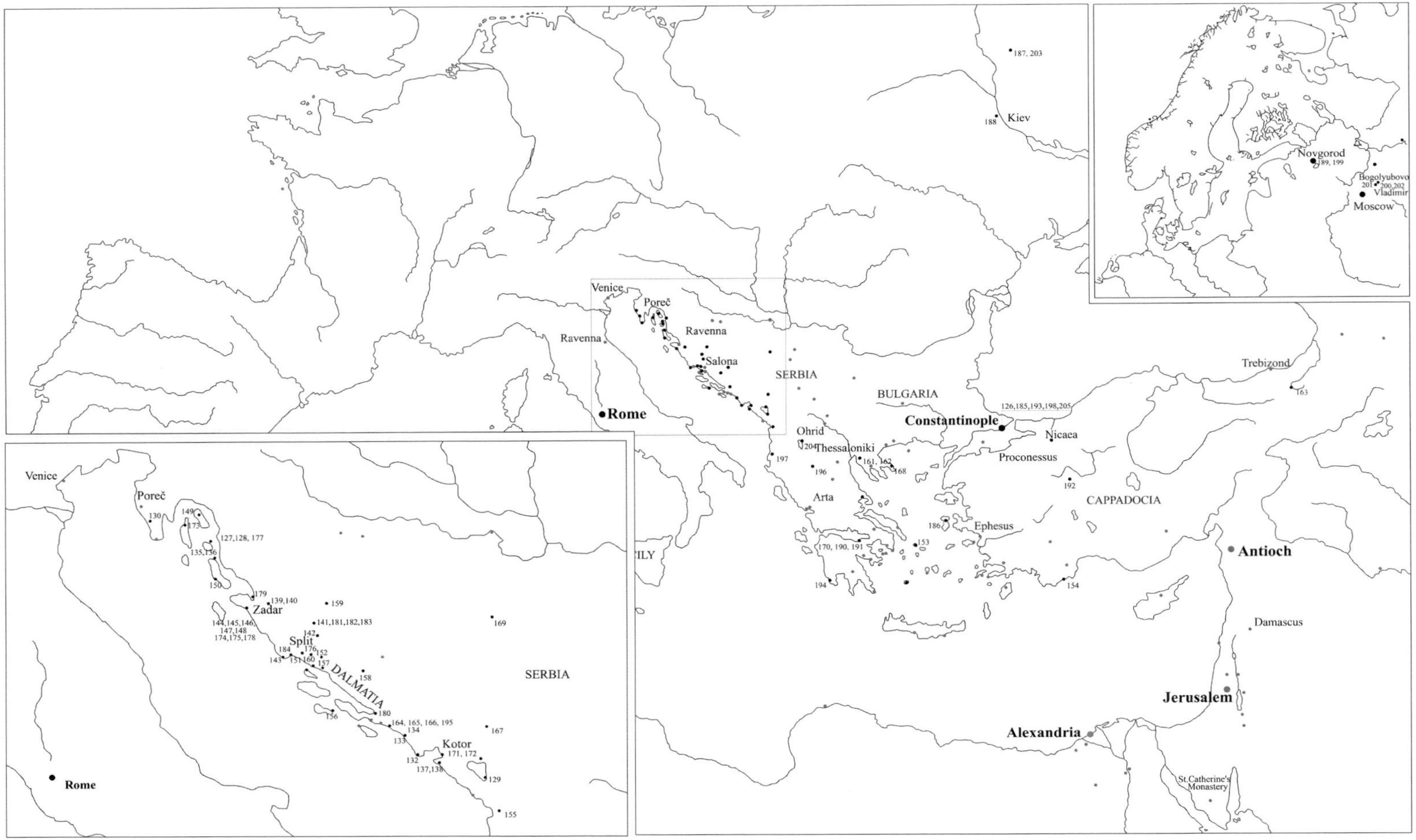

MAP 4 *Canopies in Middle Byzantine Period ca. Mid-Ninth–Twelfth Centuries*

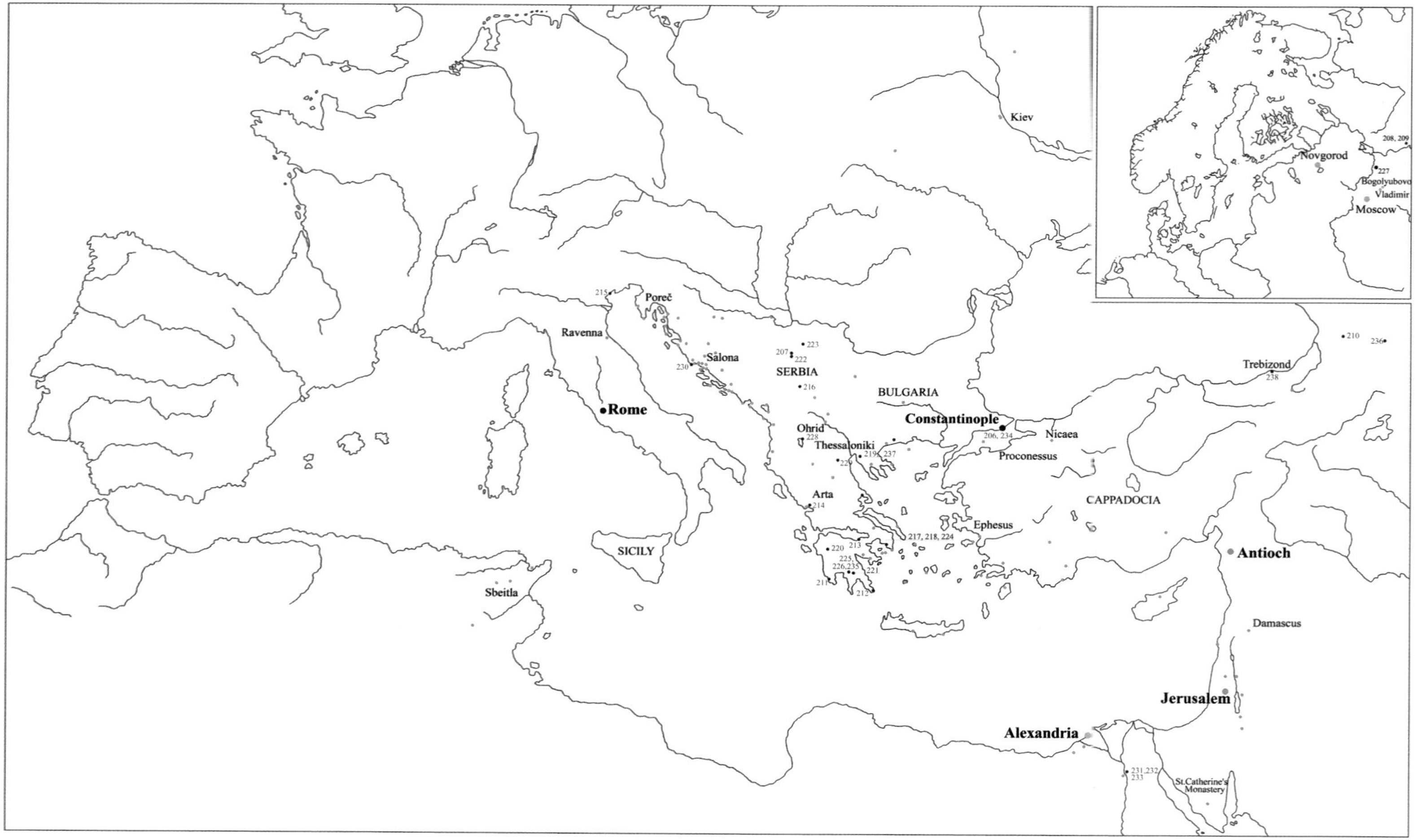

MAP 5 *Canopies in Late Byzantine Period ca. Thirteenth–Fifteenth Centuries*

Introduction

CANOPIES, CENTRALLY PLANNED COLUMNAR STRUCTURES, ARE WIDELY USED in religious and royal contexts in various cultures and historical periods—in ancient pagan, Christian, Islamic or Hindu traditions, to name but a few.[1] However, their significance and meaning is far from being fully understood. This book examines the importance of studies of canopies from archeological and architectural perspectives as a way to enhance our understanding of the idea of a Byzantine church. The discussion of canopies is focused on Byzantine tradition alone due to two major reasons. First is the need to present the empirical evidence on canopies, which would be difficult to illuminate if done across different cultures. Second highlights how the domed church, essentially an elaborated canopy, emerged as a recognizable building type in Byzantine architecture. This particularly Byzantine phenomenon of the domed church reveals that its architecture and some of the central features of its interior have the same form, and hence calls for the detailed investigation of the material evidence and the interpretations of its cultural meanings.

Canopies as integral features of Christian churches have received frequent but often superficial attention in lexicons, dictionaries, and general studies of Christian art and architecture. These studies tend to single out the formal architectural functions of canopies—as altar canopies (often called ciboria), baptismal canopies, or tomb shelters—or their visual representations in art as architectural backdrops for Biblical, hagiographical, and liturgical narratives and scenes.[2] Numerous accounts usually address early Christian, medieval, and later examples in the West, highlighting above all Bernini's famous baldachin in St. Peter's in

[1] See, for example, Smith, B. E. (1956) 107–129; Smith, B. E. (1978).

[2] For entries within dictionaries, see *DACL* vol. 3, 2; *RAC* vol. 1, 68–86; 462; *RBK* vol. 1, 1055–1065; *Dictionary of Architecture* 24, 62; *Leksikon ikonografije* 180–181; *LMA* vol. 2, 2062–2063; *ODB* vol. 1, 462, s.v. *ciborium; Coptic Encyclopedia* vol. 1, 202–203; *Modern Catholic Encyclopedia,* s.v. *ciborium; DArt,* s.v. *ciborium* (ii); *EAM,* s.v. *ciborio.*

For studies within Christian art and architecture, see, for example, Braun (1907); Wieland (1912); Braun (1924); Underwood (1950) 43–138; Soteriou (1952); Duval, N., and Lezine (1959) 71–147; Klauser (1961); Hoddinott (1963); Orlandos (1963); Orlandos (1935–1973); Grabar (1972); Badawy (1978); Kapitän (1980) 71–136; Harrison, M. (1989); Deshman (1995) 131–137; Hill (1996); Duval, N. (2003) 35–114.

Rome.[3] Canopies from the western territories of medieval Europe currently constitute the major corpus for studies of medieval canopies in general.

Canopies of the Christian East have not been included in major discussions mostly because scholarship about Byzantine canopies has habitually been limited by the lack of material evidence. This study presents the complex archeological, visual, and literary evidence for canopies in the Byzantine ecclesiastical tradition. The initial aim of assembling and presenting this information on canopies is manifold: (1) to question how much evidence we actually have and how aspects of this evidence relate to each other for a given period and/or geographic region; (2) to question whether the form of a canopy held significance and meaning; and (3) to examine to what extent canopies were imitative or non-imitative structures, and as such critical for the process of architectural design. To determine whether the main centers of intellectual thought and artistic production may have influenced the notion of canopies, I investigate canopies within the broad scope of Byzantine art and architecture (ca. 300-1500).

This broader evidence for canopies comes from structures, which were made or have remained in the territories that were once part of the Byzantine Empire and its commonwealth, based on shared Orthodox Christianity, in the Eastern Mediterranean.[4] With full understanding that the early Christian and Byzantine canopies did not develop independently from the better studied examples from Rome and western Europe and that they belonged to the same cultural and church tradition—at least until the ninth century, when the emergence of the Carolingian Holy Roman Empire directly confronted the Byzantine Empire as fully Christianized and the rightful successor of the Roman Empire, or until the official doctrinal split between the Roman Catholic and Greek Orthodox churches in 1054—my investigation focuses on canopies in churches in the east, while making recurrent references to comparable examples of canopies in the west.[5] Such an approach allows for better clarity in the overview as to how many of the canopies definitely belong to the territories directly associated with the Byzantine Empire. This approach is furthermore critical

---

[3] An excellent overview of canopies in the medieval West is offered in: *EAM* vols. 3 and 4, s.v. *baldacchino*, s.v. *ciborio*, respectively. Among literature on canopies in the West are the following titles: Kroesen (2013) 189–222; Kroesen (2009) 30–41; Weigel (2000); Weber (1990); Weiss (1995) 308–320; Spagnolo (2006); Kirwin (1997); Valverde and Fernández-Oxea (1987); Zambrano (1984); Scott (2003); Schöller (1998) 190–205; Thelen (1967); Lavin (1968) ch. 2; Pace (1991) 181–189; Pace (1992) 389–400; Pani (1976) 337–344; Morano (1980) 331–342; Ponsich (1993) 21–27; Acconci (1993) 15–41; Buis (1976) 233–245; Gatti (1987) 70–71; Moskowitz (1998) 88–102; Guidobaldi (1999) 55–69; Kreytenberg (2002) 91–126.

[4] Although Byzantine-rite churches are the focus of this study, church canopies are occasionally considered more broadly, together with examples from Syria, North Africa, and Armenia. On the eve of Iconoclastic controversies of the eighth and ninth centuries, Byzantine churches were restricted to the churches in the Patriarchate of Constantinople, its daughter churches, and Palestinian monastic churches. While still waiting for comprehensive studies on liturgical practices from the Christian East, see Taft (1992); *History of the Melkite Patriarchates* (1998–2001); Todt (2001) 239–269.

[5] Full reconsideration of material evidence from the so-called Latin West within larger medieval contexts, like restored ninth- and eleventh-century canopies previously located in the so-called *Sala bizantina*, Vatican, and canopies made in early Christian Rome, including the famous St. Peter's canopy and those in the churches of St. Andrew and St. Alexander, is wanting. *Corpus* (1974) 7 *La diocesi di Roma* 64–68, figs. 10–11; Smith, M. T. (1974) 379–414. I touched upon comparative analysis of altar canopies in Constantinople and Rome before the ninth century in an essay that confirmed the simultaneous use of canopies in churches in Rome and Constantinople at least since the fourth century, based on textual sources and further supported by coeval sixth-century archeological evidence in both centers, in Bogdanović (2002) 7–19.

in the attempts to eventually confirm that canopies were, in contrast to prevailing scholarly opinion, extensively used in the Byzantine ecclesiastical tradition, and that the use of canopies in medieval churches was a pan-European cultural phenomenon, as has been recently suggested by several important publications prepared by Justin Kroesen.[6]

During my research, I have collected archeological evidence for more than two hundred canopy-like structures, constituting a body of physical data complemented by images of more than five hundred representations of canopies in the visual arts and by testimonies in more than one hundred texts that by using various descriptive and metonymic terms mention objects known as, or surmised to be, canopies. Such extensive material, never previously examined as a whole, confirms the broad use of canopied installations in Byzantine-rite churches and challenges the prevailing opinion that after the so-called transitional period (seventh–ninth centuries), marked by socio-economic and a decline of building monumental, large architecture, canopies as architectural installations ceased to be used. Surviving textual, visual, and above all archeological evidence confirms the prolonged and continual use of canopies throughout the Byzantine realm, both in the main centers of the empire and in its periphery and neighboring countries that adopted Byzantine culture as a model. This wide geographic framework permits a better understanding of concurrent Byzantine architectural developments, not only in Constantinople but also elsewhere. By providing a short overview of the literature and the gaps in current scholarship on Byzantine architecture that often lack discussions of interior furnishings and micro-architecture in general, this book emphasizes the great potential of "soft" archeology and new methodologies in the studies of historical architecture that unveil Byzantine architecture beyond the building as a shelter.

An unpublished doctoral dissertation "The 'Ciborium' in Christian Architecture at Rome, 300-600 AD" by the late M. T. Smith (Institute of Fine Arts, NYU, 1968) remains the most critical comprehensive work addressing the subject of early Christian canopies in the West. Her work, complemented by two additional articles, is also essential as it addresses the early Christian canopies in Rome in connection with the pagan and Jewish traditions, making possible insights into further developments within the Western Christian sphere.[7] My work also touches on notions of the appreciation of the cultural heterogeneity and of the shared religious values of the Byzantines with Judeo-Christian and Hellenistic traditions and on the long-lasting creative conventions in the Mediterranean. Yet, instead of following the models and methodology of scholars who have studied canopies in Western Europe, I have taken an approach that revises the functional paradigm in order to consider theological texts as a corpus of medieval "philosophy" that informs architecture in the Byzantine realm, and to combine traditional with new methodologies. In particular, I engage with innovative studies that emerged in the 1990s and that consider sacred space—such as the so-called *hierotopy* by Alexei Lidov and the so-called iconic and spatial "turns" advanced among medievalists by Hans Belting and Myrto Veikou.[8] Such a more comprehensive approach takes into account the architectural and design principles that the

---

[6] Kroesen (2009); Kroesen and Schmidt (2009); Kroesen (2013) 189–222, with the citation of my findings from my dissertation project on p. 192, n. 11.

[7] Smith, M. T. (1970) 149–175; Smith, M. T. (1974) 379–414.

[8] For general overviews of methodological approaches in Byzantine architecture and the still prevailing preference for the functionalistic paradigm, see, for example, Mango (1991) 40–44, and Belting (1987), *passim*, esp. 32–33. On nineteenth-century scholarship that imposed preeminence of time over space in historical studies of art and architecture, see Nelson (1997) 28–40. On information coming from disciplines other than the history of art and architecture in order to support art historical narrative, thus calling for monographic studies focused on one single object or a group of similar objects from a given period or region, and leaving aside the objects that cannot fit proposed paradigms, see Kessler (1988) 166–187.

Byzantines used and offers beneficial trajectories for studies of the creation and reception of sacred space framed by canopies.

Major books on Byzantine architecture written by internationally renowned architectural historians such as Ralph Hodinott, Cyril Mango, Richard Krautheimer, Slobodan Ćurčić, Thomas Mathews, and Robert Ousterhout provide three-dimensional reconstructions of churches or floor plans with delineated locations of specific interior fittings, yet seldom discuss canopies and their relation to church design in greater detail.[9] Archeological reports occasionally mention canopies, frequently reduced to traces of their original appearance and setting within churches, and related journal articles mostly highlight carved fragments of canopies within discussions of architectural sculpture. Among numerous texts that reveal the existence of canopies in Byzantine-rite churches across vast territories and chronological spans are those written by scholars such as Andre Grabar, Laskarina Boura, Jean-Piere Sodini, Catherine Vanderheyde, Angeliki Mitsani, and Øystein Hjort.[10] The majority of Byzantine canopies are difficult to date and to locate accurately within their original settings because most of them only survive in fragments, while stylistic analysis is critical for establishing the centers of their production, yet often ineffective for precisely tracing regional differences.

Imbued with symbolic meanings, the abundant visual evidence for canopies in Byzantine paintings is complementary material in researching the meaning of canopies, yet cannot be taken as verifiable documentary evidence of actual objects. In this study I follow a new generation of scholars who, by working with small scale, portable objects such as lamps or utensils, emphasize the need for more subtle interdisciplinary approaches in the research of material culture in Byzantium. For example, Maria Parani has successfully revealed how images of portable objects can certainly provide clues about their material reality and meaning, apart from references coming exclusively from textual sources.[11] Texts in Byzantine Greek and other languages used in the Mediterranean are vague and often deemed as confusing and convoluted, especially because medieval writers were not primarily interested in material topics but rather in spiritual ones. Therefore, archeological evidence and visual representations of canopies remain invaluable references to the examination of the role of canopies in Byzantine-rite churches.

Examining the context of Gothic churches, François Bucher defined micro-architecture as miniature architectural structures frequently used as church furnishings, such as altar canopies, font canopies, saintly shrines, and reliquaries.[12] *The Framing of Sacred Space* further aims to foster studies about micro-architecture, which significantly lag behind the studies of monumental architecture despite the fact that the emphasis of Byzantine architecture was placed on its interior, spiritual space with church fittings critical in its

On new methodologies for studying sacred space, see Lidov (2015a); Lidov (2011); Lidov (2006b); Lidov (2009b); Lidov (2009a); Lidov (2004). On spatial and iconic "turns," see, for example, seminal Lefebvre (1991); then Veikou (2012); Bachmann-Medick (2006) 284–328; Belting (2001).

[9] Hoddinott (1963); Mathews (1971); Mathews (1976); Mango (1985b); Krautheimer (1986); Ousterhout (2008); Ćurčić (2010).

[10] Metsanē (1996–1997) 319–334; Vanderheyde (2005) 427–442; Hjort (1979) 199–289; Sodini (1995) 289–311; Boura (1977–1979) 63–72; Grabar (1976).

[11] Parani (2003); Parani (2005) 147–171.

[12] Bucher (1976) 71–89. Since Bucher's work, scholars have furthered studies of micro-architectural structures within both the medieval West and Byzantium. Timmermann (2013); Timmermann (2009); Kratzke (2008); Angar (2008) 433–453; Ćurčić, Hadjitryphonos, et al. (2010); Lidov (2011); Lidov (1999) 340–353.

articulation. These structures provided performative frameworks for liturgical services and paraliturgical devotional practices while at the same time they evoked Biblical architecture and space such as the Heavenly Jerusalem, the paradisiac Fountain of Life, or the Holy Sepulchre in Jerusalem. Expanding upon the definitions of micro-architecture as miniature architectural structures, micro-architecture here implies structures that assembled by a minimal number of basic architectural elements convey the sense of framed space, while their micro-architectural qualities are here understood not primarily in terms of human-based size, but rather in terms of their relative scale to the sacred space in which they are found, such as churches, and which they denote, such as the Heavenly Jerusalem. This book highlights the canopy that by virtue of its physical form represents a basic micro-architectural framing device in the Byzantine religious context. At the same time, this study challenges studies of Byzantine architecture that are limited to detailed formal typological discussions of floor plans and church design. The examined material suggests how a deepening insight into the total cultural context of ecclesiastical settings may significantly expand our current scholarly perception of canopies in Byzantium beyond merely physical evidence to include the memory image of a canopy as an architectural frame for sacred space. For example, in this work, the Tomb of Christ is considered as a seminal object for understanding Byzantine canopies and the messages they conveyed despite the fact that architecturally speaking this still partially preserved object is not a canopy, strictly understood as an open columnar structure. Similarly, another critical building in Byzantine religious thought, the Temple of Jerusalem, was only creatively recreated in Byzantine art and architecture as a canopy and certainly was not originally built as such. Probably the best-known Byzantine canopy (also named *ciborium* in Greek texts), that of St. Demetrios in Thessaloniki, was not an open columnar structure either, but rather an *aedicula*-shaped miniature building with engaged columns comparable in form to the Tomb of Christ. Hence, this book shows how like many canopies seen in illuminated manuscripts or wall paintings that denoted sacred space, the canopy in a Byzantine-rite church became a spatial, visual, and literary *topos*. Simultaneously, essential architectural elements that constitute a canopy as architectural *parti* were potent carriers of multifold religious messages in the Byzantine world.

OUTLINE OF THE BOOK

How did the Greek speaking Byzantines refer to canopy-like structures? An attempt to answer this seemingly simple question in Chapter 1 reveals that there is not a single and absolute answer, and that a critical reassessment of the applicability of the currently used term *ciborium* is needed. Moreover, the plethora of original late antique and medieval accounts on canopied structures provides two distinct bodies of evidence. One is critical for proof about the existence of actual canopies in Byzantine tradition; the other for understanding culturally determined ways of their perception. This chapter develops an analysis of the different idioms, arguments, and rhetorical strategies the Byzantines used to describe and discuss canopies in their churches. It compares the modern academic conventions of naming and describing canopies as ciboria with conventions that are related to the Byzantine tradition. The formulaic nature of ekphrasis, encomium, and other rhetorical devices allowed the Byzantines for complementary but non-hierarchical treatment of texts and structures. Such an analysis links some of scholarship's evident lacunae and misunderstandings to the inception of Byzantine studies and its antiquarian approach starting in the sixteenth century and solidified by positivistic scholarship since the eighteenth-century Enlightenment.

My research shows that the Byzantine Greeks used the word *ciborium* (in Greek κιβώριον) less often than we previously thought. Moreover, the word *ciborium* occasionally denoted various entities, not only canopies, in contexts outside of Christian ecclesiastical architecture. Textual accounts that employ Greek versions for the word *ciborium* are various, ranging from poems and texts on magic, to teaching resources such as grammars and lexicons, to hagiographies and highly complex theological writings. The term with its variant meanings remained in use until the fall of the Byzantine Empire; and yet, its meaning might have been different depending on the type of discourse or specific time-period in which it was used. Furthermore, those writers who employed the word κιβώριον recurrently provided an extended explanation of what a *ciborium* was. Potentially, the word was strange to the Byzantines as well, and the necessary explanation of *ciboria* resulted from a conflation of various pre-Christian sources, usually Hellenistic pagan and Jewish. At the same time some other, overlooked descriptive and metonymic words may have referred to canopies in the Byzantine tradition—such as πύργος [*pirgos*] meaning tower; οἰκίσκος [*oikiskos*] "small house"; ορόφιον [*orophion*] referring to roofs, usually domical ones; ἀψῖδα [*apsida*] with its meaning for the arch and vault; references to four columnar structures such as τετρακίονος [*tetrakionos*] and τετράπυλον [*tetrapylon*]; various terms for religious curtains such as τετράβηλον [*tetravēlon*], καταπέτασμα [*katapetasma*], παραπέτασμα [*parapetasma*], and πέπλα [*pepla*]; or the relatively obscure term κουβούκλειον [*koubukleion, kouvouklion*], referring to various rooms, chests, burial and funerary installations. Though used very little in Byzantine scholarship, the modern term *canopy* is the most applicable one for this study as it points to the basic architectural form behind all these various terms used in Byzantine texts. This chapter also highlights the awareness of the Byzantine intellectual elite to the changing and interrelated multi-layered terminology pertaining to canopies in the Byzantine church as a carrier of complex theological ideas that were deeply associated with the materialization, meaning, and perception of such architectural installations.

Turning more specifically to the archeological evidence, Chapter 2 establishes the prevalence of canopies in Byzantine churches—their quantity being far greater than previously thought—and then suggests that Byzantine canopies, though formulaic in execution, indeed, perhaps *because of* their generic imagery, were readily adapted for diverse contexts. This chapter details the use of altar canopies as well as canopies over baptismal and holy water fonts, over ambos and other types of church furnishings, and over tombs, shrines, relics, and icons. With the increasing interest in the so-called "soft" archeology that documents architecture not only as buildings but also carefully analyzes traces of their original settings, including various fittings and material evidence that can hint to a better understanding of religious space, new discoveries of canopies from the Christian East are additionally presented.

Recently Anastasios Antonaras published archeological findings from the Church of Hagia Sophia in Thessaloniki, which revealed the remnants of a medieval bronze canopy, hence also expanding discussions on their materiality.[13] Namely, the majority of surviving canopies from the Christian East are early examples made of fine-quality stone. Some of them were made of silver or cast in bronze, decorated with gems, semi-precious stones and glass, and sometimes gilded. Textual evidence confirms that wooden canopies may have been more common despite only a few later extant examples. Even in cases when canopies were made of wood, it is likely that many of them would have been gilded and sheathed in silver, gold, or other precious materials.

[13] Antonaras (2014) 21–22.

The decoration and inscriptions on canopies reveal their potency to act as carriers of various spiritual, proprietary, and votive meanings. Yet, the function of medieval architectural installations, including canopies, cannot fully explain their form, decoration, or meaning. Canopies of similar form did not necessarily have parallel functions in Constantinople, Thessaloniki, or elsewhere in the Byzantine domain; furthermore, canopies of similar function and location within the church proper may not have had the same form and decoration in every Byzantine church. The same is true of the spatial arrangement of canopies of the same form, function, and decoration. These can be seen most vividly through analysis of the various examples of altar and baptismal canopies, the most numerous groups of preserved canopied installations.

Chapter 3 demonstrates that Byzantine architectural design was deeply human oriented, which resulted in a peculiar version of place-making, whereby the canopy, despite its generic design, within the church space articulated singular place identity. Being most closely related to human presence and experience, canopies also effectively promoted spirituality, salvific messages, and a variety of Christian religious beliefs. Several case studies exemplify the contextualized use and experience of canopied installations, all the while highlighting how both individually and culturally constructed meanings were variously related to each other, occasionally independently of official religious or administrative directions. The analysis highlights the third-century Dura Europos baptismal canopy, the earliest canopied installation acknowledged to serve exclusively Christian purposes because the sacrament of baptism is unique to Christians. Specific examples of Byzantine canopies preserved in situ on the island of Paros and in Kalabaka, Greece, provide insights into the complexities of place-making by focusing on canopies in their original church settings and by making references to comparative structures in Constantinople and elsewhere. In 2010, I had the opportunity to provide expertise for the acquisition of a heretofore unknown and unique monolithic early Christian canopy from the Middle East for the Royal Ontario Museum, which granted me the rights to discuss it in this publication and to ask the questions raised when the original setting remains unknown. The reconstruction of the multiple canopies and their placement in the major Byzantine church, Hagia Sophia in Constantinople—which set the standards for Byzantine religious architecture—reveals the heretofore understudied, multi-focal topography of the Byzantine church as a re-creation of spatial settings and their meanings for various church practices articulated by canopies within an individual church.

A critical feature of canopies is their micro-architectural quality, which brings to light the essence of design practices in Byzantine religious architecture. Chapter 4 examines various canopies as columnar and vaulted installations and relates them to the meaning and form of the canopy as a basic spatial unit of the Byzantine church. The analysis highlights how altar canopies, for example, resulted from, among other factors, the complex circumstances of diverse liturgical needs, devotional practices, and movement-directing channels within a given church and may have originated from various concepts related to funerary (funerary altars and tomb canopies), civic (*tetrapyla* and imperial canopies), and sacred architecture (shrines and sacrificial altars). Specific case studies include the canopied shrines of Old St. Peter's in Rome and related early Christian churches in the wider Mediterranean, as well as of St. Euphemia in Constantinople, St. Demetrios in Thessaloniki, and Blessed Loukas in Boeotia. As I move from specific examples to larger trends within Byzantine domains, canopies are examined within their broader context, which includes prevailing theological concerns, piety, and liturgical practices, as well as generalized contemporary social attitudes and economic conditions for their creation and maintenance.

Most importantly, Chapter 4 emphasizes the concepts of design of the Byzantine church based on the micro-architecture of canopies on a micro-scale defined by the human body and the church building to which they belong. Specific architectural solutions reveal the various spatial relations and meanings between different canopied installations. In particular, the following relations are examined: between canopies for altars, tombs, and saintly shrines; between altar canopies, *templon* screens, and *proskynetaria*; between canopied *phialai* outside the church and vaulted chambers that served as *phialai* inside the church; between ambo canopies and two-dimensional *omphalos* disks in the nave of the church; and finally the spatial and symbolic merging of imperial canopied thrones, canopied settings for the veneration of relics, and those canopies with funerary associations as well as their further transposition into domical canopy bays of church *narthexes* and *exonarthexes* or canopied and domed chapels in the galleries above *narthexes*.

This chapter ends with an explanation of how domed bays in Byzantine churches were architectural canopies and had a crucial role in the modular transposition from domed basilica to various Middle-Byzantine solutions. Above all the longstanding nine-square problem in architectural design is revealed in the articulation of Byzantine church design and in particular in the prominent, so-called cross-in-square Middle Byzantine church. The multiple relations between various canopied installations and settings in the church point to the dynamic process of architectural modular design based on canopies as spatial units that also allowed for singular rather than generic experience of space. Hence, canopy emerged as an efficient spatial and symbolic unit in articulating the nine-square grid design, which in turn provided an impressive variety of solutions in Byzantine church architecture. When juxtaposed with the conventional studies of Byzantine architecture that examine various floor plans as defined and systematized in the twentieth century, the major contribution of the consideration of the canopy in the nine-square grid design is in revealing a more plastic understanding of the Byzantine church typology and adjusting the previously set chronological taxonomy that placed Hagia Sophia at the pinnacle of Byzantine accomplishments followed by architectural decline. On the contrary, in this proposed innovative understanding of Byzantine church design, the essential role of a canopy is in asserting the continual links between late antique and medieval Byzantine architecture, while at the same time the Middle and Late Byzantine churches can be understood as architecturally and symbolically mature rather than inferior solutions.

The sophisticated and complex concepts of total design of the Byzantine church based on canopies of different scales are examined in Chapter 5. The Byzantine church centered on the micro-architecture of canopies, as structures assembled by a minimal number of basic architectural elements to convey the sense of framed and specified space, allow for the expansion of their scale beyond a micro-scale based on human size to include a macro-scale relative to the space in which they are found and which they denote. Two ultimate architectural models for the embodiment of heavenly and earthly Jerusalem in a Byzantine-rite church are the Temple and the Holy Sepulchre. By focusing on Hagia Sophia as a building that set ideals for Byzantine architectural design, these two concepts and related architectural models are especially highlighted: first, the Biblical architectural models carried on the level of ideas—the Ark, the Tabernacle, the Temple, Heavenly Jerusalem—and second, the Tomb of Christ and the complex of the Holy Sepulchre in Jerusalem as seminal Christian sites that palpably carried the pervasive salvific messages from the holy land and holy places to the Byzantine believers. Throughout, I emphasize the inseparability of the material and spiritual aspects of canopies as carriers of meaning. Although the medieval sources—archeological, visual, and textual—may independently yield different conclusions, the potency of the canopy as a device for framing sacred space expands towards these different types of evidence in a corresponding way. The triumphant micro-architecture of the Tomb of Christ in Jerusalem, the seminal building for the testimony of the New Covenant, is detailed through several lines of investigation to reveal its overarching significance in

Byzantine-rite churches. In this chapter, we reconcile, for instance, why Byzantine theologians often describe the altar canopy as a symbol of Christ's tomb and yet testimonies about the Holy Sepulchre in Jerusalem compare it to another piece of liturgical furniture, the ambo. The typological links between the Ark of the Covenant, the Tabernacle, the Temple, and the Tomb of Christ in the Holy Sepulchre establish organic architectural, tectonic, symbolic, and sacred ties between the Old and New Covenants within Byzantine domed churches, which are essentially large-scale canopies.

At last, I summarize the major findings of this study in the conclusion, revealing the canopy as a spatial and symbolic unit of sacred space. By emphasizing the phenomenon of canopies as essential architectural and ontological constructs in the Byzantine church, the study calls for wider discussions about the additive and modular design processes in the Byzantine domain and beyond. The book claims that such a design was based on a canopy as a spatial unit and diagrammatic architectural *parti* rather than the reproducible precise two-dimensional imagery of floor plans and cross sections, which we use today when studying Byzantine architecture. The formal and conceptual integrity of canopies emphasizes the fine merging of the total design of Byzantine churches within canopies, inclusive of their form and associated values. Because canopies as micro-architectural structures are on the verge between architectural and sculptural installations, they simultaneously highlight the tectonic and aesthetic qualities of a Byzantine church. When captured in their memorable imagery and their dynamic relations to the sacred space, canopies reveal the diagrammatic reasoning behind their creation, which in turn alters our perceived aesthetics and the meaning of Byzantine churches.

ONE

Ciborium or Canopy? Textual Evidence on Canopies in the Byzantine Church

Above the all-pure table of gold into the expansive air rises a tower, reared on four arches of silver. It is borne aloft on silver columns on whose tops each of the four arches has planted its silver feet. And above the arches springs up a figure like a cone; yet it is not exactly a cone: for at the bottom its rim does not turn round in a circle, but has an eight-sided base, and from a broad plan it gradually rises up to a sharp point, stretching out its eight sides of silver. At the juncture of each to the other stand long backbones, which seem to join their course with the triangular faces of the eight-sided form and rise to a single crest where the artist has placed the form of a cup. The lip of the cup bends over and assumes the shape of leaves, and in the midst of it has been placed a shining silver orb, and a cross surmounts it all. May it be propitious! Above the arches many a curve of acanthus finely chiseled twists round the base of the cone, while rising over the edge, at the top it terminates in upright points resembling the fragrant pear fruit within the beautiful foliage, glittering with light, peeking out from the edge. Now where the sides of the base are fitted to each other are fixed silver vessels, and in each vessel is set a candelabrum like a candle yet that burns not, expressing beauty rather than giving light; for these are fashioned all round of silver, brightly polished. Thus the candle flashes a silver ray, not the light of fire. And on columns of gold is raised the all-gold slab of the holy table, standing on gold foundations, and bright with the glitter of numerous precious stones that adorn it.

Χρυσείης δ᾽ ἐφύπερθε παναχράντοιο τραπέζης ἄσπετος εὐρυκέλευθον ἐς ἠέρα πύργος ἀνέστη, τετραπόροις ἁψῖσιν ἐπ᾽ ἀργυρέῃσι βεβηκώς. κίοσι δ᾽ ἀργυρέῃσιν ἀείρεται, ὧν ἐπὶ κόρσης ἀργυρέους ἵδρυσε πόδας τετράζυγος ἁψίς. ὑψόθι θ᾽ ἁψίδων ἀνατείνεται οἷά τε κώνου εἴκελον, ἀλλ᾽ οὐ πάμπαν ὁμοίιον· οὐ γὰρ ἑλίσσει νειόθεν εὐκύκλοιο περίτροχον ἄντυγα πέζης, ἀλλά τις ὀκτάπλευρος ἔφυ βάσις, ἐκ δὲ κελεύθου εὐρυτέρης κατὰ βαιὸν ἐς ὀξυκόρυμβον ἀνέρπει, ὀκτὼ δ᾽ ἀργυρέας τανύει πλάκας· ἁρμονίης δὲ ζευγνυμένης δολιχὴ ῥάχις ἵσταται· αἱ δὲ τριγώνοις εἰδόμεναι μίσγουσι πόρους ὀκτάζυγος οἴμου εἰς ἓν ἀγειρομένους κορυφῆς σημήϊον ἄκρης·ὁππόθι καὶ κρητῆρος ὑπήραρεν εἰκόνα τέχνη χείλεά τε κρητῆρος ὑποκλασθέντα πετήλων εἶδος ἐμορφώσαντο. μέσωι δ᾽ ἐνεθήκατο χώρωι εἶδος ἐμορφώσαντο. μέσωι δ᾽ ἐνεθήκατο χώρωι ἀργύρεον στίλβοντα πόλου τύπον· ὑψόθι δ᾽ αὐτοῦ σταυρὸς ὑπερτέλλων ἀναφαίνεται ἵλαος εἴη. ἁψίδων δ᾽ ἐφύπερθεν ἕλιξ πολύκεστος ἀκάνθης πέζα διερπύζει νέατον περὶ πυθμένα κώνου. ὀρθοτενεῖς ἀκτῖνας, ἴσας εὐώδεϊ καρπῶι ὄγχνης καλλικόμοιο, διακριδὸν ὑψόθι φαίνει λαμπομένας σελάεσσιν, ὑπερτέλλουσι δὲ πέζης. ὁππόθι δ' ἀλλήλοισιν ἀρηρότα πείρατα πέζης ἁρμονίην τεύχουσιν, ἐνιδρύσαντο παγέντας ἀργυρέους κρητῆρας. ἐπὶ κρητῆρι δ' ἑκάστωι πυρσοφόρους στήσαντο, λιπαυγέα δείκελα κηροῦ, κόσμον ἀπαγγέλλοντα καὶ οὐ φάος· ἀργυρέοις γὰρ πάντοθι τορνωθέντα περιστίλβουσι μετάλλοις φαιδρὰ λεαινομένοισιν ἀπυρσεύτωι δ' ἀμαρυγῆι ἀργυρέην ἀκτῖνα καὶ οὐ φλόγα κηρὸς ἰάλλει. κίοσι δὲ χρυσέαις ἱερῆς πάγχρυσα τραπέζης νῶτα κατηρείσαντο, κατὰ χρυσέων δὲ θεμείλων ἵσταται, ἀφνειῶν δὲ λίθων ποικίλλεται αἴγλῃ.

Paulos Silentarios, poet and official of Emperor Justinian (r. CE 527–565) [1]

THIS IS HOW A SIXTH-CENTURY POET, INTELLECTUAL, AND HIGH OFFICIAL AT Emperor Justinian's court, Paulos Silentarios, elaborately described the canopy that once rose above the altar table in the sanctuary of Hagia Sophia in Constantinople. Silentarios wrote his poetic description of this impressive architectural installation in the year 562 as part of a long rhetorical praise of the famous Constantinopolitan cathedral. He presumably recited his poem before the emperor and his court and the patriarch and his clergy on the occasion of the second dedication of the Church of Hagia Sophia. The event coincided with the restoration of the massive dome of Hagia Sophia, which had collapsed four years earlier due to structural failures and earthquakes and smashed the liturgical furnishings in the sanctuary. As shown by Macrides and Magdalino, the poem subtly combined a rhetorical description of the church and its decoration with a specific historical reference to the church's restoration in the sixth century that enables the auditors to visualize the church and its furnishings.[2] Because it was originally recited as part of the ceremonial procession, the poem was meant to be experienced in movement and in the actual church space. We can imagine that when the procession reached the church sanctuary, Silentarios pointed to the sumptuously designed altar canopy made of silver. He vividly described the restored structure as a delicate four-columned installation with a pointed, octagonal, pyramidal roof. Hence, Silentarios accurately named the towering installation above the altar table πύργος, or tower. John Malalas (ca. 491–578), Silentarios' contemporary and a Byzantine orator and chronicler from Antioch, in his brief historical account of how the dome of Hagia Sophia fell and crushed the liturgical furnishing in the sanctuary, named the same installation a *ciborium* (τὸ κιβούριον).[3] These two different accounts of the same object that once stood in Hagia Sophia, the church that set the standards for Byzantine design principles, reveal that an altar canopy was an important feature of Byzantine churches, but

1 *Paulos Silentarios-a* cols. 2147–2148; *Paulos Silentarios-b* in *TLG* lines 719–753. Translation into English *Paulos Silentarios-c*, in *SD* 88 by Cyril Mango is here slightly adjusted to better respond to the original text. For the translation of this Greek poem into Italian by Fobelli and Andoloro, see also *Paulos Silentarios-d* 78–81.

2 Macrides and Magdalino (1988) 47–82.

3 Ἐν αὐτῷ δὲ τῷ χρόνῳ φιλοκαλουμένου τοῦ τρούλλου τῆς μεγάλης ἐκκλησίας, ῥήξας γὰρ ἦν εἰς φανεροὺς τόπους ἐκ τῶν γεγονότων (20) (490.) κατὰ φιλανθρωπίαν θεοῦ φόβων, αἰφνιδίως ἐργαζομένων τῶν Ἰσαύρων ἔπεσε τὸ ἀνατολικὸν μέρος τῆς προϋποστολῆς, καὶ συνέτριψε τὸ κιβούριον σὺν τῇ ἁγίᾳ τραπέζῃ. *John Malalas-a* book 18, 708B; see also *John Malalas-b* and *John Malalas-d* in *TLG*.
"In that year [558–J.B.] the dome of the Great Church was being restored, for it had cracked in several places (490) because of the shocks that had occurred through God's benevolence. As the Isaurians were working, suddenly the eastern part of the supporting dome fell and crushed the ciborium (τὸ κιβούριον), together with the holy altar." Translation by Jeffreys in *John Malalas-c* book 18, 297.

also that even contemporaries could use different terminology to denote it. Indeed, as we shall see, the seemingly simple question of what the Greek-speaking intellectual elite called canopy-like structures in their churches is actually very complex to answer. Because of the diverse terminology, arguments, and rhetorical strategies they used, a particularly difficult task is to appropriately relate the meaning of canopies from the Byzantine cultural context to our own. Starting with these reasons and expanding upon further analysis of the available evidence, in this book we will use the modern term *canopy* with its associated architectural form of a centrally planned columnar structure with a roof.[4]

Scholars frequently use the terms *ciborium, baldachin,* and *canopy* as synonyms for protective devices and markers of sacredness.[5] Of these three terms, the word *ciborium* is favored among specialists studying Christian canopies,[6] presumably because the terms *ciborium* and *baldachin* may have denoted different objects, while the terms *baldachin* and *canopy* are post-Byzantine conventions. The term *baldachin,* which was not used by the Byzantines, and the term *ciborium* are closely related.[7] *Baldachin* is a late medieval derivative from the Italian *baldocco* or Spanish *baldaquin* for the elaborately brocaded luxurious fabric imported from Baghdad that was hung as a textile canopy over an altar or doorway. It subsequently became a synonym for the freestanding canopy over an altar, tomb, or throne. Some scholars use the term *ciborium* for a fixed structure, often placed on a raised base, and the term *baldachin,* or *baldacchino,* for a portable, temporary structure. Still, the most famous and major example, that of the Baldacchino at St. Peter's in Rome built by Gianlorenzo Bernini and others, is a fixed, monumental structure, prompting other scholars to maintain that *ciborium* and *baldachin* are not easily distinguishable and to continue to use both terms interchangeably. Of these three words—ciborium, baldachin, and canopy—which we continue to use today, the Greek-speaking Byzantines only knew the word τὸ κιβώριον (*to kibōrion, to kivōrion*), and its linguistic variants—ὁ κιβώριος (*o kibōrios, o kivōrios*) and τὸ κιβούριον (*to kibourion, to kivourion*)—all related to their Latin counterpart *ciborium.* Hence, scholars examining Byzantine examples often use the term *ciborium,* assuming that it is the original term pervasively used by the Byzantines themselves.[8]

---

[4] Of various definitions for "canopy" in modern dictionaries, I find most appropriate the one offered by J. S. Curl, according to whom a canopy is a "1. Roof-like ornamented hood surmounting an altar, doorway, font, niche, pulpit . . . stall, statue, tabernacle, throne, tomb, window, aperture, etc., supported on brackets, colonnettes, etc., or suspended. 2. *Canopy of honour, ceele, ceilure, celure, cellure,* or *seele,* is a richly coloured, often gilded, and panelled ceiling above an altar, chancel, chantry-chapel, mortuary-chapel, etc. 3. *Town canopy* is a structure resembling an arcaded gabled opening . . ., like a model building, set on top of a niche or protecting a statue: the motif was adapted in funerary architecture . . ., on tomb-chests over the heads of effigies, and was later shown in incised slabs and funerary brasses. A canopy over an altar is usually called *baldacchino* or *ciborium.*" *DALA,* s.v. *canopy.*

[5] *DALA,* s.v. *canopy.* For canopies as symbols of sacred space, see Ćurčić (1991) 251–261; Underwood (1950) 43–138.

[6] See, for example, *DArt* vol. 7, s.v. *ciborium* (ii), esp. 301; *EAM* vol. 4, s.v. *ciborio; ODB* vol. 1, 462, s.v. *ciborium; New Catholic Encyclopedia* vol. 3, s.v. *ciborium*; Mirković (1995) 103; Barnea (1940) ch. 7; *Leksikon ikonografije* 180–181; *ODA,* s.v. *ciborium; ODE,* s.v. *ciborium.*

[7] *ODA,* s.v. *ciborium.* On the meaning of *baldachin,* see, for example, *Leksikon ikonografije* 180–181; *Dictionary of the Liturgy* 50–51; *New Dictionary of the Liturgy* 58–59.

[8] When interpreting some archeological remains from the Middle Byzantine church in Amorium, Turkey, C. S. Lightfoot and E. A. Ivison used the term "ciborium-like canopy," as if reflecting the problematic terminology. See Lightfoot and Ivison (1997) 291–300, esp. 296. Bakirtzis (2002) 175–192 uses the terms *ciborium* and *baldachin* as supposedly denoting two distinct objects, without providing explicit definitions of either. Talbot (1993) 243–261, esp. 247, uses the terms *baldachin* and *altar canopy* as synonyms. However,

A comparative analysis of more than a hundred surviving texts that provide literary evidence of canopies from Byzantine sources (Tables 1, 2, and 3) reveals that the word κιβώριον denoted various entities, not only canopies, while other, overlooked words may have referred to canopies in the Byzantine tradition, as our opening example of the description of the altar canopy from Hagia Sophia demonstrates. The vocalization of these diverse terms and their conflation may be the result of a particular rhetorical strategy used by the Byzantines to convey the meaning and the form of these structures. The role of the vocalized messages behind the objects is important because, not only professional orators, but also other educated Byzantines habitually pronounced aloud written words, and especially inscriptions on objects, which in turn vocalized their message to the beholder.[9] To respond to the Christian meanings, often the Byzantines expanded upon the ancient Greek sophistic and epideictic (ceremonial) rhetoric and combined it with Biblical references.[10] In ancient sophistic rhetoric, which the educated Byzantines continued to practice, authors were encouraged to engage in original compositions and arguments. Following the examples of ancient sophists, such as Hermogenes (fifth century BCE) and Gorgias (fourth century BCE) in particular, who emphasized the power of content, description, and sound in devising mnemonics so that certain themes could be remembered, and who emphasized the power of emotional presentations and the belief that obscurity can be a virtue since the ultimate truth cannot be known rationally, the Byzantines developed their own rhetorical tradition. They often conflated various sources from Biblical mnemonic references and sophistic figures of speech, which additionally combined with their belief that religious thoughts should not be profaned; these thoughts often remain obscured, highlighting that the divine wisdom can be apprehended, but not rationally understood. Quite often the meaning of certain, often conflating, terms related to the church would be complex and multilayered, and the power of the emotional presentation and the sound of rhetorical presentations were aimed at stirring the audience's will to believe. Within such a context, various conflating processes occurring in references to canopies and canopy-like objects in the Byzantine tradition point to the complexities and contradictions in the naming of and the related meaning and form of canopies. Though used the least in Byzantine scholarship, as we shall further see, the modern term *canopy* is the most applicable for our study of these architectural installations.[11]

---

non–English-speaking scholars and significantly, above all, Greek-speaking scholars give equal treatment to terms other than *ciborium* or *kivōrion* when referring to canopies. For example, Prokopios (1981) 125–128 uses terms *kiborion, ouraniskos, tholos, koubouklion,* and *katapetasma* as synonyms; and Antourakēs (1994) ch. 3 uses the terms *kiborio* and *koubuklion*.

[9] Talbot (1999) 75–90; Papalexandrou (2001) 259–283.

[10] Kennedy (1983) 183–190; Kennedy (1999) 52–132; 265–290. I thank Kevin Kalish for calling my attention to the specifics of Byzantine rhetoric relevant for this research.

[11] Hjort (1979) 199–289 quite appropriately employed the term "canopy" when naming the framing of the *proskynetaria* icons from the Chora Monastery in Constantinople, now Istanbul. M. T. Smith, in her doctoral thesis (1968) 8, 336–345, and subsequent articles (1970) 149–175 and (1974) 379–414, interchangeably used *a canopy* and *a ciborium* to describe essentially the same objects. Eventually she also recognized that *canopy* is a more fitting term. She concluded that, by the sixth century, there was no identifying term for a Christian canopy, but that from the mid-sixth century onwards, the term *ciborium* both in Latin and Greek had been widely accepted as a reference to various structures, not only altar canopies. Though I essentially agree that the term "canopy" is more appropriate than *ciborium,* Smith's conclusion on the sixth-century "standardization" of the term *ciborium* in the Christian world needs to be reassessed.

THE TERM *CIBORIUM*: Κιβώριον (*KIBŌRION, KIVŌRION*)

Modern dictionaries often define the Greek word τὸ κιβώριον as the etymological root of *ciborium* and with the meaning of *canopy*.[12] My research shows that the Byzantine Greeks used the word κιβώριον (*kiborion, ciborium*) less often than we previously thought and in contexts outside of Christian ecclesiastical architecture. Remarkably, the word τὸ κιβώριον does not appear in the Holy Scriptures, neither in the Septuagint nor in the Greek New Testament.[13] The word does not appear in most widely used and translated medieval Greek dictionaries, like the major tenth-century Souda lexicon.[14] Professional books on architecture, like Byzantine architectural treatises and textbooks comparable to Vitruvius', have not survived, yet some surviving texts such as the *Collection* by Pappos of Alexandria (fourth century) confirm that both practical and liberal arts architectural education was related to the ancient Greco-Roman traditions.[15] It is critical to note that even if canopies were not discussed in Byzantine texts from an architectural point of view, vaulted Byzantine structures provide material evidence that they were part of the overarching principles of architectural design during this time. Similarly, Vitruvius did not make any unequivocal reference to a ciborium or any other explicitly canopy-like structure, despite the fact that canopied structures did exist in ancient pagan architecture.

Textual accounts that employ Greek versions for the word *ciborium* are various, including poems and texts on magic, teaching resources such as grammars and lexicons, and hagiographies and highly complex theological writings, to name but a few (Tables 1 and 2). The writers of these texts were not primarily concerned with material objects, and the ciborium denoted various entities, some indefinable. The earliest known uses of the term come from pre-Christian antiquarian, poetical, and medical treatises. Of the fifty-three texts I analyzed, in twenty-two the word *kiborion* refers to κολοκασία (*colocasia*), a kind of Egyptian beans (Table 2).

The term κιβώριον also stood for a variety of manmade objects, such as a chalice, a dome, a reliquary shrine, or a canopy, in which case it could refer to the canopy over the altar, or over the ambo, or to the covering over the royal throne. Yet, the word frequently shows several layers of meaning. For example, by the early tenth century, Byzantine emperor Constantine VII Porphyrogenitos (r. 913–959) in his *Book of the Ceremonies*, which consisted of several contemporaneous and older texts, used the word κιβώριον to describe a canopied structure on the stepped porphyry platform erected over the throne of the emperor in the Consistory of the royal palace in Constantinople.[16] However, terms other than κιβώριον were used for this same canopied structure from the Consistory throughout this collection of various

---

[12] For example, *EAM* vol. 4, s.v. *ciborio; ODB* vol. 1, s.v. *ciborium; Leksikon ikonografije* 180–181; *ODE*, s.v. *ciborium*.

[13] See *Living Bible*, which has Hebrew, Greek, and Russian versions of the Holy Scriptures. For the Septuagint versions see *TLG* and *Lexicon of the Septuagint*.

[14] The *Souda lexicon* annotates terms Κίβος, κιβώτιον, and Κιβωτός.

[15] I have consulted the English editions *Vitruvius-a* and *Vitruvius-b*. Vitruvius' silence on canopies does not suggest the absence of canopies in ancient Roman tradition. Vitruvius speaks of domes and vaulted ceilings, some of which may have belonged to canopy-like structures. For an overview on canopies in Greco-Roman tradition, see Lehmann (1945) 1–27. On Byzantine sources for architectural practices, see Downey (1948a) 197–200; Downey (1948b) 99–118; Meek (1952) 216–220; Cutler (1966b) 27–35; Ousterhout (2008); Schibille (2009) 360–379.

[16] *De Ceremoniis-a PG* 112, col. 16. See also critical editions, *De Ceremoniis-b* and translation in French *De Ceremoniis-c*. For the translation in English by Moffatt and Tall, see *De Ceremoniis-d* vol. 1: 98, 163, 181, 232, 234, 290, 291, 406. (Table 1, T.71, this volume.)

texts, such as βῆλον (*velon*, curtain) and καμελαυκίον (*kamelauhion*, making reference to a textile installation; this term was also used for a headgear of the church prelates). A reference to the curtains and (holy) veil were also included in the explanations of the throne in the context of its use for ceremonies for great religious feasts such as Easter, thus suggesting that the throne canopy might have expressed the idea that the emperor himself is a ruler of God's kingdom on earth, rather than that the throne canopy itself reflected the original meaning and ancient use of the word in an exclusively imperial context.[17] The prolonged use of the word κιβώριον for Egyptian beans, *aedicula*-shape graves,[18] or some other entities now lost and indiscernible from textual accounts confirms two important facts (Table 2). First, the term with its variant meanings had remained in use until the fall of the Byzantine Empire in the fifteenth century; and second, its meaning might have been different depending on the type of discourse or specific time-period in which it was used.

The writers who employed the word κιβώριον usually provided an extended explanation of what a ciborium is. Potentially, the word was strange to the Byzantines as well, further implying that the word may not be of Greek origin.[19] The etymology of the Greek words for *ciborium* is obscure, both in relation to a specific object and its form, as well as to the idea that the object conveyed. The older transliteration of the Greek word for *ciborium*—τὸ κιβώριον, ο κιβώριος, is the noun τὸ κιβούριον.[20] Following the early Christian and Byzantine rhetorical practice of the importance of sound in delivering a message, when pronounced aloud, the Greek nouns ὁ κιβ (*kib, kiv*) and τὸ κιβωτός (*kibōtos, kivōtos*) on one hand, and the nouns τό ὠρίον, τό ὅριον (*orion*) or ὁ οὐράνος(*ouranos*) and the adjective οὐράνιος (*ouranios*) on the other, share the sound and the new meaning of the κιβούριον (*kibourion, kivourion*). The famous lexical encyclopedia the *Etymologicum Gudianum*, compiled in southern Italy in the tenth century and containing references and citations from now-lost ancient Greek texts, as well as church theologians such as St. Basil the Great, Bishop of Caesarea; Sophronios, Patriarch of Jerusalem; or Germanos, Patriarch of Constantinople in the fourth, sixth, and eighth centuries, respectively, used these terms in their commentaries to explain the word *ciborium*.[21] Those early church leaders were trained in various educational centers of the Classical and late antique world, and their explanation of ciboria may result from a conflation of various pre-Christian sources—Hellenistic pagan and Jewish, above all. Before the sixth century, when major Byzantine cultural concepts were formulated, various centers of thought defined the theological discourse on questions

---

[17] Scholars have searched for a possible explanation of the canopy structure and its function in the Christian church in imperial iconography. The repeated tent-like structures and canopies in the second and fourth Styles of Pompeian wall painting reveal these objects as important features of palace ceremonies and palace architecture of the Hellenistic East. Connected with the *epiphany* and *adventus*, they were later adopted in all parts of the Roman Empire. More in Smith, B. E. (1956) 121–125; *RACr* vol. 1; Lehmann (1945) 1–27.

The important juxtaposition of imperial and sacred ideas and a reassessment of previous scholarship on imperial canopies in the Christian tradition was first offered by Smith, M. T. (1968) 346.

[18] Georgios Kodinos (d. ca. 1453), a reputed author of *De Officiis*, described an *aedicula*-shaped grave monument in Constantinople. See Braun (1924) vol. 2, 192.

[19] I concur with scholars like R. Eisler, J. J. Reiske, and M. T. Smith, who concluded that the word is potentially not of Greek origin, but instead that it was based on Near Eastern and Hebrew terminology transcribed into Greek and then into Latin. Eisler (1966) 193–197; J. J. Reiske in *De Ceremoniis-b, Commentarium on De Ceremoniis-a PG* 112, col. 317, n. 29; Braun (1924) vol. 2, 193; Smith, M. T. (1968) 5.

[20] *Liddell* 578; *Lampe* 753, 1399.

[21] Four of the fifty-three Greek sources on *ciboria* I consulted provide an extended explanation: St. Basil the Great, Sophronios, Germanos, *Etymologicum Gudianum* (Tables 1, 2, and 4, T.22, T.32, T.54, T.79, this volume).

of the church, from which, by extension, we can form an idea about an actual church building and its furnishing. Those theologians, who wrote before the sixth century, offered various and vague references to a ciborium.

• • •

Theologians trained in the Alexandrian tradition understood words related to *ciborium* in a metaphysical and conceptual sense, interpreting the Holy Scriptures through their classical education. The term τὸ κιβούριον was related to the Greek noun ὁ οὐράνος (*ouranos*) and the eschatological descent from heaven to earth, the realm between heaven and earth, a vault or firmament of heaven. The opening lines of the first book of the Holy Scriptures of both Judaism and Christianity, the *First Book of Moses,* also called *Genesis,* provide a reference to the firmament as a divider between the Heaven and the Earth (Gen. 1:6ff).[22] The firmament in the Hebrew Bible was denoted by the term for a dome.[23]

Similarly, the ancient Greeks conceived οὐράνος as a vault or firmament of heaven, the sky—and hence, in formal geometric terms, as a concave hemisphere. Οὐράνος was usually understood as a dome made of solid metal, which rested on the verge of the earth, borne by the pillars of Atlas.[24] The diminutive of οὐράνος, οὐρανίσκος, with the cosmological meaning of "little heaven or sky," simultaneously signified a vaulted ceiling, especially the top of a curtained tent or a canopy.[25] The ancient Greeks used ceremonial carpets embroidered with stars and representing the "heavenly carpet," or "heavenly canopy," which they called "little heaven," οὐρανίσκος.[26] The shape of the cloth for this kind of temporary canopy was rectangular, conforming to the four-poled sub-structure. According to Christian interpretation, these curtained canopies could have been compared with the curtain-like heavens, "who covered thyself with light as with a garment: who stretched out the heavens like a curtain," as described in Psalm 104:2. That is why, in the fourth century, an Archbishop of Constantinople, Gregory of Nazianzos, who also belonged to the Alexandrian school of thought, used in his *De vita Mosis* (Table 1, T.17) yet another term when speaking of the heavenly firmament—καταπετάσματα (curtains) (Tables 1 and 3).

Church fathers understood that οὐράνος is an abode of the divine, though not containing God.[27] Clement of Alexandria (150–ca. 215) connected the noun ὁ οὐράνος and the adjective οὐράνιος, which means *eternal, heavenly, divine,* or *spiritual* (i.e., everything that is opposite from the earthly, material realm) with *manna* as heavenly bread and as the Body of Christ.[28] Thus, Clement of Alexandria provided an early liturgical reference to the Eucharist, which was performed at the altar table, presumably under a canopy, symbolizing the heavens and sacred space.

The theologians who were trained in the Antiochene school of exegesis used more literal and typological explanations in their texts than those trained in the Alexandrian

---

[22] Gen. 1:6ff: *And God said, Let there be a firmament in the midst of the waters, and let it divide the waters from the waters. . . .*

[23] On the translation of the Hebrew term for "a dome" as "the firmament" in the *Latin Vulgate,* see Pelikan (2000) 8.

[24] *Liddell* 578; *Lampe* 753, 1399. This story about Atlas holding up the sky was also known to the Byzantines. See, for example, *Joannes Malalas-c* 73, translation according to Jeffreys.

[25] *Liddell* 578.

[26] In Hellenistic Greece, the use of temporary tents and canopy structures for festivals is confirmed in *Euripides, Ion* 1121f, esp. 1129. See more on the subject in Lehmann (1945) 1–27, esp. 11.

[27] *Lampe* 978–979.

[28] *Clement of Alexandria, Stromata* 2 (2. II 139.12; *PG* 8, 985A); *Clement of Alexandria, Excerpta ex Theodoto* 13 (III.II; M.9.664B), according to *Lampe* 977.

school. They used the term κιβώριον in association with different objects, often explained as chest- and box-like. In the late fourth century, St. John Chrysostom (349–407), a priest from Antioch and later a patriarch in Constantinople, described some small objects (μικρά κιβώρια; small ciboria) dedicated to the goddess Diana at Ephesus.[29] He conflated stories about Diana and Danae, and by analogy associated these objects with Noah's ark, which symbolized the ultimate salvation rather than death (Table 1, T.21). Namely, the scriptural reference mentions silver shrines for Diana, a local trade in Ephesus: *For a certain man named Demetrius, a silversmith, which made silver shrines* [ναούς] *for Diana, brought no small gain unto the craftsmen* (Acts 19:24). The word ναός (naos) was also used for the temple at Jerusalem, for the sacred edifice or sanctuary itself, consisting of the holy place and the Holy of Holies. In classical Greek, the word stood for the sanctuary or cell of the temple. The Byzantines used the term for any shrine, and even for the Virgin, as the most sacred vessel, which God had chosen to be his Mother.[30] The familiar story of Danae as a mortal female who gave birth to a son, Perseus, after Zeus came down to her in a shower of gold, was therefore appropriated for Christian use and conflated with the story about Diana. When the gods discovered Danae and her son, they were brought to the altar of Zeus, enclosed in a chest, and cast into the sea. The chest, representing a floating coffin, was ultimately saved in a fishing net on the island of Seriphos. Besides a striking resemblance to Christ's Nativity according to the flesh, early Christians substituted the figures of Danae and Perseus with the figure of Noah and associated the chest with the Ark, which ensured, not death, but survival through water. The protective function of the chest-like, floating object known as κιβώριον was also related to the term *kiborion* used by ancient Egyptians for the floating seed-pod of the Egyptian water lily.

Because the small objects (μικρά κιβώρια; small ciboria) St. John Chrysostom mentions have not survived, we cannot know whether St. John Chrysostom was referring to actual objects or whether he was reinterpreting the references from the classical tradition and the Scriptures and conflated them to explain their Christian meaning. Prevailing opinion today is that St. John Chrysostom wrote of the small *kiboria,* which were votive objects in the shape of small silver *aediculae,* though references to silver cups and miniature shrines have also been proposed.[31] Some ancient intellectuals and early antiquarians such as Athenaeus of Naucratis from Egypt (second–third centuries), confirm that κιβώρια, presumably cup-like objects, did exist in pagan temples (Table 1, T.15). In his *The deipnosophists; or, Banquet of the learned of Athenæus,* a cup called κιβώριον was used in the temple of Athena on the Greek island Sikion.[32] Despite having a shape similar to an exquisitely made drinking cup, this κιβώριον was some kind of a religious or devotional object, since the person who drank from it defiled the cup, according to Athanaeus. However, St. John Chrysostom, being primarily concerned with theological discourse rather than the material world, may have been referring to shrines from the texts.[33] More important for our investigation is that Chrysostom's opinion on *kiboria* entered the *Catenae,* the Biblical commentaries made up from textual excerpts by early theologians (Table 1, T.30) after the fifth century, and was

[29] *John Chrysostom, In Genesim. Hom.* 42 (9.318B). *DArt* vol. 7, s.v. *ciborium* (i), esp. 299.

[30] See, for example, *Acts of the Third Ecumenical Council in Seven Councils* IV, 580E, 1253A/C, 1256B; *Epiphanius* 488CD, 492B/D, 496D; *Andrew of Crete* 868C, 1316AB. All references according to Evangelatou (2002) 189, n. 706.

[31] See, for example, *DArt* vol. 7, s.v. *ciborium* (ii); *EAM* vol. 4, s.v. *ciborio*.

[32] Pausanias also gives an account about this now-lost lost temple of Athena, in front of which the Sikion king Epopeos was buried. *Athenaeus-b* 121–210.

[33] He uses the same sentence from the Septuagint.

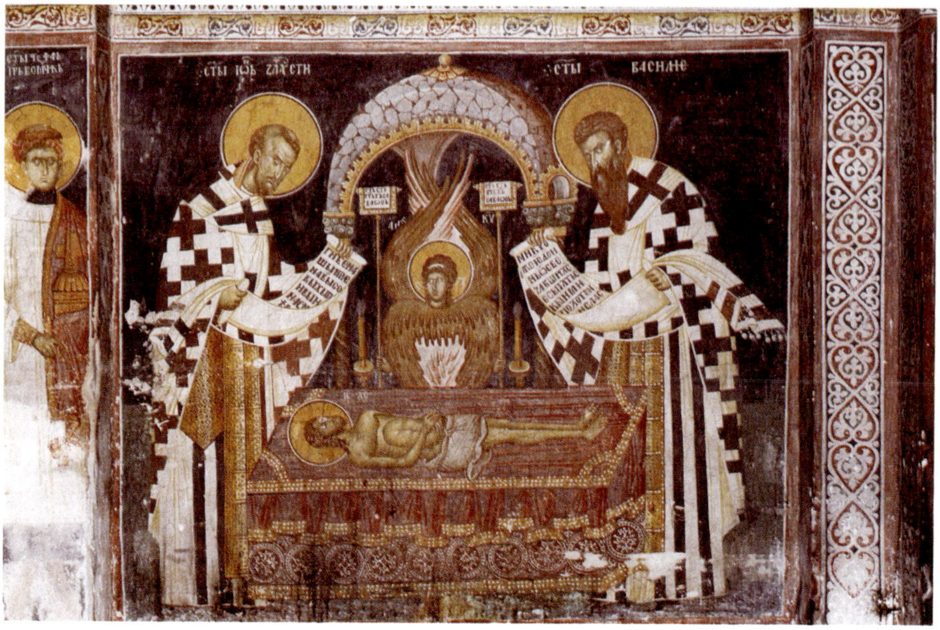

FIGURE 1.1 *Service of the Hierarchs—St. John Chrysostom (inscribed as such in Old Church Slavonic, left) and St. Basil the Great (inscribed as such in Old Church Slavonic, right) service to Christ, Lamb of God (inscribed as such in Greek, center), fresco, Church of Christ's Ascension, narthex, east wall, Monastery Dečani, ca. 1335–1348/1355.* PHOTO IVAN DRPIĆ

disseminated throughout the Christian world, thus becoming a critical reference for canopies (Table 4.3).[34]

St. Basil the Great (329–379) was, with St. John Chrysostom, one of the most important contributors to the development of Byzantine theology and liturgy. Trained in Caesarea, Constantinople, and Athens, St. Basil used the term κιβώριον in reference to Christ and to the Ark of the Covenant (Fig. 1.1).[35] In his *Historia Mystagogica,* St. Basil the Great wrote (Table 1, T.22):

> τὸ κιβούριόν ἐστι ἀντὶ τοῦ τόπου ἔνθα ἐσταυρώθη ὁ Χριστός· ἐγγὺς γὰρ ἦν ἡ τόπος καὶ ὑπόβαθρος ὅπου ἐτάφη . . . ἔστι δέ καὶ κατὰ τὴν κιβωτὸν τῆς διαθήκης κυρίου ἐν ᾗ λέγεται ἅγια ἁγίων . . . ἐν ᾗ προσέταξεν ὁ θεὸς γενέσθαι δύο χερουβὶμ . . . τὸ γὰρ κιβ ἐστὶ κιβωτός, τὸ δὲ οὖριν . . . φῶς κυρίου
>
> The ciborium is here a place where Christ was crucified; for the place where He was buried was nearby and raised on a base . . . It is related to the ark of the covenant of the Lord, which is called the Holy of Holies . . . Next to it God commanded two cherubim . . . for κιβ is the ark, and οὖριν . . . light of the Lord. (trans. J.B.)

[34] Referring to "mikra kiboria" as small *aediculae* spread relatively early in the West via Constantinople. In 498, there is a reference from the library of Byzantine emperor Athanasios I that the text was translated for Theodoric in Rome (Table 1, T.31).

[35] *Basil the Great, H.myst. 4.* According to *Lampe* 753.

The metaphorical and symbolic linguistic interpretation of the Scriptures here denoted a *ciborium* in a sense of the words κιβ, κιβωτός, meaning *tabernacle* or *ark* (cf. Ex. 25:10),[36] and ώριον, meaning the *effulgence*, or Light of God. St. Basil's interpretation resembles St. John Chrysostom's, further implying that the two words referring to *ark* and *light* could have had an origin in the Aramaic text of the Bible and that the theologians may have combined them to produce a new, Christian meaning.[37] Moreover, St. Basil the Great related *ciborium* to the Hebrew term *keber, geber*, Syrian *ke bôrâ*, and Greek ἡ κιβωτός, which all signify a tomb, grave, or chest.[38]

Sophronius (ca. 560–638), the Melkite Patriarch of Jerusalem, also provided a highly symbolic explanation for a ciborium. Like St. John Chrysostom speaking of the *kiboria* for Diana, Sophronius connected *ciborium* to Noah's ark (Table 1, T.32): Ὁ κιβώριός στιν εἰς τύπον τῆς κιβωτοῦ τοῦ Νῶε τὸ μὲν κιβ κιβωτός τὸ δὲ ὥριον τουτέστι διάταξις αὐτοῦ. *The ciborium imitates the ark of Noah; on one hand is κιβ, the ark, on the other hand is όριον (light) [that] commands to itself* (trans. J.B.). The Ark from Sophronius' writings can be visualized in various ways, though he suggests the Ark with four columns: . . . Ὁ κιβώριός ἐστιν εἰς τύπον τῆς κιβωτοῦ ˙ τὰ δέ παρακιόνα κατὰ μίμησιν τῶν τεσσάρων ζώων τῶν ὀφθέντων τῷ προφήτῃ. *The ciborium is one type of ark/chest. Its columns imitate four lives prophetically foreseen* (trans. J.B.);[39] where the columns are related to the four Evangelists, the authors of the New Testament Gospels. Sophronius' *ciborium*, hence, can be understood as a chest on four legs, as pagans, Jews, and early Christians before the sixth century depicted Danae's coffin and Noah's Ark.[40] In Greco-Roman art, Danae's chest was usually represented as a cubic, lidded box, sometimes with four feet, as on the Attic kalyx-krater by the Triptolemus Painter (ca. 480 BCE), now kept in St. Petersburg's Hermitage, or on a wall painting from Pompeii (79 CE).[41] The emphases on the feet, and, in some examples, the absence of water do not follow the literal narrative of Genesis and have not yet been properly explained. Following the text from the Old Testament, the Ark of Noah is often understood as a kind of huge houseboat. However, on the bronze Apamea-Kobotos coins struck under the emperors Septimus Severus (193–211), Macrinus (217–219), and Philip the Arabian (244–249), the Ark is represented not as a boat but as an open box.[42] The Ark is inscribed in Greek as ΝΩΕ and is shown with a raven perched on it and a dove carrying an olive branch above it. It is considered the earliest Jewish visual representation of Noah and the Ark. The fourth-century wall paintings from the catacomb of Ss. Peter and Marcellinus in Rome also depict Noah in the box-like ark.[43] In the illustrated sixth century *Christian Topography* by the merchant, traveler, and later Christian monk Cosmas Indicopleustes,

[36] Ex. 25:10: *And they shall make an ark of shittim wood: two cubits and a half shall be the length thereof, and a cubit and a half the breadth thereof, and a cubit and a half the height thereof.*

[37] Smith, M. T. (1968) 315, has already shown that, according to notes of a certain Andreas Gallamdi, which Migne published, the Chaldean words כיב *cub*, signifying ark, and ארץ *ura*, for light, were related to Biblical Aramaic.

[38] According to Smith, M. T. (1968) 344. Museums, like the Walters Art Museum, occasionally have on display exquisitely carved wooden objects or their fragments that come from monastic communities and that are also labeled *kibotia*. Though post-Byzantine, these chests, with figural carving depicting New Testament themes in a traditional Byzantine manner, presumably point to their Byzantine sources.

[39] *Sophronius, PG* 87, 3984. I am thankful to Loukas Karentzos for proofreading the translation for me.

[40] Murray (1981) 98–111.

[41] Murray (1981).

[42] Grabar (1951) 9–14; Murray (1981); Revel-Neher (1995) 405–414.

[43] Josi (1924) 108ff., figs. 56–56; Wilpert (1900) 85–97, esp. 93; Murray (1981).

the Ark of Noah, inscribed as κιβωτός, is depicted as a prismatic shrine with a gabled roof. Cosmas, who provided a theoretical and geographical model for the Christian universe, related the Ark of Noah to the Ark of the Covenant of Exodus, even though its precise shape cannot be determined from the text and probably was constructed on the visual model of existing ritual objects.[44]

Interpreting the narrative of the Old Testament as a typological prefigurement of the New Testament, St. John of Damascus (676–749) wrote about Noah's ark as a wooden chest that prefigured Christ as the chest of Life (cf. Gen. 6:14–22; 2 Moses 25:10–20; 37:1–9) (Table 5.1). Following this line of thought whereby the *ciborium* is related to the Ark, later Byzantine chroniclers, like Constantine Manasses (ca. 1130–c. 1187), continued to use the Ark of Noah (cf. Gen. 6:14–22) and the Ark of the Covenant (cf. 2 Moses 25:10–20; 37:1–9) as their prime examples to provide a way for the Byzantines to understand their allegorical significance for Christological themes.[45] In that context, a canopy-like architectural structure above chest-like objects remained an essential microcosmic symbol.

Byzantine theologians and scholars who wrote about ciboria may have considered other *kibotia*, presumably box-like containers for saintly relics, as a means for salvation. Such *kibotia* called to mind canopy-like objects and shrine installations in churches. The term *ark* (*kib, kibot*) was used in the Old Testament narrative for the receptacle of the remains of Joseph, thus suggesting its meaning for the container, possibly chest-like, of bodily remains: *So Joseph died, being an hundred and ten years old: and they embalmed him, and he was put in a coffin* (ark) *in Egypt* (Gen. 50:26). Byzantine hagiographers have called saintly shrines *kiboria* since the fifth century (Table 4.5). The words *kibotion* and its Slavic counterparts—*kibot* and *kivot*, which were both used for saintly shrines, whether they were in the form of a canopy or simply burial chests—were used throughout the Byzantine period (Table 3).[46] The same terms were used to denote canopies above specially venerated icons. The medieval Rus also called the frames of the holy icons themselves, which were depicted in the recessed inner space of a wooden panel, *kovcheg*, meaning "ark" or "chest" and pointing to the meaning and translation of the Greek term *kibotion* as an architectural frame for sacred space. In the case of two-dimensional icon paintings, the *kovcheg* itself lost its three-dimensionality, remaining a visible, almost two-dimensional form for framing the otherwise invisible and impalpable sacred. Similar to rhetorical devices used by the Byzantines, where the term *kiborion* for canopy carried multiple meanings and was meant to convey more to the audience than the term's basic definition,[47] the *kovcheg* (*kibotion*) of the icon, as shown by Oleg Tarasov, became both in physical and conceptual terms a "vehicle for delivering the visual image" and the "threshold for its perception."[48] Such multiple connections between *kiborion* (ciborium, canopy) and *kibotion* (chest) are also confirmed by the ninth-century writings of Photios I, Patriarch of Constantinople, one of the most influential and most educated Byzantine intellectuals and a major figure in the conversion of the Slavs into Byzantine Christianity (Table 1, T.62). Yet conflations of various terms and concepts in explaining the meaning of *kiborion* (ciborium), which were devised in Alexandria, Antioch, and Jerusalem at least by the sixth century, only merged in Constantinople and from there were spread throughout the Byzantine realm (Table 4.6).

---

[44] Mouriki (1970) 98; Gutmann (1989); Kominko (2013) 141–142.

[45] *Constantinus Manasses, PG* 127, col 235. (Table 5, T.2).

[46] Voronin (1961) vol. 1, 256.

[47] For rhetorical principles and the use of symbols and allusions see Kennedy (1983) 285–286.

[48] Tarasov (2011) 20–36, citation on p. 20.

CIBORIUM AS AN ALTAR CANOPY

The use of *ciborium* to denote an altar canopy dates only from the sixth century, with a definite explanation that the word κιβούριον is a canopy-like structure above the altar table. When John Malalas described the altar ciborium in Hagia Sophia in his chronicle, he also mentioned that when the Avars and the Slavs attacked Byzantine territories in Thrace in 558–559, Emperor Justinian ordered his officials to bring to Constantinople all "silver ciboria and silver altar tables that were outside the city,"[49] confirming that other churches had similar costly canopied installations over altar tables. At approximately the same time, Gregory the Great (540–604) used the word *cyburium* to describe a Christian canopy, while Gregory of Tours (538/9–594) wrote about the canopy over St. Peter's tomb in Rome as the *ciborium sepulcri.*[50]

During the time of Germanos, Patriarch of Constantinople (715–730, d. 733), various theological thoughts were combined to explain altar canopies because of the need for a unified liturgy.[51] The exchange of ideas on ciboria among theologians, not only from Constantinople, but also from Alexandria, Antioch, Jerusalem, and Rome, is still far from being fully understood, though there is convincing evidence of contact amongst them (Table 4).[52] Germanos followed the definition of *kiborion* by St. Basil, who explained it as a church furnishing standing for the place of Christ's crucifixion, burial, and resurrection. In his *Ecclesiastical History and Mystical Contemplation,* Germanos wrote (Table 1, T.58):

> Τὸ κιβώριόν ἐστι ἀντι τοῦ τόπου ἔνθα ἐσταυρώθη ὁ Χριστός ἐγγὺς γὰρ ἦν ὁ τόπος καὶ ὑπόβαθρος ὅπου ἐτζάη . . . ἀλλά διά τὸ ἐν συντομίᾳ ἐκφέρεσται, τὴν σταύρωσιν τὴν ταφὴν καὶ τὴν ἀνάστασιν τοῦ Χριστοῦ εν τῇ ᾿Εκκλησία τέτακται.
>
> Ἔστι δὲ καὶ κατὰ τὴν κιβωτὸν τῆς διαθήκης Κυρίου, ἐν ᾗ λέγεται Ἅγια Ἁγίων καὶ ἁγίασμα αὐτου ἐν ᾗ προσέταξεν ὁ Θεὸς γενέσθαι δύο χερουβὶμ ἑκατέρωθεν τορευτά τὸ γὰρ ΚΙΒ ἐστὶ κιβωτός, τὸ δὲ ΟΥΡΙΝ φωτισμὸς Θεοῦ, ἤ φῶς Θεοῦ.[53]
>
> The ciborium represents here the place where Christ was crucified; for the place where He was buried was nearby and raised on a base. It is placed in the church to represent the crucifixion, burial, and resurrection of Christ.
>
> It similarly corresponds to the Ark of the Covenant of the Lord, which is called the Holy of Holies and His holy place. Next to it God commanded that two Cherubim of hammered work be placed on either side (cf. Ex. 25:18)—for KIB is the ark, and OURIN is the effulgence, or the light, of God. (trans. J.B., according to J. Meyendorff)

Germanos' definition shows that the ciborium was conceived as both a shrine for the divine tomb, which alone offers the promise of resurrected life, and in its Old Testament context, as the Ark of the Covenant, which was a container of divine law. Such a conceptualized ciborium in the church sanctuary represented the place of divine mystery. The formal pattern, which can be deduced from Germanos' description of the ciborium as the place of Christ's death and resurrection and from the Old Testament description of the Ark of the Covenant—where God makes himself known—suggests an installation that consisted of a chest made of gold and a monolithic canopy above it formed from the outstretched

---

[49] *John Malalas-a* book 18, 708B; translation according to Jeffreys in *John Malalas-c* book 18, 297.

[50] Smith, M. T. (1968) 344.

[51] *Germanos-b* 23–52.

[52] Taft (2006) 27–52.

[53] *Germanos-a* 5; translation according to Meyendorff, *Germanos-b* 59.

wings of the cherubim covering the Ark (cf. Ex. 25:18–22).[54] The symbolic aspects of each individual object suggest a reason for which the ciborium was also made as a light-emitting, or rather light-reflecting, object, thus, the choice of silver as the material for some altar canopies, including the example of the altar canopy in Hagia Sophia and other contemporaneous Byzantine churches as described by Silentarios and Malalas in the sixth century. The great significance of Germanos' explanation lies in his quasi-official explanation of the Byzantine liturgy. Germanos' text was reproduced in at least fifty manuscripts dated between the ninth and fifteenth centuries, confirming that it was widely distributed throughout the Byzantine world.[55] Moreover, fragments of his text entered, not only other theological texts, but also teaching material like grammars, as exemplified by the tenth-century *Etymologicum Gudianum* (Table 4.4).

Germanos' explanation of the altar canopy additionally illustrates how most Byzantines understood liturgical objects at least until the fourteenth century, when a theologian, Nicholas Cabasilas (1319/23–1392), challenged some of Germanos' explanations because of the absence of the explicit emphasis on the reception of holy communion.[56] Namely, *ciborium* can be connected with the container of the holy Hosts. The relationship between these two different church objects is highly complex. In the Byzantine tradition, an altar canopy and a Eucharist chalice are not related linguistically, as modern dictionaries maintain.[57] Nevertheless, the Byzantines related the two objects by their conceptual meaning and by association of the actual physical place they occupied in the sanctuary of a Byzantine church. Moreover, some objects that we today surmise may have served as receptacles for the holy Hosts were shaped as architectural structures, suggesting that, through their shared conceptual design, the shared conceptual meanings and the location of the receptacles and altar canopies were merged.

After the sixteenth century, the meaning of *ciborium* as "canopy" was almost lost, since *ciborium* has been most often used as an anachronistic term for the *pyxis* (πύξις), originally a boxwood receptacle and, by extension, a box in which the Eucharistic Host was kept.[58] The two differently sized but similarly shaped objects, which have been used in the same or similar contexts, allowed for the possibility of linking an architectural structure with a liturgical utensil. As the architectural historian James Stevens Curl has emphasized, a "fixed canopy over a Christian altar . . . resembles an inverted cup, or the vessel in which the Eucharist is reserved, with its domed cover, so the canopy itself has a similar domed top."[59]

---

[54] Ex. 25:18–22:18: *And you shall make two cherubim of gold; of hammered work you shall make them at the two ends of the mercy seat. 19 Make one cherub at one end, and the other cherub at the other end; you shall make the cherubim at the two ends of it of one piece with the mercy seat. 20 And the cherubim shall stretch out their wings above, overshadowing the mercy seat with their wings, and they shall face one another; the faces of the cherubim shall be toward the mercy seat. 21 You shall put the mercy seat on top of the ark, and in the ark you shall put the testimonies I will give you. 22 And there I will make Myself known to you, and I will speak with you from above the mercy seat, from between the two cherubim which are on the ark of the testimony, about everything which I will give you in commandment to the children of Israel.*

[55] *Germanos-b* 9–54.

[56] *Germanos-b* 9–54; Taft (1980–1981) 45–75. See also *The Orthodox Study Bible* 98, with further references to Basil the Great and his additional interpretation of the section on the Ark of Covenant, from where God makes himself known in intimate communion, which Germanos used for the definition of the ciborium.

[57] See, for example, *DArt* vol. 7, s.v. *ciborium* (i), s.v. *ciborium* (ii).

[58] *DArt* vol. 7, s.v. *ciborium* (i). It has been already demonstrated that the use of the term *ciborium* for a cup-like vessel can be confirmed by textual evidence only from the sixteenth century (Braun [1932] 284–285), and that the fourteenth-century sources mentioned by King (1965) 112–113 are ambiguous. See more in DaCosta Kaufmann (1975) 65–71.

[59] *DALA*, s.v. *ciborium*.

Thirteenth-century sources in the West indicate that a *pyxis* could have been suspended from the top of the ciborium, an architectural structure above the altar table, and that by metaphorical, symbolic, and even formal-visual extension, the chalice-like *pyx*, which was occasionally topped by a towering architectural superstructure, and *ciborium* became synonyms.[60] Thus, the ciborium as a container for *cibus*, which in Latin literally means "food," was closely associated with the hanging *pyx* and the place of its suspension, the architectural canopy—the ciborium.[61] It may well be that, in that period, some Roman Catholic theologians started to express the opinion that the word *ciborium* derived from the Latin term for the holy gifts, *cibus*—food, which is the revivifying Body of Christ.[62] By the nineteenth century, the explanations of the original meaning of *ciborium* associated its protective function with the use of inverted leaves from Egyptian beans as chalices and covers.[63]

However, there is no evidence that in the Christian East Eucharistic doves (*peristera*) and *pyxes* were ever referred to as ciboria.[64] Such a link is likely to be post-Byzantine and derived from erroneous attributions of altar ciboria to *pyxes* by early modern scholars like Ioannis Stephani Duranti (1534–1589), Leo Allatios (1586/7–1669), and Charles Du Cange (1610–1688). Relying on texts, these intellectuals reinterpreted altar canopies from the Constantinopolitan churches of Hagia Sophia and of St. John at Studion as chalice-like ciboria. Duranti and Du Cange also reinterpreted the sixth-century account by Silentarios and the eleventh-century account of the altar canopy of Hagia Sophia as references to the *pyx*.[65] In the mid–seventeenth century, Leo Allatios claimed that Theodore of Studios (759–826), in his ode on St. John the Forerunner, spoke of the ciborium of St. John (κιβούριον τοῦ Προδρόμου) while referring to its ancient name for the *pyx*, a box for holding the Host.[66] Allatios' opinion has already been challenged and superseded by

---

[60] In the course of the fourteenth and fifteenth centuries, and especially after the Counter-Reformation, the chalice-like *ciboria* became monumental objects, occasionally topped by a towering architectural superstructure, which were placed on altars and carried in processions. King Arnulf's *ciborium* can represent an intermediate step in the development of the *ciborium* as a Eucharistic vessel in the West. DaCosta Kaufmann (1975) 65–71.

[61] DaCosta Kaufmann (1975) 65–71, provides references to such pyxes in the West—at Petershausen (Bishoff, Schatzvertzeichnisse, I.148), Culmstock (Lehmann-Brockhaus, Schriftquellen England, I.326, no. 1207), Hurst (Lehmann-Brockhaus, Schriftquellen England, I.577, no. 2170), and at Colyton, Devonshire (Lehmann-Brockhaus, Schriftquellen England, I.295, no. 1091), where we know that: . . . *Pixis as ciborium eburnea et honeste pendens sed sine sera*. . ..

[62] The mid–sixteenth century is also proposed for the development of the notion that *ciborium* is a container for a *cibus* placed below the canopy. See, *ODE*, s.v. *ciborium*.

[63] Henricus Stephanos, *TLG* 4, col. 1542–43.

[64] *John Chrysostom, De Beato Philogonio* col. 753, writes about the use of Eucharistic doves (*peristera*) in his homilies. The twelfth-century Eucharistic dove from Hagia Sophia was called a *peristerion* as well: Mango and Parker (1960) 233–245. On the Eucharistic dove from Pharos church, see Mango (1956) 123+125–140, and *Photius, The Homilies of Photius Patriarch of Constantinople-b* 177–183. For Greek text, see *Photius, The Homilies of Photius Patriarch of Constantinople-a*.

[65] Bingham (1710–1722) vol. 1, 16, pointed to the erroneous attribution of the *ciborium* to the *pyxis* in the work of Ioannis Stephani Duranti (1534–1589); Duranti (1591). Bingham further pointed to a work by DuFresne, who, essentially following the sixth-century poetic work by Paulos Silentarios, stated that *ciborium* originally denoted only an ornamented canopy over the altar. See, Bingham (1710–1722) vol. 3, book 8, ch. 6, sec. 18, 197–198. Du Cange (1688) cites an eleventh-century description of the Hagia Sophia in Constantinople, *Paulos Silentarios-a* 86, 2, col. 2223, as evidence for a vessel for the Eucharistic host, suspended from the center of a canopy over the altar. However, the vessel was not called a *pyxis*.

[66] *Allatios* 18, with reference to *Iambi de variis argumentis 42* tit. 42 in *Theodore of Studion, Iambii-a* in *PG* 99, col. 1793D.

the proposition that Theodore of Studios wrote about the altar canopy in his monastery.[67] Though Theodore of Studios was probably thinking of the altar canopy, his epigram relates the object to the altar table, but neither the chalice nor the altar canopy from the Studion monastery in Constantinople have survived to confirm this opinion.[68] In any case, no Byzantine source provides a philological reference to a ciborium as a receptacle for the Host, the argument that is so often used by scholars when associating altar *ciborium* and chalice as *ciborium*.[69] Moreover, the Byzantines usually used the term τροφή (*trophē*) as the equivalent for *cibus*, and the term *trophē* does not make any linguistic or visual reference to a ciborium (*kiborion*).[70] The connection between the altar canopy and the box for holding the Eucharistic Host did exist, but it had its own development in the Christian East.

The Byzantines had two names for the Ark-tabernacle and the Holy Gifts box; i.e., the receptacle of Host—σκηνή (*skēnē*, literally meaning *tent* in Greek and symbolizing the Tabernacle)[71] and αρτοφόριον (*artophorium*, a casket or box for holding Eucharistic bread).[72] Numerous written and visual references to *skēnē* as the Tabernacle and temporary dwelling place of God suggest not only vessels but also the entire sanctuary and its furnishings. That *skēnē* could have been in the form of a canopy is indicated by the seventh-century graffito from Kellia, Egypt, where the image of a canopied structure is inscribed with the word *skēnē*.[73] Furthermore, Byzantine writers used the word *skēnē* to describe the human body as the temporary home of the soul, as they did for the *kiborion*.[74]

---

67 *Iambii-b* 192–193.

68 Russian archeologists never revealed whether they had found elements of the *ciborium*. The Russian Archeological Institute did research and confirmed that there was a crypt below the altar, a *synthronon*, and elements of a chancel screen—missing the location of the ambo, solea, and *ciborium*. Mathews (1971) 19–27.

69 *Allatios* 18, with reference to the text by Theodore of Studios, *Iambii-a*, claims that *ciborium* refers to "myxomēlon," the corrupted version of the word "pyxomēlon" for *pyxis*, but I find his explanation problematic.

70 See, for example, *Symeon of Thessaloniki* ch. 133, col. 339.

71 Ibid., ch. 133, col. 341B–C.

72 On the term *artophorion*, literary "bread-bearer" as the Tabernacle; i.e., the dwelling place, see *Glossary of Theological Terms* 18, 181. In the Patristic dictionary, only the root of the word is recorded, ἄρτος (*artos*), which has numerous meanings, including a loaf of bread, Eucharistic bread, *manna*. *Lampe* 231–232. However, Patriarch Manuel of Constantinople (1215–1222) noted that the pre-sanctified gifts for the Easter liturgy would have been kept in *artophoria*. See *PG* vol. 119, 809A, 809D-812A. Allatios appropriately identifies *arthophorion* with a *pyxis*.

Some Latin uses of the word *turris* (tower) seem to refer to the relatively large vessel in the shape of a canopy, used as containers for the Eucharistic hosts. See *PL* vol. 71, col. 1185; *PL* vol. 88, cols. 144–145. Gregory of Tours in *De Gloria Martyrium* mentions a deacon who, as he entered the church and walked towards the altar, dropped a bronze *turris*, a vessel in which was "the mystery of the Body of Christ." See *PL* vol. 71, cols. 781–782.

73 On the *skēnē* as "tent" and its use to designate the stage-building of the ancient Greek theatre, and subsequently its meaning as tabernacle, temple, canopy, and, in general, dwelling-place of God, see: Devyver (1982) *passim*. According to Devyver, the word *skēnē* rendered several different Hebrew words that referred to the Tabernacle of Moses when the Hebrew Bible was translated into Greek, and its subsequent use in the Greek New Testament was a result of the translator's choice.

74 For *skēnē*, *Theoktistos* 125, with further references. On the "mutability of the tent (*skēnē*) of the earthly body" in Middle Byzantine poetry, see also Anderson and Jeffreys (1994) 8–18. For *kiborion*, Golitzin (2005).

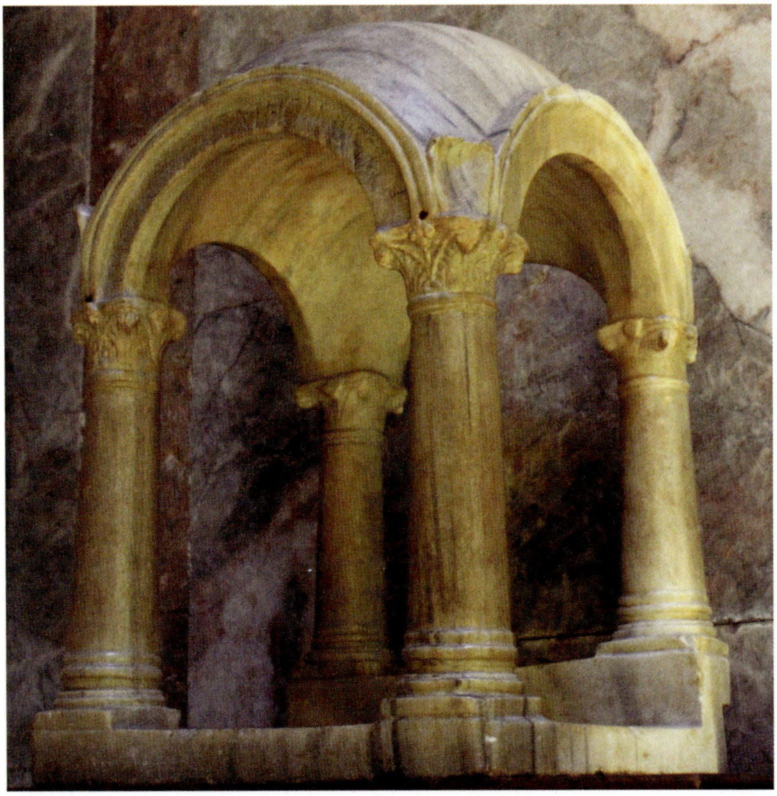

FIGURE 1.2 *Ciborium, Constantinople, sixth century (?), Treasury of San Marco, Venice.* PHOTO IVAN DRPIĆ

The receptacles for the host, *artophoria,* were box-like objects.[75] By the twelfth century, a small chest for keeping the pre-sanctified gifts and for the Eucharistic particles for the sick and prisoners became an important liturgical vessel kept on the altar table.[76] Placed on the altar table, the *artophorion* is often made in the shape of a miniature church, but other vessels and dove-patterned forms were also used. Whether *artophoria* were made in open canopy-like forms, like the medieval containers for the consecrated Host surviving in the West, remains unverifiable due to lack of material evidence.[77] However, one example of a canopy-like Byzantine *artophorion* might have been the fifth-century "ciborium shrine" currently in the treasury of San Marco in Venice (Fig. 1.2).[78] This small-scale, monolithic

[75] These receptacles of the Host were often made of wood, or silver and gold, but they could have been made of other materials as well, such as ivory or stone. Allatios confirms that, by the seventeenth century, *arthophoria* were made of wood, and "where possible, of silver and gold worked after the manner of *pyx*." *Allatios* 18.

[76] For the medieval use of *artophoria* for pre-sanctified and Eucharistic host, see Mirković (1995) 103–104.

[77] DaCosta Kaufmann (1975) 65–71. See also Timmermann (2009).

[78] The famous ninth-century King Arnulf's *ciborium,* often interpreted as a portable altar, resembles in size and general shape the *ciborium*-shrine from San Marco in Venice. An eleventh-century manuscript from Regensburg, the *Uta Codex,* even contains a depiction of King Arnulf's *ciborium* on the altar table and below a canopy. The altar canopy itself has in its interior inscriptions with strong Eucharistic symbolism. One inscription reads: "Jesus Christ the true bread from heaven [*Iesus Christus verus panis veniens de celis*]."

object was not designed to be a free-standing structure, but rather to be attached to another feature, perhaps a wall.[79] Leo Allatios informs us that *artophoria* kept the consecrated bread for the liturgy, the Body of Christ, and were "carefully enclosed in a piece of silk cloth or a small bag and reverently kept in the wall with lamps hung before it" or on a separate altar table to the north in the *bema* or in the *prothesis*.[80] The canopy from San Marco in Venice has on its two sides a votive inscription in Greek: Ὑπερ εὐχῆς κ(αὶ) σωτηρίας τῆς ἐνδοξοτάτης Ἀναστασίας ("For the blessing and salvation of the most glorious Anastasia"—trans. J.B.).[81] The reference to Anastasia has been connected with the Anastasis; i.e., the Resurrection. More likely, Anastasia was the name of a woman.[82] The inscription does not explicitly reveal the function of the object. Yet, both the flow of the text of the prayer inscribed only on two sides of the canopy and the "tongue-and-groove" end profile of one side of the canopy suggest that the object was attached to the corner of a niche or some other feature in the north wall of a church. It is exactly the northern section of the church sanctuaries where *artophoria* are located, as Allatios writes and as is still the tradition in Orthodox-rite churches. Whether the object from San Marco was an *artophorion* or some kind of reliquary, this kind of portable, canopy-like object could have been among the numerous sacred vessels donated to churches throughout Byzantine Empire. The mosaic from seventh-century church San Apollinaire in Classe depicting a Byzantine emperor with a canopy in his hands may indicate this practice of offering; yet because the image is not realistic and does not necessarily depict the object relative to the human scale, it might have been that it was an offering of an altar canopy as well (Fig. 1.3).[83]

The Byzantines—and the medieval Slavs, who followed Byzantine tradition—knew about portable objects in the shape of a church and called them *Jerusalems* and *Zions*. These luxurious objects, some of them preserved in museum collections, are still called interchangeably *Jerusalems* and *Zions* (Fig. 1.4).[84] Already in the fourth century, Ephraem the Syrian (306–373), a prolific Byzantine hymnographer and theologian, wrote of the holy containers πύργοι ("towers") in reference to Zion—Heavenly Jerusalem: Μακάριοι οὖν ἐκεῖνοι οἱ τοῦ Χριστοῦ ἀθληταί, οἱ τοῦ φωτὸς μέτοχοι καὶ τῆς ζωῆς τῆς αἰωνίου, οἱ στύλοι τῆς

A second inscription along the underside of the canopy continues this theme: "He nourishes the Church with his body through faith on earth Who nourishes the angels in the heavens through his form [*Hic pascit aec[c]lesiam corpore suo p[er] fidem in terris Qui p[er] specie[m] suam a[n]gelos pascit i[n] celis*]." A Byzantine influence has been widely observed throughout this Ottonian manuscript and implies the possibility that similar canopy-like objects, *artophoria* and *tabernacles*, were used in Byzantine churches as depicted in the *Uta Codex*. On the *Uta Codex*: Dodwell (1971) 70; Nordenfalk (1988) 213; Cohen (c2000). I am grateful to Jeremy Thompson for bringing my attention to the *Uta Codex*.

79 Ćurčić (2000) 134–142 claims that this *ciborium*-shrine in Venice potentially contained saintly relics and that it was not a free-standing object.

80 *Allatios* 18–19, citation on p. 19.

81 I am thankful to Loukas Karentzos for proofreading the inscription for me.

82 Bettini (1974) 46–47 suggests that the title "Anastasia" is a reference to the Resurrection. Because there is no reason to assume that the inscription for such a costly, luxurious object would be misspelled, I concur with A. Guillou, who advocates that Anastasia might have been a patrician lady from Justinian's court. Guillou (1995) 119–152, esp. 141.

83 Deichmann (1976) 273–279 proposes that unnamed Byzantine emperor is Justin II. On the later depictions of donors with canopies as their offerings, see also a reference to the fourteenth-century altar canopy donated by Pope Urban V to the Lateran basilica. Osborne (1991) 20–32, fig. 1.

84 Oikonomides (1980–1981) 239–247; Sterligova (1994) 46–62; Sterligova (1996) 46–62; Ryndina (1996) 69–106.

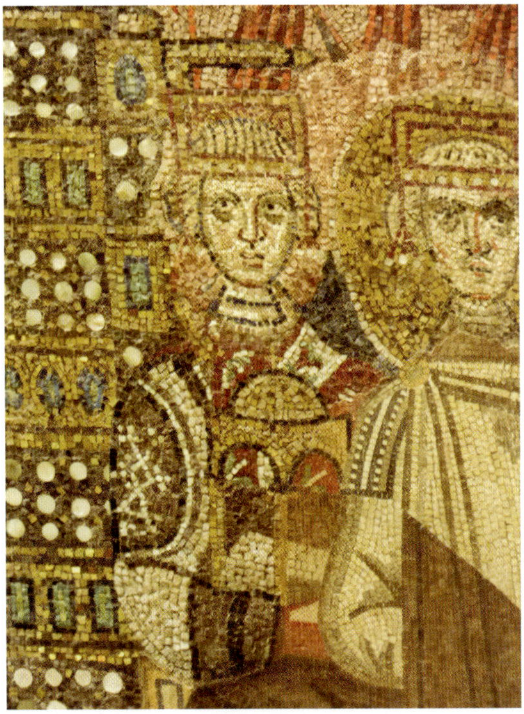

FIGURE 1.3 *Byzantine emperor (unnamed) holds a canopy as a donation; mosaic, San Apollinare in Classe, Italy, seventh century.* PHOTO IVAN DRPIĆ

πίστεως καὶ ἀγάπης σύνδεσμοι, οἱ ζῶντες θεμέλιοι καὶ πάντα συνέχοντες, οἱ υἱοὶ τῆς σεμνῆς τοῦ Χριστοῦ Ἐκκλησίας, οἱ πύργοι (τῶν βάρεων τῆς ἐπουρανίου Σιών).[85] Blessed are those athletes of Christ [martyrs—J.B.], the holders of light and the everlasting life, those pillars of faith and dear intercessors, the living foundations and always present, the sons of the Church of Christ, those towers (heavy with the heavenly Sion) (trans. J.B.).

Like the monumental chalice-like objects preserved in the West and known as ciboria, these church-shaped containers were ceremonially carried in a procession, judging by the fittings and handles still preserved on some of them. The size of these *artophoria* vessels and the possibility that they were carried during processions suggest that they were made to hold sufficient Hosts for the Communion of huge congregations, especially during the annual Easter celebration.[86] Assuming that numerous faithful would have taken Communion on Easter, the greatest feast for the Orthodox and all Christians, the relatively large size of some Late-Byzantine *artophoria*, particularly of those preserved in Russia, is understandable. Thus, although modern glossaries of theological terms in Orthodox Christianity, which stem from the Byzantine tradition, still maintain that *ciborium* (κιβώριον) denotes a free-standing canopy on columns above an altar,[87] small-size ciborium-like vessels in the Byzantine church may have been derived by metaphorical and symbolic extension

---

[85] *Hosios Ephraim* 163–175.

[86] The Byzantine and Rus *Jerusalems* and *Zions* are comparable to Easter *ciboria* from the West, like the Malmesbury *ciborium* in the Morgan Library. For the reference to Malmesbury *ciborium,* see DaCosta Kaufmann (1975) 65–71.

[87] *Glossary of Theological Terms* 32, 221.

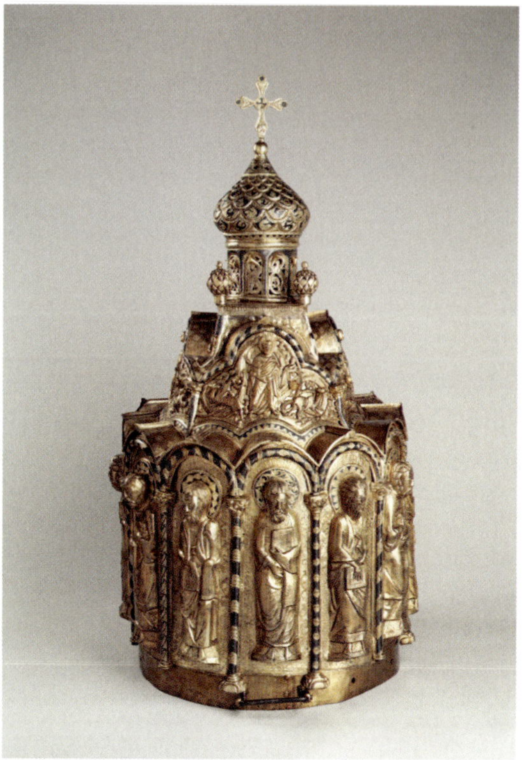

FIGURE 1.4 *Great Zion, Moscow, 1486.* PHOTO S. V. BARANOV © MOSCOW KREMLIN MUSEUMS

from canopy-like architectural installations that sheltered the Eucharistic mysteries in the church.[88]

TERMS FOR CANOPIES OTHER THAN *CIBORIUM*

The surviving texts confirm that the Byzantines and those who followed their religious traditions did not exclusively use the word *ciborium* for canopies and canopy-like objects (Table 3).[89] In addition to metaphorical, allegorical, and typological references, the rhetorical strategies that Byzantine theologians employed in their discussions of canopies also

---

[88] DaCosta Kaufmann (1975) 65–71 suggested such a development for the *ciboria*-like vessels in the West, and I would posit that such a development can also be observed in the East.

[89] Similar trends have been noticed in the West. For example, Pope Symmachus (498–514) described canopies as *tiburium* and *tegurium*, meaning "small house" or "hut." Other Latin synonyms were *tugurinum, tiburinum, tiguriam, cyburium, cipurium, ciborium, fastigium, tegurmentum, tibutium, tegimen, umbraculum, arcus,* and *arca* (*cib*). Charlemagne's Edict from 789 confirms that the term *altare tegurium,* signifying altar *ciborium,* was in use at least until the end of eighth century. Braun (1924) 185–186, 190. References to the *umbraculum* as an altar *ciborium* come from *Ordo Romanus*, according to Bingham (1710–1722) vol. 3, book 8, ch. 6, sec. 18, 197–198. For further references, see "Basilicam sanctorum Silvestri et Martini construxit, ubi et super altare tiburium argenteum fecit" in *EtLP* vol. 1, 261; Smith, M. T. (1968) 336–345; *EAM* vol. 4, s.v. *ciborio*.

allowed for extensive use of terms that are related to architectural terminology, hence providing yet another layer for understanding various canopies in their ecclesiastical settings. In approximately 100 selected texts, which use terms that might have denoted canopies and canopy-like objects but which are by no means comprehensive, numerous terms are descriptive and refer to either architectural, formal idioms such as towers, or to architectural elements that constituted canopies such as columns, domes, vaults, and arches.

Πύργος (*Pirgos*)

In our opening example, Paulos Silentarios in his encomium described the canopy that stood over the main altar in Hagia Sophia in Constantinople as a πύργος (*pirgos*), which means "tower" in Greek (Table 1, T.40).[90] In the mind of contemporaries, the word for "tower" could have evoked both literal and metaphorical meanings for the canopy, which is visually a vertical or tower-like structure. By analogy, the tall canopy on four columns from Hagia Sophia resembled a tower. Moreover, at least since the fourth century and probably earlier, the connections between columns and towers had already been established among Christians. The text *Expositions in Psalms* (*Expositiones in Psalmos*) attributed to Athanasius the Theologian spoke of columns as if they were the towers of the church (Καὶ τίνες ἂν εἶεν οἱ πύργοι τῆς Ἐκκλησίας—J.B.).[91] St. John Chrysostom compared the apostles Peter and Paul with the columns and towers of the church (Παῦλος γὰρ καὶ Πέτρος πύργοι καὶ στῦλοι τῆς Ἐκκλησίας),[92] adding an important ontological layer to architectural metaphors and our understanding of actual architectural structures. The towering structure of a canopy resembled a mountain (ορος, *oros*) and the heavenly heights (ουράνιος, *ouranios*);[93] therefore, by literal, visual, and aural extension, all of these words could effectively denote the notion of a ciborium (κιβούριον, *kiborion*). The mountain as a sacred space and symbol of the ladder to heaven where the sun god and other solar deities supposedly lived has its roots in the ancient Greek tradition.[94] These ancient terms for the mountains, *oros* and *ouranios*, in turn, by vocalization evoked the sound of the term *kiborion* (*kib-ourion*) and its meaning of the heavenly place of the Lord, high above. Such a strong rhetorical tradition among the Byzantines, which combined aural and visual thinking, would explain how contemporaries Paulos Silentarios and John Malalas effectively communicated their

---

[90] Similarly, Paulinus, Bishop of Nola, Italy (ca. 354–431), used the term *turris*, meaning "tower" in Latin, to describe a fountain canopy in the church atrium in the city. Paulinus called the fountain canopy in the atrium at St. Peter's in Rome *tholus*, which means vault (Smith, M. T. [1968] 344). According to the *Liber Pontificalis*, Pope Symmachus gave *tiburiums* (canopies) of pure silver to the basilica of St. Andrew and to Ss. Silvester and Martin (*EtLP* vol. 1, 261–262). The *ciborium* probably stood over the altar dedicated to St. Andrew, which was placed in the central of seven altar niches. *His fecit basilicam sancti Andreae apstoli apud beatum Petrum, ubi fecit tiburium ex argento purissimo et confessionem*, pens. lib. CXX; arcos argenteos III, pens. lib. LX (Smith, M. T. [1968] 164–166). The reference to St. Andrew reads: "planted its silver feet" (*SD* 88). These words, however, may not have described only canopies, but obviously a variety of structures, which acquired the meaning of "a small house." When Arculf, a native of Gaul, took a pilgrimage to the Holy Land ca. 670, he described the *aedicula* of the Holy Sepulchre as *tugurium* and *tuguriolum* (*Arculfus* in *PPTS* vol. 3, 6).

[91] *Athanasius Theol., Expositiones in Psalmos* vol. 27, 221, line 30. The linguistic analysis by Stead (1989) 65–78 concludes that the text could not have been written by Athanasius.

[92] *John Chrysostom, De prophetiarum obscuritate* vol. 56, 182, line13.

[93] *Liddell and Scotts* 578.

[94] Numerous ancient Greek sun altars of worship were on the highest acropolis. Siggh (1993) 21.

thoughts about the altar canopy in Hagia Sophia by using two different terms—*tower* and *ciborium*—which otherwise are not recorded as synonyms in Byzantine dictionaries.

Οἰκίσκος (*Oikiskos*)

The term οἰκίσκος (*oikiskos*), meaning "small house," was used to describe both the canopy-shrine of St. Demetrios (also known by the Byzantines as a ciborium) in Thessaloniki, and the canopy over specially venerated icons in the metropolis of Ss. Theodores in Serres, near Thessaloniki (Table 3, T.57, T.106).[95] These examples confirm that, if we did not have the material evidence for some of these canopy-like installations, the textual evidence for various "small houses" elsewhere might have been overlooked. Already in the fifth century, the now-lost, centrally planned columned shrine that held holy relics of St. Thecla in the eponymous church in Seleucia, Isauria (modern Turkey) was known as her *oikia*, or her "house" (Table 3, T.27). Once again, conflation in the minds of contemporaries might have resulted in such word choice that "small house" was understood not only physically but also symbolically. Neither of the two mentioned shrines in Thessaloniki and Serres housed a saint's body, but they represented a kind of symbolic house for their images—icons, valued by the faithful only second in rank after saintly relics.[96]

Ορόφιον (*Orophion*) and Other Terms Related to the Canopy Roof

Other, descriptive expressions related to the columns, arches, or roof of a canopy were used interchangeably to denote complete canopies, either of a specific kind or for different objects within the church proper, which were, however, united by their architectural solutions. A well-known rhetorical figure of metonymy, which educated Byzantines used extensively, would allow them to mention only one part, often the most symbolic, of the whole, to indicate the entire canopy-structure.[97] In the tenth century, Byzantine hagiographer Niketas Magistros called a still-preserved altar canopy on the Island of Paros an ορόφιον (*orophion*) and its cognate στέγους (*stegous*), which literally means "a roof"; i.e., a dome, thus referring only to one of its constituent parts—its cover (Table 1, T. 68).[98] Sometime between the twelfth and first half of the fourteenth centuries in the *ekphrasis* of a baptistery from the *Progymnasmata* recorded in *Marc. Gr. 444*, an anonymous Byzantine poet used the same word, ορόφιον (*orophion*), to describe an architectural structure, which most likely was a baptismal or *phiale* canopy over the font with the sanctified water (Table 1, T. 90).[99] The Greek words *orophion* (roof) and *thalamos* (a room) were used to describe

---

95 On the canopy from St. Demetrios in Thessaloniki, see Pallas (1979) 44–58. On the canopy from Serres: A. Orlandos (1949) 259–271, esp. 263. Drpić (2012) 645–694, esp. 652–660, argues that the canopy for the icon of Ss. Theodores in Serres was made after the model of the canopy-ciborium of St. Demetrios in Thessaloniki and was similarly a house-shrine for an icon located in the north section of the basilica.

96 Though the two sites in Thessaloniki and Serres are geographically close to each other, at this moment I have not determined whether "*oikiskos*" denoted canopy-shrines only in a given region, as more work is needed on the subject.

97 I thank Cristina Carile for calling my attention to metonymy.

98 *Life StTheokiste-b, SD* 104. In the similar manner, in the fourth century, Pope Silvester speaks only of the columns of the canopy-shrine that stood over the grave of St. Peter at St. Peter's basilica at the Vatican in Rome. Krautheimer (1985) 11–23; Toynbee and Ward Perkins (1956) 231, n. 20; Kirschbaum (1959) 143–164.

99 Flusin (2005) 163–181, esp. n. 32.

the framing of the space around the basin. According to the description, a low wall was placed around the water font to form a space that the anonymous author calls a "room" (*thalamos*). There is no reference to how this low wall was connected to its domical roof (*orophion*), but presumably columns were set to support such a dome, thus forming the canopy-like structure, suggesting that the entire installation was understood as a spatial unit (a room). In the early thirteenth century, the word *ouranos* ("heavenly vault") was used to denote the now-lost canopy on eight columns over the baptismal font from the eleventh-century monastery of the Theotokos Evergetis in Constantinople.[100] Some other words pointing to the roof, like καμελαύχιον (*kamelauhion*) and θόλος (*tholos*), in addition to their original references to "tall headdress" and "dome, vault," may have referred to canopy-like structures.[101] The testament of a certain monk, Maximos from the monastery at Skoteine, hence speaks of the "sacred dome," possibly a canopy, judging by a reference to small metal crosses with a censer inside this sacred dome (Σταυρία χυτὰ μετὰ θυμιατοῦ ἐν τῷ θείῳ τρούλλῳ).[102] At least since the eleventh century, inventories of the Byzantine monastic foundations have occasionally spoken of candlesticks named *kamaria*, as described in the twelfth-century *typikon* of Empress Irene Doukaina Komnene (ca. 1066–1138) for the Convent of the Mother of God *Kecharitomene* in Constantinople.[103] Today unidentified as specific objects, *kamaria*, which signified "arch and vaulting" in Byzantine mathematical treatises, were potentially massive "arched, canopy-liked candlesticks," some of which are still preserved.[104]

Ἀψῖδα (*Apsida*)

In the fourteenth century, the monk Theoktistos from the monastery of St. John the Studion used the word ἀψῖδα (*apsida*) to describe the tomb canopy of St. Athanasios I (1289–1293, 1303–1309), who was buried after 1323, presumably in his monastery in the Church of Christ Savior, now lost.[105] The same word, ἀψίδα (*apsida*), was used in the fourteenth-century Grotta Ferrata version of the medieval poem "Digenes Akrites" for the tomb of the main character after whom the poem is entitled.[106] Sometime between 1389 and 1391, an anonymous Russian traveler used the Greek word апсида (*apsida*) to describe the open, lid-covered canopy over the stone *phiale* in Hagia Sophia.[107]

Though *apsida* was a technical term for the arch or dome used by Early Byzantine authors,[108] it seems as if the word was metonymically revived in the Late Byzantine period. According to these later texts, *apsida* probably stood for an open, free-standing domed canopy. The structure may have been comparable to the canopied tomb of Alexios

---

100 Magdalino (1998) 432–447, esp. 442–443.

101 *EAM* vol. 4, s.v. *ciborio*. For the use of the word *kamelauhion*, see *RBK* vol. 1 (1966) 1055; *De Ceremoniis-d* 163, 181, 290, 291.

102 *Skoteine* in *BMFD* vol. 3, 1186.

103 *Kecharitomene* in *BMFD* vol. 2, 716.

104 Downey (1946) 22–34. For the use of the word *kamaria*, see Heath (1965) 11, 306–310, with his reference to *Kamaria*, a treatise on vaulting written ca. 250 CE by the mathematician Heron of Alexandria. This treatise, now lost, remained the foundation of Byzantine mechanics.

105 *Theoktistos* 57.

106 *Dig. Akrit.* 246–247, col. 240–245.

107 *RussTravelers* (1984) 128–154, 138–139.

108 On the use of the term *apsida*, see Downey (1946) 22–34.

IV of Trebizond (1417–1429), destroyed after 1918, or to some of the canopied installations depicted in Byzantine manuscripts.[109] The death of St. Athanasius as depicted in the fourteenth-century *Homilies of Gregory Nazianzenzus* (gr. 543, fol. 260v) resembles the illustration of the death of St. Basil found in the same manuscript (fol. 130v) and in the eleventh-century *Homilies of Gregory Nazianzenzus* (Rossikon 6, Taphou 14, f. 113r).[110] In each case, the display of the dead body of a saint was represented under canopied structures. It may be that, in illuminated manuscripts, such canopies generically represented the church interiors, following the Byzantine monastic tradition according to which the body of the deceased monk was put on display before the funeral. The canopy could create a potent conceptual memory image among the faithful that stood for the sacred space. Tombs of important personae were represented as canopies, even if in reality they were not such. The mausoleum of Halikarnassos in an eleventh-century manuscript (Taphou 14, fol. 311v 9) is one example. A fifteenth-century manuscript (Manuscript no. 771 [381], today in the National Library "Kiril i Metodii" in Sofia, Bulgaria, folio 191), presumably following the Old Church Slavonic text of the novel of Alexander the Great, also depicts the mourning for the deceased Alexander set within an open, four-columned, canopy-like structure.[111] The bed on which the body of Alexander is laid is set below a canopy curiously depicted in red suggestive of purple, an imperial color for the Byzantines, hence revealing another web of communication the Byzantines used to anachronistically relate their own with pre-Christian traditions. However, it is known that St. Gregory of Nazianzos made an oration at the outdoor tomb of St. Basil, his lifelong friend and intellectual companion, and the tomb is depicted as an open canopy in his illustrated liturgical homilies.[112] In this eleventh-century manuscript, the canopied tomb is flanked by a canopy over the Holy Scriptures, presumably inside the church, and by another open canopy, this one over the baptismal font or the *phiale,* which may have been inside or outside the church.

The open canopy over the water font from the *Homilies of Gregory Nazianzenzus* manuscript was not named. Yet *apsida* may have been both an open tomb canopy mounted over a sarcophagus and an open, free-standing canopy over a holy water font. The anonymous Russian traveler, who was not a native speaker, might have made a mistake when he called the *phiale* in Hagia Sophia *apsida,* but it is more likely that he asked native speakers what the structure he encountered was and accordingly recorded in his travel diary the word *apsida* for the open canopy over the holy water font.[113]

---

[109] See also the depiction of the Mausoleum of Halicarnassus in MS. Holy Sepulchre Jerusalem 4 f. 312v (1066–1081); Moscow State Historical Museum 146 f. 81r, Athos Panteleimon 6, f. 100r; 14th c. Paris BN Gr. 543 f. 130v; Oxford Bodleian Canon gr. 103, f. 90v. References according to Bryer (1993) 93–102. See also Mango (1995) 99–117, esp. 110.

[110] Galavaris (1969) 46ff, 240, figs. 114, 466.

[111] Maksimović (1983) 47–50, fig. 70. Similarly, a sixteenth-century Armenian manuscript (Vienna, Monastery of the Mikitaristis collection, no. 319) depicts the tomb of Alexander the Great as an open canopy. The role of the widely spread novel of Alexander the Great and the imagery from the illustrated texts in the Middle Ages merits a separate study. It has been recently suggested that it may have even influenced some formulaic depictions of the canopy-like tombs of dervishes, like the mausoleum of Seyyid Ahmed el-Rifa'i, which in reality was not a canopy tomb at all. Baha Tanman (2001) 1–37. I am grateful to Suna Çağaptay for drawing my attention to the article by Baha Tanman on Ottoman examples of canopy tombs.

[112] Bryer (1993) 93–102.

[113] *RussAnon* in *Russian Travelers* (1984) 128–154, 138–139.

Τετρακίονος (*Tetrakionos*) and Τετράπυλον (*Tetrapylon*)

By formal analogy, canopies were also associated with various four-columned architectural structures, with or without roofs.[114] Primary sources point to structures on four columns, variously called a τετρακίονος (*tetrakionos*) and a τετράπυλον (*tetrapylon*), both literally meaning "four columns" and associated with triumphal architecture as they localized ceremonial stations along the imperial triumphal way in Constantinople and other cities.[115] Symbolically, these massive structures represented imperial markers over the *locus mundi*, the "navel of the world" (Table 2).[116] Known as public monuments from the period of the Roman Tetrarchy, *tetrapyla* and *tetrakionia* are composed of four single pillars identical in size and shape, standing apart from each other and forming a coherent square plan, sometimes connected with an entablature, thus forming a massive canopy-like structure. In the Mediterranean, these late antique structures were associated with the canopied throne of the emperor in the audience hall and symbolized the presence of the Roman emperor even in his absence.[117] The emperor passing on his ceremonial route below the canopy-like *tetrapylon* would have been associated with the canopy-like throne and symbolically transformed into a divine person.[118]

Often described as synonymous structures by Byzantine authors, *tetrapyla* and *tetrakionia* could have been topped by a dome-like superstructure.[119] Therefore, these essentially pagan four-columned structures could have had a formal continuity with Christian architecture, and some of these objects could have been full canopies with roofs. For example, by the tenth century, the so-called Bronze *Tetrapylon* in Constantinople, so named because of its "bronze" (or rather, copper) revetment,[120] sheltered the relics of the Forty Martyrs

---

[114] Canopies without roofing are known in pre-Christian Greece and were occasionally depicted in Christian manuscripts, such as the canopy framing the oversized figure of the Evangelist Mark as shown in the illuminated manuscript Garret 6, fol. 54b, dated to the second half of the ninth century. For canopies on four columns without a roof in Ancient Greece, see Rupp (1974) 176. However, the term "canopy" is used in a modern sense, designating various objects with a roof, which may not have been indispensable in the Byzantine tradition as previously thought.

[115] Though essentially denoting the same architectural structures, *tetrakionia* is presumably an older term than *tetrapyla*, as exemplified by the writing of John Malalas, who mentions both terms in his *Chronographia*, but cites Pausanias for his reference to *tetrakionia* (cf. *Pausanias* Fragment 4, line 63). In the sixth century, John Malalas, who also quotes Evagrius Scholasticus, writes of a stone *tetrapylon* adorned in bronze, which was built in Antioch by a certain Mammianus, a tradesman, who became a prominent man and a member of the Senate during the reign of Zeno (474–491). The *tetrapylon* was destroyed, presumably by the earthquake of 457 or 458, as Evagrius informs us. *John Malalas-b* 232, 19; *Evagrius Scholasticus* ch. 28. On the *tetrapylon*, see also Downey (1937) 194–211 and Downey (1935) 55–72.

[116] Thiel, W. (2002) 299–326; Milojević (1996) 247–262.

[117] On the discussion of imperial canopies, exemplified by the Severan *quadrifrons* covered by a dome in Leptis Magna, see Lehmann (1945) 1–27. See also Roueche and Smith (1996).

[118] See, for example, McCormick (1986) 297–327.

[119] On the Hellenistic and Roman *tetrapyla* with domes, see Kader (1996), where she analyzes in particular the *tetrapylon* of Latakia, until now usually called a "triumphal arch" and dated to the late second or early third century CE. Kader demonstrates that the *tetrapylon* at Latakia was a propylon-like entrance to a probable sacred *temenos*, an area that could have been dedicated already to a Hellenistic ruler cult and was later the site of a Roman imperial cult. On the double *tetrapyla* in Rufianus, which were presumably in the cemeteries or contained tombs, see *John Malalas-b* 397:16ff. (T.36).

[120] On the *Chalkoun* tetrapylon, see Mango (1985a) 30–32; Magdalino (1996) 21–25; Berger (2000) 161–172.

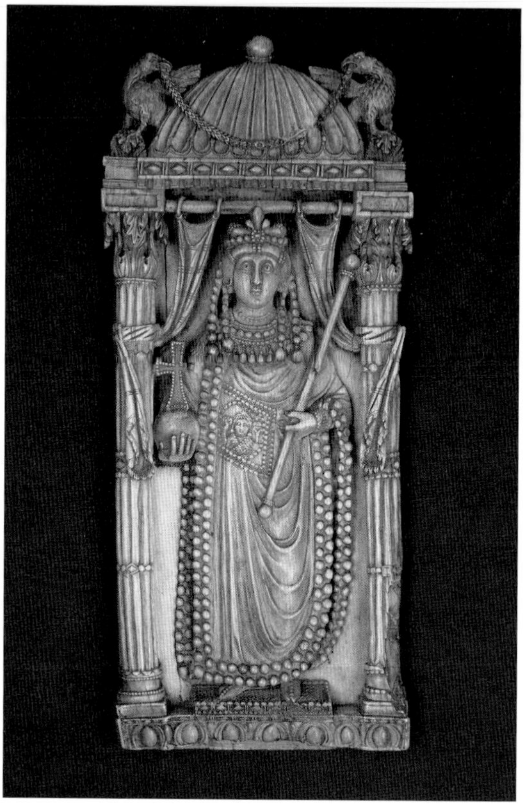

FIGURE 1.5 *Curtained canopy with a domical roof sheltering Byzantine empress. Ivory from Constantinople, sixth century.* NICOLO ORSI BATTAGLINI/ART RESOURCE, NEW YORK

of Sebastea. This practice was recorded in the tenth-century *Synaxarion,* an abridged collection of Christian Orthodox saints, and later mentioned by an eyewitness, the Castilian ambassador, traveler, and writer Clavijo, in the early fifteenth century.[121] Such a practice effectively combined the meaning of saintly shrine with the honorific meaning of the *tetrapylon,* incorporating their related architectural solutions in a Christian context.[122]

Τετράβηλον (*Tetravēlon*), Καταπέτασμα (*Katapetasma*), Παραπέτασμα (*Parapetasma*), and Πέπλα (*Pepla*)

Interestingly, a four-columned canopy was frequently described by making reference to textiles, such as το τετράβηλον (*tetravēlon*), το καταπέτασμα (*katapetasma*), το παραπέτασμα (*parapetasma*), and even πέπλα (*pepla*), the ancient Greek term for "religious curtains" (Table 3).[123] Though *tetravēlon* literally means "four curtains," the object it denoted may have been made partially of solid material, presumably with four columns enclosed by curtains. The monastic document *Kecharitomene* mentions the "curtains (*pepla*) of the four

[121] *Synaxarion CP* 356, 524; Janin (1953) 485–486.

[122] See also Bogdanović (2008c).

[123] Eighteen sources about canopies that I analyzed mention curtains. About the meaning of specific words the Greeks used for religious curtains, see also *Lampe* s.vv. *katapetasma, peplos.*

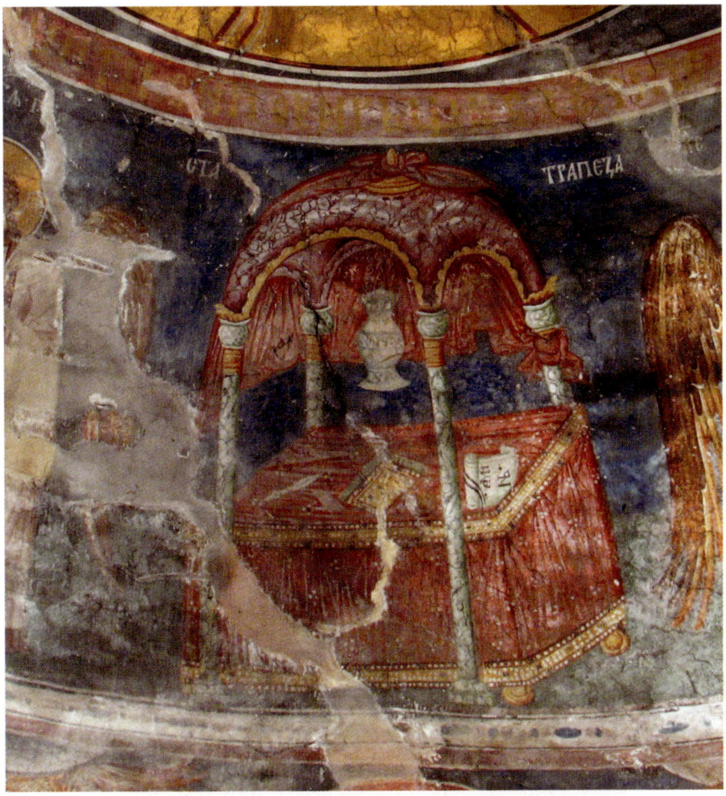

FIGURE 1.6 *Altar canopy (inscribed as Holy Table in Old Church Slavonic), Church of the Mother of God Hodegetria, Monastery Pećka Patrijaršija, fourteenth century.* PHOTO IVAN DRPIĆ

pillars . . . bearing a representation of a cross [and the] portraits . . . of [various] saints."[124] The "curtains" may refer to a *templon* (τέμπλον) screen, but also to a canopy. In the eleventh-century, a famous Byzantine philosopher, poet, and politician, Michael Psellos, who might have influenced the writer of the *Kecharitomene typikon*, writes in his manuscript *Theologica* about the curtains of the sanctuary and of a four-cornered structure, τετράγωνον ξύλινον (Table 1, T.74). Moreover, a collection of texts dating between the tenth and fifteenth centuries attributed to an official at the Constantinopolitan court, a certain Pseudo-Kodinos, explains that *tetravēlon* can resemble *tetrapylon* with some kind of a chamber (*koubukleion*) on top of the columnar installation, and that such a structure was built in imitation of an imperial structure in Rome.[125] This description implies that the entire canopy, including both its columns and roof, was made of a solid material, and that the curtains might have been hangings, presumably set on metal rods and spread between two columns, as depicted in some Byzantine ivories, manuscripts, frescos, icons, and even represented in some post-Byzantine canopies (Figs. 1.5, 1.6, 1.7).

The existence of curtains for liturgical furnishing and canopies in the Byzantine tradition has been debated; textual and visual sources are obscure, while material evidence of

---

[124] *Kecharitomene* in *BMFD* vol. 2, 716.

[125] *Pseudo-Codinus, Patria-a* book 2 sec. 55; *Patria-b* 88–91. (Table 1, T.72.)

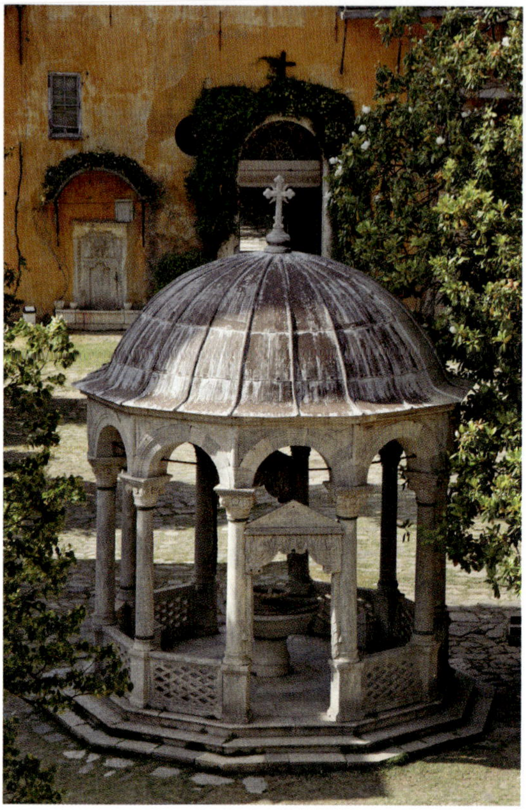

FIGURE 1.7 *Phiale, Iviron Monastery, Mt. Athos, Greece, sixteenth or seventeenth century, most likely in the place of the earlier Byzantine installation.* PHOTO NEBOJŠA STANKOVIĆ

canopy-curtains, perhaps due to the fragility of textiles, is nonexistent.[126] In accordance to the Scriptural reference in Ex. 26:32 to the veil of the desert tabernacle that hung by means of golden hooks from four pillars of acacia, which were overlaid with gold and set on four silver bases, the four columns on which these curtains would have been hung could have been placed in a straight line, thereby forming a structure like a sanctuary screen with three doors, like in most Byzantine churches.[127] Alternatively, the columns could form four corners of a square-based enclosure, the veil being hung around all four sides, with the two ends overlapping at the front to give access to the inner space. The latter possibility of structuring the canopy is attested to through numerous visual representations, generally associated with either Old Testament themes and representations

[126] Taft (2006) 27–52; Walter (1993) 203–228; Mathews (1971) 162–171. According to Khouri-Sarkis' studies on the liturgy of St. James, in addition to those on the chancel, the Syrians used curtains on the altar canopy and opened or closed them according to the demands of the liturgy. Khouri-Sarkis (1960) 363–384; Khouri-Sarkis (1962) 277–296. On evidence of the use of curtains for *ciboria* in the West, see, for example, Zchomelidse (2010) 221–262, fig. 5.

[127] The sanctuary screen was variously called *templon, diastila, kagnkelos, kankellon, kinklis, kinklides*, etc.: Taft (2006) 27–52. The term *templon* was used in the seventh century for the church of H. Artemios, supposedly the north Church of the Kalenderhane in Constantinople, today Istanbul. Mango (1979) 40–43; Walter (1993) 203–228.

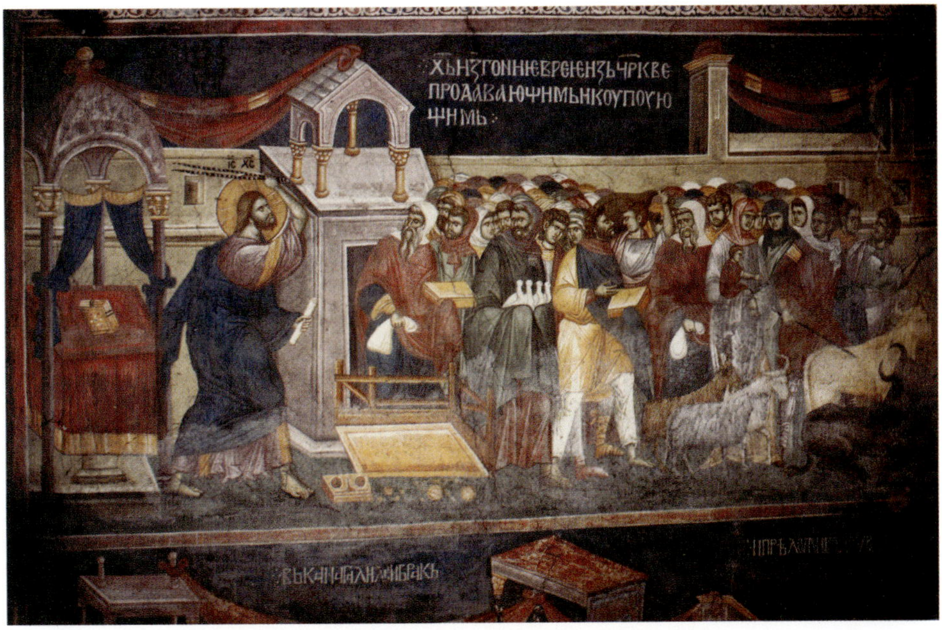

FIGURE 1.8 Purification of the Temple, *Church of the Mother of God, Monastery Gračanica, ca. 1321.* PHOTO IVAN DRPIĆ

of the Tabernacle, the Jewish Temple or the Holy of Holies or, in Middle Byzantine and later examples, with the Christian narrative related to liturgical rites and the canopied altar table (Figs. 1.6, 1.8, 1.9).[128]

Though prevailing scholarly opinion is that the curtains were used for an altar canopy in the early Christian period in Syria,[129] widespread use of the terms such as *tetravēlon, katapetasma,* and *parapetasma* across time in the wider Mediterranean challenges this observation and suggests that canopies with curtains existed in Byzantine churches as well (Table 3). The use of various terms for curtains was extended to canopies.[130]

---

[128] The Communion of the Apostles in Byzantine monumental painting is recorded in the side chapels in the early-tenth-century Church of the Nativity near Sagri on the island of Naxos. In the eleventh century, the Communion of the Apostles decorated the side walls of the sanctuary in the Church of Panagia Chalkeon in Thessaloniki (1028) and in the Cappadocian Church of Karadaş Kilise in Soğanli Valley (ca. 1060). By the mid–eleventh century, it was transferred to the middle register and in the center of the altar apse, as was the case with the fresco in the Church of St. Sophia in Ohrid and the mosaic of St. Sophia in Kiev. From the twelfth century on, sometimes on the lower level of the apsidal wall, two liturgies might be painted one above the other. The upper liturgy is the Communion of the Apostles, and the lower, that of the Holy Bishops. Among many examples of such painted liturgies in the frescoes, one can mention that of St. Panteleimon at Nerezi (1164) and St. George at Staro Nagoričino in Macedonia (1317). Gerstel (1996) 141–148; Walter (1982) 192; Wharton (1988) 44; Djurić (1974) 158. For the curtained canopies depicted within the Heavenly Liturgy in the dome of the Church of Ss. Joachim and Anna ("King's church") ca. 1313–1314 in Studenica, Serbia, see Babić (1987).

[129] Taft (2006) 27–52, with references.

[130] According to the *Deed of concession to the Genoese of certain areas of Constantinople (October 13, 1202),* the marble canopy was named *katapetasma*. Two versions of the text survive, in Greek and in Latin: *Acta et diplomata* 3, 55–57 and x–xv. (For the same reference, see *SD* 240.) See also *Alexiad-a* XII 3.6; *Nicolaus Mesarites, Descriptio ecclesiae SS. Apostolorum* 855–924, esp. 890–891.

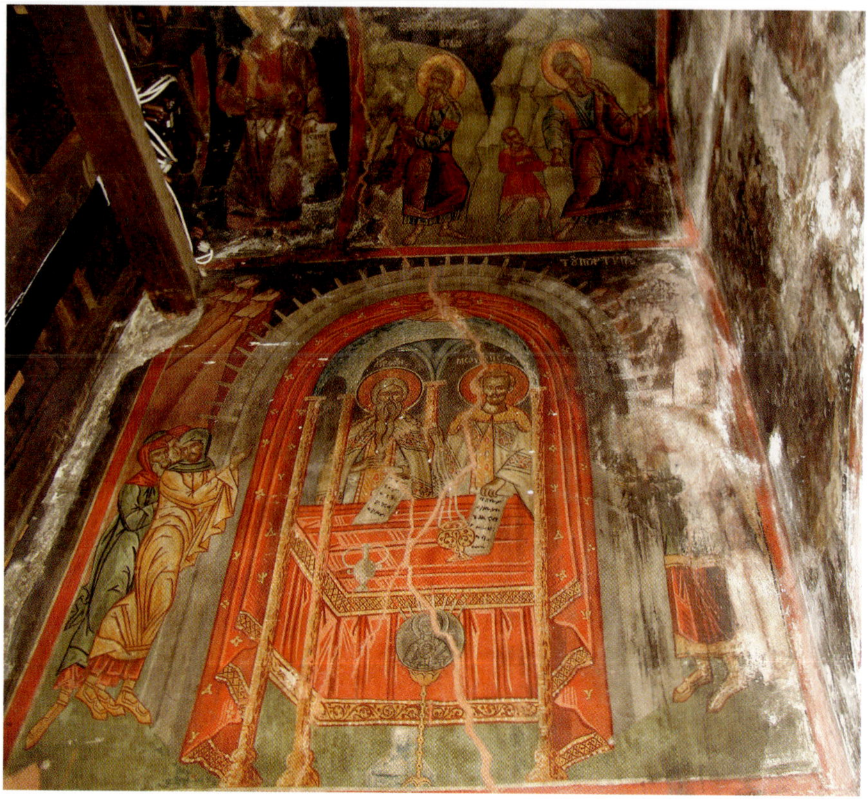

FIGURE 1.9 Ark of the Covenant, *Church of the Mother of God at the monastery of Koronas, Thessaly, Greece, fifteenth century.* PHOTO IVAN DRPIĆ

In the eighth century, Theophanes Confessor called the altar canopy in Hagia Sophia *tetravela*. In the twelfth century, Anna Komnene described an imperial canopy-tent as a *katapetasma*. In the thirteenth century, Nikolas Mesarites used *katapetasma* to describe the altar canopy in the Church of the Holy Apostles and a marble canopy from the palace church in the *Inventory of the so-called Palace of Botaniates*, part of the legal document of the Constantinopolitan Botaniates family, while Anthony of Novgorod used the Slavic version of the same word катапезма (from *katapetasma*) for the altar canopy of Hagia Sophia.

Κουβούκλειον (*Koubukleion, Kouvouklion*)

The word κουβούκλειον (*koubukleion, kouvouklion*) has been already associated with the canopy, though it has become generally disassociated from "canopy" in modern art-historical studies.[131] Besides its basic meaning of *cubicule*, room, and in essence "a box," *koubukleion* may have denoted spaces of various sizes and shapes. Because the main purpose of the spaces known as *kouvouklia* was to hide or reveal certain objects or persons during particular moments, those spaces could have taken the form of canopy-like structures, rooms with curtains, or moveable panels in place of lateral walls.[132] Medieval texts that

[131] Prokopios (1981) 125–128 uses the term *koubouklion*.

[132] In *De Ceremoniis*, the word usually stands for chambers and entire buildings, but also for the metaphorical language related to imperial affairs. See, for example, *De Ceremoniis-d* 405, 416, 441, 442.

mention *koubuklia* are often contradictory, but in the collection of texts by Pseudo-Kodinos (tenth–fifteenth centuries), a *kouboukleion* is also a structure on four columns.[133] In 1375, the Russian pilgrim Archimandrite Arsenius visited the Tomb of Christ in Jerusalem and called it the *kuviklion*, a corrupted version of the Greek counterpart.[134] Medieval pilgrims interchangeably called both the Church of the Holy Sepulchre and the Tomb *Aedicula* the *Holy Kouvouklion*, emphasizing their roles as shrines. The *Aedicula* of the Tomb of Christ has remained known as the *Holy Kouvouklion* up to the present. Similarly, the construction of the canopy-like stand for the *Epitaphios* (the icon of Christ's dead body) representing the Tomb of Christ was also named *kouvoukleion*.[135]

In post-Byzantine churches in Greece, κουβούκλι (*kouboukli*) signifies the Easter canopy with a dome, usually made of wood and richly decorated, which is used for the burial cortège on Easter Eve (Fig. 1.10). Numerous such canopies in Greek museums are marked as *kouboukli*a.[136] Byzantine examples of such canopies do not survive, and it has been suggested that they actually did not exist during the Byzantine period.[137] However, in 1247, a certain monk Maximos writes that in the *katholikon* (main church) in his, now-lost, monastery, the Mother of God at Skoteine near Philadelphia in Asia Minor, *lamnai* (presumably metal rods with candle and lamp holders) were set in front of the "sepulcher."[138] Though it remains unverifiable what kind of object the sepulcher from Skoteine might have been and whether it signified the Tomb of Christ in the church or a tomb of a specially venerated monk, a canopy-like installation inside the church could have been a viable solution. A surviving example for the canopied saint's tomb is Saint Athanasios tomb (tenth century) at Great Lavra on Mt. Athos.[139] The tomb is set in the church bay and enclosed by metal rods with lamps and votive offerings. Similarly, the post-Byzantine canopy in front of the *prothesis* chapel and abutting the north wall of the fourteenth-century Church of the Annunciation at Gračanica Monastery, Kosovo, Serbia, might have replaced an earlier church furnishing that symbolized the Tomb of Christ.[140]

The canopy-like *kouvoukli* may have acquired Christian meaning by the Byzantine association between Christ and kingship, which followed older precedents. For example, when Septimius Severus (r. 193–211) held the funeral rite for Pertinax in the second century, "a wooden platform was constructed in the Roman forum upon which was set a shrine, without walls, but surrounded by columns, cunningly wrought of both ivory and gold."[141] The description of this burial cortège echoes the post-Byzantine *kouboukli*a. Roman

[133] *Pseudo-Codinus, Patria-a* book 2, sec. 55. (Table 1, T.72.)

[134] *PG* 165, col. 517. See also Auxentios of Photiki (1999) 4–5.

[135] *Great Greek Encyclopedia* s.vv. *koubikoularios, koubikoulon, kouboukli*on. I am grateful to L. F. Kallenos for calling my attention to the reference in *Great Greek Encyclopedia*. For the term kouvoukli (koubouklion) see also, *Oxford Greek Dictionary*, s.v. *κουβούκλι*.

[136] Instructive examples are on display at the Benaki Museum in Athens or in the museum in Hosios Loukas.

[137] Taft (1975) 216–219 is of the opinion that the *epitaphia* in the form of *kouvouklia* are post-Byzantine inventions, despite the material evidence for cloths symbolizing portable altars and Christ's Tomb, which are dated to the first half of the twelfth century.

[138] For the "sepulcher" in *Skoteine*, see *BMFD* vol. 3, 1176–1195, esp. 1186. Reference to *lamnai as* metal beams with candleholders used over the *templon* and icon frames, in Boura (1982) 479–491, esp. 480.

[139] Unpublished photo material from Dumbarton Oaks Collection DO Dolger BF. P. 2002. 001198, which I was able to use for research purposes.

[140] Ćurčić (1991) 251–261, fig. 3.

[141] Smith, M. T. (1974) 379–414.

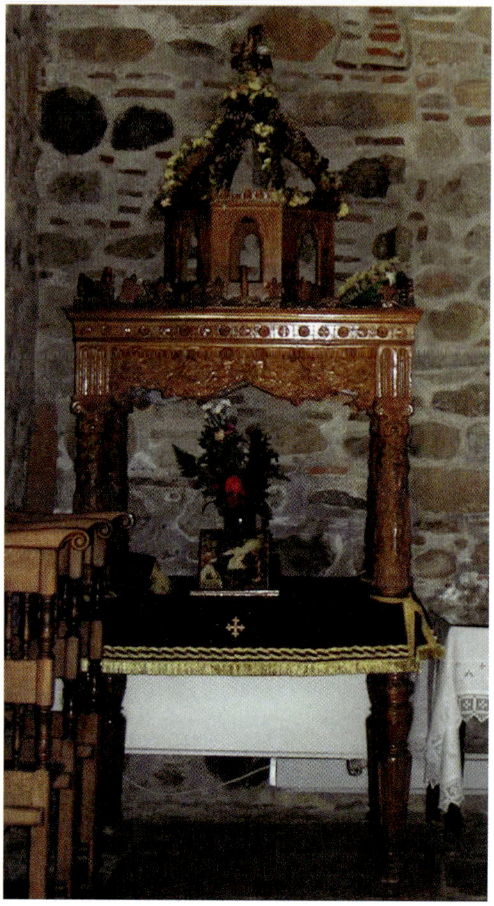

FIGURE 1.10 *Epitaphios (koubuklion), Church of the Mother of God, Hosios Loukas Monastery, Greece, post-Byzantine.* PHOTO AUTHOR

imperial architecture and funeral practices might have inspired the forms and even some of the rituals in the Byzantine church.[142] The Byzantines might have actually continued to use burial cortèges, established in pagan traditions, but revived in a Christian context as a liturgical reenactment of Christ's burial.

This overview of Byzantine terms for canopies is not intended to be exhaustive but only to illustrate the numerous terms that occur in the surviving textual evidence and whose meanings are occasionally confirmed by available archeological and visual material. Then again, some canopy-like structures have survived, but we simply do not know what the Byzantines called them. A curious canopy, projecting above the narthex roof in the thirteenth-century Church of Panagia Parigoritissa in Arta, Greece, is just one such example.[143]

---

[142] The Byzantines used the word *koubuklion* for both the royal chambers and the apartment of the royal palaces where the royal chambers and servants' quarters were found. The important feature of such chambers seems to be that they were domed and that they were frequently used in Constantinople, though none survive.

[143] Orlandos (1963) 137–140. See also Fig. 4.37 in this volume.

THE CIRCULATION OF INCONSISTENT TERMINOLOGY FOR CANOPIES

The inconsistent terminology used for canopies, now as well as in the past, seems to result from the thinking process itself intermingling rhetorical imagery and the visual embodiment of ideas. The process of copying texts and their influence on our understanding of material objects is important. For this study, I have traced just a few examples that show how terms and associated meanings for canopies circulated widely, spanning vast chronological and geographical horizons (Table 4).

For example, a Greek poet Nicander (third–second centuries BCE) from Anatolia named a kind of Egyptian beans *kiboron* (κιβώριον) in his poem (Table 4.1). Some 400 years later, another pre-Christian poet and antiquarian, Athenaus (second–third century CE) from Alexandria cited Nicander directly and expanded the meaning of the term *kiborion* to denote chalices used in pagan temples. In Alexandria, the texts obviously circulated for a prolonged time. Hence, Hesychius in the sixth century wrote a lexicon that included the term *kiborion* as used by Nicander and Athenaus and associated the term further with its phonetic and symbolic cognate *kibotion* (chest) for a saintly tomb and shrine. Yet, such distribution and appropriation of terms used for canopies was certainly not linear. In the twelfth century, Archbishop Eustathius directly cited Nicander and Homer and used the word *kiboron* for a kind of Egyptian beans, without making any reference to canopies as architectural installations or sacred objects.

The phonetic and cognate conflation of the terms *kiborion* and *kibotion* that had happened already in pre-Christian times, judging also by the medical treatise written by Dioscorides Pedianus in the first century, was expanded by Hesychius in his sixth-century lexicon and adopted by the sixth-century church prelate and historian Sophronios (Table 4.6). Later on, both Patriarch Photios in the ninth century and a Russian pilgrim, Stephen of Novgorod, in the fourteenth century would use these terms in the same manner in their theological and pilgrim accounts, respectively, for the canopies—either over the altar table in a Byzantine church or over the miraculous icon that once stood in Hagia Sophia in Constantinople. These later accounts by Patriarch Photios and pilgrim Stephen also reveal how the terms became associated with specific and distinct architectural installations of the Byzantine-rite churches.

Similarly, in the fifth century, the monk Callinicus used the word *kiborion* for a saint's shrine or reliquary, while Marcus the deacon used the same word for a Roman structure in Gaza, presumably on four columns with a dome (Table 4.5). In the seventh century, Archbishop John called the ciborium-shrine of St. Demetrios in Thessaloniki *kiborion*, even though the shrine most likely never was in the shape of an open columnar canopy. At the same time, hegumenos George named the now-lost saint's shrine of St. Theodore Syceote *kiborion*. It seems as if after the seventh century the term *kiborion* was used in hagiographies for various saintly shrines, but it was *always* used in connection with the shrine of St. Demetrios, once the term entered the Constantinopolitan *Synaxarion*. This abridged compilation of the lives of the saints was used in liturgical services in the Byzantine-rite churches and certainly developed further for the wide dissemination of the term and meaning of saintly shrines from Syria to Novgorod. At least since the tenth century, judging by the authoritative Constantinopolitan *Synaxarion*, the ciborium-shrine of St. Demetrios had also been related to the concept of his eternal house (*oikos*). After the tenth century, the word was used for various shrines and installations, including for the shrine for the sandals of Christ in Constantinople. In the fourteenth century, an anonymous Russian pilgrim used the Slavic counterpart of the term *kiborion* for saintly shrines in the Holy Apostles in Constantinople, now permanently lost with the destruction of this Byzantine imperial foundation that was replaced by the Fatih mosque under the Ottoman Turks in 1461.

This brief overview of the terminology and how the Byzantines and their contemporaries both named the canopied structures or used the same terms interchangeably for objects, which were not canopies, is critical. It reveals the importance of assessing the texts in their wider context, understanding the ways in which texts of different genres convey ideas on architecture, as well as juxtaposing the archeological and architectural evidence with the textual sources, thereby trying not to lose our grasp of the material reality of various canopies used in the Byzantine tradition.

CONCLUDING REMARKS: CANOPIES—DIVERSITY IN UNITY

Because Byzantine Greek was not a standardized language, contemporary theologians, poets, official historians, and others used various, descriptive, and versatile terms, which they copiously combined and interpolated, when writing about canopies.[144] This phenomenon can be followed on several levels. The Greek formal linguistic counterpart for a ciborium—κιβώριον (*kibōrion, kivōrion*)—potentially reveals objects of different forms and meanings. There was no "standardization" of the term *kibōrion* for canopies in the Byzantine tradition by the sixth century or by the period of Iconoclasm, as has been previously suggested.[145] Some other, mostly descriptive words, which are marginalized in current scholarship,[146] were also used to define canopies, usually in terms of their component parts. These terms include *kibotion, orophion, apsida, oikiskos, pirgos, tetravelon, tetrapilon, tetrakionia, katapetasmata, parapetasmata, ouraniskos, tholos, kouboukleion,* and *kamelauhion,* to name but a few. When describing canopies, the Byzantine elite, deeply familiar with rhetorical traditions, used diverse rhetorical strategies that allowed complementary treatment of text and structure. Some of these strategies aimed to invoke a contemplative process about the multiple meanings of canopies stretching back to the pre-Christian past. In some cases, as in Paulos Silentarios' encomium to the altar canopy in Hagia Sophia, the rhetoric included a performative aspect—the praise was recited aloud and experienced while in movement and in front of the actual canopy in the actual church. Highly efficient treatment of rhetorical figures such as metaphor, allegory, or metonymy allowed the conflation of many sources that built upon the Byzantine belief system and for a multilayered conceptual and multisensory understanding of canopies. These educated approaches allowed the Byzantines to interchangeably relate the same image and vocal associations of the whole and parts of a canopy, like its columns, roof, or curtains, thus leaving us without the possibility of developing a strict, systematic, and hierarchical overview of what a canopy meant to them or what its most decisive parts were. However, all this is not to imply that the long-term perspective provided here is suggestive of a monolithic and underdeveloped tradition in Byzantium, but rather that the chronologically and geographically focused studies actually allow for superficial, positivistic, strictly empirical systematic studies, as sporadic "revivals" of certain terms for canopies highlighted in this discussion.

Certain words for canopies may have been more frequently used at some points of time than others, as if some of them were "forgotten" and then "revived," sometimes not even with the exact same meaning, as was the case with *apsida*. My observation is that such a phenomenon most likely belongs to the general phenomenon of Byzantine "revivals" and

144 Downey (1946) 22–34 came to a similar conclusion.

145 Smith, M. T. (1968) 325–349.

146 Except in the works by Greek scholars like Prokopios (1981) 125–128.

"renaissances" that do not always overlap with each other and may be a result of the intellectual and theological trends in a given period, or of the survival of certain Christian and pre-Christian texts in certain medieval libraries or within certain educated circles, monastic or aristocratic, for example.[147] If my hypothesis is sustainable, further research by scholars in other disciplines—linguists, historians of religion, and anthropologists, above all—may clarify the use and geographical spread of these and other terms that communicated the idea and meaning of canopies, and consequently related multilayered concepts. In turn, careful reconsideration of the terms and textual evidence for canopies may significantly re[de]fine our knowledge about canopies in Eastern Christianity.[148]

Though this book points to some of the linguistic and visual ambiguities related to canopies familiar to the Byzantines, careful rereading of the sources in the future may reveal additional terms that may have been used to denote canopies. Simultaneously, by paying closer attention to the textual descriptions of canopies, including the way they build canopies in the cultural memory, we may further expand our knowledge about what these structures meant to the Byzantines. In light of the analyzed terminological issues here, the modern term *canopy,* as a reference to its recognizable basic form as a four-columned structure with or without a roof that frames a singular place, is the most appropriate and applicable for the research of canopy-like objects in the Byzantine tradition, while the terms used by the Byzantines themselves remain valid for understanding the various meanings of the actual canopies in the Byzantine church.

A possible reason for the lacunae in scholarship on Byzantine canopies in general, and especially later examples, should be sought in the beginning of Byzantine studies. Early scholarly interest in Byzantine church architecture and art was facilitated roughly after the 1450s by travelers and antiquarians from the West and by Greeks who lived in the West. Antiquarian visits in the early modern period were focused predominantly on the Greek classical past and the post-Byzantine present, and did not provide viable and verifiable evidence on Byzantine canopies as liturgical furnishings.[149] The silence of the early scholars of Byzantine churches about canopies cannot be understood to be a conclusion about whether Greek churches had canopies by that time. A recently reconstructed painted wooden altar canopy dated to the mid–sixteenth century from the Church of St. Mamas, Morphou, on the island of Cyprus revealed strong Byzantine references in its form and meaning.[150] Among possible reasons why early antiquarians did not discuss church canopies could have been that most post-Byzantine churches did not have canopies, but also that antiquarian writers did not consider it important to write about canopies. Starting from the nature of their research, the antiquarians and travelers would not find church canopies exotic enough because many churches in the West did have

[147] On the Byzantine revival in the eleventh and twelfth centuries, see Kazhdan and Wharton Epstein (1985), esp. 133–145, 158–166, 197–233.

[148] I concur with Smith, M. T. (1968) 325–349, who argued that the terminology for canopies was probably transmitted to the Western world from the East.

[149] Antiquarian interest in Byzantine architecture spread from Italy throughout Europe. Although there were many voyages to the Eastern Mediterranean from the fifteenth century on, only some post-1670s missions to the Levant provided references of Byzantine architecture *in situ*. French travel accounts by J. Spon (1679); Grelot (1683), and Tournefort (1717), to name but a few pre-Enlightenment accounts, did include Byzantine church architecture, but continued to be concerned primarily with the continuation of liturgical practices in churches, or with their transformation into mosques. See also Auzépy and Grélois (2001) 39–43.

[150] Bolman (2010) 134–162.

canopies at the time. Additional reasons could well have been related to the fact that, by the time the Westerners visited them, most churches were in ruins or had already been converted into mosques. In the case of the conversion of churches into mosques, liturgical furnishings, including canopies, were occasionally reused as building material or as *spolia* for *minbars,* as examples from the Cathedral St. Sophia in Ohrid and the imperial Pantokrator Monastery (now Molla Zeyrek Camii) in Constantinople reveal.[151]

Moreover, Charles Du Cange, who is considered the founder of Byzantine historical studies in the seventeenth century, actually had never examined architecture *in situ* himself, yet he provided numerous critical references to Byzantine architecture.[152] Though Du Cange does not list the term *ciborium* (κιβώριον) in his seminal work *Glossiarum,* the first systematic pre-encyclopedic dictionary of medieval Greek, he writes elsewhere about the altar canopy of Hagia Sophia: "Ciborium appellant Scriptores Ecclesiastici quod Ordo Romanus tegimen et umbraculum altaris."[153] Du Cange's reference to the altar canopy of Hagia Sophia comes from surviving Greek texts translated into Latin, and his interpretation is based on an analogy with altar canopies in Western Europe. Inspired by the "medieval genealogy" of the Roman Empire in the East, Du Cange's work set the course of modern historiography of the Byzantine world, yet it also established an oversimplified view of its material culture. As historian Jean-Michele Spieser explained, "Byzantium was not considered a historical reality in itself, but . . . an 'avatar' of the Roman Empire."[154]

Similarly, by translating numerous manuscripts from Greek into Latin, educated Greeks who fled the Byzantine Empire to the West after the fall of Constantinople (1453) studied the Byzantine Church philologically and theologically, rather than architecturally and archeologically. They influenced the development of Byzantine studies and raised awareness of Byzantine monuments through their interest in Greek manuscripts and collections. These intellectuals were often teachers and librarians and converts to Roman Catholicism, like Manuel Chrysoloras (ca. 1350–1415) and Jean Lascaris (?-ca. 1535), to name but two of the most prominent.[155] It is surely significant that, at about the time when Byzantine studies were originating and were focusing predominantly on texts rather than on archeological and architectural evidence, various Greek words for canopies—not only *kiborion*—were almost uniformly rendered in Latin as *ciborium.* For example, in the Latin version of the Hagiography of St. Theokiste from the island of Paros, a reference to the altar canopy, still preserved, is amended from the original text, and the word *orophion* is changed to the more "appropriate" term *kiborion.*[156] A cursory comparison of the Greek and Latin versions of the text sometimes reveals this phenomenon of free translation. Leo Allatios added numerous annotations to the translation of Migne's *Patrologia Graeca,* which are usually overlooked as burdening texts that are already difficult to read. However, his annotations often refer to the original words and occasionally to the sources he thought may have been used for a full understanding of the text. In my opinion, this fact reveals, not only how difficult it was for scholars in the sixteenth and seventeenth centuries to translate Greek into Latin, but also how difficult it was to overcome the difference between theological assumptions inherent

[151] Grozdanov (1969) 49–63; Ousterhout (2010) 432–439. See also Figs. 2.44, 2.61, and 2.62 in this volume.

[152] More about Du Cange as an antiquarian and historian with an interest in Byzantine Greek in Ostrogorsky (1969) 4 and Auzépy and Grélois (2001) 72–79.

[153] Du Cange (1937) 118–130. For the *Glossarium,* see Du Cange (1688).

[154] Spieser (2000) 199–210.

[155] *ODB* vol. 1, s.v. *Manuel Chrysoloras*; Auzépy and Grélois (2001) 17.

[156] Ὡς δὲ καὶ τῆς σεβαστῆς καὶ θείας τραπέζης τὸ ὑπερκείμενον ὀρόφιον [ὃ κιβώριον καλεῖν σύνηθες *add.* M.] εἴσω τῆς πύλης ἑωράκαμεν . . . *Life StTheokiste-a* 226.

in Orthodoxy on one hand, and those of Roman Catholicism and Protestantism on the other. Once again, like Du Cange, the native-speaking Greeks who translated Greek texts into Latin often did not have immediate knowledge of Byzantine churches *in situ*. Allatios was among the earliest scholars to provide explanations about Byzantine churches and their furnishings. Paradoxically, his knowledge of actual buildings was bound to his childhood experience on his native Chios and to his Jesuit missionary service on Chios and Crete. Occasionally he would draw conclusions by comparing Greek churches with those that served in the Latin rite, based on his experience in Rome.[157] The 1520s, when the first printed version of the Septuagint and of various religious texts translated from Greek into Latin were massively disseminated throughout Europe, marked the threshold for the development of all aspects of Byzantine studies, including those related to canopies.[158]

Though Byzantine studies have advanced since the Enlightenment, academic knowledge of textual evidence for canopies seems to have remained bound to these early positivistic inquiries. Such a state of affairs inevitably led, not only to a partial knowledge of the terminology used by the Byzantines to visualize and describe canopies, but also to some lacunae and misunderstandings in scholarship about the presence and significance of canopies in the Byzantine tradition. Genuine advancement in our knowledge of Byzantine ecclesiastical architecture cannot depend on the criteria of interpretation that were established four centuries ago. The scope of the problem is immense, and this book certainly cannot offer a comprehensive treatment, but it does address some important aspects of the terminology and methodology relevant to the studies of canopies, including their architectural properties and meanings in sacred space.

---

[157] Allatios' two letters on Greek churches, *De templis Graecorum recentioribus* written to Jean Morin (1591–1659), a French scholar and antiquarian, remain invaluable, not only for our understanding of the early methodology of Byzantine studies, but also for early modern accounts of Byzantine churches. *Allatios*; Cutler (1966a) 79–89; Ostrogorsky (1969) 2–4. On the relationship between works by Du Cange and Allatios, see Auzépy and Grélois (2001) 17ff.

[158] Two thousand copies of the Septuagint were first printed in the Complutensian Polyglot Psalter. *Bible. O.T. Psalms. Polyglot* (1516).

TWO

Canopies in the Byzantine Church

Archeological and Architectural Evidence

But when we saw the orophion ["roof" denoting "canopy" - J.B.] *over the venerable and holy altar inside the gate (of the sanctuary), we were astonished at the delightful (sight). For the carving did not seem to be made of marble nor wrought by (human) hands with (tools of) iron and skill. (It looked), instead, as if (it had been made) out of milk mixed with juice of the fig tree (in order to thicken) and had been cast in the shape of a stegous* [another word for "roof," again denoting "canopy" - J.B.]. *Made of such stone I saw once (a statue of) Selene (the goddess of moon) driving a chariot drawn by bulls. The (canopy) lay broken in pieces and we ran up to it and stood before it, uttering all manner of curses and revilement at the man who smashed it, for it was surely a treasure and an heirloom and offering worthy of the house of God.*

Ὡς δὲ καὶ τῆς σεβαστῆς καὶ θείας τραπέζης τὸ ὑπερκείμερον ὀρόφιον εἴσω τῆς πύλης ἑωράκαμεν, κατεπλάγημεν τῆς τερπνότητος· οὐδέ γὰρ ἐῴκει λίθον φύσιν ἔχειν τὸ τόρευμα οὐδὲ σιδήρῳ καὶ τέχνῃ λελαξεῦσθαι καὶ χείρεσιν· αλλ'οἱά τινι γάλακτι ὀπῷ φυραθέντι καὶ πρός τὸ σχῆμα τοῦ στέγους μεμηχαημένου τοῦ χεύματος· τοιούτῳ ποτὲ ἐγὼ λίθῳ τεθέαμαι διγρηλατοῦσαν ἐπὶ ταύροις Σελήνην· Τὸ μὲν οὖν ἔκειτο τεθραυσμένον, ἡμεῖς δὲ συνεθένμεν καὶ παριστάμεθα καταρώμενοι καὶ παντοίως τὸν συντρίψαντα λοιδορούμενοι· καὶ γάρ ἦν τι χρῆμα καὶ ἄξιον οἴκῳ Θεοῦ κειμήλιον καὶ ἀνάθημα.

Niketas Magistros, chronicler of Emperor Leo VI (r. 886–912)[1]

THIS TENTH-CENTURY ACCOUNT BY THE HIGH-RANKING OFFICIAL NIKETAS Magistros of the marble altar canopy in the still-standing sixth-century Cathedral of Panagia Ekatontapyliani (literally *Our Lady of the Hundred Gates*) on the island of Paros is the only surviving description written by a Byzantine writer about this famous and best-preserved Byzantine canopy (Fig. 2.1).[2] The text suggests the continual use of altar canopies in Byzantine churches as well as their common looting and destruction during medieval times. More importantly, this narrative graphically expresses the sensual

[1] *Life StTheokiste-a* 226. Translation according to *SD* 104. See also *Life StTheokiste-c* 104–105 (ch. 7).

[2] *Life StTheokiste-c* 97, n. 7.

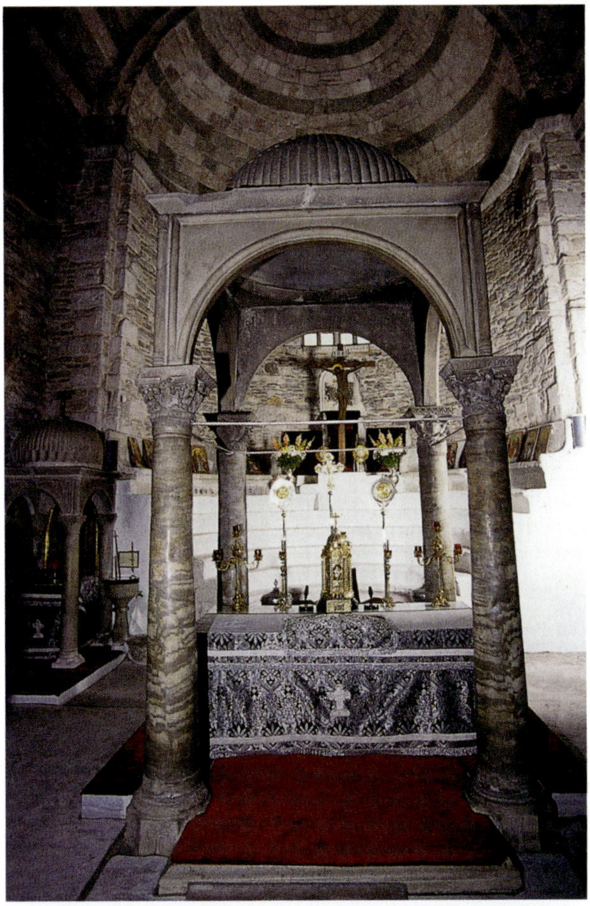

FIGURE 2.1 *Altar canopy, Paros, sixth century (?), restored.* COMMERCIAL POSTCARD

delight that canopies evoked among the Byzantines. To the Byzantine beholder, the material splendor of a canopy in its intended architectural setting in the sanctuary invoked the immaterial glory and heavenly beauty of the sacred. Visually prominent above and beyond the sanctuary screen, the canopy sheltered the holy table. Focusing on the canopy roof and describing the entire installation as an offering worthy of the house of God, Niketas Magistros, who wrote in educated Byzantine Greek, frequently making references to Homeric language, compared the beauty and skillful work of the marble of this canopy with those of a famous statue of Selene, the pagan goddess of the moon, as described by Achilles Tatius, an antique Greek writer from Alexandria.[3] The comparison of the Paros canopy with a pagan statue is critical, because the widely established notion that the Byzantines feared that demons inhabited pagan statues cannot be grasped at all from this account; rather it insists on the continuity of the sculptural quality of the church canopy with famous sculptures of classical antiquity.[4] As an object worthy of the "house of God,"

---

[3] *Achilles Tatius* 1.4.3, 6.1–2; according to *Life StTheokiste-c* 105, n. 38.

[4] On the well-balanced and critical approach to the widely accepted notion that the Byzantines believed that demons inhabited statues and the other aspects of Byzantine "superstition" and "credulity," see James (1996) 12–20, where she successfully analyzes Byzantine attitudes to classical art as seen through their accounts

the impressive canopy was inseparably intertwined with notions of sacredness, which at first may also sound somewhat unusual in light of accepted norms of Byzantine piety being reserved for holy figures. Hermit Symeon, who narrated to Niketas Magistros the episode about the Arabs' unsuccessful removal of the canopy, suggested that the canopy was both physically and spiritually too big to leave the church through the sanctuary doors. According to the narrative, an Arab named Nasiris (Nasr) was impressed by the beauty of the canopy and presumably wanted to use it in the mosque in Chandax on Crete.[5] He even measured the canopy and the width of the doors and made a plan for removing the canopy from the church. Yet the "holy and divine" canopy miraculously "grew in size" each time the Arabs attempted to remove it from the sanctuary, holy monk Symeon narrated, and as the "divine object did not deign to be defiled and become the instrument of foul sacrifices," it was eventually smashed in rage by Nasiris.[6] For his disrespect of the holy object, the notorious Nasiris was punished by divine providence as he perished with his ship beneath the sea, reported monk Symeon.[7]

The episode from Paros illustrates the destiny that many Byzantine canopies had of being plundered and reused, but it also demonstrates the expressive power that contemporaries, both Christians and non-Christians, ascribed to them. Comparably, in the twelfth century, Michael the Syrian, Jacobite Patriarch of Antioch (1166–1199), wrote about the sixth-century "Sclavene," possibly Slavic, raid into Greece, when numerous canopies were carried off from devastated churches.[8] In Corinth, one Sclavene leader even took the big church canopy and used it as his tent-like dwelling.[9] This re-appropriation and reuse of the church canopy for the regal setting is better understood in light of the widely accepted imperial connotations of canopies. Already in the 570s, the throne of the Byzantine emperor, as Christ's representative on earth, was associated with the throne of Christ. Widely circulated coins of Byzantine emperor Justin II (r. 565–574) emphasize this quasi-religious theme of the enthroned emperor. Flavius Cresconius Corippus, in his poem written on the occasion of the emperor's rise to power, wrote:

> The inner sanctum is ennobled by the imperial seat, which is surrounded by four excellent columns, above which a canopy, shining bright with solid gold in imitation of the vault of heaven, overshadows the immortal leader sitting on his throne. [The latter is] ornamented with gems and distinguished with purple and gold. Four *arcs* bend to intersect one another, and above, on the right and left side, matching victories alight with wings outspread in the air, carrying a laurel crown in their shining right hands. (trans. A. Cameron)[10]

---

on statues and demonstrates that pagan sculptures had to be distinguished from holy images. Saradi-Mendelovici (1990) 47–61, also offers a revised overview of the Byzantine attitude to their pagan past.

[5] *Life StTheokiste-c* 107 (ch. 12).

[6] Ibid.

[7] Ibid.

[8] Curta (1998) 19–34; Setton (1952) 351–362.

[9] Ibid.

[10] Corippus 11, 106; Cameron (1981) 205–234, esp. 221. According to Averil Cameron, with whom I tend to agree, the four arcs are the arches of the canopy. Mathews (1993) 105–106 offered an alternative interpretation, suggesting that they are the arched legs of the throne.

Hence, the huge church canopy is similar to a canopy over the imperial throne, and the overarching victory symbolism such installations carried possibly impressed diverse groups of people when they reused church canopies as their settings and symbols of power.[11]

This chapter examines in particular the surviving archeological and architectural evidence available on canopies in the Byzantine ecclesiastical tradition and asks how the aspects of this evidence relate to each other for a given period or geographic region. As the majority of archeological evidence on canopies is reduced to their architectural and sculptural fragments, special attention is placed on the materials used, as well as on surviving decorations and inscriptions. These remains further point to the major characteristics of the production of canopies and understanding their materiality, decoration, and inscriptions as carriers of meaning. Combined, this evidence highlights the various types of canopies used in Byzantine-rite churches and how their shape and decorative features were related to each other.

CANOPIES IN BYZANTINE ECCLESIASTICAL TRADITION: QUANTITY, CHRONOLOGICAL, AND GEOGRAPHICAL DISTRIBUTION

The question of how many canopies there were in Byzantine churches remains open and potentially unanswerable. Many of these objects were lost because of the rebuilding of churches over the prolonged time of their existence; because of their looting, demolition, and destruction due to unrest and wars; and because of natural disasters such as major earthquakes that often strike in this part of the world. Due to the conversion of churches into mosques, and especially once Islam became a predominant religion in the medieval Eastern Mediterranean, Christian canopies could have been dismantled and their parts used as raw building material or simply reused as *minbars*, which are shaped as towers, usually with pyramidal roofs. The sheer beauty of monumental canopies and the costly, luxurious materials used are perhaps the main reasons why only a tiny percentage of them have survived. As the episode of the canopy from Paros recounted before testifies, entire canopies or their marble parts were often plundered. Similarly, canopies made of silver and gold were often melted down. Some canopies were dismantled and carried off by the Byzantines themselves. When in the sixth century, at the time of the Slav and Avar invasions, Emperor Justinian ordered silver *ciboria* from non-Constantinopolitan churches to be brought inside the city,[12] he was following ancient Greek laws about the alienation of sacred objects in times of crises. Due to their monetary value, silver canopies were then melted down in order to ransom prisoners of war.[13] In the light of such complex historical circumstances, it is understandable that only a tiny fraction of the Byzantine canopies that once existed have been preserved.

---

[11] Curta (1998) 19–34; Nikolajević (1983) 801–829, esp. 803. On the symbolism of canopied thrones, see Alföldi (1950) 537–566.

[12] *John Malalas-a* 18, 708B; *John Malalas-c* book 18, p. 297. See also Mundell-Mango (1992) 123–136, esp. ns. 27, 28; and Chapter 1 of this book.

[13] Mundell-Mango (1992) 123–136. The Byzantine princess Anna Komnene (b. 1083–d. ca. 1153/1154) in her book *Alexiad* wrote about the "ancient laws and canons of the alienation of sacred objects from churches" for the ransoming of prisoners of war. She quite appropriately compared these laws with those in pagan Athens, when Pericles "borrowed" the golden necklace from the goddess Athena Parthenos and other valuables from her treasury in times of crisis. (cf. *Thucydides* ii, 13). *Alexiad-a* V 2.2; VI 3.3–VI 4.4; *Alexiad-b* 186.

My research shows that there were definitely many more canopies in Byzantine churches than we have previously thought, and that these canopies were used from the early Christian times throughout the medieval period, until circa 1500. During the course of my research of architectural and archeological evidence for canopies in Byzantine-rite churches, I was able to assemble records for more than 200 canopies (Map 1, Table 5). The physical data confirm the wide use of canopies, as is suggested by their images in more than 500 visual representations that I have collected independently[14] and by testimonies in more than 100 texts that mention canopied objects.[15]

Starting with a conventional typology based on the ways in which certain canopies framed sacred loci for the performance of many liturgical and non-liturgical rites, it is possible to distinguish several types of canopies in Byzantine-rite churches. The Divine Liturgy, the celebration of the Eucharist, is the most important service in churches, yet, as succinctly explained by Vasileios Marinis,

> the Byzantine rite, the liturgical system of the Byzantine Orthodox church, consisted of a series of services comprising the sacraments, such as Eucharist, baptism, and ordination; the Divine Office or the Office of the Hours; the daily corporate prayer services, such as Matins, Vespers, Compline; a cycle of fixed feasts and saint's days such as Christmas and Epiphany, . . . a cycle of moveable feasts such as Easter; and occasional vigils and lesser services.[16]

In the Byzantine rite, the sacraments are considered the divine mysteries, through which the recipient receives the mystery of the divine grace and perceives such mystery both sensorily and performatively. Hence the perceptible frames, including the architectural setting, are constituents of the performance of the sacraments. The sacraments in the Byzantine rite were never explicitly enumerated, though some of them became predominantly recognizable. In addition to the Eucharist and baptism, because the sacrament of confession was directly related to the receiving of the Eucharist, and chrismation (anointment) to baptism, confession and chrismation were often performed at locations adjacent to the sanctuary and baptismal fonts, respectively. Similarly, ordination and marriage could take place in the main church spaces—in the sanctuary and *naos*, respectively—and often within overlapping service of the Divine Liturgy. Hence, church canopies that were most directly related to liturgy and the two major sacraments were altar canopies that framed the holy table and the performance of the Eucharist, and baptismal canopies that enclosed baptismal fonts.[17] While similar in form and meaning to baptismal fonts, by the sixth century if not earlier, canopied *phialai* became distinct architectural installations for fonts with sanctified water, which were used daily and for ceremonies related to the blessing of holy water on the occasions of Epiphany (Theophany) on January sixth, Bright Friday (Friday of Easter Week or Bright Week), and Mid-Pentecost.[18] The readings from the scriptures and prayers were related to the ambo, which also could have been framed by a canopy, even if only a few churches in the Middle and Late Byzantine periods actually had ambos as distinct church furnishings. Other devotional and non-liturgical rites and the foci of their respective locations were occasionally marked by canopied installations over specially venerated tombs,

---

[14] Bogdanović (2008a).

[15] See also Chapter 1.

[16] Marinis (2014) 10.

[17] Mirković (1983) 24.

[18] Mirković (1983) 151–157; Patrich (1995) 273; Kandić (1998–9) 61–78; Marinis (2014) 95–97.

reliquaries, icons, bells, or episcopal thrones. To these we can add various stationary locations within and outside the church proper, those closely related to the processional character of Byzantine services, both liturgical and non-liturgical. For example, canopied church entrances or *tetrapyla* (monumental four-columned structures) in urban spaces marked the stations of religious and imperial processions. Similarly, distinct locations in the church *naos* and on church galleries could have been reserved for emperors and empresses and for members of the imperial family and retinue when they attended the church.

I have taken material comprising archeological evidence for different types of canopies and mapped and distributed the data across four crucial periods widely acknowledged for their impact on the development of Byzantine art and architecture (Maps 2–5). The first part comprises evidence from approximately the fourth through sixth centuries, also known in scholarship as the late antique and early Christian period, with the peak of early Byzantine accomplishments embodied in the famous and most-studied Hagia Sophia in Constantinople. The second section, from the seventh to the mid-ninth centuries, or the so-called transitional period, juxtaposes the evidence of canopies with marked theological and Iconoclastic controversies coupled with urban and economic decline, and hence also a decline of monumental architecture. The third period, from the mid-ninth through twelfth centuries, known as the Middle Byzantine period, is characterized by the increased building of cross-in-square domical and other types of centralized churches. These churches were generally much smaller than early Christian basilicas, which prompted suggestions about the decreased use of architectural installations such as canopies. The fourth section reveals evidence of canopies from the thirteenth through fifteenth centuries, or from the so-called Late Byzantine period, during which the limited architectural and building campaigns were focused on the reconstruction and the rebuilding of existing structures in Constantinople, ending with a complete cessation of church building after the 1330s in the capital.[19] Yet the so-called Middle and Late Byzantine periods simultaneously featured the emergence of new centers of architectural production based on Byzantine models in the Balkans, the wider Mediterranean area, and beyond. Hence, I include evidence of canopies in Byzantine-rite churches beyond the territories of the Byzantine Empire. Above all, here are included references to canopies from medieval Serbia and Rus, which were available to me. This material presented chronologically and geographically is further subdivided by various types of canopies (Table 6). The types of canopies are initially defined by their primary function based on where they were found within the church proper. Occasionally, decoration and inscriptions found on architectural segments of canopies, complemented by the knowledge of the rites and objects they may have originally framed, further point to the type of a particular canopy. When in doubt, due to the lack of evidence or due to ambiguous references, the function of a canopy is marked as unresolved.

The earliest surviving canopy-like installation in the eastern Mediterranean, which was without any doubt used in Christian ecclesiastical context as it relates to the exclusively Christian sacrament, belongs to the baptistery installation from the so-called Christian building at Dura Europos, Syria (now in the Yale University Museum); the installation itself dates to around the 240s.[20] Essentially composed of an arched niche framed by two columns and leaning against a wall, the canopy elucidates the variety of types and forms used for such installations, and that they were not necessarily always realized as four-columned structures. The Dura-Europos installation is additionally important because it predates the wide and official

[19] Ćurčić (2004) 65–94; Bogdanović (2008b).

[20] On the archeological references to the baptistery from Dura, see Gates (1984) 166–181, esp. 178; Snyder, G. F. (2003), esp. 128. See also Chapter 3.

acceptance of Christianity in the fourth century, which can be illustrated by a series of events, starting with the Edict of Milan in 313, when Roman emperor Constantine I (d. 337) proclaimed religious tolerance of Christianity, followed by his own decision to be the first Roman emperor who embraced Christianity just before he passed away, and confirmed by the official proclamation of Nicene Christianity as the state religion of the Roman Empire in 380 with the Edict of Thessaloniki under Emperor Theodosius I (d. 395).[21] Indeed, with the wide acceptance of Christianity and its status as the official religion of the Roman Empire, the number of preserved canopies in churches of the early Christian and early Byzantine period between fourth and sixth centuries is much greater. I have recorded some 100 of them, mostly altar, baptismal, and tomb canopies, constructed as architecturally fully defined four-columned covered installations, made of high-quality stone, and dispersed in the territories across the eastern Mediterranean (Map 2, Table 6).

It was assumed that, as they became more centralized and less processional, most of Middle Byzantine and Late Byzantine mid- to small-sized compact churches could not have, nor needed, architectural installations such as canopies. Scholars have highlighted the unsuccessful spatial and visual inclusion of altar canopies as being behind the changing tectonics and function of early Christian knee-high sanctuary barriers—*templon* screens, which during the Middle Byzantine period developed into the tall structures today also known as icon stands—*iconostases*.[22] While the form and use of sanctuary screens were not uniform across time and geography, by the ninth century, they were most often composed of four columns connected by waist- or chest-high parapets in the lower zone and topped by an architrave beam. These wall-like structures not only separated the sanctuary from the nave, but eventually also visually, and at least partially, concealed the altar canopies behind them. The inter-columnar spaces of sanctuary barriers were filled at first with curtains and then ultimately by panel icons, which as figurative images guided the believers during the liturgical and devotional rites. In such a setting, only the roof of the altar canopy would have been visible beyond the screen. Hence, Middle Byzantine churches differed from their early Christian precedents in terms of tectonics, size, and furnishings, which were further intertwined with changes in the liturgical and other services performed within churches. According to the archeological evidence I have collected, however, canopies existed and were continually used in Middle and Late Byzantine churches (Map 4, Table 6). More than 100 canopies can be dated to the period between the mid-ninth and twelfth centuries, suggesting their continued significant production as in the early Christian and the early Byzantine periods. Moreover, we have more evidence for canopies built in the approximately same time span of some 200–250 years and in a smaller geographical territory because the Byzantines lost significant territories in Africa and the Middle East after the emergence of Islam and its fast expansion in the eastern Mediterranean after the seventh century (Map 3). The loss of territory and church properties under Islam was partially supplanted by Byzantine diplomatic relations with the new emerging states of medieval Bulgaria, Serbia, and Rus, all of whom adopted Byzantine-rite churches along with Byzantine concepts of their design and furnishing. Accordingly, starting with the Middle Byzantine period, new evidence of canopies in Byzantine-rite churches also comes from within the expanded territories in the Balkans and the new territories in what we today recognize as Eastern Europe (Maps 4, 5).

---

[21] The literature is immense. See, for example, Forster (2008).

[22] Ousterhout (2008) 12–25; Marinis (2014) 25–48; Blaauw (2009a) 47–55.

Furthermore, more than ten different types of canopies in terms of their primary function can be observed throughout the Byzantine period: from altar canopies, to canopies that framed the spaces of a baptistery, *phiale*, tomb, shrine, reliquary, icon, ambo, episcopal throne, or church bell, to numerous other fragments of canopies, whose functions cannot be confirmed today. In each case, indeed, altar canopies remained the predominant type made for churches. More than half—i.e., 130 of some 240 canopies that I analyzed based on archeological and architectural evidence—belong to fully formed, four-columned altar canopies coming from churches throughout the wider Mediterranean basin. The overwhelming majority of these altar canopies can be divided into two almost equally large groups of approximately 60 canopies each, and can be dated to the early Christian and early Byzantine period (ca. fourth–sixth centuries) and to the Middle Byzantine period (ca. ninth–twelfth centuries), respectively (Table 6, Maps 2, 4). Most of the recognized canopies sheltered altar tables, while a much smaller, but still significant number of them were used for framing water fonts—baptisteries and *phialai* as well as tombs and shrines throughout the Byzantine realm, chronologically and geographically defined, confirming their importance as distinctive types of canopies (Table 6). Frequently, these objects were made of high-quality stone—above all, marble—but there is also evidence for canopies made of luxurious metals such as silver.

As expected, there is a noticeable decline in the production of canopies during the so-called transitional period (seventh–mid-ninth centuries). This period is marked by theological controversies, the emergence of Islam, religious and civil wars, the decline of cities and urban culture, the gradual loss of imperial control over the silver production and marble quarries in the Mediterranean, and overall economic decline.[23] This context explains the vivid decline in the production of church canopies as sumptuous objects; a few surviving examples of altar and baptismal canopies confirm the lower quality of materials used and the lower quality of execution of canopies. The closing section of this chapter and the material presented in the following chapters will address separately whether theological debates on the sacred objects used in Byzantine-rite churches during the so-called Iconoclastic controversies of the eighth and ninth centuries were also related to the symbolic meanings of canopies for framing sacred space and understanding canopies as sacred objects themselves.

Another period of decline of the production of new canopies and obvious reuse of *spolia* for making anew other canopies is evident during the Late Byzantine period (Map 5, Table 6). This trend can be related to the decline of church architecture after 1300 in Constantinople, the major architectural center of the Byzantines, as well as to the general trend of building smaller churches and *parekklesia* (lateral church buildings, usually funerary chapels in the Late Byzantine period). These smaller churches and chapels, if they had canopies, would either reuse previous installations related to the general increased use of *spolia* or were habitually made of perishable materials such as wood, as seen in medieval Rus.

Yet the mini-statistics based on the collected archeological evidence of canopies indicate that the sheer number of surviving archeological remains of some 135 canopies from the later periods is actually comparable to the some 100 canopies preserved from early Christian times. In fact, previously scholars nearly by default dated almost all extant stone

[23] Cruikshank Dood (1973); Karagiorgou (2001) 194; Sodini (2002) 129–145.

canopies to the fifth and sixth centuries, and only recently have scholars again examined the archeology of some of these canopies and independently reassigned them a date as late as the ninth century.[24] These contributions significantly change the overall scholarship of medieval canopies. Even if my corpus is not and cannot be exhaustive, my analysis definitely points to the continual use of canopies in Byzantine-rite churches, even more so because it is fair to assume that early Byzantine churches functioned over a prolonged time during the Middle Ages, and if they had canopies, they often would have continued to be used.

Textual evidence confirms the continuous, though not indispensable, use of canopies (Tables 1, 3). A couple of contemporary statements are especially revealing on the role of canopies in Byzantine-rite churches and their production. Already in 582, John, Bishop of Ephesus with a permanent residence in Constantinople, remarked that a large altar canopy was "customary in all the churches of the capital."[25] None have been preserved in Constantinople *in situ*, and only a few are confirmed archeologically. At the threshold of the eleventh and twelfth centuries, Byzantine Bishop Theodore of Andida informs us that not all churches have altar canopies, but that the hemispherical form of the *bema* (sanctuary) may have assumed the role of the canopy.[26] Theodore's statement opens the question on the meaning and form of canopies as necessarily three-dimensional objects, which are simultaneously sculpture and architecture, both literally and metaphorically. Hence, even if canopies were not required but rather recommended installations that framed sacred space in Byzantine-rite churches, Theodore's statement also implies that the Byzantines did not abandon entirely the idea of canopies as an important part of their churches. Moreover, judging by Theodore's testimony, at least by the Middle Byzantine period, the architectural segments of the church building itself, and more precisely the vaulted compartments such as the sanctuary space, could have been understood as canopies in their own right. We will turn to this important point of understanding vaulted church spaces as canopied architectural units in Chapter 4.[27]

Visual evidence of canopies as recorded by pilgrims can help us further contextualize the existence and use of canopies during the late Byzantine and post-Byzantine periods. A drawing by the Russian Grigorovich-Barskii from 1744 is remarkably informative for our understanding of the prolonged use of canopies in Byzantine-rite churches, because it clearly depicts a liturgical service in progress in the Lavra monastery on Mount Athos in Greece with the altar canopy prominent among the furnishings (Fig. 2.2).[28] Because in 1423 the Ottomans imposed a strict building regulation that forbade the construction of new ecclesiastical buildings, the depicted altar canopy implies a high possibility that some

---

[24] Piccirillo (2006) 51–113, esp. 55; Brubaker and Haldon (2001) ch. 1; Jakšić (1999–2000) 129–150; Preradović-Petrović (2002) 247–264; Vežić and Lončar (2009); Voyatzis (2011) 195–227.

[25] Mundell-Mango (1992) 123–136, esp. ns. 27, 28.

[26] *PG* 140, 417 col. 443.

[27] Significantly, in the twelfth century, Gervase (ca. 1141 – ca. 1210), a chronicler and sacristan of Canterbury Cathedral, also wrote of the ribbed vaulted compartments as "ciboria," with associated theological meanings. According to Gervase of Canterbury, "each compartment of a vault resembles a *ciborium*, and a vaulted aisle may be compared to a series of *ciboria*." Willis (1845) 49, n.e. I thank Richard Etlin (2015) for alerting me to this reference and for sharing with me his work on the symbolism of ribbed vaults and flying buttresses.

[28] Barski (1774), fig. on p. 60.

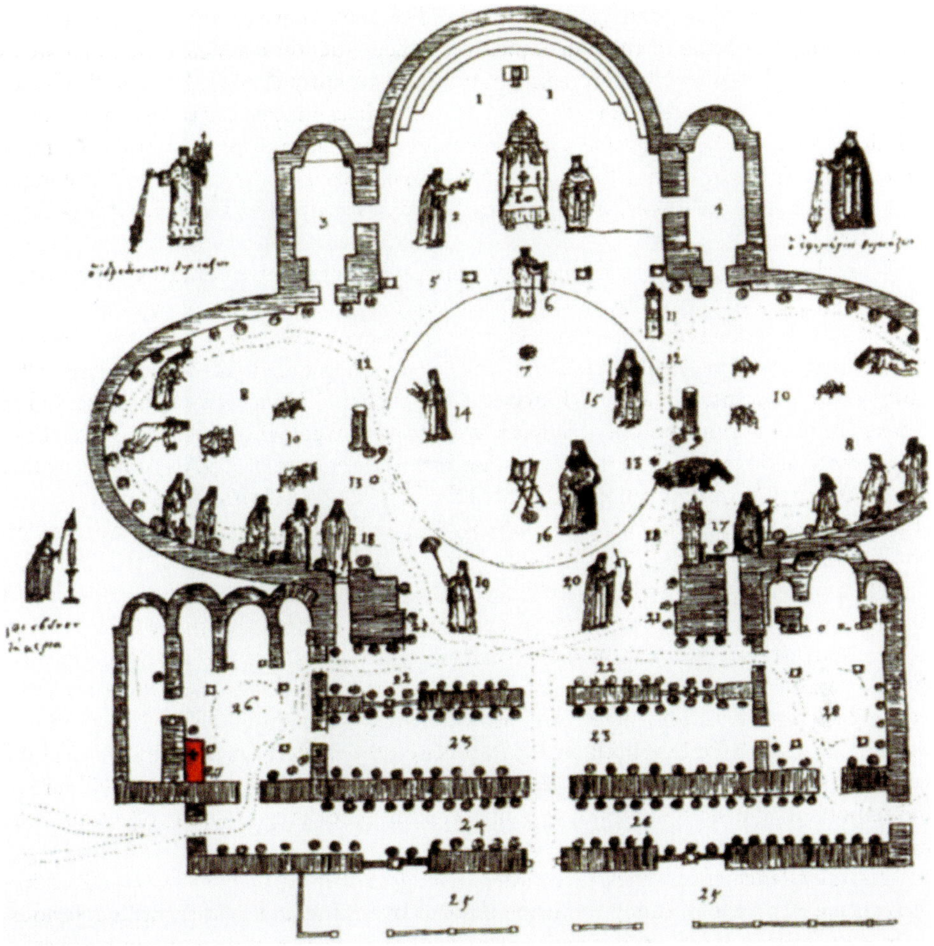

FIGURE 2.2 *Great Lavra Monastery. Architectural setting of the canopied tomb of St. Athanasios the Athonite (ca. 925–1001) marked in red and the depiction of the altar canopy in the apse.* DRAWING GRIGOROVICH-BARSKII, 1774

canopies on Mt. Athos may have been refurbished medieval installations.[29] Moreover, most post-Byzantine canopies above altar tables, holy water fonts, and icons that have been preserved in the conservative monastic communities on Mt. Athos could have simply replaced

[29] About Athonite acknowledgement of Sultan Murad II in 1423, see Fotić (2000) 108–133 and Fotić (1998) 91–102. Numerous Athonite churches have canopies; the oldest positively dated is the canopy over the *phiale* in Great Lavra monastery from the seventeenth century, while the majority of *katholika* have eighteenth- and nineteenth-century altar canopies, like in the Stavroniketa, Dohiarou, and Great Lavra monasteries. Boura (1975–1976) 85–96; Millet (1905) 104–141. The *katholikon* at the Hilandar monastery on Mt. Athos, for example, also has an altar canopy, though no work has been done on it, to the best of my knowledge.

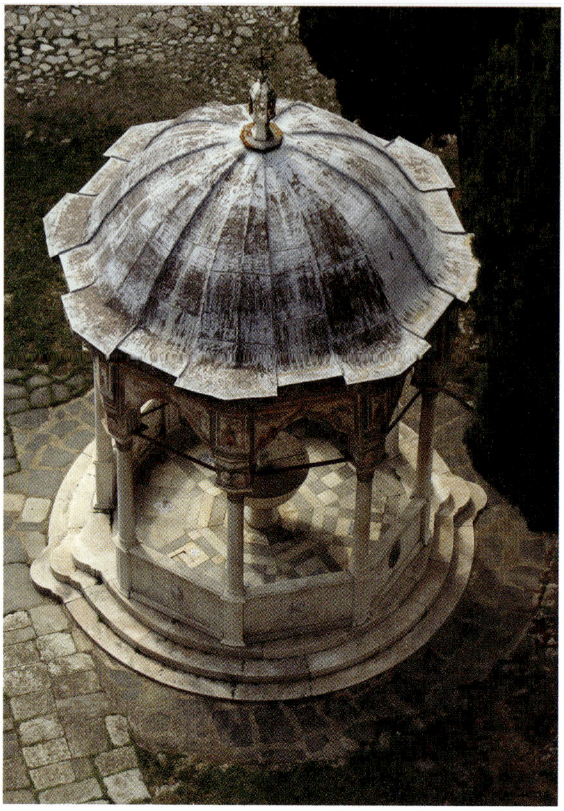

FIGURE 2.3 *Phiale, Hilandar Monastery, Mt. Athos, Greece, 1784.* PHOTO NEBOJŠA STANKOVIĆ

older Byzantine structures, the religious meaning of which was rooted in earlier traditions (Fig. 2.3).

THE LOCATION AND TYPES OF CANOPIES IN THE BYZANTINE-RITE CHURCH

By looking at the conventional typology of canopies within the church proper, canopies could frame the sacred space of the altars (holy tables); baptisteries; *phialai* (installations for the sanctified water); ambos; tombs of important individuals, including specially venerated shrines and sacred relics; venerated icons; church bells; or episcopal thrones, to name but a few. As we shall see, archeological evidence reveals that neither the location of such identified types of canopies within church spaces nor their geographical and chronological distribution were uniform. Furthermore, secondary elements of church canopies such as their materialization and decoration often cannot unilaterally point to the specific or singular use of different types of canopies.

Altar Canopies

The overwhelming majority of archeologically confirmed canopies in Byzantine churches are altar canopies. Altar canopies are placed in the Christian sanctuary over the holy table where the Eucharist, the bloodless sacrifice of the New Testament, and the presence of

Jesus Christ within the Divine Liturgy are manifested.[30] The altar table and the sanctuary represent the most sacred place in a church. Yet it is amazing that various Christian sites throughout the Eastern Mediterranean and especially those dated to the first centuries of Christianity offer no archeological proof for the existence of an altar table, presumably indispensable furniture for the liturgical function of a church.[31] Kimberly Bowes has demonstrated that in the first centuries of Christianity only a tiny percentage of the population in the Mediterranean were Christians, variously dispersed throughout cities and rural areas.[32] In other words, by the year 200 there were perhaps 200,000 Christians all together, and by the fourth century, the best estimate is that up to ten percent of the six million Roman citizens might have been Christians. Most of them practiced their faith in private homes.

Despite the limited evidence for altars in churches before the official Roman embracement of Christianity in the fourth century, the earliest altar canopies can be dated only to the fifth century (Tables 5, 6). Indeed, during any destruction or restoration of a church, the floors would often suffer first, leaving limited evidence for the footings of both the altar table and the canopy.[33] Altar canopies could be placed directly on smaller altar tables that occasionally reveal footings for a canopy at the four corners of the table top.[34] Lack of evidence for altars and related objects like canopies that framed them, which may not even have been obligatory, however, does not necessarily imply that these objects did not exist.

One valid explanation for the absence of altar tables and eventually their canopies in some churches could be that they were not made of stone but of other, less durable materials such as wood and metals. Another reason may well have been that altars and their canopies were sometimes portable. Indeed, the earliest altar in the Old St. Peter's in Rome from before the fifth century was probably portable, separated from the shrine of St. Peter and positioned somewhere in front of the shrine or near it.[35] Actually, a wooden, portable canopy had been in use in the Vatican for centuries for various purposes: to display relics periodically, to cover the pope during his public appearances, to shelter his bier, to enshrine the Holy Sacrament when it was moved within church.[36] Less is known of such practices in the Eastern Mediterranean.

Moreover, in contrast to masonry churches, which were repeatedly looted and left without interior fittings, Byzantine rock-cut churches often preserve their liturgical furnishing, including *synthrona* and ambos, which were also rock-cut, while altars are conspicuously absent.[37] For example, the rock-cut Church of St. John in Çavuşin, in Cappadocia, has preserved in its sanctuary a one-stepped *synthronon* (bench for the sitting of the clergy), a throne, and even a small cruciform crypt, but there is no archeological evidence for the altar. Therefore, its altar, indispensable and presumably among the most precious church

---

30 Mirković (1995) 103.

31 On the Christian liturgical requirements of the church since the earliest times, see, for example, Bradshaw (2002).

32 Bowes (2011) 53–57; Bowes (2008a); Bowes (2008b) 575–619.

33 The floor is one of the first elements of a church building to be altered during looting or changing of their function to non-Christian spaces. It was not uncommon for the floor to be robbed to its foundations, thus removing any trace of the church furnishings, which were only rarely recorded previously. See, for example, the case of the Episcopal basilica in Kourion, Cyprus in Megaw (1976) 345–371.

34 Déonna (1934) 1–90; Drioton (1937) 29–40.

35 Ward-Perkins (1994a) 469–489.

36 Kirwin (1997) 85.

37 Teteriatnikov (1996).

objects because of its economic and sacred value, must have been portable. Rock-cut churches in Cappadocia, variously dated from the ninth to the fourteenth centuries, show structural and architectural elements, such as columns, vaults, and domes, which are also found in masonry churches.[38] All these elements are also found in canopy structures, hence eliminating the lack of technical expertise for their making as reason for their absence. Though so little is known about the use of portable altars and portable canopies in the East, it is known that in the sixth century, Emperor Maurice (r. 582–602) sent an entire altar canopy in pieces from Constantinople to the now-lost church of his native town, Arabissos in Cappadocia.[39] This episode demonstrates, not only that some church canopies might have been portable, but also that some might have been standardly designed objects and assembled on site from pre-made pieces.

Because the altar is an indispensable liturgical furnishing in Byzantine-rite churches, it is particularly difficult to establish whether older altar canopies were simply reused over a prolonged period of time, or were (and on what occasions) built anew during the Byzantine period. The two Byzantine examples that survive *in situ* in Paros and Kalabaka suggest both possibilities. Older canopies were at times reused or reinstalled in churches and were used for a prolonged period, as was the altar canopy in Paros. In some churches, canopies might have been installed at a later point and not simultaneously with the construction of the church or the installation of its altar table. This was the case with the altar canopy from the Basilica B in Nikopolis in Epirus, where the early Christian canopy postdated the church by a century (Table 5.45). These trends can be followed throughout the millennium-long tradition and in various locales.

In some early Christian churches, a long, wide slab, with sockets for the colonnettes that would have served as a base for the permanent altar and canopy, was employed in order to avoid damaging the floor mosaics of an older building, which may or may not have served as a church previously.[40] In the fifth and sixth centuries, the design of the floor mosaics in some basilicas could have accommodated bases for stone altar canopies. This is exemplified by several surviving altar canopies located in the fifth-century Christian basilicas of Sabratha, North Africa; in the village of Mastichari, on the Aegean island Kos; in the basilica at Kourion, Cyprus (after 365 and before the seventh century); in the Church of St. George on Mt. Nebo (586); and in the Church of St. Stephen at Umm al-Rasas (ca. 756) in the Syro-Palestine region (Table 5.8, 19, 47, 71, 75).[41]

Sometimes the installation of the permanent altar table seems to be an afterthought. In the Chapel of the Mother of God of the church at Mt. Nebo (beginning of seventh century), altar columns were placed over mosaics, which were consequently damaged (Table 5.103, Fig. 2.4).[42] From an archeological point of view, it remains unclear whether such an inserted

---

38 Teteriatnikov (1996) and Kostof (1989).

39 Ruggieri (1991) 166.

40 According to the law issued by emperors Theodosios II and Valentian III, dated November 14th, 435, all pagan shrines and temples along the Mediterranean were ordered closed, although they might be consecrated as Christian churches: *Codex Theodosianus* XVI, 10, 25. However, the implementation of the law was certainly not immediate and simultaneous everywhere. The Parthenon and Erechtheum were possibly consecrated as churches just before Justinian's time: Strzygowski (1889) 272–273. Numerous sites in the western Balkans such as the Heraklea Lyncestis, F.Y.R. Macedonia, preserved pagan shrines side by side with the Christian sites up to the sixth century: Spieser (1976) 309–320.

41 Piccirillo (2006) 51–113, esp. 54–58; Duval, N. (2003) 35–114; Michel (2001) 61; Parrish (2001) 331–349; Loverance (1990) 225–243; Megaw (1976) 345–371; Bagatti (1956–1957) 64–94.

42 Buschhausen (1986) figs. 71–72.

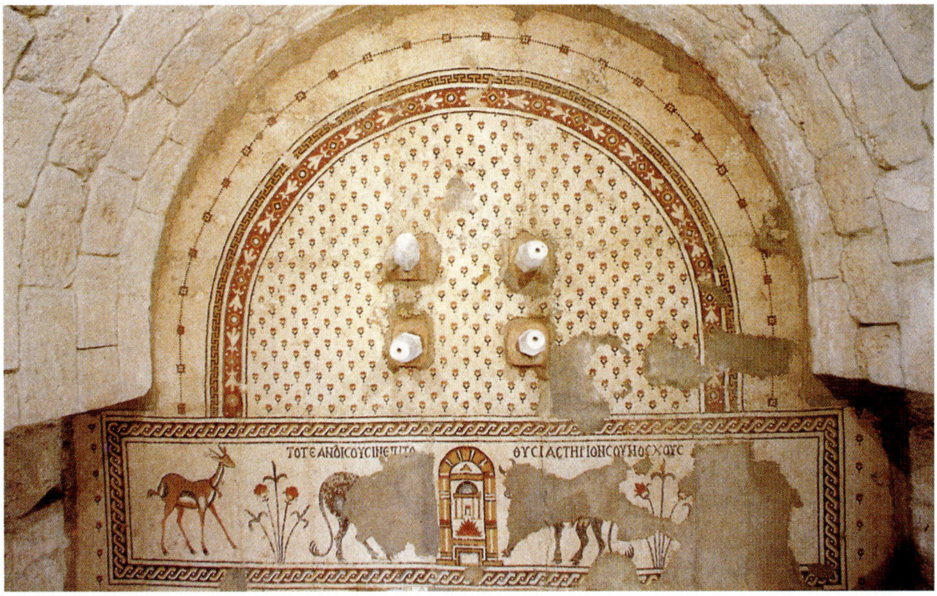

FIGURE 2.4 *Mt. Nebo Mother of God Church; Theotokos Chapel, Mt. Nebo, built in 597.* AFTER M. PICCIRILLO, *THE MOSAICS OF JORDAN* (1993), FIG. 200, P. 151. COURTESY OF THE FRANCISCAN CUSTODY OF THE HOLY LAND, MT. NEBO, AND THE AMERICAN CENTER OF ORIENTAL RESEARCH, AMMAN

permanent altar canopy would have replaced a portable one or whether it was an initial furnishing that the community installed after the consecration of the church. After the Council of Elvira in 427, figurative Christian images in floor decorations were prohibited, and motifs sacred to Christians, such as images of crosses, Biblical scenes, or saints, were placed on the walls instead of the floor as a gesture of respect.[43] With the implementation of this prohibition, indirect evidence for the existence of canopies and the relative chronology of their installation in churches, which is based upon the evidence of the floor decoration, becomes even more obscure. Moreover, canopies might have been rebuilt, often incorporating earlier architectural elements. Such a practice was pervasive throughout the Byzantine world. The rebuilding of canopies may have been not only due to the "wear-and-tear" of furniture over time, but also due to discontinuities of church practices. In the Church of St. Stephen at Umm al-Rasas, after the Muslim conquest in the eighth century, new bases for the altar canopy were incorporated into sixth-century colonnettes (Table 5.105).[44]

Then again, for some later churches, new altar canopies were made, as in the case of the altar canopy in the eleventh-century *katholikon* of the monastery of Hosios Loukas in Boeotia, Greece (Table 5.190).[45] Architectural fragments of several canopies made of marble are currently on display in the museum, the former refectory, of Hosios Loukas (Fig. 2.5). The original setting of these fragments remains unverifiable, yet the footing preserved in the sanctuary of the *katholikon* confirms that the altar canopy was planned as indispensable furniture from the outset.[46] Despite devastatingly limited archeological

[43] Vitto (1995) 281–300.

[44] Piccirillo (2006) 51–113, esp. 55.

[45] Schultz and Barnsley (1901) 29.

[46] Ibid., plate with the ground plan of the monastery.

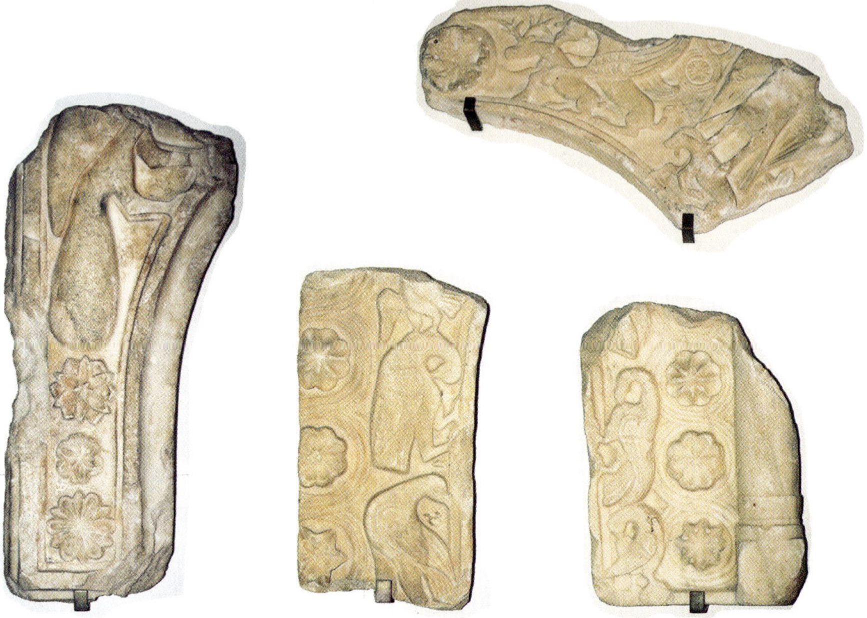

FIGURE 2.5 *Architectural sculpted fragments of various canopies from the Hosios Loukas monastery, Greece, Middle Byzantine period; now in the monastery museum, former refectory.* PHOTO AUTHOR

and architectural evidence for canopies in Constantinopolitan churches, based on remnants of footings, archeology has confirmed the existence of an altar canopy in the Church of the Holy Savior in Chora, an imperial construction from the Middle Byzantine period, which was restored and expanded by a powerful Byzantine statesman Theodore Metochites (1270–1332) in the fourteenth century.[47]

A particular question is the relationship between the sacrificial and funerary functions of altar canopies, because archeology reveals that, starting in the fifth century, monumental tombs and altars could have been combined into one installation, occasionally marked by a canopy. An example is the memoria, a martyr's shrine, at Majsan in the Byzantine province of Dalmatia (Fig. 2.6).[48] The original tomb of the local saint, Maxim (Maximus), who died in 346, was at some point enclosed by a relatively large (approximately 7.4 by 3.5 meters), rectangular, vaulted structure. Most likely by the fifth century, an altar was placed over the saintly tomb. By the sixth century, in the interior of this memoria, four massive pilasters enclosed the central location of the tomb and the altar and most likely supported a domical, canopied roof above the central locus. In several other early churches from the fifth and sixth centuries, such as in H. Leonidas in Corinth-Lechaion, in Ilisos; in Basilica A, Nikopolis; or the Eastern church in Apollonia, Libya, massive canopied structures approximately 10 by 10 meters in size were placed over *bemas*, i.e., sanctuaries, and some of these canopied constructions may also have enshrined tombs (Fig. 2.7, Table 5.25, 43, 60, 102). In the seventh century, the entire body of St. Euphemia was transferred from her original *martyrium* in Chalcedon, Bithynia, to an eponymous church in Constantinople, now lost

---

47 Marinis (2014) 28–29.

48 Ćurčić (2010) 147.

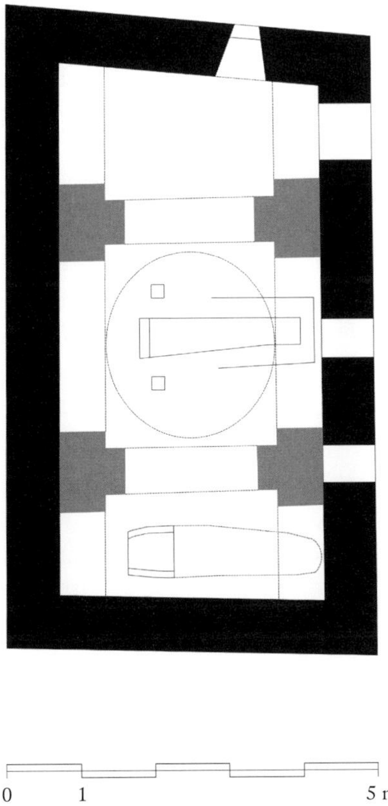

FIGURE 2.6 *Memoria, Majsan, Dalmatia, Croatia, fifth century.* DRAWING AUTHOR AND HEIDI REBURN AFTER ĆURČIĆ (2010) 148, FIG. 148

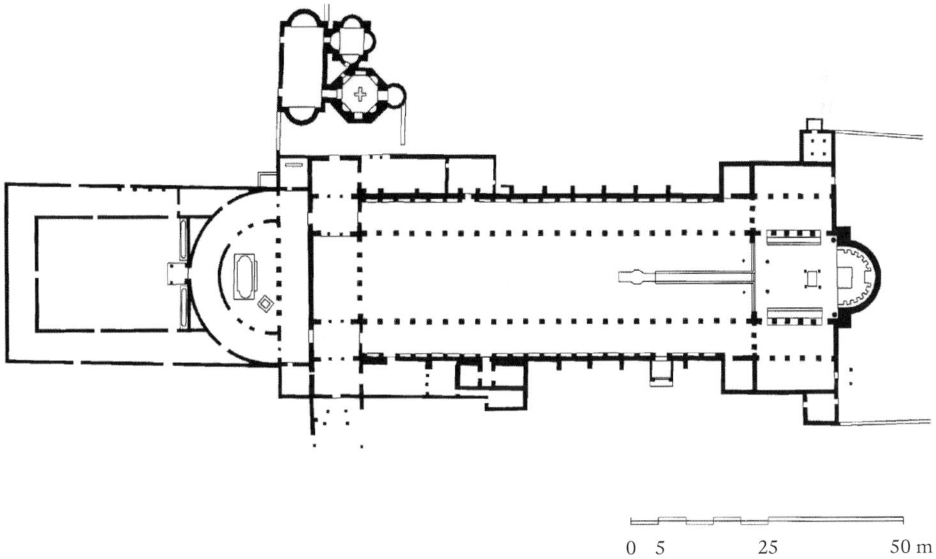

FIGURE 2.7 *Hosios Leonidas in Corinth-Lechaion, Greece, fifth century.* DRAWING AUTHOR FROM ĆURČIĆ (2010) 127, FIG. 124

(Table 5.104).[49] This centrally planned hexagonal building with deep niches embedded in the thickness of the wall was originally a secular building that, once it received Euphemia's relics, became a church. The large-size saintly shrine was presumably deposited directly beneath the altar table in the eastern niche, thus forming a box-type altar, as suggested by several pilgrims' accounts.[50] A massive four-columned canopy articulated the sanctuary installation architecturally. This phenomenon of canopied installations that simultaneously framed altars and shrines expanded upon the requirement for the consecration of altars with saintly relics, which are bodily parts and usually tiny fragments, not entire human bodies. The altar table and sacred relics are closely associated liturgically and theologically, yet archeology reveals that spatial merging and relationships between canopied altars, tombs, and reliquary shrines are extremely complex, and this will be investigated in greater detail in Chapter 4.

Baptismal Canopies

Early Christian and Byzantine baptismal canopies were often large-sized architectural installations in their own right, as can be seen in the earliest archeologically confirmed, third-century canopy from Dura Europos (Table 5.1, see also Fig. 3.1).[51] These large installations are related to the early Christian practice of baptism of adult individuals, who with their full will and understanding received the sacrament of baptism, followed by a sacramental anointing and first Communion. The practice of baptism of infants and children (*pedobaptism*) is still disputed and is generally attributed to later periods despite textual evidence of the baptism of children and infants since at least the second century.[52] Christ was baptized in the River Jordan, and baptism was always performed with natural, "living water," understood as fresh, flowing water from a stream or spring, rather than tap water from a cistern. This practice was closely related to the Biblical reference when Christ met the Samaritan woman at the well and acknowledged the power of the "living water," imbued with the grace of the Holy Spirit that leads to eternal life and spiritual rebirth (cf. John 4:5–34, esp. 4:10–14).[53] The Samaritan woman was later baptized as Photini, literally "the luminous one," derived from Greek term φως (light).[54] Similarly, the Byzantines would often name the places for performing baptism φωτιστήρια (places for illumination) for the spiritual illumination in Christ.[55]

While any day and any location with running water ("living water"), including rivers in the open and interiors of private houses, would suffice for the ritual of baptism, a practice of mass baptisms on the great feast days was especially popular between the third and sixth centuries. Above all, during Christmas, Easter, and Pentecost, the baptismal ritual would overlap with the notions of death in Adam and rebirth in Christ and of the Epiphany; a practice attested to, for example, in the writings of Tertullian in the

---

[49] Goldfus (2006) 178–197; Mango (1999) 79–87; Mathews (1971) 61–67. See also Chapter 4.

[50] Ibid.

[51] See also Chapter 3.

[52] Mirković (1983) 21. *Tertullian, De Baptismo* ch. 19, and *Gregory Nazianzus, Oratios in sanct. Baptism,* Oration 40 (*PG* 36, 396).

[53] John 4:10: . . . *If thou knewest the gift of God, and who it is that saith to thee, Give me to drink; thou wouldst have asked of him, and he would have given three living water.* . . . John 4:14: *But whosoever drinketh of the water that I shall give him shall be in him a well of springing up into everlasting life.*

[54] *Orthodox Study Bible* 1429.

[55] Mirković (1983) 24.

third and Gregory of Nazianzus in the fourth century.[56] The ritual itself could occur during the night service of the vespers before the next morning's liturgy, emphasizing the religious concept of baptism as spiritual enlightenment and the transition from darkness to light.

The shape and location of massive baptismal installations built by the sixth century meet the requirements for the performance of baptisms as set by the texts and liturgical practices. Even if a canopy was not an obligatory architectural solution, baptisteries were often centrally planned, round, six- or eight-sided buildings with a domical or pyramidal roof, emphasizing the central focus of the rite of baptism. Open columnar structures repeating the major design of baptisteries were regularly made as four-, six-, or eight-sided canopies and occasionally framed relatively deep baptismal fonts. The fonts themselves would often have two flights of triple stairs that would allow for physical movement that emphasized the spiritual transition: descent into the tub and ascent on its opposite side. These installations emphasized the notions of death and rebirth, eternity, and the Holy Trinity through triple full immersion of the full human body into water within the large baptismal tubs. The preserved large baptisteries across the Mediterranean, such as those in Albenga and Ravenna, at the apex of the dome show interlocking crosses, the sky with stars or the baptism of Christ in the River Jordan.[57] The visual program aided in the understanding of the architecture of the baptisteries, highlighting the concept of the microcosmic locale where the earthly and the heavenly overlapped. It may be reasonable to assume that the preserved columns of canopied baptismal installations elsewhere supported roofs, which were shaped and decorated similarly to baptistery domes. A now-lost columnar canopy originally framed the octagonal font at the baptistery in Albenga. Given the lavish interior decoration of the baptistery building, it is possible that the baptismal canopy was of similar shape and decoration.

Archeology confirms that the locations of martyr tombs, as in Carthage, Tunisia, and previous water installations of the baths, as in the case of the baptismal canopy from the Basilica IV, Mactaris, Tunisia, have overlapped with the construction of canopied or larger baptisteries (Table 5.37).[58] In the case of the canopied baptismal fonts over martyr tombs, the architectural design reinforced the idea of eternal salvation. In the case of the reuse of previous water installations, the design most directly responded to practical concerns about supplying running ("living") water for the ceremony of baptism.

In their location and shape, early baptismal installations can be also then related to the Biblical prescriptions when Moses instructed Aaron and his sons to wash themselves with water before they entered the Tabernacle of the congregation (Ex. 29:4)[59] and to similar water installations with steps used by the Jews for maintaining spiritual purity, known as *mikvahot*.[60] Such a *mikvah* may have originally stood outside of the Temple and may have been used by Paul and his followers before they entered the Temple (Acts 21:26)[61] and followed by Paul's appeal to his followers in the Temple to be baptized in the name of the Lord (Acts 22:16).[62] More than 80 *mikvah* installations from the Second Temple period have been archeologically confirmed.

[56] Mirković (1983) 21. *Tertullian, De Baptismo* ch. 19, and *Gregory Nazianzus, Oratios in sanct. Baptism*, Oration 40 (*PG* 36, 396).

[57] Jensen (2011) 198–208.

[58] Duval, N., and Lezine (1959) 71–147; Stevens (2000) 271–274.

[59] Ex. 29:4: *And Aaron and his sons thou shalt bring unto the door of the tabernacle of the congregation, and shalt wash them with water.*

[60] Snyder, B. (2014).

[61] Acts 21:26: *Then Paul took the men, and the next day purifying himself with them entered into the temple, to signify the accomplishment of the days of purification, until that an offering should be offered for every one of them.*

[62] Acts 22:16: . . . *Arise and be baptized, and wash away your sins, calling on the name of the Lord.*

While the ritual of baptism definitely differs from the ritual purification of the Jews, since the baptismal water was believed to be imbued with the Holy Spirit, providing both physical and spiritual cleansing as divine intervention, the recovered *mikvah* installations allowed the full immersion of the adult body and were stepped. Hence, they share some formal and symbolic features of architectural design with early Christian baptismal fonts.

In architectural terms, baptisteries, framing the fonts as the locus of baptismal ceremony, could take different shapes and sizes of one of essentially three types of canopied structures. They could have been massive, often centrally planned buildings with domical and vaulted roofs;[63] they could have been open canopied structures outside the church, as in the case of the fifth-century baptismal canopy in front of the Church of St. Theodore in Gerasa (Jerash), Palestine (Fig. 2.8, Table 5.31);[64] or they could have been a combination of both a centrally planned building and a canopied installation above the font, nested inside each other, as in the case of the fifth-century Vitalis Baptistery in Sufetula (Sbeitla), Tunisia (Fig. 2.9, Table 5.82). Vivid archeological evidence confirms the diverse locations and shapes of baptismal canopies throughout the Mediterranean region. Elaborate installations were recurrently placed in the immediate vicinity of the church, frequently to the south of the main church as in the case of the episcopal complexes at Stobi, F.Y.R. of Macedonia; at Caričin Grad, Lebane, Serbia; and at the cathedral complex in Poreč, Croatia (Fig. 2.10, Table 5.41, 58, 66).[65] However, they could

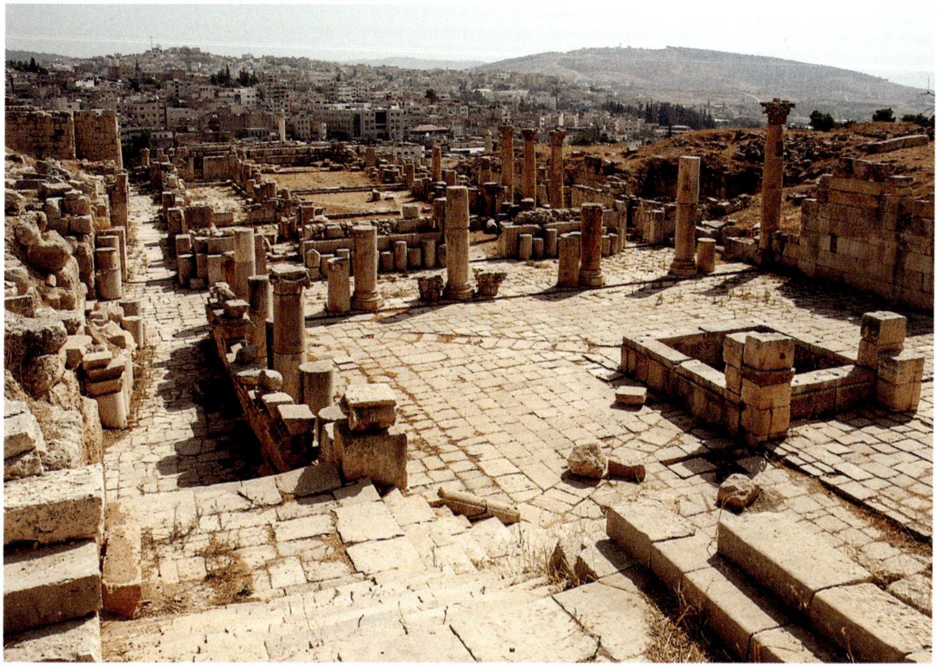

FIGURE 2.8 *Baptismal canopy, Church of St. Theodore, Gerasa (Jerash), Jordan, fifth century.* PHOTO DANIEL C. WAUGH

[63] Ćurčić (2010) 163–167.

[64] Mango (1985b) 20–23, figs. 19–2; Michel (2001) 226–237.

[65] Downing (1998) 259–280; Kitzinger (1946) 81–162; Kondić and Popović (1977) 109–129; Popović (1979) 249–311; Ćurčić (2010) 113, 163–167. The baptistery in Poreč has not survived, though some of the architectural sculpture at the site might have been used for the canopy, as Terry (1988) 12–64 has convincingly argued.

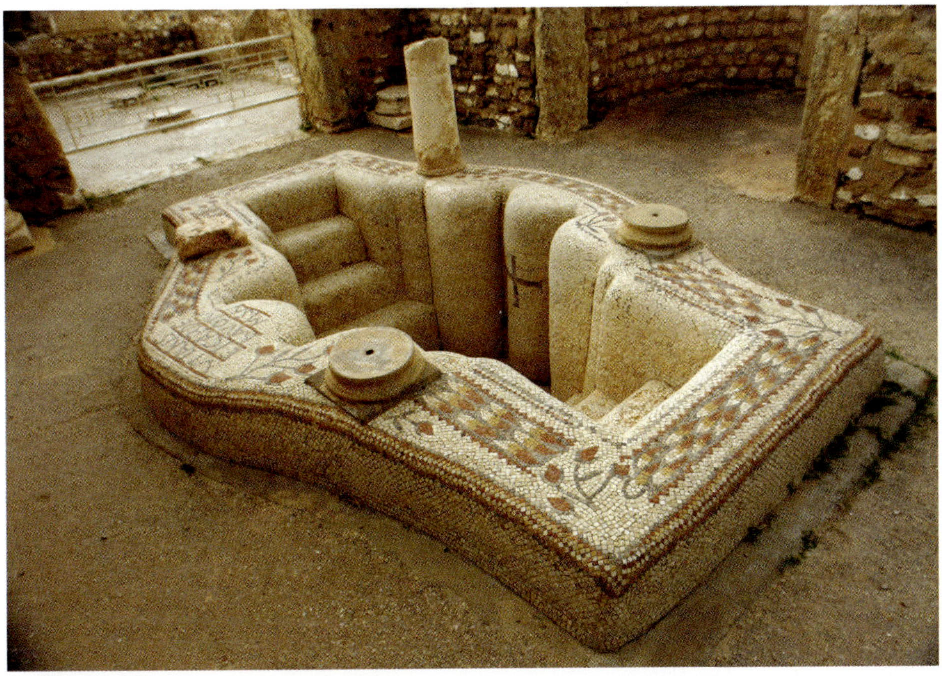

FIGURE 2.9 *Vitalis Baptistery in Sufetula (Sbeitla), Tunisia, fifth century.* PHOTO ROBIN JENSEN

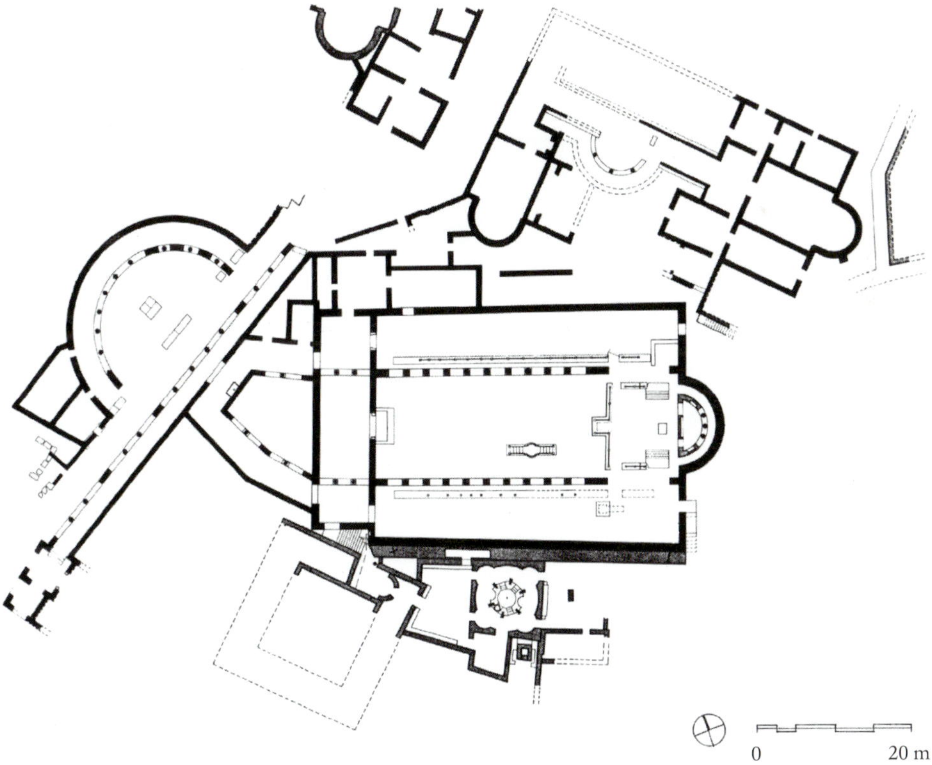

FIGURE 2.10 *Episcopal complex at Stobi, F.Y.R. of Macedonia, fifth–sixth century.* DRAWING AUTHOR FROM ĆURČIĆ (2010) 113, FIG. 111

also be located in various other positions in relation to the main space of the church—in front of or behind it—and there are several additional examples of those placed to the north. While the specific location of baptismal installations, either set in separate buildings or in chambers attached to the main body of the church within the larger church proper, may have varied, there was usually only one baptismal installation, and it was almost always separated from the major church space of the *naos* and sanctuary. At least eighteen such canopied baptismal installations from the Eastern Mediterranean can be dated to the period between the fourth and sixth centuries, revealing a number of architectural solutions (Table 6).

Sometimes a singular canopied baptismal installation would point to multiple uses and meanings attached to specific locations. An eight-sided canopied baptismal installation from the site of Bargala, F.Y.R. of Macedonia still has preserved footings for the canopy that framed the major locus (Fig. 2.11, Table 5.7).[66] This installation, attached to the north-east of the basilica, however, first marked the tomb believed to belong to a local martyr and the major reason for building the church in its immediate vicinity. At some point the tomb was reappropriated to serve as a baptismal font. The entire installation was eventually

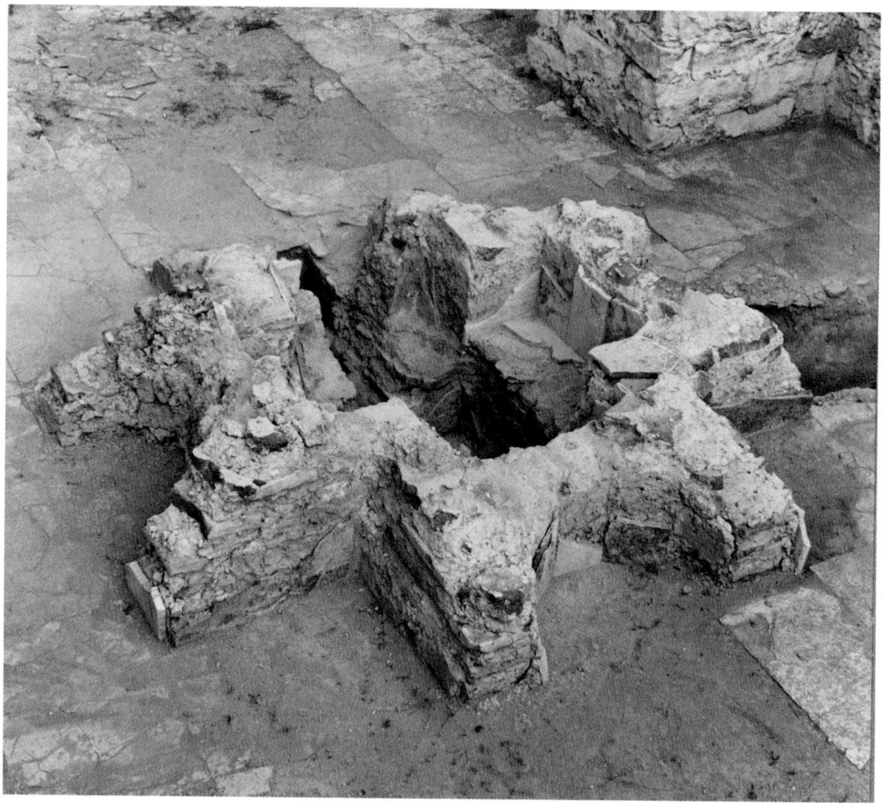

FIGURE 2.11 *Baptismal font, Basilica Bargala near Štip, F.Y.R. of Macedonia, fifth century.* PHOTO BLAGA ALEKSOVA AND CYRIL MANGO, COLLECTION: THE BYZANTINE INSTITUTE AND DUMBARTON OAKS FIELDWORK RECORDS AND PAPERS

[66] Aleksova and Mango (1971) 265–281; Ćurčić (2010) 163.

redesigned into a cruciform canopied installation enclosed by a vaulted chamber, which was directly linked to the basilica.

Because no water drainage system was found on the site of Bargala or in several other large baptisteries, scholars have raised questions as to whether these structures actually ever functioned as baptisteries. Indeed, some installations that combined a tomb and a baptistery, such as at Bir Ftouha, Carthage, Tunisia, would have had a drain at the bottom of the font (Table 5.54).[67] I would like to propose that, given the advanced Byzantine knowledge of science and their centralized, powerful, and economically strong government, especially until the sixth century, canopied baptisteries could have had quite sophisticated water installations, which did not require extensive underground water channels or similar archeologically verifiable evidence for drainage systems. The Byzantines could have used some hydraulic machines, known as "automata" and explained by Philo of Byzantium (ca. 280–220 BCE).[68] Above all, the Byzantines knew about the extremely simple and efficient water-screw or Archimedean screw, which allows water to be lifted directly inside a tilted, rotating tube by a helicoidal surface within a tube. Set within a font, or a nearby basin filled with water, this mechanism could lift the water up and release it into baptismal font from above. In the same manner, after the ceremony of baptism, the water could have been scooped back into the vessel to be disposed of. The Archimedean screw would have been a convenient mechanism, keeping in mind the ritual requirements for baptismal water. Baptismal water had to be running, "living" water; it was mixed with oil during the ceremony, and was always removed from the font after the baptism. Public mechanical fountains existed in Constantinople and were often described.[69] Less is known of their potential use for baptismal installations, though this is possible. A poem by bishop Ennodius of Pavia (511–521) describes a kind of hydraulic machine that filled the sixth-century baptistery font of San Stefano in Milan with water falling from the underside of a stone canopy:

> Behold, it rains without a cloud under the canopy—
> a rain shower in a clear sky.
> The clear face [form] of heaven provides the water;
> Flowing sacred rivers run down over marble blocks.
> See again, see! The stone brings forth water.
> Truly the dry canopy poured forth pure springs
> And born again comes above the holy water.
> Sacred water flows through the air from the vault
> built while Eustorgius was bishop.[70]

Especially beautiful canopied baptismal fonts are those from Tunisia, North Africa, including the installations from the so-called Jucundus Chapel baptistery and Vitalis baptistery, both in Sufetula (Sbeitla), and in the Basilica Clupea in Kélibia (Table 5.10, 79, 82).[71] The

---

[67] Stevens (2000) 271–274.

[68] Russo (2004) 120–125; Jensen (2011) 230.

[69] Magdalino (1987a) 28–38, esp. 32ff; Magdalino (1990) 165–188; Magdalino (1991) 2191.

[70] *En sine nube pluit sub tectis imbre sereno Et cadi fades pura ministrat aquas. Proflua marmoribus decurrunt flumina sacris Atque iterum rorem parturit ecce lapis. Arida nam liquidos effundit pergula fontes, Et rursus natis unda superna venit. Sancta per aetherios emanat limpha recessus, Eustorgi vatis ducta ministerio. Ennodius* 2.149. Translation into English from Latin adapted from Jensen (2011) 195.

[71] Michel (2001) 226–237; Jensen (2011) 210–220. Patout Burns and Jensen (2014) 103–113, 165–219, bring forward extensive material on canopied baptisteries in North Africa, some not included in this book, as I became aware of them when this project was closing. Their research also reveals manifold theological and architectural nuances related to the construction of bapisteries in North Africa.

baptismal fonts were made in an elongated, undulating, scalloped shape with a flight of stairs along the north–south axis and were lavishly decorated in mosaics. They still preserve the footings for the four columns that lifted the canopy roof above the central section of the font. In the case of the Jucundus Chapel baptistery, part of the fifth-century cathedral complex, the installation was at some later point associated with the tomb of the local bishop and martyr Jucundus, judging by the inscription in the floor and confirming the merging of the funeral and the salvific messages that baptismal installations carried. The process of merging the two different functions within one installation is here, however, different from the Bargala case. In the Jucundus baptismal chapel in Sufetula (Sbeitla), the tomb was most likely inserted after the baptistery was built. A hollow column inserted into the font of the Jucundus baptistery could have been used to conceal the saintly relics (Fig. 2.12).[72] An alternative explanation would be that it held the tube needed for the water-screw mechanism, which was well known to engineers from Alexandria and North Africa.[73] Be that as it may, in the sixth century, with the building of a new cathedral, another baptistery, the so-called Vitalis baptistery, was built adjacent to the new cathedral. It was set just behind and to the east of the sanctuary, which probably resulted in the discontinuation of the use of Jucundus baptistery. The new baptistery, consisting of a rectangular chamber, obviously had an installation for an altar, judging by the eastern niche; a practice

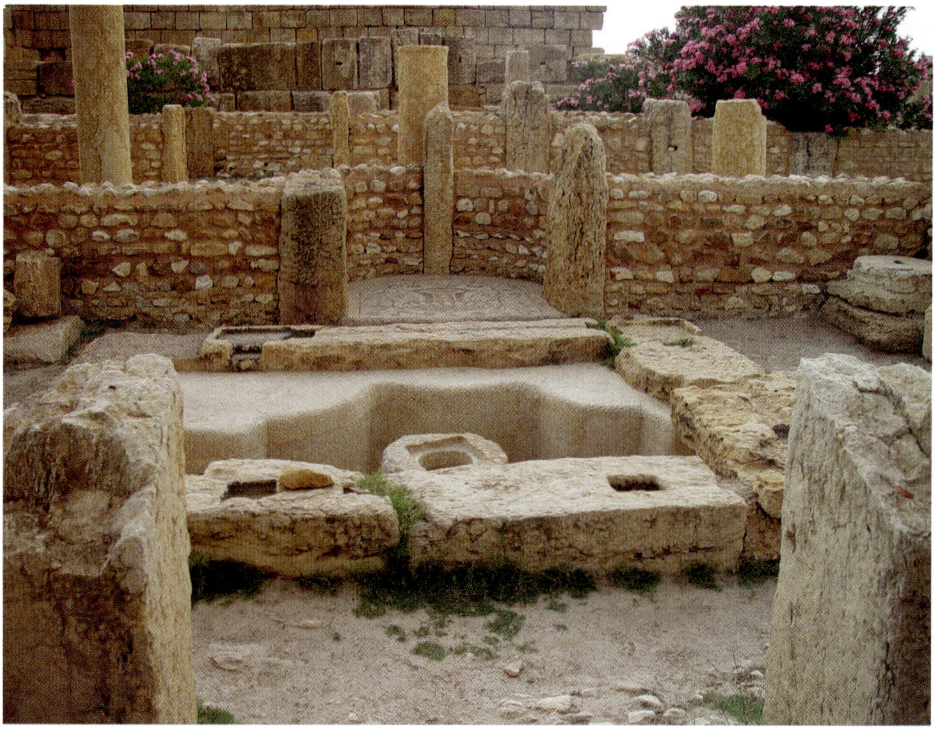

FIGURE 2.12 *Jucundus Chapel baptistery, Tunisia, fifth century.* PHOTO ROBIN JENSEN

[72] Jensen (2011) 211.

[73] I thank Robin Jensen for discussing with me the Jucundus font. See also Jensen (2011) 230; Patout Burns and Jensen (2014) 112–113.

confirmed by texts that many baptisteries were equipped with altars and were consecrated buildings.[74] The chamber itself is further articulated by four columns at the corners, emphasizing that it was a vaulted structure and a kind of a canopy in its own right. An additional canopy, whose footings are preserved, framed the central part of the baptismal font with triple lobes along the lateral sides and was lavishly decorated in mosaics with geometric, floral, and water motifs and highlighted by a cross in the central lobe of the font. In Kélibia, among several decorative motifs are the representation of the Ark and the cross under the canopy (Fig. 2.13). Such a nesting of canopied installations and their representations with multiple baptismal, funerary, salvific, epiphany, and microcosmic meanings are attested to elsewhere, indicating that a strict typology based on the singular function in Byzantine-rite churches is somewhat elusive.

From the eighth century, in addition to their locations subsidiary or complementary to the main church, baptismal installations could have been included in the major space of the church, coinciding with the slow but definite decline of the building of separate baptisteries as well as baptismal canopies.[75] Fragments of potentially five baptismal canopies from the territories of modern Greece and along the Adriatic littoral can all be dated to this transitional period between the ninth and eleventh centuries. They are found in the Church of St. Tryphon in Kotor, Montenegro; an unidentified church in Budva, Montenegro; the Church of St. Bartholomew in Galovac, Croatia; Hagios Andreas in Peresterai, Greece; and St. Mary in Biskupija near Knin, Croatia (Table 5.118, 138, 140, 153, 183; Table 6).

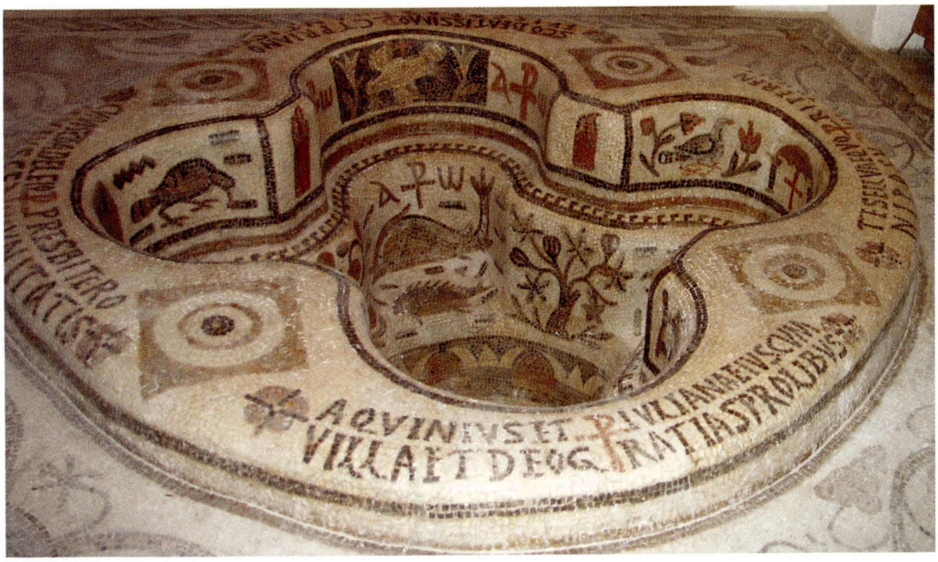

FIGURE 2.13 *Baptistery from the Basilica Clupea in Kélibia, Tunisia, sixth century.* PHOTO ROBIN JENSEN

[74] Mirković (1983) 24.

[75] Ibid.

Canopied *Phialai* (Holy Water Fonts)

In Byzantine-rite churches, canopied installations for water fonts could have served other functions than as baptismal canopies. They could have framed a *phiale,* an architectural installation that is a font for sanctified water.[76] Because baptismal and *phiale* canopies both framed water fonts, too often scholars have conflated them and have studied them as the same installation.[77] Yet these are two distinct installations that could not be interchangeably used for different church rites and practices.

Phialai were used for the rites of the blessing of water. As early as the fourth century, the rites of the blessing of water were being performed in Antioch.[78] By the sixth–seventh centuries, Jerusalem monastic *typikon* explained three distinctive rites for the blessing of water to be performed on the occasions of Epiphany (Theophany) on January sixth, Bright Friday (Friday of Easter Week or Bright Week), and Mid- Pentecost.[79] The Great Blessing of Holy Water is performed on Epiphany (Theophany), commemorating the baptism of Christ.[80] Because Christ was sinless, his baptism made water and all Creation holy, and in that context, water can become both the instrument and the sign of its original Biblical meaning—the source of life. This pervasive concept of holy water is also related to lesser ceremonies such as on Bright Friday—which in the Orthodox Christian tradition became associated with a feast of the Theotokos ("God-bearer") and her epithet the "Life-giving Spring"[81]—and on the feast of Mid-Pentecost (cf. John 4:5–34, esp. 4:10–14).[82] By the eleventh century, the rites for the blessing of waters in monastic communities were obligatory.[83] A ritual that includes prayers and sprinkling with holy water was used monthly in monastic churches and for the ceremony of the consecration of a church. In addition, holy water in *phialai* is used for ritual cleansing before entering the church, for the blessing of believers' homes, for the blessing of the sick and the needy, and for quenching one's thirst.[84]

Olivera Kandić has effectively demonstrated that, even if the rites of baptism and the blessing of water share many elements, such as the invocation of the Holy Trinity and of the baptism of Christ, and the fact that the baptism begins with a brief ceremony of the blessing of the waters, the baptismal ceremony includes pouring oil into the water, while nothing is added to the water in the ceremonies of the blessing of holy water.[85] Basing her research on primary texts and archeological evidence, Kandić explained how the same font could not have been used for these two separate rites. The baptismal water is poured out after the ceremony, while the sanctified holy water remains stored in the font. Due to the need to store blessed water, at least since the eleventh century, holy water fonts were prescribed to have lids, which is an unnecessary element for baptismal fonts.[86]

---

[76] Kandić (1998–9) 61–78 provides an extensive overview of the fonts used for the blessing of water in Byzantine and Serbian churches and effectively demonstrates that, during medieval times, terms for these installations were not standardized. Numerous terms deriving from Greek and Slavic languages would be used for these installations, such as *phiale, louter, hagiazma, apsida, atrium, kupelnica,* and *krestilnica,* yet *phiale* was most often used for fonts architecturally framed by a canopy. See also Bogdanović (2017b).

[77] For example, in Thomas, J., et al. (2012) 542–547, medieval fonts are uniformly considered baptismal fonts.

[78] Mirković (1961) 105–106; Mirković (1983) 151–157; Kandić (1998–9), 61–78; Marinis (2014) 95–97.

[79] Mirković (1983) 151–157; Patrich (1995) 273; Kandić (1998–9) 61–78, esp. 62, with references.

[80] Mirković (1983) 151–157; Kandić (1998–9) 61–78, esp. 62–64.

[81] An extremely detailed analysis of the development of the theme of Zoodochos Pege in Milanović (2004–2005) 141–165.

[82] *Orthodox Study Bible* 1429. More on lesser ceremonies of the blessing of water in Mirković (1983) 151–157.

[83] Kandić (1998–9) 61–78, esp. 62–64; Mamaloukos (2002) 9–10.

[84] Marinis (2014) 97.

[85] Kandić (1998–9) 61–78.

[86] Ibid.

Texts often do not detail the architectural form or setting of *phialai*, but archeological excavations of early Christian sites, such as those at the fifth-century basilicas at Soli and Kourion and the sixth-century Basilica of Hagia Kyriaki (Chrysopolitissa) at Paphos, have revealed the existence of separate installations for the baptisteries and other fonts, possibly *phialai*, within a single site.[87] Located in the southern portion of the atrium just before the entrance to the church or within the southwestern portions of the church—in a narthex or in a separate, southwestern chamber directly linked with the narthex—*phialai* sometimes contained a fount of streaming ("living") water or could merely be a vessel for holy water itself within these subsidiary church spaces.[88]

By the sixth century, some of these installations were canopied, as suggested by Paulos Silentarios, who described the now-lost *phiale* in the Constantinopolitan Hagia Sophia.[89] The physical space of a *phiale* could expand beyond the canopy to the atrium of larger foundations, where it stood. Perhaps this is the reason why *phialai*, placed in the atrium and articulated by columns, could have been identified with the atrium itself, as Michael of Thessaloniki specified in his twelfth-century description of the canopied *phiale* (here termed *louter*) in Constantinopolitan Hagia Sophia.[90]

The earliest archeological evidence for a canopied *phiale* belongs to a Constantinopolitan installation from the Middle Byzantine period. A large canopied *phiale* at the monastery church St. George in Mangana in Constantinople was built under Emperor Constantine IX (1042–1059). Attested to in the writings of a Byzantine monk and intellectual Michael Psellos, Russian pilgrims, and Castilian traveler and ambassador Ruy Gonzáles de Clavijo, this *phiale* framed a large marble font and rested on eight marble columns richly carved with numerous figures and supporting the domical roof.[91] Excavations in the 1920s revealed the footings of eight columns supporting a canopy, covering some 10 meters in span (Fig. 2.14, Table 5.185).[92] At least two additional Middle Byzantine canopied *phialai* have been archeologically confirmed in the monastic complexes of Studenica in medieval Serbia and Bogolyubovo in medieval Rus (Table 5.201, 207).[93] The now-lost canopied *phiale* in front of Hagios Demetrios church in Thessaloniki belonged to late Byzantine period (Table 5.237).[94]

Large and elaborately decorated canopied *phialai* from Mt. Athos, such as those in the monasteries of the Great Lavra, Iviron, Vatopedi, or Hilandar, are dated with certainty to the post-Byzantine period based on their painting programs (see also Figs. 1.7, 2.3). Due to the lack of texts and limited archeological surveys of Athonite monasteries that have been in continual service up to the present, canopied *phialai* have only been partially studied. These installations may have been initially built during the late Byzantine times, following the form and location of canopied *phialai* as attested to in younger structures in Constantinople, Thessaloniki, Rus, and Serbia. The canopied *phiale* at the Great Lavra monastery on Mt. Athos (Fig. 2.15) is a seventeenth-century installation, which may well have existed in this location and in a similar form during medieval times.[95] It consists of a large circular water basin made of marble and a water

[87] Megaw (1974) 57–85; Tsaferis (1985) 1–15; Papageorghiou (1998–).

[88] On the still under-investigated role of the southern access to the church within the liturgical rites and within the connection with the monastic refectory, briefly in Bogdanović (2012) 95–107.

[89] *Paulos Silentarios-b* as in *TLG*, lines 590–606.

[90] Mango and Parker (1960) 233–245.

[91] *RussAnon* 138–140; *Clavijo* 48. For *phialai* in Constantinople, see also Marinis (2014) 95–97.

[92] Demangel and Mamboury (1939), 23–30.

[93] Archeological evidence in Voronin (1961) 251–258. I agree with Sedov (2014) 110–111, who recognizes that the canopy over the *phiale* in Bogolybovo was built following monastic and Constantinopolitan practices.

[94] Bakirtzis (2002) 175–192. See also Chapter 4.

[95] Millet (1905) 104–141; Boura (1975–1976) 85–96; Kandić (1998–9) 61–78.

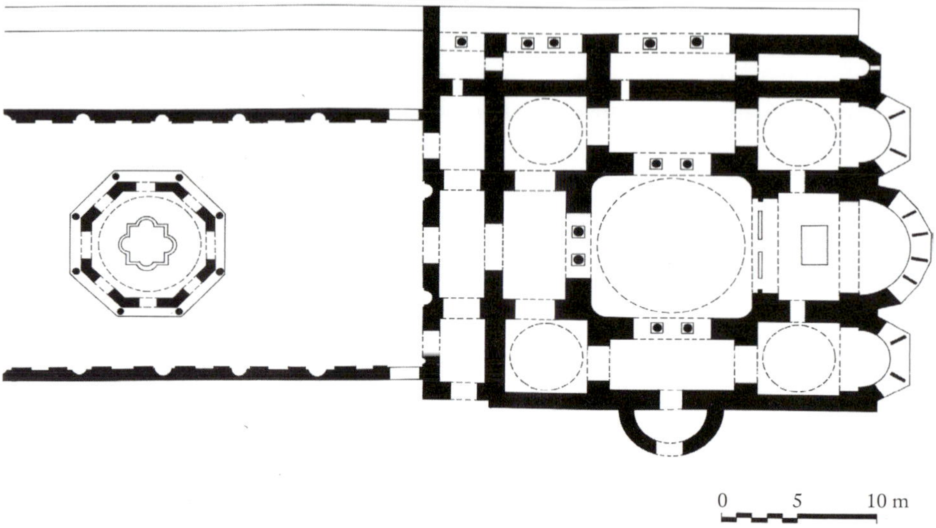

FIGURE 2.14 *St. George in Mangana, Constantinople, built under Emperor Constantine IX (1042–1059), confirmed in archeological excavations of the 1920s, floor plan.* DRAWING R. DEMANGEL AND E. MAMBOURY. *LE QUARTIER DES MANGANES ET LA PREMIÈRE REGION DE CONSTANTINOPLE*. PARIS, 1939

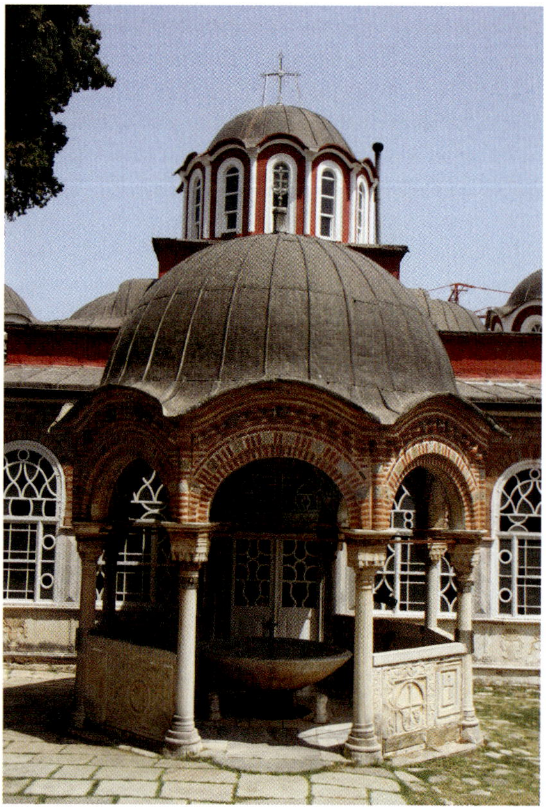

FIGURE 2.15 *Phiale and the katholikon (principal church) of the Great Lavra Monastery, Mt. Athos. The Great Lavra Monastery was founded in 963. Current installation of the phiale post-Byzantine, assembled of spolia, some of which can be dated to the eleventh century.* PHOTO NEBOJŠA STANKOVIĆ

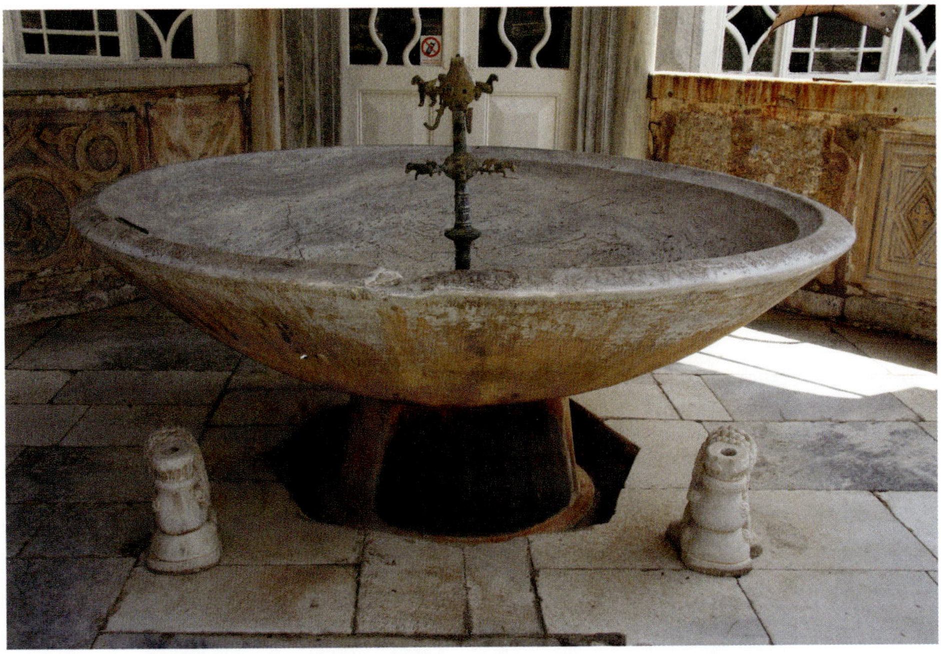

FIGURE 2.16 *The water conduit of the phiale from the Great Lavra Monastery, Mt. Athos, dated to ca. 1060s, made by the Constantinopolitan workshop.* PHOTO NEBOJŠA STANKOVIĆ

conduit (Fig. 2.16). The conduit can be dated to approximately the 1060s and was most likely done by a Constantinopolitan workshop. Marble slabs from the eleventh century have been reused to enclose the space of the *phiale*. The post-Byzantine canopied roof in the interior has preserved fresco paintings dated to 1635, possibly replicating an earlier practice of decorating the interior of *phialai*. In its present form, the Vatopedi *phiale* is a nineteenth-century installation (Fig. 2.17). Mamaloukos has demonstrated that originally it was a freestanding architectural installation in the atrium, a short distance southwest of the Chapel of St. Nicholas. The central dome and eastern wall of the Vatopedi *phiale* are original parts of the installation, while the columns of the *phiale* have monograms referring to the Kantakouzenos family, whose presence has been attested to in the fourteenth century on Mt. Athos.[96]

Large-scale canopied *phiale* fonts similar to baptismal fonts were often mistaken for them, as when de Clavijo recorded that the Mangana *phiale* was a baptistery.[97] These installations on Mt. Athos, in particular, were not and could not have been used as baptisteries. They were established when the baptism of adults had become increasingly rare;[98] large-scale installations for mass baptisms were not needed. Moreover, the relatively shallow fonts from the Athonite monasteries could not have been used for baptismal rites. They were most likely used in the past as they are used today, for the rites of the blessing of water, which have been required rites

[96] I thank Stavros Mamaloukos for discussing with me the *phiale* in Vatopedi and for sending me his material. Mamaloukos (2001) 103–104, 128–129, 211–212, 219, 220–221, 225, 226, 227, 270–271, 382, 391–392; drawings: 1–6, 13, 14, 22, 64–66, 74–79; figures: 3, 384–391; Mamaloukos (2002) 9–10.

[97] *Clavijo* 48.

[98] Gouma-Peterson (1978) 197+199–216 shows that adult baptism was rare but was still practiced in fourteenth-century Thessaloniki.

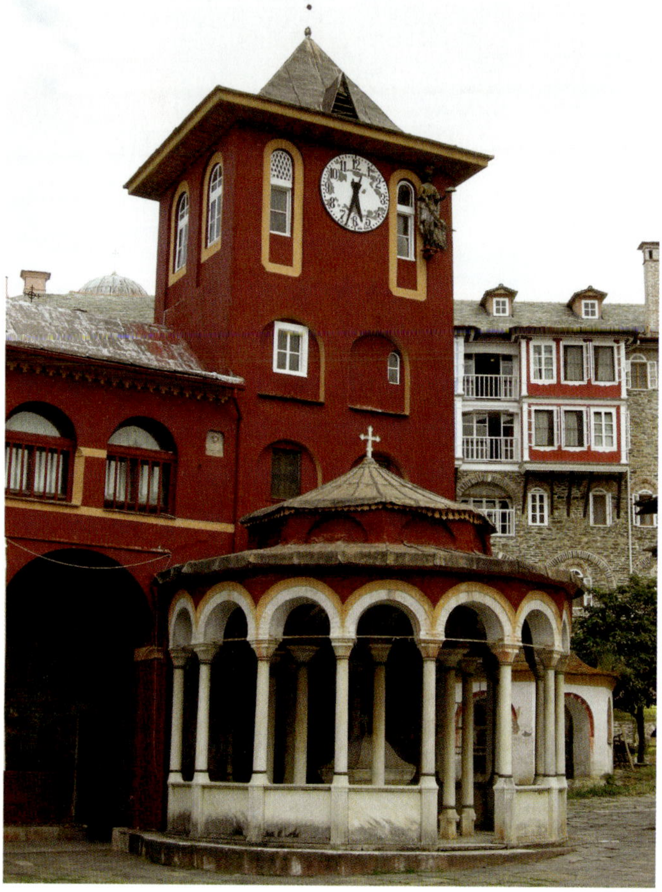

FIGURE 2.17 *Phiale from the Vatopedi Monastery, Mt. Athos. Current installation nineteenth century, the domical core at least seventeenth century, some marble elements carry the name of Kantakouzenos family from the fourteenth century.* PHOTO NEBOJŠA STANKOVIĆ

in monastic communities since the Middle Byzantine period.[99] Hence, it is highly possible that some archeological remains of canopied installations currently identified as having belonged to baptisteries actually belonged to *phialai*, especially because these installations continued to be used in the Middle and Late Byzantine churches, both in monastic and urban communities.[100]

Canopied Ambos

The ambo is one of the principal liturgical furnishings of Byzantine-rite churches. The liturgical and ritual function of the ambo is still not fully understood. It was used predominantly for readings from the Scriptures and lections at the end of the liturgy as a prayer of Thanksgiving, but also for prayers and readings related to wedding and funeral ceremonies, judging by the preserved collection of texts "prayer before the ambon," from the liturgy of St. John Chrysostom (fourth century).[101] As an elevated platform from which the Word of God is delivered, the ambo resembles the similarly designed *bema* used in ancient Greece as the orator's podium and *bemah* used for readings of the

[99] Kandić (1998–9) 61–78, esp. 62–64; Mamaloukos (2002) 9–10.

[100] Pallis (2012) 119–130; Broilo (2009) 5–24; Bogdanović (2017b).

[101] White (2015) 34.

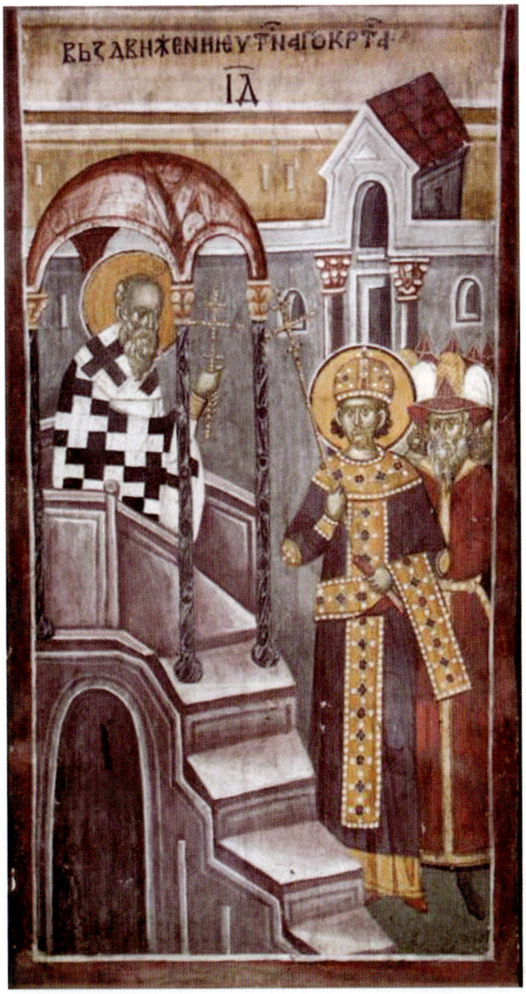

FIGURE 2.18 *The Elevation of the Cross, Church of the Mother of God, Monastery Gračanica, ca. 1321.* PHOTO IVAN DRPIĆ

Torah in Jewish synagogues. In the sixth century, Paulos Silentarios described the ambo in Hagia Sophia as an elevated platform where "the priest brings the good tidings (i.e., the Gospels Book)" as an icon of God that the faithful venerate.[102] Illuminated manuscripts, such as the tenth-century Gospels book (Par. gr. 70), would often frame the chapter heading for the Gospels by a canopy, as if suggesting both the framing of the sacred Word and the actual ambo furnishing in a church where the Gospels would be read. Constantinopolitan Patriarch Germanos in the ninth century also considered the ambo an important liturgical furnishing, signifying the stone of the Holy Sepulchre, which the Angel rolled back from its entrance.[103] It was defined as a hill (*oros*) put on a flat and leveled place, from which announcements could have been made.[104] Only clergy were allowed to climb and use the ambo during various services. A fourteenth-century fresco from the *katholikon* of the Gračanica monastery shows the priest elevating the cross as he climbs the canopied ambo, presumably mirroring the eponymous liturgical service (Fig. 2.18).

[102] Mango (1986) 95–6. On the iconic book, see Parmenter (2006) 160–189.

[103] *Germanos-b* 63.

[104] Kazhdan (1987) 422–426.

The performance of imperial ceremonies of coronation on the ambo of Hagia Sophia confirmed its sacred and elevated status.[105]

Archeological evidence has shown that the ambo—as its name suggests, *ambo* via Greek Ἄμβων, literally meaning "step, to elevate"—is a large oval platform with flights of steps leading up to it.[106] It usually stood in the middle of a Byzantine church facing the sanctuary directly, as in the fifth- and sixth-century churches of H. Leonidas, Kourion, Cyprus; Basilica B, Philippi; Hagia Euphemia; and Hagia Sophia in Constantinople (see Fig. 2.7). In these churches, the ambo was at the end of the *solea*, a raised elevated walkway leading from the bema. Such a design reveals that, architecturally and symbolically, the ambo was an extension of the sanctuary area into the nave of the church. A few examples of ambos set to the side of the nave and close to the sanctuary are also attested to in the contemporaneous churches Basilica A, Philippi; Amphipolis; Basilica B, Nikopolis; and Basilica D in Caričin Grad (Figs. 2.19, 2.20). Some of these basilicas were rather huge, more than 100 meters long, as in the case of H. Leonidas. I agree with Andrew White, who sees the location of ambos deep into the space of the nave in the early churches as necessary to meet practical and acoustical needs.[107] In a way, the ambo extended the ritual space used for liturgical services into the major nave, allowing the congregation to participate in the thanksgiving prayers and lections. If the churches were domed, quite often the ambo was placed almost directly under the dome, which served as a sound box, enhancing the acoustics. An example is the ambo in the centrally planned Hagia Euphemia in Constantinople.

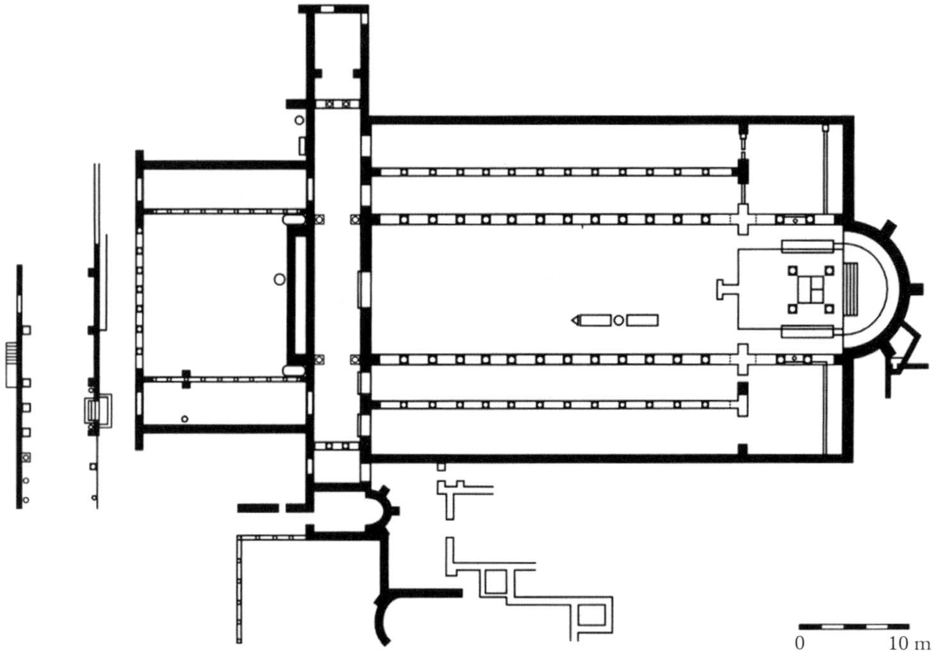

FIGURE 2.19 *Basilica B, Nikopolis, Greece, fifth century.* DRAWING JOEL KELLY FROM ĆURČIĆ (2010) 131, FIG. 130

[105] Majeska (1997) 1–11.

[106] Mathews (1971) 65, 70, 96–99; Kazhdan (1987) 422–426; Peschlow (1994) 255–260.

[107] White (2015) 34.

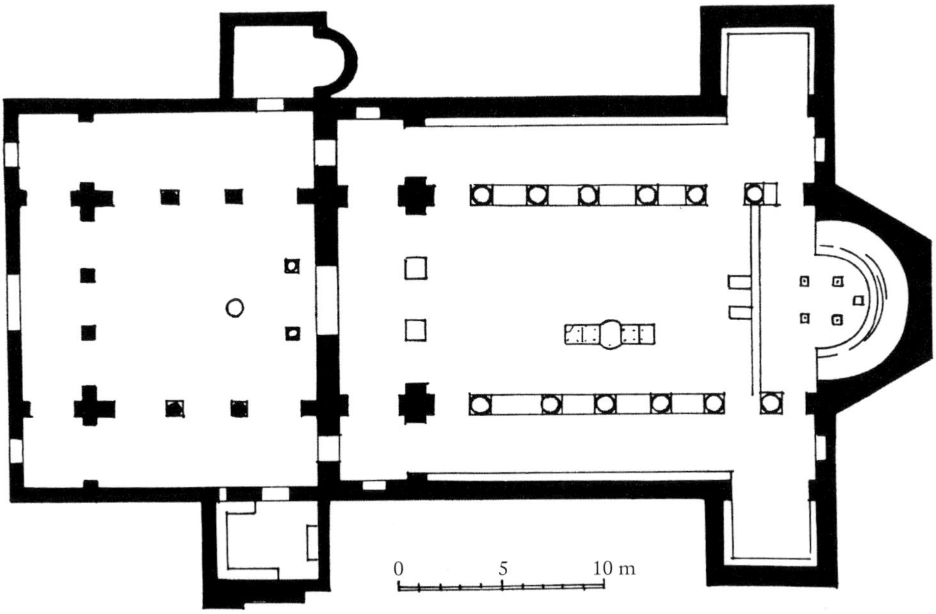

FIGURE 2.20 *Basilica D, Caričin Grad, Serbia, sixth century.* DRAWING JOEL KELLY FROM ĆURČIĆ (2010) 213, FIG. 221

Although very few ambos have been preserved, occasionally these installations were topped by a canopy, which could accommodate both standing and sitting figures (Table 5.16, 48, 49, 198, 228, 229). In a way, such canopied ambos replicated the core of the church structurally, conveying the meaning that the church core and the ambo were inhabitable, living spaces. This was the case of the ambo in Hagia Sophia in Constantinople, now lost, which was topped by a canopy roof at least since the twelfth century.[108] In the Basilica B in Nikopolis, one dome stood over the sanctuary, and the second was above the canopied ambo. Canopied ambos also existed in other Byzantine-rite churches. A three-columned canopy topped the ambo of the fifth- and sixth-century Basilica A, Thebes, while a canopied ambo most likely existed in Hagios Demetrios, Thessaloniki. In the Middle and Late Byzantine periods, when most churches became minuscule in scale, the use of monumental ambos gradually diminished.[109] Yet larger churches continued to have and use them.[110] The extraordinary preserved canopied ambo *in situ* from the Church of the Dormition of the Mother of God in Kalabaka, as we shall see, confirms its use in later periods. The canopied *ambo* was in use in the Old Cathedral, Beroia (Veria), Greece, and in St. Sophia in Ohrid, F.Y.R. of Macedonia, at least until the fourteenth century.[111]

Canopies Framing Venerated Tombs, Relics, and Icons

As church furniture, canopies above altar tables, baptisteries, holy water fonts, and ambos are closely related to the liturgy. Other canopied installations may have been

108 Mango and Parker (1960) 233–244.

109 Mango (1982) 297–313, esp. 302.

110 Kazhdan (1987) 422–426; Peschlow (1994) 255–260.

111 Orlandos (1965) 159–168; Soteriou (1962) vol. 1, 184–185, 209–213, figs. 117–118; Soteriou (1931) 86–97, fig. 107; Pazaras (1994) 251–254; Grozdanov (1969) 49–63.

related to non-liturgical, often devotional practices or could have marked the places where several different rituals merged. Canopied tombs, reliquaries, artophoria, and icons are exceptionally complex, as they are most directly associated with devotional practices, to the concepts of the body and human presence in the church, and some of them can be related to liturgical practices, as when, for example, relics are associated with the altar table.

A canopy whose poles rested on the altar table at the fifth- or sixth-century Church of St. Bacchos, Horvat Tinshemet, Palestine, is most interesting because its primary function was not to shelter the altar table itself.[112] This marble altar table (0.60 m x 0.64 m) is located in front of the apse and has in its middle a round depression with a small hole in the center, most likely for consecrated relics. In the four corners of the depression are iron nails that were probably meant to support a small canopy. A fragment of the marble reliquary lid was also discovered, thus confirming the existence of a reliquary. Thus, such small canopies fixed on the altar table would have primarily sheltered, not the altar table, but the holy relics within the altar table. In St. Gabriel's Church in Nazareth, such a small, modern canopy with its columns resting on the edges of the altar table is still in use. Though we may never be certain how widespread such a practice was during the Byzantine era, the above-mentioned examples indicate that both the variety and the spread of canopies were greater than we might even suspect. At the same time, it stands to reason that if canopies could have been attached to the top of an altar or other types of tables, such as tables for the display of relics, more churches might have had such canopies. This must have been especially true of smaller churches with more confined sanctuaries and devotional spaces, where monumental canopies could not have been accommodated. In that context, the altar canopy in such cases not only defies our understanding of its acceptable size and physical relationship to the altar table itself, but it also becomes an architectural symbol for the place of relics, combining at least two functions or types into one installation and challenging a strictly typological approach to the studies of canopies.

The canopy from Horvat Tinshemet illustrates how small-scale canopies could have served to shelter relics or to signify the location of relics. Indeed, research has confirmed through numerous examples that the most common setting for tiny saintly relics, such as bone fragments, in a Byzantine-rite church was the altar itself.[113] These relics would be inserted into the cavity of the altar table or under the altar because their presence was essential for the consecration of the Byzantine churches. Yet not all the canopies that enshrined relics were necessarily related to altar tables. Smaller relics could also have been used for veneration, and then the reliquary boxes could have been stored in various locations, including inside the bema (sanctuary with altar), chapels, and treasuries (*skeuophylakia*). Their specific placement varied, from being buried under the church floors and additionally architecturally framed[114] to being exposed on tables (not necessarily altar tables), within chests, or on specially mounted portable "towers" suggestive of canopied installations, as was recorded in pilgrims' accounts of their pilgrimages to the monastery of St. John the Baptist in Petra, in Constantinople.[115]

---

[112] This fifth- or sixth-century church dedicated to Saint Bacchus and located southwest of Horvat Tinshemet (Sheikh 'Ali Malikina; Khirbet esh-Shamiya) was discovered in 1986. Dahari (1996) 67–68, 102–104; Guérin (1875) vol. 2, 76.

[113] Hahn and Klein (2015).

[114] Yasin (2015) 133–151.

[115] Marinis and Ousterhout (2015) 153–172, esp. 160.

Canopies above venerated saintly tombs, relics, and especially venerated icons were often named *proskynetaria,* which in the Greek language stands for any "place of worship."[116] Usually full canopies or larger installations consisting of an architectural frame formed of a pair of columns supporting an arch, these structures are generally overlooked in the discussions of Byzantine canopies, despite their significant number in churches (Tables 5 and 6). Written testimony indicates that the ninth-century altar canopy from the Church of San Apollinare in Classe at Ravenna was decorated with depictions of Christ and angels.[117] The icons themselves could have been placed within a canopy or even attached to the upper part of the canopy.[118] A twelfth-century manuscript depicts an icon attached to a canopy over an ambo, confirming the possibility that, in addition to being painted, canopies might have been adorned with icons (see Fig. 2.21). Another twelfth-century miniature from the Madrid Skylitzes manuscript depicts a canopy-like four-columned structure with four icons—Christ, the Mother of God, and two archangels—attached to the upper part of the canopy.[119] Numerous Byzantine

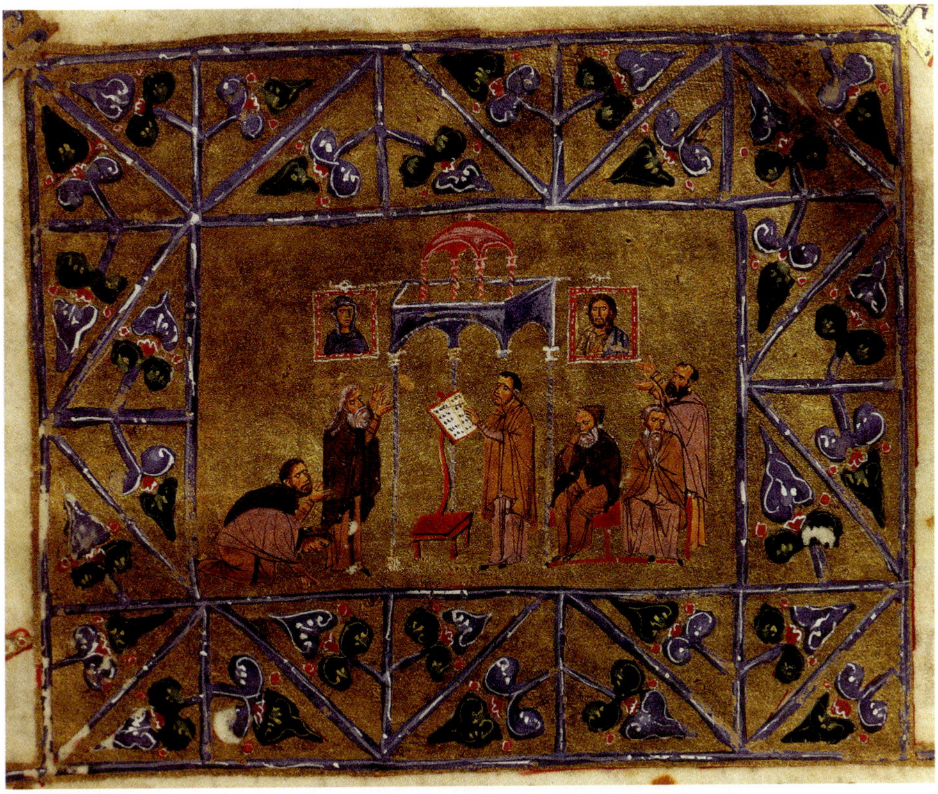

FIGURE 2.21 Monks praying and reading. *The lectern of the reader is framed by a canopy-like structure flanked by two icons of the Mother of God and Christ. Sinai gr. 418, fol. 269r. Monastery of Saint Catherine Sinai, Egypt, twelfth century* GIANNI DAGLI ORTI/THE ART ARCHIVE AT ART RESOURCE, NEW YORK

[116] Ćurčić (2000) 134–160; Marković (2009) 88; Drpić (2012) 645–659.

[117] Maksimović (1961) 32.

[118] Wybrew (1989) 147; Cormack (1985) 63, 129.

[119] Cutler (1987) 145–154 recognizes the structure as a canopy, while Sarabianov (2000) 312–359, 730–731, recognizes the same structure as a sanctuary barrier. On spatial relations and architectural design of altar canopy and sanctuary barrier, see also Chapter 4.

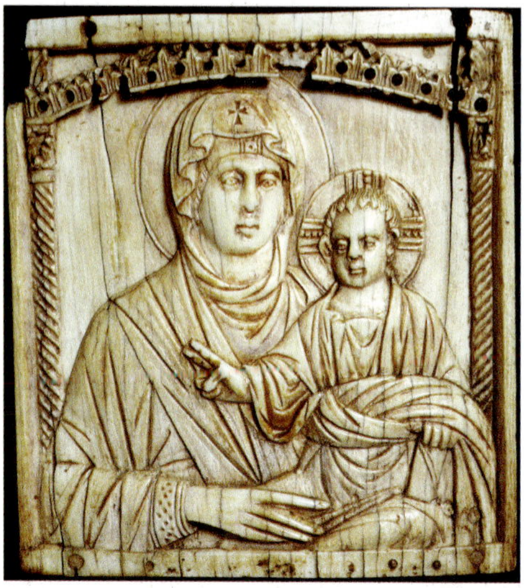

FIGURE 2.22 *Mother of God Hodegetria with Christ Child under canopy, central panel of an ivory triptych, Constantinople, second half of the tenth century.* © DUMBARTON OAKS, BYZANTINE COLLECTION, WASHINGTON, D.C.

ivories, such as a tenth-century central panel of a triptych from the Dumbarton Oaks Collection that shows the Mother of God Hodegetria with Christ child under a delicately lattice-carved canopy with spirally fluted columns (Fig. 2.22), point to the shape of *proskynetaria* canopies that once existed in Byzantine churches. Later churches that preserve comparable *proskynetaria* include the monastic church of Zoodochos Pege in Samari, Messenia (late twelfth century); Porta Panagia in Pylai, Thessaly (1283); and the *proskynetarion* in the Chora *katholikon* (1316–1321), to name but a few (Table 5.211, 221, 234).[120]

The Mother of God, Christ, and the patron saints of a church are the most common subjects of *proskynetaria* icons.[121] The icon of patron saint within eponymous Church of St. Panteleimon, at Nerezi, F.Y.R. of Macedonia, is delicately nested within the richly carved, trilobed marble frame of the twelfth-century *proskynetarion* (Fig. 2.23).[122] Framed within elaborate settings, *proskynetaria* were often physically connected to the sanctuary barriers from at least the tenth century until the end of the Byzantine Empire (Table 5.170, 194, 204, 211–213, 221, 234).[123] Frequently framed by double-knotted colonnettes and relief arches decorated with geometric, vegetal, and zoomorphic motifs, which repeat the patterns from the *templon* screen, *proskynetaria* can be carved in marble or other high-quality stone, made of stucco, or even painted, and are usually placed on the eastern piers or pilasters of a church, flanking the sanctuary barrier. *Proskynetaria* frames from Kalenderhane in Constantinople are especially instructive, because in the thirteenth century they were made of marble with horizontal entablatures, not with arches, and then replaced by frames in stucco a century later.[124] In single-aisled small

[120] Hjort (1979) 199–289; Boura (1977–1979) 63–72; Ćurčić (2000) 134–160; Kalopissi-Verti (2006) 107–134.

[121] Cecchelli (1959). On *proskynetaria* icons, see Kalopissi-Verti (2006) 107–134; Babić (1975) 3–49.

[122] Sinkević (2000) 87; Ćurčić (2000) 134–160.

[123] Kalopissi-Verti (2006) 107–134.

[124] Ćurčić (2001a) 1106–1109.

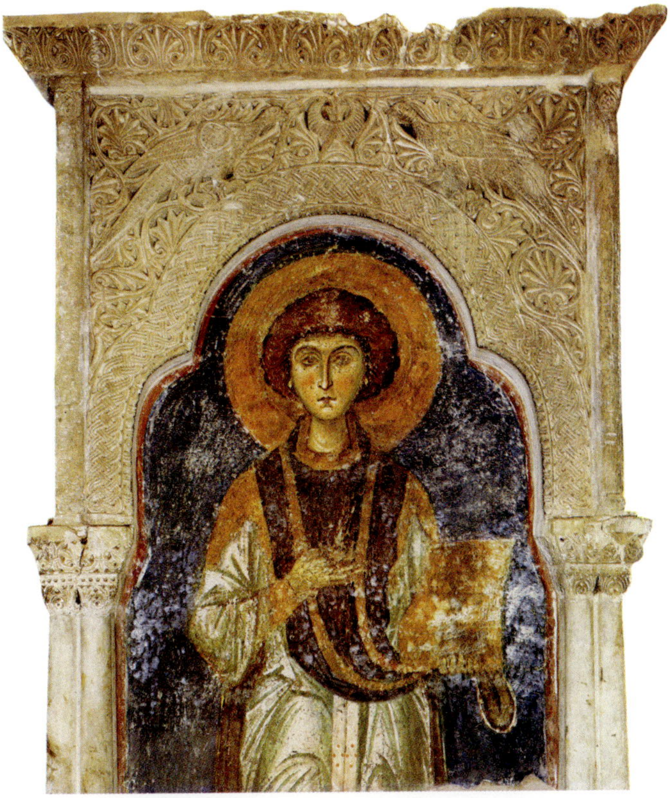

FIGURE 2.23 Proskynetarion *icon of St. Panteleimon framed by a marble canopy frame. Church of St. Panteleimon, Monastery Nerezi, F.Y.R. of Macedonia, twelfth century.* PHOTO IDA SINKEVIĆ

churches, *proskynetaria* may have been placed at the eastern ends of the south and north walls next to the sanctuary screen.[125]

A more detailed analysis of archeological evidence has shown that, in addition to flanking the sanctuary screen, *proskynetaria* could have been situated in other places in the church. For example, St. Sophia in Monemvasia (built ca. 1150) once had at least eight frames placed on each of the eight piers that supported the dome of this octagonal church, judging from the colonnette capitals used as corbels and preserved *in situ* and from fragments of arches now in the Museum of Monemvasia (Table 5.212).[126] *Proskynetaria* also might have been placed in the narthex, flanking the doors into the nave and essentially repeating the iconography of the sanctuary screen. An arched stone frame from the narthex of the Church of St. John Eleemon in Ligourio, Argolis, which was built after the twelfth century, is set next to the entrance doors to the nave and presumably once framed an icon (Table 5.213).[127] Images of the Mother of God and Christ are framed individually under marble canopies in the naos of the Chora *katholikon* (Fig. 2.24).[128] The icon of St. Paraskevi in the thirteenth-century eponymous church in Geraki is framed by a polychrome sculpted

---

125 Kalopissi-Verti (2006) 107–134, esp. 132.
126 Ibid., esp 114, figs. 10–11.
127 Ibid., esp. 123–131.
128 Hjort (1979) 199–289.

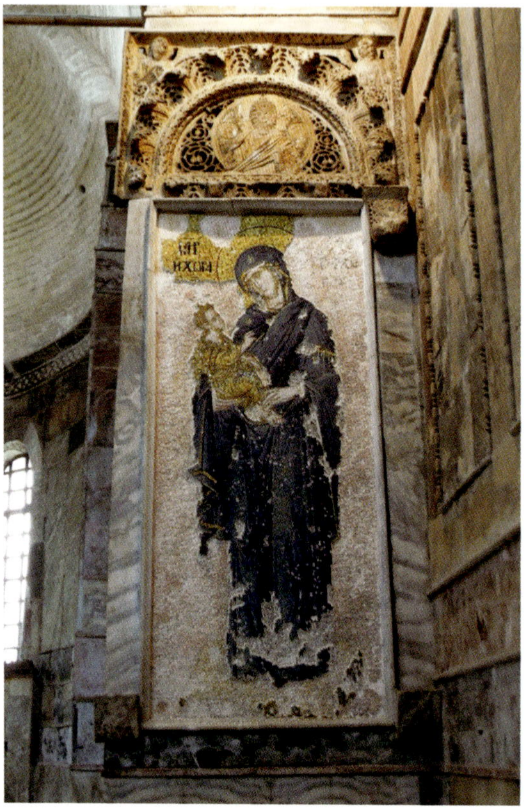

FIGURE 2.24 Proskynetarion *icon of the Mother of God with Christ Child framed by a marble canopy frame. Church of the Holy Savior, Chora Monastery, Constantinople, modern Istanbul, fourteenth century.* PHOTO NEBOJŠA STANKOVIĆ

stone frame on columns (Table 5.220).[129] Numerous similar painted representations in coeval churches in Greece, Serbia, and Bulgaria suggest that such canopies were often painted instead of sculpted, presumably emulating three-dimensional canopies by means of less expensive and more easily acquired artistic technique.[130] Examples can be found in the churches of St. George, Kurbinovo; Hagia Sophia, Trebizond; Panagia Phorbiotissa, Assinou, Cyprus; Panagia Moutoullas, Cyprus; Kakopetria, Cyprus; and others. In the fourteenth-century Church of H. Anargyroi, Kastoria, icons were even painted in the niches on the church exterior and on painted frames flanking the entrance doors. It remains to be examined further whether icons of the patron saints usually placed above entrance doors of Late Byzantine churches might somehow be related to the canopy-like frames above the main doors of sanctuary screens as described in the twelfth century in the Church of the Nativity in Bogolyubovo.[131] Moreover, the archeologically confirmed *proskynetarion* canopy in the thirteenth-century Serbian monastery Žiča, most likely exposed for veneration the relics of the True Cross rather than an icon, once again highlighting how elusive our modern typology of canopies can be when it is based strictly on the types of objects being framed.[132]

---

129 Trkulja (2004) 102–103; Kalopissi-Verti (2006) 107–134.

130 Kalopissi-Verti (2006) 107–134, esp. 123–131, figs. 21–26, 28–30.

131 Sterligova (2000) 360–381, 731–732.

132 Čanak-Medić (1998) 173–187, fig. 5.

Canopies Framing Other Church Installations (Bishop's Thrones, Bells)

In addition to canopies above altar tables, baptismal and holy water fonts, ambos, tombs, relics, and icons, material evidence, especially from the later periods, has revealed a number of other canopy types. For example, the canopy at the Georgian monastery Gelati (founded in 1106) covered the bishop's throne (Figs. 2.25, 2.26).[133] Canopies were installed over the bell tower in the Church of the Holy Cross in Aght'amar, Armenia, now Turkey (tenth century); in the Church of Panagia Parigoritissa at Arta (late thirteenth century), and in the Church of Gergeti, Georgia (fourteenth century) (Fig. 2.27, see also Figs. 4.36, 4.37). An

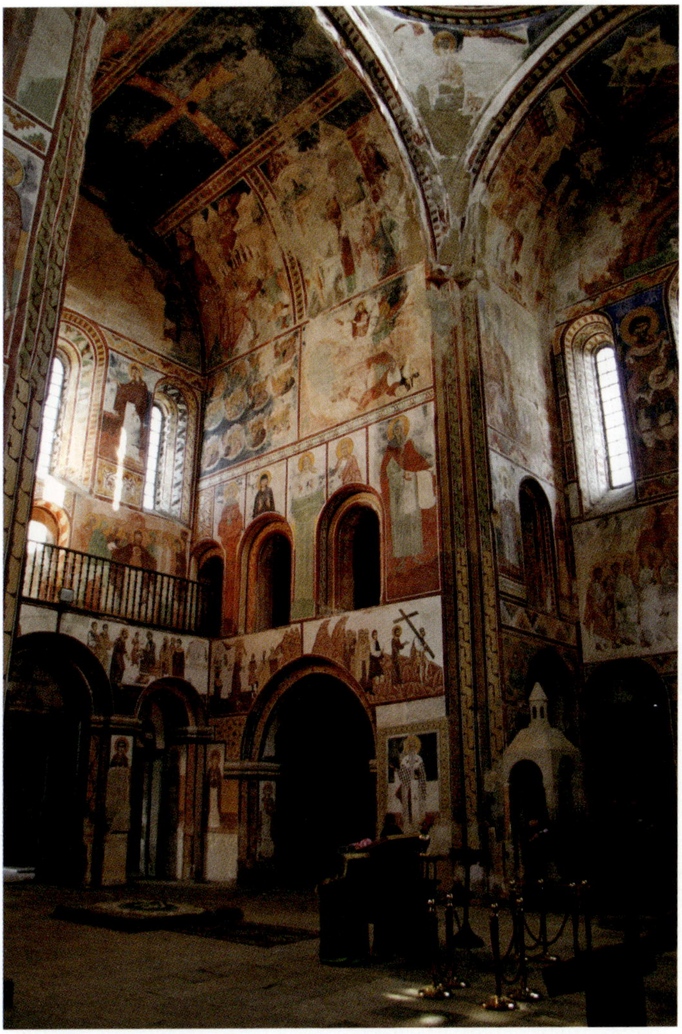

FIGURE 2.25 *Interior of the katholikon of the Gelati Monastery, Georgia, monastery founded in 1106.* PHOTO NEBOJŠA STANKOVIĆ

[133] Mepisašvili and Virsalaže (1982) fig. 54. On episcopal thrones, see also Radujko (2001) 143–178.

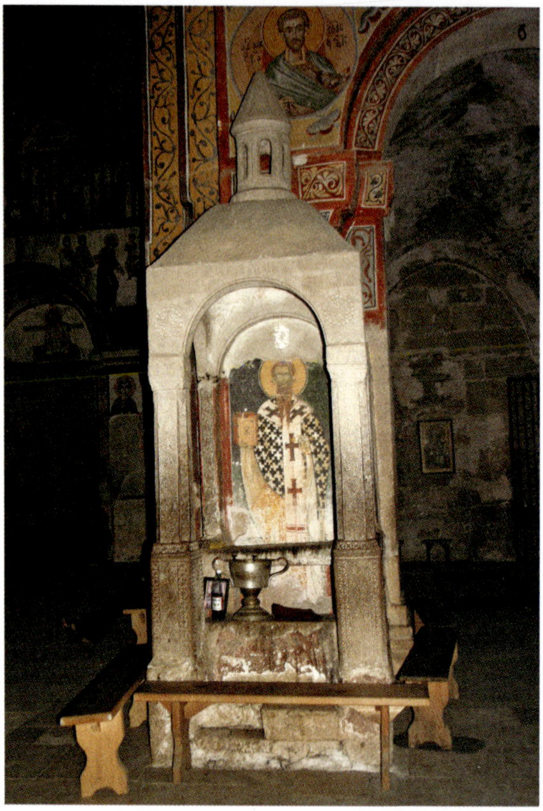

FIGURE 2.26 *Episcopal throne, Gelati Monastery, Georgia, twelfth-thirteenth century.* PHOTO NEBOJŠA STANKOVIĆ

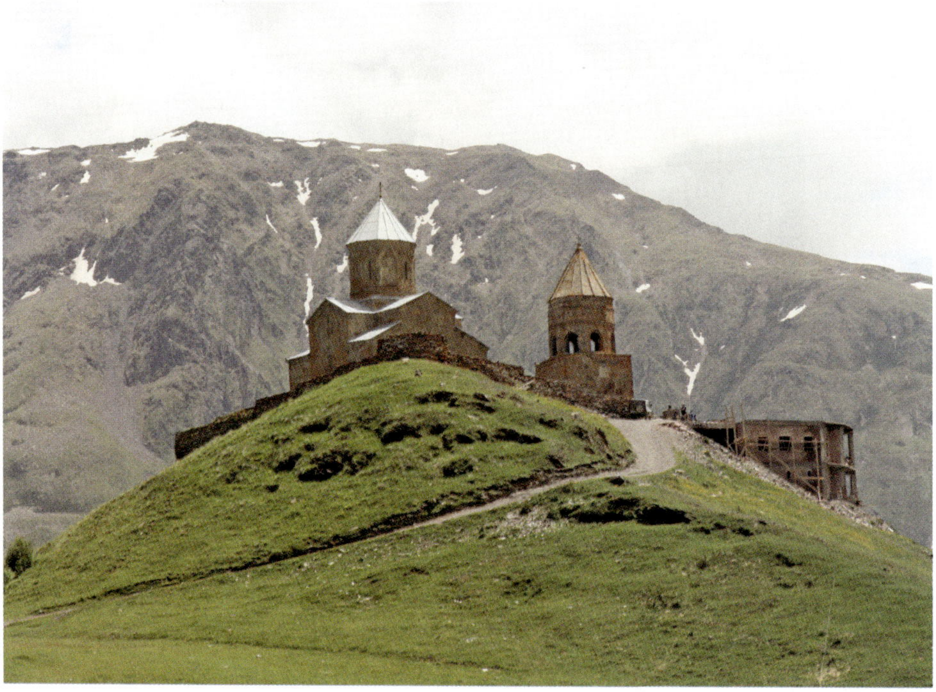

FIGURE 2.27 *Gergeti Monastery with canopied bell tower, Georgia, fourteenth century.* PHOTO NEBOJŠA STANKOVIĆ

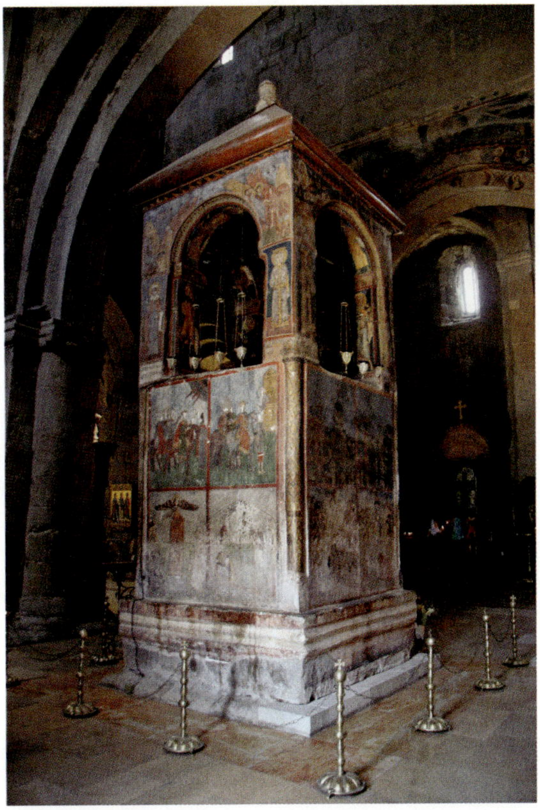

FIGURE 2.28 *Tomb of Christ canopied shrine, Cathedral Sveti Choveli, Mcheta, Georgia, fifteenth century.* PHOTO NEBOJŠA STANKOVIĆ

entire fifteenth-century canopy richly painted in New Testament narrative scenes, which symbolizes the Tomb of Christ, was built in the eleventh-century Cathedral Sveti Choveli in Mcheta, Georgia (Fig. 2.28). The stone canopy shelters the place where, according to chroniclers, the tunic (*chiton*) of Christ was buried in the archeologically confirmed, fourth-century wooden church.[134] The Cathedral of Sveti Choveli also has a seventeenth-century episcopal throne (Fig. 2.29) done in the tradition of a medieval canopied episcopal throne preserved in Gelati.[135] Similarly, tomb canopies of the founders of churches and monasteries, often dated to the post-medieval times, such as those seventeenth-century installations in the Georgian medieval monasteries of Gelati and Iqalto, may point to medieval traditions (Figs. 2.30, 2.31). Such developed canopied tombs are mentioned in medieval texts, and their existence in medieval times is confirmed by the 1916 photo of a now-lost, early fifteenth-century tomb of Byzantine emperor Komnenos IV from the

---

[134] The foundations of this fourth-century church were recovered in the 1970s during archeological works on the south end of the church, at the place of the fifteenth-century canopy. Mepisashvili and Tsintsadze (1977) 67–68, 115–116, 150–157.

[135] I thank Nebojša Stanković for sharing with me his photographic material from Georgia and for discussing with me the canopied installations preserved in medieval Georgian churches.

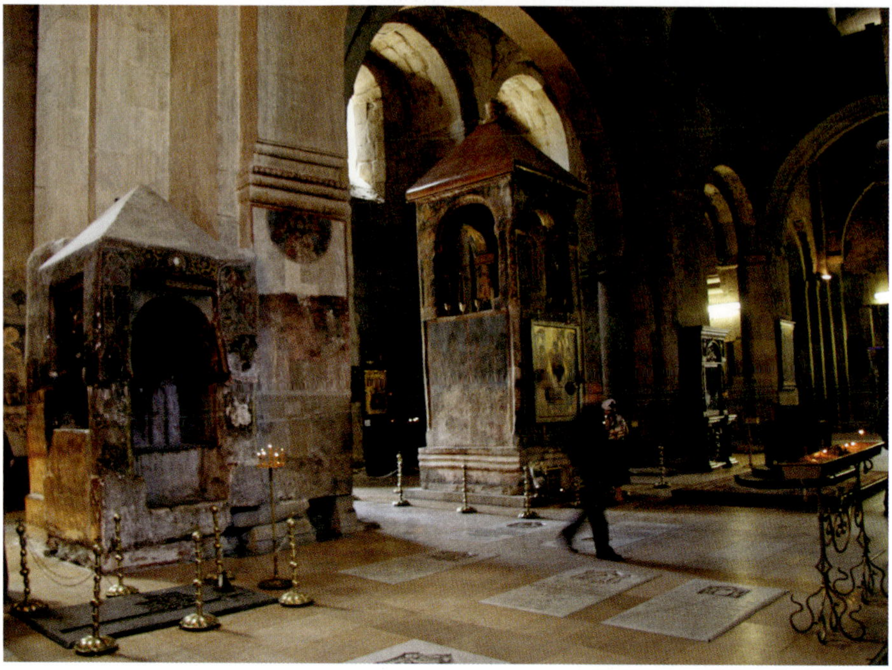

FIGURE 2.29 *Interior of the Sveti Choveli Monastery showing the fifteenth-century shrine and the seventeenth-century episcopal throne, Georgia.* PHOTO NEBOJŠA STANKOVIĆ

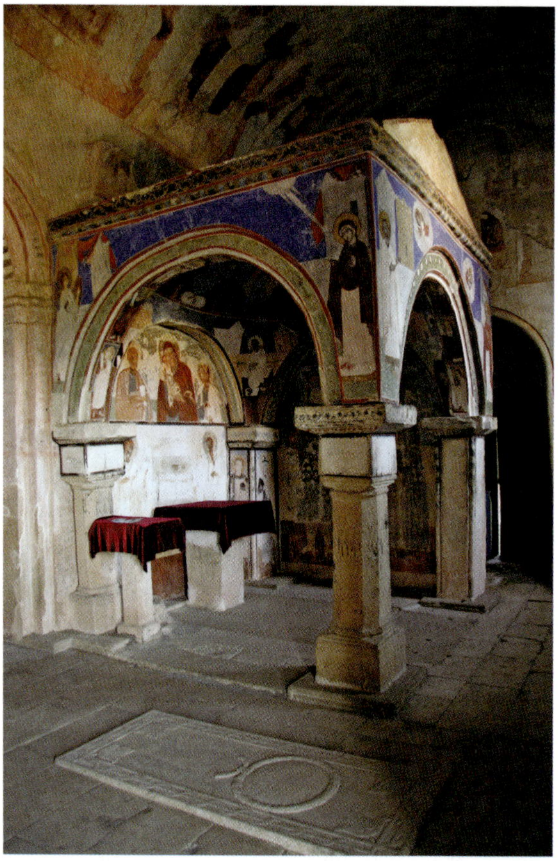

FIGURE 2.30 *Founders tomb. Gelati Monastery, Georgia, seventeenth century.* PHOTO NEBOJŠA STANKOVIĆ

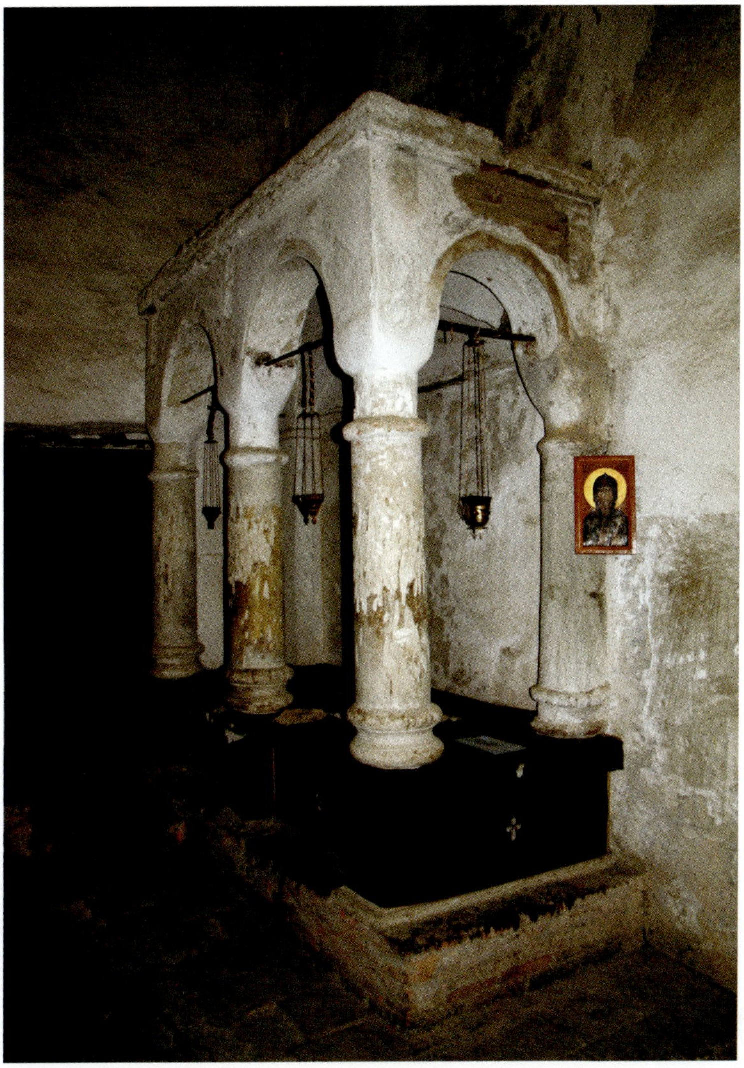

FIGURE 2.31 *Founders tomb. Iqalto Monastery, Georgia, seventeenth century.* PHOTO NEBOJŠA STANKOVIĆ

Chrysokephalos Church in Trebizond.[136] This originally freestanding imperial tomb was in its canopied construction comparable to the founder's tomb from Gelati. Despite being relatively well-preserved, these canopied installations in churches above tombs, episcopal thrones, and bells remain essentially overlooked in current studies of canopies. Because more instructive Byzantine examples have not survived, and because these canopies cannot easily fit into typological consideration and the general outlines of Byzantine architecture, the above-mentioned canopies are examined as exceptions rather than as belonging to the wider phenomena of Byzantine canopies.[137]

---

136 Bryer (c1993) 93–102. See also Chapter 1.

137 It is interesting to note that nineteenth-century churches from Metsovo, Greece—namely St. Charalambos, Holy Trinity, St. George, and St. Pantheleiomon—today exhibit canopies above belfries.

THE FORM AND MATERIALITY OF CANOPIES

While the general fragility of canopies accounts at least in part for their limited evidence, three additional concerns are crucial for understanding the limited scope of evidence that has been preserved up to the present. First, despite the significant number of archeologically documented canopies, and in particular those that were part of altar installations, in-depth analysis actually reveals a number of paradoxes and additional reasons for the limited scope of archeological and architectural evidence for various types of canopies. Above all, as we have seen, canopies could have been portable objects, or they could have been placed on the top of the altar table, raised above the floor level and cantilevered like *proskynetaria*, in each case leaving us with no or very scarce evidence of their existence. These circumstances make it extremely difficult to posit canopies in smaller-sized Middle and Late Byzantine churches. Second, though limited in scope, there was a variety of shapes used for canopies, beginning with two-columned installations projecting from the surface of the wall, as in the earliest recorded canopy from Dura Europos, and expanding into multiple variants of four- and multi-columned canopies with domical or polygonal roofs, which significantly expand the ways in which we should understand these structures in formal and architectural terms. Third, the material used for canopies is significant, since canopies made of silver, gold, and semiprecious materials, as well as those made of wood or even potentially of cloth, have not survived up to present, even though my research, coupled with texts about and images of canopies, shows that the Byzantines used these kinds of canopies as well. Therefore, in order to reveal the variety and wide geographical and chronological distribution of canopies in the Byzantine tradition, we will additionally not only highlight surviving archeological and architectural evidence for canopies and our understanding of their various types, but also consider their shape, materials, decorative features, and inscriptions as carriers of meaning.

Shape of Canopies

In considering the shape of canopies, the two most basic types of canopies in Byzantine-rite churches are four-columned canopies with either a domical or a pyramidal roof (Fig. 2.32). Combining the work of Pavuša Vežić, who analyzed a big corpus of medieval stone canopies from along the Adriatic littoral, and other archeological and textual evidence that I have assembled, the conclusion can be reached that the majority of preserved canopies were installations, not with domical, but rather with polygonal, six- or eight-sided roofs, starting with the sixth-century altar canopy in Hagia Sophia.[138] A variety of two-columned, four-columned, and multi-columned canopies existed. The shapes of canopies cannot be associated with their specific function. For example, four-columned canopies could equally frame altar tables, baptismal fonts, or ambos.

Two-columned installations, such as the *arcosolium*-like niche with two frontal columns in the Christian building at Dura Europos, are particularly critical for understanding the design process of both canopies and church buildings and their close relationships. Such "half-canopies" formed by two columns instead of four are generally under-studied, but they must have been more common than we assume today and especially in spatially confined spaces. Half-canopies in the medieval West and before the doctrinal split of the Byzantine-rite and Roman Catholic churches can be exemplified by the well-recognized, but now lost, canopy in the lower Church of St. Clemente in Rome (ninth century).[139] Canopies formed by two columns placed close to the back

---

[138] Vežić and Lončar (2009).

[139] Tronzo (1987) 477–492, figs. 4–5.

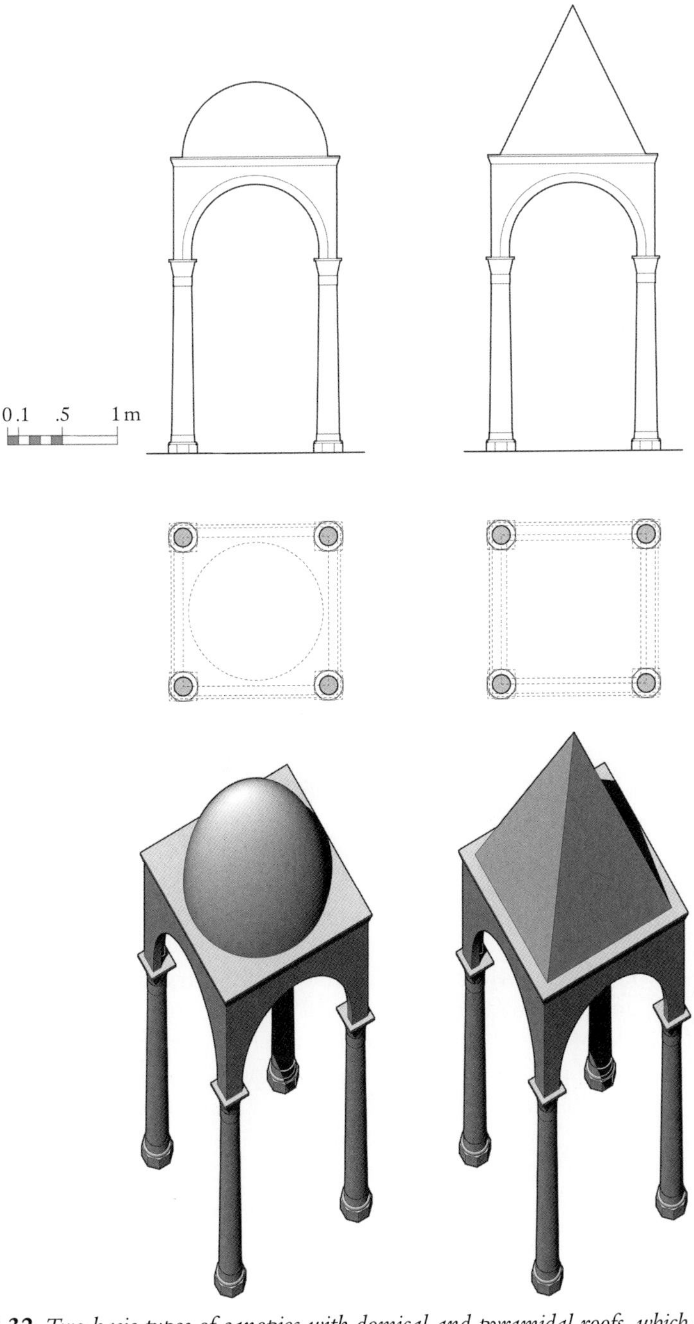

FIGURE 2.32 *Two basic types of canopies with domical and pyramidal roofs, which were used in Byzantine churches.* DRAWING ZHENGYANG HUA

wall are apparent in confirmed Byzantine-rite churches. The best-known examples are dated to later periods. The thirteenth-century tomb of Archbishop Sava II in the Church of Holy Apostles in Peć, Kosovo, Serbia, has preserved footings for the double columns on each side of the originally canopied tomb (Fig. 2.33). The fourteenth-century canopied tombs in the Chora monastery in Constantinople have also been

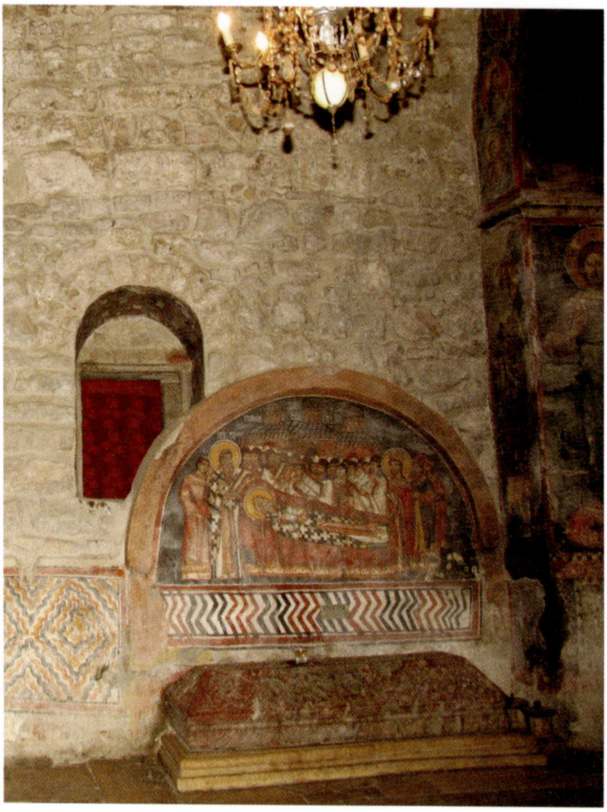

FIGURE 2.33 *Tomb of Archbishop Sava II, thirteenth century, originally within arcosolium carried by dual colonnettes set on each side of the sarcophagus. Church of Holy Apostles, Peć, Kosovo, Serbia.* PHOTO IVAN DRPIĆ

preserved without original columns, but their delicately carved arcuated frames remain (Fig. 2.34).[140] Four-columned canopies would clearly frame a rectangular perimeter and, by the virtue of their bilateral symmetry, emphasize the centrality of sacred space, yet examples of polygonal canopies with six or more columns are also recorded, including the fifteenth-century eight-sided *phiale* canopy from the church atrium of St. Demetrios in Thessaloniki, which was photographed just before its destruction.[141] A striking example of the numerous possibilities for making a canopy is the late Byzantine *proskynetarion* canopy from the Church of the Taxiarchs, Kalyvia-Kouvara, Attica, which is framed by two columns and a back wall and crowned by two polygonal roofs attached to each other side by side (Fig. 2.35, Table 5.224).[142]

After the eleventh century, while in central parts of the Byzantine Empire the design of canopies, even of those made anew, looked anachronistic, the design of canopies in the Western regions became generally more elaborate. Some canopies could have been topped by a temple or churchlike lantern, such as the altar canopy in the Church of St. Nicholas in

[140] Cvetković (2000) 3–9; Hjort (1979) 199–289.

[141] Bakirtzis (2002) 175–192. See also Fig. 4.19 in this volume.

[142] Ćurčić (2000) 134–142; Bogdanović (2008a); Drpić (2012) 645–694.

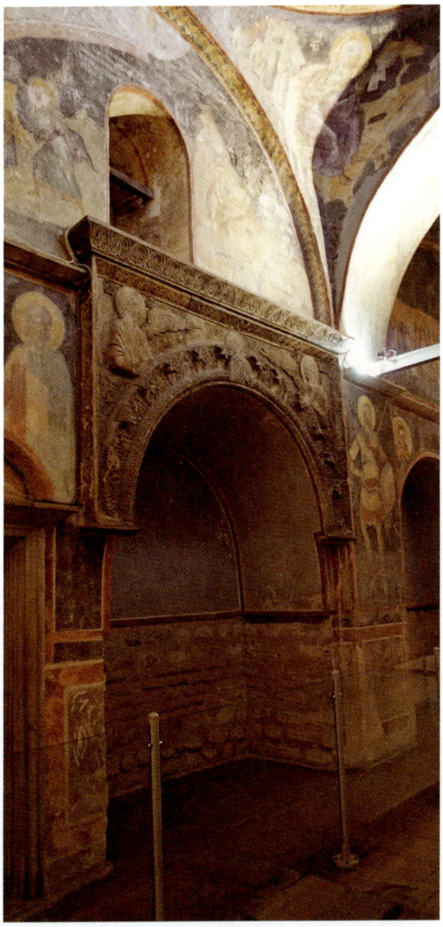

FIGURE 2.34 *Tombs in the pareklession. Church of Christ Chora, Constantinople, now Istanbul, fourteenth century.* PHOTO AUTHOR

Bari, or the fourteenth-century altar canopy still standing in the Cathedral of St. Tryphon in Kotor (Fig. 2.36) on the opposite side of the Adriatic.[143] It is usually assumed that such canopies with an additional lantern at the top and shaped in the form of a small church are later features influenced by general architectural, artistic, and liturgical trends in Romanesque and Gothic Western Europe.[144] Yet a ninth-century canopy in the basilica of Castel Sant'Elia, built by the Byzantines, was also topped by a temple-like, towered roof (Fig. 2.37).[145] Some Byzantine illuminated manuscripts, frescos, and mosaics show a canopy-like structure that nests a small house on its top (Fig. 2.38, see also Fig 2.21). Hence, the addition of the lantern at the top of Romanesque and later Gothic canopies might have resulted from concepts about the framing of sacred space, which Christians in the West shared with the Byzantines.

Then again, it is important to mention that not all Byzantine canopies had a roof. An example comes from the crypt of the Church of Hagios Demetrios in Thessaloniki.[146]

---

[143] Maksimović (1961) 32; Jurlaro (1973) 315–324.

[144] Maksimović (1961) 30–40; Blaauw (2009b) 123–140.

[145] *EAM* vol. 4, 718–735.

[146] Bakirtzis (2002) 175–192. See also Chapter 4 and Fig. 4.18.

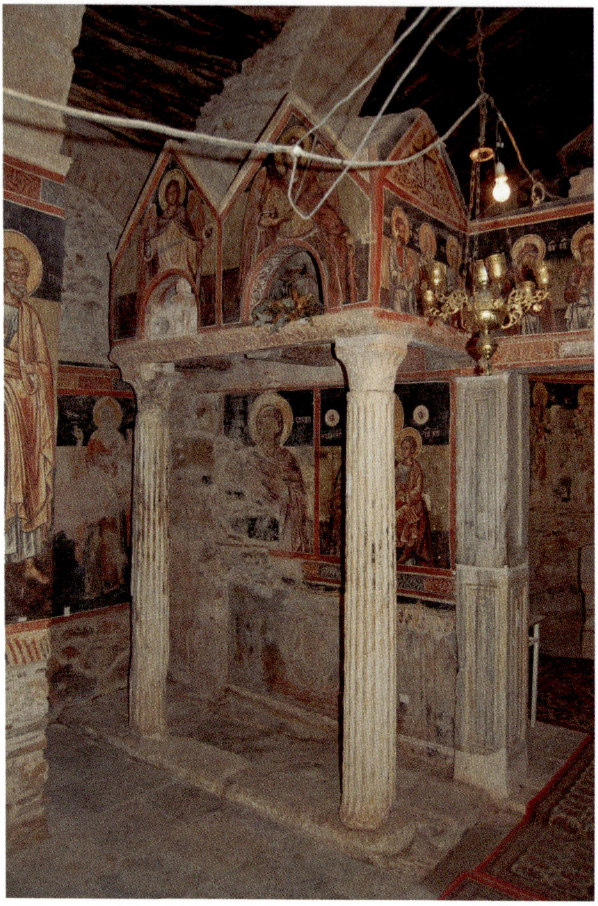

FIGURE 2.35 *Proskynetarion canopy, late Byzantine (?). Church of the Taxiarchs, Kalyvia-Kouvara, Attica, Greece.* PHOTO STAVROS MAMALOUKOS

Still *in situ*, this installation is an open-roofed, seven-columned marble canopy, which was articulated through connected arches. Established sometime after the ninth century and confirmed in texts by the eleventh century, this canopy framed the location of the believed place of a miraculous gushing of myrrh-with-water, on the location of an older bath.

Material Used for Canopies

Consideration of the material used for canopies is necessary for our full understanding of canopies in the Byzantine tradition. In addition to surviving archeological evidence for stone canopies and limited evidence for those made of metal and wood, contemporaneous texts suggest that some of them apparently were made of textiles. My analysis shows that the choice of materials for canopies was related to both the structural and symbolic properties of the selected materials and the contexts of their serial or individual production.

Stone Canopies

Archeological evidence for canopies is most often restricted to remnants of stone and marble columns, occasionally to stone and marble footings, sockets, and other fittings, which

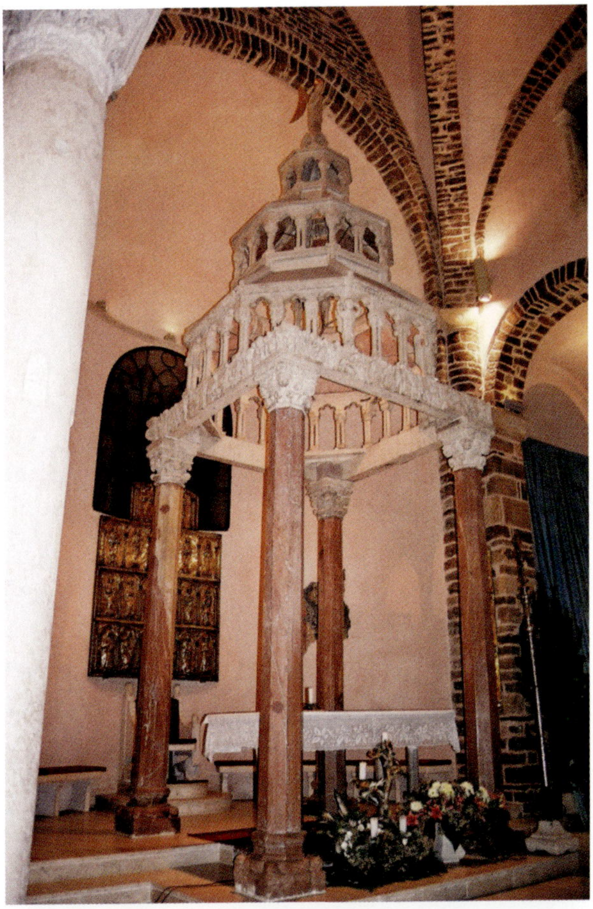

FIGURE 2.36 *Altar canopy, Church of St. Tryphon, Kotor, fourteenth century.* PHOTO NEBOJŠA STANKOVIĆ

can be recognized in church floors.[147] Numerous architectural fragments from various archeological sites, museums, and private collections, though dispersed and often without full records of provenance, may point to surviving fragments of now-lost canopies.[148] These are usually segments of relatively small-span arches (approximately 1–2 m in span), relatively thin and short columns (approximately 15–20 cm in diameter and up to 2 m in

[147] See, for example, Goldfus et al. (2000) 331–342; Bikai (2002) 271–276; Bikai and Egan (1997) 493–535; Love (1970) 149–155; Small (1980) 96–99; Pennas (2005); Mihajlovski (2007) 225–241; Peirano and Garberoglio (2013) 11–14; Peirano (2012) 25–33; Peirano (2012) 65–84; Marinković (2011a) 79–94; Ivanišević and Stamenković (2013) 22–31.

[148] Remains of canopy fragments without provenance can occasionally be noted as reused in private houses. Illustrative examples are the Middle-Byzantine canopy spandrel fragment in white marble, which was donated by a certain Recep Dinser, who stated that he found it in the ruins of an old house in Emirdag (now catalogued T952 in the Archeological Museum in Kotor), and the ninth-century canopy fragment with an inscription from an unidentified location, possibly the Church of St. Tryphon in Kotor, Montenegro, which was donated to the local museum by a certain Ljuba Ivanišević. On the canopy fragment from Turkey, see Lightfoot and Ivison (1997) 291–300; Lightfoot (1998) 323–336. On canopy fragments from Montenegro, see Vežić (2001–2002) 91–122. I am thankful to Čedomila Marinković and Dubravka Preradović for drawing my attention early on to the important work by P. Vežić. See also Almpanē (2001); Bonfioli (1979); Buzančić (1994) 39–50; Dodge and Ward-Perkins (1992); *Guide* (1980).

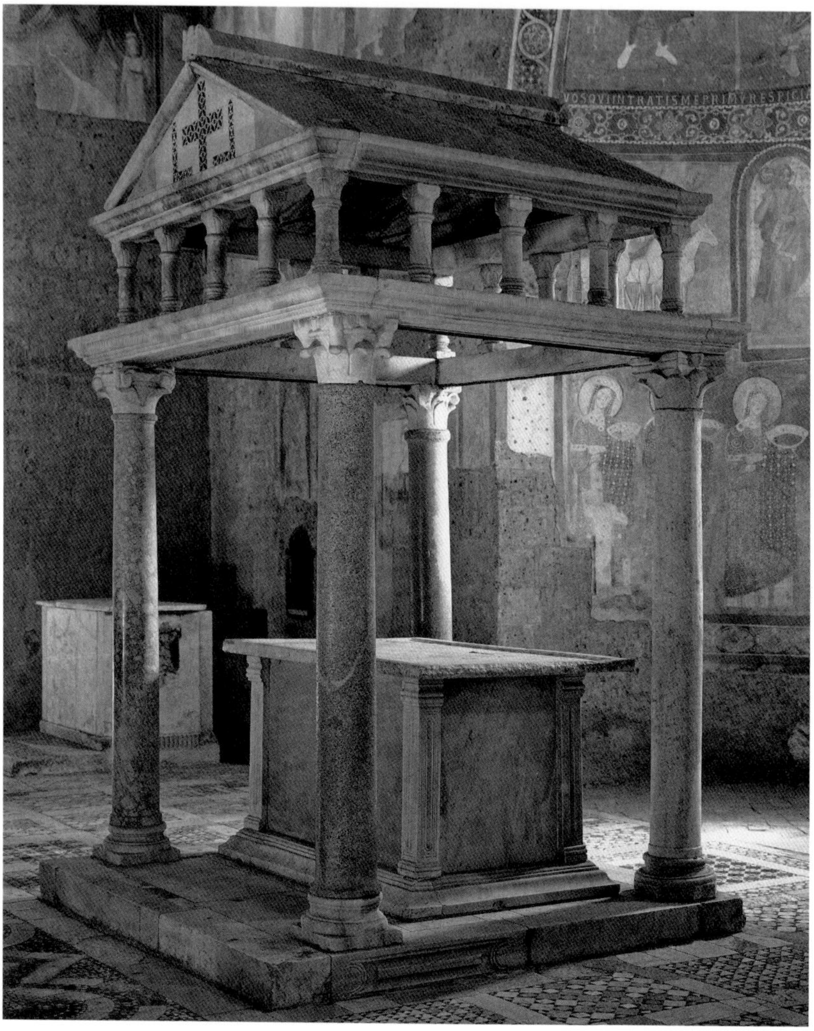

FIGURE 2.37 *Altar canopy, Castel Sant'Elia, Italy, ninth century (?) or twelfth century (?).* ANDREA JEMOLO/SCALA/ART RESOURCE, NEW YORK

height), or basket capitals with smaller bases, which are occasionally carved on three or all four sides (Fig. 2.39).

Yet it is extremely difficult to establish the acceptable size range for various structural elements of a canopy, most notably its columns and capitals, since some of the canopies were truly architectural structures in their own right, as can be seen in the surviving example from Paros or some other cases where the canopy was some 2 meters in span and more than 4 meters tall. Column shafts of approximately 15–20 centimeters in diameter may have been used for canopies, but we also know of columns from altar canopies found in sanctuary areas that have been almost 40 centimeters in diameter, as was the case with canopy columns from Hagios Polyeuktos in Constantinople, now in the Archeological Museum in Istanbul, highliting that some canopies were genuinely monumental architectural installations.[149]

Smaller and slenderer than those habitually employed for structural elements of church buildings, canopy columns are predominantly distinguished by high-quality material, usually

[149] Harrison, M. (1989) 78.

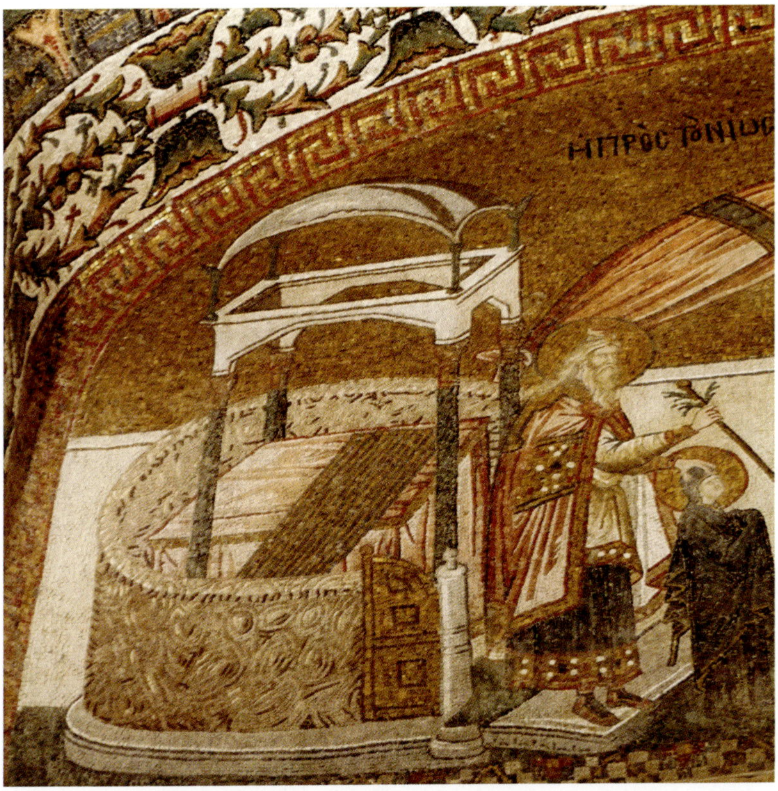

FIGURE 2.38 *Espousal of Virgin Mary, mosaic. Church of Christ the Savior, Chora Monastery, Constantinople, now Istanbul, fourteenth century.* PHOTO AUTHOR

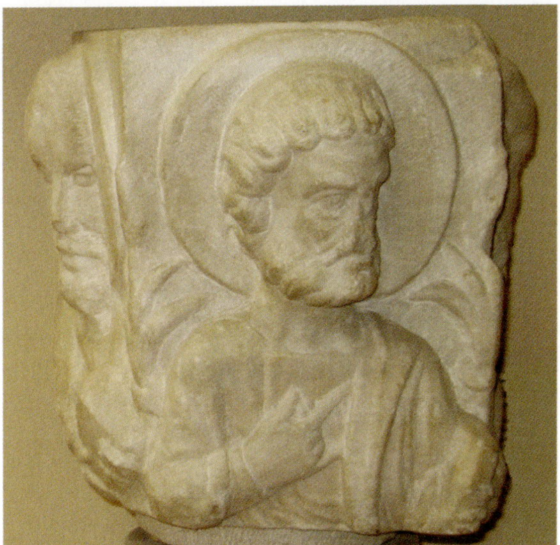

FIGURE 2.39 *Figurative capital for a canopy (?), marble, Constantinople, excavation Fethye Cammi; early fourteenth century (?); Archaeological Museum, Istanbul.* PHOTO AUTHOR

marble, and delicate decoration. Some have traces of incrustation with semi-precious stones and glass paste, like examples from the sixth-century churches Hagia Euphemia and Hagios Polyeuktos in Constantinople (Figs. 2.40, 2.41).[150] Canopies are occasionally distinguished by special carving of their elements, like spirally fluted or double-knotted columns, and then customarily used on altar and *proskynetaria* canopies that framed specially venerated icons and relics (Fig. 2.42).[151] Archeology confirms, furthermore, that Middle Byzantine and later liturgical furnishings made of stone were at least occasionally, if not frequently,

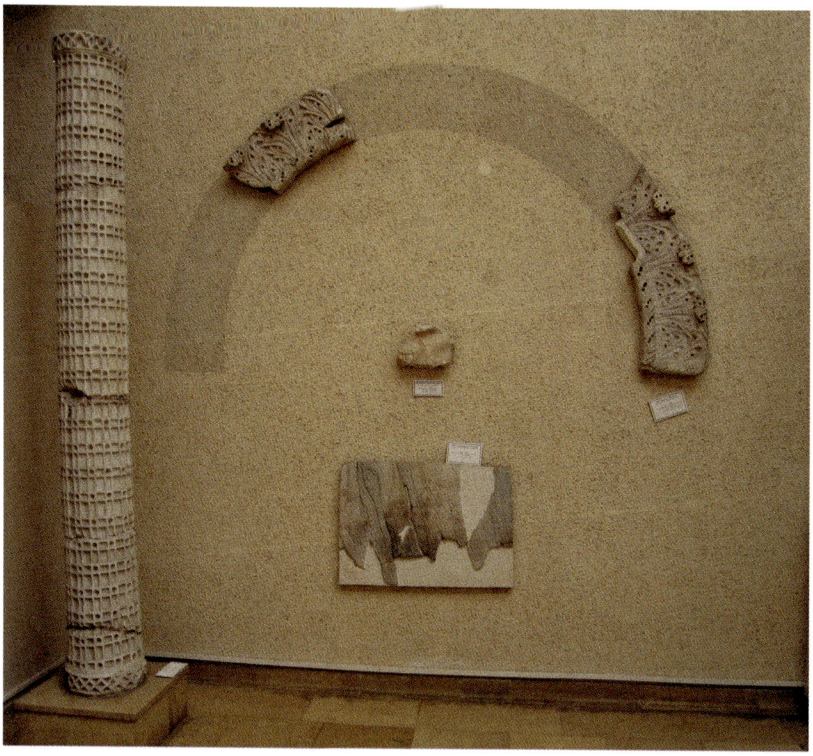

FIGURE 2.40 *Fragmentary marble arch with acanthus leaves from Constantinople and marble column (part of the liturgical furnishing, possibly, canopy) from Hagia Euphemia, today in the Archaeological Museum, Istanbul.* PHOTO AUTHOR

[150] The columns of the canopy from Hagios Polyeuktos were inlaid with squares of amethyst framed by triangles and trapezoids of opaque green glass to form hexagons and diagonal runnels with strips of gold glass. Harrison, M. (1989) 78.

[151] Benson (1959) 253–272 analyzed a number of spirally fluted columns from various archeological sites and museums in Athens, Crete, Chios, Corinth, Delos, Delphi, Eleusis, Epidauros, Kos, Naxos, Lindos, Nikopolis, Patmos, Patras, Rhodes, and Samos. All of them came from Christian sites and were mostly datable to the fifth and sixth centuries, while some could have been younger and potentially were eighth-century elements. While most of these columns are of unknown provenance, some only 15 to 20 centimeters in diameter, like the ones found at the Athens agora, Delphi, Epidauros, and Kos, along with fragments of a column in Naxos museum originally from the local church, may have been parts of canopies. Numerous slim columns, with spiral fluting from the churches in North Syria were also probably made for canopies. See also Smith, M. T. (1968) 309; Grabar (1976); Ward Perkins (1994a) 469–489.

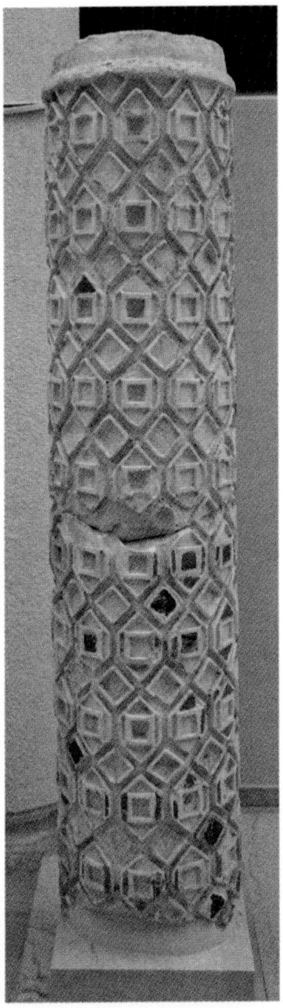

FIGURE 2.41 *Glass-inlaid marble column of the altar canopy; part of an inlaid marble column; inlay (squares of amethyst, triangles and trapeziums of green glass, and in the diagonal runnels, strips of gold glass); found in the sanctuary of Hagios Polyeuktos, Constantinople, now Istanbul, 524–527.* PHOTO DUŠAN DANILOVIĆ

painted and gilded.[152] Traces of color and gold can be seen on the architectural members of the still-extant canopy-shrine of Hosios Loukas (Fig. 2.43).

Then again, the same elements we recognize today as parts of now-lost canopies might have been used for other church elements such as architectural supports or arches above the sanctuary screens, *arcosolia*, or door and window frames. Furthermore, even if some of the innumerable architectural and sculptural fragments from the sites and museums initially belonged to canopies, once they are removed from their context, the reconstruction of their original setting is often impossible. Canopies could have been brought from earlier churches and reinstalled in later-built churches by the Byzantines themselves, as in the Pantokrator Monastery in Constantinople, where the canopy that currently serves as the

For the surviving example of the double-knotted columns for canopies, see minbar from the Zeyrek cammi in Istanbul, see Hjort (1979) 199–289, fig 116. For double-knotted columns on *proskynetaria*, see Kalopissi-Verti (2006) 107–134. For recognizable carved, architectural stone elements of canopies, see also Kalamara (2001); Voyatzis (2006) 101–114; Pallis (2006) 91–100; Voyatzis (2009) 129–140; Pejić (2012) 13–20; Fundić (2013) 141–148.

152 Ivison (2008) 487–513. Gavrilović (1999) 111–118 points to the ciborium from Rogačići, Bosnia and Herzegovina, which was painted in frescoes in the interior.

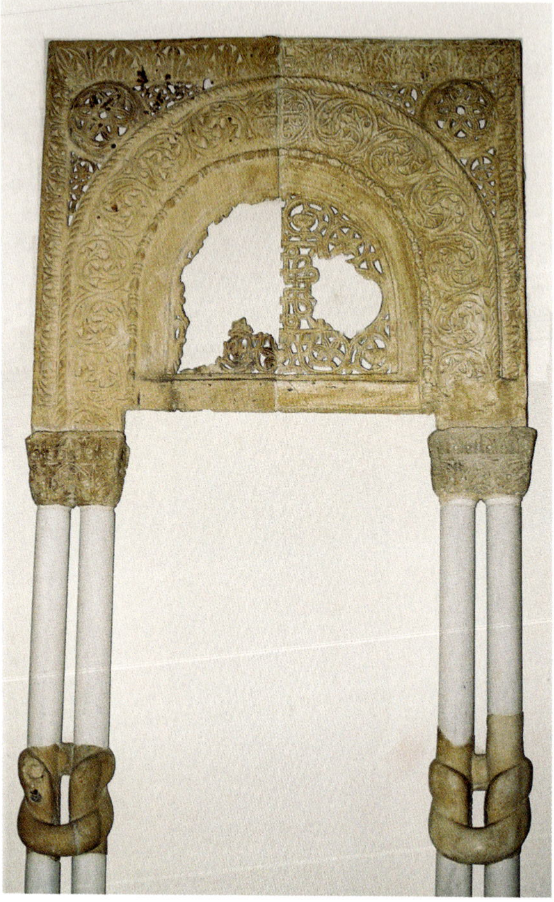

FIGURE 2.42 *Proskynetarion icon frame, Hosios Loukas Monastery, Greece, twelfth century (?).* PHOTO AUTHOR

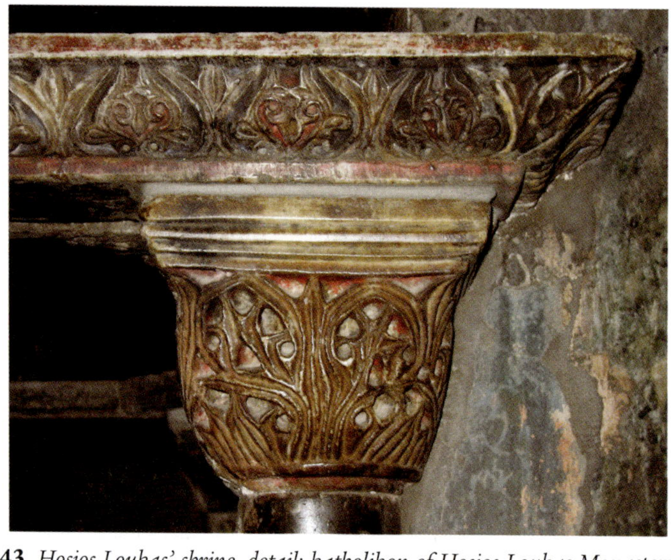

FIGURE 2.43 *Hosios Loukas' shrine, detail; katholikon of Hosios Loukas Monastery, Greece, eleventh century and later.* PHOTO AUTHOR

minbar of the Molla Zeyrek *camii* could have been reassembled from various architectural *spolia* from an older Constantinopolitan church, possibly from Hagios Polyeuktos, which was abandoned by the thirteenth century (Fig. 2.44).[153] The possibility that the architectural sculpture from the Hagios Polyeuktos was used in the Pantokrator canopy is based on stylistic grounds and can be reinforced by the fact that we have some other *spolia* from the Church of Hagios Polyeuktos inbuilt in the church walls of the Pantokrator.[154] By pointing to its double-knotted columns, known from Middle and Late Byzantine architectural sculpture of sanctuary screens, it was even proposed that the Pantokrator *minbar* was not

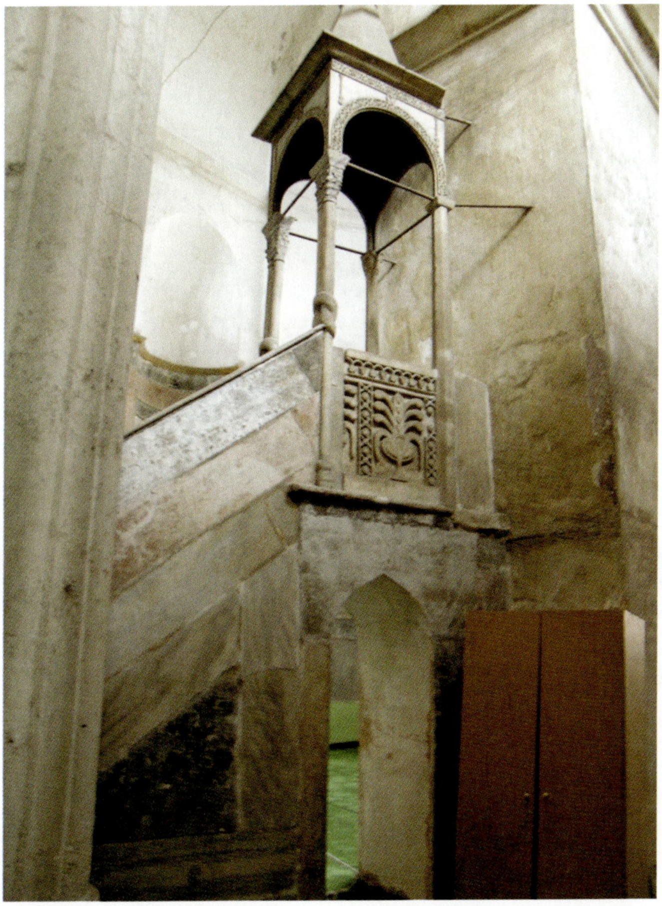

FIGURE 2.44 *Marble canopy made of spolia, reused as minbar, Pantokrator Monastery, Constantinople, now Istanbul, after eleventh century (thirteenth century?).* PHOTO ROBERT OUSTERHOUT

[153] Sodini (1995) 289–311, esp. 291–292, suggests that the Pantokrator canopy is a Middle-Byzantine installation. Ousterhout (2010a) 432–439 argues that the canopy was reassembled after the re-conversion of the church to Orthodoxy in the thirteenth century, following the Latin conquest of Constantinople. I was not able to measure and examine the canopy at close proximity myself, so for the time being I can only ascertain that the canopy was installed in the Church of the Pantokrator in the Middle Byzantine period, either shortly after its construction in the eleventh century or assembled or reassembled at some later point by the thirteenth century. I thank Robert Ousterhout for sharing with me his photographs of the canopy.

[154] Ousterhout (2001a) 133–150; Harrison (1989) 106–107; Megaw (1963) 333–364.

made from a canopy, but rather assembled from the sanctuary screen and other liturgical furnishings that once stood in the monastery.[155]

Surviving fragments of architectural sculpture that belonged to an altar canopy from Hosios Loukas are Middle Byzantine, however, and verify the use of sculpted canopies even after the ninth century and post-Iconoclastic controversies that highlighted the dematerialization aesthetics and interest in two-dimensional sacred imagery.[156] Remnants of architectural sculpture, which may have once belonged to canopies from Constantinopolitan churches, such as arches and capitals carved on three or four sides, confirm that some canopies were made anew in the Middle and Late Byzantine periods in Constantinople. For example, three small capitals (ca. 1300) decorated with the busts of three apostles carved in relief, were attributed to an iconostasis or *arcosolium* tomb in previous scholarship,[157] but the orientation of the figures—all turning to the right—suggests that they initially belonged to a centrally planned, possibly canopy-like structure (Fig. 2.45). Hans Belting and other scholars have pointed out that numerous fragments of architectural sculpture used in the interiors of Constantinopolitan churches are not *spolia* or recarved old sculpture, but were made within several decades around 1300 when stone carving following antique models was briefly renewed in the capital.[158] The remains of four canopies of the six in the Archeological Museum in Istanbul are from the fourteenth century.[159] As expressed by Niketas Magistros, when he described the Paros canopy in the early tenth century, and confirmed by the continual production, use, and reuse of sculpture in Constantinople and elsewhere, sculpted canopies reflect the Byzantine concern with continuity with their cultural past.[160]

Specially praised marbles were selected for their symbolic properties as carriers of meaning, judging by some other examples. Michael Choniates (Accominatus), brother of Nicetas Choniates and an Archbishop of Athens (1175?–1205) before it was seized by Crusaders in 1205, wrote about the altar canopy of the Church of the Mother of God (*Theotokos Atheniotissa*) on the site of the Parthenon in Athens.[161] The canopy was actually made of

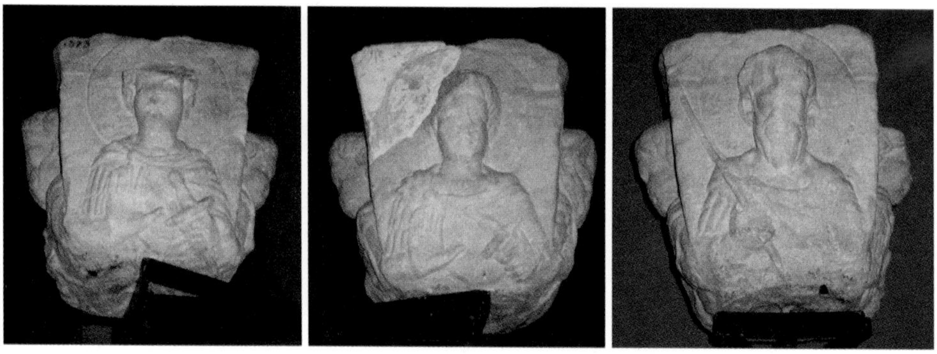

FIGURE 2.45 *Figurative capitals for a canopy (?); Constantinople, excavation Fethye Cammi; early fourteenth century (?), marble; Archaeological Museum, Istanbul.* PHOTO AUTHOR

---

[155] Megaw (1963) 333–364.

[156] Boura (1980); Boura (1977–1979) 63–72.

[157] Mango and Hawkins (1964) 319–340.

[158] Belting (1972) 63–93; Hjort (1979) 199–289; Ousterhout (1987) 137–141; Macridy (1964) 253–277; Boura (1977–1979) 63–72; Liveri (1996) 27, 36, 178–180, figs. 70, 72–73; Bogdanović (2008d).

[159] Maksimović (1961) 32.

[160] Bogdanović (2008d).

[161] Four columns of purple porphyry with smaller columns of white marble were still *in situ* in 1687. Setton (1944) 179–207. See also Kaldellis (2009) 25.

purple Egyptian porphyry, the most valued of all marbles in late antiquity and medieval times because of its high quality and imperial associations (Table 5.109, cf. Table 5.55).[162] Situated on the top of the Acropolis, a mound of white marble, the Athens canopy of purple porphyry was imported to adorn the altar table of the Christianized site. The choice of marble for the canopy in Athens was most likely deliberate, because we know that the Christians did not have any second thoughts when they used an elaborately carved seat from the Theater of Dionysus, made of ancient marble, for the bishop's throne. There were also minimal changes to the exterior of the Parthenon when it became a Christian church.[163] Such an ostentatious altar canopy, set within the premises of one of the most famous Classical temples, confirms, not only the significance that the Parthenon church had in the Byzantine period, but also the role of the canopy in establishing its Christian identity.

The slow decline in the use of marble canopies after the tenth century can be attributed also to the loss of the imperial control of the production and trade of these luxurious objects. These trends can be observed both in Constantinople and in smaller-scale churches outside major centers. During the early Christian and early Byzantine period, architectural members made in various marble workshops were used for canopies regardless of the relative nearness of the churches to the quarries; in the later periods, these would most often be reused as *spolia* for new or renewed canopies, or as raw building material.[164] Hence, marble quarried on the islands of Prokonnesos in the Marmara Sea across from Constantinople was widely used for making elements for liturgical furnishings—column shafts, capitals, bases, and other members, which were occasionally recognized as parts of canopies, ambos, and other more complex installations.[165] Premade furnishings were shipped, not only to Constantinople, but throughout the Byzantine administrative provinces in the Mediterranean basin, as far east as Georgia, as far west as Istria on the Adriatic littoral, and as far southwest as Tunisia in Africa.[166] The four-columned altar canopy from the Euphrasius basilica of Parenzo (Poreč), modern Croatia, built about 550 and rebuilt once again in the thirteenth century using the original sixth-century columns, exemplifies how far northwest we can find canopies whose fragments were made of Prokonnesian marble (Table 5.65).[167] One of the most remarkable of the sixth-century marble fragments

---

[162] Without excluding a hypothesis about taste, the insistence on the use of specific marbles may have also reflected an appreciation of certain marbles' decorative qualities, as reflected in their price. Thus we know that Egyptian purple porphyry and green porphyry from Krokeai in Lakonia were among the most valued (each 250 denarii per square foot), followed by Dokimian and yellow marble from Chemtou (200 denarii/ft2), *verde antico* (150 denarii/ft2), and ending with Prokonnesian, Lesbian, and the Sangarian marbles (40 denarii/ft2) at the lower price range. *Preisedikt* 192–193.

[163] Setton (1944) 179–207.

[164] Karagiorgou (2001) 194.

[165] A complete inventory of building components for a church may have been shipped, as was confirmed by underwater archeological finds. The Marzamemi shipwreck revealed various elements for church furnishings made of Prokonnesian marble, but also a *verde antico* (brescia stone) ambo, which was most likely loaded in a Thessalian harbor. The ship never reached its final destination, and though it sank near Sicily, no Sicilian church of that period would have waited for such rich embellishment. Therefore, the cargo was most likely intended for a church in Africa, possibly Libya, as some scholars have already suggested. Kapitän (1980) 71–136; Kapitän (1969) 122–23; Karagiorgou (2001) 194–195. On marble trade, see also Castagnino Berlinghieri and Paribeni (2011) 64–75.

[166] Kapitän (1980) 71–136; Kapitän (1969) 122–123; Sodini (1989) 163–186; Asgari (1995) 263–288.

[167] The column capitals of the altar canopy had been preserved, and were incorporated into Bishop Otto's canopy from 1277. On that occasion, the canopy was also decorated with mosaics of the Annunciation and medallions with images of Poreč martyrs. Krautheimer (1986) 280; Demus (1998) 239–244. However, Terry (1988) 12–64 has demonstrated that not all elements of the canopy were made of Prokonnesian marble.

is embedded in the wall of the southern annex of the thirteenth-century church at Ḥobi in northwestern Georgia; it is a set of monolithic columns with abbreviated versions of Theodosian capitals.[168] These columns may have belonged to a premade canopy imported from sixth-century Constantinople. A story in which a seventh-century Bishop of Thenai in Byzancena, modern Tunisia, buys an altar canopy from a ship captain confirms that trade in Aegean marble was active in this period.[169] Archeology and texts further suggest that, even where the site of the church was itself abundant in marble, the altar canopy would often have been made from imported marbles. The extant altar canopy from Paros has column shafts and capitals of Prokonnesian marble, even though the island itself is rich in high-quality Parian marble. Canopy columns in Basilica A at Nea Anchialeos and Basilica B at Philippoi were made of local, Thessalian *verde antico* marble, yet they were not used immediately after being quarried because marble quarries in Thessaly were under imperial control until the eighth century.[170] In other words, local marble elements were first shipped to Constantinople, put in a stockyard and presumably registered by bookkeepers, and then returned to be used for altar canopies in Thessalian churches.

The use of various marbles for canopies may have been the result of certain aesthetic standards or economic prosperity, and it may point to the centralized control of the building of religious edifices. Legal regulations could have induced the use of certain marbles because most quarries were under strict imperial control during the Early and Middle Byzantine periods.[171] The training of marble masons would also be critical, as they were enlisted as a distinct type of craftsmen involved in the construction projects in the tenth-century *Book of the Eparch*, a treatise compiled by a Constantinopolitan mayor that regulated activities of various guilds in the urban production and exchange in Constantinople and beyond.[172] Such a hypothesis concerning control from Constantinople would potentially explain the almost standardized structural and visual appearance of known canopies throughout the Mediterranean basin until the Middle Byzantine period.

In medieval Rus, several stone altar canopies were built in the pre-Mongol period, before the 1230s, possibly following Byzantine models (Table 5.187–189, 199–203; Map 4). The Church of the Dormition (ca. 1073) in the Pečerskii monastery (Monastery of the Caves) near Kiev had a marble altar canopy.[173] Constantinopolitan masters came to build and decorate the church, and it may be that they were responsible for the canopy as well.[174] According to the sources, masters from Byzantium came to make an altar canopy for the eleventh-century Church of St. Sophia in Novgorod.[175] However, other Russian churches had altar canopies made of local white stone by local workshops, like those in the Church of Ss. Boris and Gleb built by Vsevolod III (1171–1213) in Vladimir.[176] Though Vsevolod III, son of a

[168] Djorbadze (1984) 627–639.

[169] Sodini (2002) 129–145, esp. 134.

[170] Karagiorgou (2001) 194, has demonstrated that, although marble stocking presupposes an organized, well-developed, and active trade system, stockyards indeed functioned in late antiquity, as can be exemplified by the Marmorata Quarter in Rome and at Ostia. Despite the lack of explicit references that a similar system existed during Byzantine period, she has shown that some kind of stockyard for *verde antico* marble, and especially for relatively smaller and standardized objects, did function in Constantinople by the eighth century.

[171] Karagiorgou (2001) 194; Sodini (2002) 129–145.

[172] Ousterhout (2008) 52.

[173] Čukova (2004) 77; Voronin (1961) 251–258.

[174] Komeč (1975) 9–26.

[175] Čukova (2004) 80; Komeč (1975) 9–26.

[176] Voronin (1961) 251–258.

Byzantine princess, had strong connections with Constantinople, most likely a local workshop carved the stone canopy because its carving resembles the flat carving on the façades of the Cathedral of St. Dmitri, also in Vladimir.[177] An arch fragment, which was sculpted with geometric patterns and birds, once belonged to a canopy made of white stone that stood over the altar table in the Church of the Annunciation in Chernigov.[178] Altar canopies made of white stone were attested in the late twelfth- and early thirteenth-century churches of the Savior and the Dormition in Galich, the easternmost Byzantine-rite churches that I examined for this project.[179] Hence, both the Byzantines and those who accepted Byzantine Christianity continued to build their churches with stone canopies over a prolonged period; their production was also related to available materials and workshops.

Stone canopies were not uniquely used in churches in the main centers of the Byzantine Empire; they also were extensively used in the periphery. The research of canopies in the Western parts of the Byzantine Empire and the medieval states that emerged in the Balkans in the Middle Byzantine period is burdened by a general notion that they should be omitted from general reviews of Byzantine accomplishments because of their perceived stylistic dependence on Romanesque architecture and Carolingian artistic practices.[180] In fact, the dynamic processes of the exchange of architectural ideas and construction solutions between local and farther-flung architectural traditions in the Western Balkans actually question the traditional, but unstable stylistic terms such as *proto-Romanesque, Romanesque*, or *Byzantine style* in medieval architecture.[181] Moreover, canopies from the churches on both the Adriatic littorals and in southern Italy remained within the broader framework of Byzantine architecture, at least until the eleventh century.[182] They were established in churches that administratively belonged to the Byzantine Empire. Some of the canopies were occasionally even used to promote the Byzantine presence, either through the establishment of canopied reliquaries of the saints brought for veneration from Byzantine centers in the eastern territories, or through inscriptions on canopies that commemorated Byzantine emperors and Byzantine officials (Table 7).

Most of the stone canopies and their fragments found in the Western Balkans and along the Adriatic littoral were made of local stone and by local workshops.[183] Constructed on four or six supports of monolithic marble, granite, or limestone, they were topped with domed or pyramidal roofs. The majority of these canopies were altar, baptismal, or reliquary installations. In design and decoration, they paralleled proto-Byzantine models, as seen in canopy fragments recovered in fourth- to seventh-century basilicas in the late antique and Byzantine province of Dalmatia in modern Croatia. After the revival of building activities following the transitional period, more than forty stone canopies have been recovered in numerous ninth- to eleventh-century churches from this region (Table 5, Map 4). Some of the most

---

[177] In the local museum in Vladimir today, there are on display spirally fluted column fragments and basket capitals made of local white stone, which may have originally belonged to church furnishings and canopies.

[178] Čukova (2004) 77.

[179] The Church of the Savior in Galich (end of twelfth, beginning of the thirteenth centuries) had a canopy of white stone with slender columns 15.5–16 centimeters in diameter. Canopy capitals with the impost block (38 cm × 38 cm) were recovered in the Church of the Dormition, Galich. Čukova (2004) 79.

[180] Vežić and Lončar (2009); Delonga (2000). On textual sources and material evidence for the attribution of canopies along the Adriatic, see also Skoblar (2017).

[181] Bogdanović (2017a).

[182] On the same conclusion that the architectural developments in the Adriatic basin were dependent on main Byzantine trends by the eleventh century, see Ćurčić (2010) 436–470.

[183] See, for example, Vežić and Lončar (2009).

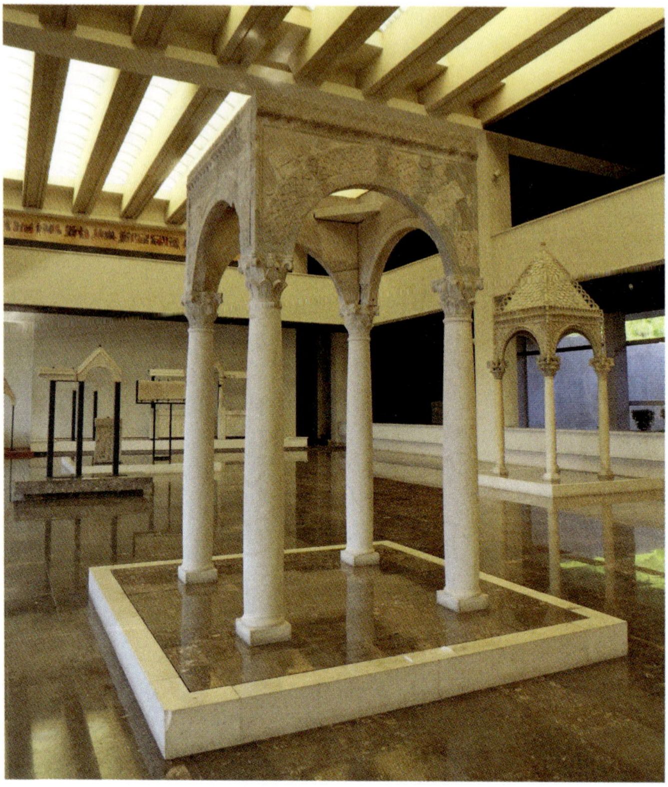

FIGURE 2.46 *Canopies from the Basilica St. Martha, Bijaće, Dalmatia, Croatia, ninth century (front), and the Church of St. Mary, Biskupija, Knin, Croatia, eleventh century (back); Archeological Museum, Split.* PHOTO JELENA PALIĆ

representative belonged to the churches in Shati in Albania; Ulcinj, Budva, and Kotor in Montenegro; or in Dubrovnik, Zadar, Split, and Novigrad in Dalmatia (Figs. 2.46, 2.47).[184]

Despite their occasionally questionable artistic quality, these canopies are increasingly important because they sometimes have inscriptions that confirm their Byzantine source (Table 7). In particular, these inscriptions reflect the recurrent diplomatic activities of Byzantine officials in the region, especially in the ninth century, when Dalmatia became a Byzantine military district (*theme*).[185] An inscription on the canopy fragment from Ulcinj, which mentions the Byzantine emperor Leo V (r. 813–820) and his son and co-emperor Constantine (r. 813–820), is the most instructive example in this regard (Table 7.114).[186] The canopy from the church in Ulcinj has been stylistically related to the workshops active in the region of Boka Kotorska and Dalmatia from the ninth to the eleventh centuries (Table 5.114–119, 129, 132).[187] The local workshop(s) produced numerous canopies for Byzantine-rite churches in the wider region. An altar canopy from the ninth-century

[184] Chevalier (1995) vol. 2, 149–152; Skoblar (2005) 7–16; Maksimović (1977) vol. 1, 237–262, esp. 243–244, figs. 21–22; 392; Vežić (2001–2002) 91–122; Vežić and Lončar (2009); Basić (2014) 21–36. See also Vežić (2002) 75–87; Vežić (1999) 7–16; Vežić (1997) 101–116.

[185] Stevović (1998–1999) 23–33; Vežić (2001–2002) 91–122.

[186] Preradović-Petrović (2002) 247–264.

[187] Vežić (2001–2002) 91–122.

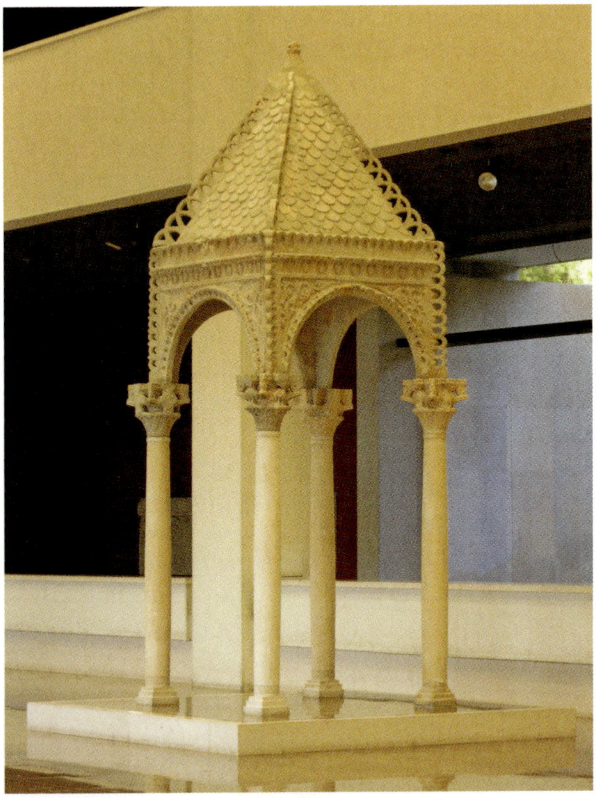

FIGURE 2.47 *Altar canopy, the Church of St. Mary, Biskupija, Knin, Croatia, eleventh century; Archeological Museum, Split.* PHOTO JELENA PALIĆ

Byzantine Church of Archangel Michael, situated deep in the medieval region of Duklja, modern Montenegro, in the village of Martinići, which is possibly the city of Lontodocla mentioned by Emperor Constantine Porphyrogenitos, is also related to canopies from the region of Kotor (Table 5.129).[188]

In Kotor, remnants of several stone canopies have been recovered in the churches of St. Michael and St. Mary Collegiate (Table 5.115–116).[189] In 809, the Byzantines brought the relics of St. Tryphon, a martyr from Phrygia in Asia Minor, to Kotor as a means of strengthening Byzantine positions in the Adriatic.[190] At least three canopies, for the altar, baptistery, and presumably the reliquary of St. Tryphon, were established in the eponymous cathedral in Kotor (Table 5.117–119).[191] Relics of at least two other saints were brought to the city of Kotor and may have been enshrined within canopied structures.[192] The relics of St. Thomas from Edessa, to whom a now-lost church in Kotor was dedicated, may have been enshrined within a canopy. Similarly, the relics of St. Andrew Stratelated from Cilicia may have been in a canopied installation because the name of the saint might have

188 Korać (2001) 78–88, 189.

189 Čuburović (1997) 139–151; Čanak-Medić (1989) vol. 2, 210–212, figs. 48, 104.

190 Stevović (1998–1999) 23–33; Preradović (2013) 187–207; Vežić (2001–2002) 91–122; Čubrović (2008) 25–42.

191 Vežić (2001–2002) 91–122; Martinović (1995) 345–355.

192 Stevović (1998–1999) 23–33.

been inscribed on the canopy arch, which was later built into the walls of the Church of St. Tryphon in Kotor. This phenomenon of the veneration of specific saints and the associated architectural framing spread from Kotor throughout Adriatic littoral. When the Church of St. Mary the Collegiate was restored in the thirteenth century, its canopy over the baptistery might have been transferred to the Cathedral of St. Tryphon.[193] Moreover, the stark similarities of the architectural design of the Church of St. Mary the Collegiate and the church in Studenica, one of the principal Serbian Orthodox medieval churches deep inland of the Balkans, have been already observed.[194] Though no original floor or liturgical furnishings from Studenica have remained, the remnants of an altar canopy from St. Mary the Collegiate suggest that Studenica initially had an altar canopy as well. These few examples of the exchange of architectural ideas and the exchange of actual canopies among various locales in the Balkans also reveal the continual importance of canopies in Byzantine-rite churches even after the definite decline of Byzantine economic power and centralized production from Constantinople.

In 1033–1036, in Dalmatia, modern Croatia, the Byzantine pro-consul Grgur (Gregorius) rebuilt the Basilica of St. Anastasia (Sv. Stošija) in Zadar on the site of an early Christian church, confirming the prolonged use of canopies in Byzantine churches in the region (Fig. 2.48; Table 5.178, 7.178).[195] Above the large crypt, on a raised platform, he also ordered a monumental stone canopy, of which eleven fragments have been preserved.

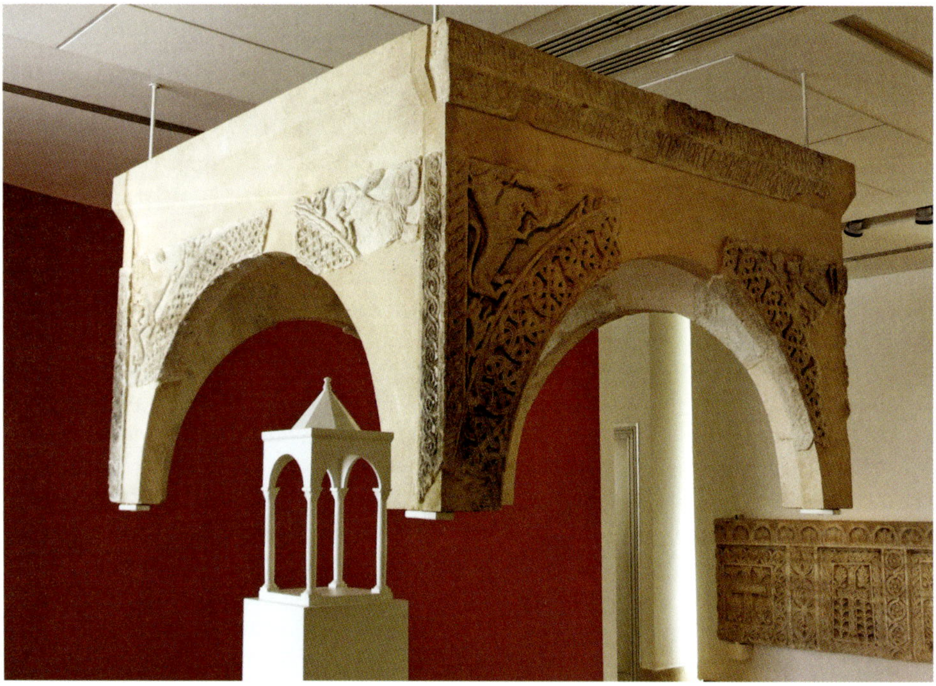

FIGURE 2.48 *Altar canopy, Church of St. Anastasia (Sv. Stošija), Zadar, Croatia, eleventh century; Archeological Museum, Zadar.* PHOTO JELENA PALIĆ

[193] Vežić (2001–2002) 91–122.

[194] Čanak-Medić (1989) vol. 2, 210–212.

[195] Ćurčić (2010) 440–452; Petricioli (1985); Petricioli (1960) 15–18; Vasić (1922) 165, figs. 123–124.

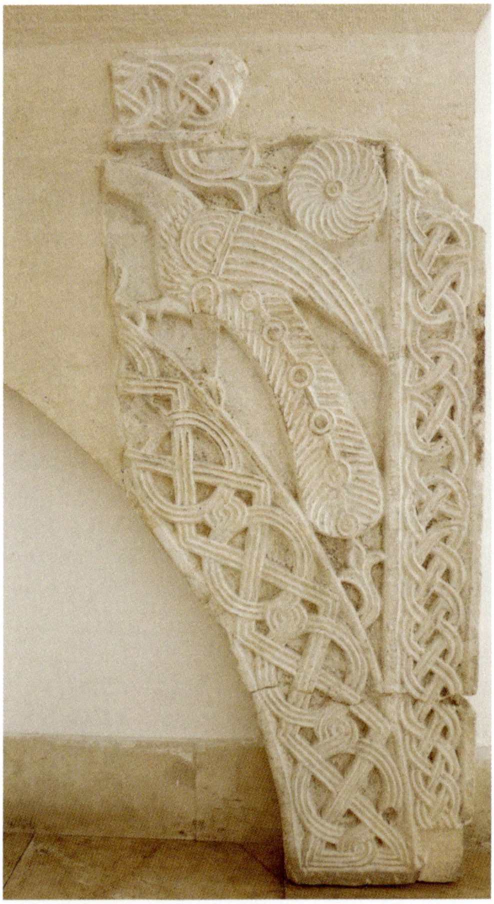

FIGURE 2.49 *Altar canopy, Church of St. Thomas, Zadar, Croatia, eleventh century; Archeological Museum, Zadar.* PHOTO JELENA PALIĆ

Elements of an altar canopy similar to the one from the Church of St. Anastasia have also been identified in the smaller Church of St. Thomas in Zadar (Fig. 2.49) and in the Church of Ss. Peter and Moses in Solin, suggesting that a local workshop may have provided canopies for numerous churches in the region.[196] The arch of a canopy with a braid design and originally painted in the interior, which was recovered in the centrally planned church (late tenth or early eleventh century) in Rogačići near Blažuj, modern Bosnia and Herzegovina, exemplifies how far to the northwest in the Adriatic basin we can observe proto-Byzantine canopies (Table 5.169, Map 4).[197]

Although most sites along the Adriatic littoral remained nominally under Byzantine administration through the twelfth and thirteenth centuries, its architecture is often studied within western European trends. The style of numerous altar canopies made of stone for both Roman Catholic and Eastern Orthodox churches after the eleventh century resembled

196 For the canopies in the churches of St. Thomas and Ss. Peter and Moses, see Petricioli (1981) 163–168; Petricioli (1995) 23–26; *Corpus* (1974) figs. 82–85.

197 Čremošnik (1953) 303–314; Gavrilović (1999) 111–118; Fekeža and Gavrilović (2000) 171–190.

comparable developments from Western Europe, but were built in territories exposed to Byzantine influences.[198] By the fourteenth century, numerous churches along the Adriatic littoral continued to have canopies, which either incorporated earlier architectural elements or were newly created. One example is the preserved altar canopy from the Cathedral of St. Lawrence (Sv. Lovro) in Trogir, Dalmatia, originally in the military province of the Byzantine Empire.[199] The altar canopy from the Church of San Marco in Venice (ca. 1290) is perhaps the best-known example of a hybrid type of a canopy made in the West but whose four alabaster columns were Byzantine *spolia* (see Fig. 3.17).[200] Similarly, the columns of the altar canopy from the Cathedral of Euphrasius in Poreč (1277) are re-employed Byzantine *spolia* as well.[201] In addition to the urban centers of Venice, Poreč, Zadar, Split, and Dubrovnik along the Adriatic, Kotor was another major urban center with established production of architecture, stone architectural sculpture, and liturgical furnishings from the ninth century on. It remained under direct Byzantine control much longer than other centers along the Adriatic.[202] The Church of St. Tryphon was serving the Byzantine-rite until the fourteenth century and was shared by Orthodox Christians and Roman Catholics long after their doctrinal split in 1054. In other words, before 1054 and often afterwards, liturgical services and religious authority from Rome and Constantinople could not be differentiating factors in distinguishing the use of canopies as either serving Western- or Byzantine-rite churches, further confirming the use of medieval canopies as a pan-European phenomenon.

Silver and Metal Canopies

Archeological discoveries, such as remnants of a bronze canopy from the sanctuary of Hagia Sophia in Thessaloniki, have expanded the discussion on their materiality and have highlighted the use of metal.[203] Canopies made of silver are often seen as imperial donations,[204] though clergy and wealthy individuals may have been responsible for some of them. Not a single fully assembled silver canopy from Byzantine times has been preserved.

A set of unique, sixth-century, delicately made silver columns currently in the Dumbarton Oaks collection, however, may have been part of a silver canopy (Fig. 2.50). Although they are usually analyzed as lampstands,[205] there is an equal possibility that these columns, more than a half a meter in height, were used for a canopied installation, perhaps standing directly on top of a silver altar table. Silver revetments of the two column shafts and three capitals are currently in the Dumbarton Oaks collection. They were part of a large silver hoard discovered in a village near Kumluca (ancient Korydalla) in Lycia, Asia Minor, in modern-day south Turkey, which included more than seventy items and liturgical objects, including a silver altar table.[206] The hoard is known as the Sion Treasury, due to the Greek inscription "Holy Sion" recovered on one of the *polycandela* (lighting devices) and because it may have belonged to the eponymous monastery founded by the sixth-century local

---

198 Ćurčić (2010) 452; Petricioli (1990). Marasović (1988) 455–461 offers a complex understanding of the cross-cultural influences in the region.

199 Ćurčić (2010) 445.

200 Brenk (1999) 143–155.

201 Demus (1998) 239–244.

202 Ćurčić (2010) 452–456.

203 Antonaras (2014) 21–22.

204 Cruikshank Dood (1973); Leader-Newby (2004) 70–72.

205 Boyd (1992) 5–38.

206 Boyd (1992) 5–38 and Bühl (2008) 90–103 provide a few entries from the Sion Treasury with important art historical and historiographical data, yet do not discuss the silver columns as elements of a canopy.

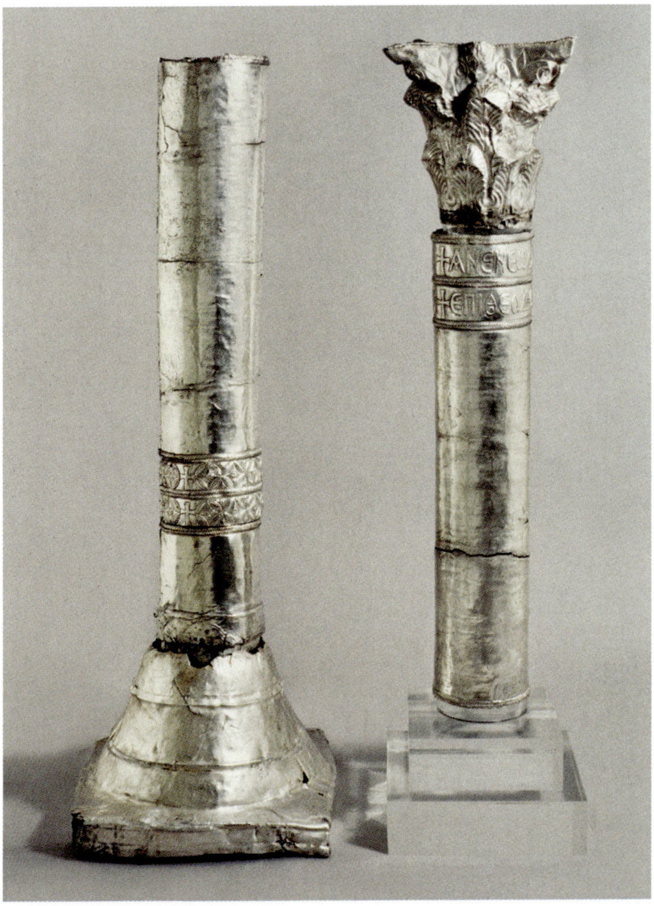

FIGURE 2.50 *Silver columns of a liturgical furnishing, possibly a canopy, from an unidentified church from Lycia, Asia Minor, sixth century.* © DUMBARTON OAKS, BYZANTINE COLLECTION, WASHINGTON, D.C.

saint, Nicholas of Sion.[207] Many objects are inscribed with personalized prayers mentioning the names of the bishops Eutychianos, Paregoros, and Theodore, the priest Zacharias, and other individuals, none of whom is otherwise known from historical sources. These silver columns were buried as wide rolled sheets of silver that were used as revetments for column shafts and carefully folded sheets of silver that composed the quasi-Corinthian capitals with acanthus leaves (Figs. 2.51, 2.52). Silver nails from the treasury suggest that these sheets were originally nailed to a wooden structure. At some point these parts were reassembled, folded, and sometimes smashed for portability, probably during the Sassanian-Byzantine wars of the early seventh century and most likely by the Byzantines themselves because of the care taken in reassembling the object.

The double-band preserved inscription on one of the column shafts reads +ΑΝΕΝΕ ѠΘΗ ΤΟ ΕΡΓΟΝ ΤΟΥΤΟ +ΕΠΙ ΘΕΟΔѠΡΟΥ ΤΟΥ ΟCΙѠΤΑΤΟΥ ΕΠΙCΚΟ[ΠΟΥ] ("This work was renewed under (in the time of) Theodore, most holy bishop") (Fig. 2.53).[208]

[207] An alternative opinion is that the Sion Treasury belonged to the Cathedral of Korydalla.

[208] Translation by I. Ševčenko, according to Boyd (1992) 5–38, esp. 31.

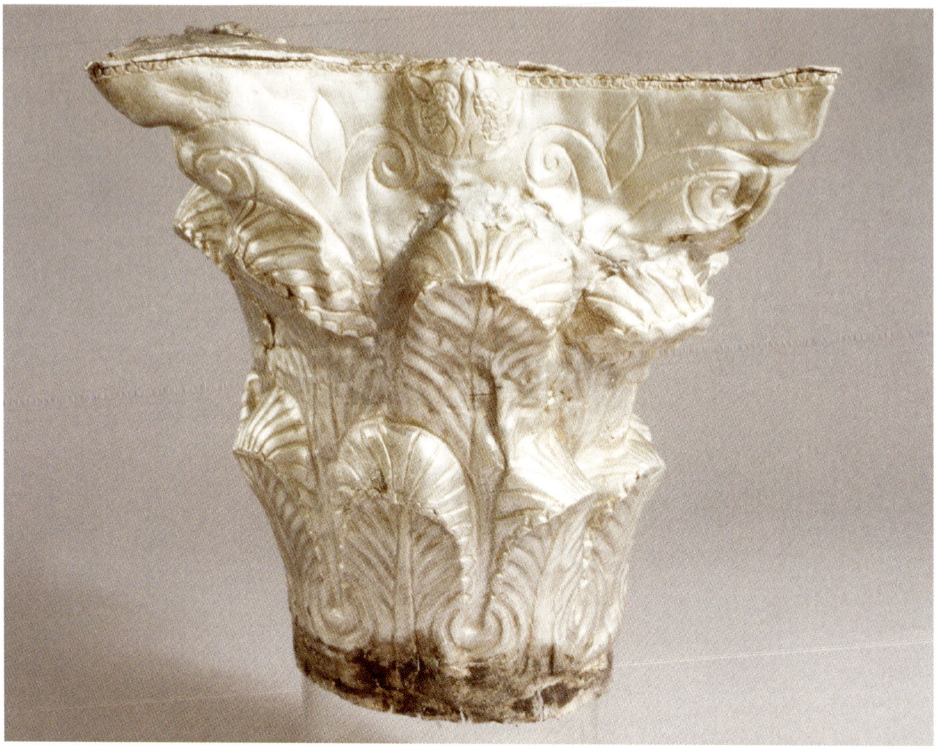

FIGURE 2.51 *Silver capital, part of liturgical furnishing, possibly a canopy, from an unidentified church from Lycia, Asia Minor, sixth century.* © DUMBARTON OAKS, BYZANTINE COLLECTION, WASHINGTON, D.C.

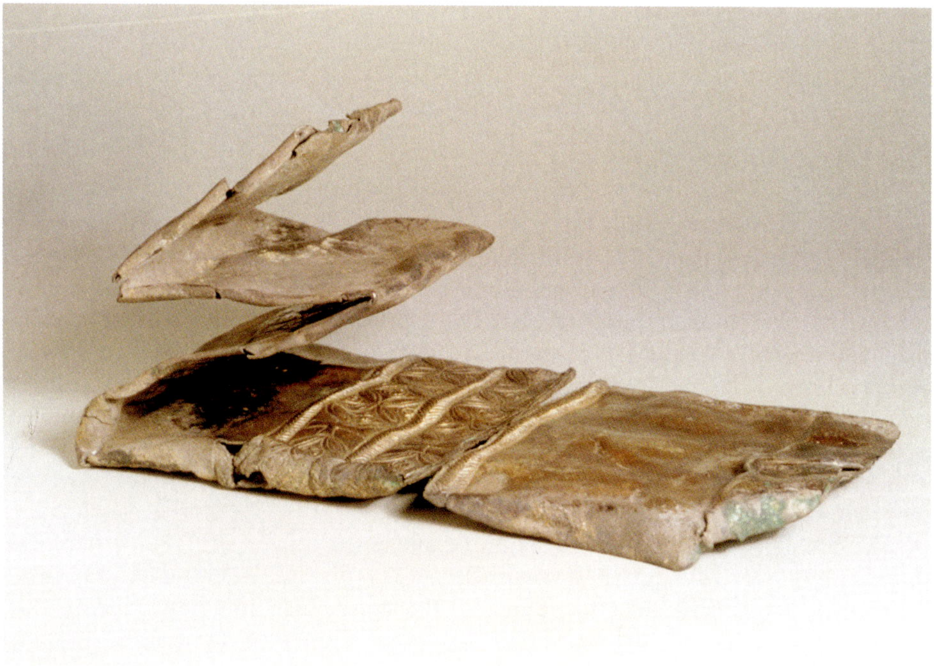

FIGURE 2.52 *Silver revetment for a column shaft, part of liturgical furnishing, possibly a canopy, from an unidentified church from Lycia, Asia Minor, sixth century.* © DUMBARTON OAKS, BYZANTINE COLLECTION, WASHINGTON, D.C.

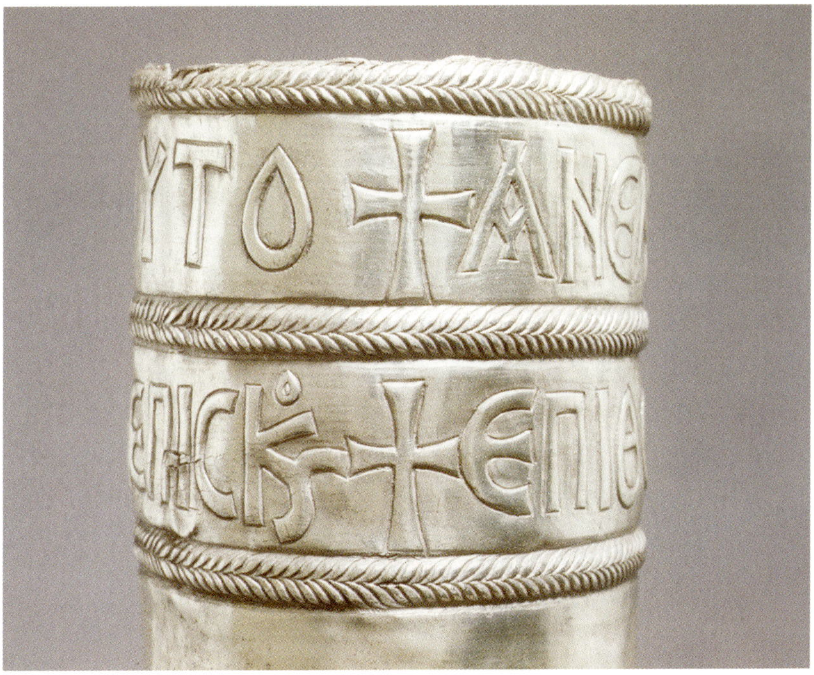

FIGURE 2.53 *Silver column with an inscription:* +ΑΝΕΝΕΩΘΗ ΤΟ ΕΡΓΟΝ ΤΟΥΤΟ +ΕΠΙ ΘΕΟΔΩΡΟΥ ΤΟΥ ΟΣΙΩΤΑΤΟΥ ΕΠΙΣΚΟ[ΠΟΥ] *("This work was renewed under (in the time of) Theodore, most holy bishop"); part of a liturgical furnishing, possibly a canopy, from an unidentified church from Lycia, Asia Minor, sixth century.* © DUMBARTON OAKS, BYZANTINE COLLECTION, WASHINGTON, D.C.

The inscription speaks of the donor of this object and of at least one of its restorations during medieval times before its final demolition, perhaps pointing to the restoration of the sacred church vessels and their reinstallation after the Iconoclastic controversies of the eighth and ninth centuries.

Especially intriguing are its spirally fluted silver revetments for a columnar structure that may have been part of the entire silver canopy installation (Fig. 2.54). Spirally fluted columns are often associated with the altar canopies from St. Peter's in Rome and Hagia Sophia in Constantinople, now lost, and both are symbolically associated with Solomon's Temple in Jerusalem. The repoussé rope-like design, spiral fluting, crosses, and the inscription on the silver columns from the Sion Treasury point to the delicate execution and high quality of silver canopies in ecclesiastical settings outside Constantinople and other major centers (Fig. 2.55).

Marlia Mundell-Mango has examined numerous texts that provide abundant references to silver canopies and liturgical furnishings in the Byzantine realm.[209] She has highlighted how the rhetorician Choricius (491–518) described the silver altar table and its colonnettes of the Church of St. Sergius in Gaza as made of silver.[210] The altar of the Martyrium

[209] Mundell-Mango (1992) 123–136, esp. 130. Furthermore, the sixth-century *Breviarus de Hierosolyma* details how, in the sixth century, Jerusalem pilgrims reported that the Holy Sepulchre, i.e., the tomb itself, had a silver and gold roof.

[210] Mundell-Mango (1992) 123–136, esp. 130.

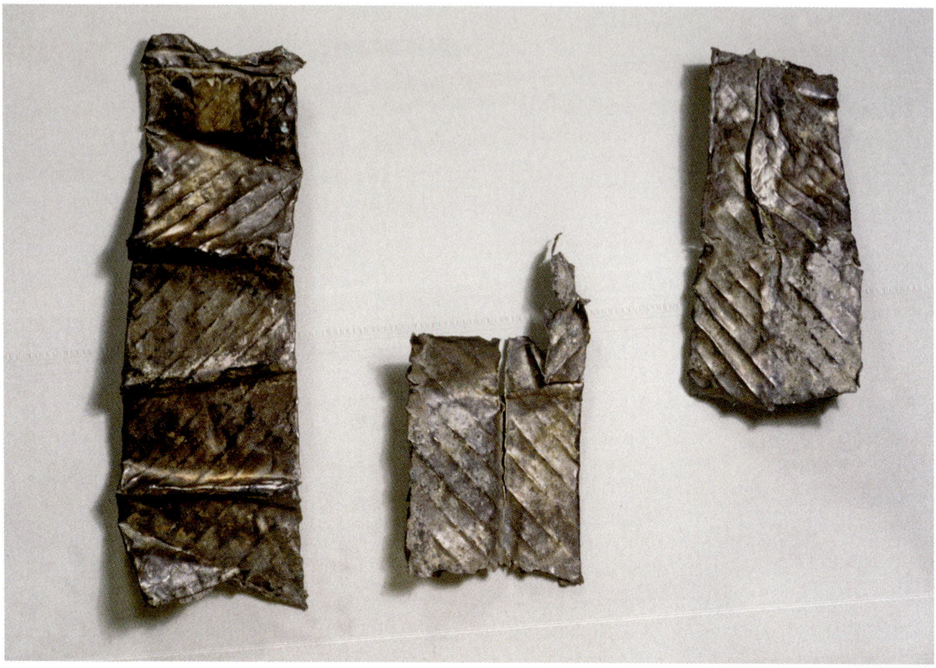

FIGURE 2.54 *Spirally fluted silver revetments for column shafts, part of liturgical furnishing, possibly a canopy, from an unidentified church from Lycia, Asia Minor, sixth century.* © DUMBARTON OAKS, BYZANTINE COLLECTION, WASHINGTON, D.C.

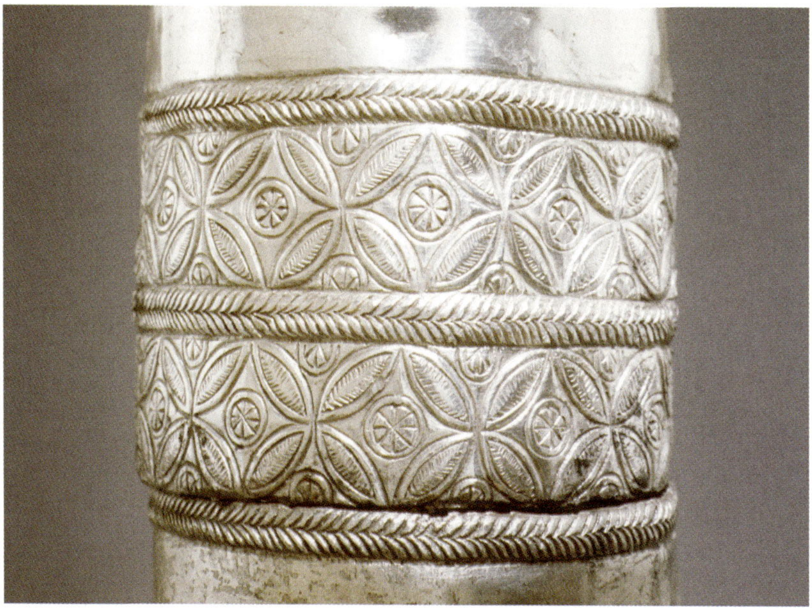

FIGURE 2.55 *Silver column with repoussé decorative design, part of a liturgical furnishing, possibly a canopy, from an unidentified church from Lycia, Asia Minor, sixth century.* © DUMBARTON OAKS, BYZANTINE COLLECTION, WASHINGTON, D.C.

in Jerusalem was made of silver and gold and was supported by nine colonnettes.[211] While these descriptions do not detail whether some of the colonnettes belonged to canopies, the fourth-century martyrium of St. Thecla in present-day Meryemlik, Turkey, had a centrally planned silver canopy above the altar, at least by the year 460 when the hagiography of St. Thecla was written.[212] A canopy (*tiburium*) of pure silver and a *confessio* weighing 120 lbs. were jointly constructed for the Church of St. Andrew the Apostle in Rome, built under Pope Symmachus (498–514).[213] The Cathedral of Edessa, rebuilt after the flood of 525, also had silver furnishings and revetments, which were described in 622 as recorded in the *Chronicle of 1234*[214] and complemented with a dedicatory hymn.[215] In addition to the ten columns of the chancel screen and the ambo in the middle of the church, silver covered the four columns of the altar canopy.[216] The sanctuary arrangement of the Cathedral in Edessa was similar to those recorded in Hagia Sophia in Constantinople and in St. Peter's in Rome. While for Hagia Sophia there is mostly textual and visual evidence for such arrangement, for St. Peter's, there is also archeological evidence about such a complex sanctuary arrangement by the sixth century.[217] Six columns from the previous construction formed a chancel screen in such a way that four columns were repositioned in a straight line and two placed centrally up front in a line with two columns behind them, hence these four columns also formed a canopy that framed the altar table (Fig. 2.56). The canopy in St. Peter's was originally made of porphyry, twisted columns brought from Greece, and the entire sanctuary was remade several times in the eighth, ninth, twelfth, and thirteenth centuries before the establishment of the still-standing Bernini's high canopy.[218] Pope Gregory III (731–741) allegedly obtained from the Byzantines a silver-plated beam decorated with holy images. The silver revetments from Rome were lost during the Arab raid of 846. There is no reason to believe that the seventh-century silver sanctuary furnishings of the now-lost church in Edessa were not rearranged in a similar manner: a four-columned altar *ciborium* and ten columns are mentioned in the hymn as supports of the canopy and forming a chancel screen.

The most famous silver canopy is certainly the one from the elaborate sanctuary installation of Hagia Sophia in Constantinople, now lost. In his encomium, Paulos Silentarios tells us that a silver canopy sheltered the main altar of Hagia Sophia; it rose on four silver columns that carried four silver arches on each side of the structure crowned by the pyramidal roof, also made of silver (Table 1, T.32; Table 5.86). The canopy was decorated with foliage, and the columns were spirally fluted. Its roof was a pyramid formed of eight triangular silver plates, which were joined in a single crest in the form of a cup and assumed the shape of leaves; at the apex were a silver globe and the life-giving cross. The four corners of the square base of the

---

211 Mundell-Mango (1992) 123–136, esp. 130, with reference to *Breviarus de Hierosolyma.*

212 Ibid.

213 Smith, M. T. (1974) 379–414. On the now-lost monumental altar canopy of St. James in Santiago de Compostela made of silver and gold, built around 1100, presumably following Italian models, see Kroesen (2009) 30–31.

214 *Chronicon 1234*. Mundell-Mango (1992) 123–136, esp. 130.

215 McVey (1983) 91–121.

216 Also see Mundell-Mango (1992) 123–136, esp. 130.

217 Mainstone (1988) 218–222 also takes into consideration the images of a silver canopy in Hagia Sophia as found in chronologically later miniatures, such as the Menologion of Basil II (ca. 1000).

218 Without entering the current discussion on the original donation of the canopy under Emperor Constantine or Constans, I summarize here the most recent, major research on the making of the sanctuary installation and its canopy in St. Peter's, based on works by Gem (2013) 35–64 and Kinney (2005) 16–47, esp. 22–24.

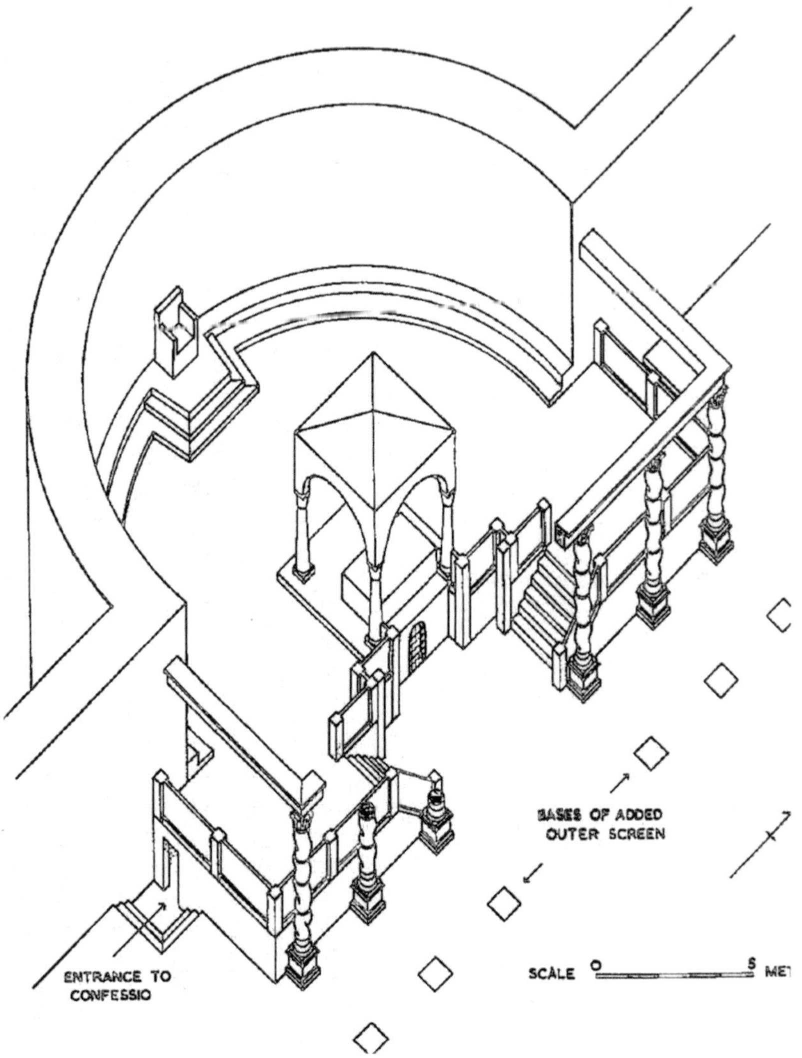

FIGURE 2.56 *St. Peter's shrine. Reconstruction drawing of the seventh-century shrine.* DRAWING FROM J. B. WARD PERKINS, *STUDIES IN ROMAN AND EARLY CHRISTIAN ARCHITECTURE*, PINDAR PRESS, 1994

canopy frame were decorated with silver bowls, candelabra, and candles, "expressing beauty rather than giving light," Paulos Silentarios further explained.[219] Prokopios, Justinian's court historian, informs us that all the original sanctuary furnishings were embellished with 40,000 lbs. of silver, of which about 10,000 lbs. were used for the altar, the chancel screen, and the ambo, and approximately 2,134 lbs. for the silver canopy that framed the altar table made of gold.[220]

---

219 *SD* 88.

220 *And as for the treasure of this church—the [vessels of] gold and silver and precious stones which the Emperor Justinian has dedicated here—it is impossible to give an exact account of all of them. I shall allow my readers to form an estimate by means of a single example. That part of the church which is especially sacred and accessible to priests only—it is called sanctuary—exhibits forty thousand pounds of silver: Buildings, I,* 1.65, 28–29. On the approximation of the silver used for the canopy over the altar table, see Mundell-Mango (1992) 123–136,

Judging from the general production of silver ecclesiastical objects in Byzantium, it may be assumed that silver canopies were widely used in the sixth century and remained in use at least until the ninth and tenth centuries.[221] A silver canopy is mentioned in the Melkite Cathedral of Antioch in 845, 967, and 1050, respectively.[222] Byzantine emperor Michael III (842–867) built his imperial palatine chapel, the Church of the Theotokos of the Pharos (864), immediately after the end of Iconoclasm.[223] On that occasion, the emperor provided the church with a silver altar canopy with a conical roof.[224] A silver altar canopy existed in the tenth-century palace church of Romanos I Lekapenos (920–944), the co-emperor of Constantine VII Porphyrogenitos (913–959).[225]

Less expensive materials such as iron or wood could have been used for canopied installations in Byzantine churches, and then they would have been eventually sheathed in precious materials.[226] Most texts actually describe pieces of precious liturgical furniture made in thin silver revetment sheets, rather than of solid stone or solid metal. Thus, Patriarch Severus, in a sermon delivered at St. Drosis in Antioch (516), appealed to the congregation to donate silver to cover the dome of the altar canopy[227] and described it thus:

> the silver columns placed about the altar which support the cupola (*hemisphaira*) placed upon their capitals which is . . . simply decorated by the iron bars as in a symbolic representation, but which has not been covered in silver.[228]

Wooden and Textile Canopies

Organic materials such as wood and textiles are fragile and perishable, so there is only circumstantial proof for the extent of the use of wooden canopies in Byzantine-rite churches. In the sixth century, Bishop Victor (537–44) replaced a wooden altar canopy with a silver one in the Basilica Ursiana (built in 370–384) in Ravenna.[229] In the eleventh-century Byzantine account *Etymologicum Gudianum*, a wooden canopy is also mentioned, though not in the context of a church, but rather in a theological and grammatical text, and thus not sufficient to verify the presence of such canopies in contemporary Byzantine churches.[230] More palpable evidence for wooden canopies comes from Byzantine-rite churches in medieval Rus and Coptic churches in Egypt.

Although no wooden churches more recent than the fourteenth century survive, most Russian churches must have been made of wood. These churches presumably also had altar canopies, known in Russian as "небо" (literally *sky*, and also denoting the canopied ceiling of the entire church) and "сень" (literally *canopy*, often made of wood), suggesting that most altar canopies in Russian churches were made of wood rather than marble,

---

esp. 129–130. The sheer value of the silver, without any work or paid labor, used for the altar, altar canopy, chancel screen, and ambo would be approximately $8,200,000 in 2015, with approximately $438,500 as the worth of the silver used for the altar canopy only.

221 Mundell Mango (1992) 123–136.

222 Ibid., esp. 130.

223 Mango (1956) 123+125–140.

224 Ruggieri (1991) 198–199.

225 Maksimović (1961) 32, with further references.

226 For revetment of liturgical furnishing in silver and occasionally gold, see Mundell Mango (1990) 245–261. On such practice of a wooden canopy resting on four iron vertical supports and entirely covered in silver sheets in fourteenth-century Spain, see Kroesen (2009) 31.

227 Leader-Newby (2004) 70.

228 *Patriarch Severus*, according to Mundell-Mango (1992) 123–136, esp. 126. Table 1, T.47.

229 *SD* 105.

230 *Etymologicum Gudianum* 365:24. Table 1, T.79.

as was customary in larger imperial Byzantine churches.[231] A footing for a four-columned wooden altar canopy has been found in the early twelfth-century Church of St. Nicetas in Yaroslavl.[232] Three additional wooden altar canopies have been confirmed archeologically in the churches of St. Savior in Chernigov (eleventh century), St. Sophia in Novgorod (ca. 1156), and in the church known as "Old Throne" in Vladimir-Volinski (second half of the twelfth century).[233] Yet archeologists have not been able to confirm whether monumental canopies replaced wooden ones, or vice versa. It seems that they coexisted during the Middle Byzantine period but that wooden examples prevailed because timber construction was prevalent in medieval Rus; the Slavs held timber as the most praised and animated material, much as marble was for Greeks.[234]

Moreover, not all wooden canopies in Russian churches built from the eleventh to the thirteenth centuries were above altar tables, as previously thought. Primary texts reveal that some of these wooden installations sheltered ambos, like the one in the church in Vshchizh (late twelfth to the first third of the thirteenth century), and some were integral parts of the sanctuary screens, like the canopy that sheltered the icon over the central doors of the sanctuary barrier in the Church of the Nativity in Bogolyubovo, as described in the *Hypatian Chronicle* of 1175.[235]

In the East, in addition to preserved archeological evidence for wooden canopies in Russian churches dating to the period after the eleventh century, there is some evidence that Coptic altar canopies in the same period may have been made of wood. Many surviving post-Byzantine Coptic canopies were made of wood and then painted, in contrast to the bare altars they framed, which were devoid of any ornament or painting. The so-called Fatimid ciborium, dating from the tenth to eleventh centuries and preserved in the Coptic Museum in Cairo (inv. no. 909), is perhaps originally from the church d'al-Mu'allaqa (Mas al-Qadima) in Cairo.[236] Three other wooden canopies still in the Church of Mu'allaqa are dated to the fourteenth century and attributed to Byzantine origins (Table 5). This evidence further supports the use of various types of canopies within the church proper across the Byzantine Empire and beyond its geographical territories, expanding into the wider cultural landscape marked by Byzantine-rite churches in Eastern Europe and the Mediterranean region.

The use of textiles for canopies is an even more delicate question. Contemporaries mention cloths with rich silk and gold embroidery that accompanied the entire altar canopy installation in Hagia Sophia.[237] One of the embroidered hangings depicted Christ standing between Ss. Peter and Paul, while others represented images of divine miracles. Scholars still debate whether these textiles were altar covers or canopy curtains.[238] While there is not enough material evidence to confirm either position, the possibility of their use as canopy

---

[231] Brumfield (2000) 694–965.

[232] Čukova (2004) 78.

[233] Sterligova (2000) 360–381, abstract in English, 731–732.

[234] Interest in wooden churches has expanded in recent decades. See, for example, Khodakovsky (2015), with extensive bibliography.

[235] Sterligova (2000) 360–381, 731–732.

[236] Jeudy (2004) 67–88, figs. 17–20. Though the majority of other surviving Coptic canopies are dated to the eighteenth century, their strong resemblance to older canopies suggests a very conservative tradition in the use of canopies: Bolman (2006) 73–106; Hunt (1989) 61–77. A relatively new wooden canopy from the fourteenth-century Church of the Annunciation at Gračanica Monastery, Kosovo, Serbia, might have replaced an earlier canopy, similarly made of wood. Ćurčić (1991) 251–261, fig. 3.

[237] In addition to Silentarios' account, see the reference from *De Ceremoniis-a* (Table 1, T.71).

[238] See, for example, Taft (2006) 27–52, esp. 45; Walter (1993) 203–228; St. Clair (1979) 127–135; Mathews (1971) 162–171, esp. 167; Speck (1966) 323–375.

curtains must remain open. Early church texts speak of the use of curtains in the sanctuary.[239] Numerous textiles fragments from Byzantium and currently in museum collections confirm the use of both curtains and large wall hangings.[240] The term *curtain* was simultaneously reserved for the philosophical meaning of the veil as a symbol, while the exact location of actual curtains on canopies was never specified.[241] Yet it is important to remark that early texts occasionally mention canopies with curtains, which is further supported by images of sanctuaries in illuminated manuscripts and monumental paintings. Curtains were used for canopies in and around Rome at least since the eleventh century, as churches of San Clemente, Sant'Andrea in Flumine at Ponzano Romano, and Castel Sant'Elia near Nepi still have iron rods and rings from which the curtains were hung.[242] The metal rods still visible on the canopy from Paros may point to a medieval tradition of the use of curtains (see Fig. 2.1). Such a practice of hanging curtains in the Byzantine tradition can be further supported by numerous visual depictions of canopies with curtains, with realistically shown metal fittings, rings, and rods, most likely used for installations with curtains.[243] Symeon of Thessaloniki (ca. 1381–1429), born and consecrated as a bishop in Constantinople, served as Archbishop of Thessaloniki, the second largest town in Byzantine Empire, and wrote of the curtained altar canopies in the early fifteenth century.[244]

Although no canopy made entirely of textile has survived, we have indirect evidence that such canopies might have existed as well. Besides canopies where curtains could have been drawn to enclose or opened to reveal their interior, in my opinion, entire canopies could have been made of textile like tents. In the twelfth-century *Alexiad*, Anna Komnene briefly writes about an imperial canopy made of curtains.[245] Canopies represented in Byzantine manuscripts with curiously depicted concave roofs may suggest actual canopies that were formed of fabric draped over or attached to a frame of poles like a tent, instead of the stable canopies composed of four columns, curtains, and a roof of stone, metal, or wood.[246] Some ancient honorific monuments, like the early imperial canopy at Sagalassos, had marble concave roofs modeled as if emulating objects made of textile.[247] Without additional evidence, however, this hypothesis is extremely difficult to advance any further.

DECORATION OF CANOPIES AND INSCRIPTIONS

Numerous canopies constructed as mini-architectural structures were carefully decorated and occasionally had inscriptions, following the long-lasting Roman imperial architectural tradition of ornamenting and inscribing important buildings and structures. Canopies made of stone usually had carved decorations, while traces of color reveal that these were also sometimes painted. Using the surfaces of canopies like skin, Byzantines placed various

[239] See Chapter 1.

[240] Parani (2003) 179–185.

[241] See also Taft (2006) 27–50, esp. 40–49, and Constans (2006) 163–183. Bolman (2006) 73–106, esp. 95, provides an important discussion on the early textual references from Egypt that mentions altar canopies with curtains but never sanctuary screens.

[242] Zchomelidse (2010) 221–262, esp. 228–229.

[243] Parani (2003) 181.

[244] Table 1, T.109.

[245] See, for example, *Alexiad-a* XII.3.6 and XIII.1.8, with references to an imperial canopy called *oikiskos*, *katapetasma*, and *skēnē*.

[246] Eusebius of Caesarea and Ammonius of Alexandria, *Rabbula Gospels* f. 2r, 6th c. For additional examples, see Underwood (1950) 43–138, figs. 34, 35, 36, 38, 44, 53, 55, and 56.

[247] Gates (1995) 207–255, fig. 21.

decorative motifs literally everywhere within the canopied installations—on the columns, arches, and roofs of canopies, on both their exterior and interior. Sodini has observed an insistence on homogenous motifs in marble and stone carving in Byzantium until the fifteenth century, proposing that it was the result of the Byzantine's rooting themselves in a dignified past and investing themself with magical associations.[248] While I am cautious about assigning these motifs magical associations, I absolutely concur that the insistence on recognizable and generic motifs participated in the Byzantine attempts to maintain the perception of a stable and long-lasting identity expressed through architecture and its holistic design.[249]

The formulaic and almost generic repertoire of canopy decoration can be observed in the image of the canopy as a whole as well as in the smallest details. My analysis of the decorative motifs that most often occur on canopies suggests that their pre-Christian origins should be sought in both the Hellenistic and Old Testament past. If made of marble or silver, canopies are occasionally distinguished by special carving on their elements, like spirally fluted or double-knotted columns. Spirally fluted and double-knotted columns have been associated with the columns from Solomon's Temple.[250] By the fifteenth century, the spirally fluted columns of the canopy in St. Peter, believed to have been donated to the church by Emperor Constantine after he acquired them from Greece, were venerated themselves because it was believed that Christ leaned against them as he preached and disputed in the Temple and drove demons from the possessed during His ministry.[251] Usually carved on three or four sides, the basket capitals of the columns are most often of Corinthian or Composite variety, both with acanthus leaves. These pseudo-Classical varieties further suggest the Byzantines' continual engagement with the architecture of the past. Regardless of the specific types of canopies, the arches of canopies frequently have carved generic geometric, vegetal, and zoomorphic motifs: crosses, various roundels, or interlaced and braid rope patterns; twisting acanthus leaves, palmettes, and lilies; confronted winged creatures such as griffins and birds, usually peacocks; and confronted quadrupeds, most often lambs and lions.[252] Among conspicuously carved canopies, the eleventh-century altar canopy of Byzantine official Gregorius (Grgur, Gregory) from the episcopal complex of St. Anastasia in Zadar, has relatively well-preserved arches that show elaborate figurative decoration (Fig. 2.57, see also Figs. 2.48, 2.59). Sculpted elements with figural confronted motifs of lambs (?), griffins, peacocks, and lions on each of the four arches were all framed with decorative checkerboard and ropelike patterns. Traces of red, blue, and yellow reveal that Gregory's canopy was originally boldly painted, following the ancient Greek tradition of painting both architecture and sculpture, further highlighting how the carvings on canopies were originally more visible than they are today.

These decorative motifs were definitely powerful carriers of meaning. Individually, geometric motifs, such as crosses and various interlocking knots, point to the religious and sacred meanings of the canopies. The ancient symbol of the cross had received its definite Christian meaning when used on canopies. Similarly, other geometric symbols were additionally enriched within the Christian context. The so-called Solomon knot, consisting

---

[248] Sodini (2002) 129–145, esp. 145.

[249] See also Greenhalgh (2009).

[250] Ward Perkins (1994a) 469–489; Haussherr (1968) 101–121; Kalavrezou-Maxeiner (1985) 95–103. See also Chapters 1, 4, and 5.

[251] This notion was highly popularized in seventeenth-century guidebooks. Kirwin (1997) 80.

[252] Mijović (1985) 91–104; Mijović (1989) 403–418; Preradović (2000); Preradović-Petrović (2002) 247–264; Vežić and Lončar (2009) 24–28; Bogdanović (2008d).

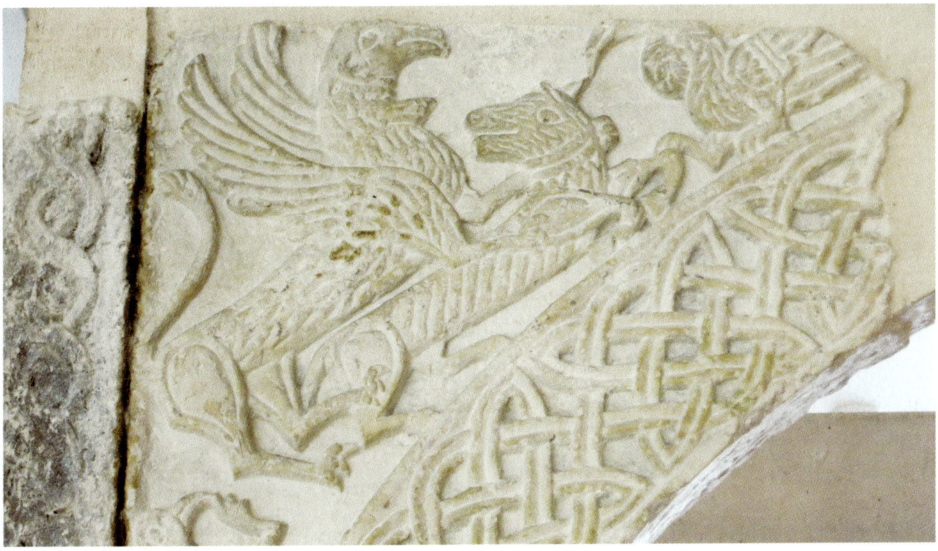

FIGURE 2.57 *Altar canopy, detail; Church of St. Anastasia (Sv. Stošija), Zadar, Croatia, eleventh century; Archeological Museum, Zadar.* PHOTO JELENA PALIĆ

of two interlocked closed loops; the so-called the Shield of David, recognizable as a six-pointed star; as well as the so-called Solomon seal, recognizable as a pentagram, are occasionally recognized on canopies.[253] Hence, the Middle Byzantine saintly shrine of Hosios Loukas has a Solomon knot on the capital of the column (Fig. 2.58). In the same church, the canopied frame for the *proskynetarion* icon has the Shield of David. The ninth-century altar canopy from the cathedral on the island of Rab has the pentagram or Solomon seal on its arch. These symbols have a wide scope of interpretations, ranging from apotropaic meanings to eternity in case of the Solomon knot, concepts of creation and unity between humans and God for the Shield of David, to the five books of the Hebrew Bible, the fifth seal as the key to the knowledge, and the five senses additionally pointing to the five wounds of Christ in case of the pentagram. Together, they confirm a more general Byzantine concern with framing and marking sacred spaces as well as making connections with the sacred Judaic traditions of the Temple.

Expanding upon the rites performed within the sacred space of the canopy, the vines, grape branches, and various vegetal motifs can be associated with the Eucharist and the Tree of Life. The images of lambs most directly point to the Lamb of God, the sacrificial lamb, the symbol of Christ and the Eucharist. Various texts, including the Scriptures and the Old Testament, reinforce the spiritual significance of other figurative images, such as those of birds and lions.[254] The birds and peacocks are related to resurrection and paradisiac themes. The motif of a lion, which is only twice mentioned in the New Testament—I Peter 5:8, when it is compared with the devil, and Revelation 5:5 when Christ is compared with the lion from the tribe of Juda—is attributed to Christ and can also refer to ideas about

---

[253] Vežić and Lončar (2009) 11–57. Dēmētrokallis (2002) 229–248, with 40 figures, provides an excellent overview of the geometric motif of the Solomon knot as it appears in Byzantine architecture, with a brief reference to the same motif in Jewish synagogues. Dēmētrokallis, however, advocates that the motif had magical power and as such was widely used in Constantinople and spread through Peloponnesus in the eleventh century.

[254] Vežić (2001–2002) 91–122; Preradović-Petrović (2002) 247–264.

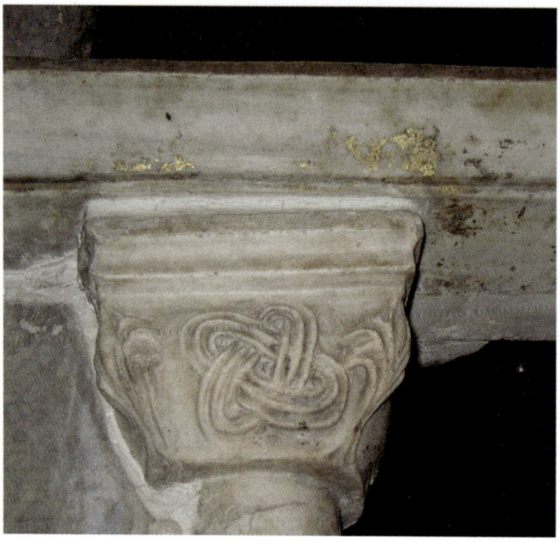

FIGURE 2.58 *Hosios Loukas' shrine, detail; katholikon of Hosios Loukas Monastery, Greece, eleventh century and later.* PHOTO AUTHOR

human will and a choice between evil and good. Moreover, the lion was closely associated with a winged mythical creature, the gryphon, which carried multiple layers of royal, solar, and guardian meanings.[255] Griffins, associated with solar motifs in both pagan and Judeo-Christian contexts,[256] were further represented within funerary Byzantine churches and installations as heavenly guardians and creatures who carried souls upward to the heavenly realm.[257]

Though generic, pillars of acacia, palmettes, lilies, ropes, confronted winged creatures, and lions are also very closely related to the framing of sacred space.[258] Interlaced and rope designs are frequently used on church elements that define liminal zones such as doors, sanctuary screens, and *proskynetaria*. The ancient use of the rope design, which is closely related to the untying or loosening of a knot, signified alighting, descending, stopping, or abiding in a place and by extension signified the dwelling of Presence, which in the Christian context could have been reappropriated to point to the Creation and the Incarnation.[259] These rope and interlaced designs are also *apotropaic* because they guarded thresholds of sacred space from the scale of a canopy to an entire building.[260] For example, interlaced patterns framing windows in Late Byzantine architecture would also be used for church furnishing, including the arch of the fourteenth-century canopy from the church

255 Goldman (1960) 319–328.

256 *RAC* vol. 10, s.v. *Grief*.

257 Ćurčić (1995) 597–601.

258 On the widespread use of the mentioned vegetative and rope motifs in Classical, Byzantine, and Islamic art, see Frantz (1934) 43–76; Trilling (1995) 59–86.

259 On the Middle-Eastern words *ḥ-l-l*, *ḥalla*, and *ḥulūl* for referencing the rope design via a scenario of being allowed to untie a knot in the desert and, by extension, for signifying abiding in a place as well as a non-technical sense of resting or dwelling, and more specifically of incarnation, see the elaborate discussion in Lobel (1999) 103–125.

260 Trilling (1995) 59–86; Boura (1977–1979) 63–72.

of Hagia Sophia in Ohrid.[261] Similarly, winged creatures like griffins were set as guardians at the thresholds of treasuries.[262] These motifs are also recognizable from the narratives of the Scriptures related to the structural elements and decoration of Solomon's Temple (cf. 1 Kgs. 7; 2 Chr. 3)[263] and the desert tabernacle made of four pillars of acacia overlaid with gold, set upon four bases of silver (cf. Ex. 26:32),[264] and guarded by the winged cherubim.

The figurative representations depicting New Testament references are rarely preserved, but these also existed. In addition to several canopies that have preserved post-Byzantine paintings, possibly repainted over older images such as those from the Middle Byzantine ambo canopy in Kalabaka and the fifteenth-century canopy shrine in the Church of the Sveti Choveli, Mcheta, in Georgia, several canopies had arches carved with images of holy figures and events from the Scriptures. Those from the collection in the Byzantine museum in Athens have in the soffits of their arches deeply carved images of holy figures, including Old Testament kings and prophets Solomon and David as well as St. John the Baptist, while the pictorial representation of the Nativity is expanded upon by references to the Christmas hymn. All of these images are identified by their inscriptions in the Greek language. The example of the richly carved columns from the altar canopy in Venice shows how impressive these canopies may have been (see Fig. 3.17). After a long debate over whether the alabaster columns with New Testament narratives and inscriptions in Latin are Byzantine *spolia* or new elements made by a local workshop in Venice, it has been proven that these are original seventh-century Byzantine historiated columns.[265] Each of the four columns is divided into nine horizontal bands with a total of 324 engraved niches populated with

---

261 Trkulja (2004) 74–87. The entwined rope motif is pertinent to the sanctuary screens in Georgian churches as well, though it has been shown that by having only one access to the apse, instead of two or three, they differed from Byzantine and Slavic examples. Mepisashvili and Vakhtang (1977) 224ff.

262 Boura (1983).

263 1 Kgs. 7:1: But Solomon was building his own house thirteen years, and he finished all his house. 2 He built also the house of the forest of Lebanon... 9 All these were of costly stones, according to the measures of hewed stones, sawed with saws, within and without, even from the foundation unto the coping, and so on the outside toward the great court. 10 And the foundation was of costly stones, even great stones....

2 Chr. 3:1: Then Solomon began to build the house of the LORD at Jerusalem in mount Moriah, where the LORD appeared unto David his father, in the place that David had prepared in the threshing floor of Ornan the Jebusite.... 3 Now these are the things wherein Solomon was instructed for the building of the house of God.... 5 And the greater house he ceiled with fir tree, which he overlaid with fine gold, and set thereon palm trees and chains. 6 And he garnished the house with precious stones for beauty.... 7 He overlaid also the house, the beams, the posts, and the walls thereof, and the doors thereof, with gold; and graved cherubim on the walls. 8... And he overlaid the upper chambers with gold. 10 And in the most holy house he made two cherubim of image work, and overlaid them with gold. 11 And the wings of the cherubim were twenty cubits long: one wing of the one cherub was five cubits, reaching to the wall of the house: and the other wing was likewise five cubits, reaching to the wing of the other cherub.... 14 And he made the veil of blue, and purple, and crimson, and fine linen, and wrought cherubim thereon. 15 Also he made before the house two pillars of thirty and five cubits high, and the chapter that was on the top of each of them was five cubits. 16 And he made chains, as in the oracle, and put them on the heads of the pillars; and made a hundred pomegranates, and put them on the chains. 17 And he reared up the pillars before the temple, one on the right hand, and the other on the left; and called the name of that on the right hand Jachin, and the name of that on the left Boaz.

264 Ex. 26:32: And thou shalt hang it upon four pillars of shittim wood overlaid with gold: their hooks shall be of gold, upon the four sockets of silver.

265 Warland (1993) 173–182; Vio (1999) 110–113.

figures that recount 108 New Testament episodes (Table 7.215). The inscriptions in Latin were added at some later point, describing each scene, occasionally with minor mistakes.

Indeed, inscriptions on canopies were not obligatory, yet they often complemented the decoration of the canopies. These inscriptions are extremely revealing, not only for suggesting the historical context of the creation and for the dating of specific installations if a historical figure or event had been mentioned, but also for further highlighting the meaning and importance canopies carried. Of some 240 canopies that I analyzed, at least twenty-four of them have preserved fragments of inscriptions (Tables 5, 7). Even if my sample cannot provide any definite assessment of how widespread such a practice was, knowing that architectural fragments with lettering would easily attract attention and often be looted and reused, as the example from Venice shows, it seems fair to assume that more than ten percent of Byzantine canopies had inscriptions, and that these installations can be associated with imperial and aristocratic donations in major urban and religious centers. For the purpose of this study, I have analyzed twenty canopies with fragmentarily preserved inscriptions on them, starting with the sixth-century small-size *artophorium* probably made in Constantinople and currently in the Venice treasury, and ending with the thirteenth-century arches of canopies, possibly funerary installations, and currently in the Byzantine museum in Athens.

Inscriptions preserved on canopies imply certain aesthetic, emotional, proprietary, and political concerns, but above all are the religious concerns. Especially telling is the now-lost ninth-century inscription on the silver altar canopy from Hagia Sophia that publicly announced the political and religious message about the restoration of religious images and the orthodoxy of Byzantine emperors. An epigram from the *Palatine Anthology*, a collection of Byzantine texts from the sixth to the tenth centuries, confirms that icons were attached to the altar canopy in Hagia Sophia, removed during the Iconoclastic Controversy, and returned afterwards when the recorded straightforward text "The images of the impostors had cast down here, pious emperors have again set up" was inscribed on the canopy.[266]

Sixth-century canopies such as the *artophorion* canopy, most likely from Constantinople and now in San Marco in Venice; the altar canopy from Basilica B, Nikopolis, Greece; and the baptistery canopies from basilicas Clupea and Sbeitla in Tunisia; ninth-century canopies from Novigrad, Bijaće, Prevlaka, and Zadar in modern Croatia, and those from Kotor and Ulcinj, Montenegro; and the canopy from the Pantokrator Monastery in Constantinople (Istanbul, Turkey) all have formulaic votive inscriptions. These occasionally disclose information on the date of the object, sometimes associated with the tenure of the Byzantine rulers and officials, the names of the donors and their family members, and the names of those to be remembered during the rites performed within the space of the canopied installation. Other inscriptions remain in fragments, but their excerpts often suggest formulaic invocations and prayers.

These inscriptions quite frequently combine references to the divine and eternal with the personal and contemporary. They are invocations in form and inseparable from the Byzantine belief that the historical moment and person mentioned should be "re-created" within sacred history and among those who have already entered the divine realm, which exists in perpetuity. To support this observation, we may turn to two inscriptions in particular: the one from the Church of St. Anastasia (Sv. Stošija) within the episcopal center in Zadar, modern Croatia, and the other from another side of the Adriatic littoral, from the unidentified church in Ulcinj, modern Montenegro—both originally in the Byzantine province of Dalmatia.

An especially beautiful poetic inscription from the equally well-designed altar canopy from St. Anastasia church commemorates its donor, Byzantine pro-consul Gregorius

[266] Oikonomides (1985) 111–115, quotation on p. 113.

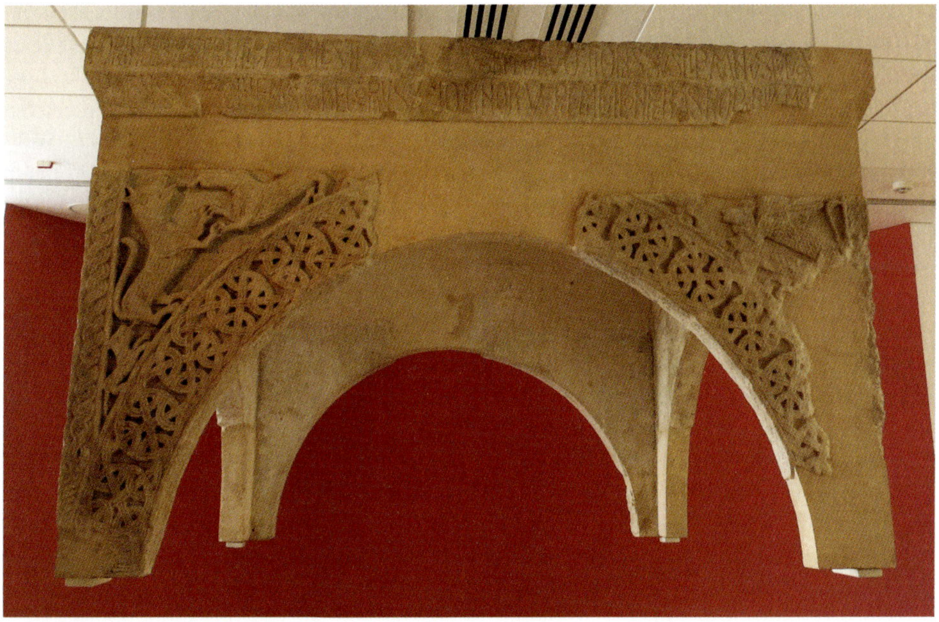

FIGURE 2.59 *Altar canopy with an inscription mentioning Proconsul Grgur (Gregory, Georgios); Church of St. Anastasia (Sv. Stošija), Zadar, Croatia, eleventh century; Archeological Museum, Zadar.* PHOTO JELENA PALIĆ

(Grgur, Gregory) (Table 7.178, Fig. 2.59). It reads, "Oh Peter, first among the leaders, Prince and the key-holder of the heavenly palace, accept this votive gift that I, lowest proconsul Gregory, vowed to give as a small token to receive in turn magnificent gifts." Made as a votive gift during the tenure of this historically attested Byzantine official, Gregory's donation is a massive, richly carved altar canopy to the church, and by ordering a poem that mentions both St. Peter and himself, he asks to be remembered during the services and to join the Christian communion in perpetuity.

In another example, pieces of the relatively lengthy inscription, which originally ran on all four sides of the Ulcinj canopy, have been preserved on four marble fragments, which have allowed scholars to assemble them and propose several alternate readings (Table 7.114). Without going into epigraphic details, each of the proposed readings recognizes the names of co-emperors Leo and Constantine; the donor's reference calling for the salvation of his wife, Gusma—a Christianized name and a corrupted version of Cosma; and a dual reference to the Savior Jesus Christ and the Lamb of God. Provided by a wealthy donor, this altar canopy architecturally framed the holiest place in the church and simultaneously honored the emperors and the local woman, the donor's deceased wife, Gusma, bringing them into communion within the liturgical rites. The text roughly reads: ". . . (in the glory of the Lord) our Saviour Jesus Christ for the salvation of [the soul?—J.B.] of my [wife?] Gusma . . . in front of the Lord and Lamb . . . because this structure was made at the time of our pious lords perpetual Augusti [Emperors—J.B.] lords Leo and Constantine" (Engl. trans. J.B.).[267]

[267] The following translation follows the main lines of the translation offered by M. Lončar in Vežić (2001–2002) 91–122, and by Preradović-Petrović (2002) 247–264.

Dubravka Preradović-Petrović has challenged the previously held opinion that the Byzantine emperors Leo and Constantine mentioned on the canopy inscription from Ulcinj are Leo III (r. 717–741) and his son Constantine V (r. 741–775) who became a co-emperor in 720.[268] She has demonstrated that the canopy should be associated with the time of the co-emperors Leo V the Armenian (r. 813–820) and his son Constantine Symbatios (r. 813–820) and hence dated to the ninth instead of the eighth century. Besides the anachronistic use of Latin, the conservative local populace anachronistically used the title *Augustos* instead of the title *Basileos*, widely used by the Byzantines in the ninth century. In addition to the example from Ulcinj, in the ninth-century church in Martinići, the surviving inscription on the sanctuary barrier is a combination of Greek and Latin, suggesting this was a trend in the wider region.[269] Moreover, similar to the early eleventh-century inscription from the canopy donated by the Byzantine pro-consul Gregorius, these inscriptions confirm the prolonged use of Latin instead of, or with the addition of, Greek script in the periphery of the Byzantine domains, where the autochthonous Christianized populace spoke Latin. By extension, these inscriptions that allowed for the redating of canopies to more recent periods also point to the already observed conservatism in the church design and furnishing. A leaf from the thirteenth-century Armenian manuscript [*Entry into Jerusalem*, The T'oros Roslin Gospels, Armenian, 1262, The Walters Art Museum, Ms. W. 539 f. 174 r.] shows a canopy-like structure with a here-illegible inscription on its eaves, further suggesting that inscriptions in various languages on Byzantine and Byzantine-inspired canopies might have been more common than we can prove today.[270]

The messages the inscriptions on canopies conveyed to the beholders and churchgoers simultaneously speak of the monumental simplicity and power of various canopied installations. Especially revealing is the ninth-century canopy from the Basilica of St. Martha in Bijaće that has two sets of inscriptions that run along the four arches, one on the exterior and the other in the interior of the canopy, thus, two texts on the canopy that differ in their location and meaning (Table 7.113; Fig. 2.60).[271] The inscription on the exterior reads: "You, worshipers of Christ, whoever enters, praise the holy[?] Trinity . . . with cheers and in honor of John [the Baptist?] and blessed Martha look at all of this new [potentially both a canopy and the building itself] built in time of [name of the donor lost]." The interior text, which is written as if a mirror image of the outer text, reads: "Here, the soul, like the bird from the trap, raises the hope of eternity. . .. We pray to Jesus Christ, trusting in help of holy [Martha?] . . . most humbly to be surrounded by God's will while we exist and to receive the eternal life. Amen." (Engl. trans. J.B.)[272]

As explained by Milenko Lončar, the inscription on the outer arch emphasizes the act of making a canopy, by whom and for whom, as well as establishing the date.[273] The inscription on the inner arch, written as if a mirror image of the outer inscription in that it follows the other direction of reading if viewed from the exterior, is more personal and spiritual and points to how the inscription is related to the "inner vision." Together, the inscriptions point to the possibility that the structure was either an altar canopy by invocation of the name St. Martha, to whom the church was dedicated, or a baptistery canopy because of the mention of St. John, possibly John the Baptist.

---

268 Preradović-Petrović (2002) 247–264.

269 Korać (2001) fig. 71.

270 Noeal and Weiss (2002) 127, fig. 8.

271 Vežić and Lončar (2009) 206–223.

272 The following translation follows the main lines of the translation offered by Milenko Lončar in Vežić and Lončar (2009) 206–223.

273 Vežić and Lončar (2009) 206–223.

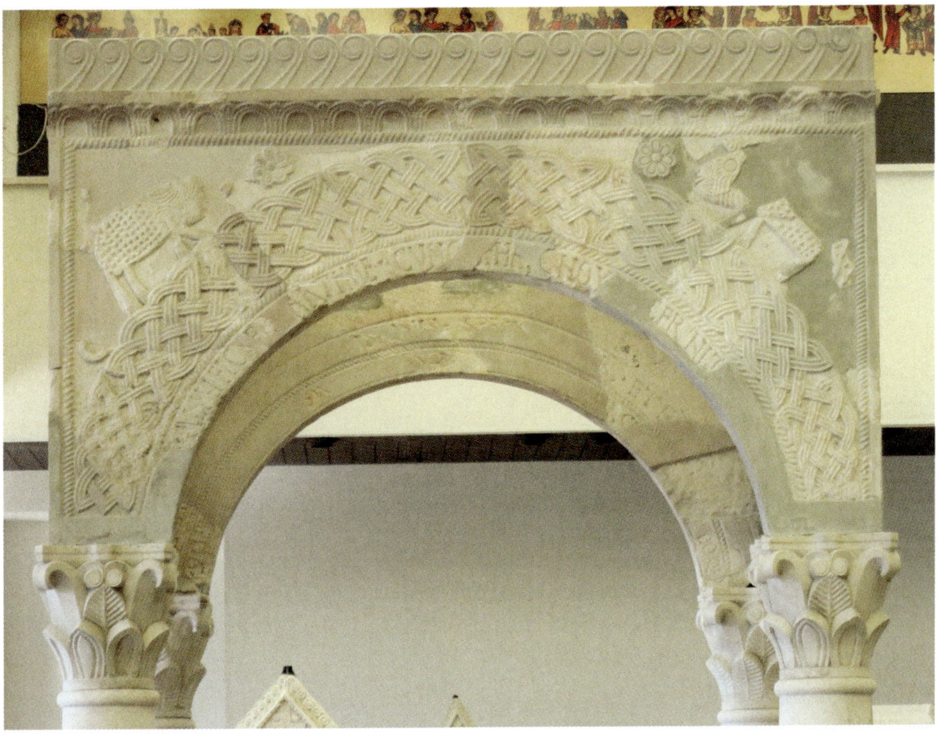

FIGURE 2.60 *Altar canopy (?); inscriptions run on both the exterior and the interior of the arches. Basilica St. Martha, Bijaće, Dalmatia, Croatia, ninth century.* PHOTO JELENA PALIĆ

It is difficult to discern the specific type of canopy based on inscriptions once they have been removed from the original context and because of the often overarching dialogue of the inscriptions that simultaneously refers to the earthly and the heavenly. We can find an example of this difficulty in the Constantinopolitan canopy from Pantokrator Monastery, today comprising the *minbar* in Molla Zeyrek camii in Istanbul (Table 7.193, Fig. 2.61, see also Fig. 2.44). Here, the fragmentarily preserved inscription is composed of a series of three inscribed disks on the interior of one of the four arches of what was presumably originally a Byzantine canopy.[274]

Roundels with monograms were quite frequently used in Byzantine art and architecture, at least since the sixth century, and can be seen occasionally on the canopies depicted in Byzantine art.[275] An interesting example is the arch fragment presumably from the marble canopy from

[274] Ousterhout (2010a) 432–439.

[275] Some of the earliest-studied monograms in roundels are from the sixth-century ivory diptychs sent by a Byzantine emperor to his consuls. These ivories depict enthroned consuls set in architectural framing with the roundel with a monogram bearing the consul's name above his figure. Netzer (1983) 265–271, figs 10–15. Roundels with monograms are used in the mosaics of Hagia Sophia, flanking the tenth-century Emperor Alexander, the third son of Emperor Basil I and brother of Emperor Leo VI. Underwood and Hawkins (1961) 187–218, figs. 4–5. Roundels with monograms engraved in stone elements of churches, usually on lintels above entrances, columns, and spandrels, are attested throughout the Byzantine Empire, as in the widely known sixth-century church in Paros, Hagia Sophia and the Chora monastery in Constantinople, the early fourteenth-century H. Apostoloi in Thessaloniki, or the little-studied fourteenth-century Church of St. John the Theologian in Poganovo, the last of which bears medallions with inscribed names of the saint and of certain nobles Konstantin and Jelena, presumably donors of the church.

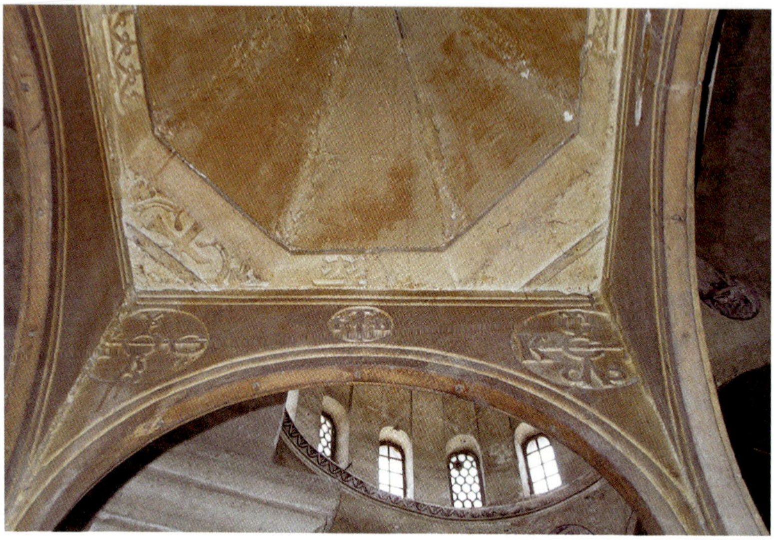

FIGURE 2.61 *Marble canopy made of spolia, reused as minbar, detail of the interior showing roundels with an inscription; Pantokrator Monastery, Constantinople, now Istanbul, after eleventh century (thirteenth century?).* PHOTO ROBERT OUSTERHOUT

Hagios Demetrios Church in Thessaloniki; it contains a roundel with an inscription related to the healing *myron* from St. Demetrios' shrine.[276] The monogram is visible on the top of the lintel of the icon canopy from the thirteenth-century Church of Metropolis in Mystra. Monograms may have also been used on tomb canopies, as suggested by two monograms inscribed in Cyrillic and reading "Asanina" and "Palaologina," embroidered within a canopy-like niche-tomb on the elaborate fifteenth-century burial shroud of Maria of Mangop (d. 1476/1477), a Moldavian princess and descendant of Bulgarian and Byzantine imperial dynasties.

Although I was not able to reconstruct the partially preserved inscription from the Pantokrator canopy, the first two roundels, when read clockwise, as seems correct to me, provide an invocation and prayer Κύριε βοήθει τῷ δούλῳ . . . ("Lord save your servant . . ."), most likely followed by a personal name. The name is difficult to decipher, but the inscription was clearly intended to personalize the sacred space of the canopy.[277] The preserved inscription is a segment, preserved only on one arch of the canopy, today set as the eastern arch of the *minbar*. The installation itself has several sixth-century marble panels, probably taken from the Constantinopolitan church of Hagios Polyeuktos, which functioned until the thirteenth century.[278] Other parts such as double-knotted columns are usually associated with *proskynetaria* icons, but another canopy from the fourteenth-century Church of Hagia Sophia in Ohrid, now reused as a *minbar*, also has them, and the architectural elements of this canopy are associated with the episcopal throne (Fig. 2.62).[279] I would suggest

[276] Bakirtzis (2002) 175–192.

[277] I have consulted Fink (1971) for the possible visual analogy of the monograms from the Pantokrator monastery and monograms he collected, which bear the names of Byzantine emperors and various invocations. However, I was not able to ascertain the personal name. Ousterhout (2010a) 432–439 claims that the three roundels carry an inscription dedicated to Ignatios Synkkelos, the famous ninth-century Constantinopolitan patriarch.

[278] Ousterhout (2010a) 432–439.

[279] Grozdanov (1969) 49–63.

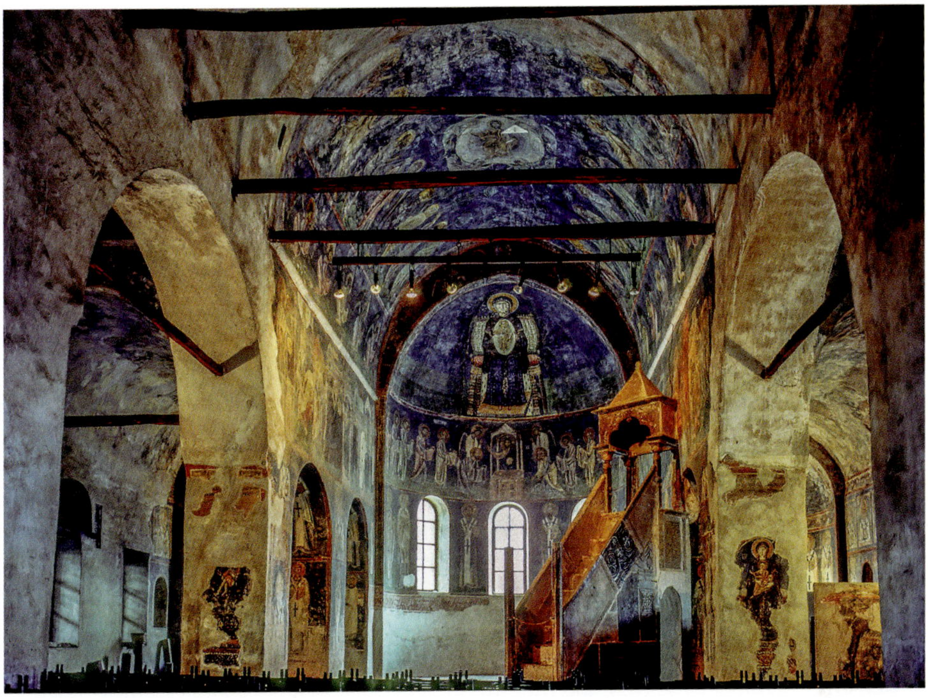

FIGURE 2.62 *Interior view of the Church of Hagia Sophia, Ohrid, F.Y.R. of Macedonia, fourteenth century. Canopied minbar is made of spolia of the episcopal throne; The Communion of the Apostles performed at the canopied altar table is represented in fresco in the sanctuary.* PHOTO DANIEL C. WAUGH

that the *minbar* was reassembled from a Christian canopy that once stood in the Pantokrator monastery, most likely as a tomb or altar canopy, based on the formulaic inscription that calls for the salvation of a donor or the deceased.[280] The inscribed prayer framed both by the roundels and the canopy—which initially may have been in honor of the deceased if it was originally a tomb canopy or may have framed the Eucharistic mysteries performed on the altar table in the case of an altar canopy—seemingly conceals complex emotional, religious, and semantic meanings.

The inscription is set on one of the canopy arches, obviously cut during the reassembling, and is currently set in the interior. Even if originally on the exterior of the arch, the inscription was not meant to be read and understood by everyone, but was intended for those initiated, presumably priests, who would not defile its power and would vocalize the dialogue with the divine, when facing east. The prayer, inscribed in three roundels with cruciform monograms, was meant to be pronounced syllable by syllable. In the first roundel, the monogram bears the inscription "Κύ-ρ-ιε βο-(ή)-θ-ει," which is read starting from the "Κύ" at the "nine o'clock" position and going clockwise. If my reading is correct, the inscription on the second roundel (*τῷ δούλῳ*) picks up at "twelve o'clock" and finishes with the name in the third roundel starting at "three o'clock." The arch of the canopy has been cut on its sides in order to conform to its new function as a *minbar*, and the beginning letter of the third roundel is illegible. It is interesting to remark that this kind of "clockwise"

[280] Ousterhout (2010a) 432–439 posits that the *minbar* is assembled from parts of the *templon*, not from the canopy, while the double-knotted columns are from a frame of the *proskinetarion*.

reading can also be seen on the two mosaic disks with monograms flanking the mosaic of Emperor Alexander in Constantinopolitan Hagia Sophia: on his right-hand side, and bearing the similar invocation "Κύριε βο(ή)θει (τῷ σῷ) δού(λ)ῳ" in the first roundel and "ὀρθοδόξῳ" in the second.[281] Reading the monograms crosswise and clockwise corresponds to the priest's movements and actions during the liturgy. The cross composed of words matches the priest's making of the sign of the cross with the Gospel book over the altar. In addition, the action of reading the entire three-circled prayer clockwise, or in other words "sun-wise," concurs with the circular movement of the priest walking three times around the altar during the liturgical services.[282] Facing east and standing at the foot of the altar table, the priest would make a prayer of remembrance of the person whose name is inscribed on the canopy during the liturgical service. The invocations were usually in a series of three. Each of the three times, the priest would start yet another circular movement of the prayer from the three inscribed disks. Following the proposed key inscription, the prayer for an individual intertwined with the liturgical service. Through the overarching divine symbolism of the cross and the disk, Christ and the sun, the secret and mystical sense of the text as the "prayer of the mind," the total symbolism of the canopy expanded into the prayers offered at the tomb or the divine mysteries presented on the altar table, which revealed the canopy to be a symbol of the Byzantine Church and a microcosm of Divine Creation.

That canopies were considered important architectural works and carriers of meaning is further supported by several other inscriptions recorded on them. Hence, the inscriptions from the sixth-century silver column that probably belonged to a canopy from an unidentified church in Lycia, modern Turkey, and from the arch of the baptistery canopy of the Cathedral of St. Tryphon in Kotor, Montenegro, read in Greek and Latin, respectively, "This work was renewed . . ." and "This work is beautifully decorated . . ." (Table 7.88, 118). The ninth-century canopies from the baptistery of the Basilica of Pelagia in Novigrad and from the Church of Archangel Michael in Prevlaka, both in modern Croatia, are identified as *the veils*, with references to the sacred veils, in their inscriptions, despite the fact that both of these structures are made of marble, thus further alerting us to impossibility of completely verbatim readings of textual sources that mention canopies (see Chapter 1, and Table 7.112, 132). The baptistery canopy from Novigrad is identified as, "This veil [canopy—J.B.] made of ornate marble for a baptistery from which radiates light and life overflows, I, Maurice Bishop, offered to the Lord wholeheartedly, with care and devotion. O, blessed John may many of our sins be destroyed, so that we learn what is in paradise, where the life rules" (Engl. trans. J.B.).[283] The fragmentary inscription on the possible altar canopy from the Church of Archangel Michael in Prevlaka reads, "The propriatory in honor of St. Michael" and refers to the *propitiation*, the mercy seat, and the veil of the Ark of Covenant (cf. Ex. 25:17–22, 26:1–37; Heb. 9:5).[284]

Even when the inscriptions on canopies are absolutely illegible—as in the case of the so-called pseudo-Kufic motifs used on canopy frames of the *proskynetaria* icons

---

[281] For the image of the inscription and its decipherment from Hagia Sophia, see Underwood and Hawkins (1961) 187–218, esp. 192, figs. 4–5. For the comparanda with the "counterclockwise" reading of texts inscribed on New Ritualist Russian icons (seventeenth–nineteenth centuries) and the significance of text for the religious experience, see Tarasov (2002) 252–254, figs. 110–111, where he particularly examines Loginov's icon *Resurrection of Christ*, which also has a cruciform inscription in a roundel. Tarasov proposes a counterclockwise "Baroque" key for its reading, though I would suggest that it is in a way "inverted" Byzantine reading, which conforms with the changes of the rituals of the New Believers in Imperial Russia.

[282] According to the Liturgy of St. John Chrysostom.

[283] Here, I follow and combine translations offered by G. Cuscito, M. Jurković, and M. Lončar. Vežić and Lončar (2009) 199; Jurković (1995) 141–149.

[284] Delonga (2000) 131.

common in Greece in the tenth and eleventh centuries,[285] or in the visual depictions of canopies denoting the Temple as in the scene of the *Presentation of Christ in the Temple* in the mosaic from Hosios Loukas (Fig. 2.63)—they seem to me to surpass merely decorative or *apotropaic* functions. Pseudo-Kufic motifs, though intelligible, also carried some deeper religious and spiritual meanings. Pseudo-Kufic letters are occasionally found represented, not only on the images of canopies representing the Temple, but also on the veil of Mary and on the cloak of the Old Testament High Priest, as in the early fourteenth-century fresco depicting the *Presentation of the Virgin in the Temple* from the Church of the Virgin Peribleptos (Fig. 2.64), and in numerous scenes that are directly related to the Ark of the Covenant, as in its representation in the fourteenth-century Serbian monastery Lesnovo, where "undulating" pseudo-Slavonic inscriptions imitate a "foreign" script on the cloak of the Old Testament High Priests Moses and Aaron.[286] Pseudo-Kufic script on canopies, which are, we should remember, church furnishings, should be rather understood as pseudo-Hebrew and not related to the Byzantines' attempts to write in Arabic, but rather intended to represent visually similar Hebrew texts, which were equally foreign to the Greek-speaking Byzantines, yet they

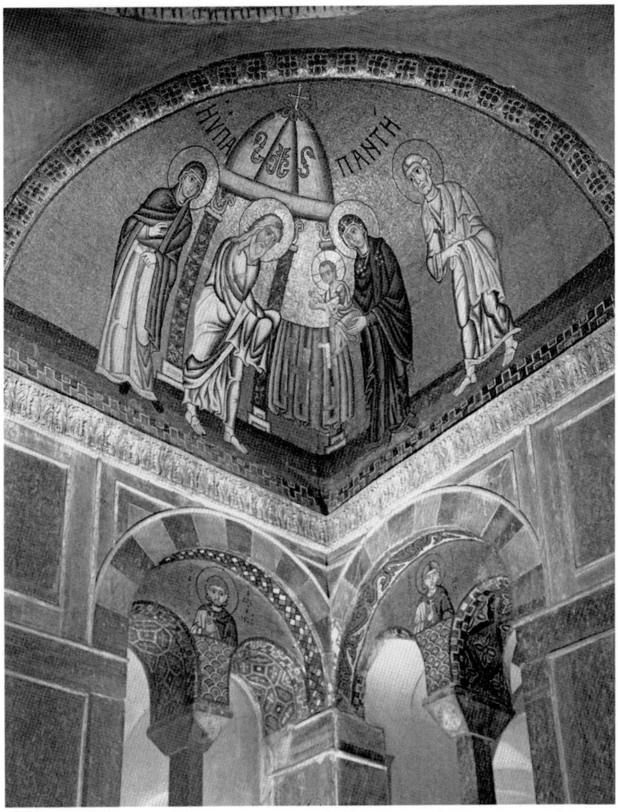

FIGURE 2.63 The Presentation of Christ in the Temple, *mosaic, katholikon of the Hosios Loukas Monastery, Greece, eleventh century.* ERICH LESSING/ART RESOURCE, NEW YORK

[285] Kalopissi-Verti (2006) 107–134, esp. 110.

[286] Gabelić (1998), fig. 81. On embroidered texts as references to holiness of Jewish vestments, see Greene (1992) 31–39.

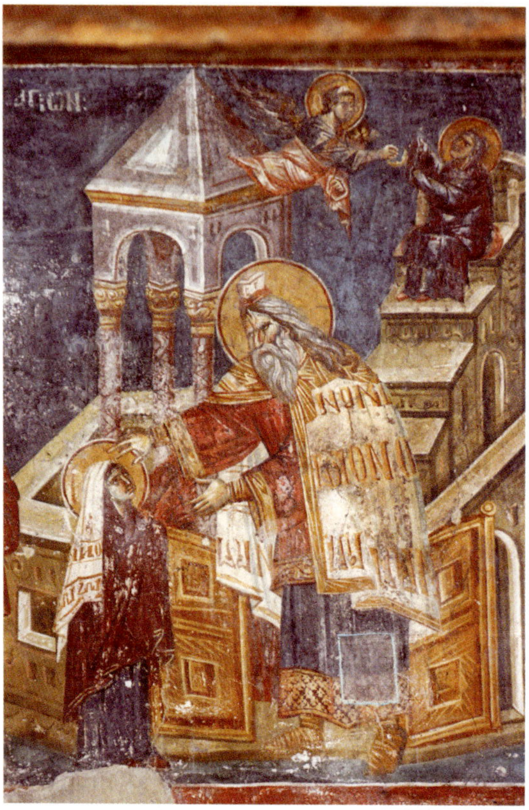

FIGURE 2.64 The Presentation of the Virgin in the Temple, *fresco, Church of the Virgin Peribleptos, F.Y.R. of Macedonia, fourteenth century.* PHOTO IVAN DRPIĆ

nevertheless had remained an integral part of their services along with the memory of the Temple and its restoration in Christian church.[287] The most obvious reference is the liturgical use of the praise "Hosanna in the highest" from the Seraphic hymn, which comes from the Hebrew Bible and was incorporated first into the Greek Septuagint without translation, and then within the liturgy by at least the mid-fourth century. The sacredness of inscriptions and exclamations related to canopies, though occasionally illegible or obscure, extended the aura of their antiquity and tradition. These remarks on the significance of inscriptions and decorative motifs on canopies point to the important role of canopies in the Byzantine tradition and the complex questions of their meaning and function.

---

[287] Solovey (1970) 226–229. Miles (1964) 1–32 has already shown that, from a plethora of pseudo-Kufic inscriptions from the Byzantine period, only a couple of them are actually written in Arabic, and furthermore, none of these can be associated with Byzantine ecclesiastical objects or architecture. Though at this point I cannot demonstrate further that the pseudo-Kufic inscriptions occasionally seen in the Byzantine images of the *Presentation into the Temple* are actually pseudo-Hebrew, it is interesting to compare my suggestion with attested Hebrew lettering from Isaiah in some early Renaissance paintings of the *Presentation into the Temple.* Haitovsky (1994) 111–120. Ilia Rodov further points to the use of Hebrew and pseudo-Hebrew inscription in Christian art and architecture with a dual role of perceived historical accuracy and sacred meaning of the objects with inscriptions. Rodov (2013) vol. 3, 642–477; Rodov (2015) vol. 11, cols. 631–37.

CANOPIES: RENEWALS OF CONTINUITY

Much as the Byzantines used inconsistent terminology to describe canopied structures, they did not develop a standardized typology of actual canopied installations, in terms of either their function or their particular location within the church proper, except perhaps for the altar canopy, the location of which was established in the sanctuary at least since the fifth century, based on available archeological evidence. The materials used for making canopies, and their shape, decoration, and inscriptions were all carriers of meaning, yet neither style nor iconography can definitively confirm the type or use of a particular canopy. The wide chronological and geographical distribution of various canopied installations in Byzantine-rite churches also precludes any possibility for the proposal of the evolution and linear development of canopies.

Though not considered indispensable furnishings, the more than two hundred examples of three-dimensional canopies from an extensive geographical and chronological range in the Byzantine ecclesiastical tradition confirm their wide and continual use (Table 5, Map 1). Most of the canopies can be dated to the periods between the fourth and sixth and then again between the ninth and twelfth centuries, during the times of economic and cultural prosperity of the Byzantine Empire. The period of changes in the quantity and quality of canopies during the "transitional period" (seventh to ninth centuries), marked by economic decline and the shrinking of urban centers and building construction in general, due to the external wars of the Byzantines with the Arabs and the Slavs, also coincides with the aftermath of Byzantine iconoclasm. Byzantine iconoclasm, which the Byzantines themselves called *iconomachy* (struggle over images), was a major internal dispute on the meaning of religious, figurative icons and their use in spaces of worship.[288] For more than a century, and emphasized by the two officially proclaimed iconoclastic policies in the eighth (ca. 726/730–787) and ninth (813–843) centuries, the controversy about images polarized Byzantine society.[289] Starting in Constantinople with the first official ban on the veneration of religious images under Byzantine emperor Leo III the Syrian "Isaurian" (r. 717–741) and the first iconoclastic church council of Hieria of 754, icons were physically destroyed, and those who made and venerated religious images were persecuted for religious and political motives.[290] From visual abundance, many churches and religious objects were stripped to visual minimalism; cross and vegetal motifs became the most acceptable decoration. Byzantine iconoclasm is usually considered a main threshold, not only for the use of religious images, but also for the liturgical and structural changes in a Byzantine-rite church.[291]

Most likely the evident decline in the material quality of canopies during and after Iconoclasm, however, did not result from the theological debates or liturgical changes, but

---

[288] The literature on the topic is immense: Brubaker (2012); Brubaker and Haldon (2011); Ivanović (2010); Brubaker and Haldon (2001); Gero (2000) 331–343; Barber (2002); Parry (1996) esp. 178–181; Giakalis (1994); Elsner (1988) 471–491; *Icon and Logos*; Cormack (1985); Taft (1992) 42; Taft (1980–1981) 45–75; John of Damascus, *On the Divine Images*; Bryer and Herrin, eds. (1975); Mango (1975a) 1–6; Barnard (1975) 7–13; Ahrweiler (1975) 21–27; Cormack (1975a) 35–44; Mundell (1975) 59–74; Cormack (1975b) 147–163; Wharton Epstein (1975) 103–111; Barnard (1974); Gero (1974); Brown (1973) 1–34; Kitzinger (1954) 83–150; Uspenski (1987) 382–394; Dvornk (1953) 67–98; Alexander (1953) 36–66.

[289] On the two different dates for the official proclamation of Iconoclasm, either in 726 or in 730, depending on various primary sources in Mango (1959) 113, 170–174.

[290] On the extent of Iconoclasm and its different layers, chronologically and geographically, more in Gero (1974); Brubaker and Haldon (2011) 109–11; 199–212.

[291] Ousterhout (2001b) 3–19; Ruggieri (1991).

rather from declining imperial control over marble quarries and silver production, and the loss of territories in Africa and the eastern sections of the empire (Map 3, Tables 5, 6). A significant number of altar, shrine, and baptistery canopies from the western sections of the Byzantine Empire along the Adriatic littoral can be dated precisely to the period between the eighth and mid-ninth centuries through inscriptions and historical documents, thus overlapping with the period of the Iconoclastic debates. This hypothesis can be additionally supported by assessing the overall use of canopies associated with icons in the Byzantine tradition until the fifteenth century, and by considering the dynamics of producing canopies and the devotional use of icons on canopies, both geographically and chronologically.

Archeological material concerning canopies reveals that there is not enough evidence to suggest the use of canopies was discontinued during the Iconoclasm. Throughout this time, a relatively small number of newly built churches could have been dedicated without sacred relics.[292] Canopies related to saintly tombs, relics, and icons could have not been used during the period, but this does not indicate the same fate for the canopies over altar tables, which sheltered the Eucharistic mysteries. The sixth-century altar decoration with representations of the Eucharist under an altar canopy from the Monophysite Church of Mâr Gabriel, near Kartman, Turkey, clearly depicts the altar table with the vessels of the Eucharist under a domed canopy, surmounted by an orb, with two censers suspended from the canopy's roof and flanked by trees (Fig. 2.65).[293] Because Monophysites like the Byzantine Iconoclasts rejected the representation of the human nature of Christ, the mosaic from Mâr Gabriel confirms that the canopy as an object could have been in use during the

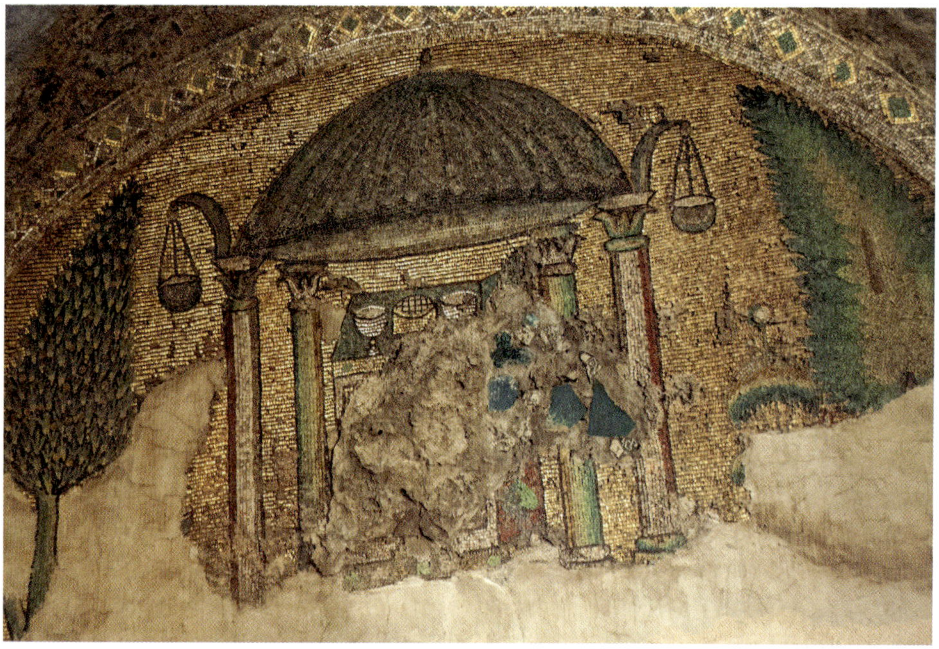

FIGURE 2.65 *Apse mosaic showing altar canopy installation, Mâr Gabriel, near Kartman (Tur 'Abdin), in Anatolia, modern Turkey, ca. 512.* PHOTO DANIEL C. WAUGH

---

[292] *Patriarch Nicephorus of Constantinople, Antirrheticus (Refutation)* 2.5; *Theodore of Studion, Orations* 9.12. According to Pelikan (1974) 92–93.

[293] Mundell (1975) 59–74; Hawkins, Mundell, and Mango (1973) 279–296; Lafli and Bru (2013) 287–303.

Iconoclastic controversy. The trend of the continual use of canopies for altar tables, baptisteries, holy water fonts, and tombs as established in the Early Byzantine period can be observed after the ninth century (Tables 5, 6, Maps 4, 5).

Not even canopy-like installations for especially venerated icons can definitely point to changes in the use of canopies after the Iconoclasm. Some canopies could have been demolished because of figurative depictions on them.[294] The text of the twelfth-century Madrid Skylitzes manuscript, which accompanies the illustration of a canopy-like installation with attached icons, explains that Iconoclast Patriarch John VII (d. before 867) removed these icons during the Iconoclasm.[295] Text from the *Palatine Anthology* records the reattachment of icons to the altar canopy in Constantinopolitan Hagia Sophia, which were removed during the Iconoclasm, and also demonstrates that the canopy itself was not destroyed. [296] Then again, surviving contemporaneous canopies from the western frontiers along the Adriatic reveal extensive figurative decoration, confirming that the removal of figurative images from canopies was not methodical across the empire, apparently not on the peripheries. This trend coincides with the similarly non-systematic removal of icons during Iconoclasm, which was centered in Constantinople.[297]

Although the earliest archeological evidence for canopies above icons can be dated to the tenth century, the phenomenon of the *proskynetaria* installations cannot be exclusively related to the post-Iconoclastic period. Visual evidence suggests that *proskynetaria* might have existed well before the tenth century. The sixth-century manuscript illumination from the Rabbula Gospels depicts a canopy, which presumably shelters an icon of the Mother of God with the Christ Child (Fig. 2.66). Texts, images, and archeology reveal that icons could have been placed either on the altar table framed by a canopy or throughout the church, independent of the altar: on the sanctuary screen as in the Church of the Nativity in Bogolyubovo, next to the sanctuary barrier as in a *proskynetaria* in St. Panteleimon in Nerezi, on piers and pillars in the nave as in the Church of St. Sophia in Monemvasia, in the church aisles as in Hagia Sophia in Constantinople, or in the narthex flanking the entrance to the nave as in St. John Eleemon in Argolis.

The types of canopies used in Byzantine churches are habitually defined by the particular ritual function they had within the church proper. While the Byzantine rite itself is a hybrid of various practices and had had its own development from the earliest times of Christianity, Marinis has effectively demonstrated that most elements of the Byzantine rite, and above all the Divine Liturgy itself, underwent minimal changes over time that would demand explicit architectural modifications, including during Iconoclastic disputes.[298] Two major features of the Byzantine rite as formulated in Constantinople gradually outlined its distinctiveness from other liturgical traditions, but these had seemingly minor relevance for altering architectural church design. One was the decline of outdoor processions after the seventh century, even if the rite remained processional in its character, and the other was its enrichment by imperial splendor and ceremony, evidently after the completion of Hagia Sophia in the sixth century. Hence, Byzantine churches after the transitional period (seventh to ninth centuries) differed from their early Christian precedents in terms of tectonics and size; as a result of which, there were changes in the liturgical and other services performed within the churches as they became more centralized, compact, and less

[294] Gero (2000) 331–343.

[295] Cutler (1987) 145–154.

[296] Oikonomides (1985) 111–115.

[297] Cormack (1975a) 35–44.

[298] Marinis (2014).

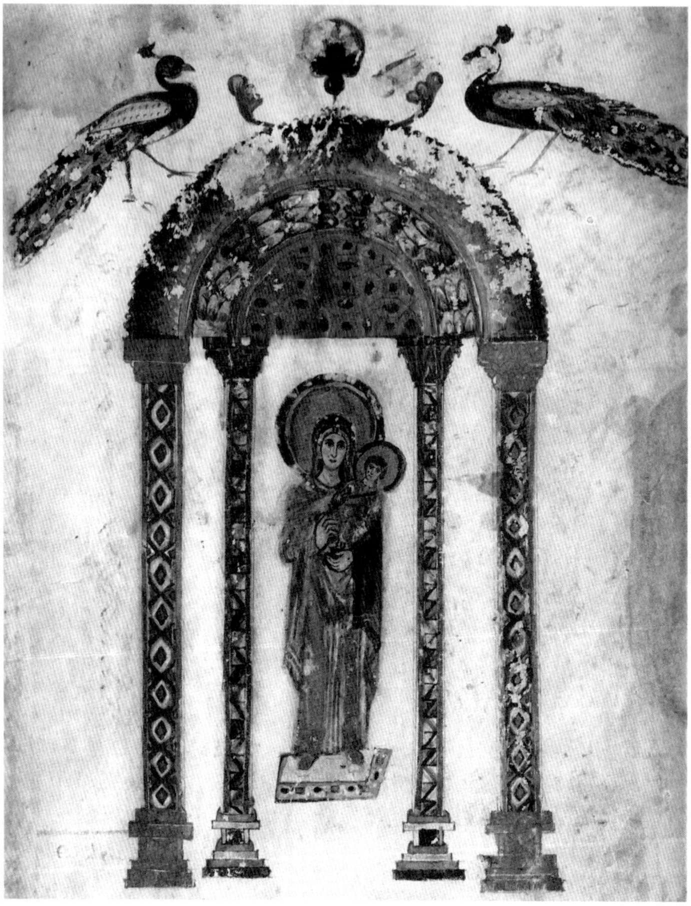

FIGURE 2.66 *Icon of the Mother of God and Christ Child under canopy,* Rabbula Gospels *fol. 1b, Syria, 586.* ALINARI/ART RESOURCE, NEW YORK

processional, and as various rites developed and became more elaborate within the church proper. Despite these changes in church space and liturgical practice, the architects of the Middle and Late Byzantine churches continued to use the potential of canopies to point to the location of these various rites and architecturally frame the sacred place and focus of the sacraments, prayers, readings, and other services.

Throughout a millennium-long tradition, within a Byzantine church and its subsidiary spaces, canopies were located at several significant locations (Figs. 2.67, 2.68, 2.69, 2.70; Tables 5, 6). *Arcosolia,* canopy-like installations in Christian houses, and fully developed canopies first sheltered baptismal basins in the third century. It is generally accepted that, as the need for adult baptism ceased in the later periods, there was no need for a full-size baptistery and consequently a large canopy above it. However, adult baptism was practiced in Thessaloniki until the fourteenth century.[299] Mass baptisms of new converts into Christianity, like the Russians, happened after the ninth century, and visual evidence suggests that these would happened within large canopied installations. Starting in at least the

[299] Gouma-Peterson (1978) 197+199–216.

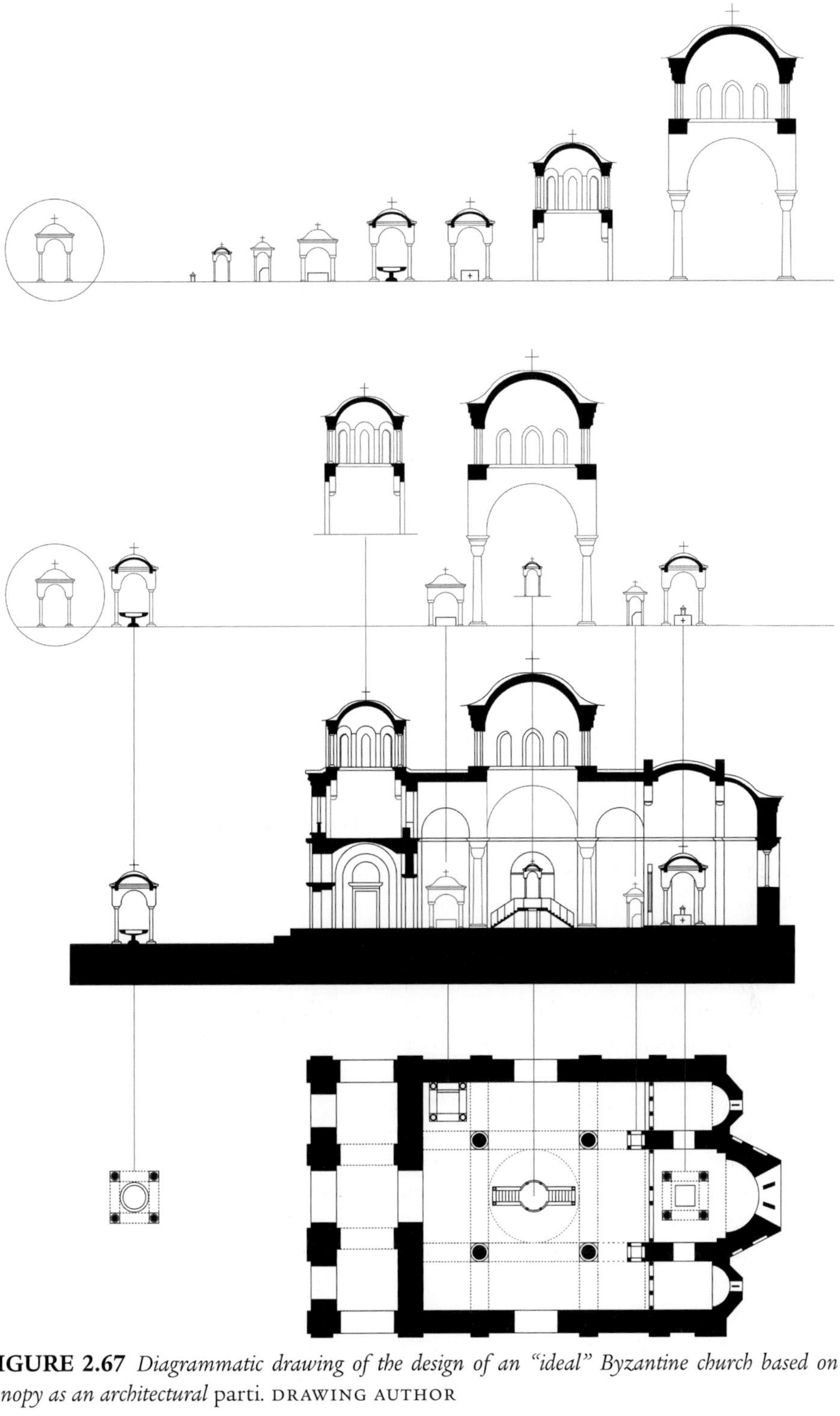

FIGURE 2.67 *Diagrammatic drawing of the design of an "ideal" Byzantine church based on a canopy as an architectural* parti. DRAWING AUTHOR

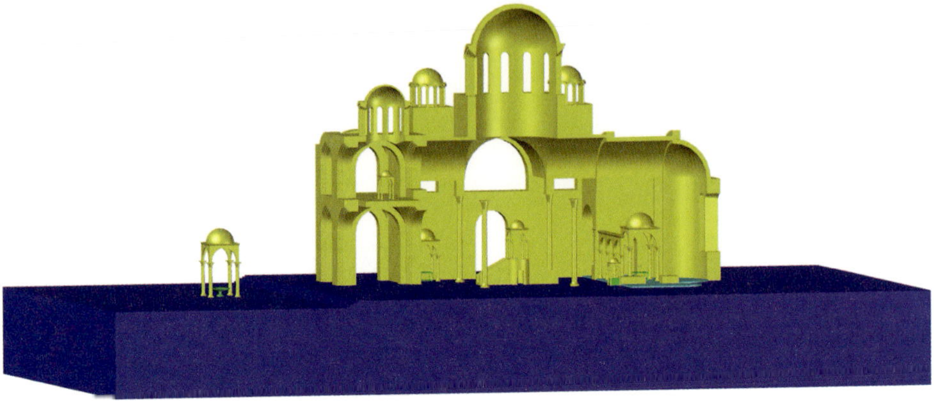

FIGURE 2.68 *Diagrammatic three-dimensional model of an "ideal" Byzantine church based on a canopy as an architectural* parti. DRAWING ZHENGYANG HUA

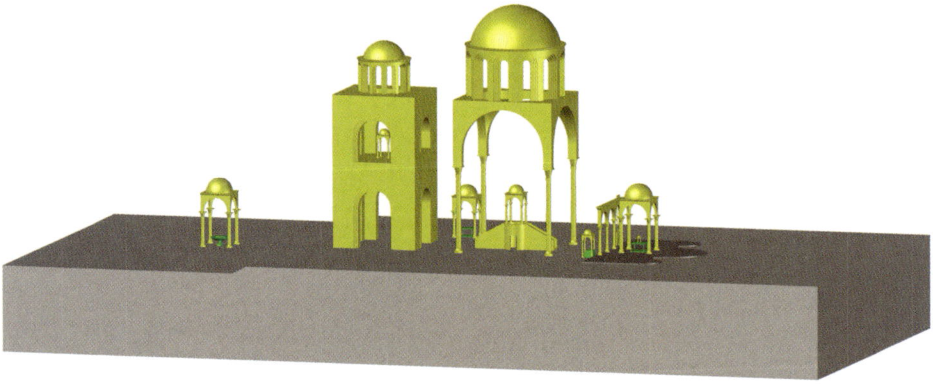

FIGURE 2.69 *Diagrammatic three-dimensional model of an "ideal" Byzantine church constituted of canopies of different size and scale.* DRAWING ZHENGYANG HUA

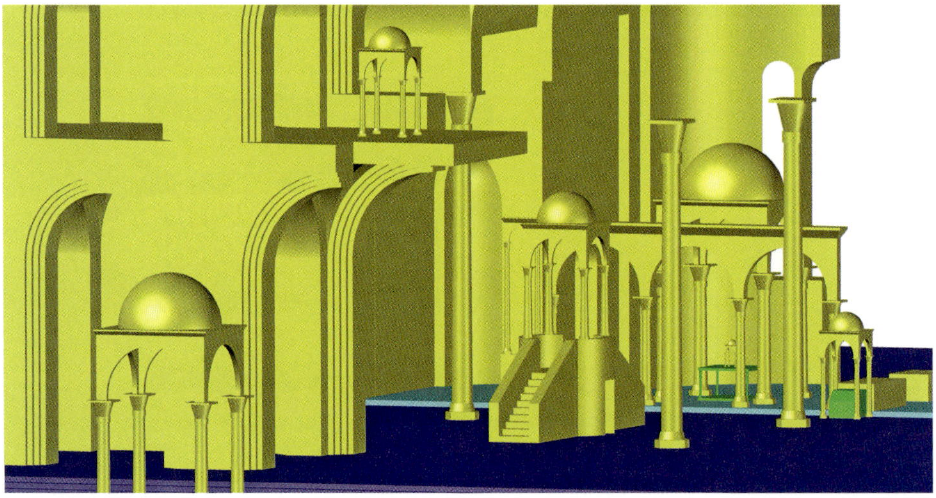

FIGURE 2.70 *Diagrammatic three-dimensional model demonstrating beholder's experience of sacred locations mapped by canopies within an "ideal" Byzantine church.* DRAWING ZHENGYANG HUA

sixth century, the ceremony of the blessing of water in a separate *phiale* was performed in the church atrium under canopies located over holy water fonts, although the eleventh-century canopy from the monastery of St. George of Mangana in Constantinople is the earliest ascertained example to archeologically verify such a practice in Constantinople. In the altar space, canopies were sheltering the holy table by at least the fifth century. At least since the sixth century, canopies were occasionally situated above the ambos in the main space of the church. This practice of using canopied ambo installations, though not widespread, continued in later periods, mostly in larger churches. Canopied installations sheltering saints' relics and the tombs of privileged individuals were used continuously throughout the Byzantine period and could have been placed in various locations inside and outside churches. Archeologically confirmed since the tenth century and potentially dating from even earlier, canopy-like installations were used in conjunction with especially venerated icons and relics (*proskynetaria*). Canopies over bells and bishops' thrones also existed in Middle and Late Byzantine churches.

The majority of known monumental canopies are altar canopies. These altar canopies can be confirmed also by their more-or-less fixed location within the church proper, in the sanctuary. Other types of canopies could have been found literally everywhere within the sacred space of the church, in both the interior and the exterior. Archeology reveals, moreover, that occasionally one canopy could serve more than one function, as when altar canopies also enclosed saintly tombs. Often it is impossible to establish the linear development of such canopied installations that belong to several types simultaneously. For example, some canopies could have framed the tomb of an important individual first and then a baptistery, as archeology confirmed in Bargala, but also the other way around, first the baptistery and then the tomb, like in the Jucundus chapel baptistery.

Seemingly various architectural forms of canopies were continuously used from the earliest archeologically verified Christian sites until the end of the Byzantine Empire. This is vividly exemplified by the third-century baptistery canopy of Dura Europos, in modern Syria, and the fifteenth-century canopy over a *phiale* in Thessaloniki, Greece. These two canopies, one a half-canopy on two columns and the other a full, four-columned canopy, are not only different in design but also significantly different in size, physical appearance, and artistic quality. The form of most canopies throughout the Mediterranean basin, regardless of their primary function, is actually limited to a narrow range of shapes. Byzantine canopies are usually centrally planned structures, most often with four columns with capitals that carry four arches that support the flat stone slab cut in the center to receive the heavy pyramidal or domical roof as a lid. The form of a canopy, however, cannot point to its specific type, commonly defined by the functional context of a particular canopy. Most altar canopies were four-columned structures. Yet four-columned canopies also framed tombs and baptisteries. Baptistery canopies were frequently four-, six-, or eight-columned installations.

The majority of known canopies were made of fine-quality stone or of silver. Some canopies were cast in bronze and iron and decorated with gems, semiprecious stones, and glass, or were sometimes gilded. Wooden canopies may have been more common, though only a few later examples have survived. When canopies were made of wood, it is likely that many of them would have been sheathed in silver or other precious materials. The choice of marble and silver for canopies suggests that canopies were considered especially valued furnishings. The use of polychromy and decorative patterns is also revealing in this regard. Occasionally, still-visible traces of color and gold on both the exterior and interior of a canopy confirm the special care given to their physical appearance as well as their potential continuity with classical sculpture and architecture, which were also painted. Later examples that survive—richly decorated and painted with figurative images and narratives from the Scriptures as in Kalabaka, Sveti Choveli in Mcheta, or in Coptic churches—presumably emphasized the special sacredness of the place they marked and enclosed within the church premises.

The repertoire of designs for canopy members is surprisingly homogenous for canopies of different kinds and canopies found in geographically distant areas. The formulaic execution of canopies can be explained by some kind of standardization of elements and the diffusion of technical and stylistic solutions. Stylistic analysis can be very fruitful in searching for the localized workshops for the production of canopies and liturgical furnishings as well as revealing their relationship to the design of entire church structures. At the same time, stylistic analysis is frequently focused on the search for the origins and evolutionary developments of canopies and the themes represented on them. Such a methodology can point to certain centers of production of canopied installations, such as the centers in Constantinople, Kotor, or Zadar; yet in terms of sources of the origins of these structures, it often presents contradictory results. For example, canopies made in Zadar were equally related to Byzantine and Carolingian sources.

After the transitional period of economic decline (seventh to ninth centuries), canopies continued to be built, many from *spolia* and a significant number of new canopies from local materials with local stylistic features. Stylistic characteristics of these later canopies seemingly betray the main trends in the Byzantine artistic tradition as known from the main centers and earlier periods. Not a single canopy from Constantinople has been preserved *in situ*; subsequently, direct comparisons are difficult to make. The canopied *minbar* from the Pantokrator monastery, even if reassembled and altered to the point that it is extremely difficult to contextualize any of its critical aspects with certainty, remains critical for understanding that canopies, new and made anew, were used in Constantinople over a prolonged period of time. These later installations, despite problematic stylistic analysis and obscure origins, testify to the continual and copious use of canopies. Multiple canopies—in the Cathedral of St. Tryphon in Kotor, Montenegro, or in some Russian churches, not only above altar tables, but also above ambos, tombs, *phialai*, icons, bishop thrones, and even above sanctuary screens as in Bogolyubovo and Uspenski Sabor in Moscow Kremlin[300]—potentially represent a mirror-image of similar trends in the major centers of Byzantine Empire, confirmed by the prolonged existence of multiple canopies in Constantinopolitan cathedral Hagia Sophia and in the churches of Hagios Demetrios and Hagia Sophia in Thessaloniki. Newcomers in the Byzantine Commonwealth presumably slavishly copied contemporary trends in the use of canopies from Byzantine churches. The greater variety in design, material, and above all quality of artistic accomplishment, which is manifest in these later canopies, suggests the definite loss of imperial control over the production and distribution of liturgical furnishings throughout the empire and its Christian neighbors, a trend that can be detected in the Early and Middle Byzantine periods.

Some later canopies that have survived, either in photographs or in fragments, are usually treated as examples of local and non-Byzantine trends, most readily Western European or Islamic. Canopies from the Adriatic littoral, whose style had earlier been unconditionally attributed to Romanesque and Gothic trends in Western Europe, can be related to wider trends within Byzantine church tradition. Surviving later canopies in Orthodox churches in the Balkans are habitually qualified as stylistically Baroque and Neo-Classical objects but are usually separated by and from humanist vocabulary and related to "Oriental" and more precisely Ottoman furniture.[301] The decline of production of monumental church

---

300 Vežić (2001–2002) 91–122; Voronin (1961) 251–258; Sterligova (2000) 360–381.

301 Hoddinott (1954) 278–283. In contrast, Baroque-looking canopies in churches in the west-northern parts of the Balkans are related to church furniture introduced under Catholic reform.

furnishings, including stone canopies, is routinely related to the emergence of wooden carved canopies stemming from high-quality Ottoman woodwork.[302] However, archeological evidence confirms that wooden canopies had already existed before Ottoman conquest. The stylistic dependence on wooden furniture in the Ottoman architecture and post-Byzantine churches is a separate question, which has never been juxtaposed, for example, with already noticed stylistic interactions between the so-called proto-Byzantine and proto-Romanesque canopies in the Adriatic littoral. More recent canopies from post-Byzantine churches support my hypothesis concerning the continual use of canopies and that previous notions about their limited use and non-inherent role in Byzantine churches must be superseded. Some of these later canopies, including several cases of canopied *minbars* reassembled from Byzantine installations and used in Ottoman mosques, could have been developed from Byzantine canopies. Similarly, the post-Byzantine canopies in churches in the eastern Mediterranean most likely extended a much older tradition, rather than being simply reintroduced into Orthodox churches as a consequence of the general intellectual and theological trends concerning the use and meaning of church canopies in the sixteenth and seventeenth centuries, as typified by Bernini's famous *baldacchino* in St. Peter's Basilica in the Vatican.[303] This hypothesis is supported by the analysis of positivistic scholarship on canopies based on textual sources, as examined in Chapter 1.

Comparative analysis of the quality of execution of canopies, coupled with stylistic analysis, may point to the centers of production of canopies and other liturgical furnishings, while the acknowledged difference in production and distribution of church furnishings, especially in the period after the sixth century, most effectively explains the demonstrable decline in the overall quality of canopies in the later periods. Within this apparent decline of imperial control over the production of canopies, the constant insistence on generic and formulaic motifs, even when the artisans were obviously less skilled and the material used *spolia* or new material often of lesser quality, suggests yet another parallel phenomenon—the emphasis on the historical continuity of the present with the sacred past, both Christian and pre-Christian, either Hellenistic or Jewish. This continuity within discontinuity can be exemplified by this chapter's opening tenth-century account of the altar canopy from Paros, which clearly draws parallels between the Christian and ancient past.

The iconographical analysis of decorative motifs cannot confirm the functional type of canopies, as sepulchral, salvific, and Christological motifs can equally suggest altar, tomb, baptismal, ambo, or *proskynetaria* canopies. Yet the content of decorative motifs and the narrative they establish within the ritual performances in the church, as well as their specific locations in the larger network of sacred space, reveal important messages that specific canopied installations carried. The delicate reference to the Christmas hymn recreated from a richly carved marble arch of a canopy, originally part of either a tomb or an altar installation, is just one example of how canopies articulated the perception of the merging of the earthly and the heavenly, the present and eternity (Table 7.217). Such spatial and temporal qualities establish canopies as markers of places of spiritual transformation.

To those who fully participated in the Byzantine religious and cultural life, canopies inclusive of their location, shape, materiality, decoration, and inscriptions provided the most nuanced ways for establishing meaningful relationships between people, various concepts, historical traditions, and sacred places. Indeed, only the faithful and educated elite could participate in all the subtleties and multiple meanings canopies provided within

---

302 Sodini (2002) 129–145.

303 On the influence of Bernini's canopy for those in Counter-Reformation Europe, see, for example, Kirwin (1997) 189–233; Moore (2017).

Byzantine-rite churches. Yet even for the illiterate many, the illegible and obscure inscriptions and decorative motifs would still denote sacredness and the importance of canopies. The opening example of the intended reappropriation of the canopy from the Paros church as a *minbar* in a mosque, and references to pagan chieftains who appropriated church canopies for their tents and thrones, confirm how impressive these micro-architectural structures were to even those coming from outside the Byzantine cultural realm.

The next chapters highlight how some already observed trends of "Byzantine humanism" and "revivals" supported by textual and archeological evidence are closely intertwined with the form and meaning of canopies in the definition of the sacred and place-making. By raising questions about places of human encounter with the sacred, canopies reveal their role in understanding Byzantine humanism and its dependence on observed conflating processes with Hellenistic and Jewish traditions, which are historically most closely related to the Byzantine Christian tradition. Various anachronistic phenomena that accompany our perception of Byzantine canopies can be explained most concisely and almost paradoxically by constant renewals of continuity in the use and meaning of canopies. Whether we can also trace these apparent changes and discontinuities within the Byzantine sense of continuity by focusing on the places canopies define is a separate question, which calls for a thematic rather than a chronological or geographical examination of canopies.

THREE

Place-Making

The Place of the Canopy in the Church

In the center of the wide church, yet tending rather toward the east is a kind of tower, fair to look upon, set apart the abode of the sacred books. Upright it stands on steps, reached by two flights, one of which extends towards the night, the other towards the dawn.

...

And as an island rises amidst the waves of the sea, adorned with cornfields, and vineyards, and blossoming meadows, and wooded heights, while the travelers who sail by are gladdened by it and are soothed of the anxieties and exertions of the sea; so in the midst of the boundless temple rises upright the tower-like ambo of stone adorned with its meadows of marble, wrought with the beauty of the craftsman's art. Yet, it does not stand altogether cut off in the central space, like a sea-girt island, but it rather resembles some wave-lashed land, extended through the white-capped billows by an isthmus into the middle of the sea, and being joined fast at one point it cannot be a true island. Projecting into the watery deep, it is still joined to the mainland coast by the isthmus, as by a cable.

...

Here the priest who brings the good tidings passes along upon his return from the ambo, holding aloft the golden book; and while the crowd strives in honor of the immaculate God to touch the sacred book with their lips and hands, the countless waves of the surging people break around. Thus like an isthmus beaten by waves on either side, does this space stretch out, and it leads the priest who descends from the lofty crags of this vantage point to shrine of the holy table.

Ἔστι τις εὐρυπόροιο κατ᾽ ἔνδια μέσσα μελάθρου ἁβρὸς ἰδεῖν καὶ μᾶλλον ἐς ἀντολίην τι νενευκὼς πύργος, ἀκηρασίοισιν ἀπόκριτος ἤθεσι βίβλων, †ὄρθιος βάθροις, διδυμάοσιν ἀμβατὸς οἴμοις, ὧν μία μὲν ποτὶ νύκτα τιταίνεται, ἡ δὲ πρὸς ἠῶ.

...

Ὡς δὲ θαλασσαίοισιν ἐν οἴδμασι νῆσος ἀνίσχει, δαιδαλέη σταχύεσσι καὶ ἀμπελόεντι κορύμβωι καὶ θαλερῶι λειμῶνι καὶ εὐδένδροισιν ἐρίπναις· τὴν δὲ παραπλώοντες ἐπολβίζουσιν ὁδῖται, ἄλγεα βουκολέοντες ἀλικμήτοιο μερίμνης· οὕτω ἀπειρεσίοιο κατ᾽

ἔνδια μέσσα μελάθρου λάεσι πυργωθεὶς ἀναφαίνεται ὄρθιος ἄμβων, δαιδαλέος λειμῶνι λίθων καὶ κάλλεϊ τέχνης. ναὶ μὴν οὐδ᾽ ὅγε πάμπαν ἀπόκριτος ἐς μέσον ἔστη χῶρον, ἁλιζώνοισιν ὁμοίιος ἤθεσι νήσων· ἀλλ᾽ ἄρα μᾶλλον ἔοικεν ἁλιρροθίωι τινὶ γαίηι, ἥν πολιοῦ προβλῆτα δι᾽ οἴδματος ἰσθμὸς ἐλαύνει μεσσατίοις πελάγεσσι, μιῆς δ᾽ ἀπὸ δέσμιον ἀρχῆς ὀχμάζων ἀνέκοψεν ἀληθέα νῆσον ὁρᾶσθαι· ἡ δὲ θαλασσαίοισιν ἐπιπροθέουσα ῥεέθροις ἴσθμιον ἀγχιάλοιο καθήψατο πεῖσμα κολώνης.

. . .

ἔνθεν ὑποτροπάδην χρυσέην εὐάγγελος ἀνὴρ βίβλον ἀερτάζων διανίσσεται. ἱεμένης δὲ πληθύος, ἀχράντοιο θεοῦ κατὰ μύστιδα τιμήν, χείλεα καὶ παλάμας ἱερὴν περὶ βίβλον ἐρεῖσαι, κύματα κινυμένων περιάγνυται ἄσπετα δήμων. Καί ῥ᾽ ὁ μὲν ἀμφιπλῆγι τιταίνεται εἴκελος ἰσθμῶι χῶρος, ἀπιθύνων πρὸς ἀνάκτορα σεμνὰ τραπέζης ἄνδρα καταθρώσκοντα βαθυκρήμνου περιωπῆς·

Paulos Silentarios, poet and official of Emperor Justinian (r. 527–565)[1]

• • •

[I return] to the floor, the sea out of which we have said the holy sanctuary has been scooped, as the sea would do it. From there is a certain isthmus; at this spot there is a passage, and the holy tribune comes to shore at the isthmus, just as though it were a cargo-vessel, and that it may rest un-tossed by the waves, it lowers from above its anchors of silver, the columns, down to the ground. And the cargo-vessel has ferried in the great quantity of silver. What should I say about the steps, by which one may go up into the tribune, and the further varied material which roofs it over-many-wreathed cones, stoas dancing in a circle, a pattern with many sides, little gates which go out and around, halves of circles and epicycles cleft in two, all of silver whose form has been wrought with gold? How should I not fall away from the mean, wishing also to describe the wings, truly golden, of the blameless dove of the church? I mean that one, opposite to us; this one that is with us. But come now, having anointed it with myrrh, I shall release the dove. And indeed, I shall be using this proverb at a timely moment. Where is the myrrh? Who else will deliver to us the oracle, if it be not David, he who would say today, "as is myrrh upon the head . . . ?"

*** πέλαγος ἐξ οὗ φαμὲν ἀποκολπωθῆναι νόμῳ πελάγους τὸ Θεῖον ἄδυτον. ἔστι τις ἰσθμὸς ἐντεῦθεν ἐκεῖ διάβασις, καὶ προσοκέλλει τούτῳ ὁ ἱερὸς ὀκρίβας, καθάπερ εἴ τις φορτίς, ἵνα δ᾽ ἀκύμαντος μένῃ καὶ ἀργυρᾶς τὰς κίονας ἄνωθεν χαλᾷ πρὸς τὸ ἔδαφος ἐνεπορεύσατο δὲ καὶ τὸν πολὺν ἄργυρον ἡ φορτίς. τί ἂν λέγοιμι καὶ περὶ πρισμάτον, δι᾽ ὧν ἀναβαίνειν ἔστι εἰς τὸν ὀκρίβαντα, καὶ τὴν λοιπὴν ποικιλίαν τῆς ὀροφούσης ὕλης αὐτόν, κώνους πολυστεφάνους, κύκλῳ χορεύοντας στοάς, πολύπλευρον σκάριφον, πυλίδιά τινα ἐκπεριιόντα καὶ κύκλων ἡμίση καὶ ἐπικύκλων διχοτομήματα, τὰ πάντα χρυσίῳ μορφαζόμενον ἄργυρον; πῶς δ᾽ ἂν μὴ ἔξωτοῦ μέτρου πέσοιμι, διαγράφειν ἐθέλων καὶ τὰς χρυσᾶς ὄντως πτερύγας τῆς ἀμωμήτου περιστερᾶς τῆς ἐκκλησίας; φημι ἐκείνην, καθ᾽ ἡμᾶς. ἀλλὰ φέρε, μύρῳ τὴν τοιαύτην χρίσας ἀπολύσω περιστεράν, καὶ τοῦτο γὰρ εὐκαίρως παροιμιάσομαι. ποῦ τὸ μύρον ; τις ἡμῖν ἄλλος χρήσει, ἐὰν μὴ Δαυίδ, ὁ σήμερον ἂν εἰπών, ὡς μύρον ἐπὶ κεφαλῆς . . .

Michael of Thessaloniki, deacon of Hagia Sophia and rector of the Patriarchal Academy under tenure of Emperor Manuel I Komnenos (r. 1143–1180)[2]

---

[1] *Paulos Silentarios-b,* lines 50–54; 224–239; 247–254. Translation into English by Cyril Mango in *Paulos Silentarios-c* 91, 95–96, and Barry (2007) 627–656, esp. 647.

[2] Mango and Parker (1960) 233–245, esp. 240.

These two literati writing six hundred years apart, Paulos Silentarios in the sixth century and Michael of Thessaloniki in the twelfth century, poetically described the now-lost ambo in Hagia Sophia in Constantinople. For both of them, the ambo, similar to the altar canopy in the same church, is a tower-like construction. Paulos Silentarios does not speak of the roof of the ambo installation, yet Michael of Thessaloniki also mentions an elaborately decorated silver roof, indicating that, at least by the twelfth century, the ambo in Hagia Sophia was canopied and visually resembled the canopied altar installation. The ambo was set in the midst of the church nave, just below the dome and elevated from the floor by a flight of stairs. It was connected to the altar installation by an isthmus, a *solea* passage. Along this linear passage, the towering ambo mirrored the altar canopy located behind the screen in the sanctuary. Spatially and symbolically, the ambo—which was in the nave, the "ark" of the church—was therefore both an extension and reflection of the altar installation in the holiest space of the church, in the sanctuary.

Both Paulos Silentarios and Michael of Thessaloniki liken the floor of Hagia Sophia, covered with Prokonnesian marble slabs with wavy, gray veining, to the sea.[3] Like an island and a cargo vessel, the ambo was in the midst of this sea. The ambo, "the abode of the sacred books" and from which the words of God were pronounced, was elevated from the floor that represented primordial sea and positioned as if suspended in midair, just below the monumental golden dome representing the heavens. Architecturally—both sensory and intellectually—the ambo framed the divinely inspired actions, starting with God's creation of the heavens and the earth and the parting of the waters as described in Genesis.[4] The waves of the sea-like floor were compared with the animated matter as it becomes alive, signifying the presence of *pneuma*, the breath of life religiously understood as the divine spirit.[5] The "living, breathing" body of the church is further likened to the waves of the faithful as they strive to honor God and touch the Holy Scriptures as the priest moves along the passage between the ambo and the sanctuary. The dynamic movement of the church community simultaneously marked the great litany and the spiritual progress of the faithful. Michael of Thessaloniki in his narrative thus pointed to Psalm 133:2–3, an ode of ascent by David: "It is like the precious ointment upon the head, that runs down upon the beard, . . . and as the dew that descended upon the mountains of Zion: for there the Lord commanded the blessing, even life for everyone."

In these accounts, the merging of the Biblical references, the liturgy, and the actions of the faithful, all in connection with a canopy, afford us a better understanding of the qualities of canopied installations in Byzantine-rite churches that provide singular experience, despite their somewhat homogenous architectural design and generic descriptions as individual objects in texts. This complex synthesis suggests that canopies, set locally and singularly defined in an ecclesiastical setting and time, aspired to encapsulate a common spiritual experience of the faithful. The analysis in this chapter will focus on specific archeologically confirmed canopies of the Dura Europos baptistery installation, the altar and ambo installations preserved *in situ* on the island of Paros and in Kalabaka, and the unique early Christian canopy from an unidentified church in the Middle East from the Royal Ontario Museum collection. The examination of these relatively well-preserved canopies will allow us to contextualize them in their setting and understand better their role in Byzantine-rite churches and in the framing of sacred space. This chapter ends with a discussion of the canopies that once existed in Constantinopolitan Hagia Sophia. Hagia Sophia served as a

[3] Barry (2007) 627–656.

[4] Schibille (2014) 101.

[5] Pentcheva (2010) 137–137.

model for Byzantine-rite churches for more than a millennium and will provide an opening program for the next chapters, which investigate several different concepts of framing space along with various symbolic meanings of the architectural design of Byzantine-rite churches based on micro-architecture of canopies.

DURA-EUROPOS BAPTISMAL CANOPY

The archeological excavations of the 1920s and 1930s at Dura Europos, a former Roman military camp in Syria, revealed one of the earliest canopies used exclusively in the Christian context in the Eastern Mediterranean and beyond.[6] A Christian house built around 232/233, based on the inscription on the plaster, was at some point, probably a decade later, converted into an ecclesiastical setting with a baptistery as a separate room. The canopy installation from Dura Europos was removed from its original context and is today preserved at Yale University (Fig. 3.1). Yet the archeological evidence of the baptistery canopy from Dura Europos is significant for several reasons. It reveals how the two-columned structures that framed sacred space can and should be considered canopies, prompting us to expand upon the usual typology that a canopy is a self-contained architectonic object and is more-or-less independent of the structure of the church. More importantly, because of documented archeological excavations, which provide a better understanding of the cultural and spatial context of this canopied baptistery, the structure reveals one of the many

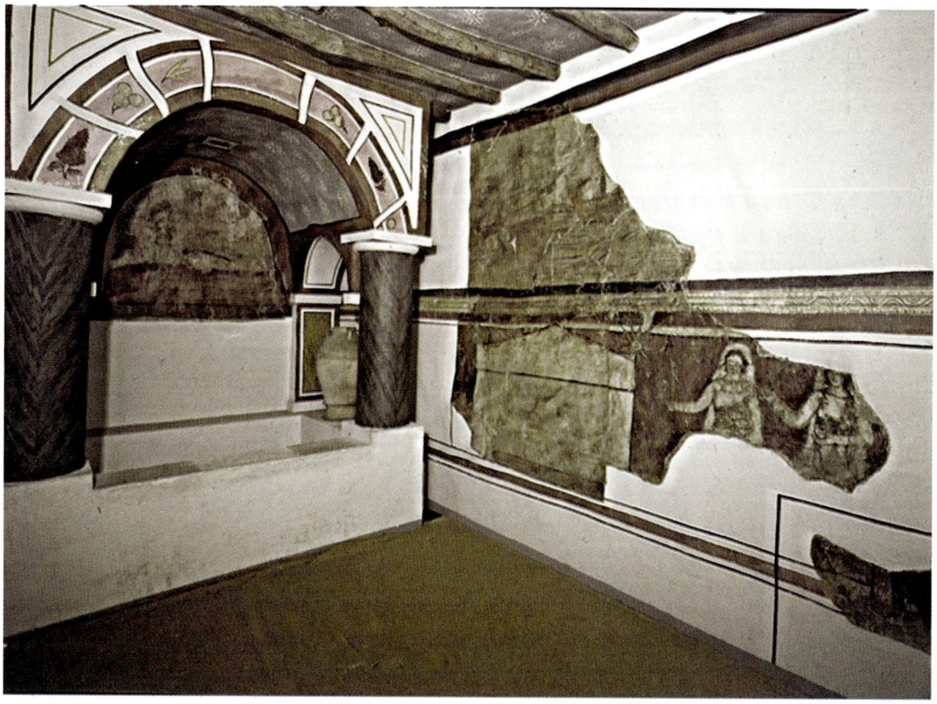

FIGURE 3.1 *Reconstruction of the Christian Baptistery at Yale University Art Gallery, Christian House, Dura Europos, Syria, third century.* COURTESY OF THE YALE UNIVERSITY ART GALLERY, DURA-EUROPOS ARCHIVES

[6] The literature is immense. See, for example, Brody and Hoffmann (2011); Wharton (1995); Weitzmann and Kessler (1990); Gates (1984) 166–181; Hopkins (1979).

sophisticated ways used to design canopies in the Eastern Mediterranean during the early Christian times.

The Dura Europos baptistery installation is made up of a baptismal tub set in a niche against the western wall; this tiny space (approximately 2.5 meters by 1 meter) was articulated with two embedded pilasters in the back wall and two frontal masonry columns spanned by arches and a barrel vault with an intrados painted in sky blue with stars. The baptismal setting conveyed the shape and experience of a canopy-framed sacred space, which was perceived as heavenly and otherworldly. The installation was itself originally set in a room with the ceiling painted as sky, suggesting, in a way, that the central focus in the space was designed to communicate the sense of merging the earthly and heavenly. The installation was used for baptisms, one of the major sacraments of the Christians. Quite in keeping with the Christian understanding that baptism marks one's death in Adam and rebirth in Christ, the entire installation takes the recognizable shape of an *arcosolium*, an arched recess resembling a rock-cut tomb and extensively used for entombments of both Christians and non-Christians throughout the Mediterranean in late antiquity. The Christian baptismal promise of the afterlife in Dura Europos is reinforced with a salvation image depicted in the lunette of the niche. It shows Christ as the Good Shepherd carrying on his shoulders a lamb, which is an allegory of the Christian soul. The idea of the Savior as the Good Shepherd was known to the early Christians from the Scriptures—in the Old Testament in the Psalms by King David (Ps. 23:1–2) and reinforced in the New Testament by Apostles John (Jn. 10:11) and Paul (Rom. 5:8; 14–17).

The salvific messages and the strength of faith that are performatively associated with the rite of baptism, intertwined with notions of literal and spiritual death, resurrection, and illumination, and Christ's epiphany, are here intensified by the surrounding images of the *Healing of the Paralytic, Christ and Peter walking on the Water*, and the *Women at the Tomb*. As shown by Charles B. McClendon, the painted program of the entire baptistery is remarkable in the way that the painted narratives mimicked the use of the room.[7] McClendon explained how, for example, the painted doors are directly opposite the doors in the south wall that connected the baptistery to the courtyard of the Dura Europos church, the feet of the women painted in the remaining decoration in the lower register of the eastern wall are represented as moving in the same direction as anyone entering the room, and the procession of the women toward the Tomb would have emphasized the main east-to-west axis of the chamber, with the baptismal font in the west. The movement through the room and the associated rites would have strongly resonated with the early Syrian testimonies of the ritual of baptism.[8] Pagoulatos further demonstrated that baptism at Dura Europos also included the Byzantine service of Christ the Bridegroom.[9] The real presence of Christ was signified by His image, which the initiated contemplated while moving through the space of the baptistery, and was fully revealed during the service. The initiated are represented on walls like the brides and their souls as birds; the women and birds moving towards the font would have been mystically united with Christ, who revealed Himself as the Bridegroom and the Good Shepherd carrying on His shoulders the saved soul of the baptized after receiving the sacrament of baptism.

Mass baptisms of grown-up individuals during early Christian times required large-sized, full baptismal tubs. The initiated catechumens would enter the room from the courtyard through the doors in the south. Before the actual baptism, the devotees would have

---

7 McClendon (2011) 155–167, esp. 160–161.

8 Ferguson (2009) 438; Brock (2005) 129–132.

9 Pagoulatos (2009).

denounced the power of Satan and been anointed. McClendon convincingly explains that the niche in the southern wall was a receptacle for the holy oil, while the image below it showing David and Goliath expands upon the Biblical narrative of how the anointed David miraculously defeated the evil giant (1 Sam. 16:1–13).[10] Then in the procession, as represented in the images, the initiated would be ritually baptized through cleansing with water three times in the font, possibly exit through the second door in the south into the intermediary room to be clothed in white garments, and then proceed to the assembly hall to receive their first Communion.

Indeed, the Syriac traditions would occasionally differ from the Chalcedonian Orthodox version of Christianity that was officially approved by the Byzantines, most directly regarding the dogmatic questions on the nature of Christ—both human and divine. Yet, like the Byzantines, the Syrian Christians also emphasized the mysteries of the sacraments of baptism, chrismation (anointing with oil), and the Eucharist, in particular, as critical for a Christian's knowing of God, while in contrast to the Byzantines, the Syrians occasionally placed theological precision and investigations as secondary.[11] These theological differences were certainly not critical for the architectural design of the places where sacraments were performed. The elaborate Dura Europos baptistery emphasized the full engagement of the participants in the space and responds to the religious framework of the architectural design of the canopied baptistery installation. Hence, even if it is not of the greatest artistic quality and execution, the sophisticated conceptual design of the Dura Europos baptismal canopy reveals its nuanced meanings that incorporated the architectural articulation of the sacred space of the baptistery through canopy design and its spatial environment and decoration that was meant to be experienced and reenacted through bodily movement.

The Dura Europos canopied baptistery is revealing, and not only as one of the earliest archeological examples of canopied installations used in an exclusively Christian context, since only Christians receive the sacrament of baptism. It is additionally important for understanding the early archeological evidence of canopies in the eastern Mediterranean, which may have developed independently from the official religious or administrative texts that mention canopies and their use, or other texts that may have been poetic, hagiographical, historical, or antiquarian in genre. Indeed, some of these structures, such as Dura Europos, may have relied on references from the Scriptures or preexisting practices of building water fonts for ritual purification, but it is critical to observe how various rites may have contextualized the use of different types of canopied installations in specific religious and spatial settings.

BYZANTINE CANOPIES *IN SITU*: PAROS AND KALABAKA

Due to the irretrievable losses and alterations of most Byzantine-rite churches, canopies still preserved *in situ* and consisting mostly of their original parts are limited to only a few canopies (Table 5). Three canopies at two remote sites in Greece, on the Cycladic island of Paros and in the village of Kalabaka below the rocks of Meteora in Thessaly, are extraordinary examples of surviving Byzantine canopies. The Church of Panagia Ekatontapyliani on Paros still retains its altar canopy (Table 5.64).[12] The Church of the Dormition of the

[10] McClendon (2011) 155–167, esp. 160–161.

[11] Michelson (2014) 144–147.

[12] The church, dedicated to the Dormition of the Virgin, has been since the seventeenth century known as Panagia Ekatontapyliani (literally *Our Lady of the Hundred Gates*) or Katapoliani (literally *in the direction of the sea*). It was built on the remains of two pre-Christian temples, possibly dedicated to Herakles and

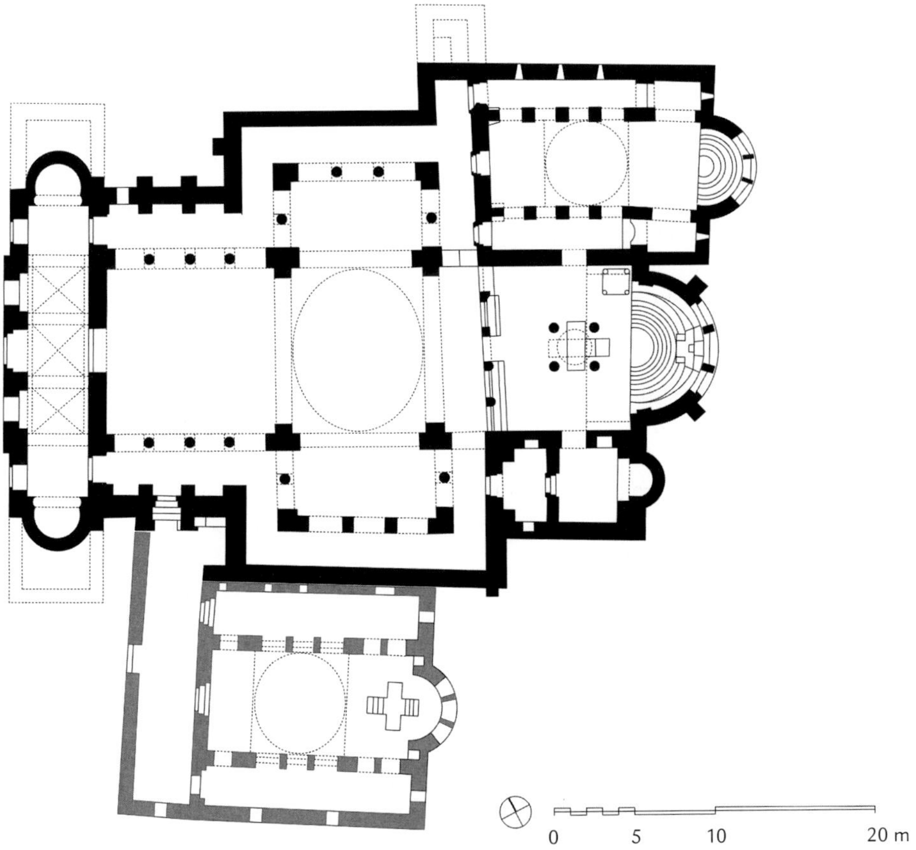

FIGURE 3.2 *Panagia Ekatontapyliani (Katapoliani), Paros, ca. 550.* DRAWING AUTHOR, FROM ĆURČIĆ (2010) 236, FIG. 251

Mother of God in Kalabaka has preserved its Middle-Byzantine altar canopy and the canopy above its ambo, which was traditionally associated with Early Christian period, but recently has been re-dated to the Middle Byzantine period (Table 5.49, 196).[13]

The restored marble canopy from Paros is a relatively big structure—some 2.5 meters by 2.5 meters in plan, and more than 5 meters in height; it is situated almost in the geometric center of the square-based sanctuary bay just in front of the semicircular apse of the basilica (Fig. 3.2).[14] The canopy in its present state is made of various materials and anachronistic elements. The column bases, arches, and roof plaque on which rests a monolithic pumpkin dome are all made of local Parian marble, while column shafts and Corinthian

the poet Archilochus. According to the legend, the church was initially built by Emperor Constantine the Great at the request of his mother, St. Helena, who en route to Jerusalem was forced by bad weather to stop on Paros. An early Christian basilica was rebuilt by the mid-sixth century by Emperor Justinian I. Orlandos (1965) 159–168; Jewell and Hasluck (1920).

13 Orlandos (1965) 159–168; Soteriou (1962) 184–185, 209–213; Soteriou (1931) 86–97. On the new dating of the ambo to the Middle Byzantine period, see Voyatzis (2011) 195–227.

14 Jewell and Hasluck (1920); AliprantĒs (1996) 51–53; Orlandos (1965) 159–168. On the restoration of the altar canopy from Paros, see also Korres (1954) 90; Orlandos (1952–1957) 471–480; Metsane (1996–1997) 319–334.

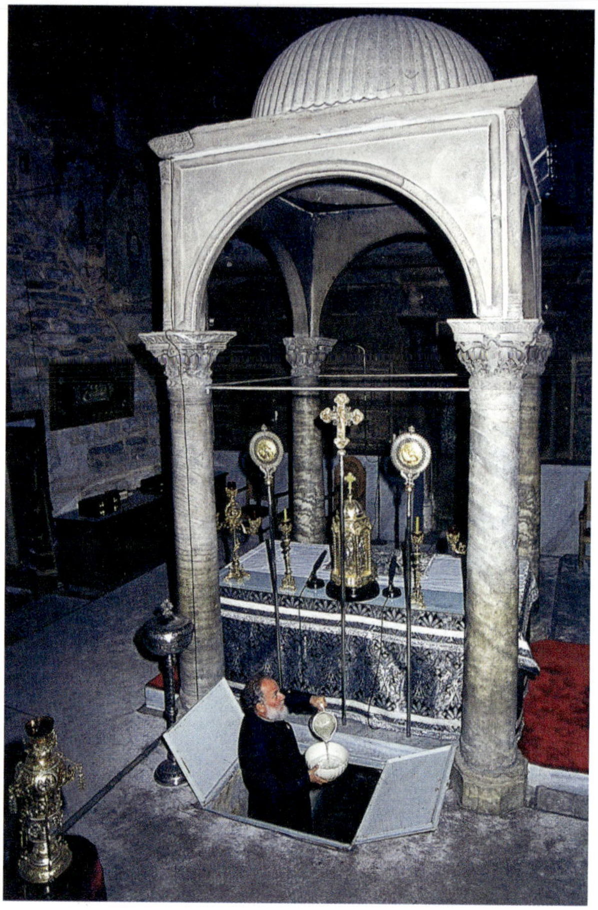

FIGURE 3.3 *Altar canopy, Paros, sixth century (?), restored.* COMMERCIAL POSTCARD

style capitals are made of grayish Prokonnessian marble (Fig. 3.3).[15] The column shafts of Prokonnessian marble are most likely sixth-century elements, while other elements of the canopy are made of local material and (especially the dome) are relatively younger. The fragments of a monolithic canopy dome, similar to the one from the altar canopy, made of local marble are today on display in the narthex of the baptistery built adjacent to the south side of the church.[16] These fragments, along with the seventeenth-century canopy above the *prothesis* table at the northeast corner of the sanctuary, which is in form a smaller replica of the main altar canopy, confirm that local masters occasionally replaced broken canopy fragments with newer ones.[17] Closer examination reveals that the altar canopy from Paros had been broken several times in the past; the earliest reference coming from the tenth century when Niketas Magistros described the Arabs' unsuccessful attempt to remove it to Crete.[18]

[15] Metsane (1996–1997) 319–334; Metsane (1998) 85–95.

[16] In the narthex of the baptistery, there are four fragments that potentially come from the earlier altar canopy. These fragments are rather big—approximately 50 cm × 60 cm, 60 cm × 30 cm, 36 cm × 27 cm, and 34 cm × 36 cm, with the thickness of some 8–9 cm each.

[17] See also Metsane (1998) 85–95, and Korres (1954) 90.

[18] *SD* 104 and *Life StTheokiste* 107. See also Chapter 2 in this volume.

The canopies above the ambo and altar table from the Kalabaka church are similarly made from various elements—reused marble fragments, which were complemented by those from the Middle Byzantine and later periods. The conspicuous canopy above the ambo in Kalabaka is the only such example that has survived, though we have indications that canopies topped ambos in other Byzantine churches (Table 5.16, 48, 49, 198, 228, 229, see also Fig. 2.18).[19] The ambo is situated along the west-to-east axis of the church, fully occupying its center and standing in front of the sanctuary. Approximately 5 meters tall, the ambo with a canopy, which can accommodate both a standing and sitting figure, is rather big and tightly set in the church interior, as if an entire house is packed into the church (Fig. 3.4). The ambo with its canopy, therefore, vividly affirms that the absolute size of the church cannot be a reliable factor for modern contentions that later and relatively smaller Byzantine churches did not have canopies.

In Kalabaka, the entire structure of the ambo topped by a canopy is made of numerous fragments, which confirm its rebuilding over a prolonged period of time.[20] The lower part of the structure is made of various kinds of white, yellowish, and green *verde antico* marble, all of which were available in nearby local quarries active in the late antique period and beyond.[21] Though the footing in the church floor allows for the possibility that an ambo stood in the early Christian basilica, on the foundations of which the present Byzantine church was built, it is not possible to prove whether the architectural elements for the ambo installation came from the earlier basilica or from somewhere else. Sotiris Voyatzis proposed that actually the early Christian basilica never existed and that the church in Kalabaka was built only in the ninth or tenth centuries during the transitional period; its liturgical furnishing made of marble fragments of secondary use sometime between the eleventh and twelfth centuries.[22] The architectural elements of the ambo canopy indeed are not uniform in design and material, and the southeastern part of the ambo is an obvious alteration. The southeastern trapezoidal segment flanking the steps of the ambo is made of a marble parapet slab that resembles the sanctuary screen typical of early Christian basilicas and Middle Byzantine churches.[23] The six-sided canopy above the ambo is made of local white stone, while the pyramidal, wooden roof is decorated with floral motifs and topped by a crest with a golden sphere. In its design, the top resembles the canopies that once existed in Hagia Sophia in Constantinople. The pyramidal roof of the canopy resonates with the sixth-century description of the eight-sided roof of the altar canopy in Hagia Sophia.[24] By the twelfth century, the ambo in Hagia Sophia also had a canopy, though contemporary accounts did not describe how exactly it might have looked.[25] The lower structure of the ambo in Kalabaka is presumably the youngest part of the entire installation, its pyramidal

[19] Orlandos (1965) 159–168; Soteriou (1962) 184–185, 209–213, figs. 117–118; Soteriou (1931) 86–97, fig. 107; Pazaras (1994) 251–254; Voyatzis (2011) 195–227.

[20] For example, six stone columns that support the canopy are not equal in size or sculptural treatment, while some sides of the basket capitals are entirely flat as if originally abutting the wall and not carved in the round to be set in open space.

[21] Karagiorgou (2001) 194–195.

[22] Voyatzis (2011) 195–227.

[23] For some comparative examples, see Sheppard (1969) 65–71, figs. 8–10; Mango and Ševčenko (1973) 235–277, figs. 50, 76, 126–129, 145, 153, 158.

[24] *SD* 88. See also Chapter 1.

[25] Mango and Parker (1960) 233–244; *Clavijo* 74. On the ambo as described in the sixth century with no reference to its canopy, see Xydis (1947) 1–24.

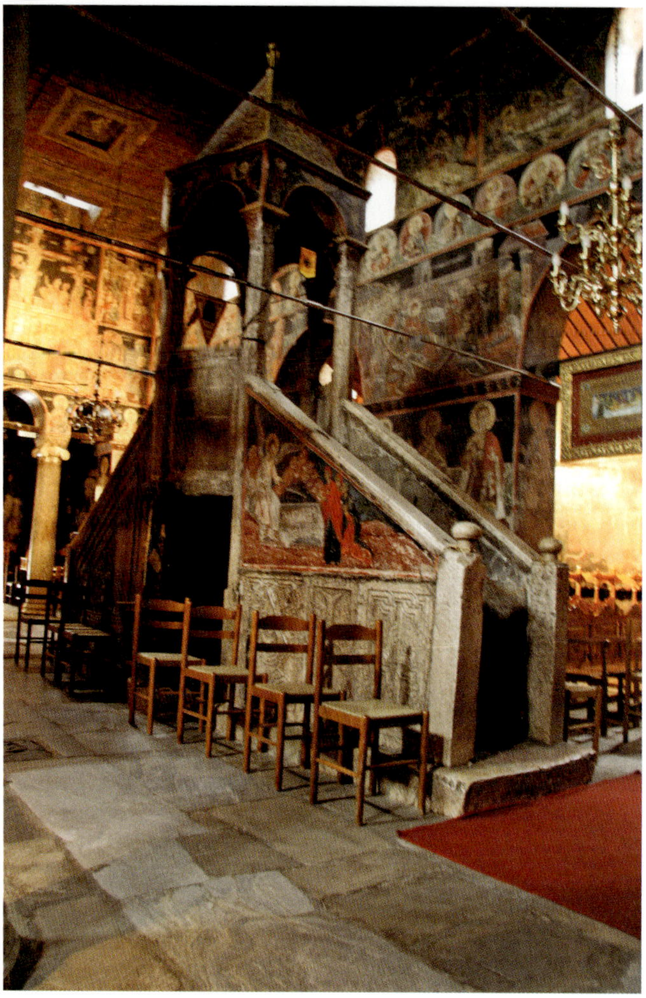

FIGURE 3.4 *Ambo canopy, Church of the Dormition of the Mother of God, Kalabaka, Greece, after tenth century (?).* PHOTO NEBOJŠA STANKOVIĆ

roof is without a doubt post-Byzantine,[26] yet the possibility that it replicated the earlier form remains, especially in light of numerous canopies with pyramidal roofs recovered along the Adriatic littoral. The readily observed similarities between the still-standing canopy in Kalabaka, other archeologically confirmed canopies, and the now-lost sixth-century canopy from Hagia Sophia as vividly described by Paulos Silentarios suggest the formulaic design of these structures across wide geographical and historical frameworks. Such close references between early Christian and later canopies might point to a monolithic, uninterrupted tradition of architectural design, a view that prevailed in most post-Enlightenment Byzantine studies of the nineteenth and early twentieth centuries. But, on the other hand, I would tend to agree with scholars who have recognized the Byzantines' active engagement with design practices and insistence on the continual

---

[26] Based on a recovered inscription, Voyatzis (2011) 195–227, dates the wooden roof of the canopy to the seventeenth century and its paintings to the eighteenth century.

revival of earlier traditions,[27] a general trend that was partially revealed through my analysis of the textual sources on canopies in particular.[28]

The anachronistic use of *spolia* in the Middle and Late Byzantine periods has already been observed, and, in my opinion, numerous examples of the use of *spolia* in Byzantine architecture verify the Byzantines' claim on and belief in an uninterrupted tradition, which conforms to the basic theological notion of order within Byzantine *oikonomia*.[29] The ambo canopy from Kalabaka made of *spolia* confirms rather than excludes the possibility that the Byzantines especially promoted some basic formulaic notions about the canopy's design and decoration. In Kalabaka, the ambo and its canopy are covered in post-Byzantine painting, which may have been repainted over earlier, medieval scenes. The triangular segment above the rectangular slab of the southeastern section of the ambo is painted with a representation of the Angel and Marys on the Tomb (see Fig. 3.4), suggesting its close symbolic association with the Tomb of Christ and with the Holy Sepulchre in Jerusalem, while the arches of the canopy are painted with Biblical narratives and Christological scenes, in both the interior and exterior. By its shape and the two flights of stairs going up to the canopied platform, the ambo is framed as a sacred place where the priest would deliver the Word of God and also points to the Tomb of Christ and Jerusalem on High.[30] Namely, the painted representation of the Angel and Marys at the open, empty Tomb is set next to the prismatic cavity of the entire ambo installation. This image alludes to the rock-cut tomb of Christ in Jerusalem, a salient witness of Christ's resurrection and the Christian belief in the hereafter in the heavenly realm, high above, which is reinforced by the massive canopy raised midair above the central section of the installation. The Kalabaka canopied ambo, its architecture and its images, hence may be derived from both topological references from Jerusalem and liturgical references in Byzantine-rite churches, as attested to in the opening verses on the ambo in Hagia Sophia.

While all the paintings on canopies in Byzantine-rite churches are chronologically post-Byzantine, it is worth mentioning how, like the Kalabaka ambo, the sixteenth-century altar canopy of the Church of St. Mamas in Cyprus has a painting, which points to the liturgical use of the canopy and the rites performed in the Byzantine-rite church.[31] Painted on the north side of the canopy of St. Mamas is the *Melismos* scene showing Christ in the Eucharistic disk, a scene used exclusively in Byzantine-rite churches.[32] The scene is depicted at the highest point of the canopy, and below it is the donor inscription. As demonstrated by Charalampos G. Chotzakoglou, the location of these images on the north side of the canopy and their content point to the *Prothesis* rite, or the Liturgy of Preparation, when the bread and wine are prepared for the Divine Liturgy and which is performed to the north of the altar. During this rite, the priest first removes and raises the Lamb (the cubical part of the holy bread standing for Christ) and ends with removing the particles that commemorate the living and the departed.[33] The examples from Kalabaka and Cyprus do not exclude a possibility that similar painted representations, with developed narratives that in a way

---

[27] See, for example, Kazhdan and Wharton Epstein (1985) 138–145.

[28] Chapter 1.

[29] On the use of *spolia* in Byzantine architecture with references to historicity, see Ousterhout (2008) 140–145; Sodini (2002) 129–145; 145f; Trkulja (2004) 109–116; Geymonat (2012) 47–65.

[30] See also Ousterhout (1981) 311–321.

[31] Bolman (2010) 134–162.

[32] Wybrew (1989) 150; Gerstel (1999) 40–48; Grozdanov (1980) 63–84; Walter (1982) 206, 220–221.

[33] Chotzakoglou (2011) 469–485. The *prothesis* or *proscomide* rite developed over time. The earliest texts that mention a prayer to be read over holy bread are from the eighth century, while *Germanos-b* 72–73 makes clear reference to the Lamb. More in Marinis (2014) 33.

simultaneously summarized both the painted programs and the rituals, existed during the Byzantine period; though due to the lack of wider evidence of canopied installations in their original settings, I cannot prove this claim.

The current altar canopy in the Kalabaka church was certainly not installed in the early Christian period, as previously thought, but sometime during the tenth and eleventh centuries.[34] It is an especially important example of Middle-Byzantine canopies as it remains in its more-or-less original setting up to the present. This canopy, some 2 meters wide and 4 meters tall, is set on four marble columns upon which rise four marble arches, approximately 10 centimeters thick, decorated with painted crosses in roundels both in the interior and exterior, and topped by a rather more recent eight-sided pyramidal roof made of wooden planks. The interior of the canopy might have been painted originally and repainted over time (Fig. 3.5) (Table 5.196).[35] The painting

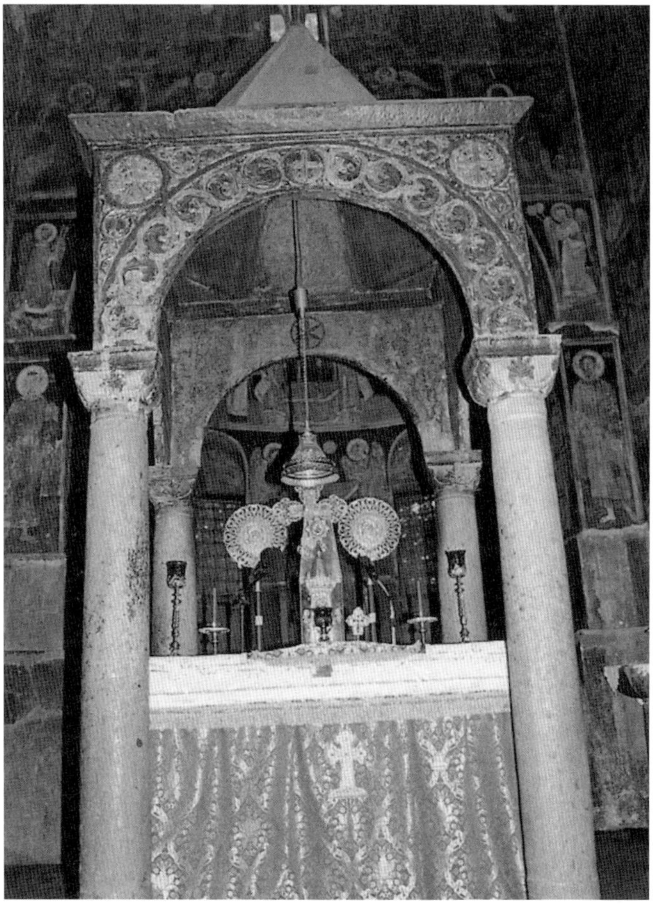

FIGURE 3.5 *Altar canopy, Church of the Dormition of the Mother of God, Kalabaka, Greece, tenth–eleventh century.* COMMERCIAL POSTCARD

[34] Vanderheyde (2005) 427–442.

[35] The interior of Coptic post-Byzantine canopies is painted with figurative Christian images. Jeudy (2004) 67–88, figs. 17–20.

of canopies has been confirmed archeologically, and medieval texts further confirm this practice. Medieval Russian chronicles even recorded that the interiors of altar canopies in the churches of Ss. Boris and Gleb (1115) and of St. John at Holm (eleventh century) were not only painted but also gilded in bronze and gold like a starry sky and heavenly firmament.[36] The altar canopy from Kalabaka, though smaller in size and different in material and artistic quality in its general form and setting, still resembles the altar canopy in Hagia Sophia as described by Paulos Silentarios: four columns supporting four arches topped by a flat roof plaque that receives the eight-sided pyramidal roof as a lid; the entire structure shelters the altar table and is placed more or less in the geometric center of the sanctuary. Because both the ambo and altar canopies from Kalabaka can be compared in design to now-lost canopies from Constantinopolitan Hagia Sophia, it is possible to hypothesize that some standardized design principles for canopies were used over a prolonged time and across the vast territories of the Byzantine Empire and its cultural domains.

CANOPY FROM THE ROYAL ONTARIO MUSEUM COLLECTION

In 2010, the Royal Ontario Museum acquired a unique and genuine architectural piece, an arcuated frame of the upper structure of a canopy, which I was able to examine in person (Fig. 3.6). Based on formal and stylistic analysis, the canopy originally belonged to an unidentified church in the Levant, possibly Syria or Armenia, and can be roughly dated to the period between the sixth and eighth centuries. My dating of this object to the early

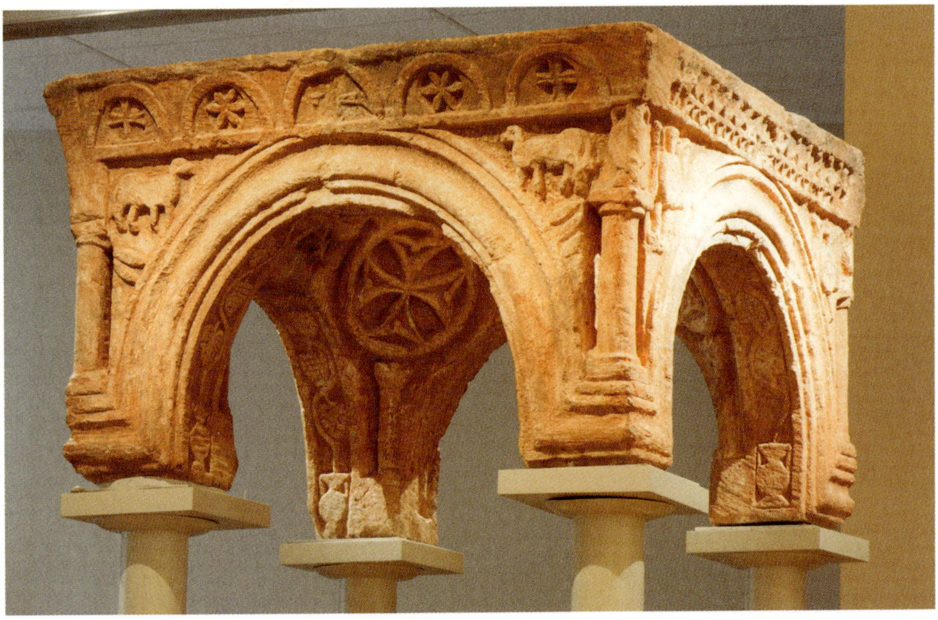

FIGURE 3.6 *Canopy from an unidentified church in the Syro-Palestine region, sixth–eighth centuries.* COURTESY OF THE ROYAL ONTARIO MUSEUM © ROM

[36] Voronin (1961) 256.

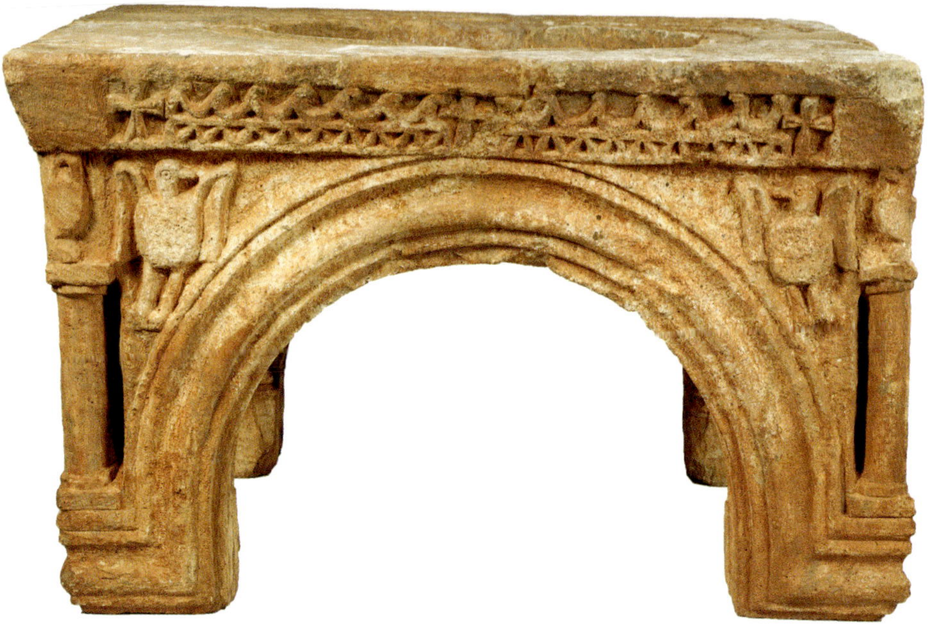

FIGURE 3.7 *Arcuated carved frame of a limestone canopy from an unidentified church in the Syro-Palestine region, sixth–eighth centuries.* COURTESY OF THE ROYAL ONTARIO MUSEUM © ROM

Byzantine period was further supported by scientific X-ray spectrometric analysis.[37] The canopy is very important due to its preserved original decoration, in this case without any narrative scenes, which points to the variety of ways in which medieval believers may have engaged with canopy-like installations and the meanings they conveyed.

Carved of a monolithic block of limestone of *bianco antico* color (typical off-white limestone color that gets an ocher patina over time), this surviving arcuated frame belongs to the upper part of a relatively large canopy (Fig. 3.7). Its external dimensions are 93 centimeters in height; width and length of 106 centimeters (bottom) by 110 centimeters (upper part); the upper part of the frame has a circular opening 59.7–60 centimeters wide with a circular groove some 7.5 centimeters wide, 5–7 millimeters deep; arches 64 centimeters wide, 43 centimeters deep; the support for columns is square, 19 (22) centimeters by 19 (22) centimeters each. Originally, the preserved frame rested on four supports and most likely had a domical (or conical) roof, judging by the circular groove on the upper part of the canopy frame (Fig. 3.8). The frame, now restored, is reassembled from numerous

[37] I thank Paul Denis, curator from the Royal Ontario Museum, for sharing with me the results of the technical examination of the canopy frame done by John Twilley, an art conservation scientist from the Ariadne Galleries in New York who specializes in analysis and material science for the preservation of cultural property. Twilley conducted stereobinocular microscopy aided by supplemental lighting and ultraviolet illumination in 2010, and independently from my own examination of the object. His analysis confirmed that the canopy frame can be attributed to the Byzantine period, approximately around 550 CE. The object was at some point fragmented, perhaps buried, followed by modern reassembly of the pieces. The material analysis of the limestone, the deposits and traces of soil, points to the high possibility that the object was buried. This may further suggest that the canopy either crashed at some point, perhaps even during the carving, and was abandoned, or that it belonged to a church that collapsed, on which occasion the canopy could have been smashed and covered by ruins.

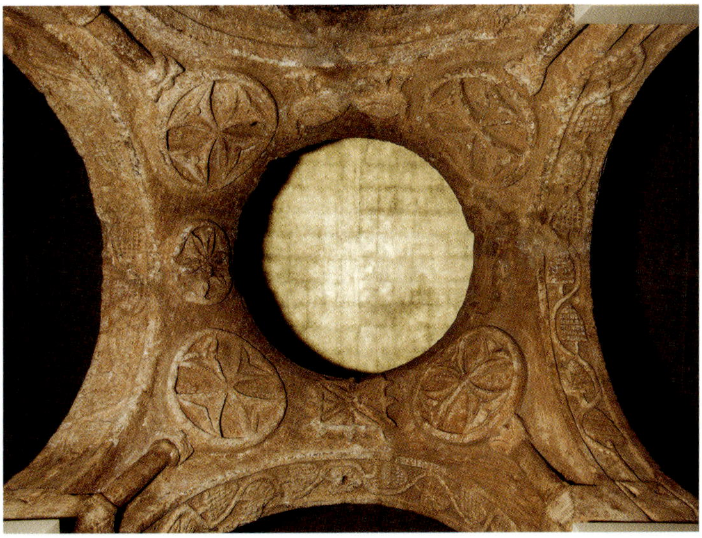

FIGURE 3.8 *Interior view of an arcuated carved frame of a canopy from an unidentified church in the Syro-Palestine region, sixth–eighth centuries.* COURTESY OF THE ROYAL ONTARIO MUSEUM © ROM

broken fragments, with minor but thoughtful additions that did not compromise the integrity of the object.[38] The examined canopy is unique in its construction in that it was made of single piece of stone as a monolithic whole, similar to the sixth-century marble canopy of Byzantine provenance today preserved in the treasury of San Marco in Venice (Fig. 1.2). In its interior, it is carved as a segment of a sphere as if to suggest a domical vault on pendentives (quasi-spherical triangles), which were used in the construction of domes in Byzantine churches. In its exterior, the canopy frame takes a prismatic shape with a rimlike protruding segment above the arches.

The canopy is richly carved and reveals the use of sophisticated geometry based on squares and circles in its production. As a whole, the frame exhibits a good level of craftsmanship and skill: its overall dimensions remain precise within several millimeters. The dimensions of this canopy frame are also consistent with the dimensions of other canopies from the Eastern Mediterranean, which are usually 1–2 meters in span. Yet surviving evidence of canopies elsewhere usually suggests their composite columnar construction of four arches assembled together to form the canopy frame, topped by an additional slab to receive the domical or pyramidal roof. Therefore, the use of this solution in the canopy now at the Royal Ontario Museum points to regional craftsmanship, while still remaining within the framework of the conceptual design of canopies, which generally consist of columnar supports, arcuated frame, and a roof.

The four arches of the examined monolith canopy, finished to various extents, are carved on their exterior, interior, and soffits. Relatively rough and unfinished carving, which shows tooth chisel marks, may point to the possibility that it was done as such to allow finishing by coats of paint. The practice of painting canopies has been confirmed in

[38] Indeed, the material analysis confirmed that the pieces were assembled, yet without any traces of modern materials or binders as well as without any alteration of the surface by mechanical or chemical treatment to simulate aging effects.

the Middle Byzantine period, and the canopy from the Royal Ontario Museum collection suggests that such a practice may have been even older.[39] The arches of the canopy are here for the purpose of description enumerated I through IV, starting with arch I carved with crosses in the exterior and going counterclockwise, mimicking the movement of the priest around the canopy in the church setting, and ending with arch IV, which is left unfinished. The four arches exhibit various decorative geometric, floral, and figural motifs, all symmetrically organized above the extrados of the arch and additionally articulated by architectural elements—colonnettes, set at corners of each arch. The four exterior colonnettes (some 30 centimeters tall) are set in corner niches and carved in the round; they have flat shafts and geometric bases and capitals. The four interior colonnettes (some 21 centimeters tall) are engaged but are also carved with flat shafts with geometric bases and with capitals of either quasi-Doric or quasi-Corinthian variety. The interior colonnettes support four deeply carved roundels (some 26 centimeters in diameter) in the pendentives. Each of these four roundels, visible in the interior of the canopy frame, has an inscribed equilateral cross with arms that taper into the center, resembling the shape of the so-called Maltese cross, known as such because it was later used by the Crusaders in the Middle East. The four arches of the canopy frame, though articulated by the same architectural elements, vary in detail, disclosing four different sides of the canopy.

Arch I shows in the exterior two deeply carved canopied arches (some 20 centimeters tall and 19 centimeters wide) with a hanging cross symmetrically placed in the spandrels of the arch and connected by a "zigzag" decorative pattern on the rim (see Fig. 3.12). The remaining surfaces of this arch remain flat and undecorated, revealing only chisel markings. The interior of this arch shows a design comprising a central motif of two overlapping birds (some sections obviously restored) carved in profile and facing outwards towards two roundels supported by two quasi-Corinthian engaged colonnettes. These two flanking roundels in the pendentives have inscribed equilateral crosses. The soffit of this arch (some 9.5–10 centimeters wide) has a simply carved vine, occasionally just left in outline, with five leaves and five grapes sprouting from two amphora-like vases carved at the springing of the arch.

Arch II is topped with a horizontal, beam-like cornice, which has a decorative design consisting of five equally spaced round arches with inscribed medallions (Fig. 3.9). The five medallions are alternatively carved with an equilateral cross and a rosette with six petals; all combined together to make three crosses and two rosettes. The spandrels of this arch are decorated with animal figures, presumably two lambs, one in each spandrel. The interior of this arch shows a geometric design composed of a central square medallion flanked by two roundels supported by two columns, carved to suggest a quasi-Doric and quasi-Corinthian variety. All three medallions are inscribed with crosses. The central medallion is square in shape and is inscribed with the two overlapping crosses: a forked, X-shaped, diagonal cross (*crux decussata*, also known as "St. Andrew's cross" because it is believed that St. Andrew was crucified on a cross of this shape) and a pointed +-shaped, equilateral cross (also known as a "Greek cross"). The flanking roundels in the pendentives have equilateral crosses. The soffit of this arch also has a carved vine, with five leaves and five grapes, sprouting from two amphorae carved at the springing of the arch. In the very center of the vine, a drilled socket reveals a fitting for some kind of hanging—potentially a cross, a votive, lamp, or similar object, now lost.[40] Maria Parani has already demonstrated

[39] On this practice of polychromatic treatment of Byzantine sculpture and canopies, see Ivison (2008) 487–513; Gavrilović (1999) 111–118.

[40] The material analysis confirmed that this anchor point for some kind of hardware is original, rather than a later addition.

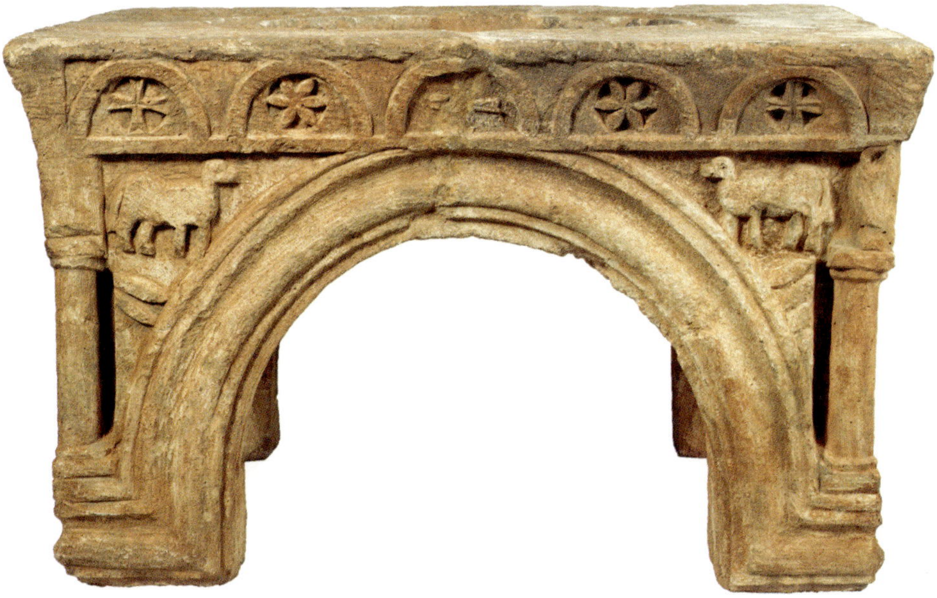

FIGURE 3.9 *Arch II of a canopy from an unidentified church in the Syro-Palestine region, sixth–eighth centuries.* COURTESY OF THE ROYAL ONTARIO MUSEUM © ROM

how some Byzantine images reveal that sanctuary lamps were fitted into some kind of a metal mount, which was suspended by chains from the metal fitting set in the soffit of the arch of the canopy.[41] These depictions are consistent with contemporary practices and material evidence of lamps and their fittings. By extension, the drilled socket from the canopy in the Royal Ontario Collection confirms the practices of fittings for hanging objects in some canopies.

Arch III shows in the exterior in the uppermost horizontal register a decorative design comprising three crosses interconnected with a geometric strip (see Fig. 3.13). The two crosses at the end of this horizontal band are equilateral with forked ends, while the central one, which was damaged and then partially restored, seems to have been very plain, a basic form of the equilateral "Greek cross." The connecting horizontal strip consists of two geometric stripes, the upper showing an "undulating wave" design and the bottom a "zig-zag" design. Here, the framing colonnettes are topped by depictions of two amphorae. The spandrels of this arch are decorated with two birds, presumably eagles, one in each spandrel. Partially restored, the birds are rendered in flight, with outspread wings; their heads and beaks are in profile with a dominant, frontally carved, large circular eye. The rounded body and two legs are also shown frontally. The representation of the two birds resembles other depictions of this extremely popular motif elsewhere during the late antique and early medieval periods. The interior of this arch also shows a geometric design composed of three roundels. The central roundel is a rosette, a six-leafed, possibly palmetto motif. This generic flower design has been used widely since antiquity in architecture, furniture, and sculpture. The soffit of this arch also has a carved vine with leaves and grapes sprouting from two amphorae carved at the springing of the arch. Like in arch II, in the very center of the vine and the apex of the arch, a drilled socket reveals a fitting for some kind of pendant, not preserved.

---

[41] Parani (2005) 147–171, esp. 154–155.

Arch IV shows a rather blank, unfinished, and undecorated exterior, except for the continual torus molding around the extrados of the arch (see Fig. 3.14). The interior of this arch shows in its central segment two confronted peacocks flanked by cruciform roundels in pendentives. The soffit of this arch is also carved differently, showing a wide, convex molding with a "knot" at each end. Rather uncarved and unfinished, arch IV points to the possibility that the canopy originally abutted a wall and was not meant to be an object standing in the round. Another option would be that this side was not finished if the canopy fragmented in the process of chiseling, but, in my opinion, this is unlikely since then the original holes for the anchorage of some kind of pendants would have not been drilled, as they most likely would have been done last.

When assembled and set on columns, the canopy and its carving would have enabled an experience of the powerful and suggestive expressive content of this architectural piece. The exterior of arch I would correspond to the interior of arch III; the exterior of arch II to the interior of arch IV; the exterior of arch III to the interior of arch I; and the "hidden," undecorated exterior of arch IV to the probably invisible interior of arch II. Hence, arch II was probably the frontal side, showing two lambs and framing the two peacocks in the interior of the canopy (Fig. 3.10). The corresponding imagery from the exterior and the interior of the canopy seemingly suggests two distinct, though closely related, messages that the entire installation would have conveyed when in use. In a way, this design principle recalls the similar solution from the ninth-century canopy from Bijaće, Croatia, which has inscriptions running on the exterior and interior of the installation and revealing two different messages.[42]

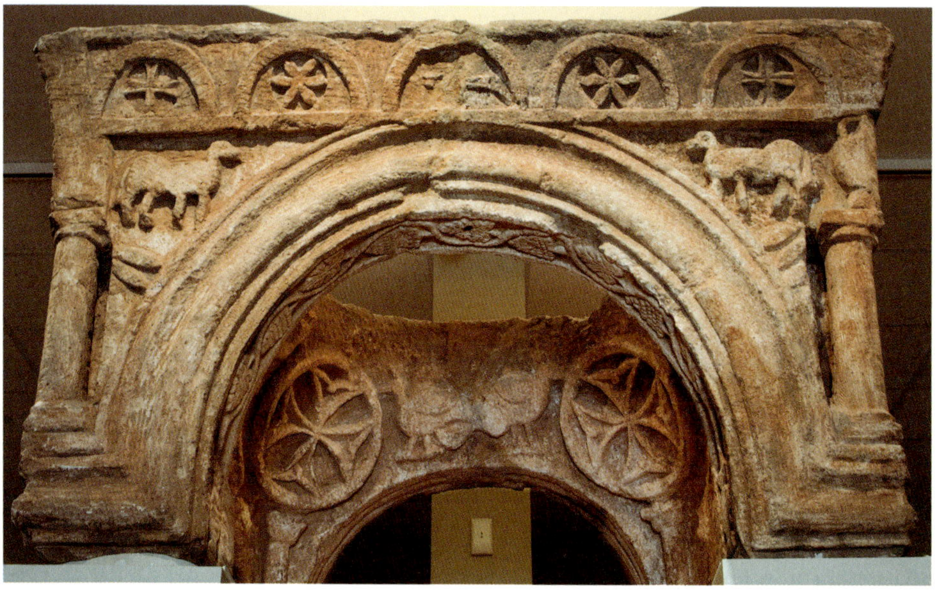

FIGURE 3.10 *Exterior of arch II and the interior of arch IV; canopy from an unidentified church in the Syro-Palestine region, sixth–eighth centuries.* COURTESY OF THE ROYAL ONTARIO MUSEUM © ROM

[42] Chapter 2, Table 7.113.

By facing the frontal side of this early Christian canopy from the Levant and moving around it, originally the officiating priest would see and contemplate the sacred, reinforced by the complex and interchangeable meanings of the carvings on the frame. The chiseled lambs on its exterior point to Christ as the sacrificial lamb and the preparation of the Lamb of the Eucharistic bread, which also symbolizes "the hidden years" of Christ's earthly life (Fig. 3.11). Thus, it is possible that this canopy could have been an altar canopy. The five-partite arcade above this representation has three crosses separated by two rosettes, and they represent the cosmological character of the divine universe and sacred space. The three crosses subtly point to the concept of the Holy Trinity, while "rosettes" sculpturally represent the whirling, heavenly wheels and perpetual spiritual movement, standing for the descent of the Logos and the grace of the Holy Spirit. Scholars have noticed the pervasive use of such "rosettes" in Byzantine architecture both in the exterior walls of the church building itself and in the interior, being part of either monumental frescoes and mosaic decorations or various church objects.[43] These whirling disks are overarching symbols of holiness. They point to the Logos, the Word of God, upon which all of creation is based; the Divine Light and the Holy Spirit; the heavenly wheels from the Vision of Ezekiel (Ezek. 1:16–18, 10:9–13); and the heavenly wheels emanating from the Word of God, spiritual and intellectual "productive powers of life" from the angelic hierarchy as explained by the theologian and philosopher Pseudo-Dionysius the Areopagite.[44] Alexei Lidov has traced the iconographic and performative use of the whirling disks in church spaces built from the fifth to the fourteenth centuries across the Mediterranean from Armenia to Serbia. He convincingly demonstrated that within a larger context they represent the cosmic symbol of the divine universe and the Heavenly Jerusalem. Whirling disks, which are essentially made of a rotating cross as in the canopy from the Royal Ontario collection and occasionally may have the letters *alpha* and *omega* or *chi* and *rho* as represented

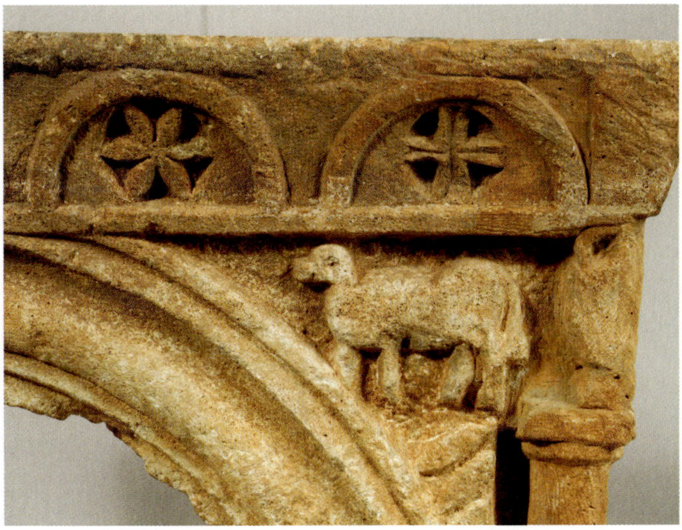

FIGURE 3.11 *Arch II, detail; canopy from an unidentified church in the Syro-Palestine region, sixth–eighth centuries.* COURTESY OF THE ROYAL ONTARIO MUSEUM © ROM

[43] Trkulja (2011) 213–246, esp. 223–228; Lidov (2015b) 127–152.

[44] *Dionysius Areopagita, CH,* ch. I, III and IX.

in the vaulted interiors of baptisteries and churches elsewhere, stand for the revelation of God through Christ.[45]

While facing the canopy in its original setting and performing the sacred rites, the officiating priest would, therefore, face the microcosmic place of the mystical divine Presence. The frontal arch of the canopy would point to the holy representation of the hidden years of Christ before the Resurrection and the Second Coming. Simultaneously he would see the peacocks flanked by crosses in roundels in the interior of the canopy frame that delineated the "revealed," inner meaning of the sacred space and its otherworldly connotations. Peacocks were believed to have incorruptible flesh, and being sacred to Hera (Juno), they became a symbol of the apotheosis of Roman empresses, as Zeus' (Jupiter's) eagle was of Roman emperors. In a Christian context, these birds signified the ascension of the sanctified soul and its union with the Lord.[46] Due to the association with incorruptible flesh, peacocks became known as paradisiac birds. Simultaneously, as further strengthened by writings of prominent Christians, such as St. Augustine of Hippo (354–430) when he wrote about the Heavenly City, the power of peacock's never-decaying flesh could have been associated with the incorruptible body of Christ of the Eucharistic hosts in the minds of believers.[47]

The lateral sides of this canopy would show arches I and III. Arch I with hanging crosses within the canopy-like arches is reminiscent of the Crucifixion and the Tomb of Christ (Fig. 3.12). This arch frames a palmetto rosette in the interior of the canopy, suggestive of paradise and the rosewater used for the anointing of the altar. Arch III has two triumphant

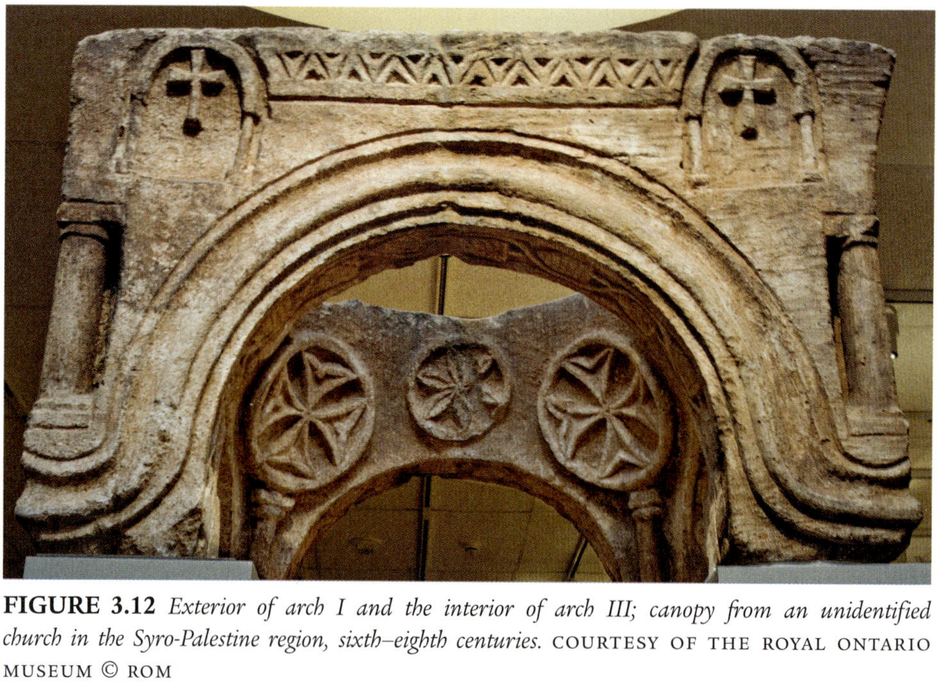

FIGURE 3.12 *Exterior of arch I and the interior of arch III; canopy from an unidentified church in the Syro-Palestine region, sixth–eighth centuries.* COURTESY OF THE ROYAL ONTARIO MUSEUM © ROM

---

[45] Lidov (2015b) 127–152.

[46] Evans (1896) 310–311.

[47] *Augustine, De Civitate Dei,* xxi.4 "Quis enim nisi Deus creator omnium dedit carni pavonis mortui ne putrescerent?" [For who, except God, the Creator of all things, endowed the flesh of the dead peacock with the power of never decaying?].

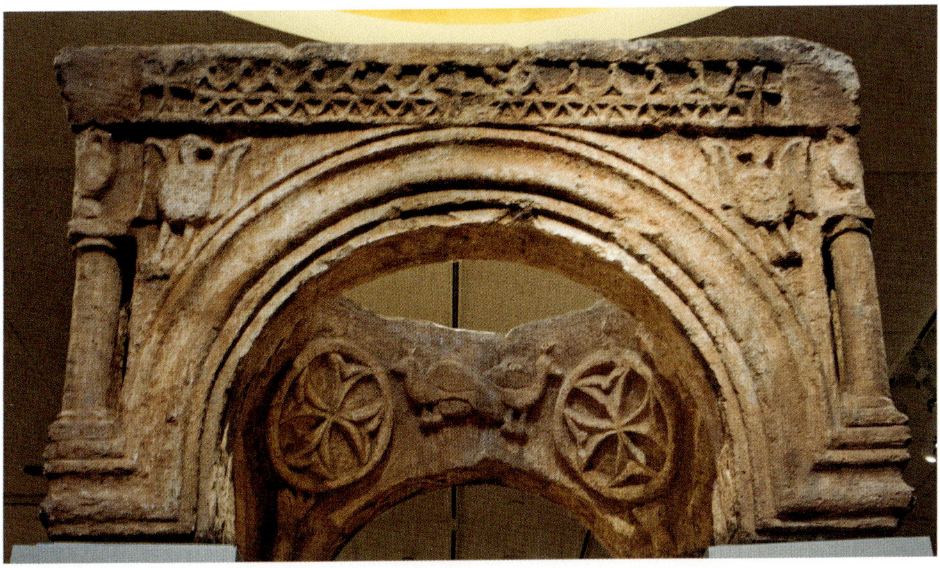

FIGURE 3.13 *Exterior of arch III and the interior of arch I; canopy from an unidentified church in the Syro-Palestine region, sixth–eighth centuries.* COURTESY OF THE ROYAL ONTARIO MUSEUM © ROM

eagles (Fig. 3.13). Eagles are symbols of the Resurrection, based on the early belief that the eagle, unlike other birds, periodically renewed its plumage and its youth by flying near the sun and plunging into the water; further borne out by Psalm 103:5, "thy youth is renewed like the eagle's."[48] This arch further frames the view towards the two paradisiac birds shown in the interior of the canopy. The rear part of the canopy probably was not meant to be seen (Fig. 3.14). Yet it would frame the most symbolic image—a double cross, or whirling cross, inscribed in a square medallion—which I suggest functioned as a kind of a "seal" of the entire installation in accordance with the rite of "sealing" or the act of anointing when an officiating priest traces a mark in the shape of cross with Holy Oil on a person or a thing during the church service, creating links to the anointment of Christ, the sealing of his tomb, and the promise of the Heavenly Jerusalem.

The carved reliefs on the arches, in that regard, effectively and in a type of multisensory dialogue framed and facilitated the perception of the exteriority and interiority of the canopy installation and the ways in which it architecturally and performatively framed a sacred space. The exact location and original function of this canopy is unknown. Yet the entire design of this canopy, whether it was used as a major altar canopy or a secondary, *prothesis* canopy, or even a shrine canopy, spatially, visually, dogmatically, and performatively reaffirms the Byzantine belief that, like the change of the substance of ordinary bread and wine into sanctified hosts—the body and blood of Christ—so, too, the change of place from the earthly to the heavenly during the Divine Liturgy happens through the grace of God and the Holy Spirit.[49] Moreover, made of stone and indicative of a cavity like the rock-cut tomb

[48] In Christianity, the eagle is also used to represent the new life begun at the baptismal font and the Christian soul strengthened by grace. "But they that wait upon the Lord shall renew their strength; they shall mount up with wings as eagles . . . ." (Isa. 40:30). Ferguson (1959), s.v. *eagle*.

[49] Taft (1975); Altripp (1998); Gamber (1985) 61–71.

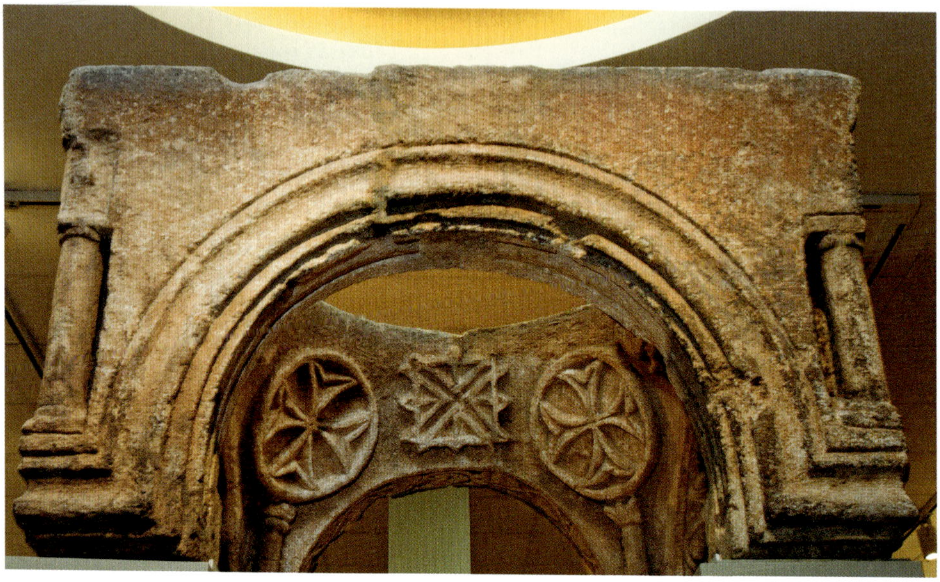

FIGURE 3.14 *Exterior of arch IV and the interior of arch II; canopy from an unidentified church in the Syro-Palestine region, sixth–eighth centuries.* COURTESY OF THE ROYAL ONTARIO MUSEUM © ROM

of Christ in Jerusalem, the soffits of this arcuated canopy frame are defined by amphorae at the springing of arches with sprouting vine with leaves and grapes, alluding to the "fountain of life" and the Resurrection of Christ.[50] Going counterclockwise, the exterior arches of the canopy combined Biblical narratives and liturgical services and presented the Crucifixion and the Tomb of Christ, the preparation of the Lamb, and the Resurrection, while in the interior the paradisiac, victorious, and salvific messages reinforced the notion that the canopy framed a sacred space beyond time and place.

The colonnettes at the corners of the examined canopy frame are further important for at least two reasons. They reveal the multilayered potency of a canopy to frame architecturally and conceptually sacred space on earth and above. Additionally, in this specific case, the iconographic features of the colonnettes may point to a fuller, more contextualized understanding of the entire canopied installation and other objects that may have been their constitutive parts. Namely, similar to the canopy of the Kalabaka ambo (Fig. 3.4) that was designed as if the canopy were suspended in midair or similar to the colonnettes at the corners of the arches and just above the structural columns of the Paros altar canopy (Fig. 3.3), the colonnettes of this arcuated frame are suggestive of the spatial qualities of such installations that point to intermediary space and allude to the transitional space between the earthly and the heavenly. I agree with Cecilia Olovsdotter, who studied numerous examples of Roman imperial and early Christian portals and gabled fronts and proposed that the architectural motifs of their upper sections, just above the pediments and arches and occasionally framed with colonnettes, denoted not only the structural-architectural qualities of such installations but also the spaces and concepts of transcendence that are associated with the rites and spaces of passage, which can also be seen in this canopy's colonnettes.[51]

---

[50] Underwood (1950) 43–138.

[51] Olovsdotter (2015).

In case of the early Christian canopy from the Royal Ontario Museum, its colonnettes also point to the similar use of decorative columns on a peculiar reliquary box from the Princeton Art Museum.[52] This partially preserved reliquary box, carved in the shape of a columnar shrine with closed doors with an original lid, now missing, that was most likely done as a pyramidal or domical roof, resembles contemporaneous funerary architecture. In material, style, and conception of design with the colonnettes at the corners of the box in the attic zone, the Princeton reliquary closely resembles the canopy from the Royal Ontario Museum. The two objects may have belonged to the same installation originally, pointing to the reliquary's possible use as an altar installation with consecrated relics or as a separate reliquary shrine. In any case, the relics were signs of the Lord, as a saint's life reflected upon the life and sacrifice of Christ.[53] The Princeton reliquary box, therefore, can be related to the canopied installation from the Royal Ontario Museum, without altering its noted Christological references; the lambs, peacocks, rosettes, and various types of crosses from the canopy indeed point to religious sacrificial and sepulchral symbolism, typical for early Christian art and architecture in the wider Mediterranean. If used as a reliquary shrine, the design of the entire installation of nesting architectural objects from the reliquary box within the canopied frame, itself set within a church space, would reinforce the concept of a saintly shrine as an eternal house for the saint in the church, as suggested in Byzantine texts,[54] overlapping with the complex sacrificial, sepulchral, and paradisiac meanings of the multilayered, nesting sacred space that the canopy denoted.

Though the carved motifs of interlace and animal design remain generic, all four arches of the canopy from the Royal Ontario Collection are additionally framed by a continual convex molding reminiscent of a rope-like design, here done in a manner typical for early Christian churches in Syria and Armenia, which are also known to be made of large stone blocks.[55] Based on the quality of material used as well as on the stylistic analysis and iconography of the carved reliefs, the production of this canopy can be roughly placed in the local workshop for churches in the Levant, possibly in the Syro-Armenian territories, and dated to the early Christian and Byzantine period (sixth to eighth centuries). The original purpose of the object, however, remains hypothetical. It is possible that the canopy sheltered the major altar table, though, in my opinion, this is less likely because of the canopy's unfinished fourth side combined with the drilled sockets for hardware pointing to its use and diminishing the possibility that the object was never finished. If the canopy abutted the church wall, such placement would prevent the full circular movement of the officiating priest around the altar as is the practice in Eastern churches. Moreover, early churches in Asia Minor and Syro-Palestine were of enormous size, and, though it is a relatively large piece by modern standards and comparable in size to some other canopies, this canopy is smaller than the middle Byzantine altar canopy from Kalabaka and would be unusually small to shelter the major altar table in an early Christian church in Asia Minor. The sockets revealed in the apex of two arches of the canopy frame[56] point to the use of hanging pendants, usually in the shape of crosses and votives, which were used for reliquary shrines and confirmed in Byzantine images. The gray discoloration of the interior of the canopy

---

[52] Ćurčić, Hadjitryphonos, et al. (2010) 248–249, cat. no. 38.

[53] Ibid.

[54] See Chapter 1 term *oikiskos*, "small house."

[55] Peña (1997) 63–86, esp. 82–86; Butler (1969).

[56] It is possible that the sockets were drilled in the apex of the other two arches as well, but concealed during the modern restoration process, as technical analysis suggested.

frame, in its upper zone around the opening for the original roof, may be a result of the aging of stone, but it could also be from the smoke from an oil lamp that could have been hung from the apex of the now-lost canopy roof. Therefore, this architectural work was a piece of liturgical furnishing meant to be used in a religious setting, yet most likely as a canopy over the reliquary or over the secondary altar for the preparation of the holy hosts, like the seventeenth-century smaller canopy in the church on the Greek island of Paros, which itself was possibly made as a replacement for a similar, older canopy (Fig. 3.15). Another possibility, especially in the light of the strong liturgical references associated with canopies that concurrently refer to tomb installations, may point to the so-called side altar shrines, archeologically confirmed in the western Mediterranean and better studied in the context of Roman Catholic rites.[57] If my hypothesis is correct, then our current typology of canopies must expand to include canopied installations for secondary altars, either *prothesis* or tomb-shrines, while simultaneously allowing for the overlapping of the different meanings that canopies denoted.

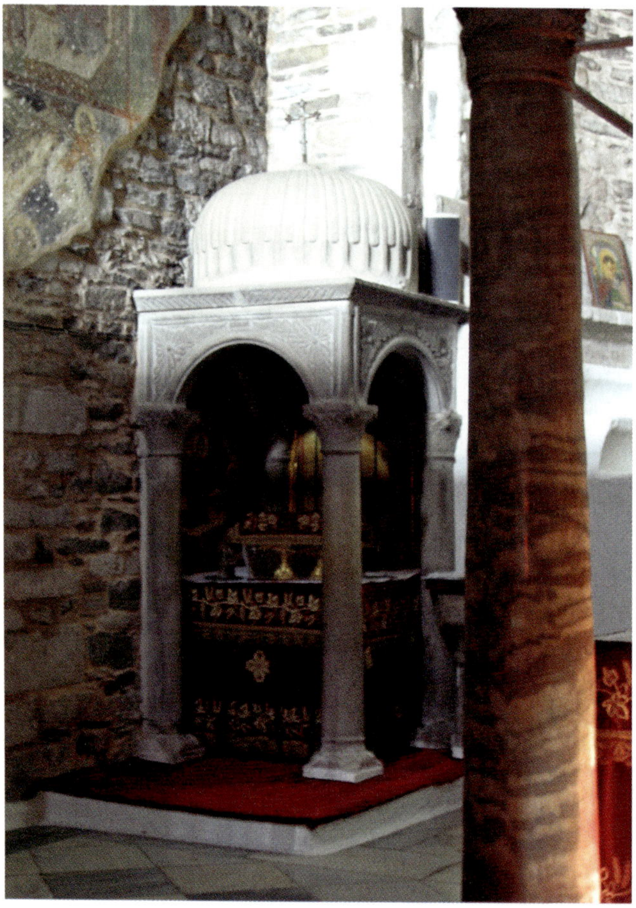

FIGURE 3.15 *Prothesis canopy, Panagia Ekatontapyliani (Katapoliani), Paros, seventeenth century, possibly made as a replacement for a similar, older canopy.* PHOTO AUTHOR

[57] Bacci (2009) 11–30.

THE CANOPIES OF HAGIA SOPHIA IN CONSTANTINOPLE

At least five different kinds of canopies once existed in the Church of Hagia Sophia in Constantinople, and they illustrate the use of multiple canopies within a Byzantine-rite church in an exceptionally revealing way. The Cathedral of Constantinople had an altar canopy, an ambo canopy, a *phiale* canopy, at least one *proskynetraion* canopy such as the one recorded to be used for enshrining an especially venerated, miraculous icon of the Mother of God, and a canopy venerated as a relic itself because it was presumably made from the wood of the Ark of Noah. These canopies were established and often reinstalled and made anew several times during the millennium-long history of Hagia Sophia as a major Byzantine church. None has been preserved *in situ*; evidence is not even available as to their exact location. However, texts, images, and archeological remains elsewhere in Constantinople and the Byzantine realm aid in the better understanding of canopies in the Constantinopolitan cathedral, which served as a model for Byzantine-rite churches.

The first altar canopy from Hagia Sophia broke when its first dome collapsed in 558.[58] It was replaced and then described by Prokopios and Paulos Silentarios in the sixth century and then again in mid-twelfth-century by Michael, rector of the Patriarchal Academy in Constantinople.[59] The silver altar canopy along with other elements of the sanctuary was pillaged by the Crusaders in 1204, but was replaced by another canopy so that the sanctuary could serve the Latin rite.[60] This new marble canopy was presumably made of elements taken from the Church of the Anastasis, now lost.[61] The altar canopy in Hagia Sophia was supposedly restored for Byzantine services some sixty years after the Latin conquest, though the thirteenth-century marble canopy, not the silver one, most likely continued to be used. The episode also confirms that churches serving both the Roman Catholic and Byzantine Orthodox rites, even after the doctrinal split, continued to use canopies in the thirteenth century.

At least by the eleventh and attested to in the twelfth century, not only the altar but also the ambo just below Hagia Sophia's dome had a canopy.[62] Byzantine illustrations, such as the painting in the Menologion of Basil II (ca. 1000) show an ambo in Hagia Sophia topped with a canopy.[63] In 1403, a Castilian diplomat and traveler Clavijo reported that a canopied ambo stood in Hagia Sophia.[64] Not enough evidence has been preserved to suggest whether this canopy underwent any changes during the Crusades. The ambo canopy from Kalabaka, which resembles the description of the altar canopy from Hagia Sophia as well as the description of the ambo by Michael of Thessaloniki, however, implies that ambo canopies were very similar to altar canopies in form and extended the meanings of the sacred space they framed.

In the sixth century, Paulos Silentarios also described the now-lost *phiale* in Hagia Sophia as a canopied installation.[65] Silentarios indicated that the blessing of water was

---

[58] *SD* 79, quoting now-lost text by John of Malalas reiterated by Thephanes, Kedrenos, and other chronicles that spoke about the earthquake of December 557 and about the collapse of the dome in 558 [*Agathias*, V, 9, 2–5; *Theophanes* 232–233]. See also Millet (1923) 599ff.

[59] Mango and Parker (1960) 233–244.

[60] On the full account of the episode with reference to primary sources, both Byzantine and Latin, see Talbot (1993) 243–261, esp. 246–247.

[61] Talbot (1993) 243–261, esp. 246–247.

[62] Mango and Parker (1960) 233–244; Xydis (1947) 1–24.

[63] D'Auito and Peréz Martin (2008).

[64] Mango and Parker (1960) 233–244; *Clavijo* 74.

[65] *Paulus Silentarios-b* as in *TLG*, lines 590–606:

Ἀλλὰ καὶ ἀμβροσίοιο πρὸς ἑσπέριον πόδα νηοῦ τέτρασιν αἰθούσῃσι περίδρομον ὄψεαι αὐλήν, ὧν μία μὲν νάρθηκι συνάπτεται, αἵ γε μὲν ἄλλαι πεπταμέναι τελέθουσι πολυσχιδέεσσι κελεύθοις. μηκεδανῆς δ' ἐρίτιμον ἐς ὀμφαλὸν

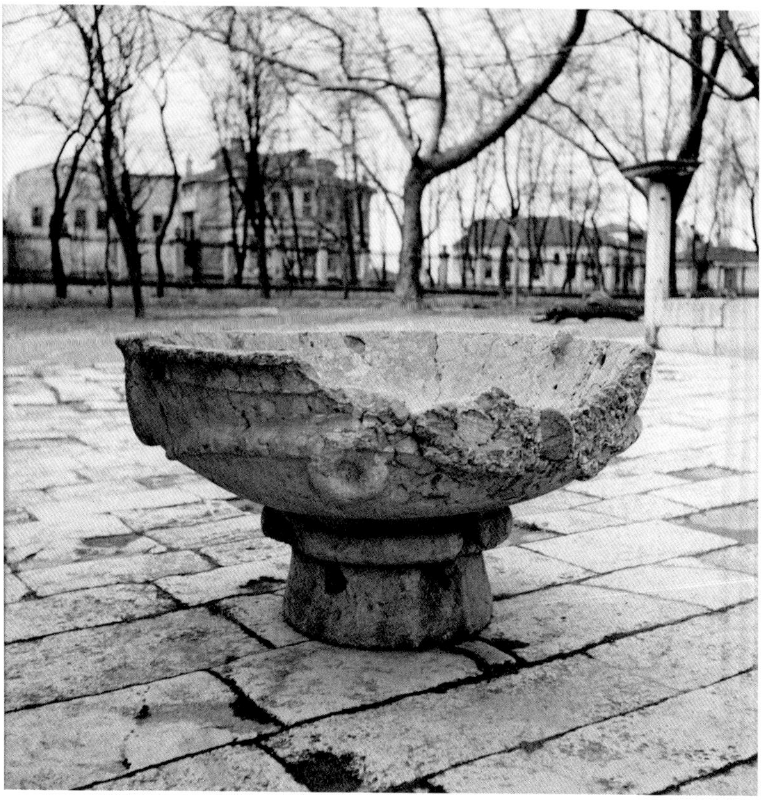

FIGURE 3.16 *Marble phiale vessel, Hagia Sophia, Constantinople, now Istanbul.* PHOTOGRAPHED BY ARTAMONOFF (ICFA.NA.0080), NICHOLAS V. ARTAMONOFF COLLECTION, IMAGE COLLECTIONS AND FIELDWORK ARCHIVES, DUMBARTON OAKS, TRUSTEES FOR HARVARD UNIVERSITY, WASHINGTON, D.C.

performed in a separate *phiale* in the church atrium and under a canopy that was placed over the holy water font, thus creating a distinct architectural installation.[66] The *phiale* from Hagia Sophia was again mentioned in accounts by the eleventh century Byzantine monk and intellectual Michael Psellos and an anonymous Russian pilgrim sometime between 1389 and 1391.[67] The anonymous Russian traveler described an open, lead-covered canopy over the stone vessel of the *phiale*, although the canopy's location at the time of his visit remains unverifiable (Fig. 3.16).[68] He revealed the *phiale* as "a great stone cup on a column in front of the church, and over the cup there is a lead-covered canopy;

ἵσταται αὐλῆςεὐρυτάτη φιάλη τις, Ἰασσίδος ἔκτομος ἄκρης, ἔνθα ῥόος κελαδῶν ἀναπάλλεται ἠέρι πέμπειν ὁλκὸν ἀναθρώσκοντα βίηι χαλκήρεος αὐλοῦ, ὁλκὸν ὅλων παθέων ἐλατήριον, ὁππότε λαὸς μηνὶ χρυσοχίτωνι, θεοῦ κατὰ μύστιν ἑορτήν, ἐννυχίοις ἄχραντον ἀφύσσεται ἄγγεσιν ὕδωρ·ἐννυχίοις ἄχραντον ἀφύσσεται ἄγγεσιν ὕδωρ· ὁλκὸν ἀπαγγέλλοντα θεοῦ μένος· οὐ γὰρ ἐκείνοις οὔποτε πυθομένοισιν ἐπέχραεν ὕδασιν εὐρώς, εἰ καὶ πουλυέτηρον ἐπὶ χρόνον ἔκτοθι πηγῆς κάλπιδος ἐν γυάλοισιν ἐελμένα δώμασι μίμνοι. Λαότορον δ' ἀνὰ τοῖχον ἐΰγραφα δαίδαλα τέχνης πάντοθεν ἀστράπτουσιν.

[66] Teteriatnikov (1998b).

[67] *RussAnon* in *RussTravelers* (1984) 128–154; Boura (1975–1976) 85–96, with references to Psellos.

[68] *RussAnon* in *RussTravelers* (1984) 128–154, esp. 138–139.

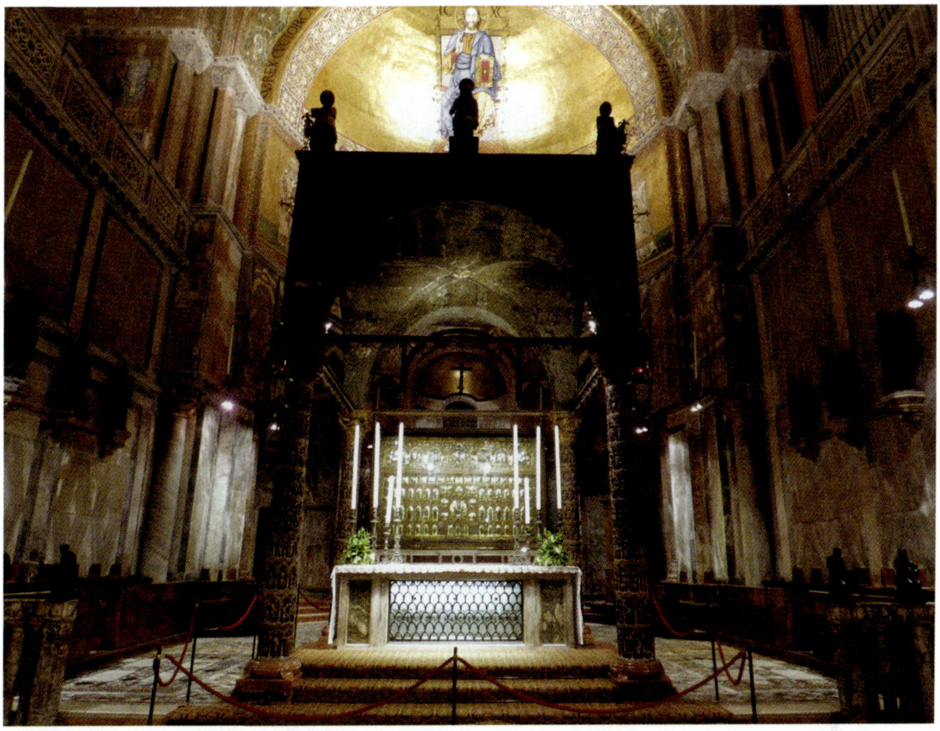

FIGURE 3.17 *Carved columns of the altar canopy, San Marco, Venice, Italy; reused Byzantine spolia, sixth or seventh century.* PHOTO AUTHOR

it is enclosed by columns with stone bars between them. The evangelists and apostles are carved on bars, and the columns are carved too."[69] The Byzantine texts record a palindrome inscription in Greek, which reads in both directions, "wash your sin, not only your face" [ΝΙΨΟΝ ΑΝΟΜΗΜΑ ΜΗ ΜΟΝΑΝ ΟΨΙΝ] and which decorated the stone font of the *phiale*.[70] Historiated carved canopy columns as mentioned by the Russian traveler did exist and had a long tradition in Byzantium, judging by the richly carved sixth- or seventh-century columns reused as *spolia* for the altar canopy in San Marco in Venice (Table 7.215, Fig. 3.17).[71]

Though now lost, the existence of a *phiale* canopy and its location in the center of the church courtyard as recounted in the Russian text coincides with the eleventh-century Byzantine accounts by Michael Psellos that describe the *phiale* in Hagia Sophia and in the eleventh-century monastic Church of St. George of Mangana, the latter confirmed by archeological excavations.[72] A reasonably accurate drawing of the western elevation of the Hagia Sophia done by Italian diplomat and antiquarian Cyriacus of Ancona (1391–1452), and copied and reinterpreted by architect Giuliano da Sangallo (ca. 1445–1516) at the end of the fifteenth century, shows a canopy centrally positioned within the courtyard of Hagia Sophia (Barberini Codex, fol. 28r). Even if the stone vessel for the sanctified water,

---

69 Ibid., 128–154, esp. 138–140.

70 Soteriou (1962) 218.

71 Klein (2004) 31–59; Klein (2006) 79–99; Dale (2010a) 159–191; Dale (2010b) 406–427.

72 For the *phiale* in St. George of Mangana, see Demangel and Mamboury (1939) 23–30. See also Chapter 2.

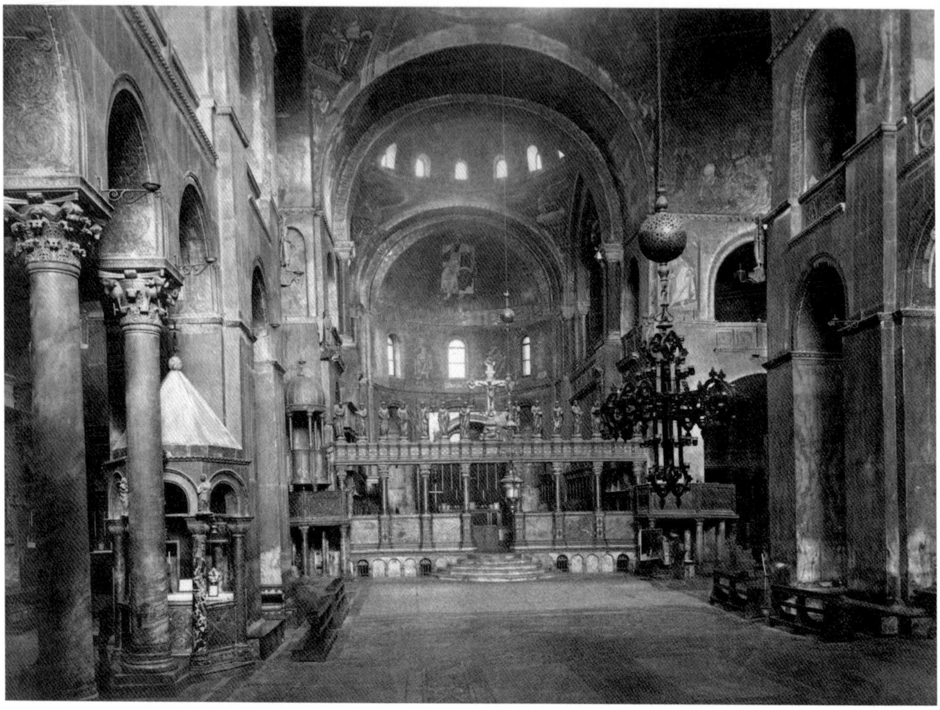

FIGURE 3.18 *Interior view of San Marco, Venice, Italy; photograph from 1915.* NGS IMAGE COLLECTION/THE ART ARCHIVE AT ART RESOURCE, NEW YORK

the *phiale* itself, is not depicted, this canopy in the drawing by Sangallo is most likely the one marking the place of the canopied *phiale* installation mentioned by Psellos and the Russian traveler.[73]

The anonymous Russian traveler wrote about other canopies in the Church of Hagia Sophia. One canopy in the north aisle enshrined the miraculous icon of the Mother of God, while a wooden canopy, believed to have been made of the wood of Noah's Ark and located at the time at the west end of the north aisle of the church, was presumably venerated as a relic itself.[74] Though these canopies mentioned by the Russian traveler could have been installed in the church after the Latin conquest of 1204, as suggested by some scholars, and the reference to the canopy made of wood of Noah's Ark is most peculiar,[75] the possibility that such three-dimensional canopies existed throughout the Byzantine period remains. I agree with Hans Belting and Thomas E. A. Dale, who proposed that the famous *il Capitello*, the thirteenth-century polygonal canopy with a pyramidal roof inserted in the easternmost intercolumniation of the north aisle of San Marco in Venice (Fig. 3.18) and which now enshrines a miracle-working wooden crucifix (Fig. 3.19), was initially designed to recreate the canopy shrine for the miraculous bleeding icon of the Mother of God and its location as it was originally in Hagia Sophia.[76] A similar arrangement of a *proskynetarion*

[73] I agree with Smith, C. (1987) 16–32, esp. 17–19, who came to the same conclusion.

[74] *RussAnon* in *RussTravelers* (1984) 128–154, esp. 132–133.

[75] For the belief that main doors of the inner narthex of Hagia Sophia were sheathed with wooden planks from Noah's ark and the reference for their removal by the Crusaders, see *RussTravelers* (1984) 207, with an extensive bibliography on the topic.

[76] Belting (1996) 197; Dale (2010b) 406–427, esp. 416; Dale (2010a) 151–191, esp. 184. See also Brenk (1999) 143–155.

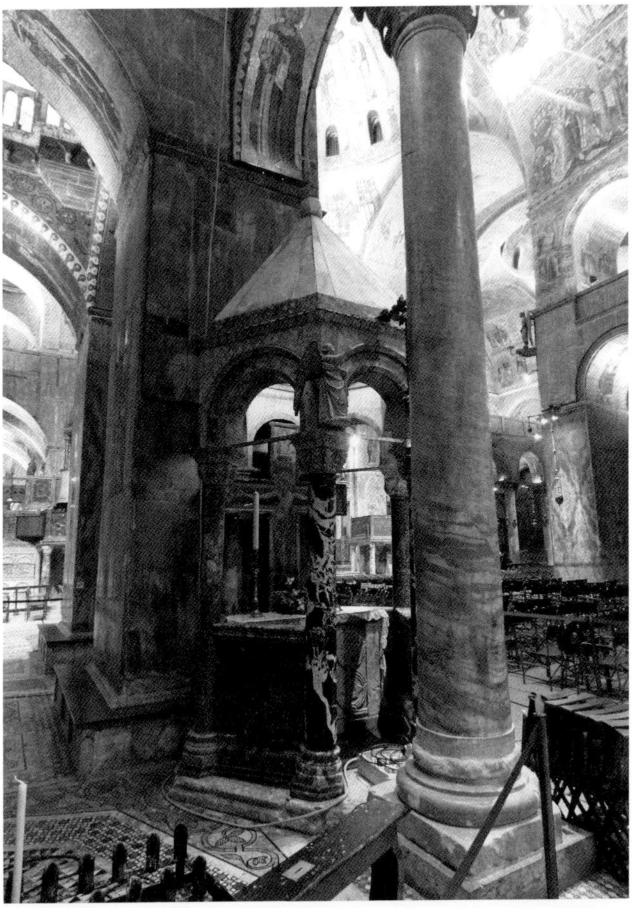

FIGURE 3.19 *Il Capitelo, San Marco, Venice, Italy, thirteenth century.* PHOTO AUTHOR

canopy, which reportedly enshrined the relics of the True Cross and a miraculous icon, was archeologically revealed in the northeastern section, flanking the iconostasis, of the Serbian monastery Church of Christ the Savior in Žiča.[77] This relatively modest church in terms of size does not resemble the famous Constantinopolitan cathedral Hagia Sophia, yet the Žiča church also served as a cathedral, and its liturgical furnishing, including this canopy, were built by Constantinopolitan builders who came to Serbia in 1219.[78] Although no relics of the True Cross are attested in the monastery of Chrysostomos at Koutsovendis on the island of Cyprus, early Christian texts record that a special canopy was built to enshrine the relic, which reaffirms the widespread use of canopied installations for the veneration of the True Cross.[79]

Numerous Byzantine texts describe the lighting of lamps in front of specially venerated icons and relics in Constantinopolitan and other Byzantine churches.[80] It is often assumed that these icons either were mounted on iconostasis screens or were enshrined

[77] Čanak-Medić (1998) 173–187; Čanak-Medić et al. (2014) 170–172, fig. 115.

[78] Šuput (1984) 157–160.

[79] Papacostas, Mango, and Grünbart (2007) 25–156, esp. 46.

[80] See, for example, references from the *Pantokrator* typikon in *BMFD* vol. 2, 725–781. On the subject, see also Boura (1982) 479–491.

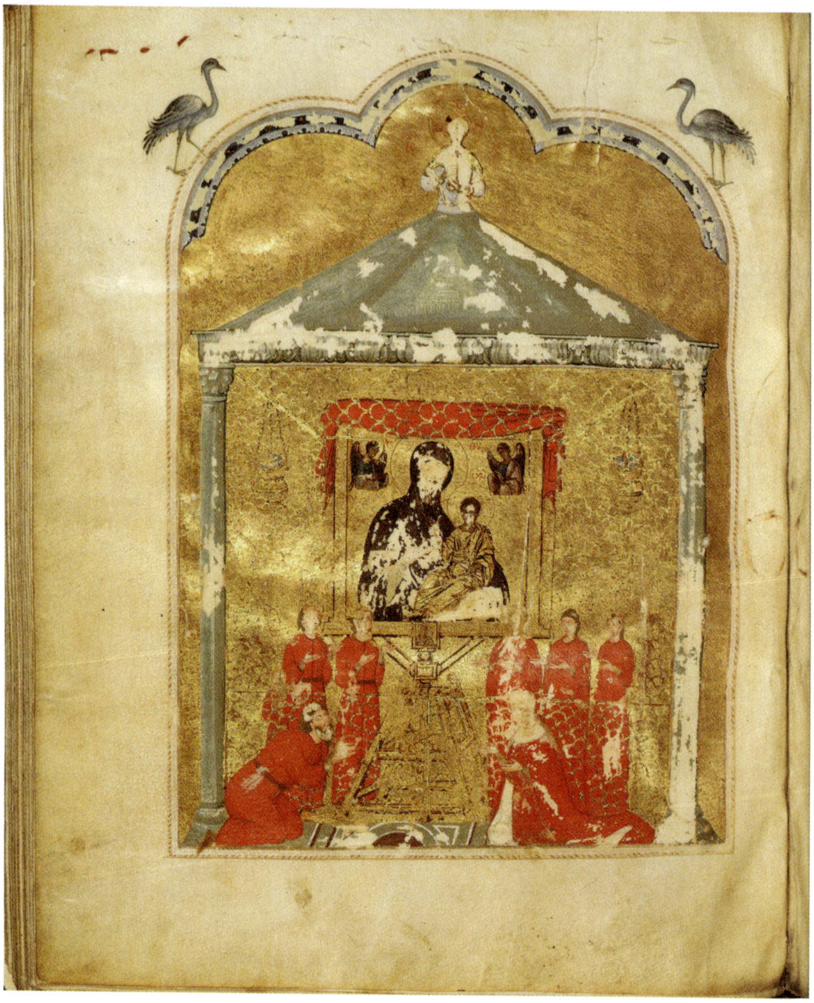

FIGURE 3.20 *Icon canopy, Hamilton Psalter, 78.A.9, fol. 39v, ca. 1300, made in Constantinople; belonged to Queen Charlotte of Jerusalem, Cyprus, and Armenia, granddaughter of Theodore Palaeologue, despot of Mistra.* KUPFERSTICHKABINETT, STAATLICHE MUSEEN, BERLIN, GERMANY/JÖRG P. ANDERS/ART RESOURCE, NEW YORK

by two-column, *aedicula*-like canopies mounted on church piers, pillars, or walls. However, the Russian traveler who described the canopy over the miraculous icon in Hagia Sophia used the Old Slavonic word *теремец* (*teremec*), which denotes a pavilion-like structure, usually any shelter on four columns.[81] An image of an icon of the Mother of God and Christ Child below a canopy in the fourteenth-century Hamilton Psalter (78.A.9, fol. 39v), found in Cyprus and made in Constantinople, provides additional visual clues as to how such icons flanked by two hanging lamps and mounted on a pedestal could have been enshrined by three-dimensional *proskynetaria* canopies and venerated by the faithful (Fig. 3.20).[82]

---

[81] *RussTravelers* (1984) 215; Voronin (1961) 254–255. The Old Slavonic word *теремец* (*teremec*) denoted "canopy" in both secular and religious architecture. Nenadović (2002) 77–78, 351.

[82] Spartharakis (1974) 190–205.

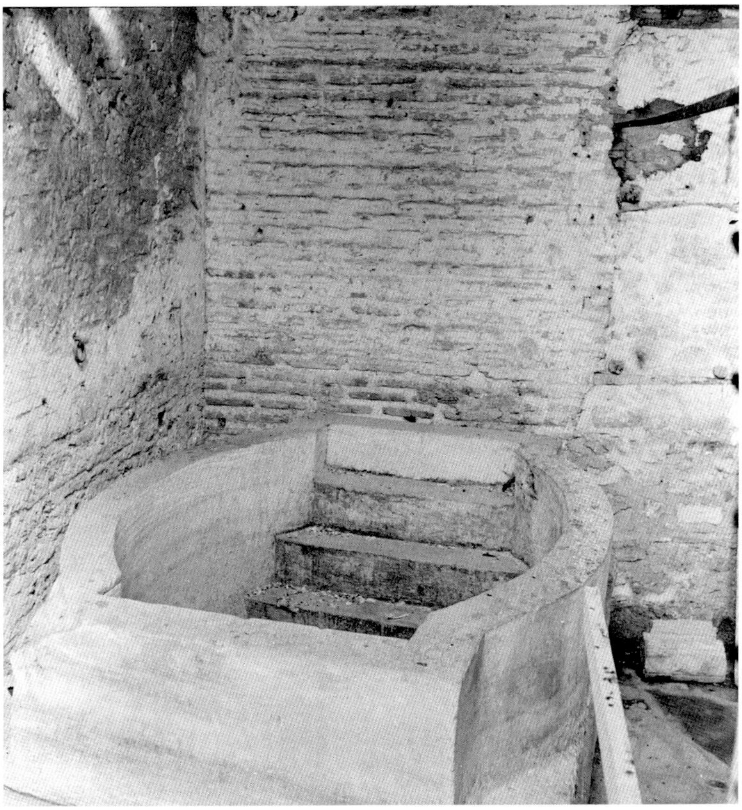

FIGURE 3.21 *Baptismal font, Hagia Sophia, Constantinople, now Istanbul.* PHOTOGRAPHED BY ARTAMONOFF (ICFA.NA.0294), NICHOLAS V. ARTAMONOFF COLLECTION, IMAGE COLLECTIONS AND FIELDWORK ARCHIVES, DUMBARTON OAKS, TRUSTEES FOR HARVARD UNIVERSITY, WASHINGTON, D.C.

We may never learn how many more canopies were in Hagia Sophia during its long history as a church. The photographs by a Russian archeologist, Nicholas V. Artmonoff, taken in 1943 clearly show a massive baptismal font that may have been originally canopied within large baptismal setting (Fig. 3.21). Mentioned in sources both to the north and to the south of Hagia Sophia, archeological evidence for the baptistery of the major Byzantine cathedral is lost; both sections to the south and north blocked with more recent buildings. It is tempting to propose that the baptistery of Hagia Sophia was similar to the still-standing "Hagiasma of H. Ioannis," which originally was the baptistery of Cathedral of Hagia Sophia in Thessaloniki.[83] This early fifth-century baptistery dedicated to St. John the Baptist was a hexagonal building, which was enlivened in the interior with six rounded niches and six massive columns in the corners between them (Fig. 3.22). Slobodan Ćurčić has effectively demonstrated that architectural articulation of the baptistery in Thessaloniki would create an impression that the six corner columns supported its dome, thus forming a huge canopy above the marble font (Fig. 3.23).[84] Such architectural design, and archeological confirmation elsewhere for early baptisteries and their relative location to the south of the major

[83] Theocharidou (1988) 189–197.
[84] Ćurčić (2010) 104–105.

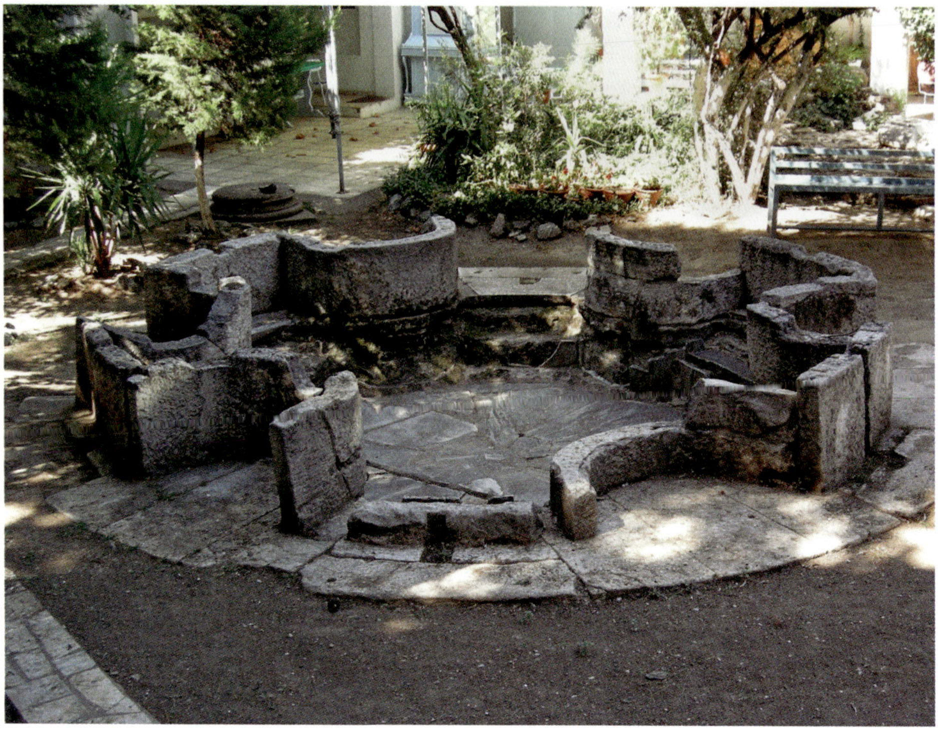

FIGURE 3.22 *"Hagiasma of Hagios Ioannis," possibly baptistery located south of the Cathedral of Hagia Sophia, Thessaloniki, fifth century.* PHOTO NEBOJŠA STANKOVIĆ

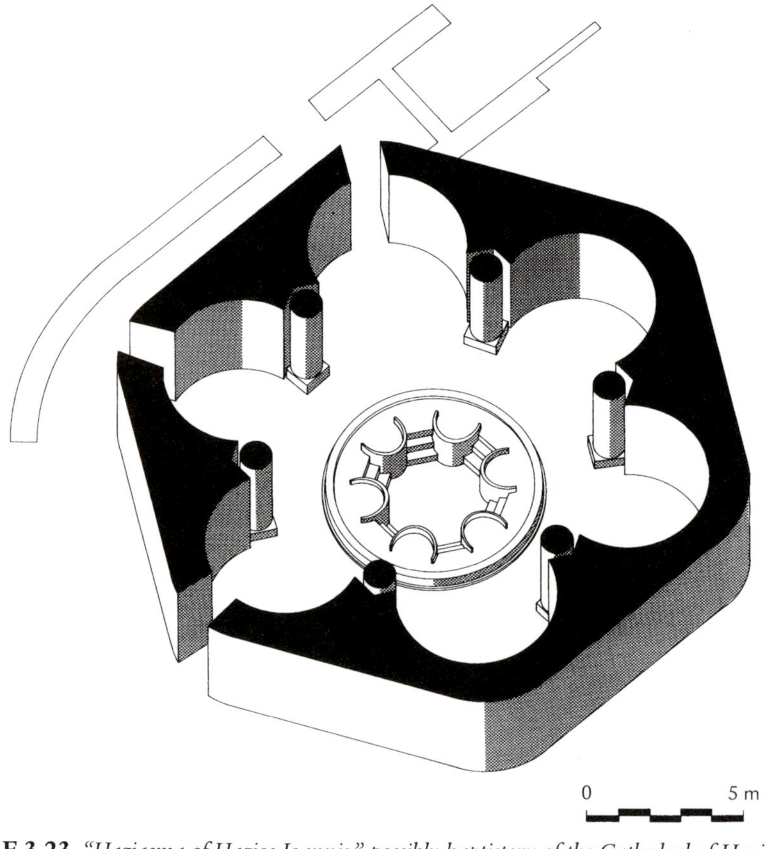

FIGURE 3.23 *"Hagiasma of Hagios Ioannis," possibly baptistery of the Cathedral of Hagia Sophia, Thessaloniki, fifth century; reconstruction drawing.* DRAWING JOEL KELLY FROM ĆURČIĆ (2010) 104, FIG. 98

church, provide an incentive to speculate that the now-lost baptistery of Hagia Sophia in Constantinople may have been a similarly designed, massive canopied structure.

The sheer number of relics that the Constantinopolitan cathedral housed or displayed for veneration during specific feasts points to a high possibility that some of these relics were enshrined in micro-architectural, canopy-like settings. It is interesting to surmise that, in addition to the above-mentioned five types of three-dimensional canopies, now lost, more canopies, including those on two columns and two-dimensional canopies, which signified three-dimensional canopies, might have existed. Some of these two-dimensional and "transitional" types of canopies can still be observed in Hagia Sophia. A canopy-like structure with curtains executed in *opus sectile* has continued to shelter the bejeweled cross on a stepped base in the western wall of Hagia Sophia's nave just above its central doors since the sixth century (Fig. 3.24). This plaque depicting the Cross within a curtained canopy is additionally surrounded with four other plaques with roundels, two in low relief and two painted, as if four circles were surrounding the main image of the canopied cross, suggesting a multi-folded framing of the sacred also recognizable through the basic outline of the canopies that have been archeologically confirmed in numerous early Christian floors, but here are seemingly inverted upright and raised on the wall.

I would, however, like to entertain the idea that this representation of the True Cross within the canopy points to potential ceremonial settings and locations for the veneration of the True Cross as attested in Hagia Sophia, since the sixth century. Holger Klein has demonstrated how numerous sources mention the veneration of small and larger particles of the True Cross, allegedly first recovered under Helena, mother of Emperor Constantine I, and then dispersed throughout Christian lands, including Constantinople.[85]

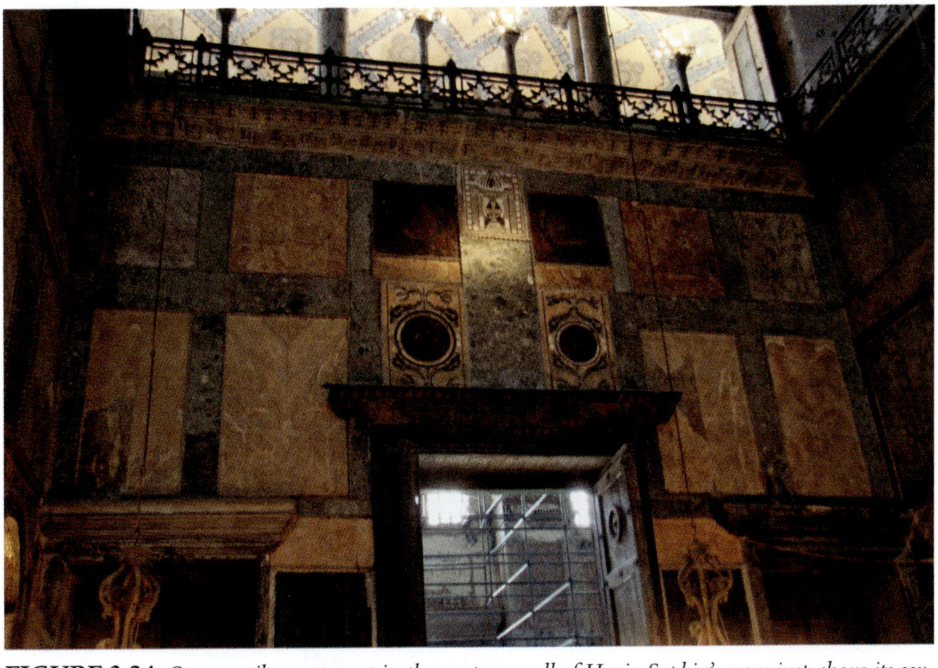

FIGURE 3.24 *Opus sectile revetment in the western wall of Hagia Sophia's nave just above its central doors, Hagia Sophia, Constantinople, now Istanbul, sixth century.* PHOTO NEBOJŠA STANKOVIĆ

[85] Klein (2004) 31–59; Klein (2006) 79–99.

Emperor Justin II (r. 565–578) ordered a precious reliquary to be made for the particles of the True Cross, presumably acquired by the city since Constantine I, and placed it for veneration in Hagia Sophia already in the sixth century, when the cathedral was rebuilt under Justinian I. By the seventh century, Emperor Herakleios (r. 610–641) regained from the Persians another, larger piece of the True Cross that had been originally kept in Jerusalem. Upon its ceremonial return to Constantinople, he placed it for veneration in Hagia Sophia for several days. After the unsuccessful return of the Cross to Jerusalem, when the Byzantines lost the city again, the emperor returned the Cross to Constantinople one more time and enshrined it in the palace, also known as the Sacred Palace.[86] The ultimate setting of the True Cross in Constantinople instigated the development of large processions before military campaigns and during Lent. These processions started at the Sacred Palace, moved along the city, and displayed the True Cross for veneration in several churches and locations, ultimately depositing it for public veneration in Hagia Sophia. Where exactly the Cross was enshrined for veneration remains unknown. Adomnán, abbot of the monastery of Iona, testified that in the second half of the seventh century, Bishop Arculf, who visited Constantinople after his pilgrimage in the Holy Land, venerated the True Cross in a "very large and beautiful chest . . . to the north of the interior of the building."[87] As the True Cross, the life-giving Cross, represented the reality of the Ark of Noah and the Ark of Covenant among the Orthodox, it seems possible that the location of the canopy-shrine of the Ark at the west end of the north aisle of the church, mentioned by the Russian traveler centuries later and also pointed to by the representation of the unveiled True Cross in the western wall of the church, just below the gallery, may refer to the place of the veneration of the True Cross by the faithful and pilgrims.

Furthermore, above this two-dimensional *opus sectile* canopy represented on the western wall of the cathedral, on the grayish marble gallery floor, there is yet another *opus sectile* canopy consisting of a big roundel of *verde antico* marble inscribed in a square. On its two western corners, it is framed by two rectangular porphyry plaques, while two *breccia verde* columns incorporated into gallery parapets delineate the two eastern corners of the roundel in square (Fig. 3.25). The two slender columns with interlaced capitals, which serve no structural role, perhaps had the now-elapsed function of framing a standing or sitting person observing the services in the naos of the church. The spot is known as the "lodge of the Empress" and spatially denotes the setting of canopied thrones known from Roman imperial architecture.[88] Though we do not have any evidence about whether the outlined squares around the axially positioned roundels marked the position of a throne canopy, the use of which has been confirmed on numerous occasions, the two columns framing an imperial personage would have created the perception of a throne canopy and also an aura of sacred appearance. Sixth-century Vienna and Florence ivories, which show empresses standing and sitting, in each case framed by a canopy-like throne, illustrate the impression created by such an architectural setting (Fig. 1.5).[89] Averil Cameron

---

[86] Carile (2012) 172–173.

[87] *Jerusalem Pilgrims* 202; Klein (2006) 79–99.

[88] Mathews (1971) 96 and 134 suggested that the floor design on the gallery of Hagia Sophia is a marking for the emperor's throne. Similarly furnished canopied thrones whose place was delineated by *opus sectile* patterns framed by four outlined corners may have existed in the imperial chamber in Luxor and in the throne room in Piazza Armerina. Kalavrezou (1975) 225–251; Karelin (2014) 6–22; Karelin (2013) 116–117; Karelin (2012) 57–82.

[89] Kalavrezou (1975) 225–251, with references to works by Lehmann, Alfoldi, and Khaler. On the sitting and standing Byzantine empress under the throne, presumably in the interior of a church or a palace, as depicted on the ivories from the Museo Nazionale, Florence Kunsthistoriches Museum, Vienna; see Delbrueck (1929) nos. 51 and 52; Maguire (2006); James (2001) 39; McClanan (2002) 168–173, figs. 7.6 and 7.7.

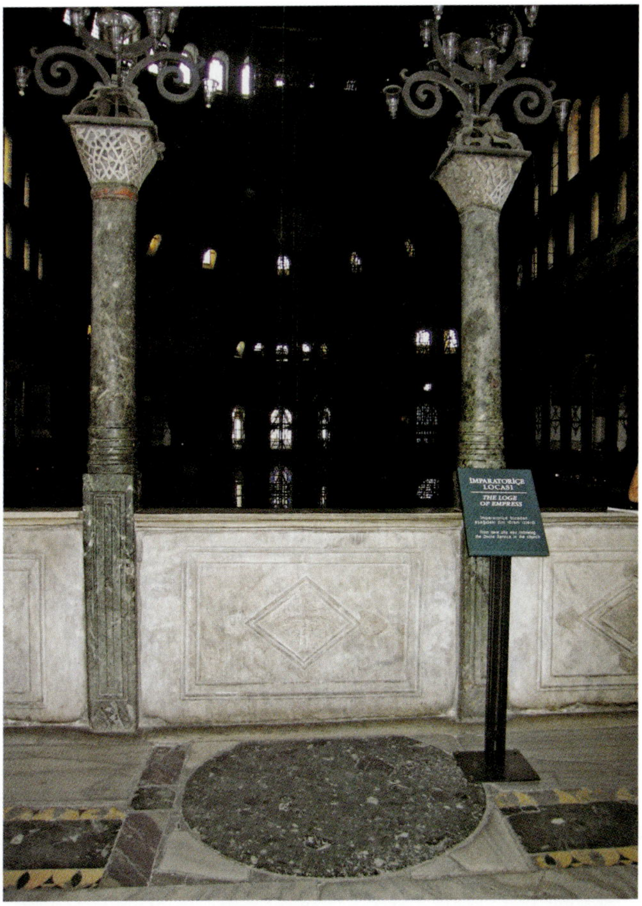

FIGURE 3.25 *"Empress lodge," Hagia Sophia, Constantinople, now Istanbul, sixth century.* PHOTO AUTHOR

has pointed out that this curtained canopy borne on columns that enclosed the empress coincides with the description by the sixth-century poet Corippus of the canopy over the throne in the Great Consistory of the imperial palace in Constantinople.[90] Such portable canopies, the position of which was marked in the church space and galleries as in Hagia Sophia, may point to various imperial connotations. For example, from the tenth-century texts, we know that the relics of the True Cross were venerated by the imperial family in the gallery of the Nea Ekklesia (New Church) built by Emperor Basil I in the ninth century.[91] The five-domed Nea was envisioned as Basil I's Hagia Sophia, and it is tempting to propose that the veneration of the True Cross in the gallery emulated an earlier practice of imperial veneration of the Cross in Hagia Sophia itself, possibly indicated by the spot of the "lodge of the Empress" in the gallery and further confirming the multiple and complex uses of canopied installations or the multiple locations marked by them within the church proper.

---

[90] *Corippus* 106, commentary on 188–191.
[91] Klein (2006) 79–99; Magdalino (1987b) 51–64; Stanković (2008).

THE CHURCH RITES AND PLACE-MAKING

The reconstructions of the various meanings that canopies revealed to the faithful within different rites performed in Byzantine churches expand beyond regularly performed liturgical services to include baptismal ceremonies as in Dura Europos or devotional practices such as the veneration of the True Cross in Hagia Sophia. The Dura Europos baptistery canopy in particular demonstrates how these installations and their environments can be understood beyond simply textual and official sources to include the reenactments of the participants of the religious rites, emphasizing that the architectural design of canopies was closely related to the living practices of the church. Though heavily restored, all three canopies from Paros and Kalabaka provide glimpses into different settings for canopies, as well as how these three have been able to be preserved *in situ* because they were located at some distance from the main urban centers throughout their history and even to this day.[92] The Paros canopy, set on a remote island far from any major urban center, further points to the complexity of historical studies based on notions of the center and the periphery. The canopy from Paros, made of marble and set in the imperial foundation, reveals the glory of the now-lost but celebrated canopies from Constantinople that were made of luxurious materials on a grand scale and by the best available artists. The rediscovery of the canopy at the collection of the Royal Ontario Museum is a unique and rare example of a relatively well-preserved canopy. Due to its rough execution and lower-quality stone, and despite its highly developed architectural decoration, the canopy from the Royal Ontario Museum offers only a taste of the different designs of canopies that once adorned churches. Its original location and use in the church remains hypothetical, however, as is the case for numerous architectural fragments of canopies reassembled or in museums. The Church of Hagia Sophia set the standards for Byzantine architecture, even if it was never repeated in design and size. In addition to Paulos Silentarios' poetic description of the altar canopy, both his verses and those by Michael of Thessaloniki on the ambo canopy in Hagia Sophia highlight the great importance Byzantines placed on the canopies in the Constantinopolitan cathedral, which gained multiple evocative meanings during church services when experienced performatively, through bodily and spiritual movements and quests. By looking at Hagia Sophia as an "ideal" Byzantine church in terms of its conceptual design and architecture, the next chapters will highlight the role of the canopy as micro-architecture and architectural *parti* in Byzantine-rite churches.

[92] For example, the island of Paros in the Aegean has been deserted for prolonged periods of time during the Byzantine period, occasionally sacked by pirates, or inhabited by hermits. *Life StTheokiste-c* 97, 105.

FOUR

The Micro-Architectural Framing of Sacred Space

Then, it seems, he entered the church and, after saying his prayers, saw the sacred and beautiful construction which is set up in the midst of the church on the left-hand side: it is hexagonal in plan, having six columns and as many partitions, shaped out of carved, assayed silver. Its roof is likewise held up all round by the six sides and terminates in a circular conjunction from the base up. At the top it bears a silver sphere of no small size, its lower part surrounded by the shoots of lilies. At the very summit flashes forth the trophy that is victorious over death: by its silver composition it amazes our corporeal eyes, while by bringing Christ to mind, it illuminates with grace the eyes of the intellect—I mean the life-giving and venerable cross of God our Savior.

Having beheld in his dream this God-given structure that is in the church—the one we call the sanctified ciborium—he seemed to be asking those around him, "What, O brethren, is this wonderful work that rises in the middle of the church's length? . . ." They replied, "We have been told by our fathers that the most glorious martyr Demetrios reposes there in divine fashion."

Εἶτα εἰσελθὼν δῆθεν ἐν τῷ ναῷ καὶ προσευξάμενος, ὁρᾷ τὸ ἱερόσκευον ἐκεῖνο καὶ περικαλλὲς δημιούργημα κατὰ μέσον τοῦ ναοῦ πρὸς τοῖς λαιοῖς πλευροῖς ἐφιδρυμένον ἑξαγώνῳ σχήματι, κίοσιν ἓξ καὶ τοίχοις ἰσαρίθμοις ἐξ ἀργύρου δοκίμου καὶ διαγεγλυμμένου μεμορφωμένον, καὶ τὴν ὀροφὴν ὡσαύτως ἀπὸ τῶν ἑξαγώνων πλευρῶν κυκλοφορικῶς ἀνίσχουσαν καὶ εἰς μίαν στρογγύλην ὡσεὶ ποδὸς ἀπολήγουσαν σύνδεσιν, σφαῖράν τε ἀργυρέαν μεγέθους οὐ μικροῦ φέρουσαν ἄνωθεν, ὑφ' ἣν ὡς κρίνου βλαστοὶ θαυμάσιοι περιέχονται, ὧν πάντων ἐπάνω τὸ κατὰ τοῦ θανάτου πεπηγὸς τρόπαιον ἀκτινοβολεῖ, τῷ μὲν ἀργυρέῳ δημιουργήματι τὰς τοῦ σώματος ὄψεις παρασκευάζον ἐκπλήττεσθαι, τῇ δὲ τοῦ Χριστοῦ νοήσει τοὺς τῆς διανοίας ὀφθαλμοὺς τοῖς οὐρανίοις καταυγάζον χαρίσμασιν, ὁ ζωοποιός, φημί, καὶ τίμιος τοῦ θεοῦ καὶ σωτῆρος ἡμῶν σταυρός.

Τοῦτο δὴ τὸ θεοδώρητον τέχνασμα κατὰ τοὺς ὕπνους ὁ ἀνὴρ ἐν τῷ ναῷ θεασάμενος, τὸ παρ' ἡμῖν καλούμενον ἡγιασμένον κιβώριον, ἐπηρώτα δῆθεν τοὺς πλησίον· «Τὸ τοῦτο, ἀδελφοί, τὸ καινοθαύμαστον ποίημα κατὰ τὸ μῆκος τοῦ ναοῦ μέσον ἐφίδρυται; οὐ γὰρ ἂν ταύτην εἰλήχει τὴν χώραν εἰ μὴ μεγάλης τινὸς ἠξίωτο τῆς προφάσεως.» Τῶν δὲ φησάντων ὡς «Ἐκεῖσε παρὰ τῶν πατέρων ἠκούσαμεν κεῖσθαι θεοπρεπῶς τὸν ὑπερένδοξον ἀθλοφόρον Δημήτριον—Ἐπεθύμουν, ἔφη ὁ ἀνήρ, τῆς κατὰ τὸ ἔνδον ὁράσεως.»

Archbishop John of Thessaloniki, seventh century[1]

• • •

The relatives took pity on her, and putting her upon an ass as if she were a lifeless burden brought her to the New Siloam—the tomb of the blessed Luke—and her son indeed followed along with her.... A little while before the tomb of the saint like a spring had exuded a sweet smelling myrrh, and the attendant [a minor official of the monastery] carefully collecting it took it and put it into one of the lamps and this he hung over the sacred tomb.

Ταύτην οἱ προσήκοντες κατὰ γένος τῆν συμφορᾶς ἐλεήσαντες καὶ οἱοωεὶ φόρτον ἄψυχον ὄνῳ ἐπιβιβάσαντες καὶ περικρατοῦντες πρὸς τὸν νέον Σιλωάμ, τὸν τοῦ μακαρίου Λουκᾶ φέρουσι τάφον, συεπομένου δηλαδὴ ταύτῃ καὶ τοῦ υἱοῦ, ἔνθα καὶ καταλιπόντες αὐτοὺς ἐπανήεσαν.... Ὀλίγῳ γὰρ πρότερον τῆς τοῦ ἁγίου θήκης πηγῇ παραπλησίως μῦρον εὐῶδες ἀποβλυσάσης, ὁ νεωκόρος ἐπιμελὲς θέμενος καὶ τούτου λαβὼν εἰς μίαν τε τῶν φωταγωγῶν ἐμβαλών, τοῦ ἱερῦ ταύτης ἀπήρησε τάφου.

An anonymous writer of the *Life of Hosios Loukas*, tenth century[2]

THE SEVENTH-CENTURY DESCRIPTION OF THE FAMOUS CIBORIUM OF ST. DEMETRIOS in his eponymous church in Thessaloniki and the tenth-century account of the canopy-shrine of Hosios Loukas in his eponymous monastery reveal the power of canopied installations to invoke various religious and spiritual concepts; to represent the entire religious foundations, buildings, or monasteries where they stood; and to evoke a variety of architectural spaces beyond them. An anonymous pilgrim, a relative of a Prefect of Illyricum in the seventh century who was seeking help from the miracle-worker St. Demetrios, accurately described the location of his hexagonal silver shrine approximately in the middle of the church, close to the north aisle—a location that has been archeologically proved. This pilgrim also believed that the structure marked the tomb of the saint, which cannot be confirmed today, as the body and relics of St. Demetrios most likely were never in this location. Above all, the pilgrim reported that the shrine of the saint was fashioned in such a manner that it invoked Christ, the True Cross, and by extension the Tomb of Christ. Similarly, in the tenth century, a miraculous healing occurred to a mother and son at another shrine, that of Hosios Loukas. Brought by their relatives to Hosios Loukas, the mother, broken with depression as if lifeless, and her son, suffering from a mental disorder and regularly inflicting wounds on himself, spent some time in front of the shrine, and just when they planned to return home, the shrine exuded myrrh that resulted in the mental and physical restoration of both the mother and the son. In the account, the saintly shrine was recorded as the New Siloam, evoking Siloam, a Biblical site in Jerusalem, the city of King David, which for Christians seeking healing had special meaning because according to the Gospel of John, Christ sent a man born blind to the Pool at Siloam to receive his physical and mental sight (Jn. 9.7–11). These medieval accounts show how various canopied installations in Byzantine churches, including those that belonged to the same type such as the saintly shrines highlighted here, might evoke different types of Biblical architecture and sacred

---

1 *Life and Miracles StDemetrios-a* Miracle 10, 87ff, lines 87(22)–88(7). Translation into English by Mango in *SD* 129.

2 *Life StLuke* ch. 69, lines 15–20; 25–28. Translation into English by Connors, *Life StLuke*, 115.

sites such as the Tomb of Christ or the Pool of Siloam. The interconnectivity between canopied installations within the sacred space in which they are found (such as the church itself) and which they denote (such as the Pool of Siloam) provided performative frameworks for discrete devotional practices and liturgical services. These examples call for a careful reexamination of diverse networks of meanings and forms of canopies in Byzantine churches.

The Constantinopolitan cathedral Hagia Sophia with the different canopied installations that once existed within it may inform the design of the "ideal" Byzantine-rite church as a space containing multiple canopied furnishings that enhanced the richly developed spatial topography of the church (see Figs. 2.67, 2.68. 2.69, 2.70). The multiple canopies within Byzantine churches, not only attested to in the Constantinopolitan Hagia Sophia, but also archeologically confirmed in cathedrals in other centers such as Thessaloniki, Kotor, Zadar, Mcheta, Bogolybovo, or Moscow, as well as in other churches that were pilgrimage or monastic centers, such as Hagios Demetrios in Thessaloniki or Hosios Loukas in Boeotia, disclose the multifocal reality of Byzantine churches and the critical role of canopied installations in framing both architecturally and symbolically the various rites and actions taking place in the church proper.[3] Indeed, these canopies could have denoted different messages to individual beholders, yet they seemingly provided meaningful settings for the various rituals and the various users—churchgoers of diverse backgrounds, clergy, theologians, pilgrims, visitors, or those seeking help. By looking at the individual canopies and their architectural settings, the historical context of the Byzantine understanding of canopies and the surviving archeological and other material evidence about actual canopied installations do not necessarily overlap and occasionally disclose the most fascinating and generally unnoticed spatial and experiential interrelations between different canopies as well as between canopies and other architectural elements of the Byzantine church. Above all, these multiple relations between various canopied installations and settings in the church point to the dynamic process of architectural modular design based on canopies as spatial units that allowed for a singular rather than a generic experience of space. The in-depth analysis of archeological and architectural evidence reveals a synthesis of two basic design processes: the inside-out process where conceptual inspirations stemming from various church practices and values, inclusive of theological, liturgical, and popular perceptions about the sacred space as the locus in the church, result in the architectural solutions for canopied installations; and the outside-in process where the architectural design was informed by the canopy as an image, which is a visually and spatially recognizable solution for framing the sacred space in the church.

Reversing the traditional approach that departs from the individual or collective experience of canopies in churches based on textual accounts, this chapter highlights the canopy as an architectural *parti*, a basic architectural module that carries the essence of the sacred and its experience. Case studies exemplify how the Byzantines used the potential of canopied installations in architectural design to achieve different solutions by rearranging, reordering, or reversing the place of canopies within church space while at the same time transposing and exchanging their symbolic meanings, which were either individually or culturally defined. The focus is on the micro scale of the canopied installations defined by human size and the human experience in selected church buildings. In particular, by examining specific architectural solutions, in the following sections I analyze the various spatial relations between canopies for altars, tombs, and saintly shrines; between altar canopies, *templon* screens, and *proskynetaria*; between canopied *phialai* outside the church and vaulted chambers that served as *phialai* inside the church; and between ambo canopies and two-dimensional *omphalos* disks in the nave of the church. I also consider the spatial and symbolic merging of imperial canopied thrones, canopied settings for the veneration of relics, and the canopies with

[3] Chapters 2 and 3.

funerary associations, as well as further transposition of canopies to the domical canopy bays of church narthexes and exonarthexes or the canopied and domed chapels in the galleries above narthexes. Finally, this chapter suggests an understanding of domed bays in Byzantine churches as architectural canopies and their transposition from domed basilicas to distinctive Middle-Byzantine solutions; above all, the so-called cross-in-square church design.

ALTAR CANOPY, SAINT'S TOMB, AND SHRINE CANOPY

One of the crucial questions for our understanding of canopies in Byzantine-rite churches is the spatial relationship between altar canopies and installations for sacred relics—the bodily remains of martyrs and saints. Because Byzantine-rite churches could not function without an altar, the sanctuary with an altar table was an indispensable part of the architectural design. The sanctuary (*bema*) was regularly spatially and visually emphasized by terminating into a grotto of a semicircular apse at the east end of the building. Starting already in the sixth century, some churches in the Balkans, and after the transitional period most Byzantine-rite churches, had a sanctuary with a tripartite apsidal arrangement consisting of a central altar space flanked by two chambers.[4] These architectural changes were closely related to the development and standardization of liturgical practices. As a result of the development of liturgical movements within the church, the side chambers known as *parabemata* or *pastophories* often had doors that opened directly into the sanctuary and into the side aisles. Most often to the north was a chamber called a *proscomide* or *prothesis,* where the eponymous service of the preparation of the Eucharist was performed (cf. Ex. 26:35) and the Eucharistic vessels were stored. To the south was a *diaconicon* that, similar to a storage space, housed liturgical vestments, sacred texts, portable reliquaries, and other sacred objects.

Throughout all liturgical and architectural changes, the sanctuary (*bema*) space with an altar remained the most important part of the church. This indispensable, most hallowed church space was used for the liturgical performance of the Eucharist, the New Testament bloodless sacrifice and the revelation of the presence of Christ. The Byzantines also followed the Biblical reference for the consecration of their altars with the relics of those who witnessed God or who suffered for their profession of Christianity: "And when he had opened the fifth seal, I saw under the altar the souls of them that were slain for the word of God, and for the testimony which they held" (Rev. 6:9). The centuries-old practice of consecrating altars with sacred relics, confirmed at least by the third century, was officially formulated by the seventh canon of the Second Council of Nicaea in 787, the last of seven ecumenical councils that formally defined practices in Byzantine-rite churches.[5]

In a Byzantine church, therefore, the altar table and sacred relics are very closely associated concepts, yet their spatial links and architectural articulation involve a controversial

---

[4] For early Christian arrangement of the single-apse sanctuary, see Mathews (1971) 105–107. For the tripartite arrangement after the transitional period, see Marinis (2014) 25–41. The development of the tripartite sanctuary was neither uniform throughout the Byzantine realm nor chronologically clearly defined. See, for example, Marinis (2014) 25–41; Ćurčić (2010) *passim*, Altripp (1998) *passim*; Gamber (1985) 61–71. Among scholarly works on *pastophoria* in Byzantine churches, see Nussbaum (1965); Stričević (1958/59) 59–65; Sodini (1984) 441–473; Smith, J. (1990) 181–204; Teteriatnikov (1996) 65.

[5] Mango (1990) 51–61 and Crook (2000) 19. Some early theologians connected the holy place with the Christian soul. *Clement of Alexandria, Stromata,* 8.5, wrote "the true temple is the assembly of Christian people," which is in line with Origen's statement, "the holy place is the pure soul." *St. Basil, Homilia in Psalmum 115* (4.112) confirmed that "he who touches the martyr's bones participates in saintliness and the grace which is there." For the post-Iconoclastic references on the altar containing the saintly relics, see, for example, 7th Canon of 7th Ecumenical Council (787) in *Seven Councils; Symeon of Thessaloniki* chs. 132–133; Mirković (1995) 102; *Seven Pillars* 157–168; Marinis (2014) 29.

question about the relationship between the altar and the tomb, especially when examining the relics that constituted entire bodies, not only tiny fragments. Without attempting any detailed investigation as to whether the canopy initially framed the altar or the tomb, the question of the formation of Christian altar-tombs sheltered by canopies remains crucial. The archeology from the early Christian martyrium at Majsan, Dalmatia, in modern Croatia and from Hagia Euphemia in Constantinople present the complexities of architectural merging of the tomb and altar and their subsequent framing by canopies.[6] At Majsan, the tomb of the local Saint Maxim (Maximus) became a venerated location, the altar was added at some later point, and the entire structure was architecturally formulated by a massive canopied installation some 3 meters in span. The installation at Majsan is congruent with the wide practice of building churches on the locations of tombs of early Christian martyrs.[7] In Constantinople, the altar and the tomb for the entire body of St. Euphemia were presumably joined simultaneously once the saintly relics reached their destination in the newly established church. Pilgrims' references to the devotional practices of venerating relics at the setting that combined both the saintly shrine and the altar raise a peculiar question, because altar installations in the sanctuaries were reserved only for clergy, inaccessible to lay people, and above all were not accessible to women. Furthermore, the Byzantine-rite liturgy requires unity of the altar and the sanctuary space, hence suggesting that the tombs with altars would originally be a tomb structure, and the altar would be established next. This phenomenon is associated with the so-called secondary altars in churches, which are recorded outside the sanctuary and were established at tombs and shrines at various locations inside churches. Such canopied shrine-altars outside of the sanctuaries have been attested to in late medieval examples, as in the Syrian-rite Church of St. George Exorinos and the Byzantine-rite Church of St. George of All the Greeks at Famagusta, Cyprus, and frequently scholars have related them to the influence of Western practices that reached Byzantium after the Crusades.[8]

The multilayered formation of the canopied installations for the altars and tombs and their merging into unique structures can be followed through several lines of inquiry, starting with the early Christian practices that combined popular piety, imperial support, and eventually approval by the religious authorities. Despite the limited archeological evidence, knowledge of Christian canopy-like architectural structures associated with tombs can be traced in the fourth century. Free-standing *aediculae* commissioned by Emperor Constantine I and his heirs sheltered the tomb of the Apostle in the basilica *martyrium* of St. Peter (begun ca. 319–322, finished ca. 333) and the Tomb of Christ (325/326–ca. 335) at Jerusalem, to mention the best-known examples.[9] These shrines initially functioned as burial markers and eternal houses. They designated important *loca sancta* and pilgrimage sites soon after being established, but originally they were not meant to function within a church or to shelter an altar. These architectural solutions would have been consistent with the older funerary traditions and current laws.

Jewish and ancient Greek altars were used for animal sacrifices and generally did not appear in funerary contexts. The only exceptions among the Greeks were the altars erected in honor of the heroicized dead.[10] Until the fourth century, the pagans might have chosen *aedicula-* and canopy-like tombs, as well as so-called funerary altars, either with a flat top or with architectural crowning elements, from a wide variety of tomb types. Two examples of centrally planned Roman *mausolea*, which were topped by a canopy-like structure—the mausoleum of the Julii at St. Rémy in France (ca. 30–20 BCE) and the tomb of the Istacidii

---

6 Chapter 2.

7 Bogdanović (2002) 7–19.

8 Bacci (2009) 11–30.

9 See, for example, Grabar (1972) 29–43, 141–152, chs. 4 and 5.

10 Kurtz and Boardman (1971) 301–302.

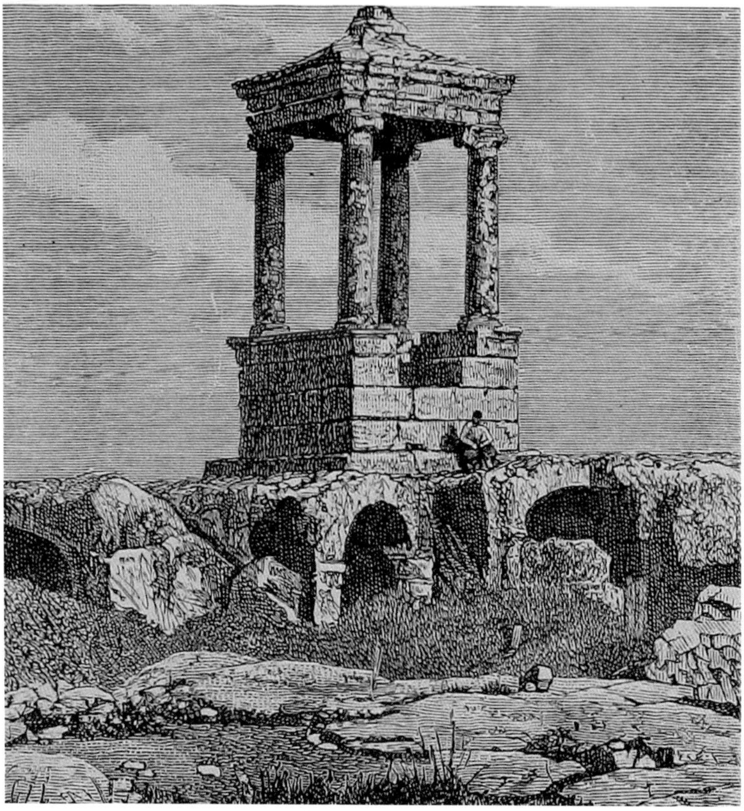

FIGURE 4.1 *Late Roman mausoleum at Dana, Syria.* DRAWING FROM E. RECLUS ET AL., *THE UNIVERSAL GEOGRAPHY: THE EARTH AND ITS INHABITANTS*, LONDON: J. S. VIRTUE AND CO., LTD., 1876. REPRODUCED FROM HTTPS://EN.WIKIPEDIA.ORG/WIKI/AL-DANA,_SYRIA#/MEDIA/FILE:ANCIENT_TOMB_OF_DANA.JPG

at Pompeii (79 CE)—confirm the fact that a canopy might have symbolized or actually sheltered the tomb.[11] Namely, over 19 meters high, the mausoleum of the Julii consists of a square base, reared in steps, an intermediate story, and a "canopy" of twelve Corinthian columns that shelters the statues of the deceased. Since no burial chamber was found at this "tomb," it was probably designed as a memorial. The so-called Pompeian canopy tomb of the Istacidii was raised on a small terrace and surrounded by a balustrade. Its rectangular base was decorated with half-engaged columns, which gave it the look of a pseudo-peripteral temple, with a vaulted burial chamber with niches cut in the inner walls. The upper structure of the tomb was a colonnaded "canopy." When reduced to the simplest form with four columns or four arches standing at a pedestal or a ground level and supporting a canopy, this kind of canopy tomb monument, like the late Roman mausoleum at Dana in Syria (Fig. 4.1), closely resembled indoor canopies that sheltered some pagan shrines and later Christian ones.[12] In any case, pagan canopy-like tombs as well as funerary altars

[11] D'Ambra (1998) 115–117; Mau (1982) 411; Marta (1985) 176–183; Toynbee (1996) 125–130; Colvin (1991) 50–100.

[12] Curl (1980) 32–33.

were burial markers rather than places of sacrifices.[13] The remains of the deceased were only rarely placed in funerary altars.[14]

The knowledge of funerary structures in a Christian context is closely related to the ceremonies performed at these settings. Until the end of the fourth century, two ceremonies might have been performed at venerated Christian tombs: first, offerings of food and wine provided by the faithful for funerary banquets, the *refrigerium*, following pagan practices of the *Parentalia*; and second, the celebration of the Eucharist, symbolizing the sacrifice of Christ for whom the martyr died.[15] Some pagan altars were surmounted by canopies to shelter a sacrifice and offerings placed on or below the altar for the *refrigerium* office.[16] In the late fourth and early fifth centuries, church leaders like St. Ambrose, Bishop of Milan, and St. John Chrysostom, patriarch of Constantinople, strongly opposed such practices at Christian tombs, which confirms that such practices were widespread.[17]

Until the mid-fourth century, laws prohibited the violation of tombs, including those of saints, which were to be venerated *in situ*; i.e., around their tombs.[18] Almost concurrently, by the early 350s, the bodily remains of St. Babylas, a bishop and martyr from Antioch, were moved less than ten kilometers from his tomb to a *martyrium* built in his honor.[19] This practice was not received sympathetically by Christian leaders and posed ethical and judicial questions. The translation of St. Babylas relics and their architectural framing initiated by popular Christian devotion was followed by the imperial translation of the relics of St. Timothy, St. Andrew, and St. Luke to Constantinople and their deposition at the Church of the Holy Apostles after 356–357.[20] From the 380s onwards, saintly relics were deposited below altar tables all around the Mediterranean—from Asia Minor, Syria, and Egypt, to Italy and Gaul.[21] By that time, theologians had already acknowledged that saintly relics were not to be understood as mere particles of dead bodies but as proof of saintly triumph over death, referring to the narrative of the book of Revelation (6:9). This notion played a role in the Iconoclastic controversy and theological debates about the relevance of relics until the end of the Byzantine Empire, ultimately resulting in the affirmation of the critical and indispensable role of relics in Byzantine churches, and by extension affected the planning of both altar and shrine canopies in churches. Yet achieved architectural solutions for tombs

---

13 Kleiner (1987) 21.

14 Toynbee (1996) 62–63.

15 Ibid., 379–414.

16 Until the end of the fourth century, the *refrigerium*, following pagan practices of the *Parentalia*, was included in Christian funerary practices. The character of Christian *refrigeria* is known both from inscriptions and from early Christian writings. Krautheimer (1960) 17–40; Smith, M. T. (1974) 379–414.

17 Schulz (1986) 14–20, 150–159. St. Augustine, Bishop of Hippo (354–430) remarked much earlier that:

> *In Africa she* [Augustine's mother] *had been accustomed to make offerings of pottage, bread and wine at the tombs of the martyrs. When she attempted to do the same here* [Milan], *she was prevented by the doorkeeper; but as soon as she learned that it was the bishop who had forbidden the practice she complied in so devoted and obedient a spirit that I marveled at the attitude she had so readily adopted . . . .*
>
> *Augustine, The Confessions* book IV 2.2.

18 Mango (1990) 51–61, with references to Byzantine laws by Emperor Constans violation sepulcri 349, which reiterated the law from 333 *Codex Theodosianus* 9.17.4. Emperor Justinian issued the same laws in *Cod. Just.* 9.19.4.

19 Mango (1990) 51–61.

20 In time, the relics from all Christendom were deposited in the Church of the Holy Apostles. Mango (1990) 51–61; Downey (1957) 855–924; Walter (1982) 156; Johnson (2009) 119–129.

21 *Philostorgius* 480; *Chronicon Pascale* col. 733; *Jerome* i.5, col. 343. According to Crook (2000) 19, n. 94.

and altars within singular settings differed and cannot point either to linear developments or a standardized approach.

The canopy for the saintly tomb and the altar: Old St. Peter's in Rome and similar solutions in early Christian churches in Constantinople and the Mediterranean

The relationship between the saintly tomb and the altar of St. Peter's *aedicula*-grave is the critical and most-studied example of the architectural merging of a tomb and shrine. The shrine of St. Peter, originally a second-century small *aedicula* to mark the traditional tomb of St. Peter within the cemetery as a pilgrimage site, was architecturally defined first by a *fastigium*, a gabled columnar frame with a pediment-like top, and then later by a large canopy in the basilica. The fifth-century grave marker of St. Peter was positioned just in front the apse of a T-shaped basilica in the Vatican, within the most privileged location within a basilica, as designated by the Roman imperial practice in which the apse was reserved for the imperial throne.[22] The four-columned tomb canopy of St. Peter was most closely related to the concept of a frame as established first by a linear *fastigium* screen. Two spiral columns at the corners of the apse, topped by the architrave, linked the backside of the four-columned canopy, thus forming, together with the canopy, a continuous curtained screen, as is visualized on an early fifth-century ivory casket from Pola (Fig. 4.2).[23] The imprints of the two rear column bases of the canopy revealed that the screen separated the apse from the transept, from shoulder to shoulder, with the canopy projecting forward into the crossing, thus over the tomb. The open canopy-like shrine with a curtained screen across the apse, in texts labeled as *fastigium*, rested on four spiral, vine scroll columns—*columnae vitineae* that Constantine brought *de Greciae*.[24] The jeweled "tower," a canopy that housed the Blessed Sacrament, as mentioned in the *Liber Pontificalis*, had a pointed roof with diagonal arching ribs surmounted by an orb, as represented on the Pola Casket. At the point of the intersection of ribs, a golden lamp was suspended in the form of a golden *corona* of lights. Four large candlesticks wrought in silver with scenes from the Acts of the Apostles accompanied other accessories.[25] Below the canopy, a rectangular enclosure was railed off and slightly raised above the floor level. The canopy stood directly over the Apostle's tomb; however, the movable altar was separated from the shrine, positioned somewhere in front of the shrine or near it.[26]

Old St. Peter's tomb was covered by a basilica. Yet this basilica did not function originally as a church. A movable altar would have been brought in only for the celebration of St. Peter's day and other important feasts, which remained more-or-less in continuity with the older Roman practice of bringing sacrificial altars to the tombs of special individuals.[27] On the Pola Casket, two figures are turned toward the Apostle's tomb in a gesture of worship, and a pair of male and female frontal *orant* figures are represented on either side of the

---

[22] Among the best-known examples is certainly *Basilica Nova* in Rome. Krautheimer (1967) 115–140. Diocletian's basilica in Luxor even has preserved archeological evidence for the imperial throne. Kalavrezou (1975) 225–251.

[23] *EtLP*; Crook (2000) 80–82; Krautheimer (1986) 56f; Ward Perkins (1994a) 469–489; Blaauw (1994) 2: 533–543; Bogdanović (2002) 7–19; Blaauw (2009b) 123–140; Gem (2013) 35–64.

[24] Ward-Perkins (1994a) 469–489.

[25] Smith, M. T. (1974) 379–414.

[26] Ward Perkins (1994a) 469–489.

[27] Kleiner (1987) 21ff.

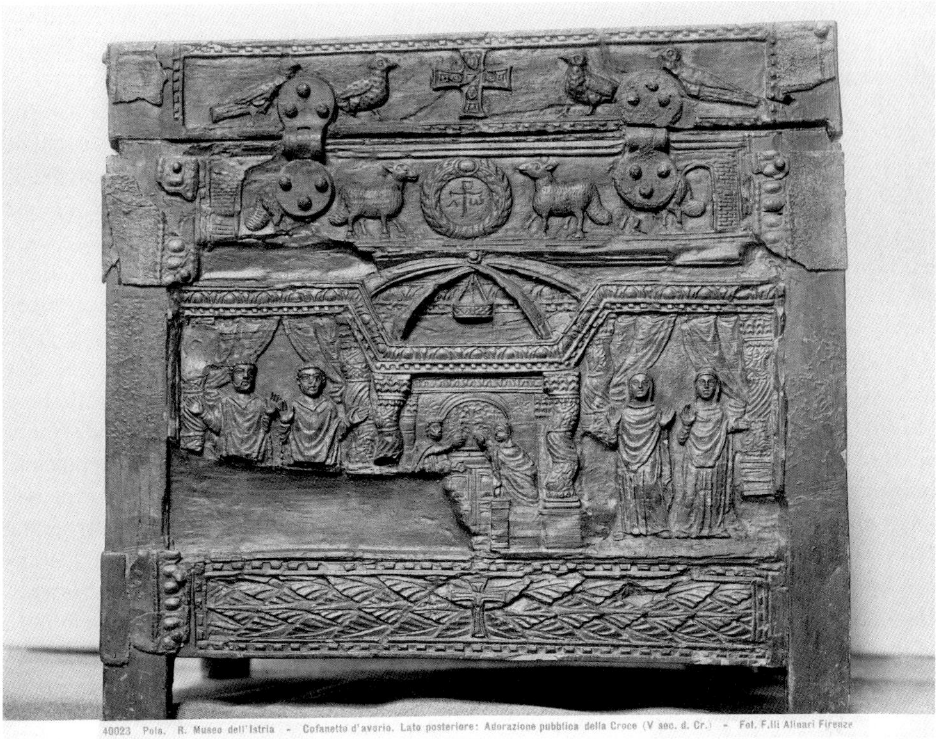

FIGURE 4.2 *Pola Casket with the representation of St. Peter's shrine, Pola, Istria, fifth century.* ALINARI/ART RESOURCE, NEW YORK

shrine. It is difficult to interpret what the figures represented on the Pola Casket are actually doing, but their gestures suggest the veneration of the saintly tomb rather than the celebration of the liturgy. Roman sacrificial altars usually had a pitcher on the left and a *pater* on the right side of the altar, respectively corresponding to the position of the chief priest at the right, and the *camillus* at the left of the altar. The priest is usually represented with his head veiled and pouring a libation from a *patera*, while the *camillus* carrying the pitcher assisted him.[28] On the Pola Casket, the two figures below the canopy leaning towards the altar may have represented a priest with his head veiled on the right-hand side and his assistant opposite him. Since the mouths of the *orant* figures from Pola Casket are open, as if they are chanting or praying, it can be assumed that a service emphasizing the divine Presence connected with the presence of the martyr's relics is represented.

Similarly, the fourth-century writings of the nun Egeria reveal that the Tomb of Christ in Jerusalem was the focal point of vespers and the resurrection vigil.[29] The Tomb of Christ was spatially separated from the sanctuary of the *martyrium* basilica where the Eucharist was celebrated. The separation of a saintly tomb from the altar is found again in sixth-century North Africa. In the *martyrium*-Church of Candidus, in Haïdra, Tunis, one four-columned canopy on the far west of the church sheltered the martyr's tomb, while the other four-columned canopy directly opposite it sheltered the altar in the east.[30] Therefore, the

---

[28] Ibid.

[29] Taft (1980–1981) 45–75. See also Chapter 5.

[30] Duval, Y. (1982) 105–115.

practice of spatially separating places for the celebration of the liturgy and the veneration of saints is consistent with the celebration at St. Peter's shrine as depicted on the Pola Casket and originally defined by the architectural setting.

The canopy-like installation sheltering the already existing *aedicula* of St. Peter's shrine was structurally and functionally unnecessary. The figures from the Pola Casket elucidate that the open canopy-shrine with curtains was used to conceal and reveal the participants at certain stages of the celebration and emphasized St. Peter's presence in the *aedicula* that stood for his eternal house. The canopy centrally positioned at the crossing of the main basilica nave and the transept would have provided access to the sacred locus on all three sides, from the nave and laterally from the transept, and may have been initially introduced also for successfully channeling the movement of the faithful.

The canopied saintly shrine and the altar were spatially associated in Old St. Peter's only in the late sixth or early seventh century, towards the end of the tenure of Pope Pelagio II (579–590) or when Pope Gregory I (590–604) returned from Constantinople and remodeled St. Peter's Tomb, widely known at this time as *ciborium sepulcri*—the sepulchral canopy (see also Fig. 2.56).[31] A platform in the apse was raised, and the area in front of it incorporated the Apostle's tomb. Thus radically rearranged, the entire architectural setting was fit for both liturgical practice and the purpose of venerating relics. The altar with its canopy on four columns was placed over the tomb, confirming that, by that time, the association between martyr's tomb and altar was established in a such a way that it demanded a spatial and physical unity of tomb and altar. This rearrangement at Old St. Peter's included one additional important change. The six vine-scroll columns from the previous canopy were moved to form a *templon*-like screen across the front of the chancel,[32] similar to the Byzantine sanctuary furnishing in Constantinople.[33]

Indeed, in the wider Mediterranean region and at least by the fifth century, canopies were critical architectural installations that might shelter both the tomb and the altar, or only one of them. Two canopies at S. Alessandro on the Via Nomentana, one above the grave of the martyr Teodolus and the other above the graves of martyrs Alexander and Eventius and the altar slab placed directly over their tombs, confirm this practice of framing tombs and altars by canopies in Rome even before the establishment of St. Peter's canopy above the tomb and the altar.[34] It seems as if the saintly shrine and church altar were related due to their references as burial markers, spatially and ritually linked in churches, and once sanctioned by imperial policy in Constantinople, such canopied installations became a pan-Mediterranean phenomenon.

Already in the fifth-century Constantinopolitan basilica of St. John the Baptist in Studios Monastery (ca. 453–454), major elements of the liturgical setting suggest the possibility that a canopy sheltered both the altar table and saintly relics, even though neither the altar nor the canopy survive. The space of the basilica's semicircular apse is extended by a Π-shaped sanctuary enclosure with three openings on each side projecting 5 meters into the nave (Fig. 4.3).[35] The small cruciform crypt, which survives under the original floor level and is centrally positioned within the sanctuary enclosure, was

---

[31] Gem (2013) 35–64; Blauuw (1994) 2:533–543; Ward-Perkins (1994a) 469–489; Kirschbaum (1959) 158.

[32] Ward-Perkins (1994a) 469–489.

[33] Mathews (1962) 73–95.

[34] Smith, M. T. (1974) 379–414; Bogdanović (2002) 7–19.

[35] The oldest archeological evidence about altars in Constantinopolitan churches from the fourth and fifth centuries locates them in the nave area in front of the apse. Mathews (1971) 11–41.

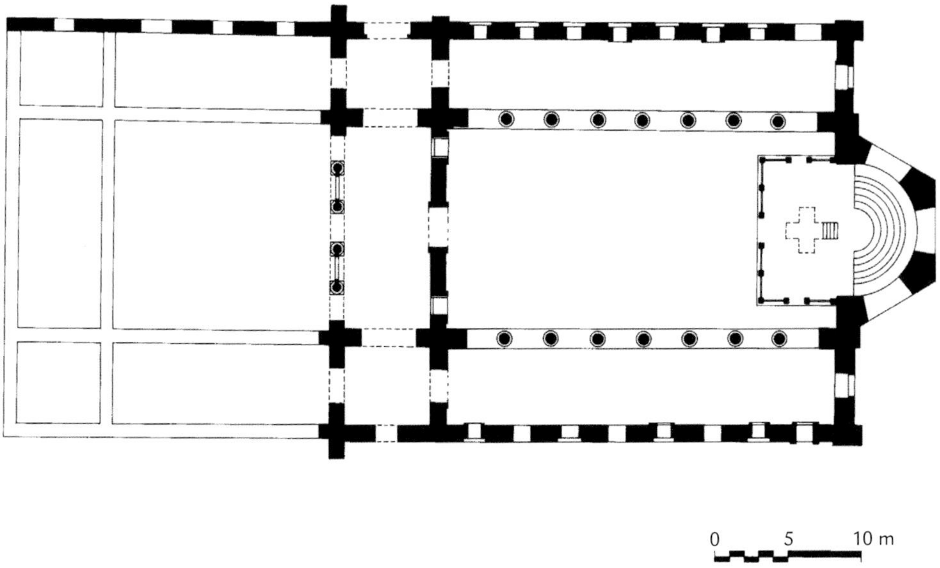

FIGURE 4.3 *St. John the Baptist in Studios Monastery, Constantinople, now Istanbul, ca. 453–454.* DRAWING JOEL KELLY FROM ĆURČIĆ (2010) 98, FIG. 91

not accessible on a regular basis and was most likely designed for accommodating saintly relics, presumably below the altar table above the crypt. Texts imply that the altar table was canopied, and by extension the canopy sheltered the tomb in the crypt below it.[36] Therefore, here the canopy marked the focal point in the church space, and was accessible to the monks from three sides, not only frontally, just as was the case with St. Peter's shrine in Rome.

The liturgical setting from the church at the Studios monastery, where the altar canopy is not in the semicircular sanctuary apse but in front of it, is not unique to Constantinople and can be observed in other coeval churches throughout the Byzantine Empire. The altar was usually set in front of the semicircular apse in the more-or-less geometric center of the sanctuary area, sometimes projecting deeply into the nave as defined by low marble parapets. Occasionally, the sanctuary may have been flanked with tiers of seats for the clergy on three sides (east, north, and south) that took the place of the *synthronon* in the semicircular apsidal area of the sanctuary. These principles can be observed in the fifth-century churches of the Basilica A, Philippi; the Episcopal Church at Aphrodisias in Caria; the Episcopal Church at Stobi; Church 3 at Diocletianopolis (Hissar); Hosios Leonidas, Corinth-Lechaion; the three-aisled basilica at Mastichari, Kos; and Basilica B at Nikopolis (Figs. 2.7, 2.10, 2.19; Table 5.14, 18, 19, 24, 36, 40, 45). The same practice was followed in such sixth-century churches as Basilica A, Nikopolis; Basilica A, at Amphipolis; Basilica tis Vardias, Aigina; and the Double Basilica of Aliki at Thasos (Table 5.59, 72, 74, 92).[37] These architectural solutions may point to attempts to spatially unify or at least closely relate the setting of the altar table in the *bema* and another focal point of singular importance within the church, including tomb-shrines.

---

[36] Table 1, T.61.

[37] Ćurčić (2010) chs. 3 and 4; Bogdanović (2008a).

The role of canopy in the redesign of a secular building into the church: Hagia Euphemia

The complex spatial relations between the saintly tomb and the altar are evident in the Constantinopolitan shrine of St. Euphemia. Here, because of the conversion of a secular building into a church, the practice of translating and enshrining saintly relics points to several critical design moments, as well as how this act might have influenced the entire spatial concept of a Byzantine church. The large hexagonal hall of the fifth-century Palace of Antiochos was converted into the Church of Hagia Euphemia, most likely when the relics of the saint were transferred from her original *martyrium* in Chalcedon, Bithynia, to Constantinople in the seventh century (Fig. 4.4, Table 5.104).[38] The conversion of the secular building into a church involved several major interventions, like the shifting of the building's axis in order to give the sanctuary apse a proper eastward orientation and the construction of a Π-shaped sanctuary enclosure, which projected deep into the domed central space. The archeologically recovered marble canopy in Hagia Euphemia was massive with a shallow, monolithic dome (Fig. 4.5). Pilgrims reported that this canopy covered both the altar and the bodily relics of St. Euphemia, forming a canopied box-type altar with a *confessio* directly beneath the altar table that allowed the faithful to touch the relics.[39]

The tactile quality of the veneration of St. Euphemia's relics is related to their affirmation of the basic Byzantine belief in both the human and the divine natures of Christ. According to her hagiography, the early-fourth-century martyr Euphemia was born in Chalcedon and was burned for refusing to deny Jesus Christ.[40] The flames could not destroy her bodily remains, and she was entombed in a small chapel, which grew into a healing shrine. In 451, the assembled church dignitaries during the Synod of Chalcedon discussed the nature of Christ. The Patriarch proposed that a book of each doctrine, one that defined Christ as having only a divine nature and the other that asserted his dual natures, be placed in the casket of St. Euphemia, where God would show where his favor rested. The casket was opened, and the two books placed in her hands, after which it was closed and the participants prayed for a divine sign to guide them. When the casket was opened again, the book on the single nature of Jesus Christ was at St. Euphemia's feet, while the book that spoke of the two natures of Christ was still in her hands. Because the veneration of the relics of St. Euphemia was most closely related to the theological debates during the Iconoclastic controversy about the nature of Christ and subsequently about the veneration of icons and relics, her relics were removed from the Church of Hagia Euphemia during the controversy. Upon the affirmation of the Chalcedonian definition of Christianity and the need for relics in Byzantine-rite churches, the relics of St. Euphemia were returned to Constantinople in 796.[41]

The canopy from the Church of Hagia Euphemia is instructive for several reasons. It confirms that shrine canopies continued to be used in Constantinople after the Iconoclasm. The canopy that sheltered both the sacred relics and the altar table within the box-type altar seems innovative for Constantinople and possibly was initiated by the practice from the

---

[38] Krautheimer (1986) 71, 77, 231 and Mathews (1971) 61–67 are of the opinion that the church dates from the sixth century. It has been suggested that the church postdated the sixth century and that the translation of relics happened in 796. Mango (1999) 79–87; Gerstel and Lauffenburger (2001) 200. On the opinion that the relics were translated in 680, see Bardill (1997) 67–95, esp. 67, n. 3. On the translation of the relics of St. Euphemia to Constantinople in the 620s, see Goldfus (2006) 178–197. I am grateful to Slobodan Ćurčić for bringing Goldfus' article to my attention.

[39] Mango (1999) 79–87; Mathews (1971) 61–67.

[40] *Evagrius Scholasticus* book 2, ch. 4.

[41] Halkin (1966) 536–538.

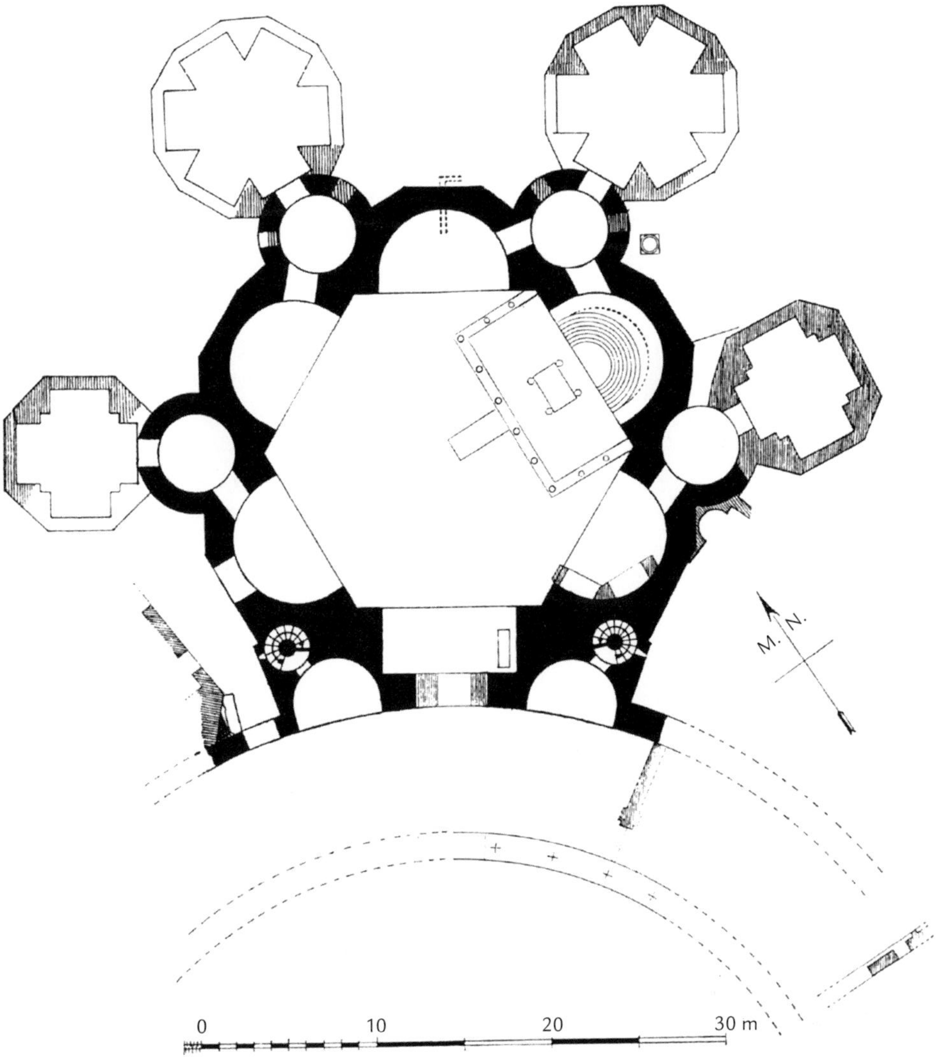

FIGURE 4.4 *Hagia Euphemia, Constantinople, now Istanbul; Palatial hall, fifth century, was converted into church by the seventh century.* DRAWING, JOEL KELLY FROM ĆURČIĆ (2010) 202, FIG. 208

original *martyrium* of St. Euphemia in Bithynia as recorded in the late fifth and early sixth centuries.[42] In Bithynia, the entire body of St. Euphemia was set in a "long silver coffin" within her saintly shrine in the domed rotunda. The casket was obviously within the shrine of her chamber, though no explicit reference to the canopy was made. A late thirteenth-century fresco in the Church of St. Demetrios in the Metropolis monastery, Mistra, records how the contemporaries remembered the original setting of the tomb-shrine of St.

[42] Mango (1999) 79–87; Halkin (1966) 536–538. In the western Mediterranean, the canopied altar *confessia*, as resting places of martyrs as confessors of faith, such as those in the Church of St. Andrew in Rome or St. Martin of Tours, can be dated only in the late sixth and early seventh centuries. Bogdanović (2002) 7–19; Smith, M. T. (1974) 379–414.

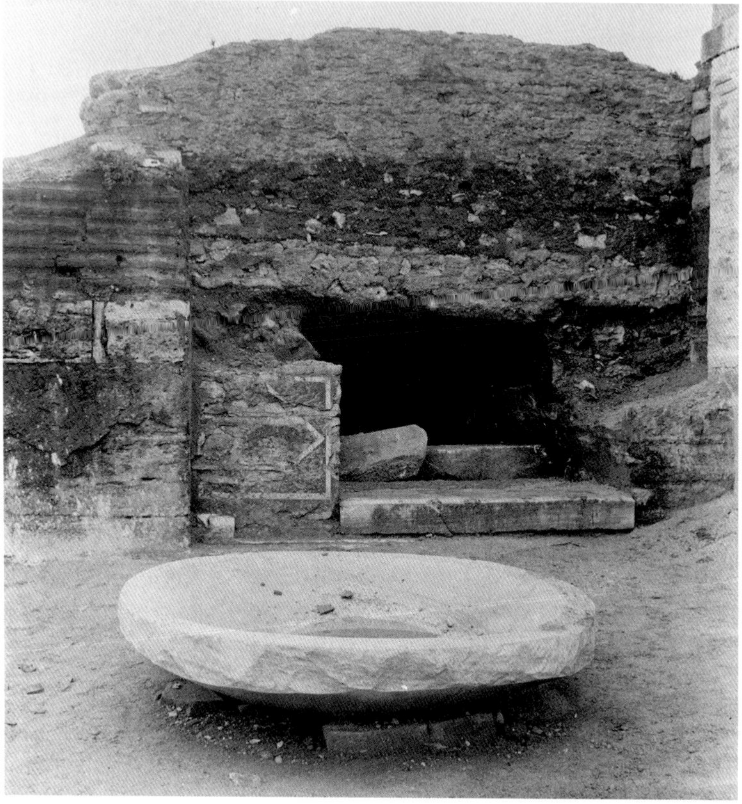

FIGURE 4.5 *Hagia Euphemia, Constantinople, now Istanbul, fragments of the canopy dome, sixth or seventh century.* PHOTOGRAPHED BY ARTAMONOFF (ICFA.NA.0289), NICHOLAS V. ARTAMONOFF COLLECTION, IMAGE COLLECTIONS AND FIELDWORK ARCHIVES, DUMBARTON OAKS, TRUSTEES FOR HARVARD UNIVERSITY, WASHINGTON, D.C.

Euphemia in Chalcedon as a four-columned canopy installation, hence merging the domed rotunda building with the four-columned canopy that simultaneously revealed the interior contents of the architectural setting (Fig. 4.6).[43] St. Euphemia's shrine in Constantinople had an aperture in the left side of the coffin, secured with small doors, through which the faithful inserted an iron rod with a sponge attached so as to reach the sacred relics and, after turning it round, drew it out, covered with stains and clots of blood. This would be consistent with the earlier practice of sending portions of blood exuding from the saintly relics from the *martyrium* in Bithynia as mentioned by Evgarius Scholasticus in the sixth century.[44] The shrine was oriented to the East, but it is not clear whether there was also an altar and, if so, what its relationship was to the saintly shrine.

The arrangement in the sanctuary at Constantinopolitan Hagia Euphemia was questioned due to the limited space in the sanctuary and the large size of such a massive canopied installation, even if in reality many archeologically confirmed altar canopies went beyond 2 meters in span, and both the canopy installation of Hagia Euphemia, which was some 3 meters in span, and the projecting sanctuary space, some 10 meters in span, were

---

[43] Millet (1910) fig. 4.

[44] *Evagrius Scholasticus* book 2, ch. 3.

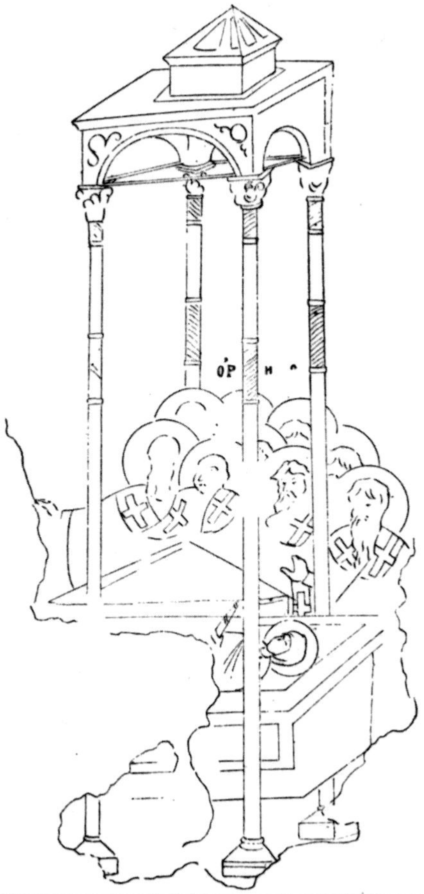

FIGURE 4.6 Miracle of St. Euphemia, *drawing of fresco, Church of St. Demetrios in the Metropolis Monastery, Mistra, thirteenth century.* G. MILLET, *MONUMENTS BYZANTINS DE MISTRA; MATÉRIAUX POUR L'ÉTUDE DE L'ARCHITECTURE ET DE LA PEINTURE EN GRÈCE AUX XIVE ET XVE SIÉCLES*. PARIS: E. LEROUX, 1910, FIG. 4

quite sizable (Fig. 4.7). Goldfus has proposed that the box-type altar contained only the head of St. Euphemia while the casket with the other body relics of St. Euphemia was actually placed in the niche-chapel north of the sanctuary.[45] The niche-chapel was articulated architecturally as an arcosolium, again a type of massive canopied, vaulted structure. The photos taken by Nicholas Artamonoff in 1945 show the interior of the presumably western chapel with richly painted scenes of the martyrdom of St. Euphemia (Fig. 4.8). The individual scenes are framed by painted columns with multicolored geometric patterns suggestive of the actual inlaid columns recovered from the sanctuary screen. Like the frescoes from the Church of St. Demetrios in Mistra, the now-lost frescoes from Hagia Euphemia in Constantinople seemingly emphasized that, for the Byzantines, such repetitive multifocal, multispatial merging of the actual setting and memory images of the settings of Hagia Euphemia's shrine only reinforced its sacred locus.

---

[45] Goldfus (2006) 178–197.

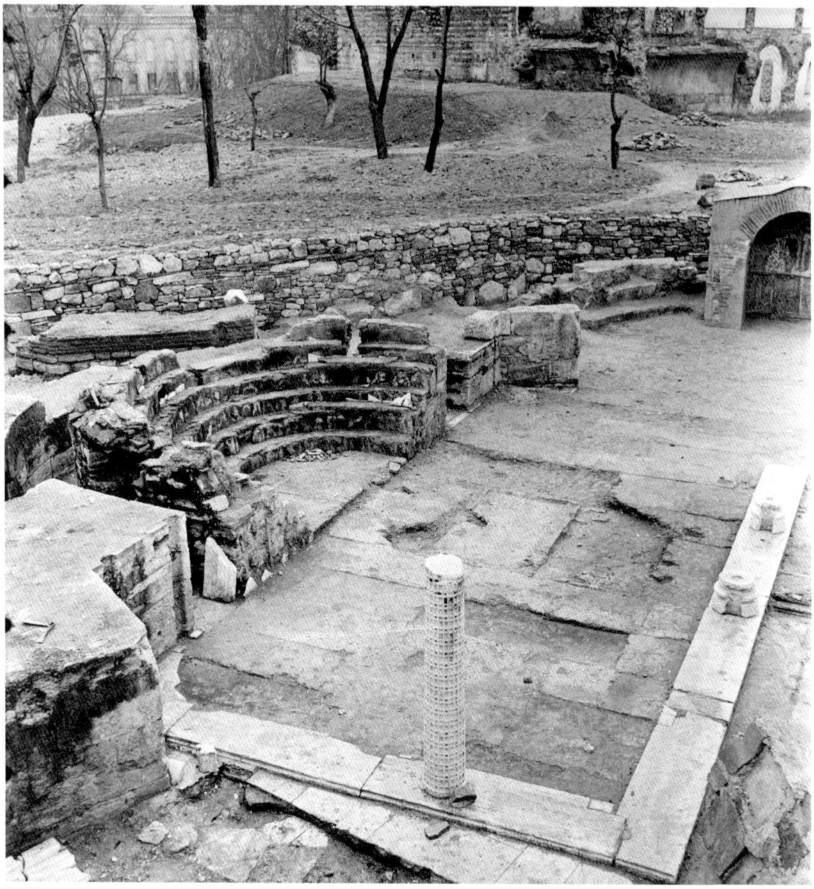

FIGURE 4.7 *View toward the sanctuary of the Hagia Euphemia, Constantinople, now Istanbul, seventh century.* PHOTOGRAPHED BY ARTAMONOFF (ICFA.NA.0286), NICHOLAS V. ARTAMONOFF COLLECTION, IMAGE COLLECTIONS AND FIELDWORK ARCHIVES, DUMBARTON OAKS, TRUSTEES FOR HARVARD UNIVERSITY, WASHINGTON, D.C.

In Constantinopolitan Hagia Euphemia, in addition to Goldfus proposal for the placement of tomb-shrine in a subsidiary chapel, another possibility is that the altar and tomb installation were a unified structure in the *bema*. The *bema* was located deep in the central space of the church and framed by the Π-shaped sanctuary screen. Hence, it formed a central focus and could allow for the coffin to be placed under the altar canopy and relatively near to the screen, allowing it to be approached from the north—i.e., the left side as reported by pilgrims. By extending the rod with the sponge, the faithful would be able to touch the relics, while not entering the space of the sanctuary reserved only for the clergy. In ca. 1200, a Russian pilgrim, Anthony of Novgorod, reported that he saw the relics of St. Euphemia in a silver reliquary in another church, but he did not describe the setting.[46] However, in the fifteenth century, Clavijo confirmed that the casket with the body of Patriarch Arsenios Autoreianos (d. 1273) was to the north of the altar in Constantinopolitan Hagia Sophia.[47] The canopy installation over the bodily remains of St. Catherine in the eponymous monastery on Mt. Sinai is

[46] Janin (1953) 455–70.

[47] *Clavijo* 56–57; Marinis (2014) 30.

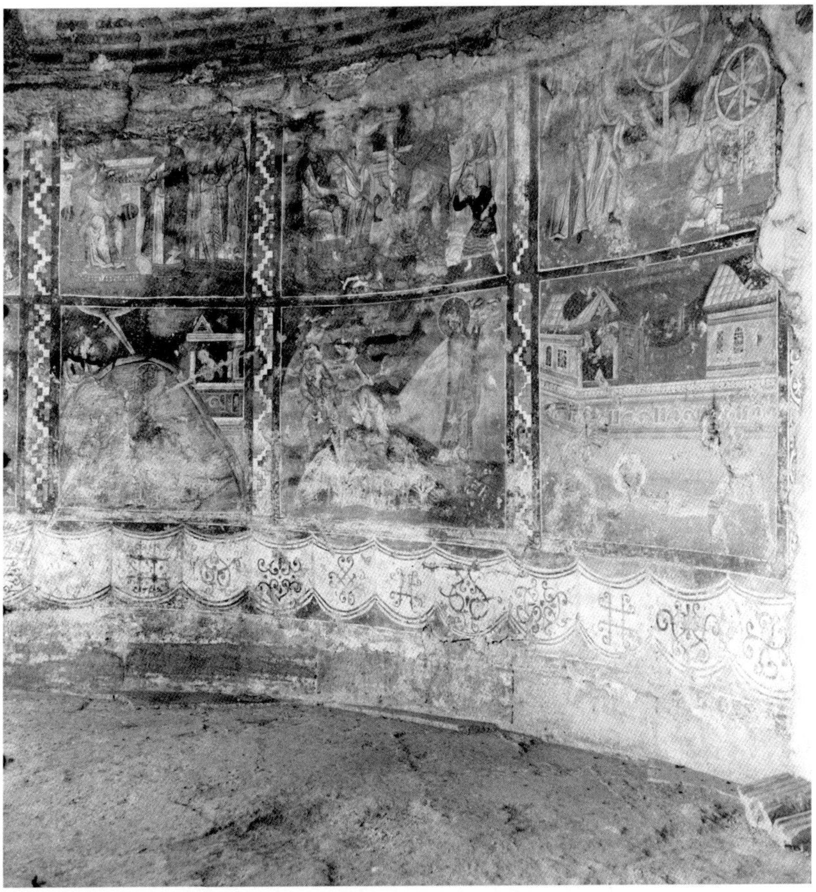

FIGURE 4.8 *Western chapel showing painted scenes of the martyrdom of St. Euphemia; Hagia Euphemia, Constantinople, now Istanbul, seventh century.* PHOTOGRAPHED BY ARTAMONOFF (ICFA.NA.0339), NICHOLAS V. ARTAMONOFF COLLECTION, IMAGE COLLECTIONS AND FIELDWORK ARCHIVES, DUMBARTON OAKS, TRUSTEES FOR HARVARD UNIVERSITY, WASHINGTON, D.C.

located just north of the altar canopy in the sanctuary. Even if post-Byzantine chronologically, the still-existing canopy-shrine of St. Catherine from Mt. Sinai, coupled with the narrative about a similar setting for the tomb of Patriarch Autoreianos in Hagia Sophia, suggest that the practice of placing the bodily relics in the sanctuary was not unique to Hagia Euphemia and could have been a long-standing, even if not common, practice in Byzantine churches.

The installation of Constantinopolitan Hagia Euphemia also points to a symbolic construct according to which the altar relics were simultaneously venerated in private and liturgical devotion, because relics used for the consecration of the altars were generally not accessible to the faithful nor used for the veneration. The merging of relics for veneration and secondary altars within church chapels provided an alternative solution. This practice has been attested to in later Byzantine churches, yet it may have been developed since early Christian times, here referring to several parallel threads of architectural designs that included canopied installations for altars and relics.[48] In Syro-Palestine, starting in the sixth

[48] Babić (1969); Bacci (2009) 11–30.

century, a reliquary—a box for sacred relics, often resembling a small sarcophagus—was sometimes placed beneath the altar, either within a stone recess, or directly on top of the floor. The saintly cult was mostly celebrated in side chambers, however, where the reliquaries were displayed for veneration. In the Church of St. Stephen at Umm al-Rasas, its north-side room, square in plan, first had a screen at the entrance, and an altar with posts was embedded in the mosaic floor later on, suggesting how this chamber became a chapel with a secondary altar in the church.[49] In the second building stage, an apse and vaulting were added to the chapel. On the central segment of the apsidal wall, an *aedicula*-shrine was built and dedicated to the cult of St. Stephen, whose remains had been brought from Jerusalem.

The deposition of relics directly under the altar, be it primary or secondary, differed from the earlier practice whereby the relics were usually buried in the crypt and eventually were related spatially to the altar above it, as was the case with the churches of St. Peter's in Rome, St. John in the Studios monastery, Chalkoprateia, and the Hebdomon, to name but a few in Constantinople and its immediate vicinity.[50]

The practice of sheltering the altar table and saintly relics by a canopy continued during the transitional period and theological controversies. Examples come from the periphery of the empire, not Constantinople, the center of imperial and official religious policies where the relics of St. Euphemia were removed from the church during the controversy and returned after it. The eventual resolution that confirmed the importance of saintly shrines and relics in Byzantine churches implies the critical role of popular Christian practices in the architectural design of canopies. Hence, the sixth-century single-apse church in the village of Massuh in the diocese of Esbus in Jordan acquired a canopy during the church's restoration in the seventh and eighth centuries. Four stone bases for the canopy above the altar table were inserted in their secondary use, and a stone cross-shape container for the reliquary was inserted beneath the altar.[51] Moreover, one of the columns of the canopy was hollowed out to create a space to insert a metal cross. Although I am not aware of any surviving example of an eastern Mediterranean canopy where saintly relics were directly inserted into the canopy itself as in the eighth- or ninth-century altar canopy from Santa Maria Maggiore in Sovana (Fig. 4.9) and the tenth-century altar canopy from San Ambrogio in Milan,[52] such an option in the Byzantine domain should not be dismissed promptly. When compared with the practice of inserting devotional crosses with saintly relics into church columns,[53] the possibility that a similar practice existed of inserting crosses with relics into canopy columns remains uninvestigated, but possible.[54]

The shrine of Hagia Euphemia further confirms that, after the theological debates during the Iconoclastic controversy, the attitudes towards relics used for private devotion and ones used for consecrating an altar may have overlapped, the relics themselves occupying similar if not the very same spatial frames. However, in my opinion, the private devotion of saintly relics and the consecration of the altar were essentially two different phenomena that continued to guide the spatial accommodation of the relics within the church altar and within a saintly shrine.[55] Indeed, the size of saintly remains, particles of saintly relics or entire bodies, but above all, the type of devotion, liturgical or private, dictated the installation of an

---

[49] Piccirillo (2006) 51–113.

[50] Mathews (1971) 67.

[51] Piccirillo (2005).

[52] *EAM* vol. 4, s.v. *ciborio*, esp. 719; Dietl (1997) 97–111, esp. 102–104, fig. 4.

[53] Teteriatnikov (1998a) 419–445, esp. 420.

[54] The canopy from the Church of Hagia Sophia, presumably made of the wood of the Ark of Noah, was venerated as a relic itself. *RussAnon* in *RussTravelers* (1984) 114–127; 128–154, esp. 132–133. See also Chapter 3, The Canopies of Hagia Sophia in Constantinople.

[55] On the opinion that the relics, places of commemoration, and the altar were usually separated in the early Christian period, see Grabar (1972) 37–43, chs. 4, 5.

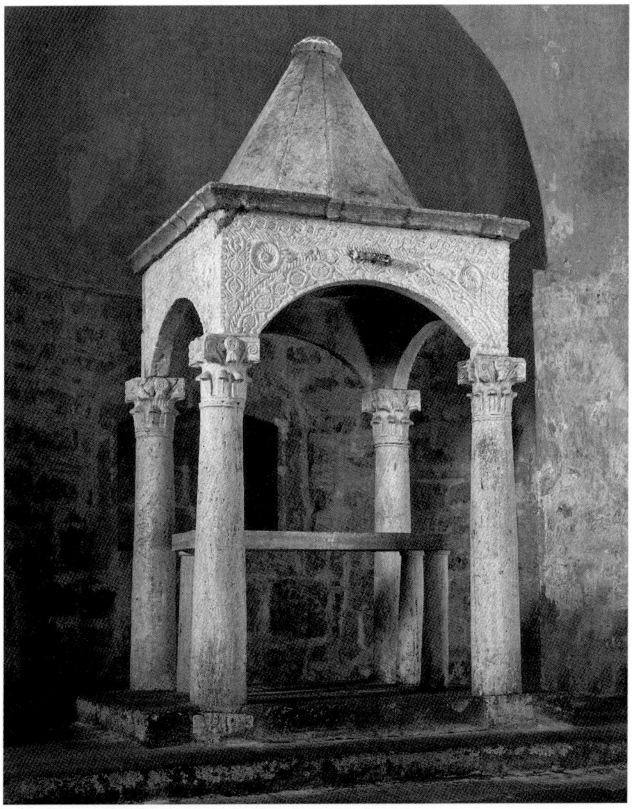

FIGURE 4.9 *Santa Maria Maggiore in Sovana, eighth or ninth century; relics are inserted into the canopy arch.* ANDREA JEMOLO/SCALA/ART RESOURCE, NEW YORK

altar canopy with saintly particles and a saintly shrine for bodily remains. These two different concepts of a relic were often reflected architecturally by two distinct installations set in different locations within a church.

The relationship between the tomb-shrine and the altar canopy in the *katholikon* of Hosios Loukas monastery

The architectural changes of the monastic complex of Hosios Loukas, which is dedicated to the eponymous local saint and healer (d. 953), reveal the dynamic processes of reshifting and rearranging the spatial and ritual relations between the installations that marked two major focal points in the *katholikon*: the tomb-shrine of Hosios Loukas and the church altar.[56] The initial information about the site and its architectural development comes from posthumous *Life of Hosios Loukas*, compiled by his anonymous

[56] The critical texts regarding the architectural provenance and dating of the Hosios Loukas monastery are: Schultz and Barnsley (1901); Stikas (1970); Oikonomides (1992) 245–255; Mylonas (1992) 115–122; Ćurčić (2010) 297–300, 383–387. Contemporaneous medieval references about Hosios Loukas, the monastery, and its architecture come from Loukas' posthumous *Life*, compiled by an anonymous disciple in *Life StLuke*. Kotoula (2007) 210–233, esp. 220–224, provides a nice and succinct overview of the major events in the life of Hosios Loukas and his monastery.

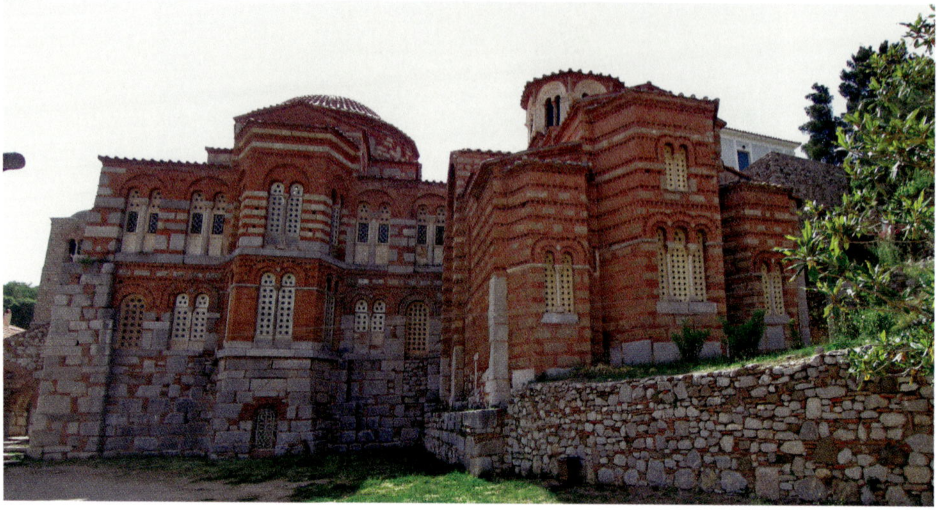

FIGURE 4.10 *Hosios Loukas, near Steiris, Phokis, Greece:* Left *or South: Katholikon (principal church), 1011 or 1022 (?);* Right *or North: Church of Theotokos, second half of tenth century.* PHOTO AUTHOR

disciple.[57] The architecture of the entire monastic complex, established by Loukas during his life, changed significantly after his death when, following the myrrh gushing and healing miracles at the tomb, the site became a major pilgrimage center.

Currently, two churches occupy the center of the monastic courtyard: to the north, the tenth-century Church of the Mother of God is accompanied and superseded by the larger early eleventh-century *katholikon* of Hosios Loukas, to the south (Fig. 4.10). According to Eustachios Stikas, the Church of the Mother of God is in the location of an even earlier church established by Hosios Loukas himself and originally dedicated to St. Barbara, an early Christian martyr whom Hosios Loukas especially venerated.[58] The younger church, the two-story *katholikon*, also contains a crypt dedicated to St. Barbara. The tomb of Hosios Loukas is marked by a non-Byzantine, possibly post-medieval cenotaph in the northern arm of this crypt. Almost axially above it, at the junction of the two churches on the ground floor of the *katholikon* and set within the narrow opening of the eastern wall of the northern arm of the *katholikon*, is a healing tomb-shrine of Hosios Loukas that is still venerated by pilgrims (Fig. 4.11, Table 5.191).[59]

The tomb-shrine is close to several important foci within the church: it is near the passage that connects the Church of the Mother of God (formerly St. Barbara's church) to the *katholikon*; it faces the *prothesis* chapel; and it is northwest of the *bema* with the altar. The tomb-shrine and altar were also related spatially by their canopied architectural framing that enhanced the importance of the two installations.

Indeed, the actual altar canopy from the sanctuary is now lost. Yet its footings are preserved in the floor, mapping the location of this sacred space, long after its architectural

---

[57] *Life StLuke.*

[58] Stikas (1970) 114–27; *Life StLuke* lines 81.5–8.

[59] The assumption about the location of the original tomb of the mid–tenth-century saint Hosios Loukas in the crypt is often taken as fact, though the architectural study of the *katholikon* showed that its crypt and the main church corpus above it is a unitary, early-eleventh-century construction. Chatzidakis (1997) 10.

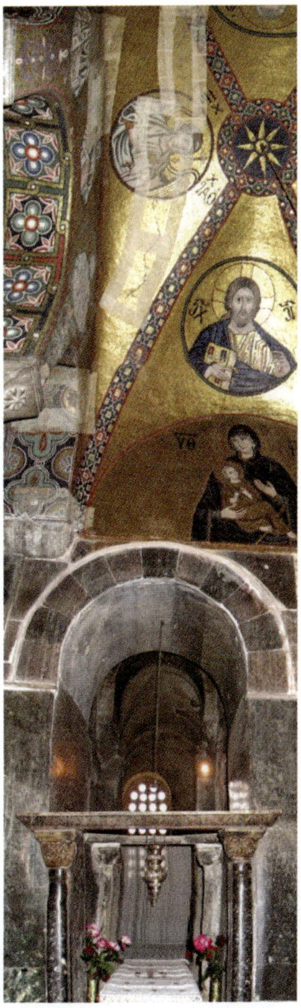

FIGURE 4.11 *Shrine of Hosios Loukas, Hosios Loukas, near Steiris, Phokis, Greece, eleventh century and later.* PHOTO AUTHOR

frame had been removed (see Fig. 4.13).[60] Richly carved marble fragments of the altar canopy are currently in the monastic museum (see Fig. 2.5). The four columns and sculpted architraves of the canopy-like shrine of Hosios Loukas still survive, while a pyramidal roof that crowned them originally is now lost.[61] Since Byzantine accounts do not refer to this shrine as a canopy, some scholars maintain that it is a rather modern installation.[62] Due to the hagiographical references from the *Life of Hosios Loukas* and the establishment of the *anakomidi* rite, the service performed on the occasion of digging the body from his original tomb and the translation of the saintly relics to the new location in the church in the eleventh century, probably in 1011,[63] as well as because the architectural sculpture of the

60 The sockets in the floor of bema for the altar of the *katholikon* were recorded by Schultz and Barnsley (1901), the ground plan, and Stikas (1974/1975) fig. 12.

61 Schultz and Barnsley (1901) 22–29, pl. 46.

62 Stikas (1970) 174–78 and Stikas (1974/5) 103–27 claims that the shrine of Hosios Loukas is an eighteenth-century addition.

63 According to the canticle from the *anakomidi*, the translation of relics of Hosios Loukas happened on May 3rd, the date that coincided with the Feast of the Ascension. In the eleventh century, such a coincidence occurred only three times: in 1011, 1022, and 1095. The author of the canticle speaks also of the "invasion

shrine that can be related to similar twelfth- and thirteenth-century architectural sculpture in Byzantine churches in Greece, I concur with the scholars who recognize it as a medieval tomb-shrine.[64] However, the architectural framing of the tomb was highly complex and developed through several distinct architectural interventions over time.

According to the *Life of Hosios Loukas*, the saint was buried under the floor of his monastic cell by a priest named Gregorios in fulfillment of the saint's wishes: "You will find fired bricks when you dig out the spot where I am lying [in his monastic cell]. Lifting these out and beautifying the place in a modest fashion take care to give dust to dust; then arrange the bricks on the surface of the earth."[65] The first reference to the shrine of blessed Loukas comes six months after his death in 953, when a monk, Kosmas from Paphlagonia, on his way to Italy had a strange dream in which he was instructed to end his journey and start serving the "new Luke."[66] According to the legend, Kosmas found the saintly tomb in the former monastic cell of Loukas. He "built it up and arranged to raise it above the level of the ground. He embellished it with slabs of the local stone, and setting lattice work in a circle around it and garlanding it, he thus made it a place not to be trodden upon or touched except by those wishing to draw near to it in faith and much veneration."[67] The reference to the stone slabs and lattice work, usually understood as a protective barrier, is a common explanation for how shrines were enclosed and beautified in the Byzantine tradition while providing controlled access to pilgrims, like the Holy Sepulchre in Jerusalem, the shrine of St. Menas in Egypt, or the shrine of St. Demetrios in Thessaloniki (Fig. 4.12, see also Fig. 4.16).[68]

The location of the monastic cell of Hosios Loukas is not specified in the *Life*. Assuming that the place of the saint's death and entombment has been preserved through oral tradition and framed by subsequent architectural structures, the present location of the saintly shrine potentially marks the original location of his monastic cell and later his tomb. Following the narrative of the miracles of Hosios Loukas, the healing-tomb-shrine was most likely in the church (*naos*), not the crypt.[69] Most telling is the account of a certain John, whose feet suffered from some malady: He "enter[ed] the divine church, prostrated himself at the miraculous tomb."[70] Neither this nor any other excerpt, however, clarifies which divine church is in question, though we may guess that it was the Church of St. Barbara, the only one mentioned in the *Life of Hosios Loukas*. Two years after Loukas' death, his fellow monks completed the monastery church and turned his cell into a "sacred oratory in the shape of a cross" which sheltered the saintly tomb.[71] The location of these buildings cannot be verified,

---

of the Scythians," a phrase that may refer to the Bulgarians, thus suggesting the dating of the canticle before the abolition of the state of the Bulgarian sovereign Samuel (r. 976–1014) and making the year 1011 as the most probable year of the translation of the relics. Chatzidakis (1969) 127–150.

64 Chatzidakis (1997) 10.

65 *Life StLuke* ch. 64.

66 Ibid., ch. 66.9

67 Ibid., ch. 66, esp. 66.16–21.

68 Ibid., ch. 66.18; Chatzidakis (1997) 10.

69 In the *Life StLuke* chs. 79.24, 82, Luke's burial place (*taphos*) is described as being in a church building, a *naos*. The tomb is variously described in the Greek text of the *Life StLuke* as: σορώς [*soros*] (ch. 81), λάρναξ [*larnax*] (ch. 82), τάφως [*taphos*] (ch. 79), or θήκη [*theke*] (ch. 74). The last term, *theke*, literally means "a box," possibly a tomb chest, but also "a room" or "a chamber" because, when the author refers to the actual sarcophagus, he uses the term *larnax* (ch. 73.9).

70 *Life StLuke* ch. 79.23–25.

71 Ibid., ch. 67.12. The Greek word for the oratory (εὐκτήριον, *eukterion*) has a wide range of meanings: chapel, church, tent, and martyr memorial, among others. *PGL*, s.v. εὐκτήριος. The *eukterion* of Hosios Loukas may well have been the entire church, and its shape of a cross may have referred to the cross-shaped plan of the church, similar to the plans of the *katholikon* or the Church of the Theotokos.

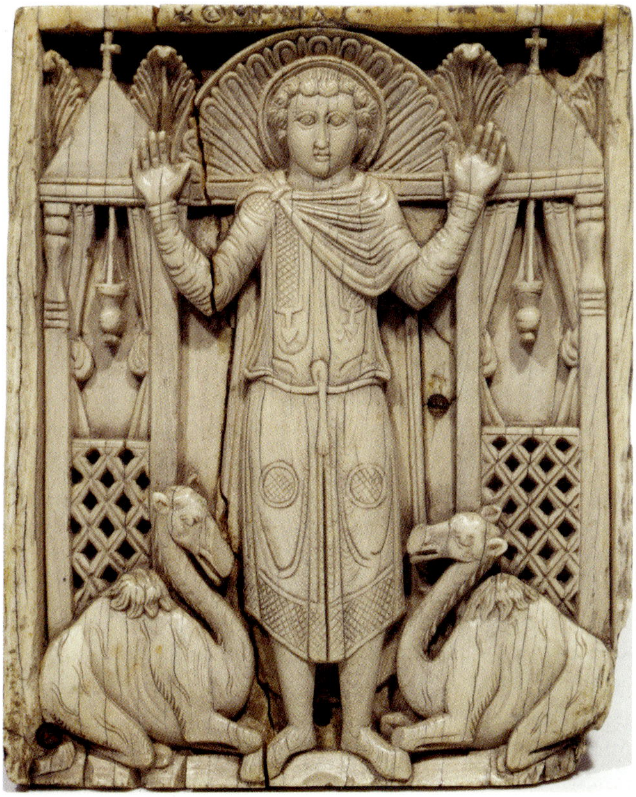

FIGURE 4.12 *St. Menas, ivory plaque from the so-called Grado Chair, from Alexandria, ca. sixth century (?), today in Milan, Ivory Inv. 1. Museo d'Arte Antica.* © COMUNE DI MILANO—ALL RIGHTS RESERVED. RACCOLTE D'ARTE ANTICA, MUSEO D'ARTE ANTICA DEL CASTELLO SFORZESCO, MILANO

and it remains unclear whether the two central churches of the monastery, those of the Mother of God and the main church with its crypt, are the two buildings mentioned in the narrative of the *Life*, namely, the Church of St. Barbara (ch. 59) and the oratory (ch. 67).[72] The Church of the Mother of God might be the original Church of St. Barbara, although the crypt under the present Church of Hosios Loukas, occasionally identified as the oratory, is dedicated to St. Barbara.[73] This certainly does not exclude the possibility that another church, dedicated to St. Barbara and predating the present Church of Hosios Loukas, might have existed at the site of the present *katholikon*.[74] The oratory, which sheltered the tomb,

[72] Mylonas (1992) 115–122; Mylonas (1990) 99–122. The existence of the two churches today certainly does not exclude the possibility that yet another church existed, the one which, according to the *Life of St. Luke*, was dedicated to St. Barbara, a patron saint of the Byzantine military aristocracy. The north church, that of the Mother of God, according to the texts and because of its material splendor, is often attributed to Byzantine emperor Romanos II (r. 959–963), who Hosios Loukas foretold "would take over the Crete" from the Saracens and who potentially honored the monastery of Hosios Loukas by a huge architectural undertaking. Boura (1980) 22–56; Connor (1992) 293–308.

[73] Mylonas (1990) 99–122 showed that the present *katholikon* is a unitary construction. See also Chatzidakis (1997).

[74] Mylonas (1992) 115–122.

would have been either the refurbished monastic chamber of Hosios Loukas attached to the Church of St. Barbara on its north side, or the entire structural complex of the cruciform Church of the Mother of God to which the chamber of Hosios Loukas was abutted on the south. In any case, the monastic cell of Hosios Loukas would be confined to the location of the north arm of the present *katholikon* and would have been initially an independent structure like the attested shrines of St. Thecla or St. Menas.[75]

The steeply inclined terrain suggests that the monastic cell of Hosios Loukas and later his tomb were within a tower-like structure. As Loukas himself established the church dedicated to St. Barbara, he potentially used the life of St. Barbara as a model for his monastic life and actions.[76] In addition to obvious similarities between the two saints, mostly in terms of their dedication to faith, chastity, and charity, St. Barbara, who lived in a tower, imprisoned by her pagan father Dioscurus, who forbade her interest in Christianity, may have inspired Hosios Loukas to isolate himself voluntarily in a humble cell within a tower-like structure—an ultimate refuge during the raids of the Muslim Arabs in the region and a typical place of retreat for Christian ascetics.[77] Furthermore, Hosios Loukas as a young monk served a *stylite* in Zemena[78] and, therefore, personally knew of the ascetic practices of those who lived within the limited enclosed spaces of elevated structures, comprised elements such as walls, columns, and rafters.

On the occasion of the translation of the relics for the yearly veneration on May third, the bodily remains of Hosios Loukas were exhumed from the tomb in his cell and translated to a new shrine in 1011.[79] According to the *anakomidi*, the construction of the present *katholikon* was complete by that time. The superb building of the *katholikon*, and its sophisticated decoration in expensive marble, *opus sectile*, and golden mosaics, point to imperial donations. During this eleventh-century enlargement of the monastery, the original tenth-century chamber, potentially the original monastic cell of Hosios Loukas within a towered building, was reconstructed and incorporated into the monastic complex as its central focus.[80] The chamber may have retained some of the features of the older structure.

---

[75] On the shrine of St. Thecla, see Hill (1996) 30–31, 208–214. On the shrine of St. Menas, see Ward Perkins (1949) 26–71; Grossman (1989); Grossman (1998) 281–302.

[76] *Life StLuke* ch. 69.

[77] Christian saints often assumed the place of walls, columns, and rafters of the church. Harvey, S. (1990) 37, 50. On the position of the monastic cells in Serbian church towers, see Ćurčić (2006) 491–514.

[78] *Life StLuke* chs. 35ff. Connor has argued that "Zemena" is Zemainas, part of the diocese of Corinth, and located near the Corinthian Gulf, to the west of Sicyon, and mentioned in the *Notitiae Episcopatuum* 494 (282); 9. 377 (302); 10.466 (323); 13.434 (361); 21.115 (420). *Life StLuke* 159.

[79] An inscription from 1014 from the sculpture in the monastery of Aliveri on Euboea, which is extremely close to the sculptural remains found in the monastery of Hosios Loukas, suggests that the *katholikon* was finished by 1011. The portrait of St. Nikon Metaniotes (active in Crete from 961–ca.1000) that is painted in the church supports the assumption that the *katholikon* may have been built in the first decades of the eleventh century. Diehl (1889) 11 hypothesized that the *katholikon* was built by Emperor Basil II, who might have visited the shrine of Hosios Loukas on his way to Athens in a military campaign of 1019. On the 1011 date, see Oikonomides (1992) 245–255.

[80] Discovered under the marble casing of the *katholikon*, a fresco depicting Jesus of Navi, an Old Testament figure, is located on the wall near the shrine, suggesting the possibility that the tower-cell was an older structure than the *katholikon*. The fresco initially belonged to the southwestern corner of the outer narthex of the Church of the Virgin, thus confirming that the Church of the Mother of God was built before the present-day *katholikon*. Stikas (1970) 174–178 and Stikas (1974/5) 103–127. It is also possible that during the early–eleventh-century reconstruction of the monastery, on the occasion of the confirmation of the saintly cult of Hosios Loukas, the original Church of St. Barbara was replaced by a new, two-story *katholikon* (?), whose crypt, potentially intended for monastic burials, retained the original dedication to St. Barbara.

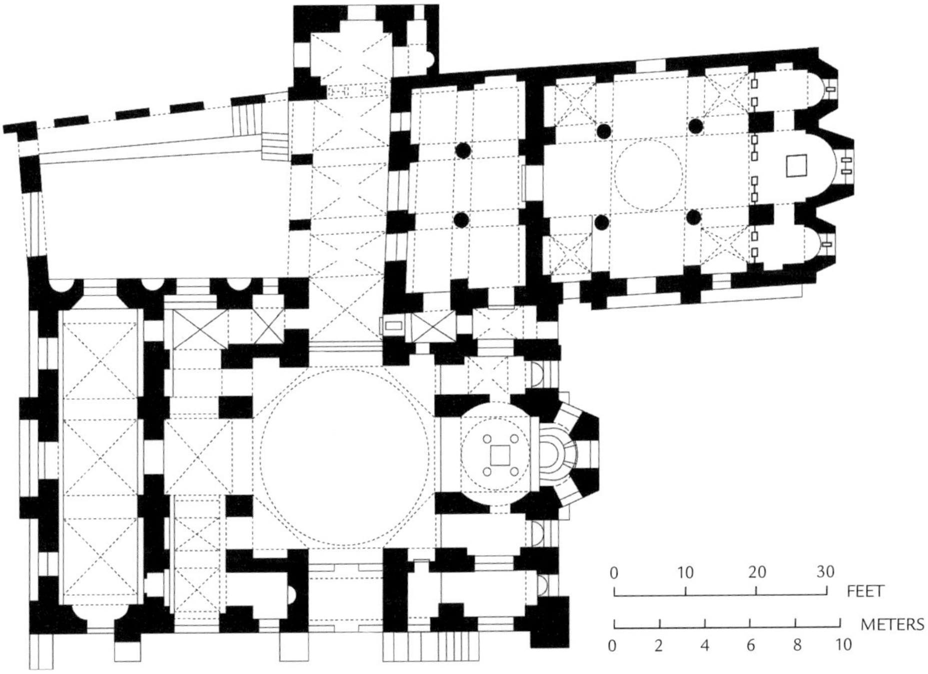

FIGURE 4.13 *Hosios Loukas, near Steiris, Phokis, Greece. South: Katholikon (principal church), 1011 or 1022 (?); North: Church of Theotokos (Mother of God), second half of tenth century, plan.* DRAWING FROM FRED S. KLEINER AND CHRISTIN J. MAMIYA, *GARDNER'S ART THROUGH THE AGES: THE WESTERN PERSPECTIVE*, INDEPENDENCE: WADSWORTH PUBLISHING, 2005, CHAPTER 9, FIG. 0919

The massive walls and the superstructure of the northern arm of the cross of the surviving main monastery church further suggest that this structure initially may have been a tower. The two surviving churches were joined to each other, so that the eastern half of the northern segment of the *katholikon* abutted the narthexes of the north church. Thus, the location of the shrine near the northern entrance to the *katholikon* became a node of communication, which enabled pilgrims to approach the shrine in an orderly manner and relatively independently from the movements within the church proper that were related to liturgical practices (Fig. 4.13).[81]

The square-like floor plan of the small-sized chamber (ca. 3.5 meters by 3.5 meters) was covered with carpet-like *opus sectile* floor.[82] The interior of this more than 5-meter-high space was encased in ash-green marble. The supporting arch of the chamber's eastern wall was possibly reconstructed so that the wall was reduced to some 4.5 meters in height. The vault and upper parts of this space were covered with golden mosaics and frescoes. A narrow opening approximately 1 meter wide and some 3 meters high is set almost in the middle of the eastern wall of the chamber and was also revetted in marble. Into this opening, the canopy-like shrine for Hosios Loukas was inserted.

---

[81] Mylonas (1990) 99–122 and Mylonas (1992) 115–22.

[82] The size of the enclosing space is comparable to the tiny room in the crypt of St. Menas, which was approximately 3m × 3m. Ward Perkins (1949) 26–71.

The shrine of Hosios Loukas marked a focal point for the pilgrims who came to the shrine to seek divine intercession from the saint, sometimes lighting candles, praying, and occasionally sleeping next to the shrine.[83] Since the location of the shrine is most likely related to the original monastic cell and later to the tomb of Hosios Loukas, the tomb-shrine took the meaning and the form of a saintly house. The canopy-shrine of Hosios Loukas and its decoration resemble the shrine of St. Menas as depicted on the ivory from Milan (see Fig. 4.12). At first, the canopy-like shrine appears simple enough, a succession of four vertical supports and horizontal beams topped by a pyramidal roof. Each element of the canopy is made of various marbles incorporated into the wall of the *katholikon*, seemingly well balanced and centrally positioned. Upon more careful investigation, the imperfections become more than obvious: the shrine is neither a coherent stylistic whole, nor centrally positioned.

The columns and architraves show different sculptural treatment and decoration as well as remnants of color and gold. The embellishment of the shrine is achieved by reused marble columns and sculpted architraves. The architrave slabs and the semi-engaged columns of the western and eastern halves of the canopy significantly differ from each other in style and material. The western architrave and columns of the canopy are made of greenish Thessalian marble. The architrave is decorated with a zone of acanthus leaves. The two columns have Corinthian capitals, set on a high, prismatic, green marble *stylobate* and red marble plinth slabs. Remnants of color are visible on the carved parts of both the architrave slab and the column capitals (see Fig. 2.43). The *stylobates* of the canopy columns resemble the *stylobates* of the *bema* screen of the *katholikon*. The eastern architrave slab and columns are made of white Prokonessian marble with gray streaks. The remains of gold are visible on the slab. The column basket-like capitals show the motif of King Solomon's knot framed by palmetto leaves (see Fig. 2.58).[84] The architectural framing and decoration, therefore, enhanced the aura of importance, tradition, and sacredness. A mosaic with the representation of the Mother of God, holding the Christ Child in her arm, is set in the lunette of the arch over the opening, with the shrine just below the arch (see Fig. 4.11).

A sophisticated set of spatial and visual contrivances provides a key to understanding the sensibilities of the Byzantine beholders, who, when approaching the shrine, would have permanently captured in their minds an encounter with the sacred. The Byzantines often linked the shining properties of marbles to saints' visions, connecting the brightness and the abundance of shining light with images of the heavenly kingdom.[85] For example, the fourth-century vision of Dorotheos visualizes the kingdom of God as a bright dwelling with radiant walls, gates, porticoes, and courtyards.[86] The veins and abstract patterns of the marble slabs were sometimes experienced as figurative images, just like painted ones.[87] This imaginative recreation of the shapes and details seen in marble was frequently stimulated by narratives about various saints and sacred places, which beholders knew about and which influenced their perception. The use of local stone for the shrine of Hosios Loukas as

---

[83] Walter (1993) 203–228, esp. 223.

[84] Chapter 2.

[85] Ex. 24:14, Ps. 18:7, Ez. 8:2, Matt. 24:27. Jn. 1, Rev. 4, 10.

[86] McVey (1983) 91–121; Bremmer (1993) 253–261; Carile (2012) 42–48.

[87] Majeska (1978) 299–308; Fobelli (2006) 48–53, with references to the *ekphrases* of St. Stephen in Gaza by orator Coricius, who explained the marbles of the church, now lost, as paintings of Hagia Sophia by Paulos Silentarios, who compared marble columns with flowers; and by Clavijo, who wrote about the images of the Mother of God with the Child and of St. John the Baptist on a marble screen in the galleries during his visit to Hagia Sophia in Constantinople.

recorded in his *Life* and the later use of marbles for the shrine and of *opus sectile* for the floor in the *katholikon* were deliberate choices made in the spirit of piety.

The tomb-shrine of Hosios Loukas was compared to the bathhouse of St. Barbara, a monastic model for Hosios Loukas.[88] The marble bathhouse was built next to the tower where St. Barbara's father imprisoned her. The baths gained extraordinary properties when she miraculously engraved the sign of the cross into the marble walls with her finger. The tomb-shrine of Hosios Loukas was also described as a new Siloam,[89] a stone pool of water in Jerusalem with healing properties, because myrrh exuded from the saintly tomb, and the moisture collected from the surface of the shrine had miraculous properties to cure various mental and physical illnesses.[90]

Hosios Loukas would often appear in a dream as a luminous body floating above the "carpeted" floor. The "carpeted floor" is the literary and architectural *topos* of the marvelous *opus sectile* floors in front of Byzantine shrines.[91] The *opus sectile* could also mark the location of prayers of the faithful who would kneel and pray in front of a shrine. Such a practice of *proskynesis* associated with liturgical and devotional rituals within the Orthodox Church is attested to at least as early as the fourth century, judging by the description of how Galla Placidia passed her night in prayer in Santa Croce in Ravenna kneeling on a central disk within an *opus sectile* floor.[92] The lavish *opus sectile* floor composed of interlaced disks and based on the rotating, or double cross, inscribed in the circle and square just in front of the shrine of Hosios Loukas, remains preserved. In the dream of a certain Christopher, who slept near the saint's shrine, the blessed appeared "at night in [his] sleep, bright and gracious."[93] Other accounts describe the gleaming apparition of the blessed Loukas as floating above ground.[94] Visions of de-materialized saints most closely resemble other accounts of saintly apparitions as well as Byzantine icons. One such icon, illustrating the Mother of God, is depicted below a canopy in the Rabbula Gospels (see Fig. 2.66).[95]

The relatively small size of the temple-like shrine in comparison to the size of the human body of Loukas conforms to ancient visions of oversized statues of pagan gods within temples or images of human figures framed by canopies as depicted in Byzantine manuscripts. The human body of the saint was of the same height as his shrine-house, dominating its interior and giving the impression of an overwhelming presence within the shrine. The disproportionate presence of Hosios Loukas was further emphasized by two monumental bust-portraits over the shrine showing him as praying towards the east. One is a fresco on the eastern wall just above the shrine, and the other is a mosaic on the western wall directly opposite the shrine. The almost lifelike mosaic portrait of Hosios Loukas shows him with outstretched arms, almost as if about to embrace the beholder within his expansive gesture

---

88 *Life StLuke* ch. 69.

89 Ibid., ch. 69.

90 Ibid., ch. 71, 72, 73, 83.

91 Glass (1969) 386–390; Pajares-Ayuela (2001) 198–209. On the comparative example of the flooring in front of the shrine of St. Thecla, see *Vita et Miraculis Sanctae Theclae* 335–337.

92 Glass (1969) 386–390.

93 *Life StLuke* ch. 82.

94 Ibid., ch. 63.53–55: "An exceedingly precious purple cloth was spread out over the earth and above it the great man was standing, gleaming wondrously and indescribably both from his body and from his clothing and seen entirely in light."

95 The image from the Rabbula Gospels is comparable to the description of Arsenios in the *Apophtegmata Patrum, Acts of James* and *Marian the Martyr*—a vision of a youth who "shone with a dazzling light" and whose "feet did not touch the earth." Rush (1941) 217f. Believers also saw St. Thecla as an apparition: *Vita et Miraculis Sanctae Theclae* 335–337, 377–379.

of prayer. This expansive presence of Hosios Loukas is spatially reinforced through his image appearing in the church many times: in the northeast and northwest chapels of the *katholikon* and above his shrine on the western side of the east wall of the north arm of the *katholikon* (Fig. 4.14). In relation to the mosaic image of the Virgin and Christ Child and the donor composition next to it, these beholders represented in icons are also perpetually "visiting" the saint in his shrine, in a way reflecting the devotional actions of the pilgrims (see also Fig. 4.11). Hence, the communication node marked by the canopy-shrine of Hosios Loukas functioned as a visual and corporeal shell for the entire site.

The architectural design of the shrine and its setting also effectively manipulated a beholder's sense of proportion and size on multiple levels. First, visitors coming to the shrine passed through the north doors of the *katholikon* and, once inside the tiny corridor, encountered the canopied shrine squeezed in the church walls and surrounded by monumental iconic representations of holy figures, Hosios Loukas and the Mother of God

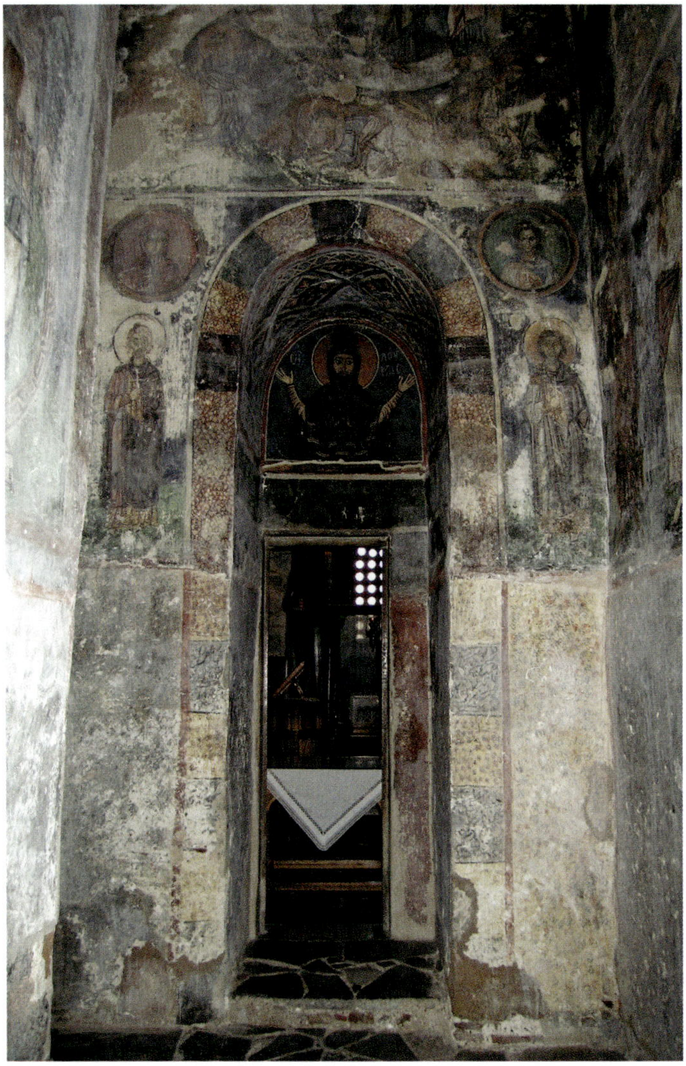

FIGURE 4.14 *View towards Hosios Loukas' shrine; fresco painting of Hosios Loukas is on the western side of the east wall of the north arm of the katholikon.* PHOTO AUTHOR

with Child above all. The pilgrims would behold the sacred on a personal, human-size level because the dimensions of the shrine perfectly accommodated a standing human figure. Then they would proceed toward the main space of the *katholikon*, eventually venerating the icons on the main sanctuary screen. Entering the open space of the *katholikon*, they would enter yet another canopy-like space, the immense space below the main church dome. Emphasized by the hovering image of Christ Pantokrator in the main dome, visitors would have been overwhelmed with the presence of God inside this church-canopy and would have become integrated with it as it surrounded them. Finally, visitors would exit the church either through the southern door or via the subsidiary space through the northwestern door of the *katholikon* (see Fig. 4.13).

The architectonics of the canopy-shrine as a recognizable solution for saintly shrines helped disclose the saint's actual presence. In the interior of the shrine, a tub-like stone container may have originally contained his bodily remains. At present, the shrine indeed shelters a wooden-frame casket with glass covers that reveal the saintly remains inside.[96] If the shrine originally contained relics, they were not displayed for continuous visual exposition. The metal fittings on the sides of the vertical columns of the canopy confirm that it was enclosed either by marble slabs alone or by marble slabs with subsequently added hanging curtains, as recorded in an early twentieth-century photograph of the shrine.[97] Screening curtains on canopy-like shrines potentially could have been removed at certain points to reveal the interior.[98] The enclosing marble panels of Hosios Loukas' shrine had window-like openings. The idea of vertical panels placed between the columns of the shrine coincides with the depiction of other Byzantine shrines, which essentially resembled small houses. The manuscript illumination of the shrine of St. Gregory Nazianzos reveals the shrine to be a small house with an opening above the marble container of the body.[99] The dividing enclosures and curtains suggest that such canopied structures were indeed understood as small houses, whose interiors could have been viewed on special occasions, during miraculous revelations and divine intercessions.

The relationship between the place of divine presence and the bodily presence of Loukas reveals that the physical presence of the saintly body was not a decisive component for divine intercession. Although most of the miracles Hosios Loukas performed did happen in the vicinity of his shrine, his actual bodily presence in the shrine was not crucial. It remains unclear whether and for how long Loukas' body was present in his shrine, especially because the bodily relics were taken by the Crusaders in the thirteenth century and returned by the Vatican only in 1986.[100] It may well be that at some point between 1205 and 1460, the northern arm of the crypt was recognized as the place of the

---

96 The enclosure slab of the sarcophagus in the north part of the crypt flanking the bema may have been originally the slab over the tomb of Hosios Loukas. The slab is cut on all four edges, thus revealing that some canopy was above it, potentially the same one on the ground floor. Schultz and Barnsley (1901) recorded the cuttings on the slab, and Boura (1980) 133 confirmed that, in its measures, it does not belong to the tomb in the crypt as it is placed today. Boura also hypothesized that it may have been the slab from the tomb of Hosios Loukas, though she connected it with the tomb on the crypt, not with the tomb-shrine.

97 Schultz and Barnsley (1901).

98 Ćurčić (2000) 134–142.

99 Ibid.

100 In 1204, shortly after the huge sequential building campaigns of the late tenth and early eleventh centuries, Boniface de Montferrat, king of Thessaloniki, drove the Orthodox monks from Hosios Loukas. From 1205 until 1308, the De la Roche family owned the monastery, and afterwards until the Turkish conquest in 1460, it was in the possession of the Catalans. Sometime during the thirteenth century, the bodily remains of Hosios Loukas were removed by the Crusaders and ultimately ended up in the Vatican. Liapis (2005) 8–10.

original tomb of Hosios Loukas, which was accompanied by two elaborate tombs in the eastern part of the crypt, flanking the altar on the north and south.[101] No archeological data confirm the existence of the actual tomb at the place of the cenotaph in the crypt. By the time the Orthodox monks reestablished the monastery of Hosios Loukas in the seventeenth century, it had been stripped of most of its church furnishings, and the memory of the shrine of Hosios Loukas was confined to the textual evidence in his *Life* and the services dedicated to him, since the monastery archives and treasuries remained empty. At that point, the saint's body had been missing from the monastery for a long time.[102] Yet the prophetic words of Hosios Loukas, when he foresaw his own death and the future glory of the monastery, emphasize the importance of the site of his death rather than the bodily presence:

> You will find fired bricks when you dig out the spot where I am lying [in his monastic cell]. Lifting these out and beautifying the place in a modest fashion take care to give dust to dust; then arrange the bricks on the surface of the earth, for God will bring glory to this place through the mysterious reasons which He Himself knows, until the end of the world, as crowds of believers come together here praising His divine name.[103]

Therefore, the physical remains failed to serve as the monumental focal point of the building. The primary reason was that the saintly body was missing from the monastery for much of its history. Another reason was that the location of the shrine was not the focus of either of the two churches, but was at a spot where the two churches join together. However, being close to the altar canopy that marked the presence of Christ during liturgical services, the canopied shrine stood as a memorial of divine providence as the Byzantines understood it. The shrine of Hosios Loukas, though visually and spatially similar to the altar canopy near it, was not made after the model of altar canopies, but had its own independent development, from a chamber to the canopy-like installation. Yet conceptually similar in conveying the messages of divine presence and actions, the two canopied installations of the altar and shrine, in the end after all the architectural changes, also achieved a close spatial connection when the shrine of Hosios Loukas was finally installed a few steps from the sanctuary and just northwest of the altar.

The multiple canopied shrines of St. Demetrios

St. Demetrios' shrines present the multiple and delicate spatial relations between canopied installations for saintly shrines, altar tables, and other singular places that marked the believed places for sacred revelations and the power of canopied structures to evoke the perception of the sacred among the beholders. As an early Christian martyr and warrior saint, protector of the Christian city, miracle worker, healer, and supporter of the innocent and weak, St. Demetrios is one of the most venerated Christian saints. The veneration of St. Demetrios was closely tied to the specially constructed shrines in his honor, on different scales and

[101] According to obviously incorrect tradition, these still-unidentified tombs are attributed to Emperor Romanos II and his wife, who were buried in Constantinople. Connor (1991) 83–93 suggests that the two tombs are those of Hosios Loukas' abbot successors.

[102] The seventeenth-century travel accounts express disappointment that the bodily remains could not be observed. It is interesting to note that the time of these missions to the Levant, which stirred late–seventeenth-century French interest in the Byzantine civilization and its architecture, coincided with interest in saintly shrines. Spon (1679) [1678]; Auzépy and Grélois (2001) 39–43; Eisner (1991) 56–57.

[103] *Life StLuke* ch. 64.

in different locations, confirming the importance of the shrines themselves.[104] Despite an abundance of textual, hagiographical, visual, archeological, and architectural material for St. Demetrios' shrines, the information about these installations based on a comparative analysis of these sources is perplexing. Numerous destructions and reinstallments of the shrines of St. Demetrios, combined with the perception of the faithful about canopied installations, reveal how the meaning of canopies was intertwined with conventional knowledge about their location within the church space and popular devotional practices.

Hagiographical texts as well as texts on miracles report that a certain Christian Demetrios was martyred in the caldarium of the public city baths and was inhumed in the furnace room where the martyrdom occurred during the early fourth-century imperial persecutions in Thessaloniki.[105] This room in the baths was probably the first location that attracted major popular veneration of St. Demetrios, as Demetrios' martyrdom was marked by numerous miracles.[106] The miraculous healing of Leontius, the eparch of Illyricum who held office in ca. 412/413, was probably the main reason that he honored and rebuilt the martyrium-shrine (οἰκία, οἰκεῖον μάρτυρα) of St. Demetrios and enfolded it within the eponymous church, also known as the "house of the saint" (εὐκτήριος οἶκος) in Thessaloniki in the fifth century.[107] Yet Leontius' interests were divided between the two capitals of Illyricum: Sirmium, modern Sremska Mitrovica, Serbia, and from 441–442 onward, in Thessaloniki, Greece.[108] Possibly Leontius built a church in both cities and within each a shrine for St. Demetrios' relics.[109] Both fifth-century basilica churches of St. Demetrios in Thessaloniki and in Sirmium have been archeologically confirmed, yet the exact location of the bodily remains in these early structures remains unconfirmed. In Sirmium, footings of a massive altar canopy, some 2 meters or 6 feet in span, set within the sanctuary space and deeply projecting into the nave, have been recovered, but not the bodily remains and relics that could have been associated with the shrine of St. Demetrios.[110] In Thessaloniki, the altar installation was never the focus of saintly veneration, nor were bodily remains ever recovered in the sanctuary.[111] Destroyed by the Avars in 582, Sirmium ceased to be the focal point of the saintly veneration by the end of the sixth century. Almost concurrently, if not earlier, the locus of the saintly veneration of St. Demetrios in Thessaloniki was transferred from the "crypt" under the transept and apse of the church, the former site of Roman baths, where according to legend Demetrios was martyred and buried, to the shrine in the main nave of the church (Fig. 4.15).[112]

---

104 On St. Demetrios and his veneration, with an extensive overview of the primary sources and controversies in scholarship, see *Life and Miracles StDemetrios-a* 10–11 and *Life and Miracles StDemetrios-c* Appendix; Grabar (1950) 1+3–28; Cormack (1985) 50–94; Popović (1998) 43–57; Skedros (1999); Woods (2000) 221–234; Bakirtzis (2002) 175–192; Walter (2003) 76–93; Popović (2004) 87–98; Bogdanović (2011a) 275–316; Bauer (2013) 143–183.

105 Primary texts suggest that Demetrios was martyred during the rule of Emperor Maximian. Both Popović (2004) 87–98 and Skedros (1999) 8–11 date the martyrdom between 304 and 308, the period that coincides with Emperor Galerius Maximianus (ca. 260–311) and his residence in Thessaloniki.

106 Skedros (1999) 149–157, appendices: The Passio Altera, Martyrdom of the Holy Great-Martyr Demetrios; Woods (2000) 221–234.

107 Popović (2004) 87–98, esp. 88; Walter (2003) 67–93; Woods (2000) 221–234; Skedros (1999) 123.

108 Walter (2003) 76–93; Popović (2004) 87–98, esp. 88; Woods (2000) 221–234.

109 Ibid.

110 Popović (2004) 87–98.

111 Walter (2003) 76–93.

112 Pallas (1979) 44–58. Bakirtzis (2002) 175–192 is of the opinion that the hexagonal shrine in the main nave of the church was there since its foundation in the fifth century.

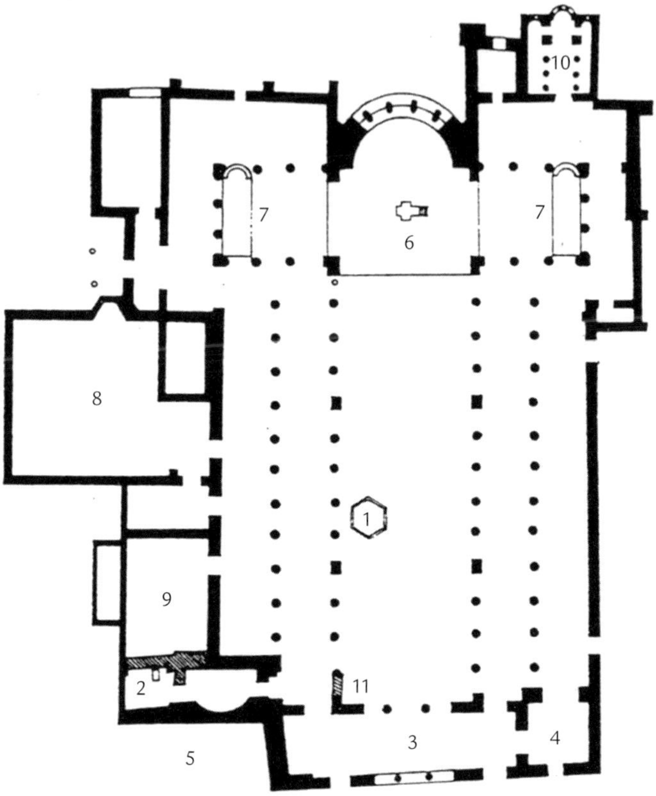

1. Ciborium
2. So-called "Tomb" of St. Demetrios
3. Narthex
4. Staircase
5. Remains of the Romans Baths
6. Altar with small crypt below
7. Transept wings
8. Chapel of St. John Prodromos
9. Auxiliary room
10. Chapel of St. Euthemius
11. Tomb of Loukas Spandounis

FIGURE 4.15 *Hagios Demetrios, Thessaloniki, Greece, fifth century and later.* CHARALAMBOS BAKIRTZIS AFTER G. A. SOTERIOU AND M. G. SOTERIOU, *HĒ VASILIKĒ TOU HAGIOU DĒMĒTRIOU THESSALONIKĒS*. ATHENS: *HĒEN ATHĒNAIS ARCHAIOLOGIKĒ HETAIREIA*, 1952

The two shrines, the two sacred *loci,* that were perceived as the places of St. Demetrios' revelations in Thessaloniki were never related to the altar canopy spatially or functionally.[113] These two saintly shrines were not only without any direct spatial link to each other, but were also known by two different terms. The "οἰκία, οἰκίσκος" [*oikia, oikiskos*], literally the "house" or "small house," marked the saint's believed tomb and the testimony of his miracles, and was within the crypt-like space below the church sanctuary, originally a two-story construction with direct access to the street.[114] The "κιβώριον" [*kiborion, ciborium*], which

[113] For the canopy above the altar in St. Demetrios church, see Hoddinott (1963) 130; Krautheimer (1986) 124; Mango (1985b) 75–79.

[114] Pallas (1979) 44–58; Cormack (1989) figs. 3–4; Cormack (1986) 547–555; Cormack (1969) 17–52, pl. 3 (black/white), pl. 7 (color); Bakirtzis (2002) 175–192; Bogdanović (2011a) 275–316.

was never an open columnar installation, was originally a six-sided enclosed shrine of the saint where his icon, not his saintly remains, were displayed.[115] The silver-gilt ciborium, some 2 meters, was in the middle of the nave length, close to its northern arcade, in a location that can still be discerned within a hexagonal outline on the floor.[116]

The ciborium of St. Demetrious in the nave of the Thessalonian basilica was replaced after fires at least twice during the seventh century alone, and both times in silver.[117] John the Archbishop of Thessaloniki records in his seventh-century miracle account that St. Demetrios himself helped in the collection of more than 115 lbs. of silver for the restoration of the silver ciborium while at the same time preventing the melting of the episcopal silver throne as originally planned.[118] It remains unknown what had happened to the silver shrine during the Saracen attack of 904, but it was certainly ransacked by the Normans in 1185.[119] Hence, sometime between the early tenth and late twelfth centuries, and possibly by the mid-eleventh century based on the octagonal replica of the ciborium in the Kremlin museums (see also Fig. 4.20), the silver ciborium was replaced by a marble canopy (Fig. 4.16), possibly octagonal in shape, judging by a number of recovered fragments that may have belonged to this Middle Byzantine installation (Fig. 4.17).[120]

By the ninth century, St. Demetrios received another canopy-like shrine within the church. In a grotto-like crypt inside the *oikia*, a seven-sided, columnar but roofless marble installation marked the remains of the public bath and the believed place of the saint's martyrdom (Fig. 4.18). Though wrongly, many faithful believed that this canopied fountain, which provided holy water to pilgrims, was physically connected to the hexagonal silver-gilt ciborium in the nave, also occasionally wrongly associated with his tomb.[121] By the eleventh century, if not earlier, the miraculous actions of St. Demetrios were associated with the production of holy water-with-myrrh at this underground shrine in Thessaloniki.[122] Bodily relics that exuded myrrh were used for the authentication of saints and saintly miracles in Byzantium, yet the body of St. Demetrios was never exposed for veneration during medieval times.[123] Rather, the veneration of St. Demetrios was related to various architectural shrines that framed the sacred places of his miracles.

Moreover, the Ottoman Turks established the veneration of St. Demetrios themselves after the conquest of the city in 1430.[124] As shown by Charalambos Bakirtzis, possibly around the 1430s, the octagonal canopied *phiale* was established some 3 meters from the

---

115 Cormack (1986) 547–555; Bakirtzis (2002) 175–192; Bogdanović (2011a) 275–316.

116 Pallas (1979) 44–58; Bakirtzis (1997) 14; Mentzos (1994) 56–67; Papamastorakis (1998) 213–230.

117 Walter (2003) 76–93; Bakirtzis (2002) 175–192; Morrisson (2002) 173–203.

118 *Life and Miracles StDemetrios-a*, Miracle 3, 75ff, lines 75(29)–82.

119 According to the *Life of St. Elias the Younger,* the ciborium was *in situ* just before the Arab attack of 904. Yannopoulos (1994) 193–221, esp. 215–216.

120 Bogdanović (2011a) 275–316; Bakirtzis (2002) 175–192; Morrisson (2002) 173–203.

121 Mango (1985b) 75–79. Cormack (1986) 547–555 advocates that the crypt became the place of veneration in the centuries after the Iconoclasm. See also Bakirtzis (1990) 140–149, esp. 147.

122 Though the myrrh-gushing may have appeared earlier, at the end of the ninth and beginning of the tenth centuries, as summarized by Walter (2003) 76–93, Bakirtzis (2002) 175–192, esp. 176, suggests that the earliest historical evidence of myrrh gushing is from 1040.

123 In 1978, Maria Theocharis recognized the relics of St. Demetrios in San Lorenzo in Campo in Italy and proposed that they were brought to San Lorenzo no later than in the early thirteenth century. The head was brought to Thessaloniki between the 23rd and 25th of October 1978, and the remains of relics were venerated in the city between the 11th and 13th of April 1980. Theocharis (1978) 508–536; Bakaros [Βακάρος] (2006) 68–91. I thank Ivan Drpić for references.

124 Bakirtzis (2002) 175–192, esp. 188.

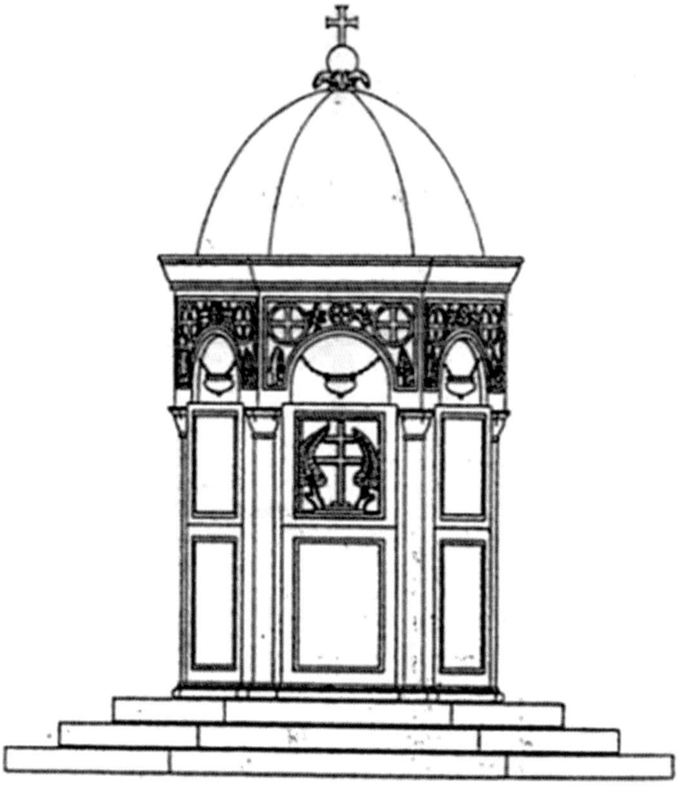

FIGURE 4.16 *Reconstruction drawing of the marble ciborium built by the twelfth century instead of the original six-sided silver-gilt ciborium-shrine of St. Demetrios; the original location of the ciborium can still be discerned within hexagonal outline on the floor, under the modern marble shrine in the Basilica of Hagios Demetrios, Thessaloniki, Greece.* DRAWING G. A. SOTERIOU AND M. G. SOTERIOU, *HĒ VASILIKĒ TOU HAGIOU DĒMĒTRIOU THESSALONIKĒS*. ATHENS: *HĒEN ATHĒNAIS ARCHAIOLOGIKĒ HETAIREIA*, 1952, FIG. 72

church entrance at a spot that according to the popular belief was close to the saint's tomb (Fig. 4.19, see also Fig. 4.15). Reportedly it was occasionally filled with a mixture of holy water and myrrh, confirming the presence and miraculous workings of St. Demetrios, in a way becoming yet another shrine of St. Demetrios used by both Christians and Muslims.

Therefore, the saintly shrines of St. Demetrios were separate installations, which were spatially, visually, formally, and functionally distinct.[125] The three saintly shrines of St. Demetrios—in the crypt, in the nave, and after the 1430s in the *phiale* outside the church in Thessaloniki—were in popular veneration often connected to the tomb of St. Demetrios. Moreover, these shrines were also compared with the Tomb of Christ. Interestingly, even if the canopied altar installation in the Church of Hagios Demetrios stood for the symbolic Tomb of Christ, as in any other church, the shrines-tombs of St. Demetrios were never related to the altar installation.

The associations between the shrines-tombs of St. Demetrios and the Tomb of Christ were related to their homologous miracles, death, and by extension the believed homologous architectural structures that framed the experience of the sacred at a tomb. This observation

---

[125] Bogdanović (2011a) 275–316.

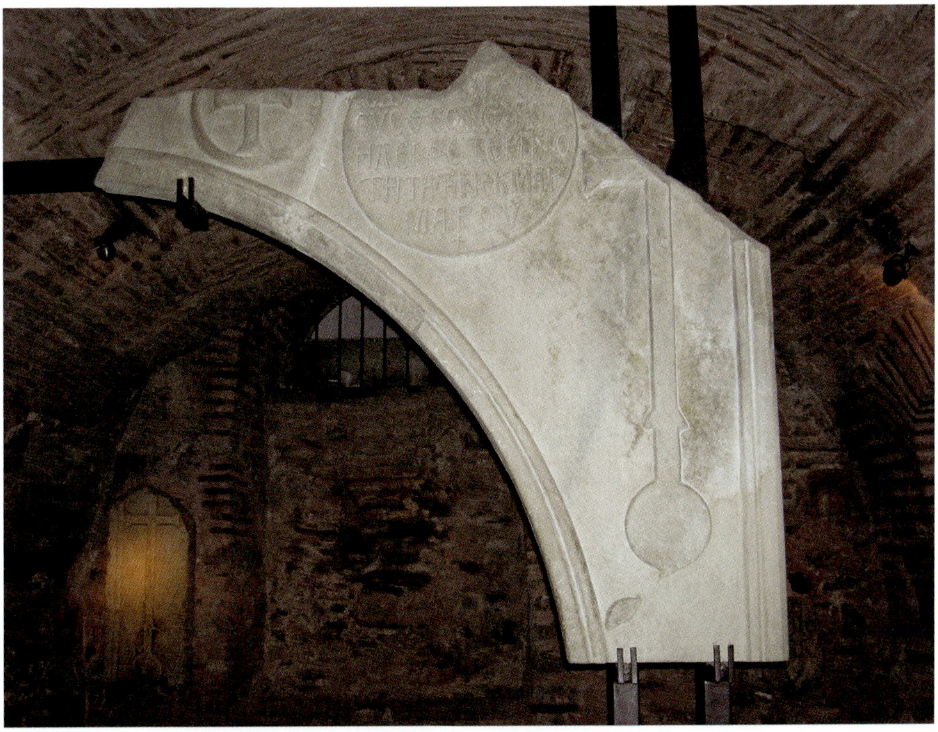

FIGURE 4.17 *Marble fragments that may have belonged to Middle-Byzantine St. Demetrios' ciborium.* PHOTO NEBOJŠA STANKOVIĆ

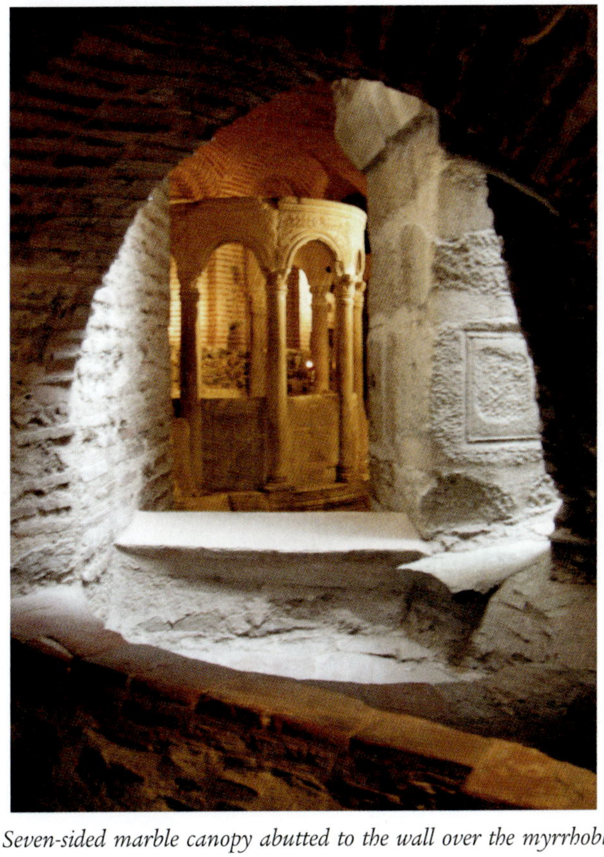

FIGURE 4.18 *Seven-sided marble canopy abutted to the wall over the myrrhobletic basin, Hagios Demetrios, Thessaloniki, Greece, after ninth century.* PHOTO NEBOJŠA STANKOVIĆ

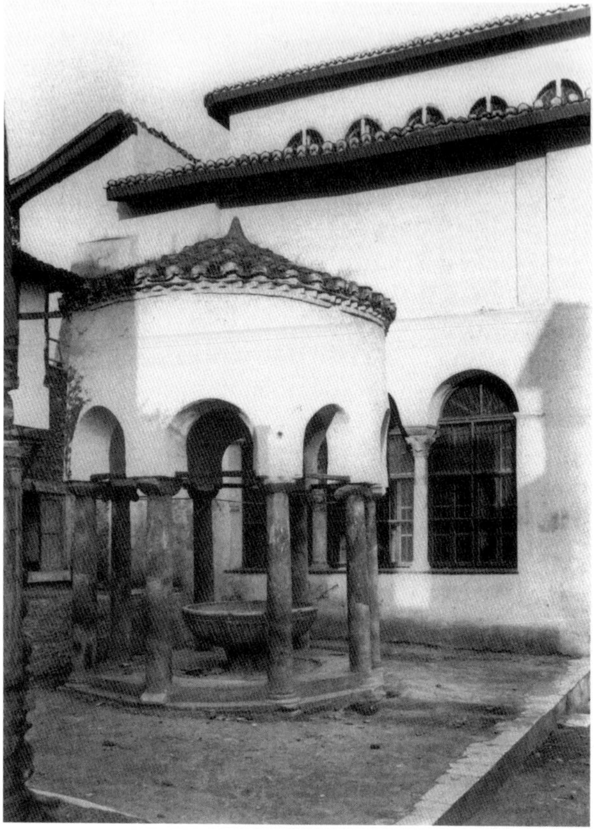

FIGURE 4.19 *Octagonal canopied* phiale *in front of the Church of Hagios Demetrios, Thessaloniki, Greece, ca. the 1430s.* PHOTO FRED BOISSONASS 1913

is particularly true for the ciborium in the nave of the Church of Hagios Demetrios. It was shaped as a miniature typical Roman mausoleum, and the faithful believed that the ciborium contained the tomb or at least functioned as a cenotaph marking the place of the underground tomb of the saint.[126]

In the seventh century, an unknown relative of the Prefect of Illyricum described the hexagonal silver-gilt shrine of St. Demetrios as having a roof topped with a sphere; the lower part of the sphere surrounded by shoots of lilies, crowned by a life-giving cross: "the trophy that is victorious over death: by its silver composition it amazes our corporeal eyes, while bringing Christ to mind, it illuminates with grace the eyes of the intellect."[127] The accounts also propose that the ciborium had its own doors, consisting of two silver panels.[128] Lamps were suspended from the canopy roof, suggesting eternal light and the mystical presence of the saint. The shrine also contained a golden votive crown of martyrdom.[129]

---

[126] *Life and Miracles StDemetrios-a*, Miracle 5, lines 88 (50)–90 (54); Skedros (1999) 91–92; Grabar (1950) 1+3–28.

[127] *SD* 129.

[128] Cormack (1985) 80–94, esp. fig. 27 on p. 87.

[129] Cormack (1986) 547–555.

In the middle of the shrine, there was a "bed" made of silver with a golden "throne," embellished by precious stones for "Christ's most glorious martyr Demetrios,"[130] and one more silver throne for the Lady Eutaxie, as depicted on icons and mosaics of the church.[131] Lady Eutaxie (literally meaning "good order") had already been associated with the personification of the Christian good order.[132] The "bed" and "thrones" most likely referred to the effigy of the saint and canopy-like *proskynetaria* installations for devotional icons.[133] The post-Iconoclastic accounts about St. Demetrios record that [the icon of (?)] the Virgin "visited" the saint in his shrine in Thessaloniki, suggesting the practice of icon processions within the developed ritual of saintly veneration.[134] Hence believers directed their prayers for intercession, not to the bodily relics, but to the sacred icons closely associated with his shrine.

The sixth-century ciborium of St. Demetrios and its subsequent replacements set in a prominent space in the church conveyed the message of the importance of this saintly house.[135] The saint would often appear to the faithful, emerging from his ciborium as he was represented in his icons.[136] Witnesses reported visions of St. Demetrios, who would appear glowing and dressed in a white *chlamys*: "the door opened to reveal the saint just inside. The observer fell to the floor at the sight of the saint, who appeared as 'on the more ancient icons' with rays of light gleaming from his face so that the observer was light with brightness. . . ."[137] The metaphor of sight and of the exchange of gazes between the saint and beholders is dominant: St. Demetrios is seen, who himself has the all-seeing eye.[138] The metaphor of the opened doors of the shrine[139] as the place of meeting between the saint and beholders is also important: the beholders occupy the same "hieroplastic"[140] space as St. Demetrios, who himself is ever-present and always the same. The metaphor of light and of the exchange of light is crucial: St. Demetrios emanates divine light, and the divine grace is transferable to the beholders, who are now enlightened.

The polygonal ciborium-shrine in the church was an essential element for the recognition of the saint and his apparitions because St. Demetrios was so closely associated with his shrine, as archeological evidence, votive mosaic panels in the church, and textual accounts corroborate.[141] The insistence on the architectural framing of the saint also implies that the

---

[130] *SD* 129.

[131] Cormack (1986) 547–555.

[132] Skedros (1999) 127; Cormack (1985) 76–77; Pallas (1979) 44–58.

[133] Pallas (1979) 44–58; Skedros (1999) 89; Papamastorakis (1998) 213–230.

[134] Belting (1996) 65–69, 184–85.

[135] Cormack (1985) 77.

[136] Bishop John of Thessaloniki, Miracle no. 10. For the English translation of the tenth miracle, see *SD* 129–130. For the references to St. Demetrios' ciborium as a silver shrine within the church, see also *Life and Miracles StDemetrios-a*, Miracle 1 page 66 line 24; Miracle 12 page 125 line 11; Miracle 15 page 162 line 9.

[137] *Life and Miracles StDemetrios-a* 145, 157, 160–161. English translation by Cormack (1985) 67.

[138] About this concept see Hahn (1997) 1079–1106.

[139] About the analysis of the metaphor of the open doors for the Church as the abode of salvation within the context of Hagia Sophia, see Lidov (2007) 135–176, 366–371, esp. 151, with reference to the Gospel of John (10:7–9): "So said the Lord: I am the door of the sheep. By me if any man enters, he shall go in and out, and find pasture."

[140] Dionysius the Areopagite introduced the term "hieroplastia" in his *Celestial Hierarchy* (CH II.1). I thank Filip Ivanović for discussing this reference with me. Here, I borrow the term "heiroplastic" as a reference to space, which is at once earthly, heavenly and beyond, from Lidov (2009a) 338; Bogdanović (2011a) 275–316, esp. n. 65.

[141] Cormack (1985) 50–94; Cormack (1969) 17–52. On comparative visual evidence from other sites, see also Koltsida-Makre (2002) 149–154; Grabar (1954) 305+307–313; Grabar (1950) 1+3–28.

ciborium, though highly visible, was accessible to the pious for private and popular devotion under controlled conditions.[142] The controlled physical access to the shrine actually fostered beholders' contemplation about the meaning of the shrine and its contents, including any spiritual messages conveyed, as reports of beholders' dreams further emphasized. For example, paralyzed and on his deathbed, Prefect Marianos, who held his tenure at the end of the fifth and beginning of the sixth centuries, had a dream in which a certain Demetrios offered a cure by inviting him to his house for a sleepover.[143] However, Marianos was cured during his contemplation about the meaning of the dream and when he acknowledged St. Demetrios' help. Only after he had been cured did Marianos actually visit the ciborium-shrine, and inside this holy "house," he recognized the engraved image of the saint on the "couch"—perhaps an effigy or an icon on the icon-stand—as the final confirmation of the miraculous intercession of the saint. The metaphor of the couch within the house and of the exchange of supine body postures between the everlasting saint and Marianos in this case emphasizes the transferable body images of sickness and death vs. physical and spiritual healing and eternal life. Moreover, St. Demetrios' miraculous healing of Marianos recalls Christ's ministry and the miracles in the Gospels and their contextual understanding. As the healing of Marianos takes place in the "home of Demetrios" and shows how spiritual healing preceded physical healing through the contemplation and intercession of the others, so the Gospel miracle of the Healing of the Paralytic (Mark 2:1–12; Matt 9:2–8; Luke 5:17–26) takes place in Capernaum, "the home of Jesus," establishing further spiritual and architectural links between Christ and St. Demetrios.

In time, the ciborium itself was invested with sacredness, and the Byzantines made various replicas of Thessalonian shrine elsewhere. A certain Kyprianos, Bishop of Thenae, after being aided by a person identical in appearance to St. Demetrios, as he was portrayed on the icon at the Thessaloniki shrine, commissioned a replica of the ciborium for his church in Thenae, now the port of Henchir Tina in Tunisia, North Africa.[144] This ciborium, made of marble, in the church in Thenae became a site of miraculous healings.[145]

The Constantinopolitan small-scale ciborium-reliquary made for Emperor Constantine X Doukas (1059–1067) and his second wife, Eudokia Makrembolitissa, today in the Armory of the Kremlin Museums, is another replica of the Thessalonian shrine (Fig. 4.20).[146] This octagonal silver-gilt reliquary references the octagonal shape of the Thessalonian shrine after the tenth century, when the silver ciborium was replaced by a marble canopy. Engraved in low relief, four narrow panels contain representations of vines and palmetto leaves, while another four panels contain images and inscriptions. One of the panels is engraved with the symbolic doors to the shrine and, on the opposite side, the other with the representation of the imperial couple being crowned by Christ.[147] The other two panels have a dodecasyllabic inscription in Greek: "I am the true image of the ciborium of the lance-pierced martyr

[142] On the limited access to the interior of the ciborium, see Skedros (1999) 91–92.

[143] Ibid., miracles 10–24.

[144] Cormack (1985) 73–74; *Life and Miracles StDemetrios-a*, Miracle 1; *Life and Miracles StDemetrios-b* 234–241.

[145] Cormack (1985) 73–74.

[146] Grabar (1950) 1+3–28; Kalavrezou (1997) 77–78.

[147] This image of Christ crowning the imperial couple is consistent with the "marriage" images of imperial couples, as the coronation was often accompanied with the marriage ceremony, which is testified to by the tenth-century Middle Byzantine and Ottonian ivories showing Christ crowning Emperor Romanos II and Empress Eudokia and Emperor Otto II and Empress Theophano. Kalavrezou (1997) 77–78 proposed that this image, in conjunction with St. Demetrios' reliquary, shows expectations for the cure of Emperor Constantine X Doukas, who was sick at the time.

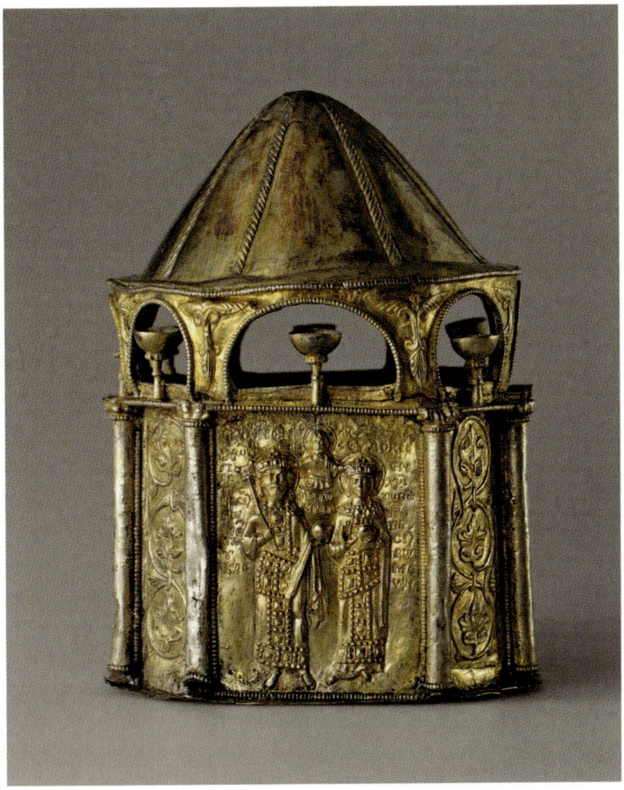

FIGURE 4.20 *St. Demetrios' Reliquary, eleventh century, made in Constantinople; Kremlin Armory Museum in Moscow.* S. V. BARANOV AND V. E. OVERCHENKO © MOSCOW KREMLIN MUSEUMS

Demetrios. On the outside I have Christ inscribed [represented], who with his hands crowns the fair couple . . . ."[148]

The principal function of the shrine of St. Demetrios in Thessaloniki and its replicas was not to expose the physical remains of the saint, but, like the Tomb of Christ, to frame active presence in physical absence. As vehicles for the transmission of the grace of the Holy Spirit, saints impersonated the presence of Christ after His Incarnation on earth, and the faithful remembered critical and often generic but memorable aspects of interconnections between the saints and Christ and the miracles they performed. The "body image" of a lance-pierced St. Demetrios recalled the "body image" of lance-pierced Christ.[149] Similarly, the form and symbolism of the ciborium-shrines of St. Demetrios can be related to the canopy-like shrine of the Tomb of Christ in Jerusalem.[150] Like the Holy Sepulchre, in which the Tomb *Aedicula* bore witness to the human ministry of Christ, the shrines of St. Demetrios confirmed that the main objects of veneration were not the physical remains of the saint. For, like the tomb-bench in Christ's tomb, the bench-like "bed" from the ciborium of St. Demetrios in the

[148] Kalavrezou (1997) 77–78, translation on p. 77. Theotoka (1941–1952) 395–413; Bogdanović (2011a) 275–316.

[149] Ksingopoulos (1975–1976) 531–553. I thank Ivan Drpić for bringing Ksingopoulos' work to my attention.

[150] Grabar (1950) 1+3–28 has already suggested a comparison of St. Demetrios' shrines with the Holy Sepulchre in Jerusalem. See also Chapter 5.

eponymous church in Thessaloniki implies the saint's presence despite his visible absence. Therefore, the ciborium of St. Demetrios as the most prominent installation in the church and a main object of veneration exposed neither the saintly body nor its fragments, and it was never its principal function to do so. Rather, it "localized" the apparitions of the saint and his miraculous actions; it provided a testimony to how divine grace became more vivid and accessible to believers. The generic architectural symbols and their conflation in various shrines did not contradict the Byzantine view of sanctity, which was typological rather than chronological or topographical, allowing the existence of several canopied shrines of St. Demetrios in his church in Thessaloniki and their conflation with the most sacred shrine, the Tomb of Christ.

ALTAR CANOPY AND SANCTUARY SCREEN

Not without significance for understanding the phenomenon of Byzantine canopies is the relationship between the altar canopy and the columnar sanctuary screen. For the Byzantines, the altar canopy framed the central locus in the church, the central place in the sanctuary that stood for the Tomb of Christ and the Ark of the Covenant, merging the major New and Old Testament architectural models and religious concepts.[151] The sanctuary screen separated the holiest place of the church, the Holy of Holies, from the nave. These subtle boundaries between the material and spiritual states, between visible and invisible creation, can be observed on both architectural and conceptual levels.

Sanctuary screens separating the *bema* and the church nave have been attested in early Christian churches across the Mediterranean region, including those in Constantinople.[152] In antiquity, various partitions, railings, and screens, known as *kinklides* (κιγκλίδες), separated the cult statues in pagan temples, and Antioch bishop Theodoret of Cyrrhus (ca. 393–466) used the same term for sanctuary screens in early churches.[153] At least since the seventh century, judging by the description of the screen in the now-lost Church of H. Artemios in Constantinople, the term *templon* (τέμπλον), potentially carrying related associations with the Temple architecture, started to supplant the previous generic and descriptive terms *kinklides* and *kankela* (κάγκελλα) used to describe sanctuary screens in Byzantine churches.[154] Merging of the meanings for the sanctuary screens, referencing both their functional properties and Temple architecture, might have developed much earlier, as the archeological evidence from the Holy Land suggests.

The actual placement of sanctuary screens in Jerusalem's synagogues and churches during the fourth and fifth centuries is especially revealing, because it points to the relocation of liturgical rites from exterior sacrificial sites to the interiors of both Jewish and Christian sanctuaries and simultaneously highlights some parallels between the liturgical services and practices.[155] At first, the movable altars might have been in the nave of Palestinian churches, similar to the one attested to in Old St. Peter's in Rome and suggested in other churches in the wider Mediterranean region.[156] The floor mosaic in front of the apse of the sixth-century chapel of the Theotokos at Mt. Nebo, where the cult of Moses was particularly strong, represents a structural motif recognized as the Jerusalem Temple (see Fig. 2.4).[157] The depicted

[151] Chapters 1, 2, and 5.

[152] Mathews (1971) 109–110.

[153] See Chapter 1. Marinis (2014) 41.

[154] Mango (1979) 40–43; Walter (1993) 203–228; Marinis (2014) 41. See also Chapter 1.

[155] Branham (1992) 375–394; Wilkinson (1979) 347–359; Saller (1941).

[156] Chapter 2.

[157] Branham (1992) 375–394.

edifice is an elongated structure, with the apse on one of its shorter sides, and it is visually recognizable as a basilica. The division among the entrance area, the part of the nave with the sacrificial altar, and the apse area reserved for the Holy of Holies is evident.

Once the altar was combined with the saintly remains, the Christian altar emphasized the salvific concept of victory over death. The canopy both sheltered the altar, which stood for the bloodless sacrifice of Christ, symbolized both His Tomb and the place of His Resurrection, and represented the eternal, triumphant house of Christ's followers. The rearrangement of the original *fastigium* screen of Old St. Peter's, which by the fifth century had a full canopy installation for the central section of the columnar screen, by the sixth or early seventh century was integrated with the tomb-shrine, and by the eighth century obtained the Byzantine silver-plated beam decorated with holy images, signals a wider phenomenon of spatial and conceptual merging of altar canopies and sanctuary screens, invested with both religious icons and theological meanings.[158]

The full understanding of the sanctuary barrier and its relationship to the altar canopy in the *bema* of a Byzantine church is highly complex and limited due to the archeological evidence that reveals the upper parts of the sanctuary screens only after the transitional period. Originally low partitions, sanctuary screens over time became taller, frequently articulated by four columns topped by an epistyle, hence replicating the architectural elements of the altar canopy framed by four columns and a roof. The three intercolumniations marked the screen in front of the central apse. In churches with tri-partite sanctuaries, the additional double columns would screen entrance to the *prothesis*, used for liturgical services and located to the north of *bema* and possibly to achieve symmetry, also the chamber to the south, which usually served as *diakonikon* and was often without liturgical significance. These intercolumniations at some point acquired curtains that could have been drawn at specific points during the services, eventually to be filled by massive, monumental icons, hence forming the icon-stand, today also known as the *iconostasis*. Religious icons were associated with the *templon* screen early on. In the sixth century, the epistyle of the sanctuary screen could have been decorated with the holy icons as in Constantinopolitan Hagia Sophia, where the icon of Christ was flanked by the images of the Mother of God, apostles, and prophets.[159] Indeed, the architrave beams of sanctuary screens in Byzantine-rite churches could have been additionally enriched by multiple rows of holy icons. These often showed the Deesis—the great prayer with Christ Pantokrator just above the central door flanked by the Mother of God and St. John the Baptist as supplicants—as well as patron saints, apostles, prophets, and, at least by the eleventh centuries, scenes from saintly lives and images of the major liturgical feasts, the so-called Twelve Great Feasts, that also marked the liturgical calendar.[160]

The tectonics of the sanctuary screen hence included both spatial and temporal aspects of liturgical rites. At least since the eighth century, following Patriarch Germanos, the setting of the liturgical mysteries in the sanctuary behind the screen was understood by the Byzantines that:

> The chancel barriers [*kankela*—J.B.] indicate the place of prayer: the outside is for the people and the inside, the Holy of Holies, is accessible only to the priest. The barriers made of bronze like those around the Holy Sepulchre so that no one might enter there by accident. (9) . . . The Entablature is the legal and holy decoration, representing the crucified Christ, the Lord by means of a decorated cross (8).[161]

---

[158] See Chapter 2.

[159] Xydis (1947) 1–24.

[160] Mango (1979) 40–43; Walter (1993) 203–228; Spieser (1999) 131–164.

[161] *Germanos-a* ch. 9, 8; *Germanos-b* 62–63.

The major scholarly focus was usually placed on the role of sanctuary screens to prevent the laity from entering the sanctuary reserved only for clergy. Christopher Walter has proposed that the profane subjects, such as animals, also seen on the sanctuary barrier, substituted for the direct view of the mysteries enacted within the sanctuary by offering a focal point for lay piety and more personal devotional practices.[162] By analyzing a significant number of masonry sanctuary screens in Greece, F.Y.R. of Macedonia, and Serbia, Sharon Gerstel has suggested that their development as icon-stands in the thirteenth century is closely related to the developments of liturgical use of processional icons.[163] Marinis has corroborated this dating with liturgical texts from the same period and has proposed that the opaqueness of icon-stands, preventing any view into the sanctuary interiors, was the result of the heightened awareness by clergy that laity should not profane the Eucharistic mystery.[164] However, it also seems that many *templon* screens were made of wood and riveted in metal, usually silver, as in case of the sanctuary barriers in Old St. Peter's and Hagia Sophia. The materiality and meaning of these screens is further supported by Germanos' reference that the epistyle beam pointed to the Cross and the bronze railing of the Holy Sepulchre as the most sacred Christian space. Wooden epistyle beams have been archeologically confirmed since the eleventh century, while the replacement of marble templa with wooden ones in late- and post-Byzantine monasteries, including those on conservative Mt. Athos, indicate their pervasive importance.[165] The preference for wood and silver could have been related to the notion that it symbolized the True Cross.

Sanctuary screens had a mixture of different images, sometimes also including the cherubim, as on the painted iconostasis from the White Church at Karan (1340–1342) or the painted columns defining the *bema* in the twelfth-century Church of the Savior at Nereditsa, Russia.[166] Despite the late date of these churches, the cherubim marking the place where the Lord appeared (Ex. 25.22; Lev. 16.2) are also mentioned in the sixth-century Syriac hymn on the now-lost Cathedral in Edessa.[167] The Edessa church had a complex multi-columnar sanctuary screen and altar installation, potentially similar to the one from St. Peter's in Rome, while the hymn also mentions the cherubim of the altar.[168] Geometric and vegetal ornaments, which often comprised various versions of Solomon knots in the shape of "pomegranate" (cf. Ex. 28:33–34),[169] are known from the descriptions of the veil of the Holy of Holies. The same motifs, including canopies with double-knotted colonnettes, decorated Byzantine sanctuary barriers, marble parapets, and *proskynetaria* icons like in the eleventh-century Church of Hosios Loukas, in Boeotia, Greece (Fig. 2.42).[170]

Within the context of the transferability of the tectonics of sanctuary barriers and altar canopies defined by different materials such as textiles and stone as well as enriched and

---

[162] According to Sozomenos, already in the fifth century, Ambrose, Bishop of Milan, forbade Emperor Theodosios to enter the sanctuary, confirming that the sanctuary was reserved for the clergy. Walter (1993) 203–228, esp. 244.

[163] Gerstel (2006) 133–162.

[164] Marinis (2014) 46.

[165] Walter (1993) 203–228. On wooden *templa* on Mt. Athos, see Melvani (2015) 305–335.

[166] Babić (1975) 3–49; Sarabianov (2005) 83–98.

[167] McVey (1983) 91–121.

[168] Chapter 2.

[169] Kalavrezou-Maxeiner (1985) 95–103.

[170] On other, less-known examples of sculpted Middle Byzantine *templa* with canopied motifs with Solomon knots, see, for example, Voyatzis (2006) 101–114; Voyatzis and Sythiakaki (2008) 207–220; Voyatzis (2009) 129–140.

connected with shared decorative motifs, the image of the *Bishops Celebrating the Liturgy* from the late twelfth-century Church of St. George at Kurbinovo, F.Y.R. of Macedonia, is particularly revealing (Fig. 4.21).[171] A depicted marble canopy frames the liturgical scene of the *melismos* that shows the Christ Child in the paten on the altar.[172] With Christ ready to be consecrated as "the Lamb," the image makes direct references to the actual liturgical service of consecrating the Eucharistic bread and cutting the cube-shaped piece, also known as "the Lamb," performed in the sanctuary space. The actual three-dimensional altar canopy and the liturgical space and liturgical rites it frames are here supplanted by the painted representation. The haptic and optic qualities of a canopy are suggested through the active use of the sanctuary wall pierced by two windows that bring light through the open columnar structure and project the light that passes through the created canopy further onto the actual altar where the Eucharist is performed. The depicted canopy is loaded with architectural and sacred meanings, which are shared with Middle Byzantine sanctuary fittings attested to elsewhere. Namely, the twin columns of the depicted canopy from Kurbinovo are interlocked in the Solomon's knots and crowned with pseudo-Corinthian capitals, as if to convey the aura of sacredness and longevity of architecture of the past by combining memorable architectural elements of the Temple through the representation of the Solomon's knot and of ancient architecture through the representation of the Classical Greek architectural order. The memorable motif of the double-knotted colonnettes is attested to in the *templon* and *proskynetaria* icons from Hosios Loukas, and double-knotted colonnettes composed the altar canopy in the Panagia Kosmosoteria (Virgin Savior of the World) at Pherrai (1152).[173] Most impressively, the dome of the depicted canopy in Kurbinovo is represented as if simultaneously made of both stone and textile. Its marble roof is subtly underlined in cloth with many crosses (*polustaurion*) of the same kind as the *polustavion phelonia*, the tent-like priestly vestments worn by Byzantine archbishops and depicted in the Kurbinovo scene as well (Fig. 4.22).[174] Hence, I would propose that ancient and Biblical architectural models, including subtle references to their materiality and decoration, are critical in understanding the Byzantine sanctuary screen and its relationship to the altar.

The veil of the desert tabernacle had been hung from the four pillars of acacia overlaid with gold, with hooks of gold, upon four bases of silver (Ex. 26.32). However, it is not clear whether these four columns were placed in a straight line or at the four corners of a square enclosure with the veil being hung around all four sides, with the two ends overlapping at the front to give the access to the inner space, which allows for the possibility that the sanctuary screen can be architecturally understood as an unfolded altar canopy (Fig. 4.23). A preserved example of a masonry sanctuary screen literally shows tectonic merging with the structure of the altar canopy. In the Syrian Church of Mar Augen, southern Turkey, founded in the early fourth century and restored in the thirteenth century, is an undated, possibly late medieval even post-medieval, sanctuary installation where the two central of the four front columns of the screen support a domical vault, which in the back is resting on the sanctuary wall (Figs. 4.24, 4.25).[175] This example from Mar Augen may point to the longer tradition as

[171] Bogdanović (2014b) 247–292. About the Church of St. George in Kurbinovo, see Grozdanov (1992).

[172] Wybrew (1989) 150; Gerstel (1999) 40–48; Grozdanov (1980) 63–84; Walter (1982) 206, 220–221. See also Chapter 3.

[173] Mango (1985b) 249.

[174] Bogdanović (2014b) 247–292.

[175] Sinclair (1989) vol. 3, 346–348, fig. on p. 347. I thank Dan Waugh for bringing the Mar Augen example to my attention and for discussing it with me.

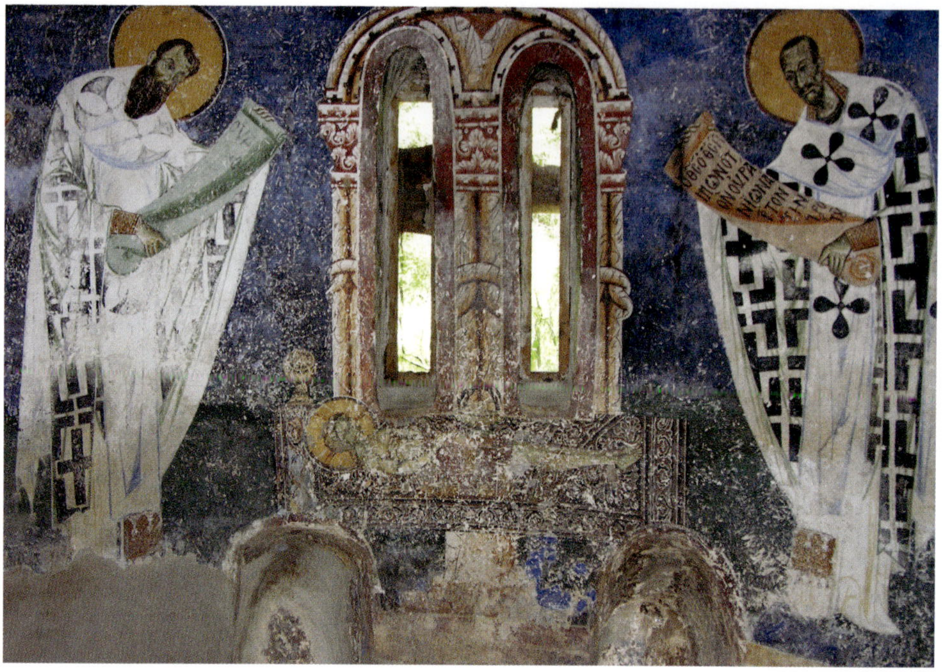

FIGURE 4.21 Bishops Celebrating the Liturgy with the Melismos, *Church of St. George at Kurbinovo, F.Y.R. of Macedonia, 1191.* PHOTO IVAN DRPIĆ

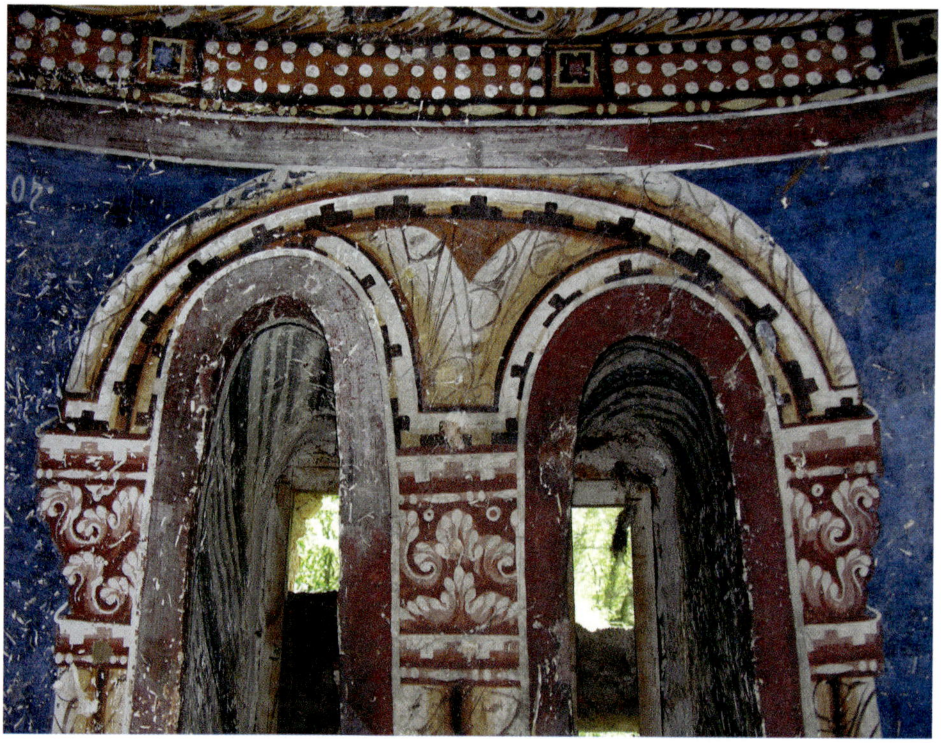

FIGURE 4.22 Canopy, *detail of the painted scene* Bishops Celebrating the Liturgy with the Melismos, *Church of St. George at Kurbinovo, F.Y.R. of Macedonia, 1191.* PHOTO IVAN DRPIĆ

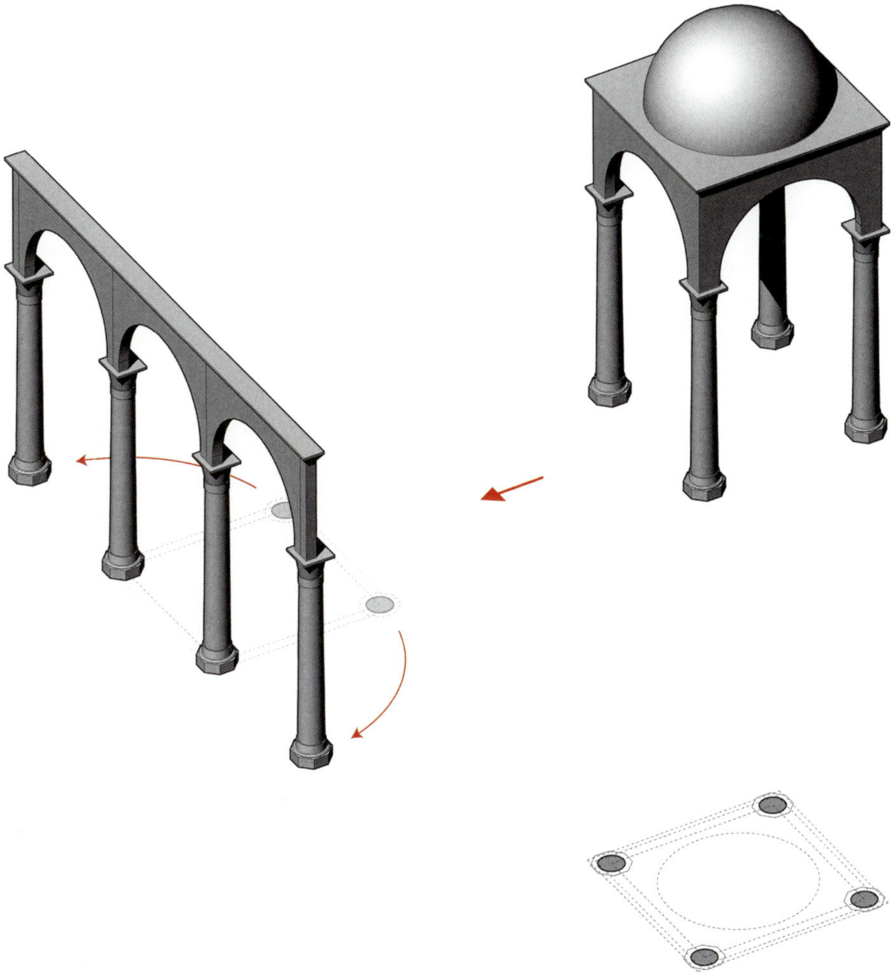

FIGURE 4.23 *Diagrammatic drawing showing the unfolding of an altar canopy into a templon screen.* DRAWING ZHENGYANG HUA

established in the Syrian cathedral in Edessa and confirmed in Old. St. Peter's in Rome during its earlier architectural phase. Such a construction might have pointed to the idea that the altar canopy corresponded to the Ark with its two cherubim forming a canopied roof in the Holy of Holies and beyond the veil in the desert tabernacle.

Byzantine images often show the Holy of Holies as a canopy on four columns, occasionally with curtains. During the liturgy, the priest would pass through the *templon*, reenacting Christ the High Priest (cf. Heb. 6:19, 9:3) as established in the Old Testament practice when the High Priest would pass through the veil of the temple.[176] By the fourteenth century, theological insistence on the sacerdotal presence of Christ during services resulted in visual representations of Christ himself as supreme hierarch, wearing the patriarchal vestment known as the *sakkos*.[177] Occasionally, even curtains for sanctuary doors would

---

176 Bogdanović (2014b) 247–292.

177 Walter (1974) 81–89; Papamastorakis (1992) 67–68. On the individual representations of Christ the High Priest, see Gabelić (1998) 68–69. On the historical context of Christ the High Priest, see Dagron (1996) 315–322.

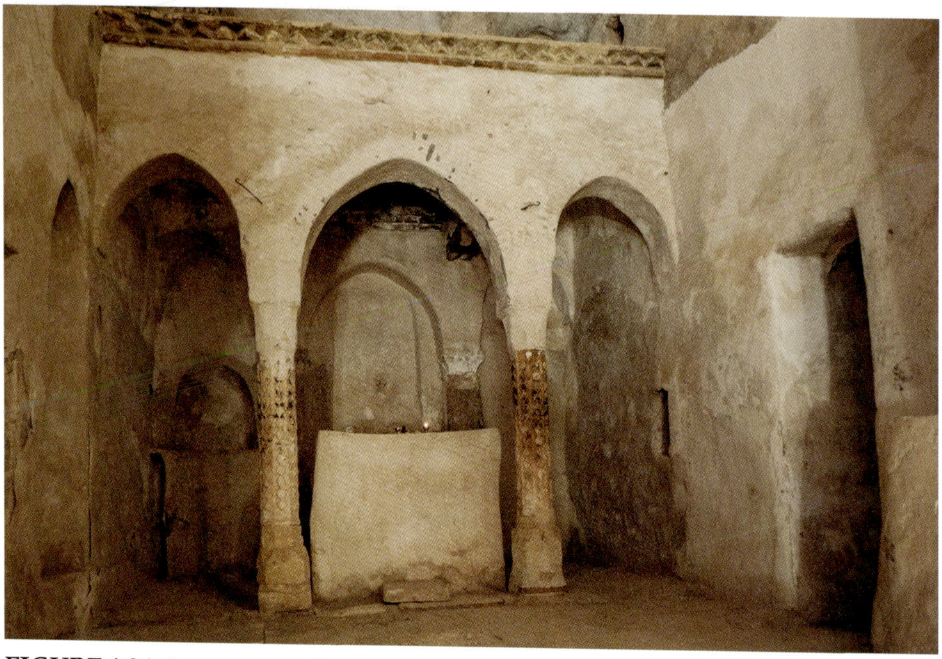

FIGURE 4.24 *Sanctuary installation that combines the altar canopy and the templon screen. Church of Mar Augen, Syria, now Turkey; founded in the early fourth century, restored in the thirteenth century.* PHOTO DANIEL C. WAUGH

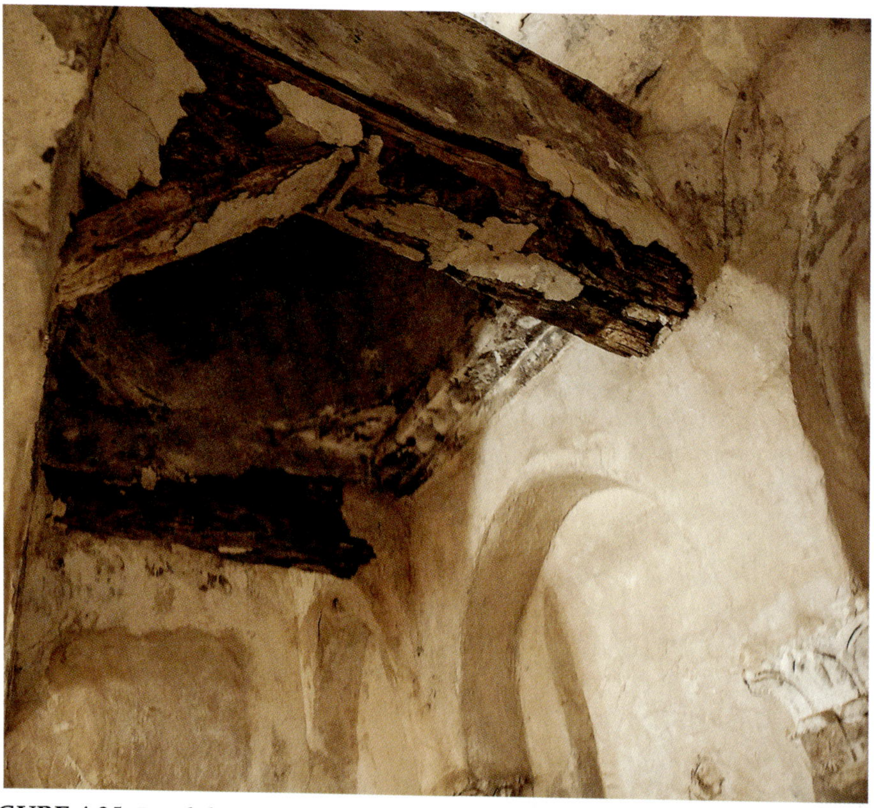

FIGURE 4.25 *Detail showing domical part of the central section of the sanctuary installation that combines the altar canopy and the templon screen in the Church of Mar Augen; the installation is late-medieval or later construction.* PHOTO DANIEL C. WAUGH

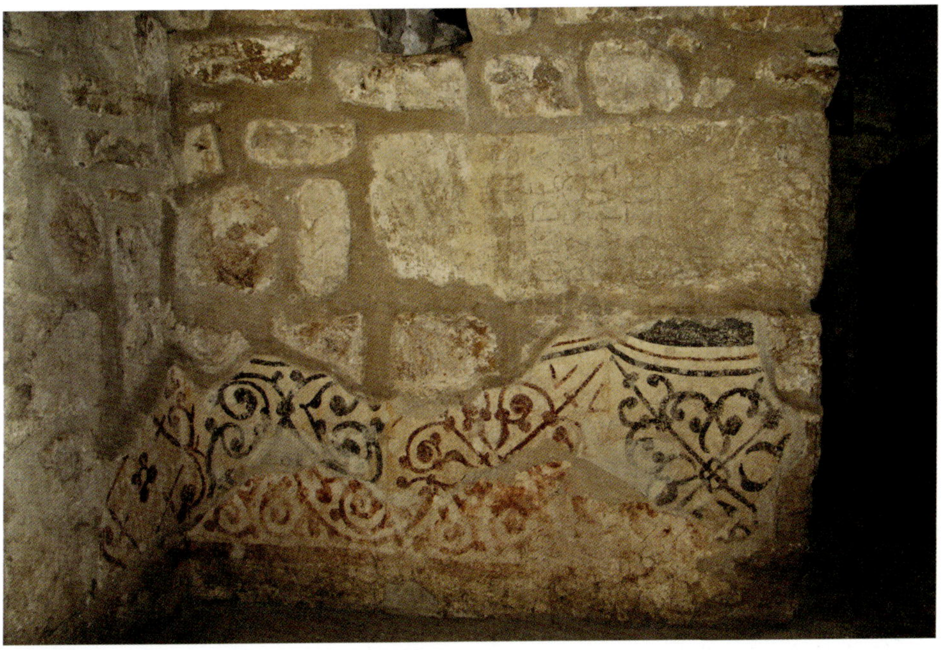

FIGURE 4.26 *Church of Ss. Peter and Paul, Ras, Serbia, ninth century; detail of the painting of the curtains on the church walls.* PHOTO NEBOJŠA STANKOVIĆ

have the "living icon" of Christ the High Priest.[178] Moreover, a few surviving Late Byzantine *sakkoi* in their tectonics and decoration are closely related to contemporaneous sanctuary screens and altar canopies.[179]

Like the *templon* screens and their curtains, the Biblical veils had decoration as a carrier of meaning. Josephus wrote that the veil of the Holy of Holies had been embroidered with flowers and patterns, but not animal forms.[180] The outer curtain was embroidered in Babylonian work. He added that the whole tabernacle represented the universe. Philo also wrote that Moses thought it right that the divine temple of the Creator of all things would be woven of such and so many things as the world was made of, being the universal temple, which existed before the holy temple.[181] According to the *Priestly Code*, the hangings of the Temple derived from those of the Tent of Meeting.[182] Thus, it seems as if Mosaic tradition preserved the memory of the holy tent as an architectural symbol of the entire universal creation, which existed even before the permanent structures of the Temple in Jerusalem.

Numerous churches, such as, for example, the ninth-century Church of St. Peter in Ras, Serbia (Fig. 4.26, see also Fig. 4.8), have hanging curtains depicted in the apsidal space in

---

[178] Bogdanović (2014b) 247–292. Smolčić-Makuljević (2000) 693–701 discusses the iconography of the curtain as a thoughtful synthesis of monumental painted programs with liturgical scenes in the altar spaces of fourteenth-century churches and draws attention to the program of the iconostasis.

[179] Woodfin (2004) 295–299; Woodfin (2012) 93–98; Bogdanović (2014b) 247–292.

[180] *Flavius Josephus* (*Ant.* 3.124), according to Barker (2003) 205.

[181] *Philo, Questions on Exodus* (2.85), according to Barker (2003) 205.

[182] Cross (1947) 45–68.

its lowest zone as if the sacred veils enclosed the sanctuary and sacred space beyond the sanctuary barrier by metaphorical extension.[183] The painted draperies possibly bore witness to the tradition of using curtains for sanctuary barriers. Although the early Christian sanctuary was separated from the laity by low parapets placed between squat pillars, which were at some point raised to carry an architrave, whether or not curtains were hung from the architrave remains debatable.[184] By the Middle Byzantine period, the sanctuary barrier of the Byzantine church was closed by dense curtains and subsequently by icon panels, which eventually formed a multi-tiered wall of icons.[185] Thus, it can be stated that the Byzantines over time symbolically replaced the veil of the Holy of Holies with the sanctuary barrier. The expression of this idea in material form varied, while liturgical practices preserved its meaning. In Coptic, Syriac, and Armenian traditions, and occasionally in Greek Orthodox churches, drawing a curtain to screen the holy place is still part of the liturgy.[186]

Yet there were two veils in the Temple. One was at the entrance to the Temple that separated the Holy Place from the outer court; the other veiled the Holy of Holies from the Holy Place. Though it is extremely difficult to demonstrate what exactly the Byzantines knew about these veils and how they eventually utilized that knowledge, it is critical, as Sophia Kalopissi Verti has demonstrated, that *proskynetaria* icons found as a part or an extension of sanctuary barriers marking the threshold between the naos and sanctuary often would have been repeated as a mirror image at the threshold between the church narthex and naos.[187] This duplication of the sacred barriers upon entering the church, first between narthex and naos and then between naos and sanctuary, resembles the use of dual veils from the Temple architecture.

A related phenomenon of the merging of canopied installations within the sanctuary screen is indeed the use of especially venerated *proskynetaria* icons. Canopy-like installations for icons are occasionally depicted in Byzantine illuminated manuscripts, like the canopy enshrining the icon of St. Basil the Great in the thirteenth-century Psalter from the monastery Dionysiou at Mount Athos.[188] The image of the saint is in this text related to the liturgy he compiled, suggesting the liturgical use of the icon. Canopy-like installations for private devotion to icons are also occasionally recorded and depicted in Byzantine manuscripts.[189] For example, the Slavic version of the works of Constantine Manasses (Vat. Slav 2, fol. 122v) shows the seventh-century Byzantine emperor Herakleios praying before the enshrined icon of the Virgin under the canopy.[190] A canopy enshrining an icon of the Virgin,

---

[183] Bogdanović (2014b) 247–292; Lidov (2014) 97–108. Such a tradition of painted veils in sanctuaries has been already noticed in ancient traditions in the Mediterranean basin. For example, the painted draperies of the *peplos* were applied to the decoration of the *cella* of Athena Polias of the Erechtheion, as a replica of the sacred tent erected for the Athenians at Delphi. Ronchaus (1886) ch. 2, with reference to *Euripides, Ion*, lines 1132–1165.

[184] Taft (2006) 27–52; Bolman (2006) 73–106; Walter (1993) 203–228.

[185] Lidov (2000).

[186] Barker (2003) 96. In the fifteenth century, Symeon of Thessaloniki *PG* 155, ch. 133, col. 341BC confirms the use of curtains for altar tables. On the use of sanctuary curtains as a consequence of monastic practices, see Taft (1975) 411–413.

[187] Kalopissi-Verti (2006) 107–134.

[188] Pelekanidis (1974) 427, color fig. 158.

[189] For example, the eleventh-century description of the veneration of the saint informs us that a supplicant had a vision, visited the saint's body, kissed it, and then moved to a separate space to venerate the icon. More in Kazhdan and Maguire (1991) 1–22, esp. 15.

[190] Pallas (1979) 44–58, fig. 5.

presumably large enough to accommodate seven people for devotion, is also depicted in the Hamilton Psalter (see Fig. 3.20).[191] Most often the sanctuary screen would have icons of Christ and the Mother of God; one of which, usually that of Christ, could have been occasionally replaced by icons of saints.[192]

It has been hypothesized already that a direct relationship exists between saintly tombs, which were frequently of an *arcosolium* type and occasionally enshrined by a canopy, and the *proskynetaria* icons enshrined by an architectural frame.[193] Indeed, occasionally the shrine canopies were placed in the immediate vicinity of the sanctuary screen. This architectural solution is suggested in the case of the Church of Hagia Euphemia in Constantinople in the seventh century. In 1343, the miracle-working relics of the holy King Stefan Dečanski (r. 1322–1331) were enshrined in the *kibotos*, a wooden chest, in the Serbian Church of the Christ Pantokrator in Dečani.[194] In the service prepared in honor of the holy king, the *kibotos* was compared to paradise and his relics within were proclaimed "more holy and honorable than the tablets of the law, the treasury of God's miracles, grace most expensive, brighter than the run rays, the source of the sweet-smelling myrrh, topaz the most honorable, the source of healing."[195] Making typological references to the Ark of Covenant, the *kibotos* of King Stefan Dečanski was created as an ark.[196] It was a holy chest richly carved with geometric interlace, vegetal palmetto, and lion and panther animal motifs; boldly painted in red and green; and gilded in gold and silver. Over time, the *kibotos* came to be filled with numerous precious objects and other relics, including Christ's hair, relics of the True Cross, and relics of other Christian saints. The *kibotos* of King Stefan Dečanski abutted the northeast column of the church and the iconostasis. The icon of the holy king was painted just above the chest, hence participating in an expanded program of the screen.

The close relationship between saintly tomb-shrines and portrait icons of the saints most likely existed well before the Iconoclastic crisis. Parallels between the tomb of St. Artemios and his image on the *templon* in the now-lost *martyrion* of St. Artemios in Constantinople have been attested in the seventh-century hagiography, while in a similar fashion, a sixth-century ivory plaque most likely depicts St. Menas in front of his canopy-like shrine (see Fig. 4.12).[197] Especially impressive is the architecture of the developed sanctuary screen in the twelfth-century Church of St. Panteleimon in Nerezi, F.Y.R. of Macedonia, where the delicately carved architectural canopies, often with double-knotted colonnettes, frame the icons of the Mother of God and St. Panteleimon, the patron saint (Fig. 4.27, see also Fig. 2.23).[198] Numerous carved frames of *proskynetaria* icons as parts of sanctuary screens are attested to in the churches of the Late Byzantine period, such as in the thirteenth-century monastery of Gradac, Serbia (Fig. 4.28). Another example is the either Late Byzantine or post-Byzantine iconostasis from the fourteenth-century Georgian monastery of the Holy Trinity, Gergeti, which exemplifies the literal merging of the canopied installations for

---

191 On icons for private devotion, see Paterson-Ševčenko (1991) 45–57, esp. figs. 2 and 5. On the devotion in front of icons as depicted in the Hamilton Psalter, see Pentcheva (2006) 180–187.

192 Kalopissi-Verti (2006) 107–134.

193 Babić (1975) 3–49; Mango (1979) 40–43; Ćurčić (2000) 134–160.

194 Todić and Čanak-Medić (2005) 32–47.

195 *Camblak, Služba Stefanu Dečanskom* 345; *Camblak, Žitije Stefana Dečanskog* 73, 81. Translation into English mine.

196 Todić and Čanak-Medić (2005) 45.

197 Mango (1979) 40–43; Ćurčić (2000) 134–160; Kalopissi-Verti (2006) 107–134.

198 Sinkević (2000) 66–67.

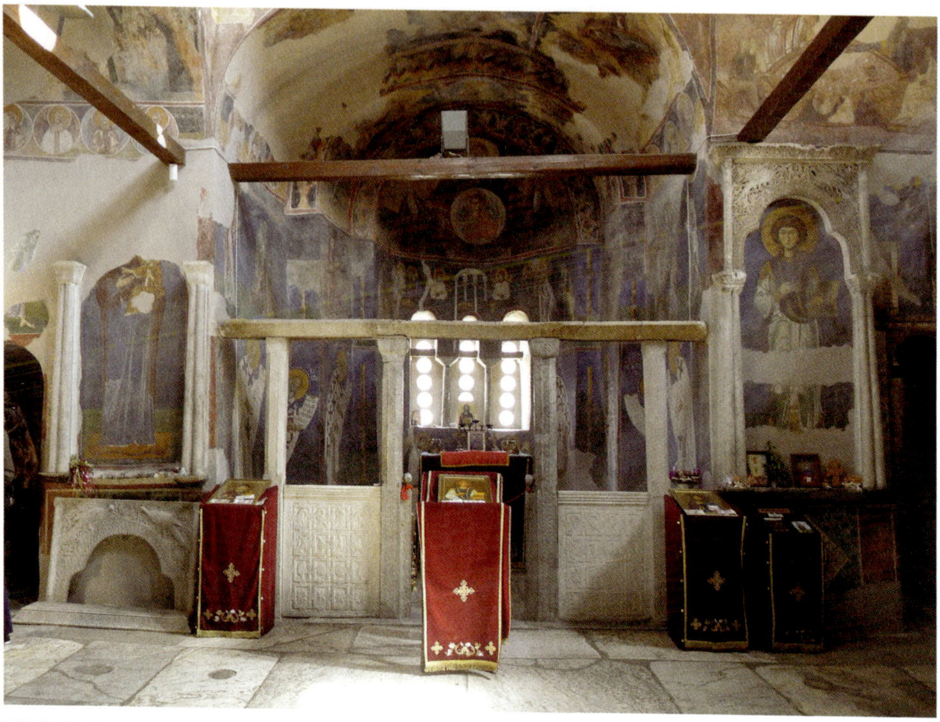

FIGURE 4.27 *Templon screen, Church of St. Panteleimon, Monastery Nerezi, F.Y.R. of Macedonia, twelfth century.* PHOTO NEBOJŠA STANKOVIĆ

icons. Here, the carved frames of the *proskynetaria* icons are shrine constructions as small houses while simultaneously a part of the *templon* screen (Fig. 4.29).[199]

In the fourteenth-century Chora monastery in Constantinople, the still-preserved richly carved frames draw focus to the *proskynetaria* icons. The threshold between the narthex and the naos is flanked by two monumental icons of St. Peter and St. Paul, and above the passage, in the lunette, is the mosaic showing Theodore Metochites offering the church to Christ Chora, entitled as "The Land of the Living" (Fig. 4.30). After passing this first threshold, the faithful would face yet another powerful threshold between the naos and the sanctuary. To the north of the sanctuary is still standing a full figure of Christ holding the Gospels in his left hand and blessing with his right hand and to the south the Mother of God with Christ Child with the inscription "The Land of the Living," subtly making dual references to the liminal space of the *templon* screen, now lost (Fig. 4.31, see also Fig. 2.24). As a sacred threshold, the *templon* pointed to the most sacred church space, the sanctuary. Through the Eucharistic sacrificial services, performed in this most hallowed space, the promise of the hereafter has been reenacted in the expectations of the Second Coming and eternal life in the paradisiac "land of the living."

The architectural design of the *templa,* associated with the liminal spaces, therefore absorbed multiple meanings stemming from theological, liturgical, and devotional practices. The holy veils referenced those known from Mosaic traditions. The architrave beam symbolized the Cross and salvation and was occasionally enriched with the images of the

[199] I thank Nebojša Stanković for discussing the Gergeti templon screen with me. For additional Late Byzantine and post-Byzantine examples, see Kalopissi-Verti (2006) 107–134.

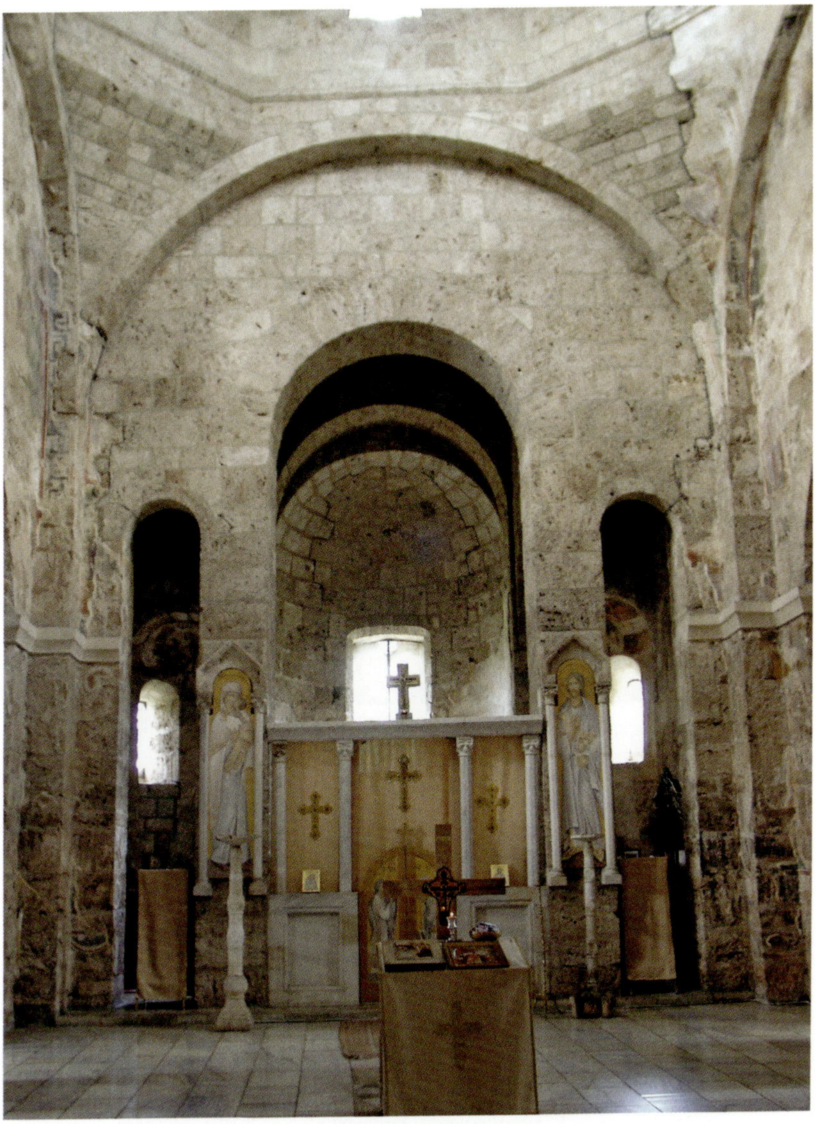

FIGURE 4.28 *Templon screen, Church of the Presentation of the Mother of God, Monastery Gradac, Serbia, thirteenth century.* PHOTO IVAN DRPIĆ

great prayer, the Deesis, the liturgical feasts, apostles, prophets and saints. The entire installation was eventually expanded with *proskynetaria* icons, so that the screen became a powerful event-place. The sanctuary screen marked the passing of the officiating High Priest through the "veil" into the most sacred space where he was spiritually reunited with Christ through the performance of the Eucharistic mystery of Christ's sacrifice for the salvation of the humankind. The *templon* also allowed the churchgoers in the naos to contemplate with their "inner eyes" the sacred space beyond the *templon* screen. Even if the space of the altar canopy remained screened beyond the *templon*, the faithful could contemplate the salvific meanings of the liturgical mysteries performed at the altar, which were often mirrored in the scenes represented high in the conch of the apse. The image of the Communion of the Apostles was regularly depicted in apsidal sanctuary spaces of Byzantine churches following

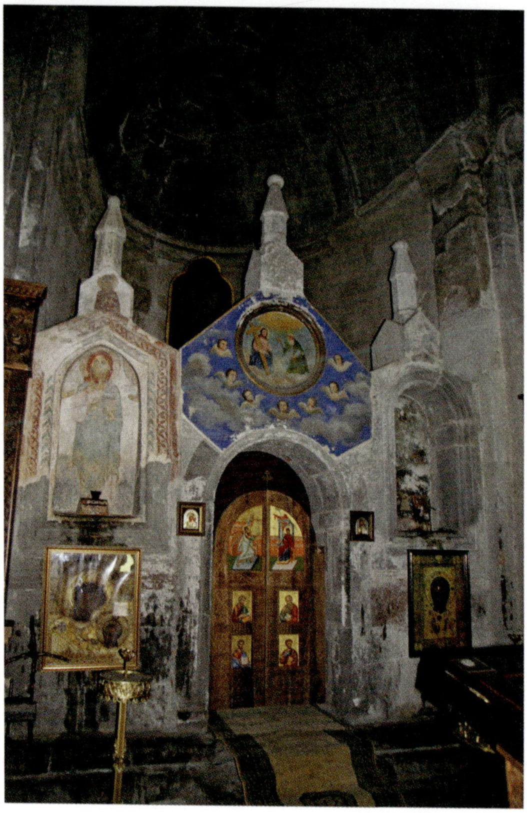

FIGURE 4.29 *Templon screen, Monastery Gergeti, Georgia, fourteenth century.* PHOTO NEBOJŠA STANKOVIĆ

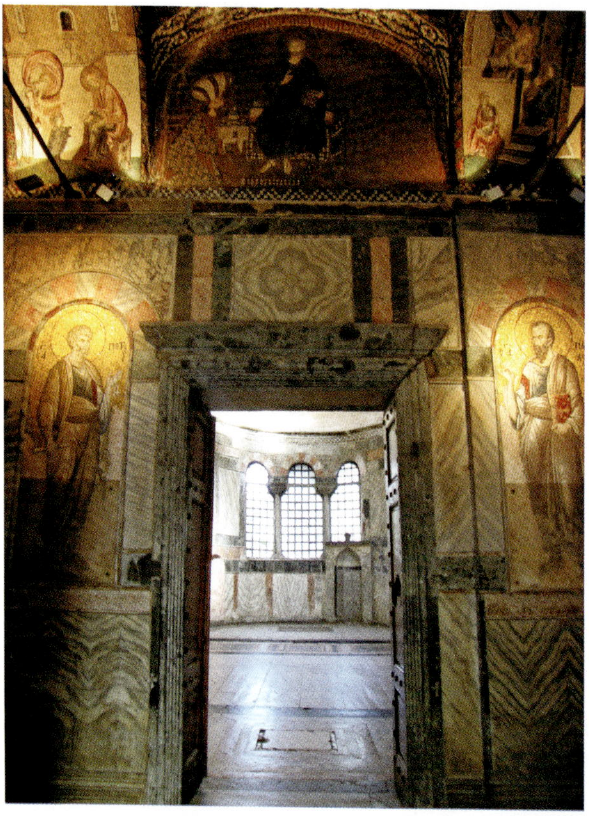

FIGURE 4.30 *Proskynetria icons flanking doors between narthex and naos, Church of Christ the Savior, Chora Monastery, Constantinople, now Istanbul, fourteenth century.* PHOTO AUTHOR

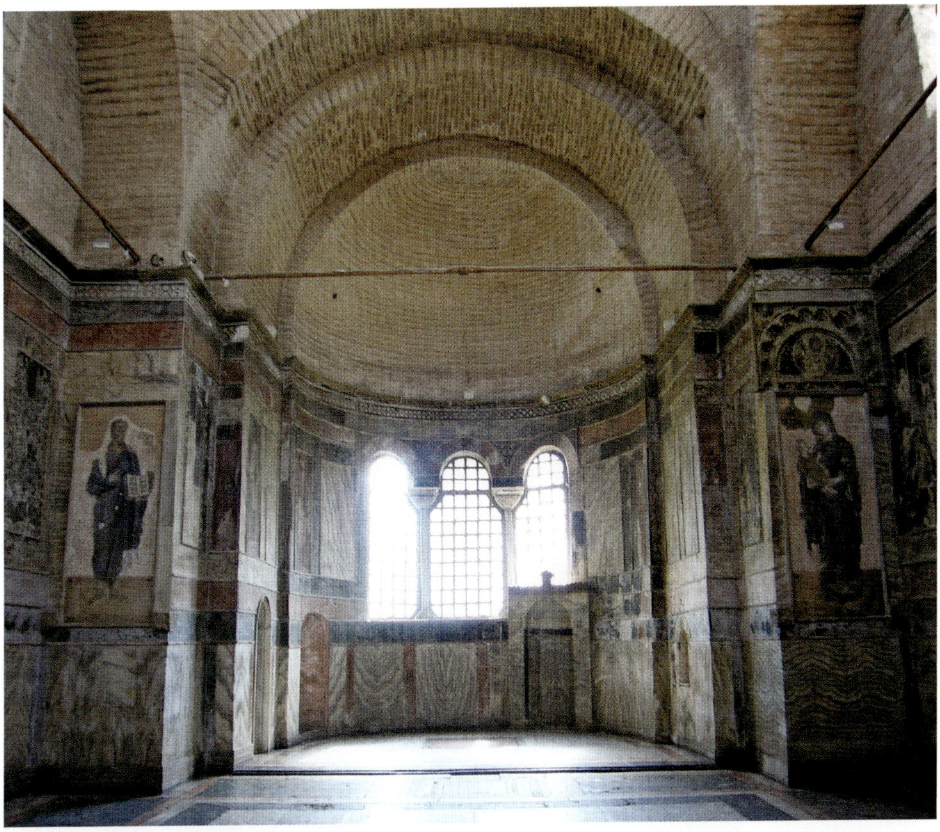

FIGURE 4.31 *Proskynetria icons, originally part of the developed templon screen, Church of Christ the Savior, Chora Monastery, Constantinople, now Istanbul, fourteenth century.* PHOTO AUTHOR

the transitional period (see Figs. 2.62, 4.27, 4.32).[200] Standing more closely in front of the icons of the *templon* itself, the faithful could pray for divine intercession and to venerate Christ, the Mother of God, and the saints whose enshrined icons and relics reminded them of holy and eternal lives. These manifold experiences of the sacred were framed within the church space by architectural and conceptual networks established between the *templon* screen, altar canopy, and *proskynetaria* shrines and icons.

AMBO AND *OMPHALOS*

In the Middle Byzantine period, church design shifted to rather compact and smaller churches; the expanded sanctuary space within the church nave as marked in Constantinopolitan Hagia Sophia by *solea* and ambo was gradually transformed into new liturgical features.[201] The *solea* became reduced to an elevated altar space, and the ambo was replaced by a central ambo-rosette just below the dome.[202] Occasionally, archeological evidence from medieval Greece and Russia confirms that the recovered round stones in the

200 Gerstel (1996) 141–148.

201 Indeed, until the fourteenth century, the Cathedral of St. Sophia in Ohrid most probably contained an ambo. However, the ambo ultimately disappeared from liturgical furnishing in the Christian East. Grozdanov (1969) 49–63.

202 Sedov (2015) 349–364; Djurić and Babić (1997) vol. 1: 134, 139, 140, 148, 159.

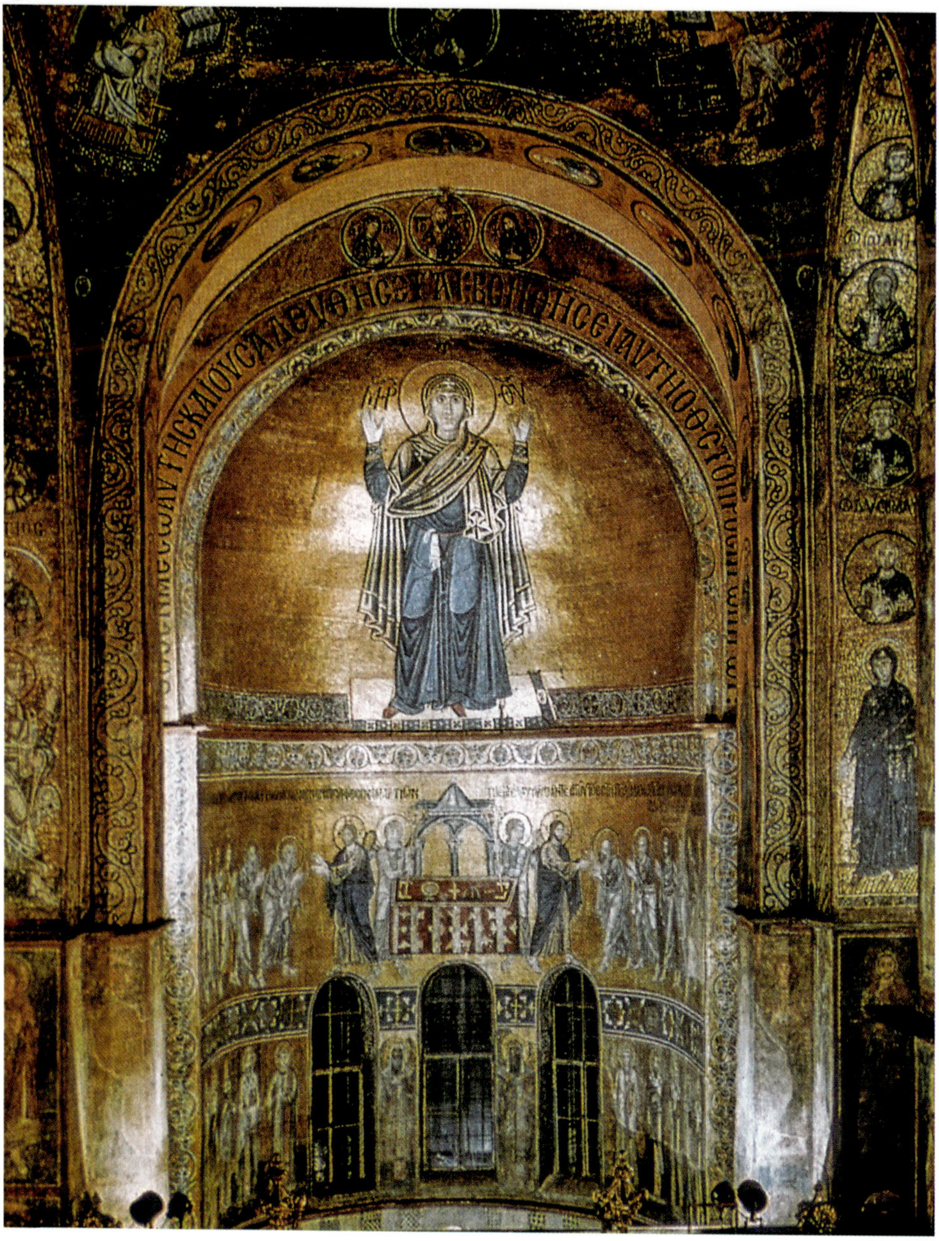

FIGURE 4.32 *Communion of the Apostles, Church of St. Sophia, Kiev, eleventh century.* PHOTO JACK V. HANEY

middle of the church were associated with the earlier location of ambos and included in the composition of the *solea* passage from the sanctuary to the ambo.[203]

The centrally placed ambo just below the church dome, and later replaced by an ambo-rosette in the same location, is associated with cathedrals that performed the so-called Cathedral office, such as the Constantinopolitan or Thessalonian churches of Hagia Sophia;

[203] Sedov (2015) 349–364.

the Cathedral of the Mother of God in the location of the Parthenon in Athens; or major monastic centers and imperial foundations such as the south Church of the Pantokrator Monastery in Constantinople or the *katholikon* of Iveron monastery on Mt. Athos.[204] Often just a plain central disk, which was occasionally framed by four circles at the corners of the square enclosing it, the ambo-rosette visually and symbolically repeated the four-columned domed framing of the church core within an approximately square ground plan. Moreover, the liturgical references to the central locus of the ambo in the church nave are seemingly seamlessly combined with references to the centrality of the church space just below the dome that symbolized the center of the world.

The central disk of decorative floors in Byzantine churches is known as the *omphalos*. *Omphalos* had stood for the navel of the human body since ancient Greek times, as mentioned in the *Iliad*, but also for the center of the world and any type of central point.[205] In the classical tradition, *omphalos* also represented both an island on the sea and a grave mount on the earth. Hence, the Byzantines could have combined the meaning and conical form of the ancient *omphalos* with a rope design with the cosmological meanings of church interlaced floor designs. For example, the sixth-century floor mosaic from the Church of St. Demetrios in Nikopolis, heavily populated by sea and earth creatures, contains an inscription that reads:

> *Here you see the famous and boundless ocean*
> *Containing in its midst the earth*
> *Bearing round about in the skillful images of art everything that breathes and creeps.*
> *The foundation of Dometios, the greathearted archpriest.*[206]

The inscription confirms the survival of Homeric notions that the ocean encircles the earth on all four sides, combined with similar concurrent cosmological concepts at the time.[207] Thus, when the believers entered the church, the earth was quite literally spread out beneath their feet. The floor would become an exact counterpart to the ceiling decorations that suggested or depicted the sky. The person entering the room was induced to yield to the perception, at least to the extent of "crossing" the outer "ocean" before reaching "land." Having reached the middle of the floor, the faithful would find themselves standing in the center of the earth—the *omphalos*. Therefore, it is not surprising that the Byzantines called the interlaced design of the central disk surrounded by four circles either the *omphalos* or the *pentaomphalon* of the church.

With no surviving evidence that in the early churches these floors had religious connotations, however, the sixth-century description of the ambo in the midst of the "sea" in Constantinopolitan Hagia Sophia, as described by Paulos Silentarios, confirms the conflation of the location and meaning of *omphalos* with an ambo as the raised island.[208] By the eleventh century, the pilgrims recorded that, in the complex of the Holy Sepulchre, in the center of the atrium just opposite the eastern apse of the Rotunda with the Tomb of Christ, a canopy or small chapel marked the *omphalos*.[209] In the early twelfth century, Abbot Daniel, a Russian pilgrim, recorded the position of the *omphalos* outside the wall of the Church of the Resurrection and connected it with the canopy and its microcosmic symbolism and divine Presence: " 'Navel of the earth,' which is covered by a small building on (the vault of) which

---

204 Alexopoulos (2015) 159–178; Sedov (2015) 349–364; Liakos (2008) 37–44.

205 Harrison, J. E. (1899) 205–251; Piganol (1945) 7–14.

206 Kitzinger (1951) 81–122.

207 See also Barry (2007) 626–656.

208 Chapter 3.

209 Patrich (1993) 101–117; Bogdanović (2014a) 1–21.

Christ is represented in mosaic with this inscription: 'The sole of my foot serves as a measure for the heaven and [my hand] for the earth.' "[210] The eleventh-century two-dimensional *omphalos*, a central disk of the highly suggestive canopied design of the *opus sectile* floor in the Iveron *katholikon* without any actual columns, but evoked by the stone roundels, has an inscription that reads in Greek, "I erected these columns and they shall not be shaken by time. George the Iberian, monk and founder."[211]

Several churches built after the ninth century in the Byzantine territories and beyond, following Byzantine models in medieval Serbia, Russia, and Italy, have retained their original stone floors, which point to the use of two-dimensional *omphaloi* or ambo-rosettes as a larger and important phenomenon.[212] The general idea of symbolically framing sacred space and using a stone disk to suggest an ambo is particularly revealing in the ninth- or tenth-century Church of Ss. Peter and Paul in Ras, Serbia. This centrally planned domed building combines the rotunda with a quatrefoil design and even has galleries despite its minuscule size, being only some 10 meters in span. However, it was a major episcopal center in Serbia, and, regardless of the crude execution of this building deep in the periphery of the Byzantine Empire, it reveals the most sophisticated understanding of the role of centrally placed ambo-rosette, here also framed by two, still-standing columns (Fig. 4.33). By the eleventh century, Psalm 33 (34) ("I will bless the Lord at all times. . .") was chanted during the distribution of the antidooron after the prayer behind the ambo, just below the main church dome.[213] Psalm 32 (33) ("Rejoice in the Lord. . .") with specific verses 13–14—"The Lord looketh from heaven; he beholdeth all the sons of men. From the place of his habitation he looketh upon all the inhabitants of the earth"—framed the bust of Christ Pantokrator in the dome of Ss. Peter and Paul in Ras, painted during the twelfth century.[214] The ritual performance of the liturgy and its location in the church illustrates the significance of the placement of ambo-rosettes and the inscribed quotations from the Psalms in a Byzantine-rite church. The central stone disk, signifying the ambo just below the dome, reveals the symbolism of a canopy as a microcosmic locus of the divine Presence, merging Old and New Testament themes with the sense of eternity within the liturgical time and sacred focus in the church space.

---

210 *Daniel* in *PPTS* 13–14. Around 1102/1103, *Seawulf* in *PPTS* 12 speaks of the "place called Compass" "at the head of the church of the Sepulchre." See also Chapter 5.

211 Liakos (2008) 37–44, citation on p. 40.

212 Sedov (2015) 349–364; Liakos (2008) 37–44; Pajares-Ayuela (2001) 11–145; Djurić and Babić (1997) vol. 1: 134, 139, 140, 148, 159. The eleventh-century revival of *opus sectile* pavement in Italy is associated with commissions of Abbot Desiderius, who invited Byzantine marble-workers to decorate the now-lost Monte Casino between 1066 and 1071. This event fueled the reemergence of *opus sectile* floors further throughout twelfth- and thirteenth-century Italy, and today is associated with the so-called Cosmatesque pavements, named after thirteenth-century marble-worker by the name of Cosmas. Similarly, ambo-rosettes in the church floors of Serbian medieval churches are attested to in the churches of the Holy Savior, Žiča (ca. 1220, with the floor from fourteenth century), Christ's Ascension, Mileševa (before 1228), the Dormition of the Virgin, Morača (1251–1252); Pridvorica (ca. 1250s); St. Nicholas near Skadar Lake (1280); St. Achilleos near Arilje (1290); Hilandar *katholikon* on Mt. Athos (ca. 1313); Holy Apostles in Peć (1330s), the Church of the Ascension in Dečani (1335); Holy Archangels near Prizren (1343–1347), and the Church of the Annunciation in Dobrun (1343), to name but a few.

213 Wybrew (1989) 137.

214 I thank Ljubica D. Popovich for bringing my attention to the inscriptions of the Psalms in Byzantine churches.

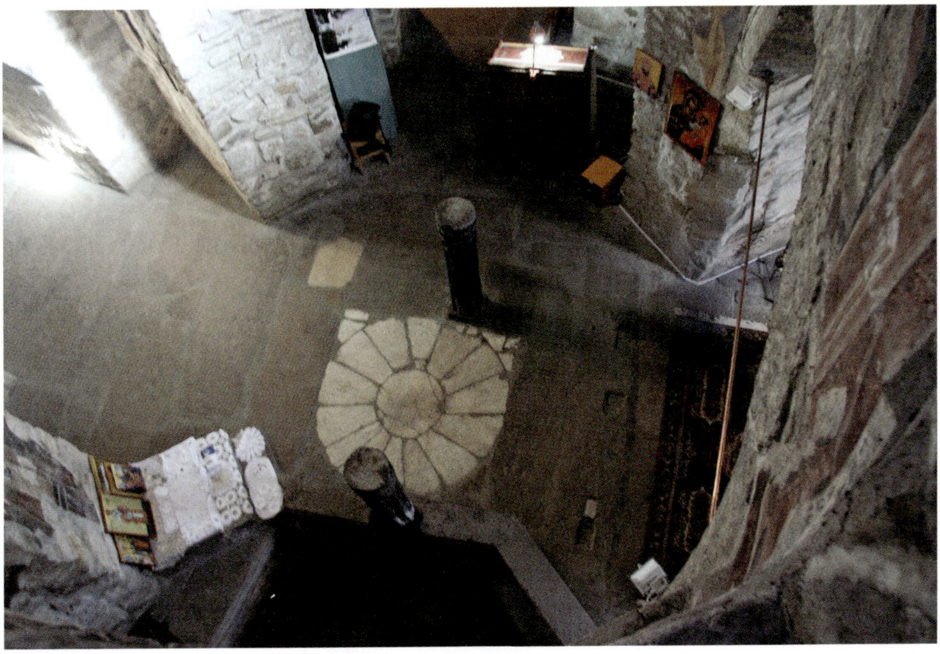

FIGURE 4.33 *Ambo rosette. Church of Ss. Peter and Paul, Ras, Serbia, ninth century.* PHOTO NEBOJŠA STANKOVIĆ

The floor of the Serbian Žiča *katholikon* was accomplished by a workshop from Constantinople that could have also worked on the *opus sectile* floor in the *bema* of the Kalenderhane, confirming that such a practice of setting a rosette in the place of an ambo together with other floor designs existed in Byzantine centers as well.[215] In Constantinople, there were no significant buildings erected during a great part of the thirteenth century, as a consequence of the Latin occupation from 1204 until 1261. Coeval examples of Constantinopolitan-quality *opus sectile* floors with interlace designs come from the Byzantine churches in Iznik and Bythinia, where the exiled Lascarids resided and presumably brought with them the best architectural practices and metropolitan marble-workers to decorate their churches.[216]

The design of the *opus sectile* ambo-rosette in the geometric center of the naos in the Serbian royal Church of Mileševa is one of the earliest surviving floors preserved *in situ*, installed before 1228, shortly after the aftermath of the Latin conquest of Constantinople. The four tangential circles of this pentaomphalon are placed on the cardinal directions, emphasizing the horizontal and vertical axes of the entire church. The pentaomphalon within the geometric center of the naos, just where the diagonal axes of the church and the two arms of the inscribed cross met, not only marked the center of the church, but also emphasized various liturgical rituals, including the celebration of Easter and the consecration of the church. Namely, after the bishop and the clergy had circled church three times, blessing it with the holy water, they would enter the church and draw a cross with censers on the axes of the church. Thus, the shape of cross made during the consecration ceremony appears in the design of the church floor.[217]

---

215 Ćurčić (2001a) 1106–1109; Djurić and Babić (1997) vol. 1, 126; Petković (1911) 3–18.

216 Eyice (1963) 373–383; Demiriz (2002) 34–38; Pinatsi (2006) 119–125; Sedov (2015) 349–364.

217 See also Etlin (2015).

In the Church of the Holy Apostles in Peć (ca. 1330s), in addition to the main ambo-rosette framed by four red square stones at the corners and positioned below the central dome, there is a pentaomphalon floor design in the northern arm of the church, just in front of the prothesis (Fig. 4.34). Within liturgical rites, the central focus of the ambo-rosette is expanded by the directional ambivalence through the inclusion of this other focus, in front of the prothesis. I would propose further that its position refers to the place of kneeling in front of the prothesis that within the church symbolized the location of Christ's Tomb and the place of the preparation of the Eucharistic gifts. During the Easter celebration, the same station could mark the location of a *kouvuklion*, the symbolic Tomb of Christ, which is left outside the sanctuary for veneration (see Fig. 1.10).

The multiple stone disks within the church proper suggest that there were multiple stations that each could have had a specific symbolic meaning, and some of these stations may have been originally enriched with canopies that carried discreet meanings. The conceptual and spatial merging of imperial canopies and canopies used for devotional and funerary rites also happened in the narthexes and exonarthexes of churches. The next section highlights this phenomenon by examining

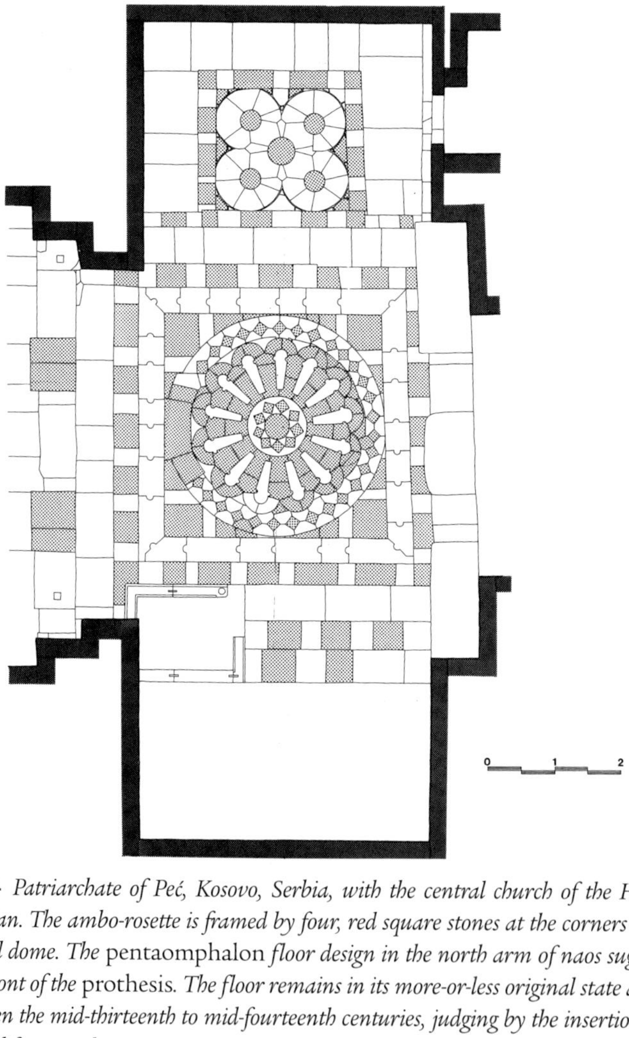

FIGURE 4.34 *Patriarchate of Peć, Kosovo, Serbia, with the central church of the Holy Apostles, ca. 1230, ground plan. The ambo-rosette is framed by four, red square stones at the corners and is positioned below the central dome. The* pentaomphalon *floor design in the north arm of naos suggests the position of a canopy in front of the* prothesis. *The floor remains in its more-or-less original state and was executed sometime between the mid-thirteenth to mid-fourteenth centuries, judging by the insertion of the episcopal throne in the mid-fourteenth century.* DRAWING ČANAK-MEDIĆ (1989) VOL. 2, 72, FIG. 121

the form and meaning of two-dimensional *opus sectile* design, three-dimensional portable imperial and funerary canopies, and the canopied bays and chambers in the narthexes and exonarthexes.

OMPHALOS, IMPERIAL CANOPY, AND DOMED CHAPEL IN THE NARTHEX AND EXONARTHEX

George Majeska has effectively demonstrated how the *opus sectile* roundels and green stripes in the floor of Constantinopolitan Hagia Sophia also served as markings for stationary places and pacing the rhythm of movement during ceremonial liturgical and imperial processions.[218] The four green stripes still visible in the floor stood for the four rivers of Paradise and were used as references during liturgical services; they marked both the placement of liturgical furnishings such as the ambo and sanctuary screen, as well as the processional rhythm, as the lines articulated the choreography of processional movement in the space.

According to Constantine Porphyrogenitos, when emperors entered the Church of Hagia Sophia in Constantinople, they would stand waiting on a porphyry disk.[219] In a similar way, in Constantine's throne room, there were special stationary places for the celebrating bishop and the ruler.[220] The lavish, essentially *pentaomphalon opus sectile* design marked by porphyry disks set in a square just southeast of the sanctuary of Hagia Sophia possibly indicated the station for the emperor and his retinue during liturgical services.[221] This station was also used for imperial coronations, often accompanied with the ceremony of marriage (Fig. 4.35). In its setting, the Hagia Sophia station is very similar to the porphyry

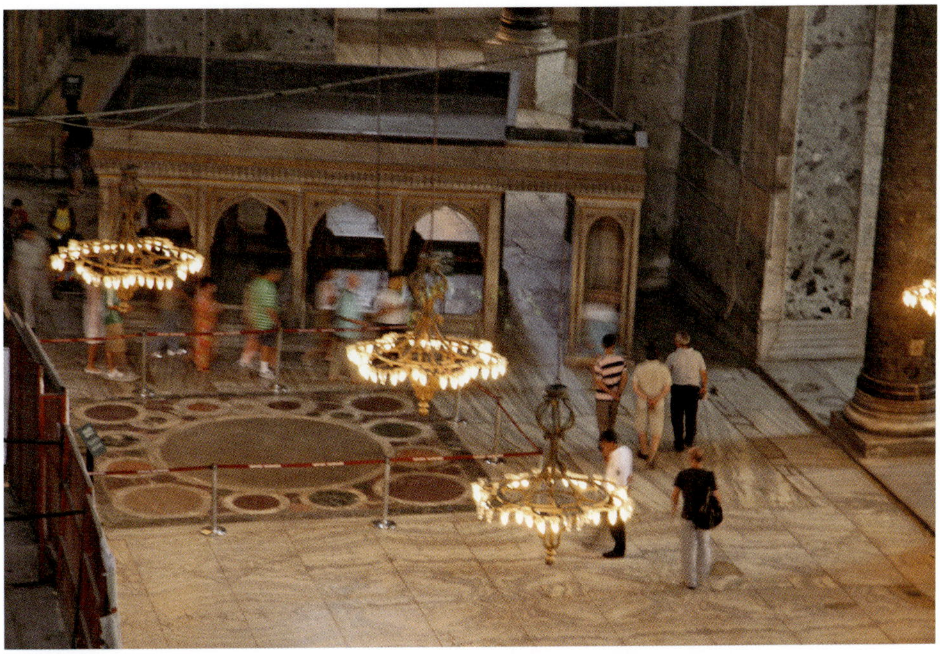

FIGURE 4.35 Pentaomphalon opus sectile *marked by porphyry disks, southeast of the sanctuary of Hagia Sophia, Constantinople, now Istanbul, sixth century.* PHOTO NEBOJŠA STANKOVIĆ

[218] Majeska (1978) 299–308.

[219] *De Ceremoniis-d* vol. 1, 10–11.

[220] Glass (1969) 386–390.

[221] Majeska (1978) 299–308; Majeska (1997) 1–11.

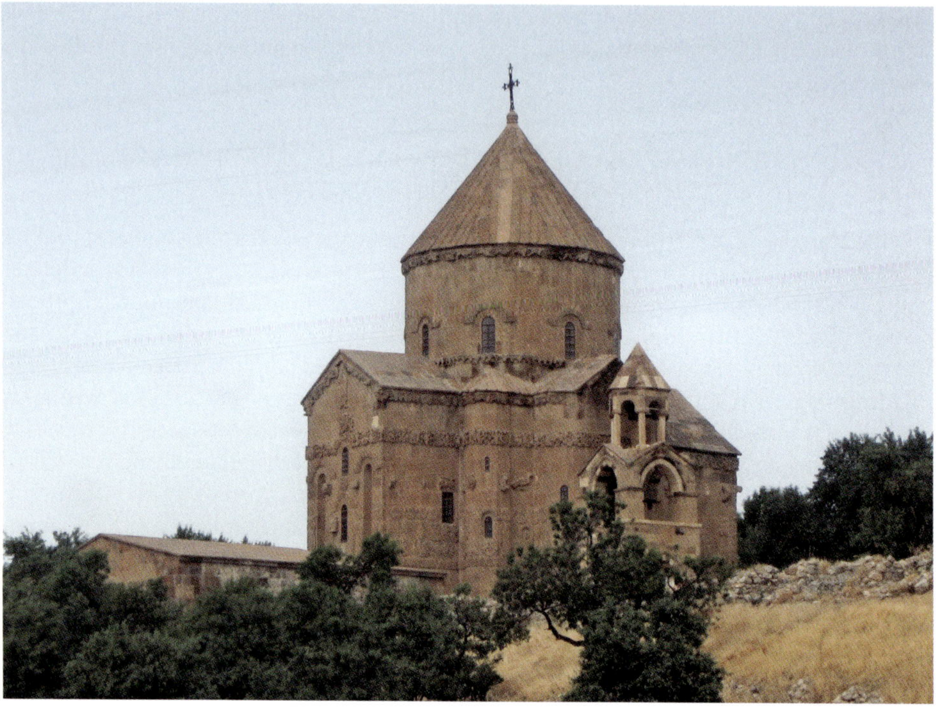

FIGURE 4.36 *Church of the Holy Cross, Aght'amar, Armenia, now Turkey, tenth century.* PHOTO BY MISHKUNDERKO, IMAGE IN THE PUBLIC DOMAIN: HTTPS://COMMONS.WIKIMEDIA.ORG

disks that marked the location of the coronation ceremony in Old St. Peter's, where a *pentaomphalon* also marked the entrance to the church.[222] The so-called "lodge of the Empress," on the gallery just above the narthex of Hagia Sophia designated by a large *opus sectile* roundel framed by two squares and two three-dimensional columns, may have been used for the placement of a portable imperial canopy (see Figs. 1.5, 3.25). The station could have also been for the portable canopy that was used to display of the relics of the Holy Cross for imperial veneration, as has been suggested by a comparative practice in Constantinopolitan Nea Ekklesia during Middle Byzantine times.[223] These references to the *opus sectile* reveal the complexities of the liturgical, imperial, and devotional meanings that such stationary places may have denoted within the space of the church.

The tenth-century palace Church of King Gagig I Artzruni (r. 908–936), dedicated to the Holy Cross, has a canopy-like vestibule (Fig. 4.36). This particular design may indicate a reinterpretation of the canopy that distinguished the place of the veneration of the True Cross and the imperial presence in the Armenian context, as it was established in Hagia Sophia in Constantinople. A hypothesis about the imperial connotations of the canopied installations on the gallery of Hagia Sophia may also point to the original imperial connotations of the curious canopied structure set just above the western gallery in the late thirteenth-century Church of Panagia Parigoritissa at Arta (Fig. 4.37). This open canopy

[222] Glass (1969) 386–90; Glass (1980) 48–52.

[223] Klein (2006) 79–99; Magdalino (1987b) 51–64; Stanković (2008). See also Chapter 3.

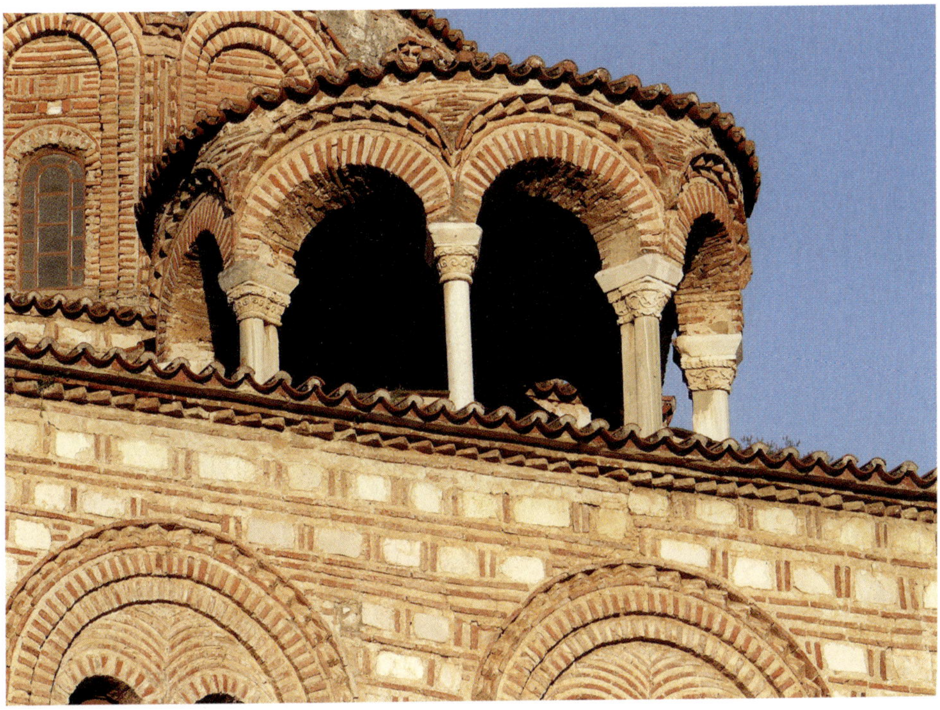

FIGURE 4.37 *Church of Panagia Parigoritissa, Arta, Greece, late thirteenth century.* PHOTO STAVROS MAMALOUKOS

may have framed the church bell.[224] However, this curious gallery canopy also may have been proclaiming the imperial status of the church in Arta. The church was a royal foundation of the despots of Epirus, who tried to reclaim the Byzantine imperial traditions during and after the Latin conquest of Constantinople.[225] The combination of sacred and imperial meanings of architecturally framed locations involving canopied structures may even point to the imperial claims of the centrally positioned domed chapels over the narthexes of numerous other Byzantine churches.[226]

Canopies at the entrances to churches or within the major thresholds within a church space, such as the canopied installation between the nave and the sanctuary marked by columns in the sixth-century episcopal basilica in Caričin Grad near Lebane, Serbia, still need to be properly explained and understood. However, they reveal the pervasive presence of stationary canopied places, mostly in imperial foundations. The eleventh-century mausoleum Church of Nea Moni on the island of Chios, built by the Byzantine emperor Constantine IX Monomachos (r. 1042–1055) and his wife Zoe, is particularly revealing, as it has domed central bays of both the narthex and the somewhat later added exonarthex.[227]

---

[224] Church bells were used in Byzantine churches since at least after the transitional period. The rule of St. Athanasios, the tenth-century founder of the monastery of Great Lavra on Mt. Athos, records the use of bells in the monastery following the model of the Constantinopolitan monastery of St. John in Studion. Bogdanović (2012) 95–107; *Ath.Rule* in *BMFD* 205–231, esp. 225.

[225] I thank Lorenzo Riccardi for discussing with me the canopy from the church in Arta. On the aims of Epirote rulers to emulate Constantinople in Arta, see also Fundić (2013) 217–250.

[226] On domed chapels, see Sinković (2002) 79–92; Babić (1969); Ćurčić (1971) 333–344.

[227] Bouras (1982) 54–75.

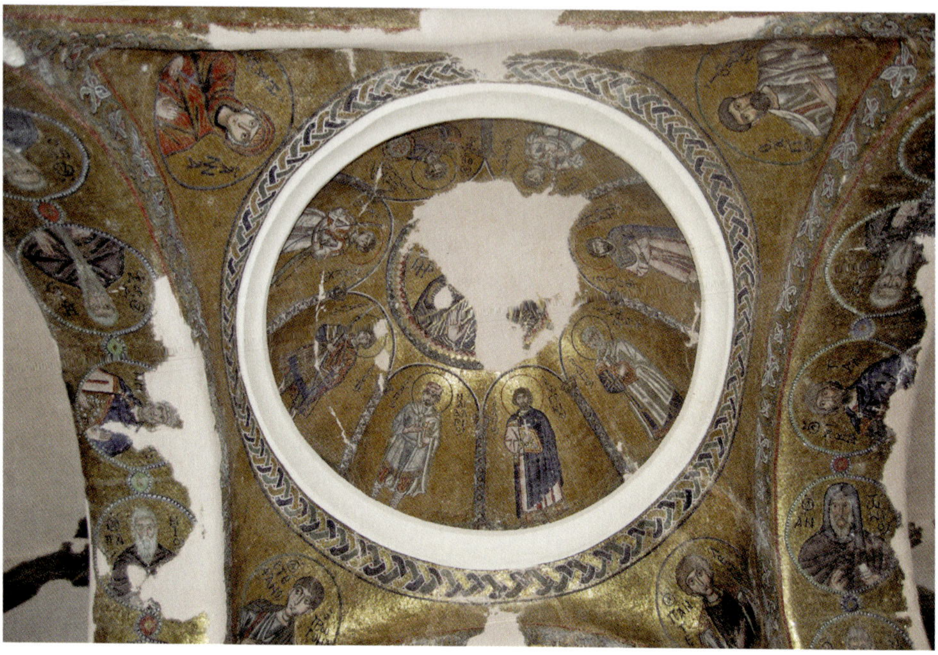

FIGURE 4.38 *Dome of the narthex, Church of the Dormition of the Mother of God, Monastery Nea Moni, Chios, Greece, eleventh century.* PHOTO STAVROS MAMALOUKOS

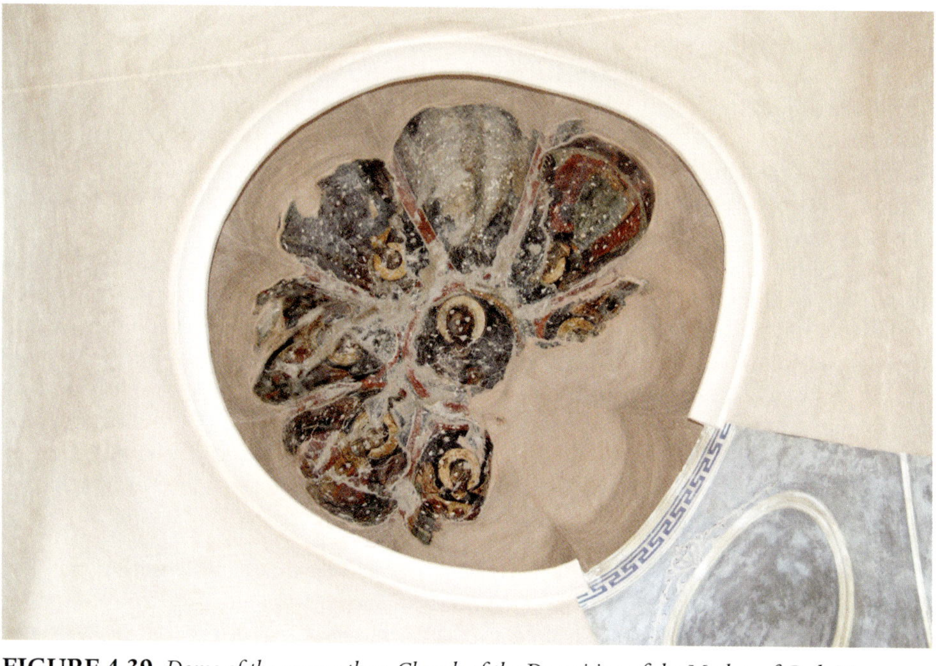

FIGURE 4.39 *Dome of the exonarthex, Church of the Dormition of the Mother of God, Monastery Nea Moni, Chios, Greece, eleventh century.* PHOTO STAVROS MAMALOUKOS

The central bay of the narthex built simultaneously with the church has an eight-sided hemispherical blind dome articulated in mosaic by eight columns (Fig. 4.38). Such a dome design, a "pumpkin" dome with elegantly curved ribs that suggest a textile covering, was repeated over the three bays of the exonarthex (Fig. 4.39).

The central bay of the exonarthex also has a *pentaomphalon opus sectile* design in the floor, which is further enlivened by an architectural canopy frame formed of four columns set close to the walls and spatially and structurally articulating the domed central bay (Figs. 4.40, 4.41). Both the two-dimensional *opus sectile* design and the nested architectural frame above it point to a highly sophisticated canopy installation.[228] The *pentaomphalon* or quincunx-in-square design—formed of five circles in a square, arranged so that four roundels in the corners envelope a central roundel, often made of a large purple, porphyry disk—are suggestive of a three-dimensional canopied structure, and Richard Krautheimer has even extended its meaning to a typical architectural design of Middle-Byzantine cross-in-square and five domed churches.[229] As shown by Paloma

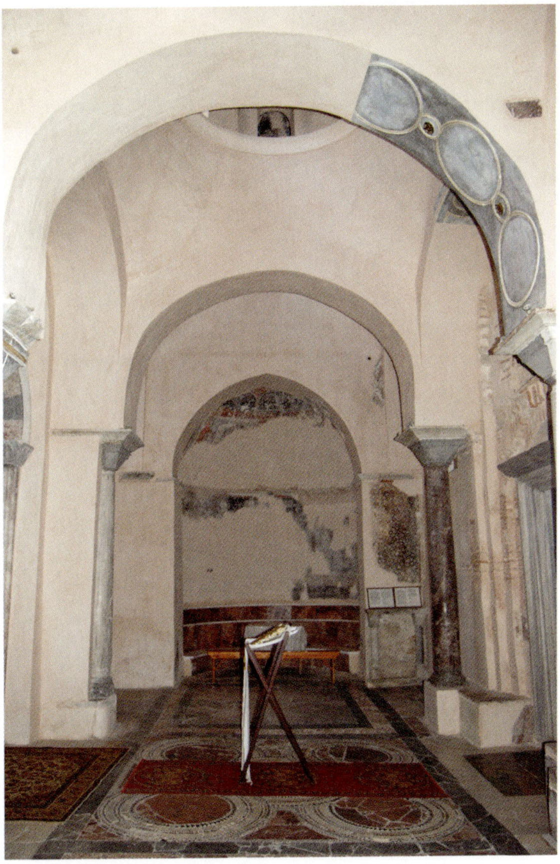

FIGURE 4.40 *The central bay of the exonarthex framed by four engaged columns and framing the* pentaomphalos *floor design, Church of the Dormition of the Mother of God, Monastery Nea Moni, Chios, Greece, eleventh century.* PHOTO STAVROS MAMALOUKOS

[228] Ibid., 153.

[229] Krautheimer (1986) 340–341, 520.

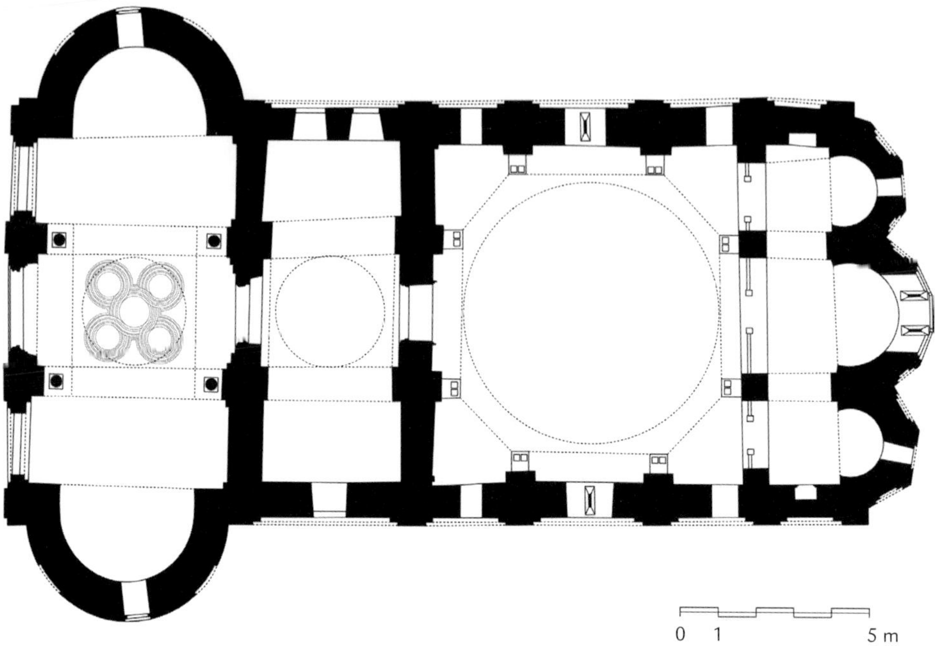

FIGURE 4.41 *Church of the Dormition of the Mother of God, Monastery Nea Moni, Chios, Greece, eleventh century.* DRAWING AUTHOR AND HEIDI REBURN

Pajares-Ayuela, the underlying geometry of quincunx-in-square design is the double cross—or the "whirling," rotating cross around a central point—set in a square, hence including the fundamental geometric and cosmic principles of the conceptual design of Byzantine architecture based on the canopy: the center, the cross, the circle, and the square.[230] The actual use of all these canopied and *opus sectile* settings remains speculative, though imperial associations are recurrent.

By the Late Byzantine period in Constantinople, exonarthexes were often major architectural commissions constructed as additions to preexisting buildings and often intended to be funerary installations. Canopied entrances within these structures could have symbolized both the long-lasting tradition of imperial thrones as well as funerary canopies, because the narthexes were critical spaces for liturgical Easter celebrations and funerary practices, above all the other services performed within.[231] The canopied central bay, fully articulated by four columns and a dome, of the fourteenth-century exonarthex of the Church of St. Andrew in Krisei—a foundation of Theodora Raouliana, niece of Emperor Michael VIII (r. 1259–1282)—or the canopied central bay of the fourteenth-century exonarthex of the Vefa Kilise Cammi—perhaps the Church of Ss. Theodores—suggest such a merging of imperial and funerary connotations.[232] These Late Byzantine exonarthexes in a way became church establishments in their own right[233] and replicated the design principles of the narthexes with the centrally domed bays of the Middle-Byzantine Constantinopolitan

---

[230] Pajares-Ayuela (2001) 196–246.

[231] Bogdanović (2008b); Bogdanović (2012) 95–107; Marinis (2014) 64–76.

[232] I thank Vladimir Božinović, who is working on the Church of St. Andrew in Krisei, for discussing with me the canopied installations in Constantinopolitan churches and their potential meanings.

[233] Bogdanović (2008b).

churches of Myralaion (ca. the 920s), Christ Pantepoptes (before 1087), and the south Church of Christ Pantokrator of the Pantokrator monastery (1118–1124), which were all imperial foundations and also served as mausolea.[234] According to the old descriptions, the sarcophagus of Emperor John I Tzimiskes (r. 969–976) was presumably in the narthex, in the upper level, of the Myralaion church, confirming both the imperial and the funerary associations of canopied installations in the central bays of narthexes and later exonarthexes of Byzantine churches. In Arta, the mausoleum basilica of H. Theodora, wife of Michael II, the despot of Epiros (r. 1230–1266 or 1268), has a centrally domed bay in the narthex. The sumptuously designed central narthex bays, acting as kinds of domed canopies, are also apparent in the fourteenth- and fifteenth-century mausolea churches of the Ravanica, Ljubostinja, and Manasija monasteries, which are the three royal foundations of Knez Lazar (r. 1371–1389), his wife Milica, and their son Despot Stefan Lazarević (r. 1389–1427) in medieval Serbia.

THE CANOPIED *PHIALE* AND VAULTED CHAPEL IN THE NARTHEX

Canopied installations for holy water fonts (*phialai*) were often located outside church buildings, yet several examples reveal how these structures could merge architecturally with the vaulted bay inside the church in several ways.[235] The Byzantine *Book of Ceremonies*, detailing protocols at the imperial court in Constantinople, provides information about the private fountain-court (*mystike phiale*) of the now-lost ninth-century edifice known as the Triconch of the Imperial Palace. This private *phiale* was used in winter due to inclement weather and was potentially an entire building or located inside a two-story building. This invaluable reference from the *Book of Ceremonies* about the alternate location of the *phiale* potentially reveals a major reason—inclement weather— for their alternate locations within the church proper, in the narthex or in a specially designated chapel.[236]

The archeological and architectural remains from the late twelfth-century monastery of Studenica, Serbia, established by a Serbian ruler, Stefan Nemanja (r. 1169–96), confirms that a massive canopied stone *phiale* was originally built in the southwest section of the monastery, just in front of the *katholikon* (Figs. 4.42, 4.43).[237] This open-space canopy was then enclosed by the spacious exonarthex built by Nemanja's grandson, King Radoslav, sometime before 1234 (Fig. 4.44). The exonarthex almost doubled the size of the church. The intervention in Studenica to enclose the architectural structure of the canopied *phiale* within the church exonarthex was most likely due to the harsh winter conditions in the western territories of the mountainous Balkans. Architecturally, this merging of the space of the *phiale* and the church resulted in a peculiar solution because the massive *phiale* was disproportionally placed in the church interior, similar to the massive canopied ambo inside the church naos in Kalabaka (see Fig. 3.4).

Within smaller establishments, where space did not allow for such "a building within a building" design, usually only the *phiale* vessel without its canopied frame was placed inside of the church, usually in the southwestern section. However, the entire architectural installation of the canopied *phiale* could have been supplanted by a vaulted bay or by a separate

234 Basic information on the here-mentioned churches in Ćurčić (2010) 275–277, 361–369, 542–543, 563–565, 674–682.

235 Chapter 2.

236 *De Ceremoniis-d* vol. 1, xxv–xxvi, xxxi, chs. 62–67 (278–303, esp. 296–301).

237 Bogdanović (2017b); Marinković (2011b) 99–110.

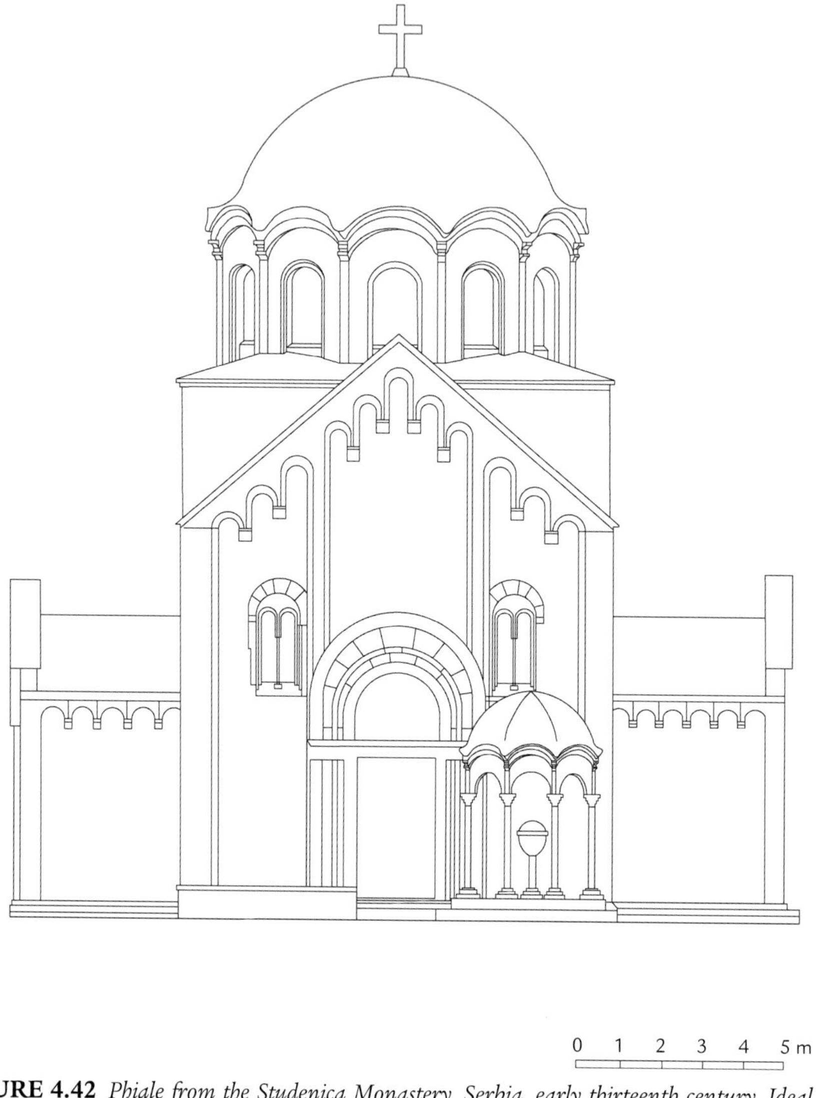

FIGURE 4.42 *Phiale from the Studenica Monastery, Serbia, early thirteenth century. Ideal reconstruction of the elevation of the phiale and the katholikon.* DRAWING HEIDI REBURN

chamber, occasionally with the apse and hence potentially also serving as a chapel and emphasizing the liturgical role of such spaces.[238] The "*phiale*," the eponymous vaulted chapel from the monastery of Hosios Loukas, is an excellent illustrative example of such merging of the space of the *phiale* and the church (Fig. 4.45). In Hosios Loukas, the vessel for the holy water is long removed from its original setting, but the name and painted program of the chapel show the essential spatial qualities of the *phiale*. At the top of the tiny vaulted bay, just above the head of the beholder, there is a depiction of the hand of God raising from the cross and making a gesture of blessing. This image essentially repeats the recognizable imagery from the interiors of preserved *phialai* designed as individual objects. The corners of the

[238] Kandić (1998–9) 61–78; Sinkević (2002) 79–92.

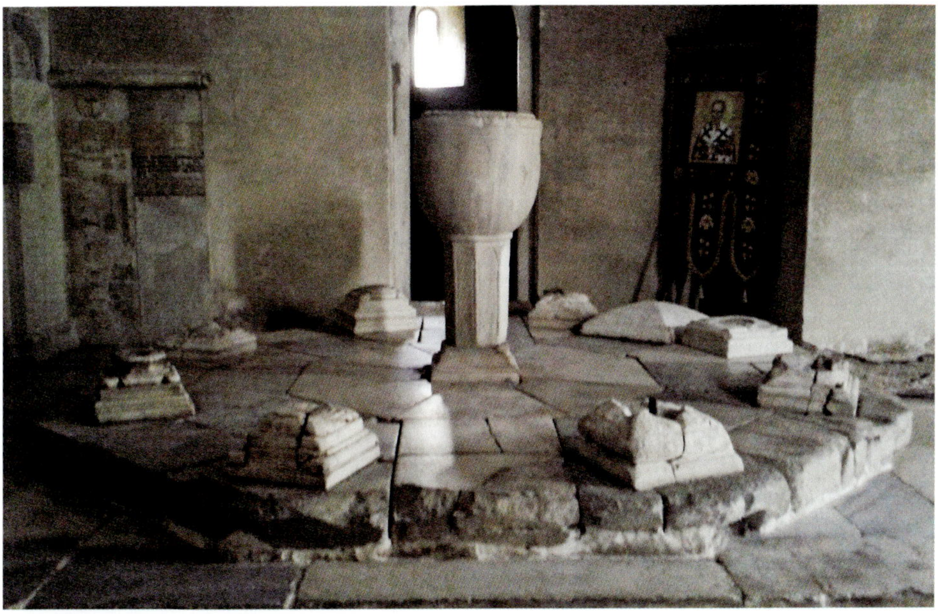

FIGURE 4.43 *Phiale from the Studenica Monastery, Serbia; the installation is possibly from the early thirteenth century.* PHOTO DUŠAN DANILOVIĆ

chapel at Hosios Loukas are further figuratively supported by four painted columns, suggesting the tectonic qualities of a canopy (Fig. 4.46). In Hosios Loukas, the canopied space of the *phiale* is on the verge between architecture and its representation and highlights the potential of a vaulted chamber with painted columns to serve as the canopied space of the *phiale* while simultaneously investing vaulted spaces and bays with theological meanings.

THE *TETRAPYLON*, TOMB-SHRINE, AND CHURCH CORE

Civic canopy-like structures also influenced the architectural design of canopies of Byzantine churches; this architectural design occurred simultaneously with, and occasionally completely independently from, other architectural processes. Architectural structures on four columns, as their names literally imply, the *tetrapyla* and *tetrakionia* had a long-established meaning as triumphal structures in the Mediterranean region.[239] Established as triumphal structures in the pagan tradition, situated at the intersection of major thoroughfares within the street grid, monumental *quadrifrons* (four-way arches) and *tetrapyla* were imperial markers over the *locus mundi*, the navel of the world.[240] These structures were additionally associated with the canopied imperial throne.[241] In Leptis Magna, Libya, the Severan *quadrifrons* covered by a dome was conceived as an enormous throne, which symbolized the presence of the Roman emperor, even in his absence.[242] This colossal *tetrapylon* resembled the canopied throne of the emperor in the audience hall. This *tetrapylon* also resembled the canopy-like *aediculae* that sheltered statues of divinities throughout the

239 Downey (1937) 194–211; Downey (1935) 55–72; Bogdanović (2008a) 34–35; Bogdanović (2008c).

240 Thiel, W. (2002) 299–326; Milojević (1996) 247–262.

241 Lehmann (1945) 1–27; Roueche and Smith (1996).

242 Lehmann (1945) 1–27.

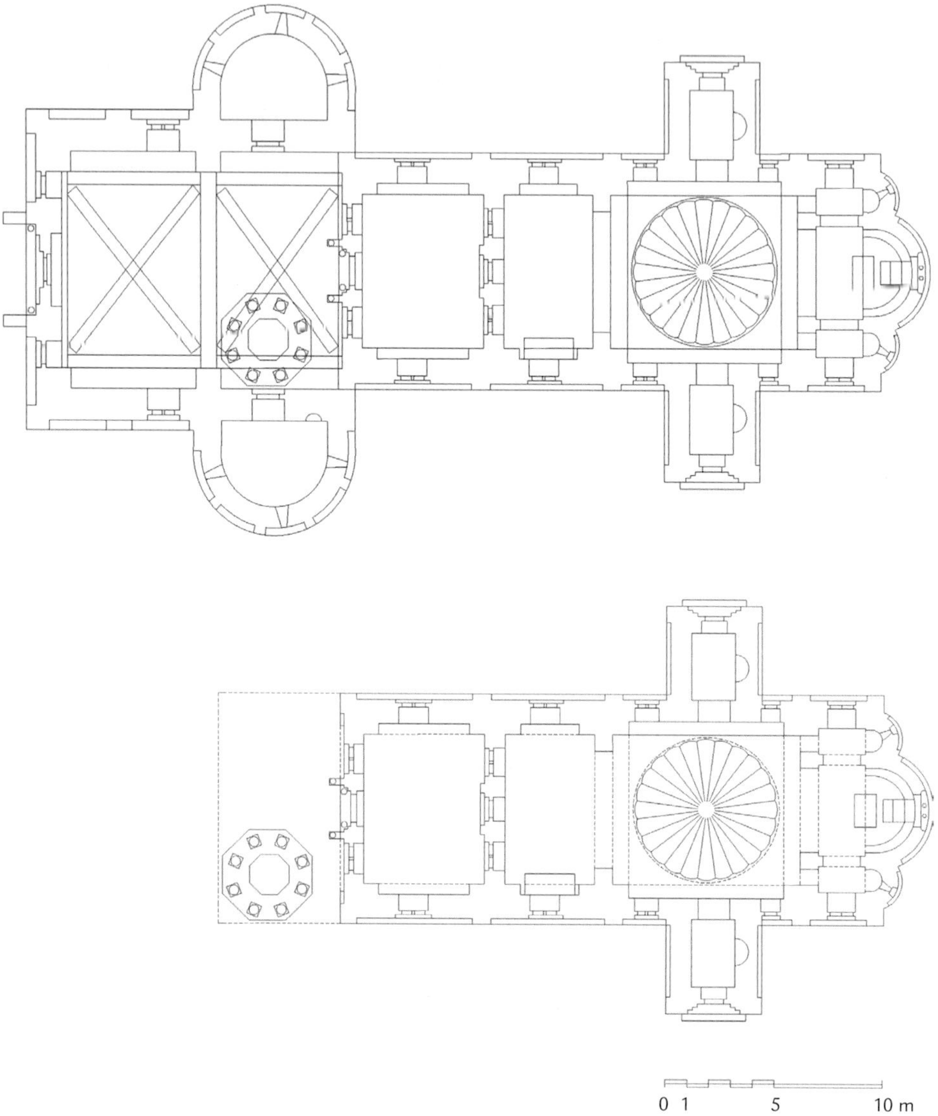

FIGURE 4.44 *Phiale within the Studenica Monastery, Serbia, first half of the thirteenth century. Floor plans of the two phases of the development of the katholikon and its relation to the phiale installation before and after it was enveloped by the exonarthex built before 1234.* DRAWING HEIDI REBURN

Roman Empire, which can be exemplified by a statue of the goddess Minerva or Roma in a canopy-like *aedicula*, as depicted in the *Codex [M]arcianus*, a manuscript copied from a Greek original.[243] Composed of four single pillars identical in size and shape, standing apart from each other, and forming a coherent square plan, sometimes connected with an entablature, and occasionally topped by domes, *quadrifrons* and *tetrapyla* were essentially colossal canopies. Their merging with canopied installations in Byzantine churches can be followed

---

[243] Nordenfalk (1973) 233–258.

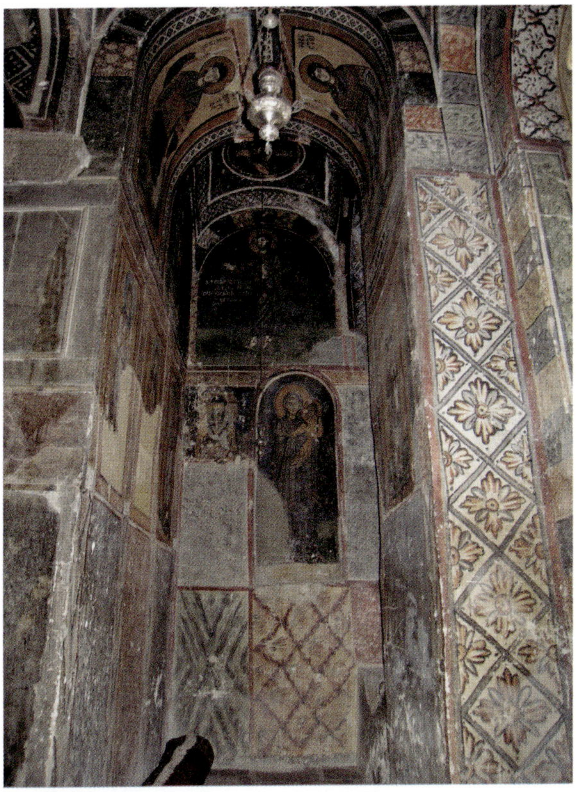

FIGURE 4.45 *The phiale chapel within the katholikon of Hosios Loukas, near Steiris, Phokis, Greece, eleventh century.* PHOTO AUTHOR

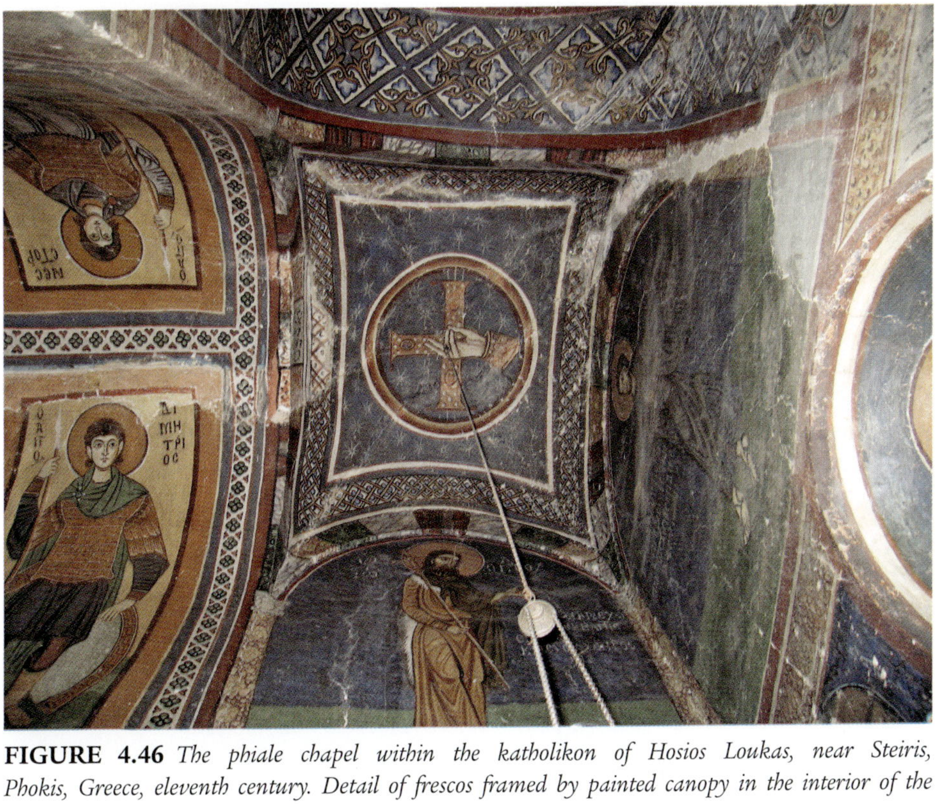

FIGURE 4.46 *The phiale chapel within the katholikon of Hosios Loukas, near Steiris, Phokis, Greece, eleventh century. Detail of frescos framed by painted canopy in the interior of the "phiale."* PHOTO AUTHOR

on at least on two levels: when they marked the tomb-shrine in the church, and when they marked the navel of the church with a monumental four-columned domed core.

The associations of monumental *tetrapyla* combined with the pagan notion of the tomb as the house of the dead were often represented by free-standing funerary *aediculae*. Such hybrid architectural installations effectively imbued the sacred place with ceremonial associations of imperial triumph, since the emperor passing on his ceremonial route below the throne-like canopy would have been symbolically transformed into a divine person.[244] The long-standing Roman association of *tetrapyla* with funerary cults and the numerous sepulchral *tetrapyla* in the Eastern Mediterranean built by the third century show how this tradition may have influenced the development of canopied saintly shrines in the Christian East, starting in the fourth century.[245] Such a practice combined the meaning of saintly shrines with the honorific meaning of the *tetrapylon*.

In 379, the remains of St. Babylas (d. ca. 250), a bishop and martyr from Antioch, were sheltered by a *quadrifrons* structure in Antioch-Kaoussie, Syria (now Turkey).[246] The L-shaped footings for the piers, approximately 3 meters by 3 meters in plan, point to a massive *quadrifrons* once covering the central space. Only at some later point was this memorial enclosed by a balustrade to prevent over-zealous pilgrims from approaching the relatively humble tomb. The central focus was architecturally defined by a massive four-columned structure and was additionally framed by an enormous cruciform building to accommodate the flowing crowds of pilgrims. A baptistery and sacristy were also added. The canopy-like shrine of St. Babylas acquired two additional tombs (of Babylas successors) and an altar within the enclosure. The entire shrine functioned like Constantine's church and mausoleum of the Holy Apostles in Constantinople.[247] The encomium of Saint Menas (mid-fourth century), written after the Arab invasion of Egypt of 640, also reveals that the faithful built a "small oratory like a *tetrapylon*"[248] over the original grave of the saint. Though archeological evidence for the oratory has not been preserved, it most likely resembled the four-arched tombs that were widespread in Syro-Palestine and Egypt, like the tomb-shrine of St. Sergios in Tetrapyrgion (Rusafa) or the *tetrapylon* of Mamianus in Antioch.[249]

By the early fifth century, archeological evidence confirms other solutions for the visual and spatial links between the saintly shrine and the *tetrapylon*. Near Athens, on the island of Ilissos, the eponymous basilica dedicated to the local martyr St. Leonidas was built in the vicinity of the site of his tomb (Fig. 4.47).[250] A large, squarish bay of a basilica, approximately 12 meters by 14 meters in plan, is delineated by four massive piers, each about 3 meters by 3 meters in size, forming an area comparable in size to other known *tetrapyla*. An altar covered by a canopy stood in the center of this *tetrapylon* core of the basilica, just in front of the large semicircular apse. However, the domed cruciform crypt with the tomb of St. Leonidas was not below the *tetrapylon*-like structure, but rather on the north, linked with the basilica, so that it could have been entered from its northern aisle. Thus, a spatial link between the *martyrium* and the church did exist, and perhaps the saintly shrine and the church sanctuary shared the same formal solution, but they were not one and the same.

---

244 McCormick (1986) 297–327.

245 Kader (1996).

246 Downey (1935) 55–72.

247 Krautheimer (1986) 75.

248 Ward Perkins (1949) 26–71; Grossmann (1989); Grossmann (1998) 281–302. I am grateful to Slobodan Ćurčić for calling my attention to the work by Grossmann.

249 Table 1, T.36, T. 38; Ulbert (1986) 33ff, pl. 49; Thiel, W. (2002) 299–326; Milojević (1996) 247–262.

250 Karivieri (2006) 895–898; Ćurčić (2010) 123–124.

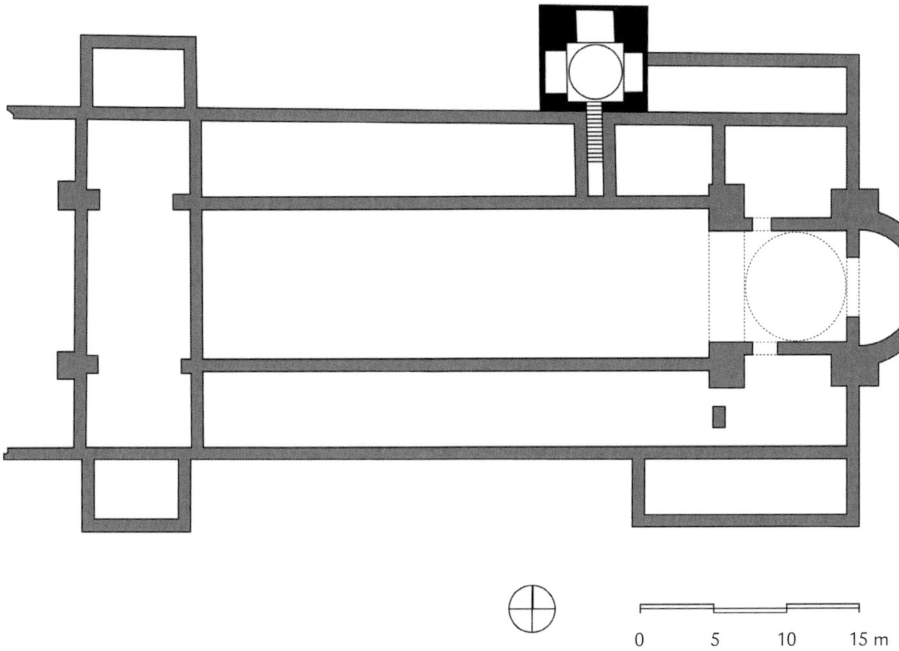

FIGURE 4.47 *Ilissos basilica, near Athens, Greece, fifth century.* DRAWING AUTHOR AND HEIDI REBURN AFTER ĆURČIĆ (2010) 124, FIG. 121

The enormous 120-meter long basilica of Hosios Leonidas, at Corinth-Lechaion (450–460), shares with the Ilissos basilica a similar design—a massive crossing sanctuary bay, which resembles a *tetrapylon* and may have been marked by a tower or a wooden dome (see Fig. 2.7).[251] In case of Hosios Leonidas at Corinth, the connection between the *tetrapylon* structure and the sacred locus was established by the almost-repetitive placing of another *tetrapylon*-like structure, a smaller-scale canopy, over the sacred locus, suggesting a peculiar architectural nesting of two canopies inside each other. Even more fascinating is that Hosios Leonidas at Corinth had a canopy, not only above the altar table in front of the semicircular apse and within the square-like *bema* framed by a *tetrapylon*-like structure, but also midway along the *solea* connecting the ambo and sanctuary, just below the "entrance" into the sanctuary. Though the meaning of this additional canopy-like structure is not clear, it is worth noting that similar framing of special locations within a church, presumably some kind of canopied *sacred loci*, can be detected in the sixth-century Basilica B in Thessalian Thebes, the Eastern Church in Apollonia, Libya, and Basilica D at Caričin Grad, near Lebane, Serbia, a foundation of Emperor Justinian I (527–565) (Table 5.61, 56, 57, 102).[252] The canopy-like structure in the episcopal basilica at Caričin Grad, indicated by four massive stone bases forming a square in the central nave, marked the center of the basilica and potentially the place of a canopied ambo or some kind of other massive canopied installation. Although it is uncertain whether another *locus* that made reference to the sacred relics was located at the center of the Basilica of Caričin Grad, the *tetrapylon*-like framing, possibly domed, certainly denotes a canopied installation of

[251] Krautheimer (1986) 131–134; Pallas (1977) 156–163.

[252] Kondić and Popović (1977) 109–129; *RBK* 222; Ćurčić (2010) 211–212.

singular importance.[253] Moreover, the episcopal basilica at Caričin Grad is distinguished by two separate chambers with apses flanking the sanctuary, most likely the *pastophoria*, serving as *prothesis* and *diaconicon*, confirming developed liturgical movements within the Byzantine-rite church. The sixth-century Church of St. Nikon at Sparta shows a similar tendency to group, formally and structurally, a sanctuary outfitted with altar table and canopy, *pastophoria*, and other chambers around and below the massive *tetrapylon*, canopy-like superstructure (Table 5.17).[254]

The survival of the late antique concept of the *tetrapylon* and its appropriation in early Christian canopies are also manifest in the well-known first Church of St. John the Evangelist, in Ephesus, Turkey, built in ca. 450 (Fig. 4.48, Table 5.27). The tomb of St. John the Evangelist, later replaced by Justinian's church in the sixth century, also contained in the center of the crossing a huge *tetrapylon*, a four-arched vaulted canopy substructure, that sheltered the martyr's grave.[255] The *tetrapylon* at the crossing of a basilica similar to St. John's at Ephesus can be detected in the sixth-century Basilica B Junca, in Byzacena, Tunis (Table 5.76).[256] In case of St. John the Evangelist, it remains unknown if at first only the canopy existed and the later fifth century church was built around the site with the *tetrapylon* at its center, positioning the altar near the apse and behind the tomb for services, or if

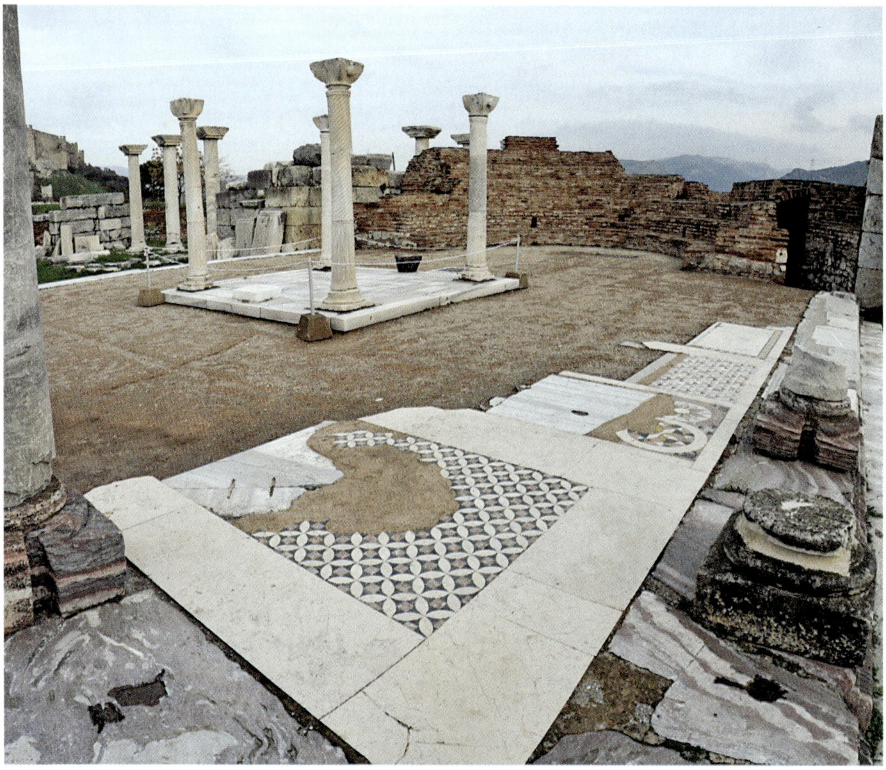

FIGURE 4.48 *Church of St. John the Evangelist, Ephesus, Turkey, fifth century.* PHOTO DANIEL C. WAUGH

[253] Popović (1979) 249–311, esp. 277–278.

[254] See also Marcattili (2011–2012) 147–174.

[255] Krautheimer (1986) 36, 106–107.

[256] *RBK* 855.

the canopy over the tomb only replicated in smaller scale the preexisting *tetrapylon*.[257] The connection of the Roman architecture of the domed *tetrapyla* with martyrs' tombs and altar canopies in the Christian East between the fourth and sixth centuries, however, is undeniable. Then again, the four-columned canopy became a structural, formal, and symbolic locus of a church, regardless of its final physical appearance, either as a basilica with multiple focal points, as in Ilissos and Caričin Grad, or as a more centralized planned structure with a central *tetrapylon* around which were grouped other parts of the church, as in St. Babylas in Antioch and St. Nikon in Sparta.

Though none of the *tetrapyla* in Constantinople have survived—neither their exact number nor their physical appearance are known—most likely these civic monuments resembled in form and function other known *tetrapyla* from the wider Mediterranean region.[258] The imperial civic program, set by Constantine I (d. 337), accomplished by Emperor Theodosius II (r. 408–450), and followed by Middle Byzantine emperors, was composed of the imperial ceremonial pathway, which was marked by *tetrapyla*.[259] The triumphal way followed the long main city avenue, known to the Byzantines as the *Mese* or central street; its two ends connected the so-called Golden and *Chalke* (Bronze) Gates at the main entrances to the City and the Great Palace, respectively. Following the Mese, Byzantine emperors on their ceremonial path to and from the Palace passed through triumphal structures, which marked special stations during a ceremonial path according to the urban topography. On the Mese, there were at least three such monumental *tetrapyla*: the domed *tetrapylon* over the Million, the urban center of the city and mile marker at the *Augustaion* square;[260] the *tetrapylon* near Sigma square, sometimes referred to as the *Golden Tetrapylon*;[261] and the so-called *Bronze Tetrapylon* (*Chalkoun Tetrapylon*), between the *fora* of Constantine and Theodosius.[262] These structures could have been redesigned into church properties, confirming the long-living tradition of the triumphal *tetrapyla* within a Christian context in the Byzantine realm.

Magdalino has demonstrated that the now-lost Constantinopolitan Church of Christ Antiphonetes (the Guarantor) was built around the domed *tetrapylon*, perhaps the Golden Tetrapylon itself, next to the temple of the Tyche at the northeastern corner of the Basilica cistern in the very proximity of Hagia Sophia.[263] Based on various chronicles such as the text by Zonaras, the biography of Emperor Heraclius (r. 610–641), as well as the epigrams from the *Palatine Anthology* (IX 696–697), Magdalino reconstructed the conversion and the rebuilding of the domed *tetrapylon* into the Church of Christ Antiphonetes in the seventh century. Though the temple of the Tyche was dismantled, sources did not record whether its material was used for the construction of the Church of Christ. Yet most likely the *tetrapylon* that originally stood next to the temple of the Tyche during the construction of the Church of Christ Antiphonetes formulated its central four-columned domed core with its associated imperial and triumphal meanings.

---

257 Thiel, A. (2005) 63–66.

258 Thiel, W. (2002) 299–326; Milojević (1996), 247–262; Kader (1996); Bogdanović (2008a) 34–35, 129–134; Bogdanović (2008c).

259 Mango (2000) 173–188.

260 Müller-Wiener (1977) 216–218.

261 *Notitia urbis Constantinopolitanae* 243.

262 On the *Chalkoun Tetrapylon*, see Mango (1985a) 30–32; Magdalino (1996) 21–25; Berger (2000) 161–172. There are also suggestions that the *Tetraplyon* stood between the forum of Theodosius (ancient Forum Tauri) and the *Philadelphion*. Janin (1964) 101, 104, 208, 210, 328–329.

263 Magdalino (2015). I thank Paul Magdalino for discussing the material with me and for allowing me to cite his work before its publication.

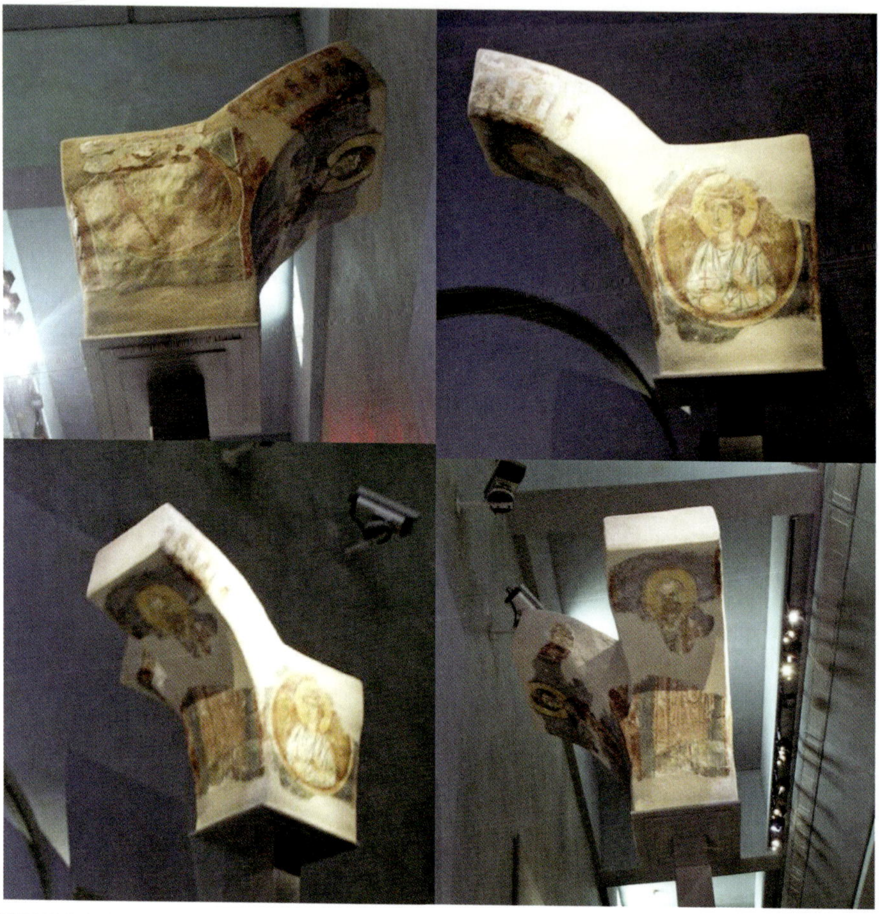

FIGURE 4.49 *Fragments of the arcosolium tomb from the southeast pier of the church core, Church of St. Sophia, Thessaloniki, thirteenth century.* PHOTO IVAN DRPIĆ

The original concept of a *tetrapylon* as a triumphal monument, however, survived in the Byzantine tradition in various forms. Recorded in the tenth-century *Synaxarion* and mentioned by Clavijo in the early fifteenth century, a bronze *tetrapylon* with acquired relics of the forty martyrs of Sebaste was a public monument in Constantinople.[264] A *tetrapylon* from Aizanoi in Bithynia was turned into a Byzantine chapel in the eleventh and twelfth centuries, sheltering still-unidentified tombs, including a privileged tomb located in a reused second-century marble sarcophagus.[265] These examples of the monumental civic *tetrapyla* that acquired relics and chapels under Byzantine interventions bespeak the architectural role of canopies for framing sacred space outside churches.

The eleventh-century shrine of Hosios Loukas embedded in the northeastern arm of the central core of the *katholikon* of Hosios Loukas (see Figs. 4.11, 4.13) and the thirteenth-century four-columned tomb originally embedded within southeastern pier cluster that supports the dome of the Cathedral of St. Sophia in Thessaloniki (Fig. 4.49) exemplify the extremely

---

[264] *Synaxarion CP* 356, 524; Janin (1953) 485–86.

[265] On Aizinoi *tetrapylon*: http://www.kultur.gov.tr/EN/BelgeGoster.aspx?17A16AE30572D3137EE1F1486EE5030E3143C82B0599388A. Accessed January 2006.

sophisticated survival of the concept of a *tetrapylon*, which sheltered the tomb of a privileged individual within the canopy-core of a church.[266] Little is known about the architectural process that led to the incorporation of the tomb into the pier cluster in St. Sophia in Thessaloniki. The analysis of the making of the canopy shrine of Hosios Loukas from an individual chamber to a tower-like canopied shrine embedded into the wall and structural core of the church indicates that the final solution may have derived from the larger concept of design of Middle Byzantine churches. Belonging to the so-called Greek-octagon church, the overall design of Hosios Loukas is based on a centralized design of a massive domed structure over the central square bay with corners bridged by squinches, which can be related to both centralized memorial imperial structures and to the structural merging of four-columned principal core with thick walls within the so-called abbreviated design of cross-in-square churches.[267] These examples do not suggest that the concept and use of *tetrapyla* from the late antique period was seamlessly integrated into the architectural design of later periods, yet they support the observation of "revivals" of various forms of canopies as critical in Byzantine church design and based on different concepts. As the building of monumental basilicas ceased over time, the original concept of a *tetrapylon* was seemingly superseded by a four-columned church architecture, typical for the Middle and Late Byzantine periods.

FROM BASILICA TO DOMED CHURCH: THE CANOPY AND THE NINE-SQUARE GRID IN BYZANTINE ARCHITECTURAL DESIGN

Following official acceptance of Christianity, early ecclesiastical architecture is generally associated with the use of massive structures known from Roman imperial traditions such as monumental basilicas and large, centrally planned rotundas. Their spacious interiors allowed for the gatherings of the faithful and the performance of various liturgical and church rites.[268] As the building of monumental church basilicas and massive centrally planned baptisteries ceased over time, most Byzantine churches after the transitional period became smaller in scale, simplified in form, and more intimate in atmosphere, making the church itself a highly symbolic sacred space encompassing the symbolism of the heavenly sphere and the Heavenly Jerusalem.[269] The development of the so-called four-columned churches in relation to their canopied core, based on four supports topped by a dome, has already been associated with sixth-century experiments with domed church design.[270] The radically innovative design of the domed basilica of the Constantinopolitan Hagia Sophia, which combined a basilical structure with a centrally positioned massive dome, is regarded as the greatest achievement of Byzantine architecture. The Byzantines never repeated its design in other buildings. The unique place of Hagia Sophia in Byzantine architecture was usually attributed to its extremely complex architectural design with the demanding statics of a large-size domed basilica as well as to the lack of financial resources and the decline of architectural education and practice during and after the transitional

---

[266] Mylonas (1992) 115–122; Ćurčić (2010) 297–300, 383–387; Kissas (1996) 36–49, figs. 2–4; Theocharidou (1994) 52–57.

[267] Mihaljević (2012) 99–119; Ćurčić (2010) 433–436; Ousterhout (1992) 48–60; Bouras (1982) 46–101; 132–142; Mango (1972) 189–193; Krautheimer (1974) 251–253; Mathews (1974) 22–29; Mango (1975b) 385–392.

[268] Krautheimer (1986) 39–237; Ćurčić (2010) 146–167, 216–247; Johnson (2012) 278–297.

[269] Mango (1975a) 1–6; Ousterhout (1998) 81–120; Ćurčić (1992) 16–38; Ćurčić (2010) 247.

[270] Ćurčić (1992) 16–38; Krautheimer (1986) 238–257.

period. Indeed, from the sixth to the ninth centuries, the basilica with a dome on four columns was transitional in scale and form, and was ultimately superseded by the generally small-sized, four-columned Middle-Byzantine church.[271] However, I would like to propose, not only that Hagia Sophia set the high standards of Byzantine architecture, but also that its design based on a canopied unit inspired further architectural solutions and established a strong link between late antique and Byzantine architecture.

The main spatial unit of Hagia Sophia—its canopied central core comprising four piers that supported a massive dome via spherical triangles known as pendentives—became the major architectural *parti* of Byzantine churches. Canopies not only defined the interior focal points of significance and the developed spatial topography of Byzantine churches, but they also defined the basic design principles of entire church buildings (see Figs. 2.67–70). Krautheimer and Ćurčić have demonstrated that, between the fourth and sixth centuries in Constantinople and other centers of the empire, structural experimentations fueled the development of Byzantine architecture.[272] The engagement in large and costly projects for religious, funerary, and civic buildings, such as vaulted cisterns, resulted in the selection of a simple, easily comprehended, structurally sound vaulted square bay as the standardized spatial unit of Byzantine structures. During their experimentations with vaulting systems, the Byzantines ingeniously altered building material from Roman concrete to brick and supported the vaults with marble columns instead of Roman brick and cement piers. By employing the most basic and structurally sound forms of vaults, either groined or domical, on four supports, the Byzantines created a standardized building module and increased the efficiency of Byzantine architecture by applying additive design principles. The use of marble or granite columns reduced maintenance costs and practically utilized a bay modular system. Similarly, groin vaults as attested to in Constantinopolitan structures, such as the Basilica, the Binbirdirek underground cisterns, and Hagia Sophia, were made of pitched-brick type with bricks laid upright with their longer sides in a curve and without the use of any formwork, which was additionally an economical solution in areas that lacked wood (Fig. 4.50). Domical or sail brick vaults as used in the fifth-century Constantinopolitan cistern of Theodosius may have influenced sixth-century experimentations with domical structural units in churches. These "blind" domical vaults have a flatter profile than true domes, and as they sprang from a square plan, their construction in thin shells of brick may have influenced practical solutions for the dome on pendentives that was used in many Byzantine churches, including the famous Hagia Sophia. Indeed, for domes that spanned larger areas, the canopy-like unit was structurally supported by clustered piers, additional lateral supports, while massive arches carrying the dome could have developed into true barrel vaults.[273] Yet the Byzantines experimented intensely with the tectonics of their structures that merged structural and compositional relations of building parts, which may also account for the preference for the smaller-sized design of churches in later periods.[274]

Following the sixth-century design of Hagia Sophia and the standardization of the tripartite sanctuary, which was probably due to the need for architectural and structural symmetry combined with liturgical requirements for the *prothesis* chamber usually located to the north of the *bema*, the greatest variation of the church planning was related to the naos of the church. The naos of the church can be defined in architectural terms as a nine-square vaulted grid (Fig. 4.51).[275] Hence, even if after the transitional period Byzantine churches

---

[271] Krautheimer (1986) 331–353.

[272] Ćurčić (1992) 16–38; Krautheimer (1986) 238–257; Bogdanović (2008e).

[273] See, for example, Mainstone (1988) 185–217; Çakmak et al. (2009) 693–698.

[274] See also Krautheimer (1986) 238–257.

[275] The nine-square grid, still used as a theoretical and practical tool in architectural education, has a long history in the Mediterranean and is evident in both the built and landscape architecture of the nine-part gardens and courtyard houses in particular.

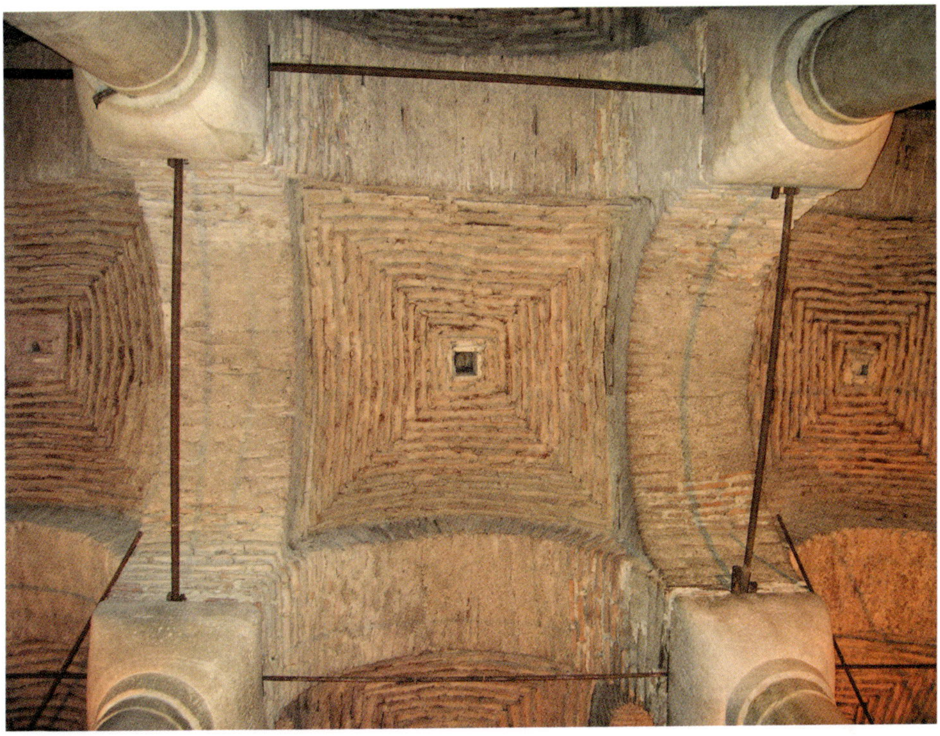

FIGURE 4.50 *Binbirdirek Cistern, Constantinople, now Istanbul, fifth–sixth centuries; detail showing groined vault.* PHOTO AUTHOR

became smaller in size, the multiple combinations resulting from the nine-square grid based on a canopied unit provided an impressive diversity of architectural solutions.

Namely, the canopy allowed the definition of a unique architectural space. While every place is singular by definition, by making boundaries, the canopy, even if it remained a simple, open, columnar structure, made an architectural and experiential distinction between various places inside and outside the church proper and enhanced the experience of the canopied place by virtue of its meaning as a frame and marker of sacred space.[276] Based on the canopied square bay as an architectural *parti*, the geometry of a Byzantine church and its structures was based either on a one-square or a nine-square diagrammatic design, as they both allowed for hierarchy.[277] A singular canopy allowed for the design of centralized one-chamber structures without any subdividing elements, which could have been used for baptisteries, *phialai*, or tombs. The nine-square grid was a preferred solution for Byzantine churches; it provided a centralized plan with a clear hierarchy and ordering of space based on the coupling of the central, middle canopied squared bay with the peripheral zone made of the surrounding eight squares. In additive modular design used by the Byzantines,[278] singular units based on the one-square principle could have been incorporated as individual vaulted chambers and chapels with their established baptismal, funerary,

[276] On the singularity of space see also, Malpas (2006); Malpas (2015) 65–92.

[277] The combination of four squares in a grid also allows for defining the architectural space, yet it is essentially non-hierarchical, because it eliminates the connecting centralized space, and as such was not used in Byzantine churches.

[278] Ousterhout (2008) 110–116 disagrees on the use of grid but highlights the additive design process in Byzantine architecture, based on both textual and archeological evidence.

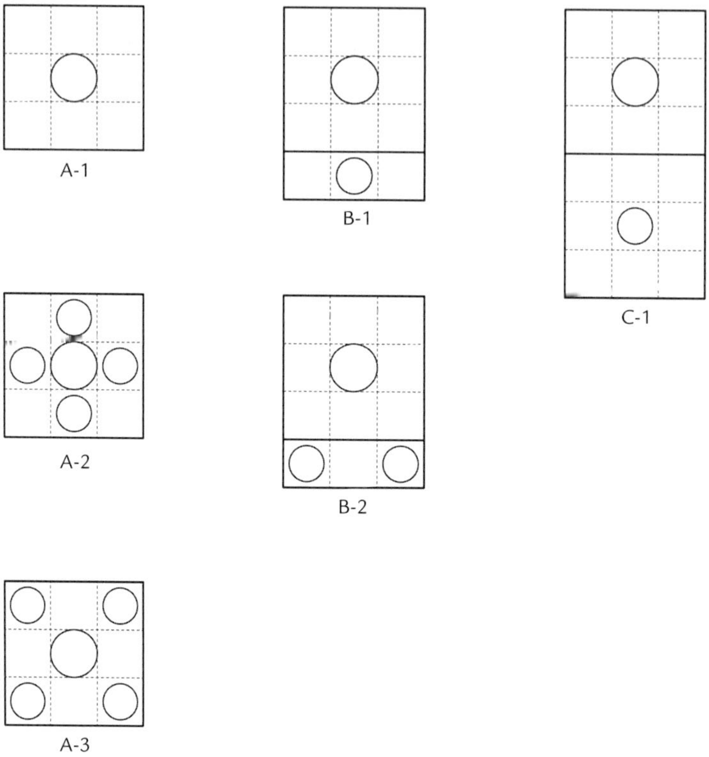

FIGURE 4.51 *Nine-square grid design: A-1, basic solution with the centrally positioned canopied bay that allows for the hierarchical articulation of the entire church structure, either reduced to a central one-square or fully developed to a nine-square grid as the eight bays enveloped the church core. A-2, cruciform hierarchical articulation of a nine-square grid that allows for the design of various church solutions such as the cruciform, cross-inscribed, cross-in-square, tetraconch, and triconch churches, as well as domed basilicas and basilicas with developed domed bemas. A-3, hierarchical placement of canopied bays in the four corners of the nine-square grid that often results in five-domed churches. B-1, merging of the narthex with central, canopied bay axially aligned with the church naos and its central canopied bay, often seen in imperial foundations. B-2, merging of the narthex with two canopied bays at the corners with the church naos with central canopied core; often seen when side bays of the narthex serve as chapels or funerary spaces. C-1, extensive development of the narthex based on the six- or nine-square grid that doubles and in a way replicates the proper of the church; this arrangement is often seen in monastic contexts where spatially developed narthexes placed adjacent to the church were used for extensive monastic services; these narthexes are known as the lite after the eponymous services performed in their space. The additions of parekklesia and enveloping ambulatoria around the central core of the church (defined as a nine-square core) would often follow various combinations of A, B, and C solutions.* DRAWING ZHENGYANG HUA

or other associations into the nine-square design of larger structures and churches. This phenomenon of merging a one-square with a nine-square grid design, indeed, happened especially with the post-sixth-century decline of building massive baptisteries and monumental tombs that had been known from early Christian times.[279]

[279] Ćurčić (2010) 247. On the late antique imperial mausolea and spatial transformation of the Holy Apostles in Constantinople from a centrally planned, possibly rotunda mausoleum structure to a cruciform ecclesiastical complex with multiple units, see Johnson (2014) 119–129.

The nine-square grid design based on a canopied spatial unit allowed for the hierarchy of the space and focused on the central domed bay and the development of multiple church types. It may be claimed that all Byzantine types of buildings, as systematized in the twentieth century to allow for chronological taxonomy, essentially belong to the nine-square grid. Indeed, domed and vaulted basilicas such as the Constantinopolitan Hagia Sophia and Hagia Eirine, as well as large centrally planned structures such as Ss. Sergios and Bachus, continued to be used in later periods, and they also partake of the concept of the nine-square grid design. In the case of Hagia Eirine, the central domical unit was surrounded by eight clearly articulated bays surrounding the massive core, while in case of Ss. Sergius and Bachus, the central octagonal core was wrapped by eight corresponding spatial units that were architecturally merged in the unique space (Fig. 4.52). The innovative architectural types that emerged after the sixth century, and today are recognized by the so-called cross-in-square, cross-domed, cruciform, tetraconch, triconch, domed octagon or Greek-cross octagon design, were all achieved by utilizing the nine-square diagrammatic grid. The so-called cross-in-square design is the most obvious solution in that regard. The naos of the church is divided into nine bays. The central bay, comprising a canopy unit on four columns crowned by a dome, provides the focus and the pivotal element for volumetric modeling of the entire building, as the central core is braced on four sides by high vaults, while corner bays are articulated with either lower vaults or additional domical units, as when the cross-in-square design becomes a five-domed church (Figs. 4.53, 4.54). In the

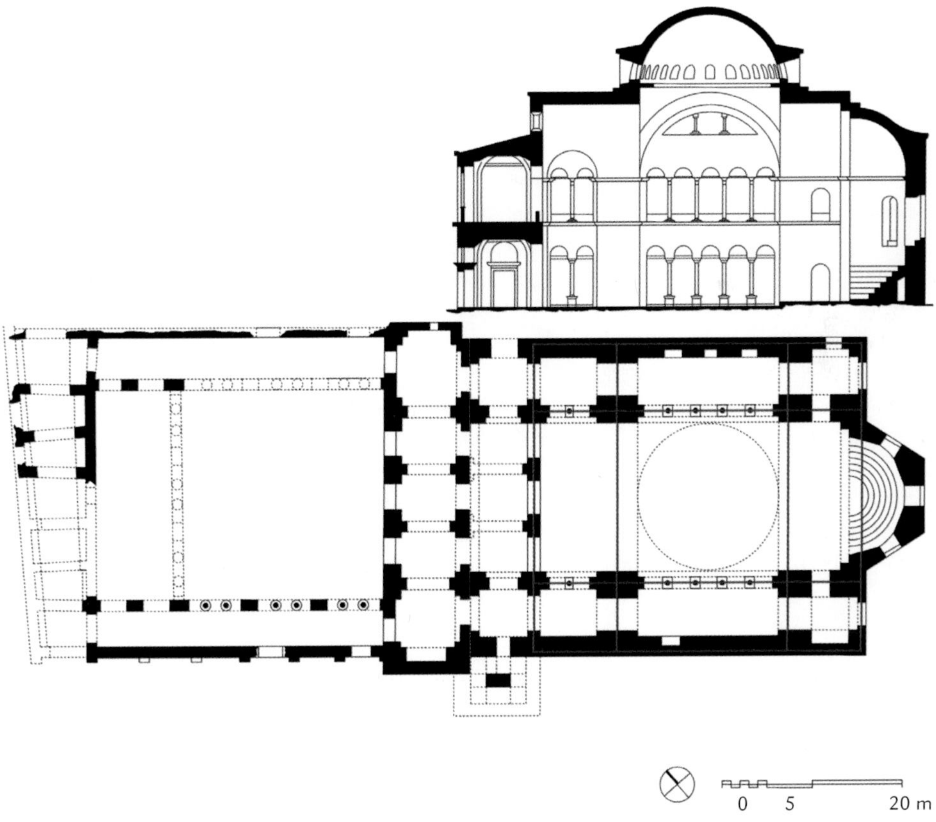

FIGURE 4.52 *Hagia Eirine, Constantinople, now Istanbul, sixth century, plan and cross section; outline of the nine-square grid added by the author.* DRAWING AUTHOR AND HEIDI REBURN AFTER ĆURČIĆ (2010) 191, FIG. 196

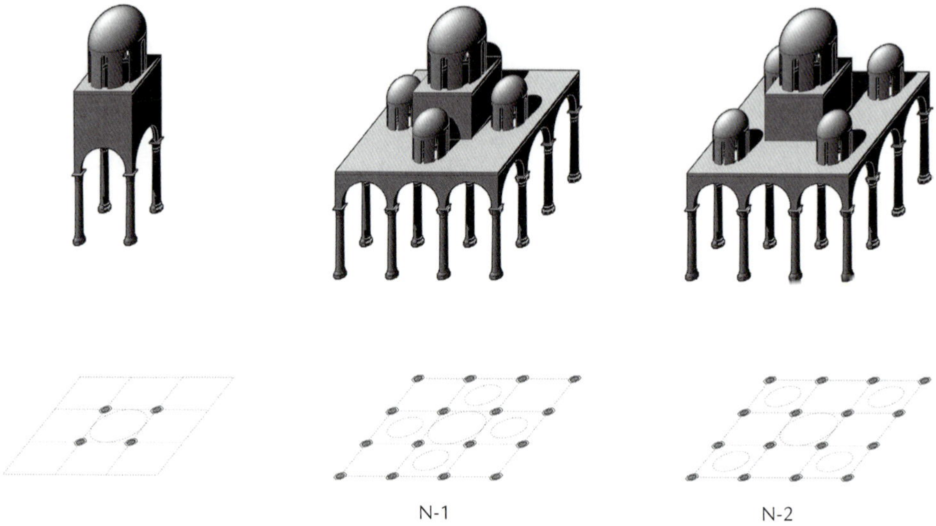

FIGURE 4.53 *Tectonic and hierarchical design of cruciform, cross-inscribed, and cross-in-square churches, often resulting in five-domed Byzantine churches; the design is based on a nine-square grid starting with a central canopied spatial unit: N-1, domes or domical vaults are placed along the cardinal directions; N-2, domes or domical vaults are placed in the corner bays of a nine-square grid.* DRAWING ZHENGYANG HUA

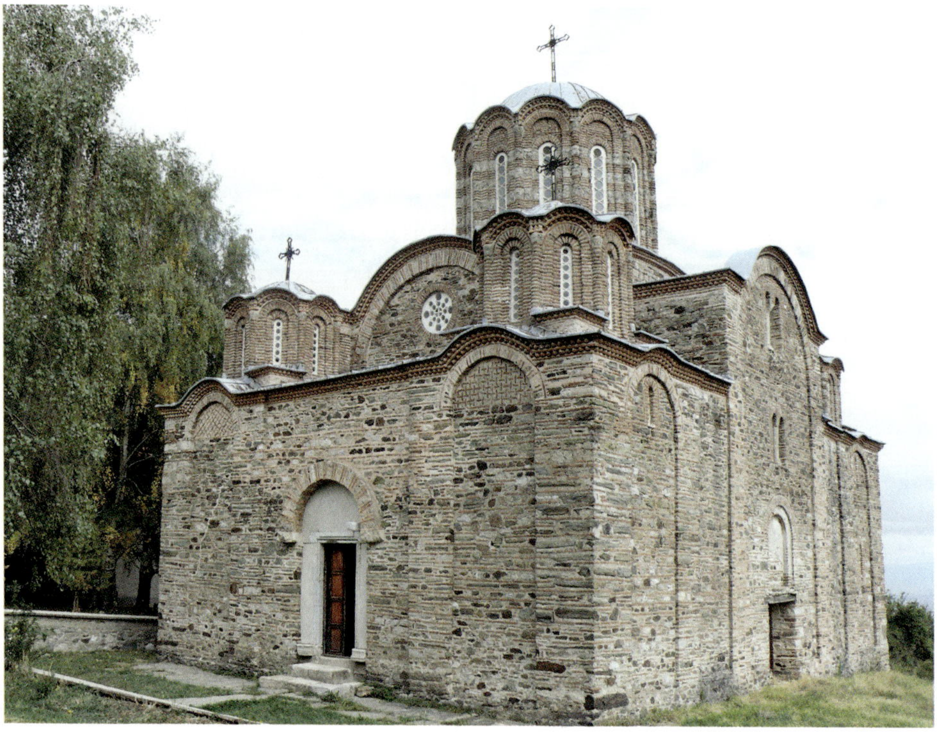

FIGURE 4.54 *Five-domed katholikon of the Matejič monastery, Skopska Crna Gora, F.Y.R. of Macedonia, ca. 1350.* PHOTO IVAN DRPIĆ

case of cross-domed churches, the central core is not resting on columns or piers, but is in its lower zone articulated by a massive corner wall or clustered pier supports. The cruciform or the so-called atrophied cross design results from eliminating corner bays or even the lateral bays, while the central canopied core remains fully tectonically integrated into the building. The tetraconch or triconch design results from geometric replacement of square bays with half-cylindrical units, which are structurally integrated in essentially a cross-in-square design. Similarly, by expanding the size of the major dome and the central canopied unit, the domed-octagon design is characterized by a changing geometry and tectonics of the central square bay that acquired octagonal shape in its upper, transitional section where the pendentives are replaced by corbels and squinches. In the process, the central bay may become the major volumetric feature, as in the atrophied cross-in-square design, or it can be surrounded by eight spatial units that would formulate the cross with equal arms for the Greek-cross octagon design.

Many Byzantine churches, and especially Late Byzantine buildings, have narthexes and exonarthexes.[280] Originally, entry vestibules, narthexes, and exonarthexes could have been built simultaneously with the main church building and its naos, or added later. Over time, narthexes and exonarthexes became smaller. With the development of liturgical and paraliturgical rites performed within them, narthexes and exonarthexes provided space for an increasing number of functions, including important liturgical services related to Easter, Christmas, and Pentecost; expanded baptismal and funerary services; services such as the Washing of the Feet; regular performance of matins and the midnight office in monastic churches; the lighting of candles, or even for the holding of church councils.[281] While seemingly generic in design and understood as architecturally independent additions, occasionally doubling the size of the church proper and serving as churches in their own right, the articulation of narthexes and exonarthexes by canopied bays subtly points to their additional meanings. For example, a central bay articulated by four corner columns that support a blind domical vault, often in a shape of a pumpkin dome to recall textile canopies as seen in Nea Moni (see Figs. 4.40, 4.41), or the central bay of a gallery above the narthex articulated sometimes as an open columnar canopy, as seen in the case of Church of Parigoritissa in Arta (see Fig. 4.37), may indicate the imperial and royal connotations of the selected foundations. The twin-domed solutions in corner bays of the narthexes, in addition to architecturally articulating the overall massing of the building, usually point to the inclusion of chapels, often with funerary functions.[282] The combination of both a domed central bay and a twin-domed structure, with the associated imperial and funerary functions of these spaces, can be exemplified by the Athonite monastery of Hilandar, the foundation of Serbian medieval royalty (Fig. 4.55).[283]

The architectural design of Byzantine domed churches based on the principles of the nine-square grid and canopy as a basic spatial unit inevitably points to the sophisticated process that involved proportioning systems and a good understanding of scale.[284] In this process, most critical is the transition from small-scale canopies as church furnishings and fittings to their use in building design. Indeed, standardization was part of this process,

---

280 Ćurčić (2004) 65–94; Bogdanović (2008e).

281 Bogdanović (2012) 95–107; Marinis (2014) 64–76.

282 Ćurčić (1971) 333–344; Ćurčić (1977) 95–110; Ćurčić (1978) 17–27.

283 Ćurčić (1989) 55–68; Ćurčić (2001b) 477–488; Bogdanović, D. (1997).

284 I agree with Hadjitryphonos (2010) 113–154 and Mihaljević (2012) 99–119, who highlighted various aspects of highly sophisticated Byzantine architectural practices that allowed for design based on diagrammatic principles.

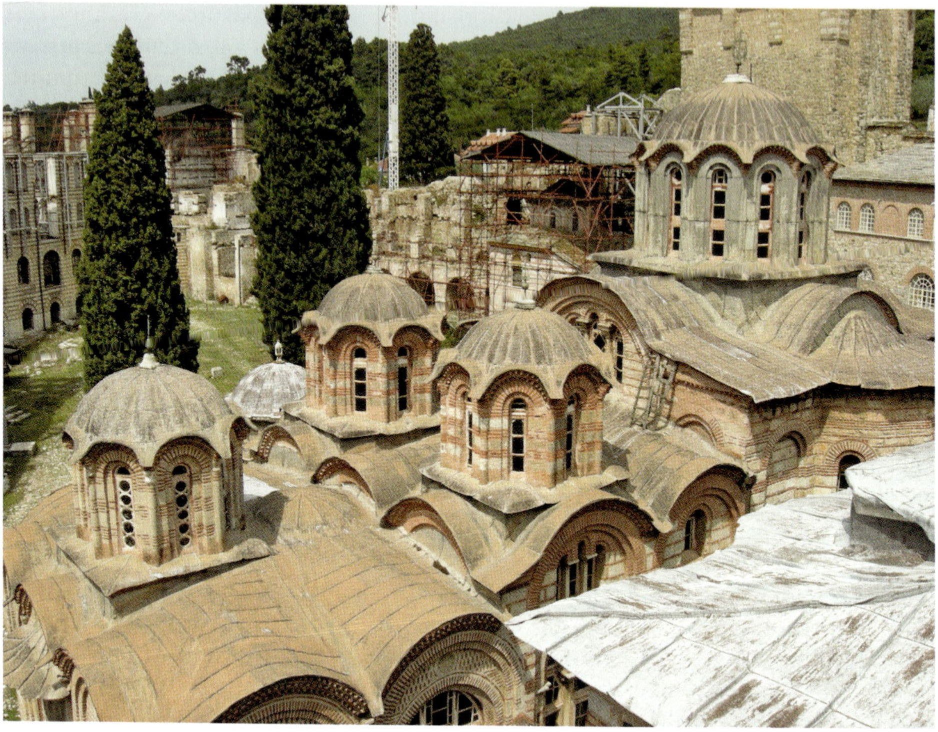

FIGURE 4.55 *Roof lines of the katholikon of the Monastery Hilandar showing the major dome of the katholikon, the twin domes of the narthex, and the central dome of the exonarthex.* PHOTO NEBOJŠA STANKOVIĆ

yet it went beyond mere replication of established schemes without a deeper engagement with the larger contexts of architectural design.[285] Only some kind of standardization of both the elements and structural design of canopies that circulated widely can explain how a canopy from a sixth-century church on Paros closely resembles a Middle-Byzantine canopy in the significantly smaller church in Kalabaka on the opposite side of Greece. The two altar canopies differ in the quality of execution and materials used for their construction, but they are closely related in size, construction technique, shape, and location within the sanctuary. Both these canopies, like the majority of others, do not employ pendentives or squinches for the transition from the four columns to a domed roof, though by the sixth century, Byzantine architects were demonstrably capable of designing church domes on squinches and pendentives.[286] The training of those who made canopies is unknown, as is whether they were considered builders, sculptors, or carpenters. For most canopies, being much smaller in size in comparison to the church domical core, there was no structural need for pendentives or squinches. Nevertheless, at least two canopies, one currently in the treasury of San Marco in Venice and the other in the Royal Ontario Museum collection, even if significantly smaller in number than the majority of studied canopies, have a construction of an arcuated domical frame on pendentives

[285] On opposing views on the Byzantine architectural design processes, see Krautheimer (1986) 238–257; Ousterhout (2008) 58–127; Hadjitryphonos (2010) 113–154; Mihaljević (2012) 99–119; Bogdanović (2017a).

[286] Ćurčić (1992) 16–38.

(see Figs. 1.2, 3.6), thus confirming that structural concerns and training cannot fully explain the way Byzantines built their canopies as church fittings. Most canopies that the Byzantines used or depicted in their manuscripts are without pendentives or squinches, and occasionally even without arches, but almost all of them have a flat plaque upon which a pyramidal or domical roof rests as a lid (see Figs. 2.32, 3.3, 3.4, 3.5). Therefore, those who built canopies and those who built churches, despite working on structurally similar architectonic forms—frequently four-columned structures with a roof—could have been trained in different workshops.[287] Yet this observable difference in the construction of smaller-sized canopies that did not require structural treatment as in church construction also resembles the long-lasting architectural practice whereby small-scaled models are made to convey the essence of the conceptual design, independently of the actual construction on a larger scale.

The subtle changes in the design of the canopied bays of Byzantine churches can be observed through the volumetric changes achieved over time with a particular focus on the modeling of the central domed core. Hagia Sophia's dome, despite being a marvel of engineering, did not have a drum and resulted in a rather squat volumetric. The use of impost blocks for columns in order to achieve more voluminous spaces has been observed already in the fifth-century construction of Constantinopolitan cisterns.[288] In order to increase the central canopied bay of their churches, Byzantine architects also inserted a wall zone above the massive arches that carried the dome and eventually included the drum, which rested on the canopied sub-structural frame and elevated the dome further, while giving the entire building better proportions (Fig. 4.56).

Diagrammatic design based on a canopy and a nine-square grid was not only a practical strategy for proportionally well-balanced and structurally sound church design, but also a potent carrier of architectural knowledge. The lack of surviving textual evidence for architectural training and theoretical education of the Byzantines cannot imply their nonexistence. Anthemios of Tralles, one of the two architects of Hagia Sophia, was well trained in theory and even wrote a treatise on descriptive geometry.[289] Even if no such texts have been preserved from later periods, achieved architectural accomplishments point to engagements with theory.

The neo-Platonic philosophy enriched with Christian thinking through the pervasive legacy of Dionysius the Areopagite informed the Byzantine understanding of critical theoretical concepts in architecture such as hierarchy and symbolism.[290] In particular, Dionysius *Celestial Hierarchy* presents detailed, ontological explanations of three three-fold groups of angels circling around God and organized them spatially in triplets from top to bottom.[291] Angels as pure intellects and mediators between God and humankind allowed for an ontological merging of the understanding of space, both intellectually and experientially, through senses and rites. Within such an expanded theoretical construct of space, Dionysius philosophy provided sophisticated reasoning on the hierarchical organization of space and a method for interpreting visual and spatial church elements as symbols that reveal information and communicate meanings of various forms of realities of the church building—celestial, ecclesiastical, and ontological.

---

[287] In the Middle-Byzantine *Book of the Prefect,* XXII, marble workers were distinguished from those who built domes and vaults. *SD* 206–207.

[288] Krautheimer (1986) 238–257; Bogdanović (2008e).

[289] Ousterhout (2008) 72.

[290] Bogdanović (2011b) 109–134.

[291] *Dionysius Areopagita, CH* VI.1–IX.4, 200C–261D.

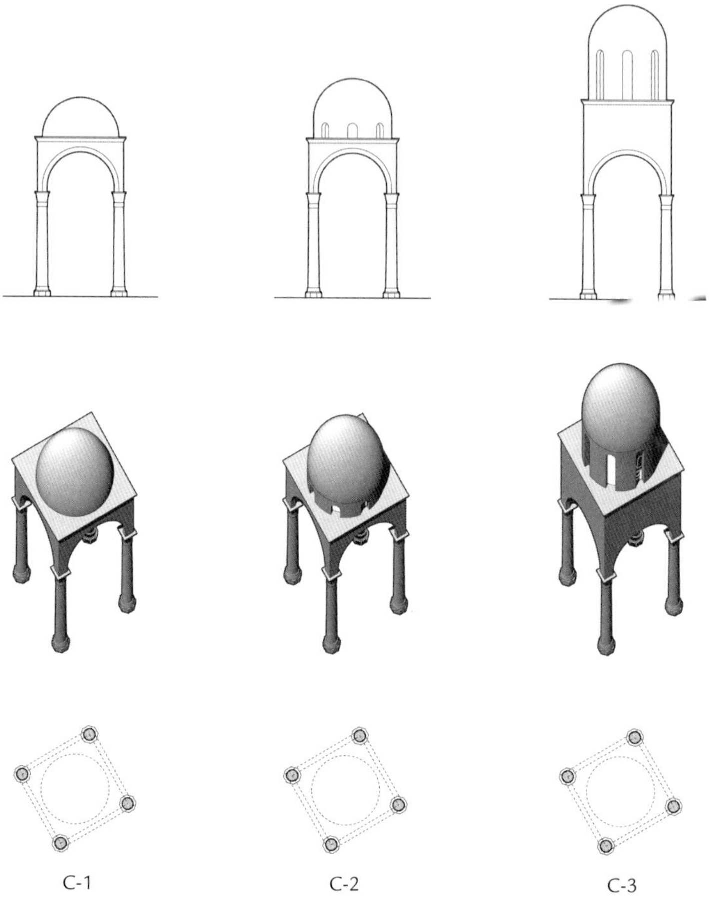

FIGURE 4.56 *Tectonic development of the church core: C-1, basic canopied unit; C-2, stilting the dome and opening of windows in the lower zone, which simultaneously provides better structural properties of the core; C-3, inserting the wall above the arcuated frame and raising the dome on the drum.* DRAWING ZHENGYANG HUA

The sophisticated designs of church installations based on modularity and the transposition of canopies, as examined through various relations between altars, tomb-shrines, *proskynetaria*, *templon* screens, ambos, or *phialai*, certainly reveal the potentials of micro-architectural qualities of canopies to articulate various aspects of sacred space in a Byzantine church (Fig. 4.57). Richard Etlin has demonstrated how, in Gothic church design, medieval people understood the canopy of the high altar as a vaulted compartment, or *ciborium*, while they compared the entire vaulted aisle to a series of *ciboria*.[292] Similarly, Byzantine bishop Theodore of Andida revealed that not all Middle Byzantine churches have altar canopies, but explained that the hemispherical form of the sanctuary assumed their role.[293] Canopied units as vaulted bays and constitutive architectural elements of church installation and entire church design correspondingly carried associated theological meanings, articulated by the neo-Platonic Dionysian concept of symbolism.

[292] Etlin (2015).

[293] *PG* 140, 417 col. 443.

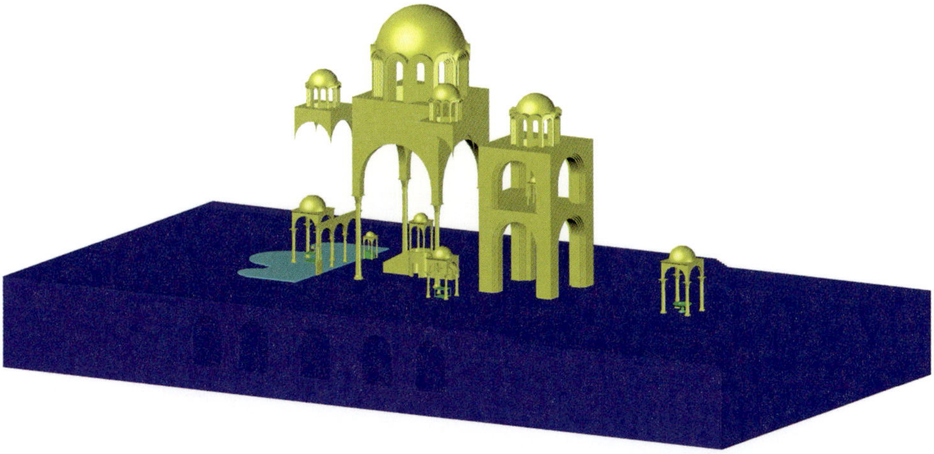

FIGURE 4.57 *Integration of various canopies as modular and spatial units within a Byzantine church.* DRAWING ZHENGYANG HUA

Dionysian symbolism allowed for the transferability of meanings from one installation to another, including those unverifiable architectural models such as the Biblical Ark of the Covenant.[294]

The Dionysian hierarchy based on angelic triplets allowed for the sophisticated interior organization of entire church spaces. In his seminal work on the monumental program of Byzantine churches after the transitional period, Otto Demus demonstrated the ideal, codified, and hierarchically organized interior decoration of a Byzantine church.[295] The Byzantine church tectonics, understood as a relationship between the architectural design and the treatment of the structural form and its surface, is divided into three major zones, with the most sacred at the top. The upper zones of the church, consisting of the cupolas, high vaults, and the semi-dome of the apse, represented the heavenly realm and were consequently adorned with images of Christ, the Mother of God, angels, prophets, and apostles. The central church dome usually had a representation of Christ Pantokrator (literally, "the Ruler of All") ruling the universe He created and redeemed. Some Byzantine churches, such as the Virgin Olympiotissa at Ellason, Thessaly (1295–1296), even have a preserved image of Christ surrounded by two concentric zones with angels as described in Dionysian Celestial Hierarchy. The middle zone, composed of vaults and the wall areas of the cross-arms belonging to the bays encircling the central church core, was usually reserved for narrative scenes of the life and ministry of Christ. The third and lowest zone was filled with images of apostles, martyrs, saints, prophets, and patriarchs in busts or full-size standing figures, often unframed, which created the perception that they occupied the same space as the congregation in the church. These images, when combined with the Divine Liturgy, coalesced into a complex entity within the sacred space of the church. The sacred space of a Byzantine church was arranged following a hierarchical-cosmic ordering of the Christian universe; a topographical system in which the church became an image of the earthly life of Christ (God-incarnate); and a liturgical-chronological scheme in which religious images were arranged on the wall surfaces in the sequence of church festivals.[296]

---

294 Bogdanović (2011b) 109–134, esp. 124–129.

295 Demus (1976) 16–30; Bogdanović (2011b) 109–134, esp. 119–124.

296 Ibid.

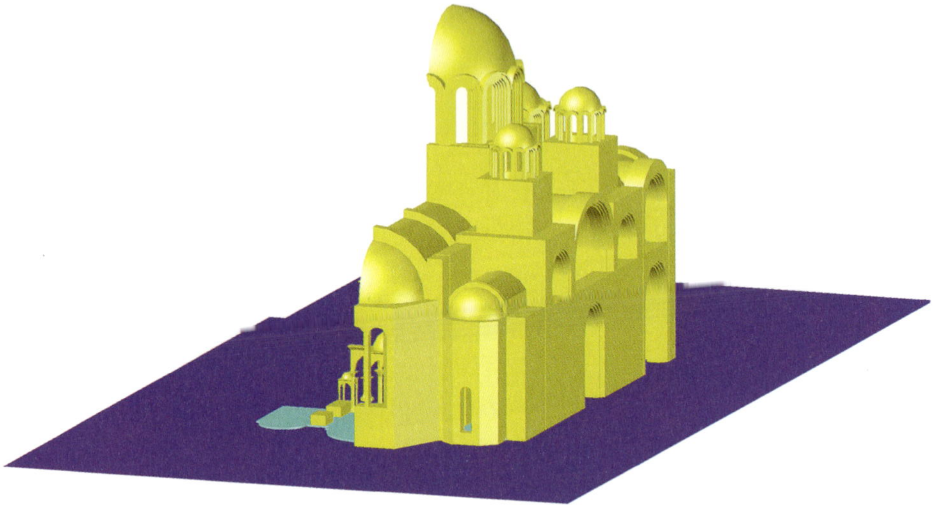

FIGURE 4.58 *Development of pyramidal composition and volumetric modeling of Byzantine churches based on a nine-square grid.* DRAWING ZHENGYANG HUA

It can be argued that the nine-square grid architectural design principle responds to the three-fold Dionysian hierarchy. As I have already suggested, the soaring system of a typical nine-bay or cross-in-square Byzantine church is the expression of a highly sophisticated hierarchical system that intertwined architectural design with the hierarchical ordering of the Christian universe (Fig. 4.58).[297] By the Late Byzantine period, some five-domed churches, with pyramidal composition and an attenuating vertical design, emphasized the coinciding of the hierarchical monumental decoration with architectural design. An impressive example is a five-domed church at Gračanica (ca. 1321), where in its interior the angelic hierarchy is distributed on the central dome and on four smaller domes with the images of thrones, seraphim, and angels (Fig. 4.59).[298] Compactly proportioned so that four smaller and lower domes are more-or-less an equal distance from the central dome and a vertical focus of the church, the church simultaneously maintains the developed tripartite horizontal hierarchical organization: narthex–nave–triple sanctuary.[299] Gračanica and similar churches such as the Hagioi Apostoloi in Thessaloniki (1310–1314), therefore, indicate an increasing level of sophistication of church design that reveals highly complex questions of spatial hierarchy resulting from theoretical and practical concerns. The Dionysian concept of hierarchy understood as the graded order may be related to the elongation of proportions of Middle Byzantine and Late Byzantine churches, masterfully accomplished in the south Church of Christ Pantokrator in the Constantinopolitan Pantokrator monastery. Yet, this interest in height and a progressive verticality is different from contemporaneous Gothic architecture. Byzantine churches with centralized, compact shapes and domical canopied forms as their basic architectural units seemingly responded better to the Dionysian concept of an "all-inclusive" hierarchy as "a radiant display that reaches out from God throughout the whole of the created order and draws it back into union with him."[300]

---

[297] Bogdanović (2011b) 109–134, esp. 119–124.

[298] Todić (1988) 80–98.

[299] Ćurčić (1988) 100–129.

[300] *Dionysius Areopagita, CH* 3.164D–165A.

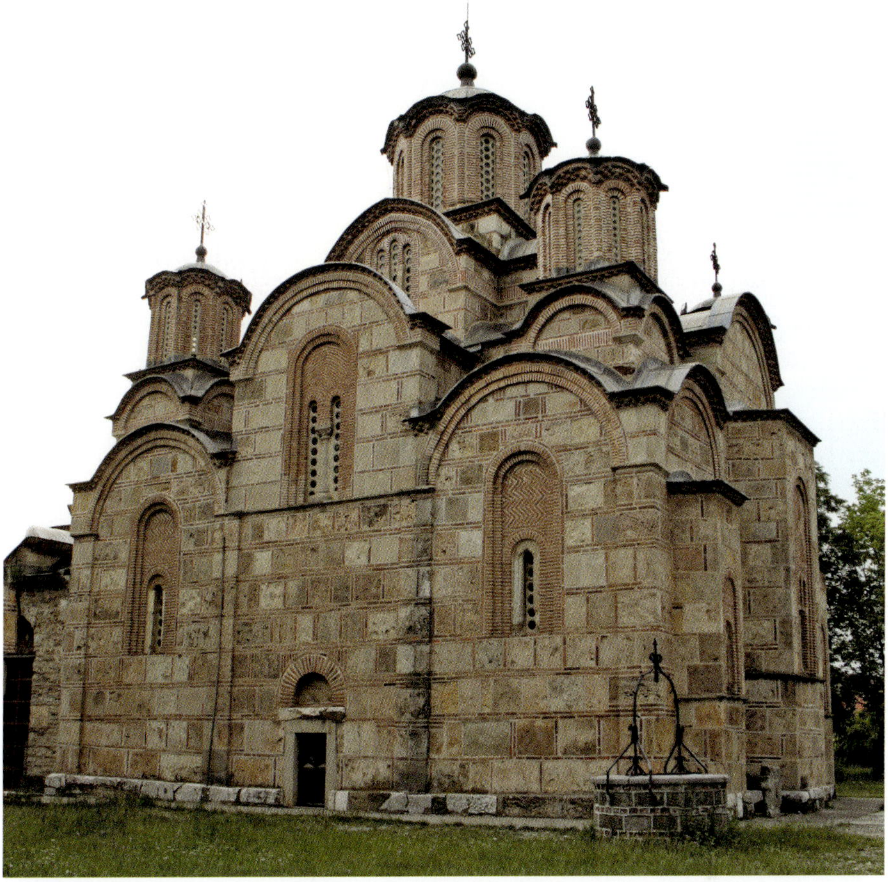

FIGURE 4.59 *Church of the Mother of God, Monastery Gračanica, fourteenth century.* PHOTO IVAN DRPIĆ

Conceptual theological, liturgical, and performative aspects of church design based on canopies also generated the experience of being and presence within the space that gave interiority and essence to a Byzantine church.[301] As micro-architectural *parti*, the canopy became a fully integrated ontological module. As shown by modern theorists of space, such as John Malpas, in such an overarching context, the singularity of place could be recreated in every church when the canopy marked the extraordinary important places, as seen when pilgrims sought healing associated with the tomb-shrine of Hosios Loukas with the New Siloam, or when for the faithful, the altar table simultaneously stood for the Tomb of Christ and the Ark of the Covenant.[302] It is my understanding that in its inclusive design based on canopies, the Byzantine church on a macro scale embraced, above all, the two major spatial models, those of the Earthly and Heavenly Jerusalem.

[301] Malpas (2006).

[302] Malpas (2006); Malpas (2015) 65–92.

FIVE

Nested in Its Own Shape

The Canopy and the Byzantine Church

The church is the temple of God (cf. 1 Cor. 3:10–17; 2 Cor. 6:16), *a holy place* [*temenos*—sacred ground within the church walls - J.B.], *a house of prayer* (cf. Isa. 56:7; Matt. 21:13; Mark 11:17; Luke 19:46), *the assembly of the people, the body of Christ* (cf. 1 Cor. 3:10–17, 12:27; Col. 1:24; Eph. 2:19–22). *Its name is the bride of Christ. It has been cleansed through the water of His baptism, it has been sprinkled with His blood, it is adorned like a bride* (cf. Rev. 21:2, 9—with the references to the Heavenly Jerusalem), *and it has been sealed with the fragrant oil* [myrrh, referring to the anointment - J.B.] *of the Holy Spirit, according to the prophetic saying: "Your name is perfume poured out"* (Song of Sol. 1.3.2), *and "We shall run after you into the (sweet) fragrance of your myrrh"* (Job 1.4.2; Song of Sol. 1.4.2), *because it is "Like the precious ointment upon the head, that ran down upon the beard, the beard of Aaron"* (Ps. 132:2 [Ps. 133.2]).

The church is an earthly heaven, where the heavenly God dwells and walks about (2 Cor. 6:16; Lev. 16:12; Deut. 23:5). *It represents the crucifixion, the burial and the resurrection of Christ. It is glorified more than the tent of witness (tabernacle) of Moses, in which are the mercy seat and the Holy of Holies* (cf. Ex. 25–27). *It is prefigured by the patriarchs, foretold by the prophets, founded by the apostles* (cf. Eph. 2:19), *adorned by the hierarchs, and fulfilled by the martyrs.*

. . .

The ciborium represents here the place where Christ was crucified; for the place where He was buried was nearby and raised on a base. It is placed in the church to represent the crucifixion, burial, and resurrection of Christ.

It similarly corresponds to the Ark of the Covenant of the Lord, which is called the Holy of Holies and His holy place. Next to it God commanded that two Cherubim of hammered work be placed on either side (cf. Ex. 25:18)—*for KIB is the ark, and OURIN is the effulgence, or the light, of God.*

Ἐκκλησία ἐστὶ ναὸς Θεοῦ, τέμενος ἅγιον, οἶκος προσευχῆς, συνάθροισις λαοῦ, σῶμα Χριστοῦ· ὄνομα αὐτῆς νύμφη Χριστοῦ· τῷ ὕδατι τοῦ βαπτίσματος αὐτοῦ καθαρθεῖσα, καὶ τῷ αἵματι ραντισθεῖσα τῷ αὐτοῦ καὶ νυμφικῶς ἐστολισμένη, καὶ τῷ τοῦ ἁγίου Πνεύματος μύρῳ σφραγιζομένη κατὰ τὸν προφητικὸν λόγον· «μύρον ἐκκενωθὲν ὄνομά σοι»

(*Cant.* 1.3.2) καὶ «εἰς ὀσμὴν μύρου σου δραμοῦμεν» (*Jb* 1.4.2), ὅτι «ὡς μύρον ἐπὶ κεφαλῆς τὸ καταβαῖνον ἐπὶ πώγωνα, τὸν Ἀαρών» (*Ps.* 132.2.1).

Ἐκκλησία ἐστὶν ἐπίγειος οὐρανός, ἐν ᾧ ὁ ἐπουράνιος Θεὸς ἐνοικεῖ καὶ ἐμπεριπατεῖ, ἀντιτυποῦσα τὴν σταύρωσιν καὶ τὴν ταφὴν καὶ τὴν ἀνάστασιν Χριστοῦ· δεδοξασμένη ὑπὲρ τὴν σκηνὴν τοῦ μαρτυρίου Μωσέως, ἐν ᾗ τὸ ἱλαστήριον καὶ τὰ Ἅγια τῶν Ἁγίων· ἐν πατριάρχαις προτυπωθεῖσα, ἐν προφήταις προκηρυχθεῖσα, ἐν ἀποστόλοις θεμελιωθεῖσα, ἱεράρχαις κατακοσμηθεῖσα καὶ ἐν μάρτυσι τελειωθεῖσα.

. . .

Τὸ κιβώριόν ἐστι ἀντι τοῦ τόπου ἔνθα ἐσταυρώθη ὁ Χριστός ἐγγὺς γὰρ ἦν ὁ τόπος καὶ ὑπόβαθρος ὅπου ἐτςάη . . . ἀλλά διά τὸ ἐν συντομίᾳ ἐκφέρεσται, τὴν σταύρωσιν τὴν ταφὴν καὶ τὴν ἀνάστασιν τοῦ Χριστοῦ εν τῇ ʼΕκκλησία τέτακται.

῎Εστι δὲ καὶ κατὰ τὴν κιβωτὸν τῆς διαθήκης Κυρίου, ἐν ῇ λέγεται ῞Αγια ʽΑγίων καὶ ἁγίασμα αὐτου ἐν ῇ προσέταξεν ὁ Θεὸς γενέσθαι δύο χερουβὶμ ἑκατέρωθεν τορευτά τὸ γὰρ ΚΙΒ ἐστὶ κιβωτός, τὸ δὲ ΟΥΡΙΝ φωτισμὸς Θεοῦ, ἤ φῶς Θεοῦ.

Germanos, Patriarch of Constantinople (d. 733) in his *Ecclesiastical History and Mystical Contemplation,* on the church and the altar canopy[1]

IN THE EIGHTH CENTURY, IN THE MAJOR TEXT *ON THE DIVINE LITURGY*, WHICH the Byzantines used most frequently to explain their church settings and rites, Germanos, Patriarch of Constantinople, writes about the Byzantine church and the canopy by combining highly complex theological symbols subtly intertwined with Biblical architecture and the notion of the place of the sacred.[2] Replete with Biblical quotations, Germanos' writing emphasizes that the place of the sacred is revived through the participation of the church community within liturgical and paraliturgical rites performed in the church. The reality of the church as a "being-place," both the community and the building, is firmly established by typological references to the Old Covenant that pointed to its ontological fulfillment in the New Covenant, which attested to the dual nature of Christ, both divine and human. Hence, Germanos explains the church as the temple of God, a holy place, a house of prayer, an assembly of people, and the Body of Christ. The Old Testament references to the Song of Songs as the love between husband and wife expands towards the understanding of Christ's love for His bride, the Church, as a Christian assembly and manifested through the rites of consecration and baptism in the church as a Christian place of worship.[3] Similarly, the Great Litany and spiritual advancement of the church assembly that mark the beginning of liturgical services and literally all sacraments, often starts after the reading of the psalms, and Psalm 132 (133), written by King David, the first anointed-king, makes a powerful reference to the abundance of the precious ointment and divine grace received by the first-anointed Old Testament High Priest Aaron.[4] By explaining the church as an earthly heaven, Germanos essentially reestablishes earlier theological explanations, such as those in the seventh-century text *Mystagogia* by Maximus the Confessor, who likened the church to the image of the universe composed of both invisible and visible entities, of both an incorporeal intelligent realm and a corporeal world of senses.[5] In this macro-scale ordering

---

[1] *Germanos-a* and in *TLG* lines 1.1–1.15; 5.1–5.9. Translation from Greek into English is adjusted according to translations by *Germanos-b* 57–59 and Marinis (2015) 753–770, esp. 755.

[2] See also Chapter 1.

[3] *Orthodox Study Bible* 882. See also Marinis (2015) 753–770 and Chapter 3 in this volume.

[4] Chapter 3; *Orthodox Study Bible* 765.

[5] *Maximus Conf.-a,* with translations into English in *Maximus Conf.-b,* and into French in *Maximus Conf.-c.*

of the church that points to the space beyond the earthly realm, the place of the Tomb of Christ as the place of His crucifixion, burial, and Resurrection emerges as the critical corporeal architectural model, which, according to Germanos, was glorified more than the Tabernacle known as the moveable tent from Mosaic tradition.

The same architectural models used to define the church building—the Tomb of Christ and the tent of Moses (the Tabernacle) that was replaced by the Ark of the Covenant in the Temple—define the altar canopy, the most hallowed installation nested inside the church. Hence, the canopy, according to Germanos, represents the place of Christ's death and Resurrection, tangibly materialized in the church space (note the reference "The ciborium represents 'here' the place where Christ was crucified"). At the same time, the canopy also represents the Ark of the Covenant, the most sacred object in the Holy of Holies, which disappeared at the time of the destruction of the First Temple,[6] but was vividly preserved by oral and written tradition ("it is called; it is written") including its major spatial pattern defined by the two cherubim.[7] The overlapping notions and spatial models for the church and its canopy, which is, architecturally speaking, a mini church, reveal a highly sophisticated design that in each case points to the Tabernacle as its ultimate architectural model, given to Moses by God himself, the ultimate and universal Creator (cf. Ex. 25:40).[8]

Germanos' explanation is bound to its historical context of the transitional period between the seventh and ninth centuries, which was marked by the political and economic decline of the Byzantine Empire and theological controversies, when the influences of Islam and a number of Christian doctrines, which rejected material images and the human nature of Christ, culminated in imperial promotions of Iconoclasm.[9] An iconophile, who was disdained and exiled from Constantinople during the first Iconoclastic crisis, Germanos actually reasserted the early Christian explanation about the meaning of the altar canopy as the place of Christ's Crucifixion and burial and its relationship to the Ark of the Covenant; an explanation which St. Basil had offered already in the fourth century.[10] The narrative of Christ's Incarnation, Resurrection, and kingship in heaven—all embodied in the locus of the Tomb of Christ—represents the very core of the Byzantine interpretation of the mysteries performed at the altar and of the promises of the afterlife. This theology became firmly established after the Iconoclastic Controversy, in a way solidifying the meanings and use of canopies and their role in the church.[11]

Germanos confirms that a canopy was considered a regular part of ecclesiastical furniture. Due to the changing conditions after the transitional period, not all churches could secure altar canopies, being expensive and large church installations. Their role and presence could have been supplanted either by painted imagery or by vaulted elements of the church buildings. This concept, wherein an individual canopy partakes in the design of the church building and points to the realm it denotes beyond its own, further reveals the many layers of the overall design of the Byzantine church. As late as the fifteenth century, Symeon of Thessaloniki wrote in his *De Sacro Templo* about the altar canopy in the church, confirming this pervasive idea that the canopy and the Byzantine church embraced the architectonics and spiritual meanings of the Earthly and Heavenly Jerusalem embodied in the Holy Sepulchre and the Temple.[12]

---

[6] Regarding the First Temple, see Meek (1995) 34–35.

[7] See also Laderman (2013); Laderman (2003) 97–125; Rosenau (1979); Golitzin (2005).

[8] Ex. 25:40: "And see to it you make them according to the pattern shown to you on the mountain."

[9] See also Chapter 2.

[10] Chapter 1; Table 1, T.22.

[11] *Germanos-b* 16–54.

[12] *Symeon of Thessaloniki* ch. 101, col. 309D; ch. 133, col. 341B–C.

To examine how these religious concepts of framing the sacred Presence and sacred space were embodied in church spaces, this chapter focuses on the Constantinopolitan cathedral Hagia Sophia as the church that set standards for Byzantine architecture. The analysis highlights the typological links between the Church of Hagia Sophia and the Temple as well as between their most sacred fittings—the altar, the Ark of the Covenant, and the Throne of the Lord flanked by cherubim. These architectural models examined through the example of the altar canopy of Hagia Sophia, will reintroduce the question of the Tomb of Christ in Jerusalem and its role in the definition of the altar canopy and the Byzantine church. Indeed, as shown through the analysis of Byzantine texts on canopies, rhetorical images of canopies are complex and often metaphorical, and do not make explicit references to definite forms.[13] Yet they pose the question of whether and to what extent the canopy was visually or spatially related to what it symbolized; the traditional sites in Jerusalem of Christ's crucifixion, burial, and Resurrection; and the believed place of the Lord in the Holy of Holies.

THE TEMPLE AND DIVINE WISDOM: HAGIA SOPHIA IN CONSTANTINOPLE

The sixth-century building project for the Church of Hagia Sophia in Constantinople, built as a structure with a central dome, defined the model for four-columned Byzantine church architectural design based on a nine-square grid and a canopy as a spatial unit.[14] According to Byzantine texts, the church itself was built on the holy model of the Temple. It was dedicated to Holy Wisdom (Sophia), an epithet and the creative agency of the Lord, ultimately related to God and Christ Himself.

According to the legendary account from the *Patria*, a Byzantine collection of various texts compiled in the late tenth century, Emperor Justinian rushed to the ambo and boasted at the dedication of Hagia Sophia: *Solomon, I have outdone Thee!*[15] This exclamation echoes the imperial and religious ideals of the Byzantines to make a church that matches the monumental Temple built by Solomon in Jerusalem. The notion that a church is a temple, which is built on earth as an intelligible image of the invisible, stretched back to the fourth century when Eusebius of Caesarea described the new church at Tyre (317), a foundation of Emperor Constantine I: . . . "[It] is therefore a great Temple, one of those that have been built all round the earth—that is to say this world is lightened by the sun. By his own Word the mighty Creator of the Universe commanded it to be built on earth as an intelligible picture of things, which lie beyond heaven's vaults . . ." (cf. 1 Cor. 2:9).[16] Robert Ousterhout advanced studies on the Byzantine understanding of the Temple by pointing out that the Tabernacle of Moses, Solomon's Temple, Zerubbabel's Temple, Herod's Temple, and the visionary temple of Ezekiel were often conflated into a singular notion of "the Temple."[17] I agree with Ousterhout that the Temple was understood diagrammatically, and hence, its basic architectural features, including numbers, dimensions, and proportions, were extracted from Biblical references, while the major ambition was to preserve the sanctity and the presence of the Temple within the Byzantine-rite church.

---

[13] Chapter 1.

[14] Chapter 4.

[15] *Pseudo-Codinus, Patria-b* 4.27, esp. 266–267. See also *Pseudo-Codinus, Narratio de aedificatione templi Sanctae Sophiae* 143.

[16] *Eusebius, VC* 10.4, 69f.

[17] Ousterhout (2010b) 223–253. See also Krinsky (1970) 1–19.

Indeed, the sixth-century experimentations in church design in Constantinople disclose that the Church of Hagios Polyeuktos (524–527), built immediately before Justinian's rebuilding of Hagia Sophia (532–537), might have been an attempt to reestablish the Temple of Solomon in Constantinople.[18] The basilica dedicated to the holy martyr Polyeuktos (d. 259) was built for Anicia Juliana (ca. 462–528), the last descendant of the former Imperial house before Emperor Justinian I.[19] Hagios Polyeuktos was the largest, and perhaps the most impressive, church built in Constantinople before Justinian's Hagia Sophia and may have served as a model for its construction.[20] The recovered architectural sculpture and general architectural outline of the Church of Hagios Polyeuktos is suggestive of Solomon's and Ezekiel's Temple as described in the Scriptures.[21] The church had a dedicatory poem to Solomon's Temple inscribed along the church building on the exterior of its narthex and in the interior along the entablature in the church nave, which remains preserved in architectural fragments. The opening lines of this long poem that the church visitor would have seen before entering the church include the text: "Solomon, I have vanquished thee."[22] These lines inscribed on Hagios Polyeuktos finished at the very outset of Emperor Justinian's reign also echo the emperor's exclamation and evoke a vivid historical and political scene in Constantinople, a stage for wealthy patrons employing the best talents in the empire to accomplish never previously seen architectural marvels as houses worthy of God.[23]

While little remains of Hagios Polyeuktos itself, which was in ruins already by the thirteenth century, surviving fragments of glass-inlaid marble columns of a massive canopy from the church extend the picture of richness and liturgical opulence in sixth-century Constantinople. Unique in a style typical for Middle Eastern traditions, the architectural sculpture of Hagios Polyeuktos was made on-site especially for the church, possibly by a Sassanian workshop.[24] The choice of Persian builders would be deliberate, since the Second Temple of Solomon was probably built by a Persian building workshop as well (cf. 1 Kgs. 5:30).[25] Date-palm trees, twisting vine-grape leaves, pomegranates, and peacocks, carved in deep relief, decorated the walls of Hagios Polyeuktos. A peacock, the bird of Juno and Byzantine empresses, in the case

---

[18] Harrison, M. (1986); Harrison, M. (1989); Ousterhout (2010b) 223–253. Bannister (1968) 3–32 proposed that the architectural design of Old St. Peter's in Rome, with its volumetric cube containing the canopy and the underground space where the relics of St. Peter's were deposited, measured 20 cubits; its numbers, dimensions, and proportions being directly related to the Temple in Jerusalem. I thank Richard Etlin for calling my attention to the work by Bannister. See also Etlin (2015).

[19] Harrison, M. (1989); Harrison, M. (1986).

[20] The possibility that Hagios Polyeutkos was domed was first promoted by Harrison, M. (1989) 130–131, and accepted by Ćurčić (1992) 16–38; Ćurčić (2010) 189. Bardill (2006) 339–370 contends, however, that the church was built without a dome. As not enough archeological evidence remains to confirm either possibility, I am still more inclined towards the idea that the church was built with a dome, especially in the light of the general trend of the experimentations with domed basilicas and massive domed structures in sixth-century Constantinople.

[21] Harrison, M. (1989) 138–139.

[22] χρόνον δ' ἐβιήσατο μούνη, καὶ σοφίην παρέλασσεν ἀειδομένου Σολομῶνος, νηὸν ἀναστήσασα θεηδόχον, οὗ μέγας αἰὼν οὐ δύναται μέλψαι χαρίτων πολυδαίδαλον αἴγλην·

She [Anicia Juliana] *alone has overpowered time and surpassed the wisdom of the celebrated Solomon, raising a temple to receive God, the richly wrought and gracious splendour of which a great epoch cannot celebrate.*

Lines 48–50 of the dedicatory poem, inscribed at the entrance to the church outside the narthex of Hagios Polyeuktos. Whitby (2006) 159–188; Harrison, M. (1989) 8–9, 137–139.

[23] See also Mango and Parker (1960) 233–245. On the political connotations of the references to Solomon's Temple in sixth-century Constantinople, see Ousterhout (2010b) 223–253.

[24] Harrison, M. (1986); Harrison, M. (1989) 122–123.

[25] Sharon (1987) 21–42.

of Hagios Polyeuktos, probably also stood in the place of zoomorphic cherubim with wings and numerous eyes, suggested by the eyes on the peacock's tail feathers. The entire visual repertoire resembled the imagery from the Temple veil and a model of the Heavenly City.[26]

The sculptural decoration of the canopy of Hagios Polyeuktos also resembled the gem-studded architecture associated with the heavenly models (see Fig. 2.41). The design of the canopy columns from the sanctuary of Hagios Polyeuktos is comparable with the representations of canopies depicted in the fifth-century mosaics of Hagios Georgios in Thessaloniki, a canopy structure from the sixth-century Syriac *Rabbula Gospels,* fol. 1b (Fig. 2.66), and the inlaid marble columns of the canopy from the Church of Hagia Euphemia in Constantinople and Hagios Ioannes in Hebdomon (Fig. 2.40).[27] The incrustation on these columns points to Solomon's Temple garnished "with precious stones of beauty" and gold (2 Chron. 3:6) and St. John's depiction of the Heavenly City embellished in jasper, sapphire, chalcedony, emerald, sardonyx, sardius, chrysolite, beryl, topaz, chrysoprasus, jacinth, amethyst, gold, and transparent glass (cf. Rev. 21:19–20). The last three—amethyst, gold, and transparent glass—have been actually recovered from the canopy columns found in the Hagios Polyeuktos.

As demonstrated by Martin Harrison, the dimensions of the Church of Hagios Polyeuktos were very closely related to the dimensions of the Temple as presented in Biblical sources.[28] The church foundations were exactly 100 Byzantine royal cubits in length, replicating the 100 cubits of Solomon's Temple, and were 100 Byzantine royal cubits in width, replicating the dimensions of the 100 cubits of the Temple platform (cf. 1 Kgs. 6–7; 2 Chron. 3–4; Ezek. 41:13–14). The church sanctuary of 20 cubits in span replicated the dimensions of the Holy of Holies in Solomon's and Ezekiel's Temple (cf. 1 Kgs. 6:19; Ezek. 41:4).

In Hagia Sophia, Justinian could have emulated and advanced the architectural concept of Hagios Polyeuktos and its decorative splendor, invoking the heavenly realm in many respects. Above all, by daring to build Hagia Sophia with its dome that was 100 Byzantine feet wide, Justinian potentially made reference to the Temple in Heavenly Jerusalem. Hagia Sophia was also an enlarged and structurally improved version of Hagios Polyeuktos, which had aimed to replicate the lost Temple in Jerusalem.[29] Moreover, even if the architectural decoration and inscriptions in Hagios Polyeuktos acknowledged it as the Temple for Byzantium, the church was dedicated to a Christian martyr-saint, just like the largest and most venerated contemporary churches in Rome were dedicated to St. Peter and other apostles and saints. The Church of Hagia Sophia, in contrast, was at least from the fifth century, if not from its inception, dedicated not to a person, but to a concept—to Holy Wisdom (Sophia)—where Byzantine wisdom replete with the wisdom of Solomon and Biblical revelation interacted to produce a full-blown Christian humanism.[30]

Hagia Sophia, the most-celebrated church of the entire Byzantine Empire, is dedicated to the concept of Wisdom, which in Eastern Orthodox Christianity is considered to belong to its holy tradition and texts.[31] The texts of the *Book of Proverbs* and the *Book of Wisdom,* both attributed

---

[26] Harrison, M. (1989) 137–144; Barker (1998) 1–21; Lidov (1999) 340–353; Lidov (2007) 135–176, 366–371.

[27] According to Lidov (1999) 340–353, the canopied structures from Hagios Georgios are part of the architectural assembly of the Heavenly Jerusalem, as described by St. John (Rev. 21:18–21). For the facsimile of the Rabbula Gospels, see Cecchelli (1959). See also Chapter 2.

[28] Harrison, M. (1989) 137–144.

[29] Ćurčić (1992) 16–38.

[30] Cf. Wis.; Cor. 1:21f, 2:1ff.

[31] The *Book of Wisdom* is found in the Septuagint as a part of the Old Testament and is included in the Eastern Orthodox Books.

to Solomon, open complex and subtle relations between Sophia (Wisdom) and the Lord, and in turn raise questions about how an elaborate canopied core and altar canopy from the Church of Holy Wisdom in Constantinople was related to such complex concept. Namely, theological-philosophical cosmogony opened the relationship between the cosmological and cosmogonic idea of uniqueness and oneness of the Almighty Creator and Father.[32] Subsequently, because the Creator in Genesis is represented like an architect, the creative agency embodied in the concept of Sophia opens philosophical questions on the materiality, form, beauty, and meaning of architectural elements of the church. Sophia was "the radiance that streams from everlasting light, the flawless mirror of the active power of God, and the image of His goodness. Though she is one she can do all things; So while remaining in herself, she renews all things; And in every generation, she passes into holy souls and makes them friends of God."[33]

The first altar canopy from Hagia Sophia, which was crushed when the first dome of the church collapsed, might have been similar to the coeval altar canopy from Hagios Polyeuktos, which, being made of multi-gemmed marbles, suggested heavenly models. The first canopy from Hagia Sophia was part of the sanctuary installation, which was done in sardonyx, sapphire, mother of pearl, gold, crystal, and silver, [34] and was replaced by a canopy that was sheeted in silver and decorated in precious stones.[35] The choice of silver is worth noting.[36] In the Old Testament and in antiquity, silver was used for a great variety of purposes and was treasured for its commercial value (cf. Gen. 13:2; 23:15–16). Following the narrative of the Scriptures, silver may have been used for altar canopies in emulation of the silver used for the vessels for the sanctuary (cf. Ex. 26:19; 27:17; 2 Kgs. 12:13) and especially for the sockets, ornaments, and hooks for the pillars of the Tabernacle (cf. Ex. 26:19; 27:17; Ex. 27:17; 38:19). Motifs of embroidery, ropes, acacia, and silver columns are recognizable from the narratives of the Scriptures related to the structural elements and decoration of Solomon's Temple (cf. 1 Kgs. 7, 2 Chron. 3) and the desert tabernacle made of four pillars of acacia overlaid with gold, upon four bases of silver (cf. Ex. 26:32). The canopy installation is suggestive of a tent, a basic, free-standing, and portable architecture that temporarily marks the place, and as such closely associated with the notion of the sacred tent, the Temple veil, the Tabernacle (2 Sam. 7:6), and the common meaning of the place of the Holy of Holies (cf. 1 Kgs. 6:19), believed to be the place of meeting with the Lord,[37] and the Judeo-Christian prototype of the dynamic sacred space activated by the human encounter with the divine (see Fig. 1.9).[38]

---

[32] About the influence of Plato's *Timaeus* on the vocabulary and philosophical notions in the *Book of Wisdom*, more in Pelikan (2000) 67–87.

[33] Wis. 7:26–27; cf. Jn. 15:15.

[34] *Pseudo-Codinus, Patria-b* 4.28 (268–269). See also Fobelli (2006) 48–53.

[35] *Paulos Silentarios-a* cols. 2147–48; *Paulos Silentarios-b* in *TLG* lines 719–753. See also Chapter 1; Table 1, T. 40.

[36] See also Chapter 2.

[37] The word "tabernacle" is a derivative from the Latin *tabernaculum* (tent). Tabernacle in Greek was construed as *skene* (tent). Tabernacle in Hebrew is referred to by *'ohel* (tent), *'ohel mo'ed* (tent of meeting), *'ohel ha-'eduth* (tent of testimony), *mishkan 'ohel* (dwelling), *mishkan ha-'eduth* (dwelling of testimony), *mishkan 'ohel* (dwelling of the tent), *beth Yahweh* (house of Yahweh), *godesh* (holy), *miqdash* (sanctuary), and *hekal* (temple). The various expressions in the Hebrew text for the Tabernacle make it possible to form an idea of its construction, and the description of a "portable tent-like sanctuary" seems the most accurate. Morganstern (1945) chs. 6 and 7; *Modern Catholic Encyclopedia*, s.v. *tabernacle*; Meek (1995) 30–39.

[38] Lidov (2007) 135–176, 366–371, esp. 144, has already pointed to the Hebrew term *tavnit* ("copy, pattern"), which was used for the entire design and creation of the Tabernacle as a prototype of sacred space and space-paradigm.

The use of silver and selected motifs for the altar canopy in Hagia Sophia give rise to a hypothesis that Emperor Justinian not only wished to emulate the canopy-ark, but wanted to go a step farther, and also simultaneously materialize the idea of the Throne of Wisdom. The canopy's four silver columns and arches may have referred to the expression of one faith sustained by the four columns of the Evangelists,[39] who were the pure words of the Lord "as silver tried in a furnace of earth, purified seven times" (Ps. 12:6). Justinian's canopy conceptually and visually alluded to the embodiment of the Lord through His Son and sublime references to the human body and nature of Christ.

When in the sixth century Paulos Silentarios described the silver canopy from Hagia Sophia, he emphasized that each of the fixed silver bowls outfitting the canopy expressed beauty and were set in a kind of candelabrum, similar to a candle but that "burns not"; "the candle flashes a silver ray, not the light of fire."[40] The streams of such ethereal silver light, reflecting from the canopy, contrast with the "light of fire," or earthly light, and recall "the radiance that streams from everlasting light" known from the apocryphal description of the Holy Wisdom (Wis. 7:26). The ninth-century illumination of *Prudentius Psychomachia* (Leiden, University Library, *Codex Burmannorum* Q.3 fol. 148v), known as *Sapientia seated in the Temple*, presumed to be a copy of the late antique original, depicts the personification of Wisdom (*Sapientia*) seated on a throne in the form of a globe.[41] The freestanding globe-throne is sheltered by a domed, temple-like structure. The canopied throne is centrally set within an open courtyard with twelve towers and twelve gates, three on each side positioned in the cardinal directions, providing a sub-textual reference to the Heavenly Jerusalem as described by St. John (cf. Rev. 21:12–13). The iconographic motif is similar to representations of Christ in Majesty, as in another of Justinian's churches, San Vitale in Ravenna, whose apsidal mosaic shows Christ in Paradise enthroned on a globe.[42]

The architectural concept of Wisdom on a canopy-like throne is consistent with the altar canopy from Hagia Sophia crowned with a silver orb, as described by Silentarios.[43] The orb on top of the canopy is consistent with the imagery of a place of epiphany and the throne of Christ at the time of His Second Coming when Christ will be in the center of the heavenly sanctuary (cf. Rev. 4). The size of the orb did not matter because the meaning of the sphere was, I would suggest, related to the geometric and supra-spatial ideas the Greeks had nourished since antiquity.[44] The orb as a singular, supra-spatial signifier of the place of propitiation is, therefore, placed above the canopy that frames and signifies the sacred space in the other, earthly realm.

Silentarios confirms that the life-giving cross at the top of the globe was the place of propitiation (ἵλαος, *ilaos*).[45] When Silentarios described the cross surmounting the canopy in Hagia Sophia, he alluded to the appearance of God in the heavens and the "mercy seat" (ἱλαστήριος), where the Lord appeared above the Ark of the Covenant in the Tabernacle (cf. Heb. 9:5, Ex. 25, 26, etc.). One is reminded of the Ark cover, a place of expiation (Heb. *kăpparā*) or God's throne as related to the cherubim and their touching wings. The

---

39 *Paulos Silentarios-a* cols. 2224–2225.

40 Table 1, T.40; Chapter 1.

41 Ćurčić (1996) 55–59.

42 Brenk (1980) 39–52.

43 Table 1, T.40; Chapter 1.

44 Downey (1946) 22–34, with extended references including those to Timaeus. On the terminology of "supra-spatial" attributes of God in Orthodox Christianity, see Stăniloae (1994) 171–184. See also *Symeon of Thessaloniki* 292A, 337–340.

45 Table 1, T.40.

Ark supported the mercy seat, a single slab of gold decorated with two attached golden-winged cherubim, with their faces turned towards the seat.[46] When stretched and joined, their wings formed a hemispherical shape.[47] Placed in the inner, closed part of the sanctuary, the Holy of Holies, the Ark symbolized the Sign of Meeting, an actual dwelling place of the Lord, who invisibly manifested His Presence and communicated His will enthroned between the cherubim.

As shown by Elisabeth (Elisheva) Revel-Neher, the Ark was often depicted in gold above two cherubim as in the Middle Byzantine manuscripts that copied the sixth-century text of Cosmas Indicopleustes (Vatican copy of Cosmas Indicopleustes, folio 48r).[48] In the *Seraglio codex fol. 333r, Smyrna octateuch fol. 154r,* and *Vatican graecus 746 fol. 325v,* the Ark of the Covenant is sheltered by a canopy, to which the Bible makes no reference, suggesting that the cherubim were replaced in the motif of the Ark by a domed canopy.[49] In some cases, such as in the *Vatican graecus 746, fol. 281r,* the canopy over the Ark is topped with a cross.[50] Since the Divine Presence, the *She'kinah,* spoke to Moses from between the cherubim, the canopy roof obviously assumed the role of the missing cherubim. The sixth-century Syriac hymn dedicated to Hagia Sophia, the Cathedral of Edessa, describes the "cherubim of its altar."[51] This columnar canopied installation was either ornamented with carved representations of a pair of cherubim, or it also may be that the domed lid of a canopy represented cherubim, just as the ten columns of the sanctuary installation only symbolized but did not actually depict the ten apostles. Thus, the touching wings of the cherubim in a three-dimensional space would have easily acquired the form of a domical or conical roof of a canopy, confirming the most frequent shape of archeologically preserved canopies.[52]

It has been already contemplated that the Byzantines drew imagery of the Ark from Torah shrines rather than from Biblical descriptions, though I would propose that both sources inspired the Byzantines.[53] At the fourth-century Hamat Tiberias, at Husifah, at the sixth-century Beth Alpha and Na'aran, the motif of the Ark is accompanied with a motif of the zodiac wheel—two concentric circles inscribed within a square, so that the central circle depicts Helios riding on a chariot with the moon and the stars in the background, and the outer is divided into twelve segments for the zodiac signs and their names.[54] Texts by early rabbis interpreted Helios as the *She'kinah* in the center, while the signs of the zodiac reveal striking analogies with contemporary liturgical poems from synagogues and point to the Ark as the place of the divine Presence.[55] The

---

46 On the varying accounts of the cherubim in the Old Testament (Gen. 3:24; Ex. 25:18f) and in the description of the Temple (1 Kgs. 6:29; 1 Kgs. 7:29, 36; Ezek. 1:1ff, Ezek. 10:1ff, Ezek. 41:20): Farbridge (1970) 264–265; Woudstra (1965) 75.

47 *Philo, De Cherubim* 7.

48 Revel-Neher (1995) 405–414; Gutmann (1971) 22–29 [reprinted in: Gutmann (1989)]; Mouriki (1970) 92.

49 Revel-Neher (1995) 405–414.

50 Ibid.

51 McVey (1983) 91–121, esp. 95, 105.

52 See Chapter 2.

53 Mouriki (1970) 98–100; Hoppe (1994) 19, 31; Meek (1995) 67–73. See also Rodov (2010) 65–98.

54 Some scholars have interpreted the zodiac as a liturgical calendar, although a fixed calendar was not introduced until about 325, and the zodiac wheel cannot be understood as a calendar in the modern sense. On the problem, see Hoppe (1994) 59.

55 *The Holy One Blessed-Be-He showed Abraham all of the mazalot (zodiac) surrounding his shekinah (Divine Presence); . . . and said: Just as the zodiac surrounds Me, with My glory in the center, so shall your descendants multiply and camp under many flags, with My shekinah in the center.*—Midrash Devarim Rabbah, according to Gutmann (1984) 1313–1342.

correlation between zodiac signs and the Ark has analogies in Christian contexts, too. A mid-fourteenth-century illustration of Psalm 148 from the church in the monastery of Lesnovo, which shows the zodiac signs inside of a Byzantine church, confirms the continuity of the tradition that envisages the Ark as the microcosmic dwelling place of the divine Presence beyond the earth and heaven.[56] The depiction of Christ inside of a double medallion, with a rayed nimbus, and seated on the cherubim, recalls the Old Testament notion that the Lord appears between the cherubim that guarded the Ark of the Covenant and represented His throne.

The Byzantine imagery of the Ark, therefore, embraced traditional conceptions of the throne of Wisdom and the heavenly throne of Christ. The models could have been enriched with those from the Torah shrines of Jewish synagogues and the Roman imperial tradition, where thrones extended the aura of deified emperors. In an eleventh-century illuminated copy (Florence Laurenziana MS. Plut. IX.28, fol. 129v) the Ark of the Covenant in the Tabernacle is accompanied by a text that simultaneously defines the Ark as the place of propitiation (ἱλαστήριον, mercy seat) and a "type of the Lord Christ according to the flesh."[57] Thus, the canopy can be seen as a furnishing that both emphasizes Christ's Incarnation and even signifies the reality of His Presence in absence. This symbolism is strikingly resonant in the Tomb of Christ, which was conceived as a focal place of divine dwelling, even though it remained empty after His Resurrection.

JERUSALEM ARCHITECTURE AND THE BYZANTINE CANOPY

Germanos' eighth-century explanation of the altar canopy, repeating St. Basil's fourth-century reasoning, emphasizes the long-standing Byzantine notion that the altar canopy represents the holy sites in Jerusalem—Golgotha and the Tomb of Christ, and the Ark of the Covenant.[58] Golgotha and the Tomb of Christ remained palpably present in Jerusalem during medieval times, while the Ark of the Covenant was lost during the destruction of the Temple in the first century. In several important texts on the Tomb of Christ and the Temple in Jerusalem, Robert Ousterhout underscores the architectural differences between the two structures and how, through philosophical and theological transformations from the Old to the New Covenant, the Tomb of Christ became the new Ark of the Covenant.[59] He highlights that this complex idea was enriched by Byzantine liturgical practices and the development of the church as a Christianized Temple that in turn shaped the perception and memory of these major holy sites. The relations between specific solutions in Byzantine churches and known architectural elements of the Tomb of Christ and Golgotha and the Temple were mostly conceptual, yet seemingly dependent on the contexts of the turbulent history of these sites in Jerusalem and the Byzantine perception of their decisive architectural features for the theological and physical modeling of altar canopies.[60] Altar canopies simultaneously stood for all these sites in Jerusalem and merged them into a singular space within churches. Therefore, a particular question is how and to what extent experiences

[56] More in Gabelić (1998) 183f, pl. LIII.

[57] Mouriki (1970) 93.

[58] See Chapter 1.

[59] Ousterhout (1990) 44–53; Ousterhout (2010b) 223–253.

[60] For example, St. Basil the Great wrote about ciborium in his *mystagogic* history, a theological work, and by its nature, questionable to what extent he was referring to the physical appearance of the holy sites in Jerusalem.

from Jerusalem reflected upon the architectural framing of Golgotha and the Tomb of Christ and memories of the architecture of the Temple and further resonated with concurrent Byzantine canopies and churches.

The Holy Sepulchre, the Tomb of Christ, and the Byzantine Canopy

The Holy Sepulchre in Jerusalem remained empty after Christ's Resurrection (*Anastasis*), marking the place in which Christ was believed to be bodily present after His death upon the Cross. Golgotha (literally "the place of the skull") and the Tomb of Christ are acknowledged as two separate places in the Gospels, the earliest references to the sites of Christ's Passion and Resurrection.[61] Despite frequent remodeling, the places commemorating the Cross upon which Christ was crucified and His Tomb remained two crucial foci at the Holy Sepulchre complex.[62]

In the fourth century, following the discovery of the True Cross by Empress Helena, she and her son, Emperor Constantine, supported a massive architectural campaign in Jerusalem, which resulted in the building of the Anastasis-Golgotha complex, consisted of two buildings: the Anastasis Rotunda and the Martyrium basilica.[63] In the process, the Tomb of Christ, originally a rock-cut tomb, was established as a freestanding *aedicula* inside the Anastasis Rotunda, while the Golgotha rock was incorporated into the inner atrium located just outside the sanctuary apse of the basilica (Fig. 5.1). The complex was frequently destroyed and rebuilt after the seventh century, marked by the emergence of Islam in the Middle East as well as Persian and Arab conquests of Jerusalem.[64] If not a church during the restoration under Patriarch Modestus in 626, by the 670s the Rotunda served at least as a chapel, and it definitely served as a church by the ninth century.[65] The architecture of the entire complex significantly changed after its destruction under the Fatimid Caliph al-Hākim bi-Amr Allah (996–1021) in 1009, when he also set the Tomb of Christ on fire.[66] Despite Byzantine interest in Jerusalem, they never reestablished a political presence there.

---

[61] The evangelists recorded that Jesus was crucified on Golgotha (Matt. 27:33; Mark 15:22; Luke 23:33; John 19:17; cf. Heb. 13:12), was buried, and resurrected from his Tomb. Christ was buried in an unused rock-cut tomb, which was sealed by a great stone rolled in front of the door (Matt. 27:59ff; Mark 15:43ff; Luke 23:53ff; John 19:40ff). The tomb was in a garden at the site of the Crucifixion (John 19:41–42) outside the walls of Jerusalem but relatively close to the city (John 19:20).

[62] The literature on the history and architecture of the site is immense: Vogüé (1860); Macpherson (1892) 417–436; Vincent and Abel (1926) vol. 2: 337–360; Harvey, W. (1935); Ovadiah (1970); Coüasnon (1974); Wilkinson (1974) 83–97; Corbo (1981–1982); Ovadiah and de Silva (1982); Ovadiah and de Silva (1984); Ousterhout (1989) 66–78; Ousterhout (1990) 44–53; Patrich (1993) 101–117; Hoppe (1994); Ward Perkins (1994b); Folda (1995); Biddle (1999); Krüger (2000); Pringle (2007) vol. 3: 6–72; Marković (2009) 28, 188–210; Ousterhout (2010b) 223–253.

[63] *Eusebius, VC* III, 33.1; Davies (1957) 171–173; Krautheimer (1986) 60–63, 462–463; Kühnel (1987) 81; Wilkinson (1993) 23–27; Patrich (1993) 101–117; Hoppe (1994) 111.

[64] Canard (1965) 16–43; Ovidiah and de Silva (1982) 122–170; Wilken (1988) 214–217, 233–237; Ousterhout (1989) 66–78; Patrich (1993) 101–117; Hoppe (1994) 108–109.

[65] Arculf, who visited Jerusalem ca. 670, mentions two altars made out of the stone rolled from the Tomb of Christ, which are also later recorded in ninth-century and subsequent documents. *Arculfus* in *PPTS* 3 (1897) 8–9; *Jerusalem Pilgrims* 258–259.

[66] Canard (1965) 16–43. The only known contemporary official Byzantine source that mentions the demolition of the Holy Sepulchre is the eleventh-century Skylitzes, *Synopsis historiarum* for the years 811–1057, while its thirteenth-century illustrated version omits the episode. Tsamakda (2002). According to Biddle (1999) 77–78, Skylitzes account is consistent with independent accounts by a Christian Arab observer, Yahya ibn Sa'id of Antioch, and by the Persian traveler Nasir-i-Khusrau, who reported the Church of the Holy Sepulchre as completely restored in 1047. Michael Psellus in *The Chronographia*, when describing the years 976–1078, made no mention of the event.

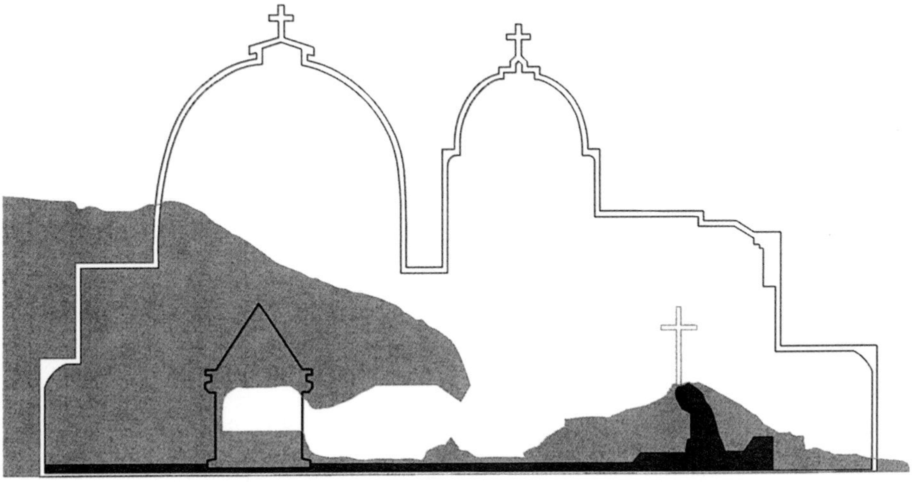

FIGURE 5.1 *The Holy Sepulchre and the Tomb-shrine of Christ in Jerusalem, ca. fourth–twelfth centuries, cross-section showing the locations of the living rock of Golgotha upon which Christ was crucified, and the Tomb of Christ, first enclosed by an aedicula in the fourth century; the general outline of the church is from the Crusader, twelfth-century period and later.* DRAWING HEIDI REBURN

By the 1040s, their reconstruction of the site resulted in the rebuilding of the Rotunda and the Tomb-shrine within it, while the basilica ceased to exist after the eleventh century (Fig. 5.2).[67] The entire complex thus became much smaller, with the main entrance to the complex and subsequently to the Rotunda, relocated to the south of the courtyard. The Rotunda gained a massive sanctuary apse on the east. With newly added galleries and chapels, the Rotunda church was filled with relics and established as a typical contemporaneous Byzantine-rite church with multiple sacred foci within.[68] During the medieval building campaigns by Crusaders, from 1099 onward, the essential architectural program established by the Byzantines remained intact, while these later constructions reestablished the church to serve the Latin rite. A new choir replaced the eastern apse of the Byzantine church; its chapels on the east were supplanted by chapels with the same dedications surrounding the new apse; but no significant changes were made to the Tomb-shrine itself.[69] Byzantine imperial donations for the Tomb continued during that period, though not to support significant architectural interventions.[70] By the twelfth century, the knowledge

[67] Bogdanović (2014a) 1–21; Krsmanović (2001) 1–32; Talbot (2001) 97–110; Hoppe (1994) 108–109; Ousterhout (1989) 66–78; Canard (1965) 16–43. The Crusaders' emphasis solely on the recovery of a relic of the True Cross in 1099 and the elaborate descriptions of the processions in the Church of the Holy Sepulchre underscore that both the Rotunda and the Tomb-shrine of Christ were largely in use by the end of the eleventh century. Folda (1995) 34ff; Biddle (1999) 76f.

[68] Corbo (1981–1982) 230; Ousterhout (1989) 66–78; Ousterhout (1990) 44–53; Wharton (1992) 313–325; Patrich (1993) 101–117. By the eleventh century, a tradition had already been established in Constantinople of rebuilding churches that essentially served as huge reliquaries, exemplified by the churches of Ss. Sergios and Bachos, Myralaion, Mangana, and most famous of all, the Church of the Virgin of Pharos. Lidov (2005) 1–26; Magdalino (1987b) 51–64; Mango (1956) 123+125–140.

[69] The only significant change of the Tomb *Aedicula* occurred in the 1120s, when King Baldwin II (r. 1118–1131) re-encased the shrine in marble. Corbo (1981–1982); Hoppe (1994) 108–109; Ousterhout (1989) 66–78; Folda (1995) 53–82.

[70] For example, late in the twelfth century, Manuel I Komnenos (1143–1180) donated a golden cover for the burial bench of the Tomb of Christ. *Phocas* in *PPTS* vol. 5, 21; Kurtz (1907) 104–107, esp. 102; Ousterhout (1989) 66–78; Folda (1995) 75.

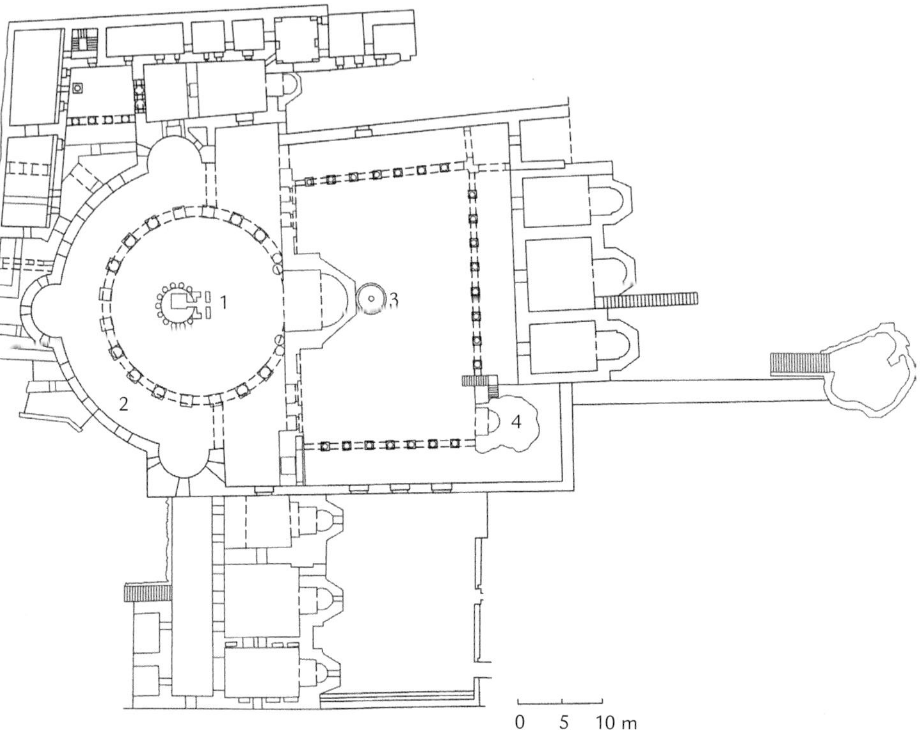

FIGURE 5.2 *The Holy Sepulchre and the Tomb-shrine of Christ in Jerusalem, ca. seventh–eleventh centuries, plan: 1. The Aedicula Shrine—Tomb of Christ; 2. Church of the Holy Sepulchre (also known as the Church of Anastasis/Resurrection)—Rotunda; 3. Omphalos; 4. The Rock of Golgotha.* DRAWING HEIDI REBURN

held by the people of Constantinople and all across the Byzantine Empire about Jerusalem and the Holy Tomb had diminished, as if the physical reality of the Holy Sepulchre was detached from the Byzantine imperial and historical realm.[71] Therefore, by that time, the knowledge of the architecture in Jerusalem was mostly based on shared but dissimilar memories, pilgrimage accounts, and *eulogiai* (objects and images that carried blessings from the site) that were often representations of the eyewitnesses.[72]

For the Byzantines, the Holy Sepulchre was both the *aedicula* shrine of the Tomb of Christ and the Rotunda Church of the Resurrection, which architecturally framed the Tomb as the place of burial and Resurrection of Christ.[73] Both the Rotunda and the Tomb-shrine were known by their generic, diagrammatic features. Medieval visitors and modern scholars generally agree on the major architectural form as well as the conceptual and spatial (even if not necessarily strictly geometrical) centrality of Christ's Tomb in the Anastasis Rotunda, which

[71] In the twelfth century, George Kedrenos and John Zonaras mainly copied Skylitzes account of the negotiations between the Byzantines and the Fatimids after al-Hakim's destruction. Byzantine princess Anna Komnene also mentioned the Holy Sepulchre, but mostly in reference to the Crusaders who officiated in the church, revealing a Byzantine imperial non-presence on the site. Though Anna Komnene speaks of the death of the Latin King Godfrey (ca. 1060–1100), who was buried in the Church of the Holy Sepulchre, it seems as if she was unaware of the fact and only mentions his death in Jerusalem. *Georgius Cedrenus; Zonaras; Alexiad-a* XI 8.1.

[72] Grabar (1958); Vikan (1982) 20–25; Kühnel (1987) 93–95; Ousterhout (1990) 44–53; Talbot (2001) 97–110; Ousterhout (2010b) 223–253; Hoffmann and Wolf (2012); Kühnel et al. (2014); Bogdanović (2014a) 1–21.

[73] Bogdanović (2014a) 1–21.

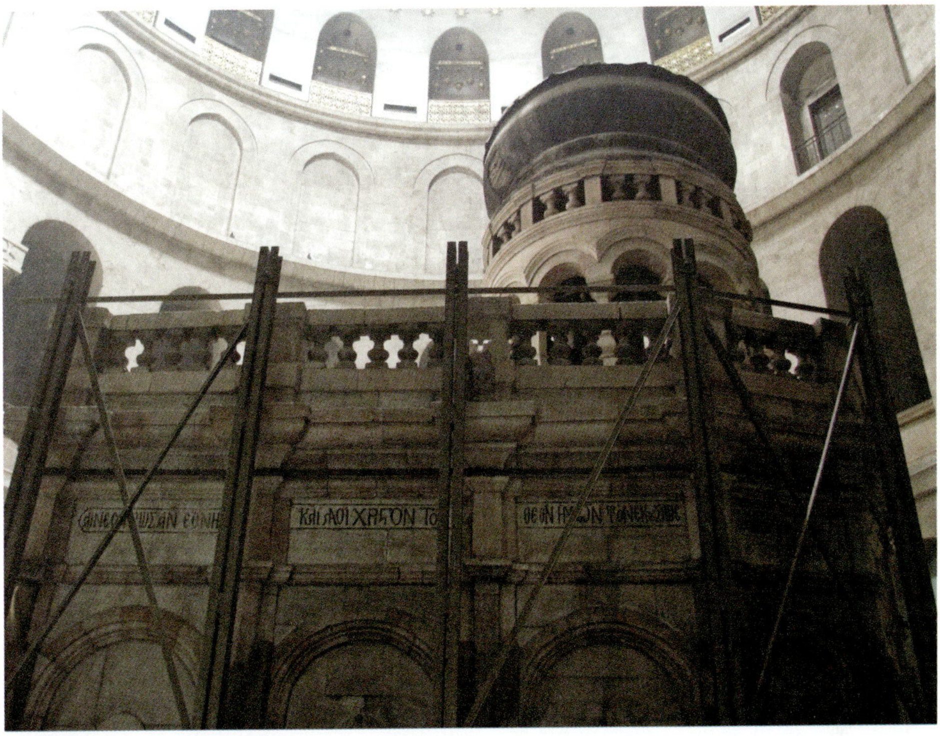

FIGURE 5.3 *The Aedicula Shrine—Tomb of Christ within the Church of the Holy Sepulchre in Jerusalem, nineteenth century with twentieth-century steel shoring.* PHOTO SVETLANA SMOLČIĆ MAKULJEVIĆ

remained unchanged from the time of Emperor Constantine I.[74] Everything else related to its architecture is more-or-less hypothetical.[75] The Anastasis Rotunda was made in the form of two concentric cylinders, the central one being the higher of the two.[76] The canopy-like core of the Rotunda sheltering the Tomb, most probably originally a chamber, was enveloped by an *ambulatorium*.[77] Following a series of rebuildings, the Tomb *Aedicula* of Christ is today essentially a nineteenth-century installation with a canopy on its top (Fig. 5.3).[78] Yet it seems that

---

74 Smith, B. E. (1956) 16–29; Kühnel (1987) 81; Hoppe (1994) 111; Biddle (1999) 28ff. Already in the seventh century, Arculf, a pilgrim from Gaul, left a schematic drawing of the Tomb chamber in the center of the Rotunda [Adomnan's *De locis sanctis* (ninth century) in Biddle (1999), fig. 25]. Byzantine sources *Jerusalem Pilgrims* 258–259 and *Abbot Daniel* 10 also speak of the centrality of the Tomb. Krautheimer (1986) 60–61 assumes that the Tomb had been in the very center of the Rotunda since its inception. Colvin (1991) 115 suggested the possibility that the Tomb was slightly off-center, towards the west, in the light of more recent research on Constantinian architecture. Kroetch (2013) 21–22 brings forward a valuable seventh-century account by an Armenian pilgrim, which highlights that the Tomb was not in the exact center of the Rotunda. The reconstruction drawings of the Anastasis Rotunda confirm this geometric off-centeredness of the Tomb. Bogdanović (2014a) 1–21.

75 Regarding the architecture of the Tomb, for example, scholars have proposed at least five distinct types: a rock-cut tomb chamber, an empty sarcophagus, a canopy-like structure, and a two-story, and a single-story architectural structure. *Egeria* 173–175; Ward Perkins (1954) 81; Krautheimer (1960) 17–40; Smith, M. T. (1968) 34–35; Barag and Wilkinson (1974) 179–187; Biddle (1999) 21ff; Johnson (1986) 80–91; Johnson (2014).

76 Wilkinson (1974) 83–97; Biddle (1999) 66; *RBK* vol. 3, s.v. *Jerusalem*.

77 Imperial *mausolea* of the period are also distinguished by the central core rising higher than the enveloping structure. Johnson (2014); Colvin (1991) 115.

78 Biddle (1999) 76f.

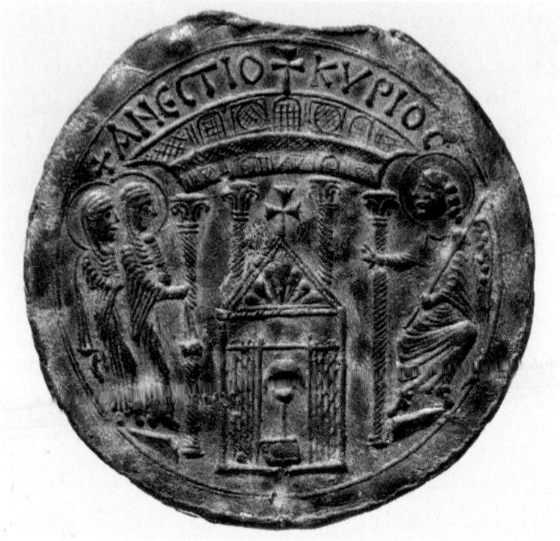

FIGURE 5.4 *Pilgrim's ampulla no. 18, reverse.* © DUMBARTON OAKS, BYZANTINE COLLECTION, WASHINGTON, D.C.

the canopy was not incorporated into the architecture of the *aedicula* shrine before the ninth century.[79]

Wilkinson's reconstruction of the Tomb as it might have looked between the fourth and sixth centuries suggests that it was an enclosed shrine, recurrently named by contemporaries as an *aedicula* ("small house"), and that it was spatially and visually similar to St. Demetrios' ciborium without any open columnar canopy as a constitutive element. Wilkinson based his reconstruction on the Tomb descriptions by an early pilgrim to Jerusalem, the nun Egeria (381–384); visual representations on the sixth-century *ampullae* from the Monza and Bobbio collections; and a stone model of the Tomb of Christ in Narbonne (Fig. 5.4).[80] According to this proposed reconstruction, the Tomb-shrine was a single-story structure with two separate spaces—an antechamber and a tomb-chamber. The burial bench was in the north part of the tomb-chamber, which had a square plan in the interior.[81] The exterior of the Tomb was oval, freed on all sides from the living rock, covered with marble and decorated with columns. The structure had a slightly pointed, conical or pyramidal roof, with an orb surmounted by a cross at the top.[82] The roof rested on columns, which were depicted with spiral fluting in numerous representations on pilgrims' *ampullae*.[83] The existence of a canopy resting on columns and set on the top of the *aedicula* that is proposed by Wilkinson is difficult to prove.[84] The porch of the Tomb was possibly a prism with a gabled roof and a pediment with a scallop shell motif. The pediment was supposedly supported by columns with spiral fluting, as represented on most Christian pilgrims' flasks. The entire *aedicula* was enclosed by railings, and thus additionally framed

---

79 Bogdanović (2014a) 1–21.

80 *Egeria* 173–175; Wilkinson (1974) 179–187; Bonnery (1991) 7–41; Biddle (1999) 21ff; Sekules (2005).

81 Willibald, a pilgrim at the end of 724, described the basic shape of the tomb as a square, which may be related to the square-like plan of the inside of the burial chamber as it has been preserved until the present. Biddle (1999) 71.

82 Smith, B. E. (1978) 16–29.

83 See also Chapter 2.

84 Smith, B. E. (1978) 16–29; Patrich (1993) 101–117, esp. 107.

within the central space of the Rotunda. Little is known about the architecture of the Holy Sepulchre after its reconstruction by Patriarch Modestus in 626. Armenian pilgrim HovsĒp did not discuss the architectural features of the shrine, yet another seventh-century pilgrim, Frankish pilgrim Arculf, mentioned its marble casing and gold plating and spoke of the Tomb as a *tugurium* ("little house").[85]

Some architectural changes to the Tomb most likely did occur during the transitional period between the seventh and ninth centuries. These changes are reflected in the contemporary accounts and how they named the Tomb-shrine an ambo instead of an *aedicula*. The earliest representations of the Tomb of Christ reveal repetitive motifs such as railings, scalloped shell niches, (spiral) columns, a lamp suspended from the top of the tomb, and occasionally hangings suspended from the entrance to the Tomb.[86] The elements that were not mentioned after the seventh century are the seashell hood of the shrine and its curtains. Columns, lamps, the enclosure, and the stone rolled from the entrance are recorded consistently. The high-quality materiality of the shrine, which included marble, silver, and copper plating, were also memorable features throughout the long-standing history of the Tomb. It is my understanding that these motifs were loaded with rhetorical capacity and were carriers of meanings to the Byzantine elite, while the pervasiveness or loss of some of the ornamental features also reflected shifts in the memory and cultural perceptions about the major messages the Tomb carried.[87]

For example, the scalloped shell motif known from the earliest phase of the Tomb-shrine decoration was a potent theme in pagan and Jewish traditions. It might have recalled the origin of the niches in semicircular form of the natural grottoes, as in the cave-tomb of Christ.[88] The rounded top of the Jewish depictions of the Ark and of the Roman funerary altar was very often in the form of a scallop shell.[89] Among the Greeks, the shellfish was sacred to Aphrodite, and closely related to her birth in a conch, illustrating the mystical relation between the goddess and love that she symbolizes. Therefore, as attested on numerous Roman funerary monuments, the shell was a symbol of birth and of regeneration and, subsequently, within the Christian artistic tradition, a symbol of the Resurrection.[90] Emperor Constantine had the Holy Sepulchre complex constructed on the site of a demolished shrine of Aphrodite,[91] a fact that suggests that some of the seashell sculptural fragments of the pagan shrine might have been reemployed in the decoration of Christ's Tomb, albeit for a new, distinctively Christian message.

In the Greek pagan tradition, shells alluded to the soul's voyage across the Ocean to the Blessed Isles and to the cosmic significance of water as the celestial path to the afterlife,

---

[85] Kroetch (2013) 21–22; *Arculfus* 6.

[86] *Egeria* 173–175; Biddle (1999) 21ff; Bonnery (1991) 7–41; Bogdanović (2014a) 1–21.

[87] Bogdanović (2014a) 1–21.

[88] The motif is also known from ancient shrines and from exotic architecture represented in the Second and Fourth Pompeian wall painting style. *Roman World, passim.*

[89] Kleiner (1987) 31ff; Toynbee (1996) 44–45. As a symbol of the renewal and continuation of life, the date-palm tree is known from the ancient Assyrian and Babylonian traditions and was used by the Hebrews as a symbol of the righteous man. The architectural decoration of Ezekiel's heavenly Temple (cf. Ezek. 40:16ff; 41:18ff) and Solomon's Temple (cf. 1 Kgs. 6:29ff) with the flourishing palm trees were highly suggestive symbols of the righteous (cf. "the righteous shall flourish like the palm-tree" Ps. 92:12). Farbridge (1970) 27–49. Moreover, the Greek terms for the phoenix and date palm are the same (φοῖνιξ), referring to the renewal of life. Evans (1896) 127.

[90] Déonna (1917) 312–416, esp. 309, 408.

[91] *Eusebius, VC* II, 26.3.

which in Christianity acquired the meaning of rebirth in the rite of baptism.[92] St. Cyril of Jerusalem (ca. 315–386) interpreted the Biblical story of the Flood as the prefiguration of Christ's baptism, in which Noah stood for Christ and the Ark for the Church outside of which no salvation is possible: "salvation came in the time of Noah by the wood [the Cross] and the water, and there was the beginning of a new creation."[93] The funerary liturgy that developed in Alexandria emphasized the same motifs of seashells, eagles, peacock tails, palmettos, and light.[94] By the ninth century, the Rule of the Monastery of St. John Stoudios in Constantinople provided remote topographical reflections of Christ's baptism and Resurrection associated with the seashore and the office of lamp-lighting during the Easter season.[95] The symbolic significance of seashell decoration perhaps preserved the symbolism of corporeal salvation, in which death is followed by rebirth, and the symbolism of spiritual rebirth, in which death is reversed by spiritual resurrection.[96]

Few archeological fragments from churches and synagogues in Palestine reveal the combination of seashell design and lighting devices. The top of the Ark *aedicula* discovered in the early Palestinian synagogue of Nabratein contains a small hole just above the scalloped shell design.[97] It was presumably made to accommodate a chain-held lamp, which was always burning in front of the scrolls housed in a synagogue. This archeological fragment confirms that lamplight was an important constituent of the Ark, referencing the Biblical descriptions of the lighting of the Ark of the Covenant (Ex. 26:32; 2 Chron. 4:20) and indicating that the light in the sanctuary symbolized the light of the *She-kinah* (God's Presence) itself.[98] A marble plaque from the Church of Sustia, east of the Sea of Galilee, has a rare depiction of a canopy-like arch.[99] A lamp suspended from its seashell top suggests that the Ark-*aedicula* and its symbolism enriched with Christian references were known to the early Christians in Palestine. In the Book of Revelation of St. John the Divine, the presence of Christ upon His Second Coming is manifested in the midst of seven

---

[92] The "Island of the Blessed" was a place of departure for the souls of the deceased who had won the favor of the gods, and was the future home of all mankind. The idea of the "Island of the Blessed" is recognizable already in the Gilgamesh epic, where Gilgamesh, as the Babylonian Noah, was granted eternal life. Early Roman ideas describing the world where *Manes* (souls) dwelt are not explicitly recorded. In time, two distinct places came to be dwellings of the dead. According to some beliefs, all human souls went to the Blessed Isles across the Ocean, while according to the others, they went to the sky and hemispheres. Farbridge (1970) 216–217, with further reference; Kleiner (1987) *passim*; Toynbee (1996) 36–38, 44–45.

[93] *PG* 33, col. 982 A–B.

[94] Evans (1896) 310–311. See also Chapter 3. All of these motifs were connected with the soul's departure from the body, and its journey to a heavenly destination in the paradisiacal fields, beside the waters, in the light of the saints:

. . . nourish them in a place of pasturage beside the waters of comfort, in the paradise of joy, whence sorrow and sighing and weeping have fled away, in the light of saints. Raise up their flesh also in the day which thou hast appointed according to thy true promises that cannot lie: grant them the good things of thy promises. . . . – Liturgy of St. Mark, according to Thomas, T. (2000) 51.

[95] *Next morning, at the second hour of the day when the precentor knocks three times, we assemble in the Church of [St. John] the great Forerunner. Vested in their priestly robes, the priests and all the brothers take up the venerable crosses and the holy icons. We circle the vineyard close to the monastery with all of us saying in a loud voice the "Christ is risen." Then, we go out in the same manner to the shore of the sea. —Studios* in *BMFD* 101.

[96] Wharton (1992) 313–325.

[97] Hoppe (1994) 31.

[98] For the example, Solomon through building the Temple brought the Lord from thick darkness; i.e., through building the Temple (faith), the Lord's light (presence) is kept burning (2 Chron. 6:1).

[99] Piccirillo (2006) 51–113, fig. on p. 73.

candlesticks (Rev. 1–4). Paulos Silentarios and Germanos both described the altar canopy as the "ark of light," a model for the Christian image of the Ark of the New Law in Christ.

Hangings, possibly curtains suspended before the entrance to the Tomb of Christ, depicted on some *ampullae,* are mentioned by the pilgrim Etheria who tells us that veils decorated with gold were hung for the occasion of the Feast of the Epiphany.[100] The representations of curtains on Monza-Bobbio *ampullae* corroborate the use of festal veils on Christ's Tomb at Epiphany and adding the suggestion that they were also used at Easter and on the *dies enceniarum,* the consecration day of both the Martyrium and the Anastasis Rotunda.[101] Veils at the Tomb may have been votive offerings as well, as Antonius the Martyr, a native of Placentia, reported in ca. 570.[102] Curtains at the Tomb of Christ were not mentioned in surviving sources, yet the feast of the *enceniarum* (*enkainia*) for Hagia Sophia as the Holy Sepulchre is attested by the eleventh century, which conceptually identified Hagia Sophia as the Holy Sepulchre, emphasizing the importance of the complex in Jerusalem in Byzantine liturgy.[103]

With the Byzantine rebuilding of the Tomb of Christ in the seventh century, decorative features such as the seashell motif known from the early representations of the Tomb were not reused, and their original meanings were lost. What continued to be mentioned are generic but highly recognizable forms, like a lamp suspended from the top of the Tomb, or twisted columns, which fostered group identity and a sense of sacred presence.[104] Luxury materials with shining qualities like marble, copper, or silver mentioned in the descriptions of the Tomb could have been easily related to the imaginative visions of Heavenly Jerusalem that reflected heavenly glory. The railings, which according to eyewitnesses were either wooden or bronze, indicated the division between the heavenly and earthly realms. Significantly, when Germanos wrote his liturgical text, he also associated the bronze railings with the Holy Sepulchre and the sanctuary screen.[105]

As the Anastasis Rotunda served either as a chapel or a church, probably since the seventh century, the meaning of the Tomb of Christ was charged with liturgical meanings and devotional practices known from Byzantine-rite churches. The stone in the Tomb-shrine, which according to the Evangelists initially enclosed the Tomb of Christ and was rolled away by an angel, was split into two parts and displayed for veneration.[106] During the Easter celebration, the stone also served as an altar, thus making the Tomb of Christ a church within the church. However, the Tomb of Christ did not look like coeval altar canopies in Byzantine churches, and its association with them was more conceptual and symbolic.[107]

At least since the late ninth century, judging by the description of Constantinopolitan Patriarch Photios (858–867, 877–886) who wrote about the Tomb based on eyewitness accounts, the Byzantines called the Tomb-shrine of Christ an ambo.[108] When the Russian abbot Daniel of Chernigov visited Jerusalem between 1105 and 1107, just after the Crusader

---

[100] Smith, M. T. (1968) 46.

[101] *Jerusalem Routes* chs. 3–8, esp. 76, 101. Smith, M. T. (1968) 45–46.

[102] *Antoninus* in *PPTS* vol. 2, 15.

[103] Ousterhout (2010b) 223–253.

[104] Gray (2001) 91–97.

[105] See Chapter 4.

[106] *Jerusalem Pilgrims* 258–259; Bogdanović (2014a) 1–21.

[107] Even visual representations of altar canopies are rarely associated with the Holy Sepulchre in Jerusalem. An extraordinary example is the early thirteenth-century fresco of the Communion of the Apostles in the apse of the *katholikon* of Akhtala monastery in North Armenia, where the upper part of the depicted altar canopy can be associated with coeval imagery of the Tomb of Christ. Lidov (1999) 340–353.

[108] *Jerusalem Pilgrims* 258–259; Bogdanović (2014a) 1–21. On Photios, see also Dvornik (1953) 67–98.

conquest, he similarly called the Tomb-shrine an ambo.[109] Associations of canopied tombs with the ambo in the Holy Land went beyond the Tomb of Christ. In the twelfth century, Joannes Phocas described the tomb of the Virgin in Gethsemane also as an ambo: "in the midst of the church stands the tomb, which is like a pulpit (*ambon*) wrought of stone in the shape of a building composed of four arches."[110] However, the ultimate source seems to be the Tomb of Christ according to John of Wurzburg, who in the same century compared the Virgin's tomb to Christ's.[111] All these eyewitnesses were aware of the lack of human bodies in such canopied "ambo-tombs," which also suggests that their understanding was guided by liturgical references, Gospels, and hymnography.[112] Indeed, Patriarch Germanos considered the ambo an important liturgical furnishing, signifying the stone of the Holy Sepulchre, which the Angel rolled back from its entrance.[113]

The descriptions of the Tomb as redesigned by the Byzantines by the ninth century also mention its canopied top. Photios spoke about the chimney-like structure on the roof, and Russian abbot Daniel of a "turret resting on pillars, and terminating in a cupola."[114] Numerous visual representations of the Tomb-shrine of Christ dating from the eleventh to the sixteenth centuries may actually refer to the Byzantine reconstruction of the Tomb-shrine as an installation with a canopied top.[115] The majority of the surviving depictions of the Tomb represent the Tomb-shrine as a massive two-storied structure with a domed canopy over the burial chamber, in a way also referencing surviving examples of massive canopied ambos, like the ambo from Kalabaka recently re-dated to the Middle Byzantine period.[116] The canopied roof of the Tomb of Christ in Jerusalem most likely was related to the miracle of the Holy Fire (Ἅγιον Φῶς, literally meaning in Greek "Holy Light"). This miraculous event preceding Orthodox Easter, when light emanates in the Cave of the Holy Sepulchre and forms a column of fire that is used to light the church candles, was attested to in both Arabic and Christian sources since the late ninth century when the major architectural reconstruction of the Tomb possibly happened.[117]

The first accounts of the miraculous fire at the Holy Sepulchre coincide with the time of persecutions of Christians in Palestine and with the period of the final formulation of the liturgical rite for Holy Saturday, which celebrates the burial of Christ, His descent into Hell, and His Resurrection. A number of seventh- to eighth-century hymnographers, all linked with Syro-Palestine and above all with the monastery Mar Sabas just outside Jerusalem, had established

---

[109] *Daniel* in *PPTS* vol. 4, 10–14.

[110] Phocas also described the tomb of Rachel as "being formed in the shape of a vault supported by four arches." *Phocas* in *PPTS* vol. 5, 21, 31.

[111] *John of Würzburg* in *PPTS* vol. 5, 51–52.

[112] See also pilgrims' accounts by *Daniel* in *PPTS* vol. 4 and *Phocas* in *PPTS* vol. 5, who both combine their descriptions of the holy sites with excerpts from the Scriptures and the hymnography of the liturgical celebrations of the feasts related to the specific holy places, events, and people.

[113] *Germanos-b* 63.

[114] *Jerusalem Pilgrims* 258–259; *Daniel* in *PPTS* vol. 4, 14.

[115] Biddle (1999) 100ff and fig. 31 on p. 31.

[116] See Chapter 3.

[117] References to the miraculous lighting of Paschal lamps and the light ceremony in Jerusalem in previous periods that were recorded by Eusebius and the nun Egeria should not be related to the phenomenon of the Holy Fire, which is always associated with the cave within the shrine of the Tomb of Christ. *Eusebius, Eccl.Hist-a* 45–906; *Eusebius, Eccl.Hist-b* VI. 9, 249; *Egeria* 90. Some of the earliest dated sources dealing with the Holy Fire are from the ninth-century writings by the monk Bernard and by Arab witnesses. *Palestine Pilgrims* xiv; *Jerusalem* 262. On the Holy Fire, see also Auxentios of Photiki (1999) ch. 1; Lidov (2006a) 58–70.

the general pattern for the Byzantine liturgical rite of Holy Saturday.[118] Thus, the Byzantine paschal hymnography of the ninth century repeatedly alludes to Christ's victory over death and the place of His burial through images of light. The ceremony of light that occurs at the Holy Sepulchre in conjunction with the celebration of Christ's Resurrection in Byzantine churches as developed by the ninth century are parallels too obvious to be dismissed.

In the Holy Sepulchre, which by the ninth century unquestionably served as a church, for Holy Saturday, the rite of the Holy Fire must have gained a special meaning. The vigil lamps inside the shrine of the Cave of the Holy Sepulchre and the other lamps in the church would be extinguished, and then the Holy Sepulchre would be sealed and remain in complete darkness. Before entering the tomb, the Patriarch would be searched for any implements that might ignite a flame.[119] After the supplications of the Patriarch inside the Tomb and the faithful outside, it was believed that the Holy Fire spontaneously ignited the lamps.[120] With this light the Patriarch would have ignited his candles, exited into the dark Rotunda, and passed the light to the faithful. Thus, the Holy Fire expresses the universal theme of renewal, the triumph of light over darkness, and becomes a powerful sign of the Resurrection, the promise of the Second Coming and of eternal life in the Heavenly Jerusalem. The Patriarch would reiterate the imagery of Christ as light and the theme of His victory over death, which in the context of the Easter celebration offers an alternative to mortality, Christ becoming the incarnate hypostasis of the eternal God.[121]

Therefore, for the Byzantines, the miracle of the Resurrection would transcend the splendor of the liturgical cycle and the imagery of the hymnography. The festal greeting "Christ is Risen!" would take the faithful back to the tomb-cave and the eager expectation of His Second Coming. The total effect of the liturgical rite is to recreate mystically the event of the Resurrection. The relics of the Tomb of Christ, the True Cross, and the Holy Fire are seen to transcend their own materiality, and the past is brought into line with the present, not just as history, but as revelation. In this moment, the end of history and the apocalyptic future of God's kingdom, as announced by Christ, were already made accessible. The symbols of the liturgy thus became mediators of the paradoxical transformation of time into eternity.[122]

In other words, at least since the ninth century, the Byzantine understanding of both the Tomb of Christ in Jerusalem as an ambo and the Tomb's canopied top was closely related to their understanding of the Tomb of Christ as the place of the Resurrection of the Incarnate

---

[118] St. Sophronios, Patriarch of Jerusalem (d. 644), St. John of Damascus (ca. 680–ca. 740), and St. Kosmas of Maiuma (ca. 685–ca. 750) took part in formulating the rite of Holy Saturday, which assumed its more-or-less present form in ninth-century Constantinople. Two monks of the monastery of Studios in Constantinople, St. Theodore (759–826) and St. Joseph (762–832), later an Archbishop of Thessaloniki, compiled and edited the general pattern of the rites for the entire period of Lent. *Lenten Triodion* 40–43. On the concise historical development of the liturgical rites for Easter, see *Great Lent* 119–122. Sophronios in his collection of verses writes of the light of Christ's Resurrection that shines from the Sepulchre, and he identifies the Light of the Tomb with Christ Himself: *PG* 137, cols. 3920–25.

[119] Auxentios of Photiki (1999) 28–37; Canard (1965) 16–43.

[120] Two twelfth-century accounts of the Holy Sepulchre that mention the Holy Fire, those by a certain Perdikos, a *protonotarios* from Ephesus, and an anonymous pilgrim, simply record that the Holy Fire descends and lights the lamps of the Holy Sepulchre: *PG* 133, cols. 965, 976.

[121] According to the life of Saint Meletios the Confessor, a thirteenth-century monk, when he visited the Holy Sepulchre, he "found worthy to behold the grace-filled light which in those days continually radiated from the Life-bearing Tomb." *Meletios Conf.* 1. The reference also reveals that the Byzantines did not associate the grace-filled, miraculous light exclusively with the rite of the Holy Fire. *Daniel* in *PPTS* vol. 4, Appendix.

[122] Eliade (1961) 172.

Lord and as a channel of communication with God. The narrative from Exodus 40:34 and Leviticus 10:1–2 with Old Testament references about God's appearance in the form of fire was occasionally depicted in Middle Byzantine manuscripts, sometimes even revealing that miraculous fire could have been collected and held in vessels and could provide visual counterparts to the Byzantine understanding of the Holy Fire in Jerusalem.[123] By that time, the Byzantines understood the Tomb of Christ as a shrine for two powerful relics, the Holy Tomb in which He was interred and from which He rose, and the Holy Fire that visibly and palpably confirmed that Christ is Risen. Therefore, it is also understandable why Orthodox pilgrims called the *aedicula* the holy *kouvouklion* from at least the fourteenth century and possibly much earlier.[124] At some point between the early eleventh and early twelfth centuries, the interior of Tomb was also remodeled and acquired the three holes on the side cover of the tomb bench, following models of the shrines for private veneration.[125] In that overarching construct, the canopied Tomb was a reliquary, an ambo, and also functioned as an altar. These changes indicate a possibility that, after the ninth century, the architectural and religious framing of the Tomb reflected the overarching meanings of canopied installations in contemporaneous Byzantine-rite churches.

As explained by Germanos, both the church and the canopy also reflected upon the place of Christ's crucifixion. Two canopies in the complex of the Holy Sepulchre were related to the notion of Golgotha. At least by the tenth century, if not earlier, a canopy installation that marked the location of the Cross of Golgotha existed in the complex of the Holy Sepulchre, judging by the tenth-century descriptions by Western pilgrims and confirmed by the twelfth-century account of Abbot Daniel (see Fig. 5.2).[126] The practice of the veneration of the relics of the True Cross enshrined by canopy installations in Constantinople, Cyprus, Serbia, and Venice confirms shared ideas that canopies served as architectural memorials of the Cross and Golgotha.[127] Another canopy or small chapel, in the center of the atrium just opposite the eastern apse of the Rotunda in Jerusalem, also marked the *omphalos*, literally the navel or the traditional place of the center of the World.[128] The navel of the World was associated with the site of Adam's tomb, although the location of Adam's skull was also related to the site of Golgotha and the Crucifixion, both within the same complex but at another location.[129]

To return to Germanos' explanation of the altar canopy as the single place of Christ's crucifixion, burial, and Resurrection, it remains unquestionable that various sites from the complex at Jerusalem were conflated and symbolically transferred to and framed by a single altar canopy nested inside the Byzantine church. This notion is additionally supported by visual evidence, such as the representation of the canopy from a stone plaque from

---

[123] Lidov (2006a) 58–70.

[124] In 1375, the Russian pilgrim Archimandrite Arsenius called the Tomb of Christ the *kuviklion*. *PG* 165, col. 517. See also Chapter 1, term *kouvuklion*.

[125] Beliaev (1998) 203–219. In addition to round openings on the marble slabs encasing the Holy Sepulchre, the same apertures on the slabs enshrining the Manger of the Nativity of Christ and the shrine of the sacred Tree from which the Cross for Christ's crucifixion was made are mentioned by the twelfth-century Russian pilgrims Abbot Daniel and John Phokas, a monk. *Daniel* in *PPTS* vol. 4, 51; *Phokas* in *PPTS* vol. 5, 32. See also Chapter 4.

[126] *Daniel* in *PPTS* vol. 4, 10–14; Milner (1996) 77–99.

[127] See Chapter 3 on Hagia Sophia.

[128] On the *omphalos* in the eleventh century, see Patrich (1993) 101–117.

[129] *Daniel* in *PPTS* vol. 4, 13–14; *Seawulf* in *PPTS* vol. 4, 12.

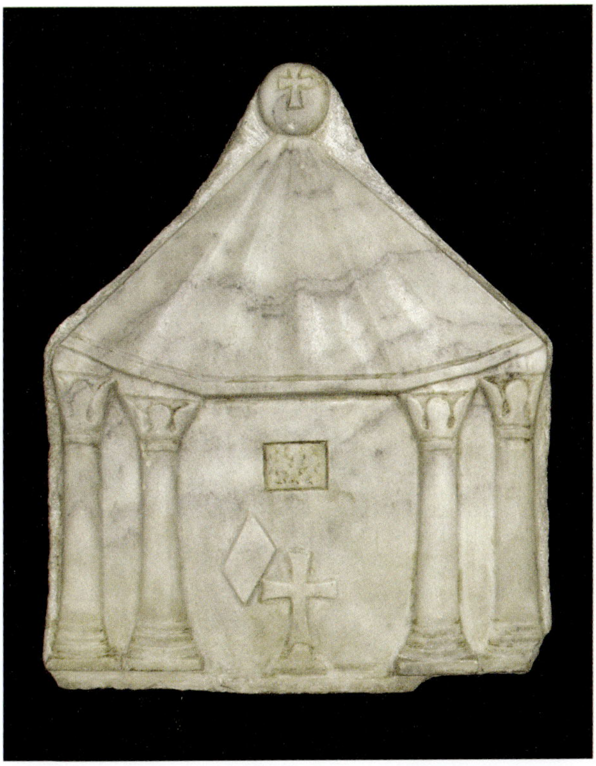

FIGURE 5.5 *Marble plaque, Holy Sepulchre and Cross of Golgotha (?) under the canopy topped with a cross (on the reverse side of the plaque is carved the sea shell), late sixth or early seventh century.* © DUMBARTON OAKS, BYZANTINE COLLECTION, WASHINGTON, D.C.

the Dumbarton Oaks Collection, often identified as the Tomb of Christ (Fig. 5.5).[130] A square-like hole engraved below a canopy symbolizes the square chamber of the Tomb. However, the Cross of Golgotha is also depicted and confirms that the Byzantines conflated the two sites of the Tomb *Aedicula* and the Cross of Golgotha by depicting them under a single canopy. Moreover, such a thesis confirms the possibility that one church could have multiple canopies, as the Anastasis complex itself had. Multiple objects, such as ambos and altar canopies, could share similar topology, and under the power of symbolic association, their potential meanings and functions could expand. The Tomb-shrine in the Anastasis church in Jerusalem, after the transitional period, looked like and was known as an ambo and occasionally served as a chapel with its own altar. The canopied ambo from Kalabaka, though with a post-Byzantine painting of the Entombment of Christ on its eastern flight of stairs, suggests that the Tomb of Christ could have been associated with the ambo in the Byzantine tradition, both literally and architecturally (see Fig. 3.4).[131] Yet other canopies symbolizing Christ's Tomb, such as those found in the Church of Dečani, Kosovo, Serbia, and Sveti Choveli, Georgia, were independent structures. In each case, these canopies designating the Tomb of Christ extended the hallowed sanctuary space beyond the sanctuary barrier into the nave of the church (Fig. 5.6).

---

[130] Underwood (1950) 43–138, figs. 39, 40; Evangelatou (2003) 181–204.

[131] See also Ousterhout (1981) 311–321, fig. 7.

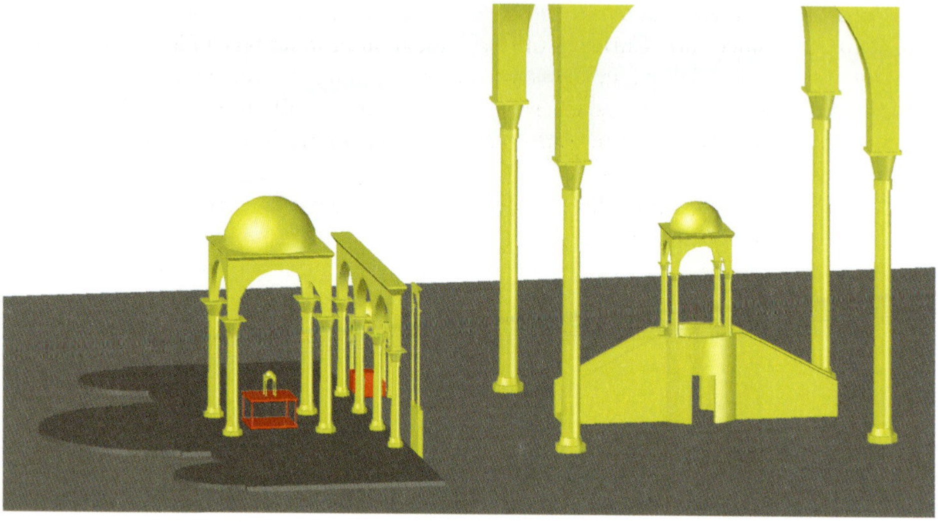

FIGURE 5.6 *Diagrammatic reconstruction of the spatial relationship between the altar canopy and the ambo in a Byzantine church.* DRAWING ZHENGYANG HUA

The Jerusalem Temple, the Tomb of Christ, and the Byzantine Canopy

In a Byzantine symbol-system, where the Church becomes a Christianized Temple, the relevance of the Temple of Jerusalem cannot be overstated. The physical presence of the Ark and the Tabernacle symbolized the covenant between God and the people of Israel (1 Sam. 4:3), and from Davidic times on, when the tent of Moses (Ex. 25–40) was replaced by the Temple made of stone (Deut. 12:2–27), Jerusalem represented the associated meaning of the covenant and of the heavenly realm.[132] As the Tomb-shrine of Christ has been identified with the Anastasis Rotunda, similarly the Ark of Covenant was often related to the Temple.[133]

The symbolic union within the Christian edifice of two distinct segments of the Jerusalem Temple—the altar area and the Holy of Holies featuring a Torah shrine—can be interpreted both spatially and liturgically. The Christian church appropriates architectural symbols of the Jewish Temple and expands their meanings to fit into a Christian typology. Thus, the Holy of Holies is seen to be Christ's Tomb, the menorah becomes the lamp burning inside the tomb, and the altar on Mt. Moriah, to which Abraham led his son for sacrifice, becomes the Rock of the Crucifixion, to which God conducted his own first-born son as the only pure sacrifice.[134] Furthermore, the stone that the angel rolled away from the Tomb of Christ after the Resurrection perhaps has a specific link to the Ark of the Covenant and to the Ark of Noah. For exegetes did not describe it as round, a shape that would fit the description that the stone was rolled, but as cubical, a shape that brings it closer to the shape of the two Arks, which preceded the fullness of salvation and the Heavenly Jerusalem.[135]

---

[132] Different aspects of the Covenant between God and his people and the union of the Ark, the Temple, and Jerusalem are elaborately treated in Kühnel (1987) 17–28.

[133] Rosenau (1979) 19–25.

[134] Ousterhout (1990) 44–53; Grabar (1979–1980) 62–63, 105–141; Evangelatou (2002) ch. III. 2. *Christ's Resurrection;* Taft (1980–1981) 45–75.

[135] Ousterhout (1990) 44–53 connects the cube with the Altar of Incense at the Temple, but I would like to extend the hypothesis that it referred to the form of the Ark as suggested by those trained in the Antiochene school of exegesis. See Chapter 1. On the cubic shape of the Heavenly Jerusalem, Carile (2012).

Although theologians and pilgrims have occasionally conflated the Temple and the Holy Sepulchre since early Christian times,[136] not all interpretations uniformly agree with descriptions from the Holy Land. Photios' account illuminates his understanding of the relationship between the Holy Sepulchre, the Temple, and the Byzantine church. In the first place, he clearly distinguishes the Temple of Solomon from the Tomb of Christ:

> The court of Solomon, itself the ancient Holy of Holies, but now occupied by the godless Saracens and providing them with a site for a mosque, has not been familiar to any one of the Christians in Jerusalem, for Christians cannot enter the places kept holy by Saracens. But the saving Tomb of the Lord of all is one bowshot away from the ancient Jerusalem, which is said to be "High," the meaning of "Sion," which means the distance is two stades. For the ancient city surrounded Sion, which served as a watchtower and a garrison, like a large city wall surrounding a smaller place.[137]

Photios confirms that a mosque was constructed on the remains of Solomon's Temple and was closed to Christian veneration, and that the Tomb of Christ across the mosque assumed the place and meaning of Zion.[138] This association of the Tomb of Christ with Zion is most vividly expressed through small-size liturgical vessels that served as receptacles for the Eucharistic host, which were often made in the shape of churches and were known as *Jerusalems* and *Zions* (see Fig. 1.4).[139] Kathryn Blair Moore has demonstrated how in the medieval West, at least until the twelfth century, the Temple was represented by the Dome of the Rock, which as a domed centrally planned building served as an inspiration for the depiction of Mary's life in the Temple.[140] In Byzantine tradition, Mary's life is also represented in the context of canopy-like structures that stood for the memory image of the Temple (see Figs. 2.38, 2.64). The Temple was variously represented as a canopy with both domical and pyramidal roofs, and rather than from Byzantine experience of sacred architecture in Jerusalem, these images of the Temple most likely came, as Ousterhout has also suggested, from the notion of the altar canopy and vaulted *bema* of the Byzantine church, their meaning closely intertwined with liturgy and hymnography.[141]

The Tomb of Christ, the Canopied Reliquary, and the Dome of a Byzantine Church

The architectural elements of the lantern of the Tomb of Christ as established by the ninth century potentially shared the vocabulary of coeval and later Byzantine church domes. By the Middle Byzantine period, the general trend in ecclesiastical architecture, even though greatly reduced in scale in comparison to Constantinian and Justiniac architecture, was to make a centralized church with a core that essentially was a dome on four columns.[142] Even the so-called atrophied cross-domed churches, such as the later remodeled twelfth-century core of the Constantinopolitan Church of Christ Savior in Chora; the twelfth-century

---

136 *Jerusalem Pilgrims* 176–77; Kühnel (1987) 102–110; Brubaker (1999) 291–302; Evangelatou (2002) 185–187.

137 *Jerusalem Pilgrims* 258–259.

138 For the topographical significance of these Jerusalem sacred places for the Muslims, Christians, and Jews, see Grabar, O. (2005) esp. chapter titled "Space and Holiness in Medieval Jerusalem."

139 See Chapter 1, altar canopy.

140 Moore (2017).

141 Ousterhout (2010b) 223–253.

142 Ćurčić (1978) 17–27.

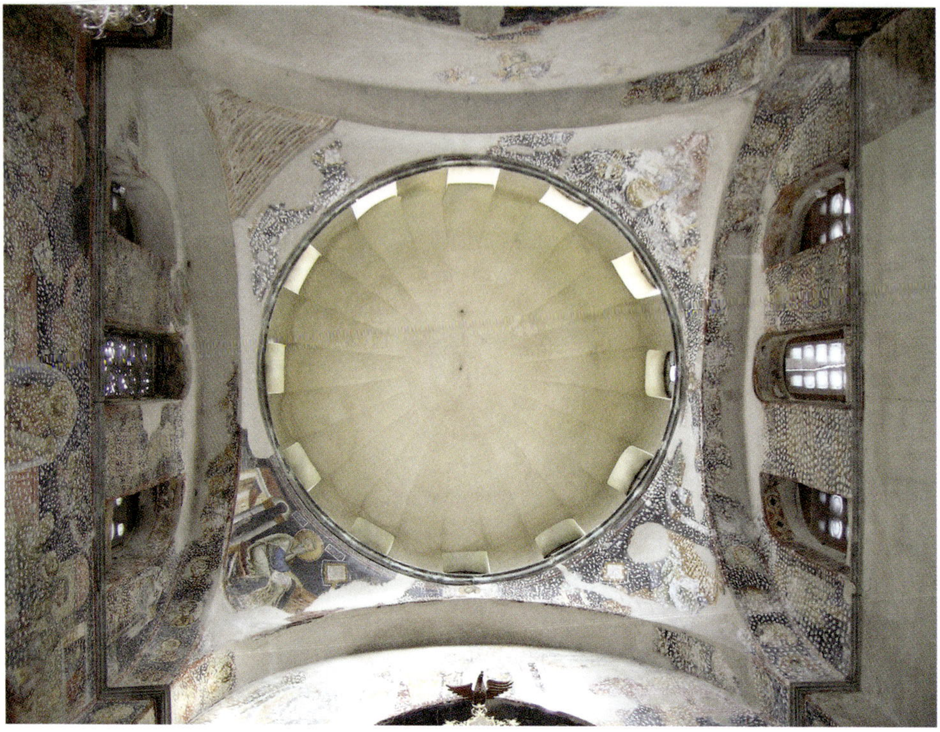

FIGURE 5.7 *Mother of God, Studenica monastery, Serbia, begun in 1183; interior view showing fresco decoration and scalloped dome.* PHOTO IVAN DRPIĆ

Church of the Mother of God at Studenica, Serbia; and the fourteenth-century King's Church of Joachim and Anna, also at Studenica, essentially resemble a canopy contained within a cubic volume of the central part of the naos (Fig. 5.7).[143] The most prominent feature of the Byzantine church acquired the structural appearance of a canopy structure.[144] All other architectural units were clustered around the canopy-like core of the church according to a defined hierarchy, by which the central dome raised on a drum became elongated and attenuated (see Fig. 4.59). The external masonry wall of the drum of the dome with engaged or painted colonnettes created a visual illusion of a relatively light, domed canopy (Fig. 5.8). The main church dome was usually topped by a sphere and crowned with a cross. The material reality of a "canopied" dome gained the potent symbolic meaning of the heavenly realm that, it seems to me, expanded in light of the symbolism of the heavenly throne. This symbolism was established by the altar canopy of Hagia Sophia and by Christ's Tomb as it appeared after Byzantine reconstructions of the Holy Sepulchre.

Little survives of the original church domes built in Constantinople, and not a single original dome survives from the first half of the eleventh century when the last significant Byzantine reconstruction took place at the Tomb of Christ in Jerusalem. The internally scalloped dome from the tenth-century Church of Myralaion, built by Romanos I Lakapenos

143 Ousterhout (1987); Babić (1987) 27–35.

144 While flexible, the Middle- and Late-Byzantine church plan was obviously associated with sanctity that surpassed the structural or functional roles, since, for example, rock-cut Cappadocian churches also had elements such as columns and domes, although structurally unnecessary. Ousterhout (1998) 81–120.

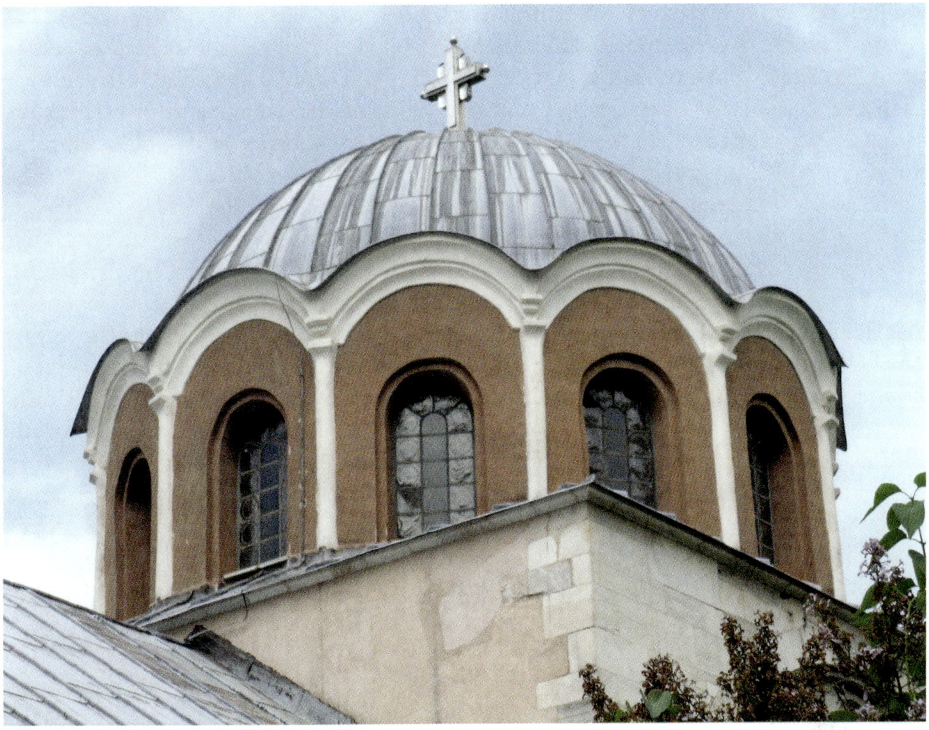

FIGURE 5.8 *Mother of God, Studenica monastery, Serbia, begun in 1183; exterior view, detail of the dome.* PHOTO DUŠAN DANILOVIĆ

in the 920s, has a cylindrical drum on the outside with eight quasi-triangular protruding supports.[145] An octagonal dome drum perforated by eight windows and decorated with slender cylindrical colonnettes supported an internally scalloped dome of a church of forgotten dedication, built ca. 1000 and today known as Vefa Molla Gurani Kilise Camii.[146] In Asia Minor, on the islands of Chios and Rhodos, at Constantinople, and as far away as Byzantine Macedonia and medieval Serbia, the dome drums of numerous churches include engaged colonnettes, executed in marble or high-quality stone, or, in a later tradition, painted columns at angles, which give the dome the appearance of a canopy.[147] The dome drum of the tenth-century Church of the Mother of God in the monastery of Hosios Loukas features engaged marble colonnettes topped by additional stone colonnetes, suggestive of a canopy, as well as, between them, representations of the Cross of Golgotha raised on a three-stepped base (Fig. 5.9). The unique feature of the paired columns supporting the dome, as occasionally depicted in reference to the Tomb of Christ, is comparable to the paired, freestanding marble colonnettes of the dome in Nea Moni and later churches such as Parigoritissa in Arta, Panagia Krina and Hag. Apostoloi at Pyrgi, both on Chios, as well as the Church of Fountoukli on Rhodos (see Fig. 4.37).[148] The churches of Nea Moni on the island of Chios, built by Emperor Constantine IX Monomachos, and of Parigoritissa in Arta, established by Epirote

145 Hallensleben (1965) 208–217; Krautheimer (1986) 356–358; Mango (1985) 113; Striker (1997).

146 Ćurčić (2010) 360–361.

147 Bouras (1982) 106–110, 152; Ćurčić (2010) 358–437; Bogdanović (2014a) 1–21.

148 On Byzantine examples of the dome with paired columns, see Bouras (1982) 109.

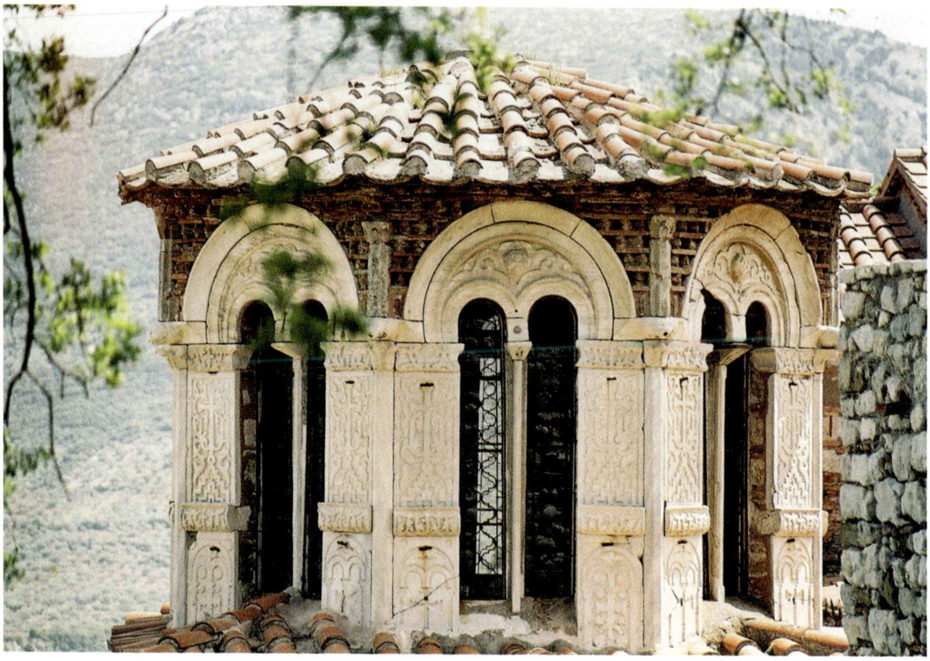

FIGURE 5.9 *Mother of God, Hosios Loukas, near Steiris, Phokis, Greece, tenth century; the dome.* PHOTO AUTHOR

despot Nikephoros I Komnenos Doukas, use columns extensively and paired columns in direct contact with the interior walls, which, examined in the context of Jerusalem architecture, potentially point to both the earthly and the Heavenly Jerusalem (Fig. 5.10).[149]

In the context of the canopy at the top of the Tomb of Christ, the place of the Resurrection and Divine Presence, the canopy-looking domes of Byzantine churches could have been related to the Holy Sepulchre. Even if the Anastasis Rotunda were domed, an architectural feature, such as a dome, could have been the repetitive physical manifestation of the Tomb of Christ. In this respect, the domes both of the Rotunda and of the Tomb would mean the same thing for the faithful, and conceivably referred, not only to the structure that sheltered the rock-cut tomb, but also to the enlarged structure of the Anastasis church that sheltered the Tomb itself.[150] Some tenth- and eleventh-century Constantinopolitan churches, such as Pharos, Mangana, and Nea Ekklesia, as well as reliquary shrines in the shape of miniature churches with domes set on drums with engaged paired colonnettes like the Reliquary of Saint Anastasios the Persian (960–970, now in the cathedral treasury of Aachen, illuminate the contemporary approach of resizing and multiplying canopied structures with special, sacred connotations.[151] The reliquary of St. Anastasios the Persian even bears inscriptions referring to the Heavenly Jerusalem and the Resurrection, as if it were a small-scale "City

[149] Bouras (1982) 106–110.

[150] Twelfth-century replicas of the Holy Sepulchre in the West, like those in Cambridge, England, ca. 1130, Santo Stefano Rotondo in Bologna, Italy, ca. 1150, and Sto. Sepúlcro Torres del Rió, Spain, also twelfth century, all have dome drums with engaged colonnettes and refer to architecture of the Holy Tomb in Jerusalem. Ousterhout (1981) 311–321.

[151] See, for example, Saunders (1982) 211–219; Ousterhout (1997) 460–461; Oikonomides (1980–1981) 239–247.

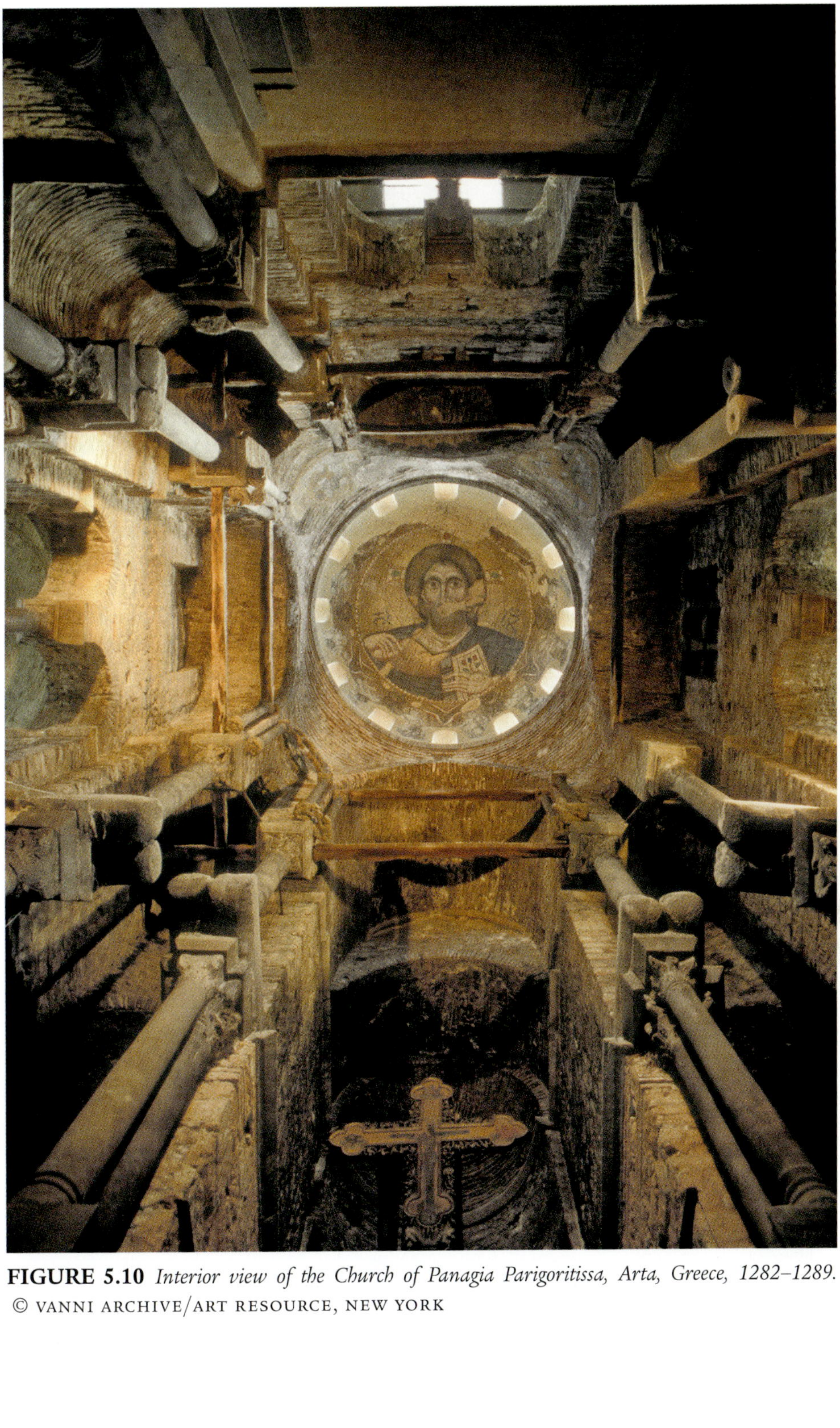

FIGURE 5.10 *Interior view of the Church of Panagia Parigoritissa, Arta, Greece, 1282–1289.*

of God."[152] Since the early Christian period, the meaning of the Tomb of Christ was understood, not as the natural extension of the tradition of ancient Greek *heröon* architecture and Roman imperial *mausolea* as tomb places, but as the place of divine majesty and of honor given to the Lord.[153] In light of the semi-religious character of the *heröon*, part shrine and part tomb, the Tomb of Christ can be closely associated with Christian shrines. The anachronistic use of the ancient term *heröon* for some Middle Byzantine churches and especially *mausolea,* as for the Church of the Archangel Michael, the mausoleum of the Komnenian dynasty in the Pantokrator Monastery in Constantinople, confirms the sacred connotations between the Tomb of Christ, reliquaries, and Byzantine domed churches built as massive tomb-reliquaries.[154] Namely, coeval and architecturally similar to the later Crusaders' rebuilding of the Holy Sepulchre and Crusaders' mausolea built as replicas of the Holy Sepulchre during the reign of King Baldwin II of Jerusalem (r. 1118–1131),[155] the *heröon* at Pantokrator monastery shared with the Holy Sepulchre yet another feature: both structures accommodated precious relics related to Christ's death. Apart from the Tomb of Christ, the fragments of the True Cross were kept at the Holy Sepulchre, while the Church of the Archangel Michael at Pantokrator monastery in Constantinople housed the tomb of Emperor Manuel I, which was closely associated with the "Red Stone of Ephesus," the stone slab upon which Jesus was believed to lie after the Deposition from the Cross, a holy relic brought by Manuel from Ephesus.[156]

It is impossible to ascertain whether preexisting or contemporary architectural forms influenced the reconstruction of Christ's Tomb by the Byzantines, or indeed to what extent the architectural forms of Christ's Tomb and of other sacred sites in the Holy Land fostered symbolic and material expression in Byzantine ecclesiastical architecture and furnishings. Yet there is a crucial similarity between the canopied, columnar features of the Tomb-shrine and those of the domes of Byzantine churches during the Middle Byzantine period. This period overlaps with the imperial policies of the Komnenian dynasty, when the Byzantines were once again very concerned with the significance of the sacred places in the Holy Land.[157] However, as it was clear that they could not regain their imperial presence in the Holy Land, the significance of the relics seemed to expand, and their presentation was diversified by display in luxurious reliquaries whose form reflected the form of a church exterior and yet another diagrammatic variation of the theme of the canopy that framed the central dome of the church building itself.[158]

THE CANOPY AS A MICROCOSMIC PLACE OF PRESENCE

The canopy as an architectural *parti* of the Byzantine domed church was a powerful design concept that allowed for the nesting within of two major spatial concepts—the heavenly and earthly Jerusalem. Architectural similarities between the canopy and the domed

---

[152] Grabar (1968) 427–433; Saunders (1982) 211–219.

[153] Ward Perkins (1981) 490, 495–516.

[154] In the *typikon* of the monastery, the mausoleum was called *heröon: Pantokrator* in *BMFD* vol. 2, 725–774, esp. 756. The terms *naos* and *ekklesia,* both meaning "a church," were interchangeably used for mausolea during the Middle Byzantine period. Bouras (1982) 141. Although the *heröon* generally ceased to be used by the twelfth century, *John Skilitzes* (eleventh–twelfth centuries) *Synopsis historiarum, Life of Emperor Nicephoros,* sec. 23.28; *Theodorus II Ducas Lascaris* (thirteenth century) *Epistulae,* Epistle 141; and *Georgios Pachymeres* (thirteenth–fourteenth centuries) *Συγγραφικαὶ ἱστορίαι* 87.5, used the word ἡρῷον (*heröon*) in their works.

[155] Folda (1995) 53–54.

[156] Ousterhout (2000) 265–270; Ousterhout (2001a) 133–150; Janin (1953) 525–523, 564–566; Mango (1969–1970) 369–375.

[157] Magdalino (1987b) 51–64.

[158] The *verde antico* lid of Manuel I Komnenos' sarcophagus was in the shape of a multi-domed church. It may have actually been part of the sarcophagus of Basil I, which symbolically and formally resembled

Byzantine church examined through micro-architectural framing[159] can be enriched with the notions of Jerusalem(s) and their architecture. Theological explanations, liturgical and devotional practices related to canopied installations, and the powerful typological links between the Tomb of Christ in Jerusalem and the Ark of the Covenant, the Tabernacle, and the Jerusalem Temple established by the Byzantine-rite church, all merged into the notion of the Heavenly Jerusalem. The Byzantine domed churches, essentially large-scale canopies, by embracing these typological links, further established palpable organic, tectonic, symbolic, and sacred ties between the Old and New Covenants.

As Germanos explained and the design of Byzantine churches confirmed, the Tabernacle, made of textile (Ex. 25–40) and then replaced by the Temple made of stone (Deut. 12:2–27), were both made to hold the Ark of the Covenant and are the only architectural installations designed according to instructions given by God Himself. They thus acquired their status as the iconic prototype of sacred space and place, which in a Christian context became the Church both as a building and the body of Christ.[160] By reassessing questions on the significance of the Temple and the Tomb of Christ in Jerusalem in the design of Hagia Sophia, the ultimate church-model for Byzantine-rite churches, and the relevance of the sacred architecture in Jerusalem, it emerges that Jerusalem architecture was mostly understood in conceptual terms. Even the Holy Sepulchre in Jerusalem acquired critical architectural features from the architectural design of Byzantine churches, following the transitional period when the essence of the Byzantine-rite church was firmly established. Hence, the Tomb *Aedicula*, essentially an enclosed chamber, was modified during the periods of reconstruction under the Byzantines into a chamber whose roof acquired a canopy-like form. The changes of devotional practices at the Holy Sepulchre after the eighth- and ninth-century Iconoclastic crises may account for the change in the physical appearance of the Tomb-shrine. Moreover, the meaning of elements employed in various stages of the architectural history of the Tomb of Christ, and especially its references to a canopied ambo, further reveal the Byzantine understanding of the relationship between the Holy Sepulchre and the Byzantine church and their interrelationship with the sacred. The canopied top of the Holy Sepulchre after its rebuilding under the Byzantines reestablished the long-living importance of the canopy as a *parti*.

Changing Byzantine perceptions of the Tomb-shrine illuminate changing notions of the church, the temple, and the sacred in general. Any resemblance of the Tomb of Christ to the Temple and its features during the Byzantine reconstructions was essentially conceptual, not material. The canopy-like crowning of the Tomb of Christ was probably inspired by the need to accommodate and to express architecturally the meaning of the Holy Fire. The miracle of the Holy Fire, after the Iconoclastic controversies, acted as a powerful vehicle for strengthening the Byzantine belief in the Incarnation,[161] additionally stimulating the flow of pilgrims to Jerusalem, and induced controversial disputes about the superiority of the faith of the Byzantines over the faith of the Muslim landlords in the Holy Land.[162] These

---

the Nea Ekklesia church. The reuse of marble decorative elements for the churches of the monastery of Lips, Christ Pantokrator, the so-called Kalenderhane Camii, and the Monastery of Chora (1316–1319) suggests a continuous appreciation of luxurious church-like and canopy-shaped objects among imperial patrons. Krsmanović (2001) 69; Karagiorgou (2001) 193; Bogdanović (2014a) 1–21.

159 Chapter 4.

160 Bogdanović (2011b) 109–134; Lidov (2007) 135–176, 366–371, esp. 144; Barker (2003).

161 Evangelatou (2003) 181–204 demonstrated the significance of the Holy Sepulchre for fostering *iconophile* arguments on relics.

162 In his tenth-century letter to the emir of Damascus, a certain Aretheos from Caesarea used the miracle of the Holy Fire as a polemical argument to show the superiority of Christianity over Islam. More in Canard (1965) 16–43, with references. In the 1360s, Monk Joasaph, former Byzantine emperor John VI

may have been the reasons why Caliph al-Hākim ordered the destruction of churches in the Holy Land in 1009, when the Holy Sepulchre was almost completely destroyed.[163] During the Byzantine reconstruction, placing a canopy, a powerful and recognizable solution for the framing of sacred revelations, on the Tomb *Aedicula* confirmed the meaning of the Holy Sepulchre as the place of the Resurrection and Divine Light.

After the transitional period and the Iconoclastic controversies, throughout the Mediterranean basin, the four-columned Byzantine church, with a dome on the drum with engaged colonnettes, and similarly shaped reliquaries with canopy-like tops, all resembled the memory image of the Holy Sepulchre and spatially, visually, conceptually, and literally emphasized the Byzantine belief in the Incarnation. References to the human nature and the Body of Christ through the Tomb of Christ and other canopy-like structures in Jerusalem and the Holy Land are recurrently present in surviving Byzantine records. The identification of the Holy Sepulchre as an ambo shows how theological and spatial principles subtly result in the conflation, not only of two liturgical furnishings but also of canopied furnishings within an entire church. The material reality of Christ's Tomb at Jerusalem, which was theologically connected to the altar canopy, was related to the ambo in the actual church, even when most Byzantine churches became minuscule in scale, and the use of monumental ambos gradually diminished.[164]

Like in the Constantinopolitan Hagia Sophia or at the Anastasis church, the most characteristic feature of the Byzantine church was the naos with a centrally positioned dome that created a directional ambivalence, a central focus, and a vertical axis. This novel organization of space corresponded to the exigencies of worship of the mature Divine Liturgy, which saw a reduction in the processions characteristic of the early Christian service. As the liturgy was reduced to a series of appearances, the most sacred activities were restricted to the *bema*, centered in the altar and sheltered by a canopy, and to the central space of the naos below a dome.[165] The refocusing, or rather multi-focusing, architecture of the church building seems to be closely linked to the church rites. Canopies as micro-architectural structures nested within the church placed a critical role in architecturally defining the multifocal essence of the Byzantine church.

Kantakouzenos (ca. 1295–1383), also used the miracle of the Holy Fire at the Tomb of Christ as an argument in his apologetic treatise on the Muslim faith. *PG* 154, col. 517.

[163] Canard (1965) 16–43; Biddle (1999) 73. A certain Radulfus Glaber (ca. 985–ca.1048) witnessed both the rite of the Holy Fire and the destruction of the Holy Sepulchre. More in Auxentios of Photiki (1999) 30–37, n. 102.

[164] Chapter 2, ambo; Chapter 3, Kalabaka, and Chapter 4, ambo and *omphalos*.

[165] As a reminder, important parts of other Byzantine rites—such as marriage, coronation, and funerary rites—took place below the dome or domical vaults of a church and in the context of specific smaller-scale canopies within the church, although they were not exclusively confined in these locations.

Conclusion

Canopies played a major role in the dynamic architectural design of Byzantine-rite churches. Since the inceptions of Christian spaces of worship, these columnar vaulted structures marked the most sacred places within the church proper, as exemplified by the earliest attested canopy used exclusively by Christians in the third-century Dura Europos baptistery. Despite the limited number of surviving churches and their furnishings in the Eastern Mediterranean, more than two hundred preserved canopies across vast geographic and chronological spans attest to their importance in church design. Medieval texts and church practices further elucidate how canopies carried and communicated multiple sacred meanings to the beholders. This potential of canopies to convey multiple messages despite their generic form was critical in the process of architectural design that privileged their use as essentially non-imitative structures capable of providing a singular experience of sacred space. Canopies framed various sacred locations in Byzantine-rite churches, from the altars to specially venerated icons, yet it is their modularity and transposition that allowed the full synthesis of the various sacred meanings attached to these structures into the church design on the level of the entire building.

While many scholars would consider the sixth-century Constantinopolitan Hagia Sophia the pinnacle of Byzantine architecture, which was then characterized by a decline of architectural innovation, this book suggests that the canopy core of Hagia Sophia remained a pervasive model of a canopy as a spatial and symbolic modular unit of Byzantine churches, recognized by their domes. This dynamic principle of architectural design based on canopied units also allowed that no two Byzantine churches were ever built the same architecturally, further confirming canopies as non-imitative structures that carried the essence of a Byzantine-rite church.

The cultural role of the canopy emerges as a major feature in the Byzantine domain. The canopy and the Byzantine church enriched the profound experience of the sacred. This singular experience of the sacred was greatly enhanced by liturgical celebrations focused on canopies and their spatial prominence. Setting canopy within canopy in Byzantine churches, where the domed church building as a container takes the evolved form and meanings of the critical features and furnishings of the interior it contained, allowed for the materialization and palpable experience of the major cultural values and beliefs in the Eastern Orthodox world. The spatial arrangement of the nesting canopies, and the interconnectivity between canopied installations within the sacred space in which they are found and which they denoted, provided extensive performative frameworks for various devotional practices, and liturgical and paraliturgical services in the Byzantine cultural context. Culturally rich contextualized meanings of a canopy were therefore deeply rooted in religious lives of the people and their spiritual experiences. This interconnectedness of the Byzantine *oikoumene* connected people with the worldly and otherworldly realms of their beliefs and practices; it allowed the faithful to transcend time and spatial constraints and to actively participate in the life started by Christ and His disciples. The extraordinary formal and conceptual cohesiveness of the canopy and the Byzantine church allows us to look at the Byzantine tradition anew.

The micro-architectural qualities of canopies and their role in church design were deeply understood by the Byzantine intellectual elite. Indeed, they did not speak of the canopy as micro-architecture nor as architectural *parti*. Yet the essence of the meanings of canopies was evident in Byzantine reasoning about space and the frame.

The ideas about frame and framing that stem from within Byzantine culture essentially come from Biblical sources that refer to a *frame* as an architectural frame, an embellishment, as well as divine Providence and "goodly frame."[1] These ideas were then reflected and further formulated in various Byzantine scholastic texts such as *Letters* by St. Athanasius of Alexandria (fourth century) or *An Exposition of the Orthodox Faith* by St. John of Damascus (seventh–eighth centuries).[2] These theologians maintained that the ultimate Framer is God, who framed the Universe and all creation, which by extension relates to architecture as well. St. Athanasius of Alexandria established the notion of *frame* as an ontological "being-place," which ultimately results from God, the "Framer of the world," and through Christ, "the Son of Framing it," all creation is framed (made) and imbued with fitting properties.[3] St. John of Damascus wrote about the framing of the universe by divine Providence, imbuing aspects of the divine and earthly in overlapping spaces, each within the other, and yet also distinct.[4] Within Byzantine thought, the canopy and the Byzantine church can be related to human activity "in accordance with the plan implanted in it in a creative manner by the Cause that framed the Universe" as St. John of Damascus wrote.[5] This thinking reveals that the Byzantines understood a canopy as a human-made construct that framed the spaces in which the divine and earthly aspects merged, yet they understood that essentially the concept of framing was ultimately established by the Framer (God).

The Byzantines understood the canopy-frame and the divine Presence within it as a single symbolic whole. The canopy-frame was a subtle boundary between the sacred and the earthly. Yet the unitary material basis of the canopy frame and the content within the canopy, often emphasized by shared features of decoration or inscriptions, suggest that the canopy and its framing were more related to the sacred "supra-spatial" realm than to the worldly. A canopy framing the sacred body or framing the sacred place was charged with the significance of sacred time, wherein the present moment recapitulates the total past, present, and future within the framework of a given church space.[6] By communicating

[1] Ex. 26:15–30, cf. 36:20–34; 25:25, cf. 37:12.

[2] *Athanasius Theol., Letters; John Damascus, Orthodox Faith.*

[3] *Athanasius Theol., Letters* book 2, ch. XVIII; book 2, discourse II; letter 2461.

[4] *John Damascus, Orthodox Faith* book 2, ch. 29 on Providence: "He willed that all things should be and they were. He wills the universe to be framed and it is framed, and all that He wills comes to pass;" and later, in book 3, ch. 15 on energies of Jesus Christ: ". . . it is in accordance with plan implanted in it in a creative manner by the Cause that frames the universe. Wherefore, also, when they [holy fathers] spoke of it along the divine nature they called it energy."

[5] *John Damascus, Orthodox Faith* book 3, ch. 15.

[6] See also Smith, J. Z. (1987) 113.

the divine Presence, canopies in the Byzantine ecclesiastical tradition acquired the twofold function of internalizing the material world and sublimating its spiritual reality, and of externalizing the spiritual world and materializing the sublime.

The two-sided relations between the earthly and the divine were reinforced through the micro-architectural arrangements within the larger space of the church. During liturgical and other religious rites, the divine Presence and the believers would occupy the same "hieroplastic space," which is at once earthly, heavenly, and beyond. "Hieroplastic space" in which spiritual phenomena are visually presented was introduced through the concept of "hieroplastia," understood as a fragmented trace of theophany by Dionysius the Areopagite, the legendary student of Apostle Paul, whose preserved writings can be dated to the sixth century.[7] Canopies are then spatial icons that architecturally frame theophany while, as further explained by Dionysius the Areopagite, their meaning could be extracted via human intellect from the appearances (phenomena) they put forward.

Similar to modern theories of architecture that analyze the multilayered relations between architectural forms and their meaning through representational qualities, the meaning of a canopy as an architectural frame can be followed on at least three levels.[8] First, a canopy as frame was most obviously representational when it had painted or sculpted decoration and inscriptions as carriers of meaning. Selected decorative, often generic and repetitive, motifs reinforced the perception of canopies as long-standing important structures. The inscriptions on canopies additionally highlighted their significance and suggested their historical accuracy, either real or perceived, all while merging the aura of tradition with present and future. Second, by virtue of being literally a three-dimensional frame, a canopy as a basic architectural structure, even before any decoration or inscriptions, provided a dominant architectural focus and significance in church space. Third, through developed philosophical reasoning about a canopy as a carrier of meaning, it could represent something of its own kind such as another canopy or a building, or another structure, or itself in a former or future existence, as demonstrated by the strong Byzantine associations of canopies with the Ark, the Tabernacle, the Temple, and the Heavenly Jerusalem.

The reaction of the faithful to a canopied space involved both an emotional response and contemplative experience. When Paulos Silentarios described the altar canopy in Hagia Sophia, he reflected upon the sensory experience of the churchgoers, whose movements within the church and knowledge of it was deeply obtained through participatory experience of church rites that were marked by canopies and a sequential understanding of their micro-architecture and constitutive parts.[9] The simple form of the four columns with a roof was charged with powerful mental and real images. The canopy as an architectural structure thus became a powerful signifier for the communication and connection between the interior and outer worlds, on both metaphysical and more literal, physical levels. A link between the two worlds, in one case seen from the inside, in the other from the outside, was made possible by a canopy frame for both the church and its furnishings.[10] Whether it took the form of a dome or an elongated pyramidal cup, the canopy top designated a sacred space below and remained a very evocative head-like form, reminding the faithful that there is always something above. Similarly, canopy columns delineating the limits of

---

[7] *Dionysius Areopagita, CH* II.1 introduced the term *hieroplastia*. I thank Filip Ivanović for bringing this reference to me. On theophany as a philosophical concept, see Perl (2007). See also Chapter 4.

[8] Davies, C. (2011) 14.

[9] Smith, C. (1987) 16–32 provided a fantastic analysis of the drawings of Hagia Sophia made by Cyriacus of Ancona in the fifteenth century that mirror the movement of the visitor through space and reflect the Byzantine *ekphrasis* of church architecture that confirms a sequential understanding of space.

[10] Nordenfalk (1973) 233–258.

the sacred place within the church proper reminded them of the space beyond. The architectural form of the canopy, therefore, resolved the problem of how un-representable space, which in the minds of the Byzantines is the supra-space of God, constitutes the discursive conditions for creation and the articulation of places on earth, which can be appropriated and understood repeatedly in different contexts.

Sacred space was not just an architectural metaphor for the Byzantines. St. John of Damascus confirms their highly sophisticated philosophical understanding of the divine manifestations determined by place, time, and mental comprehension. In his critical chapter entitled "Concerning the place of God: and that the Deity alone is uncircumscribed," St. John of Damascus writes on place and its framing (the "limits"):

> Place is physical, being the limits of the thing containing within which the thing contained is contained. The air, for example, contains and the body is contained, but not all of the containing air is the place of the contained body, but only those limits of the containing air which are adjacent to the contained body. And this is necessarily so, because the thing containing is not in the thing contained.
>
> He also highlights that the intellectual, spiritual place is. . . where the intellectual and incorporeal nature is thought of as being and where it actually is. There it is present and acts; and it is not physically contained, but spiritually, because it has no form to permit it to be physically contained. Now, God, being immaterial and uncircumscribed, is not in a place. For He, who fills all things and is over all things and Himself encompasses all things, is His own place. However, God is also said to be in a place; and this place where God is said to be is there where His operation is plainly visible . . . . Thus, the place where God is said to be is that which experiences His operation and grace to a greater extent. For this reason, Heaven is His Throne, because it is in Heaven that the angels are who do His will and glorify Him unceasingly. For Heaven is His resting place and the earth His footstool, because on the earth He conversed in the flesh with men.

And St. John further provides an intellectual understanding the church and sacred places as

> . . . the place of God, because we have set it apart for His glorification as a sort of hallowed spot in which we also make our intercessions to Him. In the same way, those places in which His operation is plainly visible to us, whether it is realized in the flesh or out of the flesh, are called places of God.

Ultimately, he points to the universal ordering and macro-scale of the sacred space:

> Moreover, one must know that the Divinity is without parts and that He is wholly everywhere in His entirety, not being physically distributed part for part, but wholly in all things and wholly over the universe.[11]

The canopy, therefore, acquired a general meaning of the marker of sacred locations in churches, and its interpretation was recurrently typological as the theologians and churchgoers compared them to various Biblical structures or seminal Christian buildings that mapped Byzantine spiritual realities and landscapes. As suggested in the theological Neoplatonic texts by Dionysius the Areopagite or liturgical commentaries by Maximos the Confessor and Germanos, which all addressed the possibilities of contemplation

---

[11] *John Damascus, Orthodox Faith* book 1, ch. 13.

and understanding of the spiritual, a church building and its fittings had a critical role in understanding sacred space.[12] Within universal, cosmological, liturgical-chronological, and topographical contexts, the church represented the ordering of the Christian universe, provided a space on earth for the reenactment of sacraments in the expectation of the Second Coming, and recreated the topography of the Holy Land and the earthly life of Christ. In that regard, the generic form of a canopy and the Byzantine domical church it denoted allowed for a universal experience of a canopy in ecclesiastic settings among the faithful who belonged to the Byzantine cultural realm. The particular meanings of individual canopies and churches where they were found resulted from the anagogical process that allowed individual engagement with canopied structures during various rites and experiences in various settings, where canopies not only marked the focal points, critical in place-making in relation to human presence, but also allowed for the singular, non-repeatable personal experience of spiritual space.[13]

The liturgical celebrations of the Byzantines thus preserved the spiritual meanings of the archetypal architecture of the Ark of the Covenant, the Tabernacle, and the Temple that otherwise might not have been known among Christians living in later centuries. Moreover, the Byzantines embraced the complex meanings of canopies, both stationary and moving, as places of divine Presence, and understood them within liturgical and other church rites. In continuation of a tradition that made the liturgy the principal indication of the Incarnation, divine grace was seen to cooperate with the human body to achieve a potent symbolic meaning for the canopy regardless of its location or form—whether a liturgical furnishing or a tomb-shrine, made of stone or wood, a fully developed architectonic object or reduced to its two-dimensional representation. The canopy acquired the sacred meanings of a holy tent and a tabernacle: a portable tent-sanctuary, recalling the Biblical Ark of the Covenant of the Israelites during the Exodus; the Biblical Temple and the Tomb of Christ, representing the presence of God; the architecture for an icon; and the human body considered as a place housing the soul or principle of life.[14] Furthermore, though canopies and related sacred objects with similar shapes or meanings multiplied in the Byzantine church after the transitional period and Iconoclastic controversies, this was not a sign of an intellectual decline in the quality of Byzantine iconography, but rather of an embrace of all its complex meanings in subordination to the ecclesiastical rites. Examined in their performative use, Byzantine canopies effectively exemplify how for the Byzantines *historia* connected the liturgical rites to the history of salvation, while *theoria* was a contemplation of liturgical realities beyond the material world.

The canopy thus becomes a symbol for what is built, what is not built, and what cannot be built—the visible, the invisible, and the un-representable to the eye of the beholder. The central focus and dominant vertical axis that the canopy provides are connected principally to the centrality and primary importance of the ritual content of the Byzantine church, not to its multifocal material reality and spatial organization. In conceptual terms, all Byzantine canopies could have been understood simultaneously as being central objects of sacred focus and as unified with one another.

---

[12] *Dionysius Areopagita, EH-a, -b, -c* (I, 2; II, 3, 2; III, 3, 13); *Germanos*-a 1–10; *Germanos*-b 56–63; *Maximus Conf.-a* ch. 2–4; *Maximus Conf.-b* 57–120; *Maximus Conf.-c*. See also Mueller-Jourdan (2005).

[13] Malpas (2015) 65–92.

[14] On the various meanings of the Tabernacle, see also Friedman (1980) 241–248; Hurowitz (1995) 127–151; Schwarzer (2001) 474–484.

Appendix

TABLE 1 Texts with References to Ciboria or Canopies

T.1: *Orphica, Hymni.* Hymn P, line 39.
T.2: Hegesander, *Fragmenta.* 21:3–5.
T.3: Nicander, *Fragmenta.* Fragment 81, line 3.
T.4: Callixenus, *Fragmenta.* Fragment 1, line 148. (Hist.)
T.5: Agatharchides, *Fragmenta.*; Volume-Jacoby, 2A, 86, F Fragment 19, line 88.
T.6: Diodorus Siculus, *Bibliotheca historica* (lib. 1–20). Book 1, ch. 34, sec. 6, line 4. (Hist.)
T.7: Strabo, *Geographica.* passim.
T.8: Claudius Iolaus, *Fragmenta.* Fragment 1 line 13. (Hist.)
T.9: Dioscorides Pedanius, *De materia medica.* Book 2, ch. 106, sec. 1, line 7. (Med.)
T.10: Soranus, *Gynaeciorum libri* iv. Book 1, ch. 57, sec. 1, line 7. (Med.)
T.11: Galenus Med., *De alimentorum facultatibus* libri iii. Vol. 6, 623:12
T.12: Pseudo-Galenus, *De theriaca ad Pamphilianum.* Vol. 14, 303:3 (Med.)
T.13: Herodianus, Περὶ ὀρθογραφίας. Vol. 3.2; 533:22. (Gramm.)
T.14: Pausanias, *Fragmenta.* Fragment 4, line 63. (Hist.)
T.15: Athenaeus-a, *Deipnosophistae.*
T.16: Eusebius, *Demonstratio evangelica.* Book 6, ch. 18, sec. 41 and elsewhere. (Theol.)
T.17: Gregory Nazianzes, *De vita Mosis.* Ch. 1, sec. 50:1.; Ch. 1, sec. 61. [cf. Philo, *De vita Mosis.* Book 2, sec. 81:1.]
T.18: Cyrillus Alexandrinus, *De adoratione et cultu in spiritu et veritate.* Vol. 68, p. 620ff; Cyrillus Alexandrinus, *Commentarius in xii prophetas minores.* Vol. 2, p. 516; Cyrillus Alexandrinus Theol., *Commentarii in Joannem.* Vol. 1, p. 574. (Theol.)
T.19: Athanasius Theol., *Expositiones in Psalmos.* Vol. 27, 221:30.
T.20: John Chrysostom, *In Acta apostolorum.* Vol. 60, 54:10; John Chrysostom, *1 Cor. Hom.* 36.5: Vol. 61, p. 104, line 63.
T.21: John Chrysostom, *In Acta apostolorum.* Vol. 60, 297:13.

TABLE 1 Continued

T.22: Basil the Great. *H. Myst.* 4:258.18.

T.23: Oribasius, *Collectiones medicae* (lib. 1–16, 24–25, 43–50). Book 12. (Med.)

T.24: Marcus Eremita, *De baptismo*. Sec. 4, line 91.

T.25: Agnellus, XXVI, *De Victore* c. 66.

T.26: Theodoretus of Cyrrhus, *Historia Ecclesiastica*. 988C.

T.27: *Vita et Miraculis Sanctae Theclae*. libri ii. Book 1, sec. 28; Book 2, sec. 30.

T.28: *Vita sancti Hypatii*. Ch. 28, sec. 3.

T.29: *Vita Porphyrii episcopi Gazensis*. Ch. 75, line 15.

T.30: Catenae (Novum Testamentum), *Catena in Acta.*

T. 31: Anastasius (the Librarian), *LIII. Sanctus Symmachus.*

T.32: Sophronius, *Historia liturg. 2.*

T.33: John Malalas, *Chronographia* [PG 97, 18.708B]

T.34: John Malalas-b, *Chronographia*. Ch. 18, 232:19; John Malalas-d. (Chronogr.)

T.35: John Malalas-b, *Chronographia*. P. 223, line 3, cf. p. 232, line 19; John Malalas-d. (Chronogr.)

T.36: John Malalas-b, *Chronographia*. P. 397, line 16; John Malalas-d. (Chronogr.)

T.37: Evagrius Scholasticus, *Historia ecclesiastica*. 56:20. (Scr. Eccl.)

T.38: Evagrius Scholasticus, *Historia ecclesiastica*. 125:4. (Scr. Eccl.)

T.39: Evagrius Scholasticus, *Historia ecclesiastica*. 5:21. (Scr. Eccl.)

T.40: Paulos Silentarios-a, *Descriptio S. Sophiae*; translation by Mango in Paulos Silentarios-c.

T.41: Aëtius, *Iatricorum libri*. Iatricorum liber i, Ch. 199.

T.42: Stephanus Byzantius, *Ethnica*. P. 60, line 2. (Gramm.)

T.43: Simplicius, *In Aristotelis quattuor libros de caelo commentaria*. Vol. 7, 417:9. (Phil.)

T.44: Cos. Indicopl., *Topographia Christiana*. Book 2, sec. 81, line 7. (Geogr.)

T.45: Hesychius, *Lexicon*. Alphabetic letter kappa entry 2603, line 1; entry 4338, line 3. (Lexicogr.)

T.46: Hesychius, *Lexicon*. Alphabetic letter kappa entry 2604, line 1. (Lexicogr.)

T.47: Patriarch Severus. *Les Homilae Cathedrales de Sévère d'Antioche. Homélies VCIX CIII.*

T.48: *Vitae Symeonis Stylitae Junioris*. Ch. 129, line 107.

T.49: *Chronicon 1234*. [Also in Mundell-Mango (1992) 123–136; K. E. McVey, "The Domed Church as Microcosm: Literary Roots of an Architectural Symbol," DOP 37 (1983) 91–121]

T.50: Emperor Maurice (r. 582–602) sent an entire altar canopy in pieces from Constantinople to the church in his native town, Arabissos in Cappadocia. [Ruggieri (1991) 166.]

T.51: *Vita Joannis Eleemosynarii episcopi Alexandrini*. P. 360, line 6.

T.52: *Life and Miracles StDemetrios-a*. Miracle 1, p. 66, line 24; Miracle 6, p. 93, lines 2ff; Miracle 10, p. 115, lines 3ff; Miracle 12, p. 125, line 11; Miracle 15, p. 162, line 9.

T.53: *Chronicon paschale*. P. 713.

T.54: *Vita sancti Theodori Syceotae*. Sec. 162, line 79.

T.55: *Vitae et Miracula Sancti Anastasii Persae. Miracula sancti Anastasii Persae,* Sec. 7.

TABLE 1 Continued

T.56: *Life and Miracles StDemetrios-b.* P. 239, line 25; p. 240, line 6.

T.57: Shrine of St. Demetrios, Thess. [Pallas (1979) 44–58.]

T.58: *Germanos-a; Germanos-b*, 58–59.

T.59: Theophanes Confessor, *Chronographia.* 494:29. (Chronogr.)

T.60: Theophanes Confessor, *Chronographia.* P. 232–331. (Chronogr.)

T.61: Theodore of Studion, *Iambii-b.* PG 99.1793D

T.62: Photius, *Epistulae et Amphilochia.* Amph. epistle 318, line 2. (Theol., Scr. Eccl. et Lexicogr.)

T.63: Photius, *The Homilies of Photius Patriarch of Constantinople-a* and Photius, *The Homilies of Photius Patriarch of Constantinople-b.* Homily 10, p. 102. (Theol., Scr. Eccl. et Lexicogr.)

T.64: Georgius Choeroboscus, *De orthographia.* P. 233, line 29. (Gramm.)

T.65: *Vita sanctorum Davidis, Symeonis et Georgii Mitylenae.* Sec. 14, line 7.

T.66: *Vita Eustratii.*

T.67: *Synaxarion* CP. *Synaxarium mensis Martii* Day 9, sec. 1, line 42; *Synaxarium mensis Augusti* Day 1, sec. 2, line 5; *Synaxarium mensis Septembris* Day 30, sec. 1, line 91; *Synaxarium mensis Novembris* Day 1, sec. 4, line 8; *Synaxarium mensis Decembris* Day 29, sec. 7, line 2; *Synaxarium mensis Januarii* Day 26, sec. 2, line 10. [Note: This canopy is mentioned by Clavijo in 15th c. as in ruins (Janin [1953] 485–86). The canopy is also mentioned in the Typicon of Hagia Sophia from the 9th–10th c. (*Typicon of Hagia Sophia* 2–386.)]

T.68: *Life StTheokiste-b.* Ch. 3f.

T.69: *Synaxariom CP. Synaxarium mensis Octobris* Day 26, sec. 1, line 110.

T.70: *Vita Eliae Junioris.* Sec. 69, line 1512.

T.71: Constantinus VII Porphyrogenitus, *De cerimoniis aulae Byzantinae* (lib. 1.84–2.56); Porphyrogenitus also mentions a canopy on silver columns and with golden curtains in the palace of Bonus constructed by Emperor Romanos I Lekapenos (920–944) dedicated to Emperor Constantine I—celebration of 21st of May and the veneration of the Cross (p. 534, line 16); as well as a canopy in Consistorium (Vol. 2: p. 1, line 15). [*De Ceremoniis-c* 1:1–179; 2:1–187; also, *De Ceremoniis-d* 98, 163, 181, 232, 234, 290, 291, 406.]

T.72: Pseudo-Codinus, *Patria-a.* Book 2, sec. 55. Also Pseudo-Codinus, *Patria-b* 88–91. (Hist.)

T.73: Pseudo-Codinus, *Patria-a.* Also Pseudo-Codinus, *Patria-b.* (Hist.)

T.74: Michael Psellus, *Theologica.* (Phil., Theol., Polyhist., Epist. et Hagiogr.)

T.75: Michael Psellus, *Laudatio in Joannem Crustulam.* Line 39. (Phil., Theol., Polyhist., Epist. et Hagiogr.) [cf. Michael Psellus, *Epistula ad Michaelem Cerularium-a.*]

T.76: *Vita Simeonis Novi Theologici.* Sec. 93, line 13. [cf. Nicetas Epist. Constantinopolitanus. Epistle 3, line 16.]

T.77: *Vita et Miracula Niconis.* Ch. 55, line 25.

T.78: *Miraculis sancti Eugenii.* Line 497.

T.79: *Etymologicum Gudianum.* 321:21, 365:24.

T.80: Georgius Cedrenus, *Compendium historiarum.* Vol 1: p. 677, line 1. (Chronogr.)

T.81: Zonaras, *Epitome historiarum* (lib. 13–18). P. 170, line 16. (Hist. et Gramm.)

T.82: Theordous Andidensis, *De divinae Liturgiae symbolis ac mysteriis, Comentatio liturgica*: 441–444.

T.83: Eustathius, *Commentarii ad Homeri Iliadem.* Vol. 3: p. 519:8. (Philol. et Scr. Eccl.)

TABLE 1 Continued

T.84: *Kecharitomene* in *BMFD* vol. 2, 716.

T.85: Michael Accominatus, an Archbishop of Athens (1175?–1205) [Setton (1944) 179–207.]

T.86: *Alexiad-a*. Book 12, ch. 3, sec. 6, line 18.

T.87: Nicolaus Mesarites, *Descriptio ecclesiae SS. Apostolorum*. Ch. 38, sec. 6. (Rhet.)

T.88: Nicolaus Mesarites, *Seditio Joanni Comneni*. P. 35, line 12. (Rhet.)

T.89: Nicetas Choniates, *Chronographia* 357.

T.90: Anon. *Marc. Gr. 444* [Flusin5 (2005) 163–181.]

T.91: Anthony of Novgorod, *Pilgrims Book*. [Majeska (2002) 93–108; Janin (1953) 455–70.]

T.92: Deed of concession to the Genoese of certain areas of Constantinople (October 13, 1202) with the *Inventory of the so-called Palace of Botaniates* [*Acta et diplomata Graeca mediiaevi* Vol. 3: 55–57, and x–xv.; in *SD* 240]

T.93: *Skoteine* 1186.

T.94: Gregory Palamas, *Capita physica, theologica, moralia et practica* [also known as Grigorios of Thessaloniki. Φυσικά, Θεολογικά, Ἠθικά τε καὶ πρακτικά] ch. 5.

T.95: Isidorus Glabas, *Homiliae in sanctum Demetrium*. Homily 1, p. 26.

T.96: *Theoktistos* 44–123.

T.97: *Dig. Akrit.* Grotaferrata version. 246–247, cols. 240–245.

T.98: Stephen of Novgorod in *RussTravelers* (1984) 15–47, 36–37.

T.99: Stephen of Novgorod in *RussTravelers* (1984) 15–47, 42–43.

T.100: RussAnon in *RussTravelers* (1984) 128–154, 138–139.

T.101: RussAnon in *RussTravelers* (1984) 128–154, 132–133.

T.102: RussAnon in *RussTravelers* (1984) 128–154, 132–133.

T.103: RussAnon in *RussTravelers* (1984) 128–154, 148–149.

T.104: RussAnon in *RussTravelers* (1984) 128–154, 148–149.

T.105: RussAnon in *RussTravelers* (1984) 128–154, 138.

T.106: Oikiskos John Prodromos in Serres, Thess. [Orlandos (1949) 259–271.]

T.107: *Chronicon Moreae*. Line 7792.

T.108: Gennadius Scholarius, *Grammatica*. Part 2, p. 457:32. (Theol.)

T.109: Symeon of Thessaloniki, *De Sacro Templo*. Ch. 133, col. 342 B/D.

T.110: *Fragmenta Alchemica*. Vol. 2, 379:21.

T.111: *Papyri magicae*. Number 4, line 1110.

This table presents a sample of the primary textual sources consulted in this study on canopies in the Byzantine church. Each source is numbered for easy reference in the major text of the book and other devised tables to aid the understanding of the chronological and geographical emergence and distribution of these sources (Tables 2 and 3). Each source is presented by the title and pointed to the line from the original text, where ciborium or other terms used for canopies are mentioned. Full bibliographic entries for each source can be found in the Bibliography. For more detailed references and further context, the readers may consult the TLG online reference or modern editions and translations of these sources.

TABLE 2 Texts with References to κιβώριον

TEXT. no.	DATE	PLACE	WORK	REFERENCE to κιβώριον						REMARKS
			Title and type of work	Egyptian beans	chalice	altar canopy	ambo canopy	reliquary or shrine	other	
T.2	3 BCE	Delphi	Hegesander, *Fragmenta.* Historical; Antiquarian	?					?	
T.3	3–2 BCE	Lydia, Anatolia	Nicander *Fragmenta* *The poems and poetical fragments* Poems	X						Text written by the Priest of the temple of Apollo
T.4	3–2 BCE.	Rhodos	Callixenus Hist., *Fragmenta* Historical; Antiquarian						X	
T.5	2 BCE	Knidos	Agatharchides Geogr., *Fragmenta* Historical; Geographical; Antiquarian	X						
T.6	1 BCE	Agyrium (now Agira), Sicily.	Diodorus Siculus Hist., *Bibliotheca historica (lib. 1–20).* Historical; Antiquarian	X						
T.7	1 BCE.–1 CE	Nysa, Anatolia Rome	Strabo Amasiotes Geogr., *Geographica* Geographical; Historical; Antiquarian	X						

TABLE 2 Continued

TEXT. no.	DATE	PLACE	WORK	REFERENCE to κιβώριον					REMARKS
T.8	1 CE?		Claudius Iolaus Hist., *Fragmenta* Historical; Antiquarian	X				?	
T.9	1 CE Post-1 CE	Anazarbus, Cilicia	Dioscorides Pedanius Med., *De materia medica*	X				X	κιβώριον = κιβώτιον
T.10	1–2 CE	Ephesus	Soranus Med., *Gynaeciorum libri iv*	X				X	
T.11	2 CE	Pergamon, Anatolia	Galenus Med., *De alimentorum facultatibus libri iii.* Medical	X					
T.12	2 CE		Pseudo-Galenus Med., *De theriaca ad Pamphilianum* Medical	X					
T.13	2 CE	Alexandria, Rome	Aelius Herodianus et Pseudo-Herodianus Gramm. et Rhet. Grammatical						Κιβώριον = κιβούριον
T.15	2–3 CE	Naucratis, near Alexandria, Egypt	Athenaeus Soph. *Deipnosophistae* Poetical, Antiquarian	X	X				
T.21	4–5 CE	Antioch Constantinople	John Chrysostom *In Acta apostolorum* *Patriarch,* Exegetical, Homiletic		?		?		κιβώρια μικρὰ
T.22	4 CE	Cappadocia, Asia Minor	St. Basil the Great *Historia Mystagogica* Theological			?			τὸ γὰρ κιβ ἐστὶ κιβωτός, τὸ δὲ οὔριν . . . φῶς κυρίου

T.23	4 CE	Pergamon, Anatolia	Oribasius Med., *Collectiones medicae* (lib. 1–16, 24–25, 43–50) Medical	X					
T.28	5 CE	Monastery of Rufinianae, near Bosphoros	Callinicus, *Vita sancti Hypatii* Monk Hagiography				?	?	The text also refers to double tetrapylon from the Hellenistic past as propylaeum to sacred precinct; The author probably comes from Syria
T.29	5 CE	Gaza	Marcus Diaconus *Vita Porphyrii episcopi Gazensis* Diacon, Hagiography				?		Roman structure in Gaza, presumably tetrapylon-like with a dome
T.30	Post-5 CE		*Catenae* (Novum Testamentum), *Catena in Acta* Exegetical		?		?		κιβώρια μικρὰ
T.31	5–6 CE	Rome	Sanctus Symmachus. *Anno Christi 498*		?		?		κιβώρια μικρὰ
T.32	6 CE	Jerusalem	Sophronius *Historia liturg. 2* Theological			?			ὁ κιβώριός στιν εἰς τύπον τῆς κιβωτοῦ τοῦ Νῶε τὸ μὸν κιβ κιβωτός τὸ δὲ ὥριον τουτέστι διςταξις αὐτοῦ
T.33	6 CE	Antioch	John Malalas, *Chronographia* Historical, Antiquarian, Theological			X			
T.41	6 CE	Amidenus	*Aëtius Iatricorum libri i-vi* Medical	X				X	

TABLE 2 Continued

TEXT. no.	DATE	PLACE	WORK	REFERENCE to κιβώριον				REMARKS
T.42	6 CE	Constantinople	Stephanus Gramm. Byzantius, *Ethnica* Lexicographic, Grammatical, Geographical, Antiquarian	X				
T.43	6 CE	Athens	Simplicius Phil. *In Aristotelis quattuor libros de caelo commentaria* Philological, Natural History, Commentaries, Antiquarian.	X				
T.44	6 CE	Alexandria	Cosmas Indicopleustes, *Topographia Christiana.* Theol., Geog., Antiq.	X				
T.45	6 CE	Alexandria	Hesychius Lexicogr., *Lexicon.* Lexicon	X	X			He also mentions that κιβώτιον is a saintly tomb (λάρναξ) of wood (ξυλίνη) or a shrine (σορός)
T.52	7 CE	Thessaloniki	Joannes I, *Miracula sancti Demetrii.* Archiepiscop., Hagiography				X	
T.53	7 CE	Constantinople	*Chronicon paschale.*	X		?	?	κιβούρια
T.54	7 CE	Syceota	Georgius Syceota Theol., *Vita sancti Theodori Syceotae* Hegoumenos, Hagiography				X	
T.56	Post-7 CE		*Vita et Miracula Sancti Demetri* Hagiography			?	X	
T.58	8 CE	Constantinople	Germanos *Ecclesiastical History and Mystical Contemplation* Patriarch, Theological			X		τὸ γὰρ ΚΙΒ ἐστὶ κιβωτός, τὸ δὲ ΟΥΡΙΝ φωτισμὸς Θεοῦ, ἤ φῶς Θεοῦ.

T.59	8–9 CE	Constantinople, Samothrace	Theophanes Confessor *Chronographia* Confessor; Historical, Antiquarian		?	X	?			Silver ciboria but with reference to chalices
T.61	9 CE	Constantinople	Theodore of Studion Theological Hymnography		?	?			?	Κιβούριον τοῦ Προδρόμου Chalice of St. John the Baptist? Or altar canopy above the relics of St. John the Baptist?
T.62	9 CE	Constantinople	Photius Theol., *Epistulae et Amphilochia* Patriarch; Epistol.; Theol.; Antiq.	X						κιβώτιον = κιβώριον
T.64	9 CE	Constantinople	Georgius Choeroboscus *De orthographia.* Diacon; Grammatical	?						Κιβώριον = κιβούριον
T.65	9 CE	Lesbos	*Vita sanctorum Davidis, Symeonis et Georgii Mitylenae* Hagiography			X		?		
T.66	9–10 CE	Jerusalem?	*Vita Eustratii* Hagiography					X		Seven-sided ciborium shrine!
T.69	10 CE	Constantinople	*Synaxarium: Octobris, 26* Synaxarion cf. Hagiography					X		The shrine is also considered a house (οἶκος) of St. Demetrios
T.70	10 CE		*Vita Eliae Junioris* Hagiography					X		
T.71	10 CE	Constantinople	Constantinus VII Porphyrogenitus *De cerimoniis* Emperor Historical; Church History; Ecclesiastical; Antiquarian			X			X	Silver columns and golden curtains. Reference to canopy in the Consistorium Palace Compilation of texts 6–10 CE
T.73	10–15 CE	Constantinople	Pseudo-Codinus Hist., *Patria Constantinopoleos.* Historical, Antiquarian					X		Shrine for the sandals of Christ, in the Chalki of the Savior

TABLE 2 Continued

TEXT. no.	DATE	PLACE	WORK	REFERENCE to κιβώριcν	REMARKS
T.77	1047	Sparta? Peloponnesus?	*Vita et Miracula Niconis* Hagiography	X	Textual borrowings from the Life of St. Luke of Phocis, the saint is depicted in the mosaics! Other editions 15–17 CE
T.78	11 CE	Constantinople, Trapezunt	Joannes VIII Xiphilinus, *De miraculis sancti Eugenii* Patriarch, Nomopylax Hagiography	X	Lamps on the canopy-shrine, over the tomb
T.79	11 CE		*Etymologicum Gudianum.* Grammatical, Theological	?	Κιβώριον, τὸ κὶβ σημαίνει κιβωτὸς, τὸ δὲ ὤριον φωτισμὸς, ἢ . . . . Λεκτίκιον, παρὰ τὸ λέχος, ὃ σημαίνει τὴν κοίτην·κιβώριον ἐκ ξύλων, ὃ ἔχουσιν αἱ παρθένοι πρὸς τὸ καλύπτεσθαι αὐτάς. wooden canopy.
T.80	11–12 CE	Constantinople	Georgius Cedrenus, *Compendium historiarum.* Monk; Histor., Chronogr.; Antiq.	X ?	
T.81	11–12 CE	Constantinople	Joannes Zonaras, *Epitome historiarum* Monk; Histor.; Antiq.	X ?	

T.82	11–12 CE	Andida, Pergamon, Anatolia	Theodore of Andydas Pg. 140, 417, col. 443–44 Episcope Theological		X			Not all churches have *kiboria*; however, the hemispherical form of the *bema* can suggest the sky (*ouranos*) above the holy table.
T.83	12 CE	Thessaloniki	Eustathius Philol., *Commentarii ad Homeri Iliadem.* Archiepiscope Commentaries; Antiq.	X				
T.94	14 CE ~1340	Thessaloniki	Grigorios of Thess. *Phisica, Theologica* *Philokalia*		?		?	Earth no. 4, Explained in the context of Heavens—circle
T.107	14 CE	Frankish Morea	*Chronicon Moreae*		X		X	
T.108	15 CE	Constantinople	Gennadius Scholarius, *Grammatica* Grammatical; Theological				X	
T.109	15 CE	Thessaloniki	*Symeon of Thessaloniki* *De Sacro Templo*		X			Curtained altar canopy
T.110	?		*Fragmenta Alchemica* Alchemical	?			?	
T.111	?		*Magica, Papyri magicae* Magic			?	?	

This table summarizes the chronological and geographical emergence of various textual sources that mention the term κιβώριον [ciborium], which are often associated with canopy-like installations in the Byzantine-rite churches. Each source is numbered for easy reference in the major text of the book and other tables (Tables 1 and 3). Each source is presented by the title, date, and place of production when known; then, the original meaning of the term κιβώριον [ciborium] is explained when known. For more detailed references and further context, the readers may consult the TLG online reference or modern editions and translations of the examined sources.

TABLE 3 Terms for Canopies

TEXT NO.	DATE	PLACE	WORK	WORD	TYPE OF CANOPY	REMARKS
T.1	6 BCE and older		*Orphica, Hymni*. Hymn P, line 39.	τετρακίονος	?	
T.2	3 BCE	Delphi	Hegesander, *Fragmenta.*	κιβώριον	?	Historical; antiquarian text
T.3	3–2 BCE	Lydia, Anatolia	Nicander *Fragmenta*	Κιβώριον	?	Not a canopy but kind of Egyptian beans Text written by a priest of the temple of Apollo
T.4	3–2 BCE	Rhodos	Callixenus Hist., *Fragmenta*	κιβώριον		
T.5	2 BCE	Knidos	*Agatharchides Geogr., Fragmenta*	Κιβώριον	?	Not a canopy but kind of Egyptian beans
T.6	1 BCE	Agyrium (now Agira), Sicily	Diodorus Siculus Hist., *Bibliotheca historica*	Κιβώριον	?	Not a canopy but kind of Egyptian beans
T.7	1 BCE –1 CE	Nysa, Anatolia Rome	Strabo Amasiotes Geogr., *Geographica*	Κιβώριον	?	Not a canopy but kind of Egyptian beans
T.8	1 CE?		Claudius Iolaus Hist., *Fragmenta*	Κιβώριον	?	Not a canopy but kind of Egyptian beans
T.9	1 CE Post–1 CE	Anazarbus, Cilicia	Dioscorides Pedanius Med., *De materia medica*	Κιβώριον κιβώριον = κιβώτιον	?	Not a canopy but kind of Egyptian beans κιβώριον = κιβώτιον
T.10	1–2 CE	Ephesus	Soranus Med., *Gynaeciorum libri iv*	Κιβώριον	?	Not a canopy but kind of Egyptian beans
T.11	2 CE	Pergamon, Anatolia	Galenus Med., *De alimentorum facultatibus libri iii*	Κιβώριον	?	Not a canopy but kind of Egyptian beans

T.12	2 CE		Pseudo-Galenus Med., *De theriaca ad Pamphilianum*	Κιβώριον	?	Not a canopy but kind of Egyptian beans
T.13	2 CE	Alexandria, Rome	Aelius Herodianus et Pseudo-Herodianus Gramm. et Rhet.	Κιβώριον = κιβούριον		Κιβώριον = κιβούριον
T.14	2 CE		Pausanias Hist., *Fragmenta*	τετρακίονος	altar canopy?	Influenced Malalas, who uses same textual reference in his writings
T.15	2–3 CE	Naucratis, near Alexandria, Egypt	Athenaeus Soph., *Deipnosophistae*	Κιβώριον	Chalice	Not a canopy but kind of Egyptian beans; Also a reference to a chalice used in pagan temples
T.16	3–4 CE		Eusebius, *Demonstratio evangelica*	Καταπέτασμα		With reference to the Temple veil
T.17	4 CE	Nyssenus	Gregory Nazianzes, *De vita Mosis*	Καταπετάσματα		With reference to the Temple veil from the Scriptures
T.18	4 CE	Alexandria	Cyril. Alexandr., *De adoratione et cultu in spiritu et veritate*	Καταπετάσμα		With reference to the Ark and the holy tent from the Scriptures
T.19	4 CE		Athanasius Theol., *Expositiones in Psalmos.*	πύργος		With reference to Zion
T.20	4 CE	Antioch	John Chrysostom 1 Cor. Hom. 36.5, Eph. Hom. 3.5	παραπετάσμα	canopy?	Curtains around the altar table—canopy?
T.21	4–5 CE	Antioch, Constantinople	*Joannes Chrysostomus, In Acta apostolorum*	κιβώρια μικρὰ	?	Silver chalices or shrines
T.22	4 CE	Cappadocia, Asia Minor	St. Basil the Great *Historia Mystagogica*	Κιβώριον	Altar canopy?	Theological text

TABLE 3 Continued

TEXT NO.	DATE	PLACE	WORK	WORD	TYPE OF CANOPY	REMARKS
T.23	4 CE	Pergamon, Anatolia	Oribasius Med., *Collectiones medicae* (lib. 1–16, 24–25, 43–50)	Κιβώριον	?	Not a canopy but kind of Egyptian beans
T.24	4–6 CE	Egypt, Palestine	*Marcus Eremita, De baptismo*	Καταπετάσματα	Baptistery canopy?	With reference to the Temple veil
T.25	5 CE	Ravenna	Agnellus XXVI, *De Victor*		Altar canopy	Altar canopy, made of silver replaced by wooden; St. Ursiana church
T.26	5 CE	Antioch	*Theodore of Cyrrhus, Church History*	παραπετάσμα		Imperial hangings around the altar in the Anastasis Basilica in Jerusalem
T.27	5 CE	Seleucia Isauria	Basilus Seleuciensis, *De vita et miraculis sanctae Theclae*	κοινὸν	Saintly shrine	Canopy over St. Thecla shrine Connected to the concept of *oikia* (small house): κοινὸν τάφοις καὶ εὐκτηρίοις οἴκοις
T.28	5 CE	Monastery of Rufinianae, near Bosphoros	Callinicus, *Vita sancti Hypatii*	Κιβώριον	Shrine?	
T.29	5 CE	Gaza	Marcus Diaconus, *Vita Porphyrii episcopi Gazensis*	Κιβώριον	Saintly shrine?	
T.30	After 5 CE		*Catenae* (Novum Testamentum), *Catena in Acta*	κιβώρια μικρὰ	Chalices or shrines	From St. John Chrysostom
T.31	5–6 CE	Rome	*Sanctus Symmachus. Anno Christi 498*	κιβωρια μικρά	Chalices or shrines	
T.32	6 CE	Jerusalem	Sophronius *Historia liturg. 2*	Κιβώριον	Altar canopy?	Reference to the Ark of Noah

T.33	6 CE	Antioch	John Malalas, *Chronographia*	Κιβώριον	Altar canopy	Reference to the destruction of the altar canopy in Hagia Sophia
T.34	5–6 CE	Antioch	Joannes Malalas, *Chronographia*	τετρακίονος		On ancient canopied structures
T.35	6 CE	Antioch	Joannes Malalas, *Chronographia*.	Τετραπύλου		On imperial canopy in the public city space
T.36	6 CE	Antioch	Joannes Malalas, *Chronographia*	Τετραπύλου		Reference to the tetrapylon of the monastery of Rufinianus (T.28)
T.37	6 CE	Antioch	Evagrius Scholasticus Scr. Eccl., *Historia ecclesiastica*.	Τετραπύλου	Baptistery canopy	With reference to the rite of baptism
T.38	6 CE	Syria	Evagrius Scholasticus Scr. Eccl., *Historia ecclesiastica*	Τετραπύλου		Reference to the earthquake that destroyed *tetrapylon* of Mamianus in Antioch
T.39	6 CE	Syria	Evagrius Scholasticus Scr. Eccl., *Historia ecclesiastica*	παραπετάσμα	altar canopy?	Curtains around the altar table, possibly from the altar canopy
T.40	6 CE	Constantinople	Paul the Silentary. *Descriptio S. Sophiae*	πύργος	Altar canopy	Altar canopy in Hagia Sophia
T.41	6 CE	Amidenus	Aëtius, *Iatricorum libri*	Κιβώριον	?	Not a canopy but kind of Egyptian beans
T.42	6 CE	Constantinople	Stephanus Gramm. Byzantius, *Ethnica*	Κιβώριον	?	Not a canopy but kind of Egyptian beans
T.43	6 CE	Athens	Simplicius Phil., *In Aristotelis quattuor libros de caelo commentaria*	Κιβώριον	?	Not a canopy but kind of Egyptian beans
T.44	6 CE	Alexandria	Cosmas Indicopleustes, *Topographia Christiana*	Κιβώριον	?	Not a canopy but kind of Egyptian beans

TABLE 3 Continued

TEXT NO.	DATE	PLACE	WORK	WORD	TYPE OF CANOPY	REMARKS
T.45	6 CE	Alexandria	Hesychius, *Lexicon.*	Κιβώριον	?	Not a canopy but kind of Egyptian beans
T.46	6 CE	Alexandria	Hesychius, *Lexicon.*	κιβώτιον	Saintly tomb	Reference to the wooden burial chest (*larnax*)
T.47	6 CE 516	St. Drosis in Antioch	*Patriarch Severus Sermon*	hemisphaira	Altar canopy	Reference to the silver domed canopy
T.48	6–10 CE		*Vitae Symeonis Stylitae Junioris*	Καταπετάσματα		Comparison with the four veils of the altar
T.49	7 CE	Cathedral of Edessa	*Chronicle of 1234*		Altar canopy	Altar canopy made of silver Dedicatory hymn of 622
T.50	7 CE	Arabissos in Cappadocia				E. Maurice (r. 582–602) sent an entire ciborium in pieces from Constantinople to the church in his native town, Arabissos
T.51	7 CE	Cyprus	Leontius, *Vita Joannis Eleemosynarii episcopi Alexandrini*	Καταπετάσματα	Altar canopy?	Katapesmata in reference to sanctuary and the holy veil of the Temple
T.52	7 CE	Thessaloniki	Joannes I, *Miracula sancti Demetrii.* Archiepiscop	Κιβώριον	Saintly shrine	Shrine of St. Demetrios, Thessaloniki
T.53	7 CE	Constantinople	*Chronicon paschale.*	κιβούρια	[Altar] shrine canopies	*Vel Chr. Alexandrinum, vel Chr. Constantinopolitanum, vel Fasti Siculi*—on the Arab destruction

T.54	7 CE	Syceota	*Georgius Syceota, Vita sancti Theodori Syceotae*	Κιβώριον	Saintly shrine	Shrine of St. Theodore Syceotae; Text also mentions curtains [καταπετάσματα] in the sanctuary above the holy doors
T.55	7–10 CE		*Vitae et Miracula Sancti Anastasii Persae*	Τετραπύλον	Saintly shrine	Shrine of St. Anastasius the Persian
T.56	after 7 CE	Thessaloniki Constantinople	*Vita et Miracula Sancti Demetri*	Κιβώριον	Saintly shrine	Shrine of St. Demetrios, Thessaloniki
T.57	after 9 CE	Thessaloniki Constantinople	*Vita et Miracula Sancti Demetri*	οἰκίσκος	Chapel-canopy?	Shrine of St. Demetrios, Thess.
T.58	8 CE	Constantinople	Germanos *Ecclesiastical History and Mystical Contemplation* Patriarch	Κιβώριον	Altar canopy	Influential theological text
T.59	8–9 CE	Constantinople Samothrace	Theophanes Confessor, *Chronographia*	Τετράβηλον	Canopy?	*Tetravila* of the Hagia Sophia, possibly curtains for the canopy
T.60	8–9 CE	Constantinople, Samothrace	Theophanes Confessor, *Chronographia* Confessor	Κιβώριον	Chalices? Altar canopy?	Silver *ciboria*
T.61	9 CE	Constantinople	Theodore of Studion	Κιβούριον τοῦ Προδρόμου	Altar canopy	Altar canopy above the relics of St. John the Baptist rather than a chalice
T.62	9 CE	Constantinople	Photius, *Epistulae et Amphilochia* *Patriarch*	Κιβώριον	?	Not a canopy but kind of Egyptian beans κιβώτιον = κιβώριον
T.63	9 CE	Constantinople	Photius, *Homiliae*. Hm. 10	στυλίσκοις ὑπωρόφοις ὄροφος	Altar canopy	Altar canopy from the church of Pharos

TABLE 3 Continued

TEXT NO.	DATE	PLACE	WORK	WORD	TYPE OF CANOPY	REMARKS
T.64	9 CE	Constantinople	Georgius Choeroboscus, *De orthographia*	Κιβώριον		Not a canopy but kind of Egyptian beans Κιβώριον = κιβούριον
T.65	9 CE	Lesbos	*Vita sanctorum Davidis, Symeonis et Georgii Mitylenae*	Κιβώριον	Altar canopy Shrine? Reliquary?	Most likely altar canopy
T.66	9–10 CE	Jerusalem?	*Vita Eustratii*	Κιβώριον	Seven-sided canopy-shrine	Saintly shrine
T.67	10 CE	Constantinople	*Synaxarion* CP	Τετραπύλον	Saintly shrine	Bronze canopy over relics of the 40 martyrs of Sebaste The canopy is mentioned by Clavijo in 15th c. as in ruins
T.68	10 CE	Constantinople	Nicetas Magister, *Vita S. Theoctistae Lesbiae*	ορόφιον	Altar canopy	altar canopy at Paros, still *in situ*
T.69	10 CE	Constantinople	*Synaxarion* CP, *Synaxarium mensis Octobris, Day 26*	Κιβώριον οἶκος	Saintly shrine	Shrine of St. Demetrios, Thessaloniki
T.70	10 CE		*Vita Eliae Junioris*	Κιβώριον	Saintly shrine	Shrine of St. Demetrios, Thess.
T.71	10 CE (6–10 CE)	Constantinople	Constantinus VII Porphyrogenitu, *De cerimoniis aulae Byzantinae (lib. 1.84–2.56)* Emperor	Κιβώριον	Altar canopy	Multiple meanings: Altar canopy; canopy on silver columns and with golden curtains in the palace of Bonus constructed by Emperor Roman Lacapene I (920–944) dedicated to E. Constantine I—celebration of 21st of May and the veneration of the Cross; imperial canopy in Consistorium

T.72	10–15 CE	Constantinople	Pseudo-Codinus, *Patria Constantinopoleos*	Τετραπύλου Τετράβηλον	Canopy	Identifying tetrapylon and tetravelon as the same object
T.73	10–15 CE	Constantinople	Pseudo-Codinus, *Patria Constantinopoleos*	Κιβώριον	Saintly shrine	Shrine for the sandals of Christ, in the Chalki of the Savior
T.74	11 CE	Constantinople	Michael Psellus, *Theologica.*	Καταπέτασμα	Shrine canopy?	Curtains above the Cross reference to Mosaic law.
T.75	11 CE	Constantinople	Michael Psellus, *Laudatio in Joannem Crustulam.*	Καταπέτασμα		
T.76	11 CE	Constantinople	Nicetas Stethatus, *Vita Simeonis Novi Theologici*	Καταπετάσματα		
T.77	11 CE 1047	Sparta? Peloponnesus?	*Vita et Miracula Niconis*	Κιβώριον	Saintly shrine	Other editions 15–17 CE
T.78	11 CE	Constantinople, Trapezunt	*Joannes VIII Xiphilinus, De miraculis sancti Eugenii*	Κιβώριον	Saintly shrine	Lamps on the canopy-shrine over the tomb
T.79	11 CE		*Etymologicum Gudianum*	Κιβώριον	Altar canopy	
T.80	11–12 CE	Constantinople	Georgius Cedrenus, *Compendium historiarum*	Κιβώριον	Altar canopy Ambo-canopy?	
T.81	11–12 CE	Constantinople	Joannes Zonaras, *Epitome historiarum*	Κιβώριον	Altar canopy Ambo Canopy?	
T.82	11–12 CE	Andida, Pergamon, Anatolia	Theodore of Andydas	Κιβώριον	Altar canopy	Information that not all churches have canopies (*kiboria*)
T.83	12 CE	Thessaloniki	Eustathius, *Commentarii ad Homeri Iliadem*	Κιβώριον		Not a canopy but kind of Egyptian beans
T.84	12 CE 1110–1116	Constantinople	*Typikon* of the *Kecharitomene*	Π<έπλ>α	Canopy?	Π<έπλ>α τῶν δ' διαστύλων τ. . . . τύπον ἔχοντα σταυροῦ εἰκονισμεν. . . . Curtains of the four columns?

TABLE 3 Continued

TEXT NO.	DATE	PLACE	WORK	WORD	TYPE OF CANOPY	REMARKS
T.85	12 CE	Athens	*Michael Accominatus*		Altar canopy	Church of the Mother of God (Theotokos Atheniotissa) on the site of Parthenon in Athens
T.86	12 CE	Constantinople	Anna Komnene, *Alexiad.*	Καταπέτασμα	Imperial canopy	
T.87	12–13 CE	Constantinople	Nicolaus Mesarites, *Descriptio ecclesiae SS. Apostolorum*	ὀρόφιον	Altar canopy	Altar canopy of the Holy Apostles in Constantinople
T.88	12–13 CE	Constantinople	Nicolaus Mesarites, *Seditio Joanni Comneni*	καταπέτασμα	Altar canopy?	
T.89	12–13 CE	Constantinople	Nicetas Choniates, *Chronographia*	Καταπετάσματα	Altar canopy	Altar canopy in Hagia Sophia
T.90	12–14 CE before 1360		Anon. *Marc. Gr. 444*	ορόφιον	Baptismal canopy	Baptismal canopy from the *Progymnasmata*; now lost
T.91	13 CE d. 1232	Novgorod	Anthony of Novgorod	Катапезма Slavic version of the Greek word Καταπετάσμα	Altar canopy	Curtained altar canopy in Hagia Sophia
T.92	13 CE	Constantinople	*Deed of concession to the Genoese of certain areas of Constantinople (October 13, 1202)*	Καταπέτασμα [harmosphenion]	Altar canopy [icon canopy?]	from the *Inventory of the So-called Palace of Botaniates*

T.93	13 CE 1247	Skoteine, near Philadelphia, Asia Minor	*Testament* of Maximos for the Monastery at Skoteine	θείο τρούλλο	Canopy?	Small metal crosses with a censer in the sacred dome (potentially a canopy).
T.94	14 CE ~1340	Thessaloniki	*Grigorios of Thessaloniki, Philokalia*	Κιβώριον	Canopy?	Reference to structure of the canopy and microcosmic symbolism: Earth—4-square, Heavens—circle
T.95	14 CE	Constantinople Thessaloniki	Isidorus Glabas, *Homiliae in sanctum Demetrium*	Καταπετάσματα	Canopy	
T.96	14 CE	Constantinople	*Theoktistos the Stoudite*	Apsis apsida—άψῖδα	Tomb canopy	Tomb canopy of St. Athanasios I (1289–1293, 1303–1309), who was buried sometime after 1323 presumably in the Church of Christ Savior in Athanasios' monastery on Xerolophos, now lost
T.97	14 CE	Trebizond	Anonymous Epic poem	Apsida—άψίδα	Tomb canopy	Tomb of Digenes Akrites
T.98	14 CE (1348–9)	Novgorod	Stephen of Novgorod, From the "Wanderer of Stephen of Novgorod"	Canopy—кивот Old Church Slavonic version for the Greek word *kibotion*	Canopy over the icon—in the open space	Reference to the Tuesday miracle in Constantinople with the icon
T.99	14 CE (1348–9)	Novgorod	Stephen of Novgorod From the "Wanderer of Stephen of Novgorod"	Canopy—киотъ Old Church Slavonic version for the Greek word *kibotion*, ark, chest	Canopy over the icon	According to Stephen—the miraculous icon of Christ Savior in the Church of the Holy Apostoloi, Constantinople stabbed by the unbeliever—Jew

TABLE 3 Continued

TEXT NO.	DATE	PLACE	WORK	WORD	TYPE OF CANOPY	REMARKS
T.100	14 CE (1389–1391)	Novgorod?	*RussAnon*	Apsida—ἁψίδα Apsida—Slavonic version of the Greek word	Canopy over phiale	Open lid-covered canopy over the stone phiale in Hagia Sophia
T.101	14 CE (1389–1391)	Novgorod?	*RussAnon*	Canopy—теремецъ Old Church Slavonic	Canopy over the icon	Canopied shrine over the miraculous icon of the Mother of God in the north aisle of Hagia Sophia
T.102	14 CE (1389–1391)	Novgorod?	*RussAnon*	Canopy—Russian word for columns	Canopy shrine	Canopy made of wood (of Noah's Ark!) at the west end of the north aisle of Hagia Sophia. The canopy itself was venerated as a relic
T.103	14 CE (1389–1391)	Novgorod?	*RussAnon*	Canopy—кивор Slavic version of the word *kiborion*!	Canopy shrine	Canopy over the body of St. Polyeuktos in the Church of Holy Apostles in Constantinople. The body must have been in the nearby church until the eleventh century and then moved to the Holy Apostles.
T.104	14 CE (1389–1391)	Novgorod?	*RussAnon*	Canopy—кивор	Canopy shrine	Canopy over the body of St. Spiridon in the Church of Holy Apostles in Constantinople, located north to the sanctuary which was in the center of the church

T.105	14 CE (1389–1391)	Novgorod?	*RussAnon*	Canopy—теремець Old Church Slavonic	Canopy over the phiale	Canopy over the phiale in the monastery of St. George of Mangana in Constantinople
T.106	14 CE	Thessaloniki		οἰκίσκος	Canopy over the icon	Canopy of John Prodromos in Serres, Thess.
T.107	14 CE	Frankish Morea	*Chronicon Moreae*	κιβούριον	Altar canopy	
T.108	15 CE	Constantinople	Gennadius Scholarius, *Grammatica*	Κιβώριον	?	
T.109	15 CE	Thessaloniki	*Symeon of Thessaloniki De Sacro Templo*	Κιβώριον	Altar canopy	
T.110	n.d.		*Fragmenta Alchemica*	Κιβώριον	?	Possibly Egyptian beans
T.111	n.d.		*Magica, Papyri magicae*	Κιβώριον	Shrine?	

This table summarizes the chronological and geographical emergence of various textual sources that mention ciboria and other terms, which can be associated with canopy-like installations in the Byzantine-rite churches. Each source is numbered for easy reference in the major text of the book and other tables (Tables 1 and 2). Each source is presented by the title, date, and place of production when known; the original term used in reference to ciboria and various canopies is mentioned and, when applicable, additional remarks are made to better understand the original context and importance of the source. For more detailed references and further context, the readers may consult the TLG online reference or modern editions and translations of the examined sources.

TABLE 4 Copying Texts with References to Ciboria or Canopies

1.	
Cat. nos.	T.3 → T.15 → T.45 → T.83
Date:	3–2 BCE →2–3 CE → 6 CE → 12 CE
Place:	Lydia, Anatolia → Naucratis, near Alexandria, Egypt → Alexandria, Egypt → Thessaloniki, Greece
Work:	Nicander Fragmenta. → Athenaeus Soph. Deipnosophistae → Hesychius Lexicogr., Lexicon. → Eustathius Commentarii ad Homeri Iliadem.
Type of work:	Poems → poetical, antiquarian → lexicon → commentaries, antiquarian
Remarks:	Nicander uses the word κιβώριον for a kind of Egyptian beans; Athenaeus cites directly Nicander and expands the meaning of the word to a chalice used in pagan temples; Hesychius uses the word κιβώριον in his lexicon and combines it with the word κιβώτιον, a saintly tomb (λάρναξ) of wood (ξυλίνη) or a shrine (σορός); Archbishop Eustathius cites directly Nicander and Homer, and uses the word κιβώριον for a kind of Egyptian beans
2.	
Cat. nos.	T.8 → T.42
Date:	1 CE (?) → 6 CE
Place:	? → Constantinople
Work:	Claudius Iolaus, Fragmenta → Stephanus Gramm. Byzantius, Ethnica
Type of work:	Historical, antiquarian → lexicographic, grammatical, geographical, antiquarian
Remarks:	Claudius Iolaus uses the word κιβώριον for a kind of Egyptian beans; Stephanus Gramm. directly cites Claudius Iolaus
3.	
Cat. nos.	T.21 → T.30 → T.31
Date:	4–5 CE → after 5 CE → 498–514
Place:	Antioch and Constantinople → Mediterranean basin → Rome
Work:	John Chrys., In Acta apostolorum → Catenae (Novum Testamentum), Catena in Acta → Pope Symachus, Anno Christi 498, Anastasii Imp. 8 Theodor. Regis 5.
Type of work:	Exegetical, homiletic → exegetical → commentaries, antiquarian
Remarks:	John Chrysostom uses the expression κιβώρια μικρὰ for either chalices or reliquaries; Pope Symachus adopts explanation by Chrysostom; Chrysostom's explanation enters catenae.
4.	
Cat. nos.	T.22 → T.58 → T.79
Date:	4 CE → 8 CE → 11 CE
Place:	Cappadocia, Asia Minor → Constantinople → Constantinople

TABLE 4 Continued

Work:	St. Basil the Great, Historia Mystagogica → Germanos, Ecclesiastical History and Mystical Contemplation → Etymologicum Gudianum
Type of work:	Theological, exegetical → theological, exegetical → grammatical, theological
Remarks:	St. Basil the Great explains the ciborium, possibly referring to the altar canopy: τὸ γὰρ κιβ ἐστὶ κιβωτός, τὸ δὲ οὔριν . . . φῶς κυρίου; Patriarch Germanos adopts explanation by Basil the Great: τὸ γὰρ ΚΙΒ ἐστὶ κιβωτός, τὸ δὲ ΟΥΡΙΝ φωτισμὸς Θεοῦ, ἤ φῶς Θεοῦ; By the 11th c., the explanation enters Etymologicum Gudianum: Κιβώριον, τὸ κὶβ σημαίνει κιβωτὸς, τὸ δὲ ὥριον φωτισμὸς, ἤ . . . ; however, it is combined with additional explanation of wooden canopies, suggesting that there are also wooden canopies in Byzantine churches: Λεκτίκιον, παρὰ τὸ λέχος, ὃ σημαίνει τὴν κοίτην·κιβώριον ἐκ ξύλων, ὃ ἔχουσιν αἱ παρθένοι πρὸς τὸ καλύπτεσθαι αὐτάς. Germanos' work was widely published and remained quasi-official explanation for the ciborium until the 15th c.
5.	
Cat. nos.	T.28/T.29 → T.52/T.54 → T.56/T.57 → T.65 → T.66/T.69/T.70 → T.73 → T.77/ T.78 → T.103/T.104
Date:	5 CE/5 CE→ 7 CE/7 CE → after 7 CE/after 9 CE → 9 CE → 9–10 CE/10 CE/10 CE → 10–15 CE → 11 CE/11 CE → 14 CE/14 CE
Place:	Monastery of Rufinianae, near Bosphoros; the author probably comes from Syria/Gaza → Thessaloniki/Syceota → Constantinople → Lesbos → Jerusalem?/Constantinople → Constantinople → Sparta? Peloponnesus?/ Constantinople, Trapezunt → Novgorod- Constantinople/ Novgorod- Constantinople
Work:	Callinicus, Vita sancti Hypatii/Marcus Diaconus Scr. Eccl., Vita Porphyrii episcopi Gazensis → Joannes I Scr. Eccl. et Hagiogr., Miracula sancti Demetrii/Georgius Syceota Theol., Vita sancti Theodori Syceotae → Vita et Miracula Sancti Demetri → Vita sanctorum Davidis, Symeonis et Georgii Mitylenae → Vita Eustratii/Synaxarium Ecclesiae Constantinopoleos, Octobri 26/Vita Eliae Junioris → Pseudo-Codinus, Patria Constantinopoleos → Vita et Miracula Niconis/Joannes VIII Xiphilinus, De miraculis sancti Eugenii → RussAnon/RussAnon
Type of work:	Hagiography, monastic tradition/hagiography, monastic tradition → hagiography/hagiography → hagiography → hagiography → hagiography/ hagiography/hagiography → historiographical → hagiography/ hagiography → pilgrim diary, antiquarian/pilgrim diary, antiquarian
Remarks:	In the 5th c., Callinicus uses the word κιβώριον for a saint's shrine or reliquary, while Marcus the deacon uses the same word for Roman structure in Gaza, presumably on four columns with a dome;

TABLE 4 Continued

	In the 7th c., Archbishop John uses the same term κιβώριον for the ciborium-shrine of St. Demetrios in Thessaloniki, which most likely never was in the shape of a canopy. At the same time, hegumenos George uses the same term κιβώριον for the saint's shrine of St. Theodore Syceote; After the 7th c., the term κιβώριον is used in hagiographies for various saints' shrines, but always in connection with the shrine of St. Demetrios, once the term entered the Synaxarion CP. At least from the 10th c., judging by the Synaxarion CP, the ciborium-shrine of St. Demetrios was also related to the concept of his eternal house (οἶκος); After the 10th c., the word was used even for the shrine for the sandals of Christ in Constantinople. In the 14th c., Russian anonymous pilgrim uses Slavic version of the word κιβώριον for saints' canopies in the Holy Apostles in Constantinople.
6.	
Cat. nos.	T.9 → T.32/T.46→ T.62 → T.98/T.99
Date:	1 CE (after 1 CE) → 6 CE/6 CE → 9 CE → 14 CE/14 CE
Place:	Cilicia → Alexandria, Egypt/Jerusalem → Constantinople → Novgorod-Constantinople/Novgorod-Constantinople
Work:	Dioscorides Pedanius Med., De materia medica → Sophronius, Historia liturg. 2/Hesychius Lexicogr., Lexicon. → Photius Theol., Epistulae et Amphilochia → Stephen of Novgorod, "Wanderer of Stephen of Novgorod"
Type of work:	Medical treatise → church history/historical, antiquarian → epistolary, church history → pilgrim diary, antiquarian/pilgrim diary, antiquarian
Remarks:	Dioscorides Pedianus conflated the words κιβώριον and κιβώτιον in the 1st c. The combination of the two words with references to shrines and wooden reliquaries is attested in the 6th c. in Hesychius' lexicon and Sophronios' history of liturgy ('Ο κιβώριός ἐστιν εἰς τύπον τῆς κιβωτοῦ · τὰ δέ παρακιόνα κατὰ μίμησιν τῶν τεσσάρων ζώων τῶν ὀφθέντων τῷ προφήτη 2 PG 87, 3984). The conflation is attested in the 9th c. by Constantinopolitan Patriarch Photios. In the 14th c., Stephen of Novgorod used the Slavic version of the word κιβώτιον to describe the canopy over the miraculous icon in Constantinople.
7.	
Cat. nos.	T.14 → T.35/T.36 → T.38 → T.67
Date:	2 CE → 5–6 CE → 6 CE → 10 CE
Place:	Asia Minor → Antioch/Antioch → Syria → Constantinople
Work:	Pausanias Hist., Fragmenta Fragment 4 → Joannes Malalas, Chronographia → Evagrius Scholasticus, Historia ecclesiastica → Synaxarion CP

TABLE 4 Continued

Type of work:	Geographical, historical, antiquarian → historical, antiquarian → church history → synaxarion, liturgical calendar
Remarks:	In the 6th c., John Malalas, who also quotes Evagrius Scholasticus, write of stone tetrapylon adorned in bronze, which was built in Antioch by a certain Mammianus, a member of the Senate during the reign of Zeno (474–491), by repeating the words from Pausanias. Bronze canopy (tetrapylon) over relics of the 40 martyrs of Sebaste in Constantinople was a public monument mentioned in the Synaxarion from the 10th c. onward. In the 15th c., the canopy from Constantinople was mentioned by Clavijo as in ruins.

This table showcases some examples of chronological and geographical distribution of the terminology related to canopies and how associated meanings of these objects were transmitted through texts of various genres and in different contexts (see also Tables 1, 2, and 3,). Though certainly not comprehensive, this sampling is also important because, when these references are juxtaposed with archeological and architectural evidence, they highlight how the intellectual elite responded to the changing and interrelated terminology related to canopies, and at the same time point to potential contradictions and complexities for understanding the role of canopies as architectural installations within Byzantine churches.

TABLE 5 List of Archeologically Attested Canopies in the Byzantine Ecclesiastical Tradition

CAT. NO.	DATE	LOCATION	CONTEXT REMARKS	TYPE OF CANOPY
1	3 CE	Dura Europos, Syria	Two-columned "arcosolium-type" canopy	Baptistery canopy
2	after 4 CE	Basilica at Metropolis, Gortyn, Greece	*Opus sectile* flooring	Altar canopy
3	4–5 CE	Morgorjelo, Dalmatia, Croatia		Tomb canopy?
4	5 CE	Memoria, Majsan, Dalmatia, Croatia	Tomb of a local saint Maxim (Maximus), who died in 346, in the 5th c., added altar and the entire space canopied	Tomb and altar canopy? One installation
5	5 CE	St. John the Baptist, in the Studion, Constantinople		Altar canopy
6	5 CE	Bargala, F.Y.R. of Macedonia		Altar canopy
7	5 CE	Bargala, F.Y.R. of Macedonia	Tomb site converted into baptistery; covered by an eight-sided canopy	Tomb and baptistery canopy one installation
8	5 CE	Basilica Sabratha in Tunisia, North Africa		Altar canopy
9	5 CE	Basilica Sbeitla, Tunisia, North Africa		Altar canopy
10	5 CE	Basilica Sbeitla, Jucundus Chapel Baptistery, Tunisia, North Africa	Tomb of Bishop Jucundus incorporated into the baptistery; elongated undulated marble font decorated in mosaics	Baptistery and tomb canopy one installation
11	5 CE	Basilica at Tigzirt, Algeria		Altar canopy
12	5 CE	Hagiasma of H. Ioannis, near Hagia Sophia, Thessaloniki, Greece	Six columns set at corners of a six-lobed baptistery and framing the central marble font; massive canopy structure	Massive Baptistery canopy
13	5 CE?	St. Demetrios Thessaloniki, Greece	Marble footings of a six-sided canopy visible in the main nave of the church	Shrine canopy

14	5 CE	Basilica A, Philippi, Greece		Altar canopy
15	5 CE	Basilica A, Thebes, Thessaly, Greece		Altar canopy
16	5–6 CE	Basilica A, Thebes, Thessaly, Greece	Three-columned canopy	Ambo canopy
17	5 CE	Basilica H. Nikon in Sparta, Greece		Altar canopy
18	5 CE	Church 3A in Diocletianopolis (Hissar), Bulgaria		Altar canopy
19	5 CE	H. Ioannis on the Aegean island Kos		Altar canopy
20	5 CE	East Basilica, Xantos, Lycia		Altar canopy
21	5 CE	Heraeon Basilica at Samos, Greece		Altar canopy
22	5 CE	Basilica in Sirmium (Sremska Mitrovica), Serbia		Altar canopy
23	5 CE	Venice, Italy (from Constantinople?)	Inscription [in Greek] on two sides only; canopy most likely abutted to the north wall	Small-scale canopy artophorion?
24	5 CE ca. 450–60	Hosios Leonidas in Corinth-Lechaion, Greece		Altar canopy
25	5 CE ca. 450–60	Hosios Leonidas in Corinth-Lechaion, Greece	At the crossing of the church	Tetrapylon canopy
26	5 CE ca. 450	St. John the Evangelist, Ephesus, modern Turkey		Altar canopy
27	5 CE ca. 450	St. John the Evangelist, Ephesus, modern Turkey	At the crossing of the church	Tetrapylon canopy
28	5 CE ca. 450	St. John the Evangelist, Ephesus, modern Turkey	Tomb-canopy in the north apse of the baptistery; column fragments *in situ*	Tomb canopy
29	5 CE ca. 490	Abu Mîna or St. Menas, Egypt		Altar canopy

TABLE 5 Continued

CAT. NO.	DATE	LOCATION	CONTEXT REMARKS	TYPE OF CANOPY
30	5 CE ca. 494–6	St. Theodor at Gerasa (Jerash), Jordan		Altar canopy
31	5 CE ca. 494–6	St. Theodor at Gerasa (Jerash), Jordan		Baptistery canopy
32	Late 5 CE	Cilician Basilica A in Corycus (Kizkalesi), Turkey		Altar canopy
33	5 CE	East Church, Mampsis, Negev desert, Palestine		Baptistery canopy
34	5–6 CE	Petra Baptistery, Jordan		Baptistery canopy
35	5–6 CE	Basilica of Bir al-Knissia at Carthage, Tunisia		Altar canopy
36	5–6 CE	Episcopal church at Aphrodisias in Caria, Asia Minor		Altar canopy
37	5–6 CE	Basilica IV in Mactaris, now Makhthar, Tunisia	Canopy over baptistery that replaced older baths	Baptistery canopy
38	5–6 CE	North Africa; unidentified location	Arch of a canopy; inscription; figure of Daniel in the Lion's Den	Tomb canopy? unresolved
39	5–6 CE	Basilica Philiatra Messenia, Peloponnesus, Greece		Altar canopy
40	5–6 CE	Episcopal Basilica, Stobi, F.Y.R. of Macedonia		Altar canopy
41	5–6 CE	Episcopal Basilica, Stobi, F.Y.R. of Macedonia	Six-sided canopy over baptismal font	Baptistery canopy
42	5–6 CE	Nessana, Negev desert, Palestine	Two-columned canopy	Baptistery canopy

43	5–6 CE	Church of Ilisos, Greece	Canopy-like structure above bema, approx. 20m x 20m	Massive tetrapylon canopy Altar canopy?
44	5–6 CE	Basilica in the village Massuh, diocese of Esbus in Jordan		Altar canopy?
45	5–6 CE	Basilica B, Nikopolis, Epiros, Greece	Canopy postdates the church; inscription	Altar canopy
46	5–6 CE	Church of St. Bacchus, Horvat Tinshemet, Palestine	Canopy placed on the altar table	Altar canopy
47	5–6 CE	Basilica in Kourion, Cyprus		Altar canopy
48	5–6 CE?	St. Demetrios, Thessaloniki, Greece	Fragments in Istanbul Museum; not enough evidence to confirm that the ambo was canopied	Ambo canopy?
49	5–6 CE?	Church of the Virgin, Kalabaka, Greece	*In situ*; several later additions (recently re-dated to the Middle Byzantine period)	Ambo canopy
50	5–6 CE	The Basilica of the Dormition of the Holy Virgin in Velushina, F.Y.R. of Macedonia	Marble	Altar canopy
51	5–6 CE	The Basilica on the Acropolis, Lassos, Caria (Asia Minor)	Marble	Altar canopy
52	mid-5–6 CE	East Church of Halutza (Elusa), Negev desert, Palestine		Altar canopy
53	5–6 CE	Basilica at Carthagenna, Carthage, Tunisia		Baptistery canopy
54	5–6 CE	Basilica at Bir Ftouha, Carthage, Tunisia	Canopy marked both the baptistery and martyr's tomb	Baptistery and tomb canopy One installation
55	after 5 CE	Church of St. George on the Acropolis, Athens, Greece	Former Hephaisteon	Altar canopy? unresolved

TABLE 5 Continued

CAT. NO.	DATE	LOCATION	CONTEXT REMARKS	TYPE OF CANOPY
56	6 CE	D-Basilica Caričin Grad, Lebane, Serbia		Altar canopy
57	6 CE	D-Basilica Caričin Grad, Lebane, Serbia		Two-columned canopy in the entrance zone
58	6 CE	Episcopal Basilica Caričin Grad, Lebane, Serbia	Four-columned canopy-like structure framing the baptismal font; columns set at the corners of a quatrefoil baptistery	Massive baptistery canopy
59	6 CE	Basilica A, Nikopolis, Epiros, Greece		Altar canopy
60	6 CE	Basilica A, Nikopolis, Epiros, Greece		Tetrapylon-like structure of the bema
61	6 CE	Basilica B, Thessalian Thebes, Greece?		Four-columned structure at the entrance to the bema, altar canopy? unresolved
62	6 CE	Basilica, Knidos, Greece	Marble sockets	Altar canopy
63	6 CE ca. 540	Basilica B, Philippi, Greece		Altar canopy
64	6 CE ca. 550	Panagia Ekatontapyliani, Paros, Greece	*In situ* marble canopy; restored	Altar canopy
65	6 CE ca. 550	Cathedral complex, Poreč, Croatia		Altar canopy
66	6 CE ca. 550	Cathedral complex, Poreč, Croatia	Fragments; lost	Baptistery canopy
67	6 CE	Il-Anderin church, Syria	Lost	Altar canopy
68	6 CE ca. 583	It-Tuba church, Syria		Altar canopy
69	6 CE	Moses Basilica on Mt. Nebo, Jordan		Altar canopy
70	6 CE	Moses Basilica on Mt. Nebo, Jordan		Baptistery canopy

71	6 CE ca. 586	St. George on Mt. Nebo, Jordan		Baptistery canopy
72	6 CE mid 6 CE?	Basilica A, Amphipolis, Greece		Altar canopy
73	6 CE	Basilica A at Nea Anchileos, Greece		Altar canopy
74	6 CE	Basilica tis Vardias, on the island of Aegina	Today known as Church of Agia Photeini	Altar canopy
75	6 CE ca. 574–603	Church of St. Stephen at Umm al-Rasas, Syria		Altar canopy
76	6 CE	Basilica B Junca Byzacena, Tunisia	Comparable to the one in St. John of Ephesus	Tetrapylon-canopy at the crossing
77	6 CE	Basilica Juvenes, Maktar, Tunisia	Canopied structure above altar table in front of the apse, delineating the bema	Altar canopy?
78	6 CE	Basilica Lariscus, Byzacena, Tunisia		Baptistery canopy
79	6 CE	Baptistery of the Basilica Clupea, Kélibia, Tunisia	On the site of a 4th c. quatrefoil font; footings for the four-columned canopy in mosaic; mosaics; inscription	Baptistery canopy
80	6 CE	Baptistery of the Cathedral La Skhira, near Gabès, Tunisia	Footings for a four-columned canopy around the cruciform font	Baptistery canopy
81	6 CE	Oued Ramel Baptistery, near Zaghouan, Tunisia	Footings for a four-columned canopy over the cruciform font	Baptistery canopy
82	6 CE	Vitalis Baptistery, Basilica Sbeitla, Tunisia, North Africa	Four-columned canopy; column bases and fragment of a stone column; elongated undulated marble font decorated in mosaics with inscriptions. The baptistery itself has four columns at the corners	Baptistery canopy
83	6 CE	Basilica at Haidra, Tunisia		Altar canopy
84	6 CE	Basilica at Haidra, Tunisia		Tomb canopy

TABLE 5 Continued

CAT. NO.	DATE	LOCATION	CONTEXT REMARKS	TYPE OF CANOPY
85	6 CE ca. 524–527	Hagios Polyeuktos, Constantinople	Glass-inlaid marble columns	Altar canopy
86	6 CE	Hagia Sophia, Constantinople	Lost; replaced in mid-12 CE	Altar canopy
87	6 CE	Holy Apostles, Constantinople	Lost; destroyed in 15 CE	Altar canopy
88	6 CE	Unidentified church from Lycia, Asia Minor (either monastic or urban)	Segments of a silver installation; two columns and three capitals recovered; part of the "Sion treasury"; inscription	Altar canopy? unresolved
89	6 CE?	St. Demetrios Thessaloniki, Greece	Six-sided wooden canopy sheathed in silver replaced an earlier marble cancpy; now lost; footings preserved	Shrine canopy
90	6 CE	Ss. Cosmas and Damian, Gerasa (Jerash), Jordan		Altar canopy
91	6 CE	St. John the Baptist, Gerasa (Jerash), Jordan		Baptistery canopy
92	6 CE	Double Basilica at Aliki, Thasos, Greece		Altar canopy
93	6 CE	Double Basilica in Srima, Dalmatia, Croatia		Altar canopy
94	6 CE	Basilica in Salona, Dalmatia, Croatia		Altar canopy
95	6 CE	Blagaj, Dalmatia, Bosnia and Herzegovina		Altar canopy
96	6 CE	Cim, Dalmatia, Croatia		Altar canopy
97	6 CE	Doboj, Bosnia and Herzegovina		Altar canopy
98	6 CE	Gata, Dalmatia, Croatia		Altar canopy
99	6–7 CE	Church of St. Vid, Dalmatia, Croatia		Altar canopy
100	6–7 CE	Cathedral of Arnithi on Rhodes, Greece		Altar canopy
101	6–7 CE	Central Church Apollonia, Libya	Approx. 2m x 2m	Altar canopy

102	6–7 CE	Eastern Church Apollonia, Libya	Canopy-like structure above bema, approx. 10m x 10m	Massive canopy-like structure over bema
103	e. 7 CE	Chapel of the Mother of the Church at Mt. Nebo, Jordan		Altar canopy
104	e. 7 CE?	Hagia Euphemia, Constantinople	Marble columns	Altar canopy with the large shrine reliquary below; one installation
105	6–8 CE	St. Stephen at Umm al-Rasas, Palestine		Altar canopy
106	6–8 CE	Church at Rehovot in the Negev desert, Palestine		Altar canopy
107	6–8 CE	Unidentified church in the Syro-Palestine region	Currently in the Royal Ontario Museum, Canada	Altar canopy? unresolved
108	7 CE?	Hagia Sophia, Thessaloniki, Greece	Bronze canopy	Altar canopy? unresolved
109	After 6 CE	Church of the Virgin on the Acropolis, Greece	Parthenon; still *in situ* in 12 CE	Altar canopy
110	4–9 CE	Shrine of St. Menas, Maryût, Egypt	Octagonal baptistery at the shrine of St. Menas	Baptistery canopy
111	8–9 CE	Basilica St. Andrew, Betika, Istria, Croatia	Fragments of a four-sided canopy	Altar canopy? unresolved
112	8–9 CE	Basilica St. Pelagia, Novigrad, Istria, Croatia	Fragments of a six-sided canopy; inscriptions	Baptistery canopy? unresolved
113	9 CE	Basilica St. Martha, Bijaće, Dalmatia, Croatia	Fragments of a four-sided canopy; inscriptions	Altar canopy? unresolved
114	9 CE	Unidentified church (St. Savior?) in Ulcinj, Montenegro	In fragments; arches with inscriptions—Leo V; Constantine; National Museum, Belgrade; Museum in Boka Kotorska	Altar canopy

TABLE 5 Continued

CAT. NO.	DATE	LOCATION	CONTEXT REMARKS	TYPE OF CANOPY
115	9 CE	St. Mary Collegiate, Kotor, Montenegro	Stone fragments	Altar canopy
116	9 CE	St. Michael, Kotor, Montenegro	Fragments of a four-sided canopy; white-yellowish sandstone, inscriptions	Altar canopy
117	9 CE	St. Tryphon, Kotor, Montenegro	Stone fragments; arch with an inscription	Altar canopy
118	9 CE	St. Tryphon, Kotor, Montenegro	Stone fragments; inscriptions	Baptistery canopy
119	9 CE	St. Tryphon, Kotor, Montenegro	Stone fragments; inscriptions	Reliquary canopy
120	9 CE	The Cathedral of the Virgin, Dubrovnik, Croatia		Altar canopy
121	9 CE	The cathedral of Pula, Dalmatia, Croatia	Fragments of a six-sided canopy	Altar canopy
122	9 CE	Church of St. Felicità, on the location of an early Christian basilica, Pula, Dalmatia, Croatia	Fragments of a four-sided canopy	Altar canopy? unresolved
123	9 CE	From an unknown church, now in Split, Croatia	Fragments of a marble canopy	Altar canopy? unresolved
124	9 CE	Basilica of the Nativity of the Mother of God? Zadar, Croatia	Fragments of a four-sided canopy	Altar canopy? unresolved
125	9 CE	Church of St. Lawrence, Zadar, Croatia	Fragments of a canopy	Altar canopy? unresolved
126	9 CE ca. 864	Pharos Church, Constantinople	Lost	Altar canopy
127	9 CE	Cathedral of the Holy Mary on the island of Rab, Dalmatia, Croatia	Six-sided canopy with later additions	Altar canopy
128	9 CE	Church of St. Peter, Rab—Supetarska Draga, Dalmatia, Croatia	Fragment of a four-sided canopy	Altar canopy? unresolved

129	9 CE	Basilica of Archangel Michael in Martinići, near Skadar Lake, Montenegro	Fragments	Altar canopy
130	9 CE	Basilica of the Virgin, Bala, Istria, Croatia	Fragments of a four-sided canopy	Altar canopy? unresolved
131	9 CE?	unidentified location; fragment from the Walters Art Museum	Fragments; arch of a canopy in the Walters Art Museum, Baltimore	Altar canopy? unresolved
132	9 CE	Archangel Michael, Prevlaka, Croatia	Stone fragments of a four-sided canopy; inscriptions	Altar canopy
133	9 CE	St. Andrew, Dubrovnik, Croatia		Altar canopy
134	9 CE	The Church of the Holy Spirit (on the site of a Byzantine basilica), Komolac, Croatia		Altar canopy
135	9 CE	Basilica of St. Mary, Novalja, Dalmatia, Croatia	Fragments with inscriptions	Altar canopy
136	9 CE	Basilica of St. Mary, Novalja, Dalmatia, Croatia	Fragments of a smaller canopy	Reliquary canopy? unresolved
137	9 CE	Unidentified church, on a site of an Early Christian basilica Budva, Montenegro	Stone fragments, four-sided canopy	Altar canopy
138	9 CE	Unidentified church, on the site of an Early Christian basilica, Budva, Montenegro	Stone fragments, six-sided canopy	Baptistery canopy
139	9 CE	Church of St. Bartholomew, Galovac, Dalmatia, Croatia	Fragments of a four-sided small canopy; perhaps placed directly on the altar table	Altar canopy? unresolved
140	9 CE	Church of St. Bartholomew, Galovac, Dalmatia, Croatia	Fragments of a six-sided canopy	Baptistery canopy? unresolved

TABLE 5 Continued

CAT. NO.	DATE	LOCATION	CONTEXT REMARKS	TYPE OF CANOPY
141	9 CE	Church of St. Bartholomew, Knin, Dalmatia, Croatia	Fragments of a four-sided canopy	Altar canopy? unresolved
142	9 CE	Church of St. Martin, Lepuri, Dalmatia, Croatia	Fragments of a four-sided canopy	Altar canopy? unresolved
143	9 CE	Cathedral of St. Domnius, Split, Dalmatia, Croatia	Fragments of a canopy	Altar canopy? unresolved
144	9 CE	Episcopal complex with the Basilica of St. Anastasia (Sv. Stošija), Zadar, Dalmatia, Croatia	Fragments of a four-sided canopy	Altar canopy
145	9 CE	Church of St. Demetrios, Zadar, Croatia	Fragments of a four-sided canopy	Altar canopy? unresolved
146	9 CE	Church of St. Chrysogonus, Zadar, Croatia	Fragments of a four-sided canopy	Altar canopy? unresolved
147	9 CE	Church of St. John, Zadar, Croatia	Fragments of a four-sided canopy	Altar canopy? unresolved
148	10 CE?	Church of St. Peter, Zadar, Croatia	Fragments of a four-sided canopy	Altar canopy? unresolved
149	9–11 CE	Krk, Dalmatia, Croatia		Altar canopy
150	9–11 CE	Pag, Dalmatia, Croatia		Altar canopy
151	9–11 CE	Unidentified church from Solin or Split, Dalmatia, Croatia		Altar canopy
152	9–11 CE	Birčina-Polača Dalmatia, Croatia		Altar canopy
153	9–11 CE	Hagios Andreas, Peresterai, Greece		Baptistery canopy
154	9–11 CE	Church of St. Nicholas, Myra, now Turkey	Column fragments *in situ*	Altar canopy

155	9–11 CE	Shati, Albania	Fragments of marble arch	Altar canopy
156	9–11 CE	Lopud, Dalmatia, Croatia		Altar canopy
157	9–11 CE	Church in Omiš, Dalmatia, Croatia	Fragments with inscriptions	Altar canopy
158	9–11 CE	Potoci, Dalmatia, Croatia		Altar canopy
159	9–11 CE	Vrba, Dalmatia, Croatia		Altar canopy
160	9–11 CE.	Založje, Dalmatia, Croatia		Altar canopy
161	9–11 CE	St. Demetrios, Thessaloniki, Greece	Eight-sided marble canopy; somewhere in the main part of the church; small-size replicas preserved; marble carved arch fragments, preserved in the crypt; possibly from this octagonal marble canopy	Shrine/tomb and icon canopy? unresolved
162	After 9 CE, confirmed by texts in 11 CE	St. Demetrios, Thessaloniki, Greece	Seven-columned marble canopy without roof and abutted to the wall; framed the myrrhobletic basin in the crypt; on the location of older bath, *in situ*	Canopy shrine
163	10 CE 915–921	Church of the Holy Cross, Aght'amar, Armenia, now Turkey		Canopy over a bell-tower
164	10–11 CE	Church of St. John, Dubrovnik, Croatia	Fragments of a four-sided canopy	Altar canopy? unresolved
165	10–11 CE	Church of St. Peter, Dubrovnik, Croatia	Four-sided canopy	Altar canopy
166	10–11 CE	Church of St. Stephen, Dubrovnik, Croatia	Fragments of a four-sided canopy	Altar canopy? unresolved
167	10–11 CE	Church of St. Nicholas, Nikoljac, near Bijelo Polje, Montenegro	Fragments embedded in the church walls ca. 14th c.	Altar canopy? unresolved

TABLE 5 Continued

CAT. NO.	DATE	LOCATION	CONTEXT REMARKS	TYPE OF CANOPY
168	10–11 CE	Great Lavra, Mt. Athos, Greece	Canopy-like tomb of St. Athanasios, the founder of the monastery	Tomb canopy
169	10–11 CE	Church in Rogačići near Blažuj, Bosnia and Herzegovina		Altar canopy
170	10 CE and later	Church of the Virgin, Hosios Loukas, Greece		Icon canopy
171	11 CE	St. Tryphon, Kotor, Montenegro	Fragments of a four-sided canopy	Altar canopy? unresolved
172	11 CE	St. Tryphon, Kotor, Montenegro (now in the sacristy of St. Mary of Rijeka)	Fragments of a canopy	Unresolved
173	11 CE	Unknown church on the island Cres, Croatia	Fragments of an acroterion of a canopy	Unresolved
174	11 CE	St. Thomas, Zadar, Dalmatia, Croatia	Archeological Museum, Zadar	Altar canopy
175	11 CE	St. Paraskevi, Zadar, Dalmatia, Croatia	Fragments of a four-sided canopy	Altar canopy
176	11 CE	Ss. Peter and Moses in Solin, Dalmatia, Croatia		Altar canopy
177	11 CE	Church of St. Andrew, Rab, Dalmatia, Croatia		Altar canopy
178	11 CE ca. 1033–1036	Basilica of St. Anastasia (Sv. Stošija) Zadar, Croatia	Fragments of a four-sided canopy; inscriptions	Altar canopy
179	11 CE	Basilica of the St. Mary, Nin, Dalmatia, Croatia	Stone canopy	Altar canopy
180	11 CE	Church of St. Michael Ston, Dalmatia, Croatia	Stone fragments	Altar canopy

181	11 CE	Church of St. Mary, Biskupija, Knin, Croatia	Two same-size canopies from the same church, Croatian Academy of Sciences and Art—Sculpture Museum	Altar canopy
182	11 CE	Church of St. Mary, Biskupija, Knin, Croatia	Two same-size canopies from the same church, Croatian Academy of Sciences and Art—Sculpture Museum	Altar canopy? unresolved
183	11 CE	Church of St. Mary, Biskupija, Knin, Croatia	Fragments of a six-sided canopy	Baptistery canopy?
184	11 CE	Kaštel-Gomilica, Dalmatia, Croatia		Altar canopy
185	11 CE ca. 1050s	St. George in Mangana, Constantinople	Canopy over quatrefoil phiale comparable with post-Byzantine phialai on Mt. Athos	Phiale canopy
186	11 CE	Nea Mone, Chios, Greece	Four-columned structure in the narthex supporting the dome	Tetrapylon-type of canopy
187	11 CE	St. Savior in Chernigovo, Russia	Wooden	Altar canopy
188	11 CE ca. 1073	Church of the Dormition in the Pečerskii monastery (Monastery of the Caves) near Kiev, modern Ukraine	Marble altar canopy, lost	Altar canopy
189	11 CE	St. Sophia in Novgorod, Russia	Marble altar canopy, lost	Altar canopy
190	11 CE and later	Hosios Loukas, Greece	Sculpted fragments	Altar canopy
191	11 CE and later	Hosios Loukas, Greece	Sculpted, painted, gilded; *in situ*	Canopy shrine
192	11 CE and later	Amorium church, Turkey	Canopy fragments, arch, inscription	Altar canopy?
193	11 CE and later	Church of the Pantokrator, Constantinople	Canopy fragments; *spolia* from H. Polyeuktos?; incorporated into minbar of the Zeyrek camii, Istanbul; inscriptions	Altar canopy? tomb canopy? unresolved

TABLE 5 Continued

CAT. NO.	DATE	LOCATION	CONTEXT REMARKS	TYPE OF CANOPY
194	11 CE and later	Androusa, Samarina, Greece		Icon canopy
195	11–12 CE	Church of St. Peter, Dubrovnik, Croatia	Replacing the earlier one in the same location	Altar canopy
196	11–12 CE	Church of the Virgin, Kalabaka, Greece	*in situ*	Altar canopy
197	11–12 CE	Church of the Dormition, Apollonia, Albania		Altar canopy
198	12 CE	Hagia Sophia, Constantinople	Now lost	Ambo canopy
199	12 CE ca. 1156	St. Sophia in Novgorod, Russia	Wooden	Altar canopy
200	12 CE	The church "Old Throne" in Vladimir-Volinski, Russia	Wooden	Altar canopy
201	12 CE ca. 1165	Bogolyubovo, Russia	Reconstructed	Phiale canopy
202	12–13 CE ca. 1171–1213	Ss. Boris and Gleb, built by Vsevolod III in Vladimir, Russia	Local stone	Altar canopy
203	12 CE ca. 1186	Church of the Annunciation in Chernigov, Russia		Altar canopy
204	12 CE	St. Panteleimon, at Nerezi, F.Y.R. Macedonia		Icon canopy
205	12 CE	Chora *katholikon*, Constantinople	Footings archeologically confirmed	Altar canopy
206	12–13 CE	Kalenderhane camii, Constantinople		Altar canopy?
207	12–13 CE ca. 1196–1235	Church of the Mother of God, Studenica, Serbia	Canopy above the phiale; later included in the exonarthex of King Radoslav	phiale canopy
208	12–13 CE	Church of Savior, Galich, Russia		Altar canopy

209	12–13 CE	Church of Dormition, Galich, Russia		Altar canopy
210	12–13 CE	Monastery of the Virgin, Gelati, Georgia	*in situ*	Episcopal throne canopy
211	late 12 CE	Zoodochos Pege in Samari, Messenia, Greece		Icon canopy
212	12 CE and later	St. Sophia in Monemvasia, Greece		Icon canopy
213	after 12 CE	St. John Eleemon in Ligourio, Argolis, Greece		Icon canopy
214	13 CE	Panagia Parigoritissa, Arta, Greece	*in situ*	Canopy over the bell
215	13 CE	San Marco, Venice, Italy	Alabaster columns; early Byzantine spolia; inscriptions added in Latin	Altar canopy
216	13 CE	Church of Holy Apostles in Peć Monastery, Kosovo, Serbia	*Acrosolium* tomb-canopy of Sava II; lost	Tomb canopy
217	13 CE	From unidentified church in Athens, Greece	Arch fragments with inscription with reference to the Christmas hymn	Tomb canopy? unresolved
218	13 CE	From unidentified church in Athens, Greece	Arch fragments with inscriptions	Tomb canopy? unresolved
219	13 CE	Hagia Sophia, Thessaloniki, Greece	Painted; originally set within the walls; *arcosolium* in the south aisle of the church; fragments in Athens Museum	Tomb canopy
220	13 CE and later	St. Paraskevi, Geraki, Greece		Icon canopy
221	13 CE	Porta Panagia in Pylai, Thessaly, Greece		icon canopy
222	13 CE	Gradac, Serbia		Icon canopy
223	13–14 CE	Church of Christ's Ascension, Žiča monastery, Serbia	Fragments of fittings for the Stone canopy installation on northeastern pillar of the church	Icon or reliquary canopy

TABLE 5 Continued

CAT. NO.	DATE	LOCATION	CONTEXT REMARKS	TYPE OF CANOPY
224	13–14 CE	Church of the Taxiarchs, Kalyvia-Kouvara, Attica, Greece	Two-columned canopy abutted to wall; painted; *in situ*	Proskynetarion canopy
225	13–14 CE	St. Demetrios–Metropolis, Mystras, Greece		Icon canopy
226	13–15 CE	St. Demetrios–Metropolis, Mystras, Greece		Altar canopy
227	14 CE	Church of St. Nicetas, Yaroslavl, Russia	Wooden	Altar canopy
228	14 CE	St. Sophia, Ohrid, F.Y.R. of Macedonia	Throne of Archbishop Grigorije; re-used fragments for the minbar	Canopy of episcopal throne? ambo canopy? altar canopy? unresolved
229	14 CE ca. 1300–1317	Old Cathedral, Beroia (Veria), Greece	Canopy fragments	Ambo canopy?
230	14 CE	St. Lawrence (Sv. Lovro) in Trogir, Dalmatia, Croatia		Altar canopy
231	14 CE	d'al-Mu'allaqa (Mas al-Qadima) Hanging Church, dedicated to St. Mary, Cairo, Egypt	One of the three different wooden canopies (perhaps on the location of a 10–11 CE installation)	Altar canopy
232	14 CE	d'al-Mu'allaqa (Mas al-Qadima) Hanging Church, dedicated to St. Mary, Cairo, Egypt	One of the three different wooden canopies (perhaps on the location of a 10–11 CE installation)	Altar canopy
233	14 CE	d'al-Mu'allaqa (Mas al-Qadima) Hanging Church, dedicated to St. Mary, Cairo, Egypt	One of the three different wooden canopies (perhaps on the location of a 10–11 CE installation)	Altar canopy
234	14 CE	Chora *katholikon*, Constantinople		Icon canopy
235	14 CE	Church of Perivleptos in Mystra, Greece	Richly carved; inscriptions	Icon canopy

236	15 CE	Cathedral of Sveti Choveli, Mcheta, Georgia	Painted canopy, built in the 15th c., cathedral begun in 1010; *in situ*	Shrine canopy; "Tomb of Christ"
237	15 CE	St. Demetrios, Thessaloniki, Greece	Eight-sided canopy in the church atrium; destroyed	Phiale canopy
238	15 CE ca. 1417–1429	Trebizond, Turkey	Tomb-canopy of Alexios Komennos IV, Trebizond; the tomb was next to the north apse of the Chrysokephalos church; destroyed	Tomb canopy
		NOT DATED		
239	n.d.	Ascension, Mt. Olive, Israel	Octagonal altar canopy, which also surmounted the rock with the footprints of Jesus; destroyed	Altar canopy with the rock with Jesus' footprints below—no other relic
240	n.d.	Es-Sesah, Egypt	Marble columns	Altar canopy
241	n.d.	The Tower of Winds in Athens reused for Christian purposes during Byzantine period	Eight footings in the floor indicate that some kind of canopy was installed in the ancient structure by Christians who also included *spolia* with crosses in the floor	Baptistery canopy? phiale canopy? unresolved
242	n.d.	Athens, Greece	Only arch preserved inscription, human figure; Museum	Tomb canopy? unresolved
243	n.d.	Unidentified medieval church, Jajce, Bosnia and Herzegovina	Canopy fragments, including acroterion	Altar canopy? unresolved
244	n.d.	Natrun, Egypt—two different, unidentified churches	Marble	Altar canopy

TABLE 5 Continued

CAT. NO.	DATE	LOCATION	CONTEXT REMARKS	TYPE OF CANOPY
245	n.d.	Natrun, Egypt—two different unidentified churches	Marble	Altar canopy
246	n.d.	Dylon, Egypt	Small canopy placed on the altar table	Altar canopy
247	10–11 CE or later?	D'al-Mu'allaqa (Mas al-Qadima), Hanging Church, dedicated to St. Mary in Cairo, Egypt	Wooden "Fatimid ciborium" from the d'al-Mu'allaqa (Mas al-Qadima) in Cairo, Egypt Coptic Museum in Cairo (inv. no. 909)	Altar canopy? unresolved

TABLE 6 Types of Canopies in the Byzantine Ecclesiastical Tradition and Their Distribution over Time

TYPE	ALL	NOT DATED	3rd c.	4th–6th c.	7th–8th c.	9th–12th c.	13th–15th c.
Altar	131	5		60	5	54	7
Baptistery	24		1	18	1	4	
Phiale	4					3	1
Ambo*	3			2 (1)		0 (1)	1
Tomb	7			3		1	3
Shrine/reliquary/artophorion	7			3		3	1
Icon	13					6	7
Bell Tower	2					1	1
Episcopal throne	1					1	
Tetrapylon, bema, and other massive canopied structures	6			5		1	
Dual functions altar—tomb	1			1			
Dual functions baptistery—tomb	3			3			
Fragments; unresolved	45	4		6	2	29	4
All	247	9	1	101 (100)	8	103 (104)	25

**Note: Kalabaka ambo initially dated to the Early Christian period was re-dated to the Middle Byzantine period; hence two numbers reflecting this change*

TABLE 7 Canopies with Inscriptions

Cat. no.:	23
Date:	6 CE
Place:	From Constantinople, now in Venice treasury
Canopy:	Small-scale canopy, artophorium (?)
Inscription:	Ὑπερ εὐχῆς κ(αὶ) σωτηρίας τῆς ἐνδοξοτάτης Ἀναστασίας For the blessing and salvation of the most glorious Anastasia (Engl. trans. J.B.)
Remarks:	Votive inscription
Bibliography:	Guillou (1991) 119–152, esp. 141

Cat. no.:	45
Date:	6 CE
Place:	From Basilica B, Nikopolis, Greece
Canopy:	Fragment of an arch of a canopy, possibly an altar canopy
Inscription:	Καὶ τοῦτο τὸ καλὸν Δουμετίου And all of good Dometios (Engl. trans. J.B.)
Remarks:	This could be a votive inscription. Kitzinger suggests that Dometios is the individual who donated the piece of furnishing, potentially an altar canopy to a church. Dometios' name is given in the form of a monogram, which is read in the cruciform key starting from 6 o'clock up.
Bibliography:	Kitzinger (1951) 81+83–122, with further reference.

Cat. no.:	79
Date:	6 CE
Place:	Baptistery of the Basilica Clupea, Kélibia, Tunisia
Canopy:	Baptistery canopy
Inscription 1:	SCO BEATISSIMO CYPRIANO EPISCOPO ANTISTECUM SCO ADELFIO PRESBITERO HUIUSCE UNITATIS AQUINIUS ET IULIANA EIUS CUM VILLA ET DEOGRATIAS PROLIBUS TESELLU[M] AEQUORI PERENNI POSURUNT Dedicated to most blessed holy Saint Cyprian, Bishop and High Priest with the Holy Adelhius, a priest in unity with him. Aquinius and Juliana, his [wife], with their household and—thanks be to God—their children, Built these mosaics for the placid waters of eternity. (Engl. trans. Robin Jensen)
Inscription 2:	PAX FIDES CARITAS Peace, faith, love (Engl. trans. Robin Jensen)
Remarks:	Votive inscription
Bibliography:	Jensen (2011) 213–215

TABLE 7 Continued

Cat. no.:	82
Date:	6 CE
Place:	Vitalis baptistery, Basilica Sbeitla, Tunisia, North Africa
Canopy:	Baptistery canopy
Inscription:	VITALIS ET CARDELA VOTUM SN Vitalis and Cardela fulfilled their vow (Engl. trans. Robin Jensen)
Remarks:	Votive inscription
Bibliography:	Jensen (2011) 212

Cat. no.:	86
Date:	6 CE
Place:	Hagia Sophia, Constantinople
Canopy:	Silver altar canopy, now lost
Inscription:	Ἃς οἱ πλάνοι καθεῖλον ἐνθάδ' εἰκόνας ἄνακτες ἐστήλωσαν εὐσεβεῖς πάλιν The images of the impostors had cast down here, pious emperors have again set up.
Remarks:	Inscription on the silver altar canopy after the Iconoclastic controversy, now lost. The inscription on the canopy can be dated to the ninth century. The same inscription was recorded on the conch of the apse of Hagia Sophia.
Bibliography:	Oikonomides (1985) 111–115, esp. 113–114, n. 31.

Cat. no.:	88
Date:	6 CE
Place:	Unidentified church, either Cathedral of Korydalla or the katholikon of the Monastery of Holy Sion, Lycia, Asia Minor, modern south Turkey
Canopy:	Altar canopy?
Inscription:	+ΑΝΕΝΕѠΘΗ ΤΟ ΕΡΓΟΝ ΤΟΥΤΟ +ΕΠΙ ΘΕΟΔѠΡΟΥ ΤΟΥ ΟCΙѠΤΑΤΟΥ ΕΠΙCΚΟ[ΠΟΥ] This work was renewed under (in the time of) Theodore, most holy bishop. (Engl. trans. I. Ševčenko)
Remarks:	Votive inscription on one of two columns and three capitals made of silver; part of the "Sion Treasury."
Bibliography:	Boyd (1992) 5–38, esp. 31.

Cat. no.:	112
Date:	9 CE
Place:	Baptistery of the Basilica Pelagia, Novigrad, Croatia
Canopy:	Baptistery canopy
Inscription:	+ HOC TIGMEN LVCEFLO ALMLOQVE

TABLE 7 Continued

	BAPTISTERIO DIGNO MARMORE [. . .] MAVRICIVS EPISCOP O[. . .]VLI DO SVMMO E STVDIO DEVOTE PECTORE TOTO BEATE IOHANIS V ER[?]R[. . .]ER[?]RE SE DELEARIS PLURA NOST[. . . . .]SA SE COGNOSCAMV IN QVID NOS [. . .?] IN PAR/ADISI VITALIS/ REGNA
	+ Hoc tigmen lucefluo almoque baptisterio digno marmore [erecto ego?] Mauricius episcop[us] o[bt]uli D(e)o summo e studio, devote, pectore toto. Beate Iohanis, [. . .] er erili me rore [or erre], se delearis plura nost[ra crimina] sa, se cognoscamu(s) in quid nos [vehas/? niti oporteat, se veniamus?] in par/adisi vitalis/regna
	This veil (canopy—J.B.) made of ornate marble for a baptistery from which radiates light and life overflows, I Maurice Bishop offered to the Lord wholeheartedly, with care and devotion. O, blessed John may many of our sins be destroyed, so that we learn what is in the paradise, where the life rules. (Engl. trans. J.B.—according to G. Cuscito, M. Jurković, M. Lončar)
Remarks:	Five arches out of six of the baptismal canopy have been preserved. All of them have inscriptions. The first arch has the beginning of the inscription and the ending of the text is inscribed just below it, over the figurative reliefs. There are several propositions as to which order to read them in. Here, I follow and combine translations offered by G. Cuscito, M. Jurković, and M. Lončar.
Bibliography:	Vežić and Lončar (2009) 199; Jurković (1995) 141–149
Cat. no.:	113
Date:	9 CE
Place:	Basilica St. Martha, Bijaće, Dalmatia, Croatia
Canopy:	Altar canopy [?]
Inscription 1:	+ V[. . .]OMN[. . .] CPI · CO[. . ./// . . .]OIT C[. . ./// . . .]TE · TRINVM . . .]IINIVB[. . .]T[. . ./// . . .]HANIS · NECNE [. . .]SPIT[.]V[. . . . . .]ALMIFICAE MARTHAE CVNC[.]A · HA[.]C NOV[. . .]CERNIT[. . .///] +TEMPO[. . ./// . . .]VD: V[. . . /// . . .] M[. . .]RI[. . .] OP[.]
	possible reading: + V[os] omn[es] chri(sti)co[lae? quicumque? intr?]oit, c[arum? lauda?]te trinum [. . .?]i in iub[ilo?. . .e?]t in [honore? beati? Io]hanis, necne [. . .?] almificae Marthae cuncta ha[e]c nov[a] cernit[e dicata?] + Tempore [N.N. factum est? ist?) ud v(. . .?) m(ise?)ri(cors?) op(us?)

TABLE 7 Continued

	You, worshipers of Christ, whoever enters, praise the holy? Trinity . . . with cheers and in honor of John (the Baptist?) and blessed Martha look at all of this new (potentially both the canopy and the building itself) built in time of (name of the donor lost) (Engl. trans. J.B.—according to M. Lončar)
Inscription 2:	+HIC A[. . .///. . .]SI[. . .]IS · SPES[. . .]R ETE[. . . + QVES[. . .///. . .]SV[. . .]BNIX[. . .///. . .]A· CI[. . .///. . .]DOQ: · .]C A E[. . .///. . .]MPE HVL [.]IM[. . .///. . .]S·V[.]DVM[..]BSISTIMVS DI M[.]REMVR VOLVNTAT[. . . . . .]EITVI[.] PER VLV [. . .]R · VITA MEREAMVR [. . .]ER[. . .]C·AM[..]N Possible reading: +Hic a[nima? de laqueo? qua?]si [av?]is spe s[urgitu?]r (a)ete[rnatis?]/Hic a[nima. . .? Dei prom?]i(s)si[on?]is spe s[urgitu?]r e te[nebris?]. +Qu(a)es[umus Christe Ie]su[. . .bnix?. . .?]a c[. . .]doq(ue) [san?]c(t)ae [Marthae?. . . .]mpe hu(mi)l[l?]im[e? . . .]s u[t?], dum subsistimus, dei m[o?u?] remur voluntate [. . .]et tui p(er) flu[enta?] vita(m?) mereamur [aet]er[nam?]. Am[e?]n. Here, the soul, like the bird from the trap, raises the hope of eternity We pray to Jesus Christ, trusting in help of holy (Martha?) . . . most humbly to be surrounded by God's will while we exist and to receive the eternal life. Amen. (Engl. trans. J.B.—according to M. Lončar)
Remarks:	The four arches of the richly carved canopy have highly fragmented inscriptions both in the exterior (Inscription 1) and interior (Inscription 2), hence suggesting two texts that differ in their location and meaning. The inscriptions point to the possibility that the installation was either an altar canopy by invocation of the name St. Martha to whom the church was dedicated, or a baptistery canopy because of the mention of St. John (the Baptist?). Here, I follow and combine translations offered by G. Cuscito, M. Jurković, and M. Lončar.
Bibliography:	Vežić and Lončar (2009) 206–223
Cat. no.:	114
Date:	9 CE
Place:	From the Church of St. Savior (?), now lost, Ulcinj, Montenegro
Canopy:	Altar canopy? Several fragments with inscriptions

TABLE 7 Continued

Inscription: 1 . . .]ISALVATORINOSTRIIhVXR[IC]ONIVGEMEAGVSMV PROREMEDIOANI[. . .
2 . . .S]ANI
3 . . .S]IDEMDIETAGNIQVIAOCEDIFICVMEDIFICATVMES. . .
4 . . . SUBTEMPORIBVSDOMINIOSTRIPISPERPETVOAGVSTIDNLOETDNCS

Possible reading (a):
SALVATORI NOSTRI IhV XR[I] [C]ONIVGE MEA GVSMV PRO REMEDIO ANI[ME] S IDEM DIE TAGNI QUIA OC EDIFICVM EDIFICATVM ES(t) SUB TEMPORIBUS DOMINI NOSTRI PI[I]S PERPETUO A[V]GUSTI D[OMI]N[I] LEO ET D[OMI]N[I] CONSTANI
Our Savior Jesus Christ for the salvation of my (wife?) Gusma (Christianized name, corrupted version of Cosma) [obscure, perhaps T Agni] (refers to the transfiguration) of the Lamb (?—J.B., with reference to the Eucharistic mystery performed on the altar table) . . . this structure was made at the times of our pious lords perpetual Augusts (Emperors) lords Leo and Constantine
(Engl. trans. J.B.)

Possible reading (b):
. . . (ad honorem domin)I SALVATORI NOSTRI INV XR(i) (c)ONIVGE MEA GVSMV PRO REMEDIO ANI(ME). . . S ANT(e) SIDEM D(e)I ET AGNI . . . QUIA (h)OC EDIFICVM EDIFICATVM ES(t). . .SVB TEMPORIBVS DOMINI NOSTRI PI(i)S PERPETVUO A(u)GVSTI D(omi)N(i) L(e)O ET D(omi)N(i) C(on)S(tantini)
. . .(in the glory of the Lord) our Savior Christ for the salvation of (the soul?—J.B.) of my (wife?) Gusma . . . in front of the Lord and Lamb . . . because this structure was made at the times of our pious lords perpetual Augusts (Emperors) lords Leo and Constantine
(Engl. trans. J.B.)

Possible reading (c):
(Adquiscite sermonibus?/verbi?). . . S ANI S IDEM D(e)I ET AGNI . . . QUIA (h) OC EDIFICVM EDIFICATVM ES(t). . . SVB TEMPORIBVS DOMINI NOSTRI PI(i)S PERPETVUO A(u)GVSTI D(omi)N(i) L(e)O ET D(omi)N(i) C(on) S(tantini). . . . . (ad honorem?) SALVATORI (s) NOSTRI IHV XR(ist) (ic)ONIVGE MEA GVSMV PRO REMEDIO ANIM(a)E. . .
(Greet?) at the same time God and the Lamb because this structure was made (by name lost) . . . OR (followers greet?) the seat of God (cf. reference to the throne of God in "Concerning the place of God: and that the Deity alone is uncircumscribed" by John of Damascus, *Orthodox Faith*, book 1, ch. 13) and of the Lamb because this structure was made (by name lost) . . . made at the times of our pious lords perpetual Augusts (Emperors) lords Leo and Constantine . . . (in the glory of the Lord) our Savior Christ for the salvation of (the soul?—J.B.) of my (wife?) Gusma . . . (Engl. trans. J.B.—all three translations according to D. Preradović-Petrović and M. Lončar).

TABLE 7 Continued

Remarks:	Inscriptions run on all four sides of the canopy, which survives only in fragments. It is a votive inscription, which mentions Byzantine emperors Leo and Constantine. Several readings have been proposed. Here I combine the propositions by D. Preradović-Petrović and M. Lončar.
Bibliography:	(a) Preradović-Petrović (2002) 247–264 (b) M. Lončar in Vežić (2001–2002) 91–122 (c) Vežić and Lončar (2009) 143–147; 224–231

Cat. no.:	116
Date:	9 CE
Place:	Church of Archangel Michael, Kotor, Montenegro
Canopy:	?
Inscription:	+ (i)N N(o)M(ine) D(o)M(ini) D(e)I ET SALV(atoris) N(ostri) III(es)V(s) XRI(sti) In the name of our Lord and Savior Jesus Christ (Engl. trans. J.B.)
Remarks:	Inscription on a fragment of a canopy
Bibliography:	Preradović-Petrović (2002) 247–264

Cat. no.:	117
Date:	9 CE
Place:	Cathedral of St. Tryphon, Kotor, Montenegro
Canopy:	Altar canopy [?]
Inscription:	ANDREE S(an)C(t)I AD HONOREM SOCIORVMQ(ue) MAIOREM+ St. Andrew for the greater honor and the allies (Engl. trans. J.B.)
Remarks:	Canopy arch embedded in the walls of the Cathedral of St. Tryphon. Reference is to St. Andrew Stratelated from Cilicia, whose relics were translated to Kotor in the ninth century.
Bibliography:	Stevović (1998–1999) 23–33

Cat. no.:	118
Date:	9 CE
Place:	Cathedral of St. Tryphon, Kotor, Montenegro
Canopy:	Baptistery canopy
Inscription:	+ HOC OPVS EST LABO(r) . . . TAM PVLCHRE DE (coratum +) This work is so beautifully decorated by his labor (name lost) . . . (Engl. trans. J.B.)
Remarks:	Fragments of the baptistery canopy from the cathedral of St. Tryphon. The baptistery font has two surviving fragments: one depicting two confronted peacocks drinking from the chalice and framed by two solar, "whirling" disks; other a lion and a bird (eagle or dove) flanking the Tree of Life.
Bibliography:	Vežić (2001–2002) 91–122

TABLE 7 Continued

Cat. no.:	119
Date:	9 CE
Place:	Cathedral of St. Tryphon, Kotor, Montenegro
Canopy:	[Shrine?] canopy
Inscription:	(N)IKIFORVS N (. . .) Nikephoros (personal name)
Remarks:	Fragment of the unidentified canopy. Reference is to a certain Nikephorios, either Byzantine emperor Nikephoros (806–812) or a local nobleman (n) IKIFORVS N(obilis cathari).
Bibliography:	Vežić (2001–2002) 91–122

Cat. no.:	132
Date:	9 CE
Place:	Church of Archangel Michael in Prevlaka, Croatia
Canopy:	Altar canopy (?)
Inscription:	(p)ROPISIATORIVM AD ONORE BEAT[i Michaelis. . .) CVM CONIVGE ME. . . . . .ORE DN [most likely (temp)ore d(omi)n(i)] The propiatory in honor of St. Michael When my wife in the time of (Engl. trans. J.B.—according to V. Delonga and M. Lončar)
Remarks:	Reference to the propiatory and the veil of the Ark of Covenant (cf. Ex. 25:17–22, 26:1–37; Heb. 9, 5)
Bibliography:	Delonga (2000) 131; Vežić and Lončar (2009) 138

Cat. no.:	178
Date:	11 CE
Place:	Church of St. Anastasia (Sv. Stošija) in Zadar, Croatia
Canopy:	Altar canopy
Inscription:	+ O PRINCEPS PETRE PRINCIPVM CAELESTIS AVLAE CLAVIGER DEVOTIONIS SVSCIP MVNVSCVLV(m) Q(uod) VO(veram) PROCONSVL EGO INFIMVS GREGORIVS Q(ui) NOMINOR VT PIE MICHI CONFERAS PRO PARVIS M(a)G(na) (munera). O princeps Petre principum caelestis aulae claviger devotionis suscipe munusculu(m) quod vo(veram) proconsul ego infimus Gregorius q(ui) nominor ut pie michi conferas pro parvis m(a)g(na) (munera). Oh Peter, first among the leaders, Prince and the key-holder of the heavenly palace, accept this votive gift that I, lowest proconsul Gregory, vowed to give as a small token to receive in turn magnificent gifts. (Engl. trans. J.B., according to Glavičić, Rapanić, and Lončar)

TABLE 7 Continued

Remarks:	Reference to the Byzantine proconsul Grgur, who built the basilica of St. Anastasia in Zadar; several readings have been proposed; here I follow and combine the three translations provided by Glavičić, Rapanić, and Lončar.
Bibliography:	Vasić (1922) 165, figs. 123–124; Vežić and Lončar (2009) 143–147; 224–231. 204–205

Cat. no.:	192
Date:	Middle Byzantine/after 11 CE?
Place:	Amorium church, Turkey
Canopy:	Altar canopy (?) Canopy spandrel fragment (T952) in white marble
Inscription:	το κ(αὶ) κοπιακότη το κ(αὶ) τ
Remarks:	Illegible inscription, part of the enumeration sequence ...
Bibliography:	Lightfoot and Ivison (1997) 291–300; Lightfoot (1998) 323–336

Cat. no.:	193
Date:	After 11 CE? [secondary use?]
Place:	Church of Pantokrator, Constantinople, Zeyrek camii, Istanbul
Canopy:	Altar canopy (?), tomb canopy (?), now minbar, with the inscriptions in monograms in roundels
Inscription:	Κύριε βοήθει (in the first roundel) τῷ δούλῳ (in the second roundel)... personal name (in the third roundel) Lord save your servant ... (Engl. trans. J.B.)
Remarks:	Inscription is a sequel of three cruciform monograms in roundels. The first two monograms are the beginning of a formulaic invocation widely used from the sixth to the sixteenth centuries. The reading of the cruciform monograms is similar to the monogram from Basilica B in Nikopolis (cat. no 45). I was not able to read the name and epithet in the monograms. The name, which comes close to the monogram in the third roundel, is "Alexios," which was common among the Komneni family. R. Ousterhout suggests that the name in the second and third monogram refers to Ignatios Synkkelos, ninth-century patriarch of Constantinople, and that the inscription reads "Lord help Ignatios Synkkelos." The formulaic reading "Κύριε βο(ή)θει" is usually followed by the designator and epithet and then by personal name, as seen, for example, in the inscription for humble proconsul Grgur (cat. no. 178). The inscription deserves further attention.
Bibliography:	Ousterhout (2010a) 432–439

TABLE 7 Continued

Cat. no.:	215
Date:	13 CE
Place:	Church of San Marco, Venice, Italy
Canopy:	Altar canopy
Inscription:	Inscriptions in Latin identifying the scenes carved on columns. Column 1 1) + YSACHAR PONTIFEX DESPEXIT IOACHIMET MVNERA EIVS SPREVIT. 2) •ADHORTATVR A(N)G(E)L(VS) IOACHIM ET ANNAM P(RE)DICENS EIS FILIAM NASCITVRAM 3) + ITEM FATVR ANGEL(VS) AD IOACHIM ET AD ANNAM DE FECVNDITATE (CON)FERENDA 4) + IOACH(IM) (ET) AN(N)A • MATERDEINASCITVR MVNERA • OFFERVNTVR IN TEMPLO 5) + OFFERTVR SACRIFI[CI]VM DEO PRO BEATA PROLE RECEPTA 6) + MATER SALVTIS NOSTRE DVCITVR CVM MVNERIBVS IN TE(M)PLVM 7) + MVNERA CVM LAMPADIBVS OFFERVNTVR DEO PRO VIRGINE NATA 8) + YSACHAR VIRGINE(M) RECIPIT IN TEMPLO Q(VE) N(V)LLO IVVANTE P(ER) SE G(RA)D(VS) ASCENDIT 9) + VIRGA IOSEPH APPARVIT Column 2 1) • ANNVNTIACIO• SVSPITIO D(E) MARIA• MARIA IT AT HELISAB(ETH)• NATIVITAS IHV (Iesu) CRISTI. 2) • ANGEL(VS) AD PASTORES NVNTIAT• SCRVTATIO P(RO)PHETIE P(RO) STELLA• HERODES 3) • MAGI VENIVNT AD CRISTVM• INVITATVR AD NVPTIAS CHANA GALILEE 4) • NVPTIE IN CHANA GALILEE• VOCATIO DISCIPVLORVM IN MARE GALILEE 5) • DE AQVA VINVM• EIECTIO DE TEMPLO• IHS (Iesus) LOQVITVR SAMARITANE 6) • ZACHEVS ASCENDIT• IHS (Iesus) VENIT A<D> ZACHEV(M)• REGVL(VS) ORAT P(RO) FILIO 7) • ITEM DE REGVLO• LVTVM FECIT D(OMI)N(V)S (ET) VNXIT ODVLOS CECI NATI 8) • SANAT(VS) TOLLIT GRAVATVM• QVATRIDVABV(M) D(OMI)N(V)S LAZARV(M) SVSCITAT 9) • SATIAT DE QVINQ(VE) PANIBVS• ORAT CHANANEA• LVNATIC(VS)• SANAT(VR) FILIA CH<A>NANE<E> Column 3 1) • SCRIBA DIX(IT) SEQVAR TE• DOMINE P(ER)MITTE ME PRIMVM SEPELLIRE PATRE(M) MEVM

TABLE 7 Continued

2) • SANAT IESVS EGROTOS I(N) GRABATIS DE VICIS SEV VILL(IS) AD EV(M) DEPORTATOS

3) • CVRAT PRALITICV(M)• CECI CLAMANT• VOCAT MATH(EV)M• MVRMVR PHARISEORV(M)

4) • SIMON I(N)VITAT IHS (Iesus; Iesum)• RIGANTVR PEDE<S> IHV (Iesu)• I(N)TRAT NAVIM. IMP(ER)AT VENTIS

5) • VENIT IN TER<R>AM GENESANORVM• DEMONES MITTIT IN PORCOS

6) • YAIRVS PRINCEPS ORAT PRO FILIA INFIRMA• ET SANATA EST

7) • TANGIT FIMBRIAM• MITTIT DISCIP(V)LOS• SEQ(VI)T(VR) ME TOLLAT CRVCEM

8) • STAGNVM GENESARET• IC.XC (Iesus Christus)• TRAHVNT RETE• IHS (Iesus) CVM SIMONE

9) • LEP(RO)S(VS) CVRATVR[ATVR]• XPS (Christus) MARIA (ET) M<A>RTHA• EXIT DEMON• DE ADVLTERA

Column 4

1) • TVRBA OBVIAT IHV (Iesu) CV(M) RAMIS PALMARVM• IHS (Iesus) LAVAT PEDES• CENA DOMINI

2) • AP(OSTO)LI DORMIV(N)T• XPS (Christus) ORAT• IVDAS P(RE)CIO RECEPTO PRODIT IHM (Iesum) OSCVLO

3) • A{P}MPVTAT AVRE(M)• DVCVNT IHM (Iesum) CAPTVM• SCINDIT VESTEM• ANDILLA PETR(VS)

4) • GALL(VS) CANIT• FLET PETR(VS)• INTERROGAT IEASVM PILATVS• REDDIT IVDAS PRECIVM

5) • LAQ(VE)VS IVDE• TRADTVR IHS (Iesus) MILITB(VS) FLAGELLATVS• LAVAT PILATVS MANVS

6) • XPS (Christus) DVCIT(VR) AD CRVCIFIGE(N)DV(M)• AGN(VS) CRVCIFIGIT(VR) CV(M) INIQ(VI)S•CVSTODIT SEPVLCHRV(M)

7) • SVRGV(N)T CORP(OR)A S(AN)C(T)O(RVM). EXPOLIATIO I(N)FERI• APPARITIO DOMINI AD DISCIPLOS

8) + ASCENSIO CRISTI AD CELOS APOSTOLIS CV(M) MIRATIONE ASPICIENTIBVS

9) + IHS (Iesus) SEDET IN GLORIA CELESTI ADSTANTIBVS ORDINIBVS ANDEL(ORVM)

Remarks: Richly carved alabaster columns are historiated with nine horizontal bands containing 324 niches populated with figures that recount 108 New Testament episodes. They are early Byzantine, seventh-century spolia. Inscriptions were added in Latin at later point, most likely in the thirteenth century, when the current altar installation was assembled. Inscriptions are carved on the bands above the figurative representations, but are occasionally misleading in their interpretation of the depicted scenes.

Bibliography: Weigel (2000); Weigel (1997) 286–302.

TABLE 7 Continued

Cat. no.:	217
Date:	13 CE
Place:	From Athens, Greece
Canopy:	Arches from a [tomb?] canopy
Inscription:	ΟΙ ΜΑΓΙ ΤΑ ΔΩΡΑ; ΟΙ ΑΓΓΕΛΟΙ ΤΟΝ ΥΜΝΟΝ; ΟΙ ΠΟΙΜΕΝΕΣ ΤΟ ΘΑΥΜΑ; ΙΩΣΗΦ The Magi, the gifts; angels, hymn; rejoicing the miracle; Joseph
Remarks:	Fragmentary inscription runs on the arch of a canopy, presumably a tomb canopy. The inscription makes reference to the Christmas hymn and the so-called Akathist hymn. The Akathist hymn literally means, in Greek, "without sitting," as the entire congregation remained standing in reverence. The inscriptions point to the hymn that honors the Mother of God and the holy event of the Nativity. Since the seventh century, the Akathist hymn has been officially part of the Orthodox services chanted during Great Lent and part of spiritual preparation for the Holy Week and Easter services. Hence, the inscription could have been also on a shrine, reliquary, or even an altar canopy. The inscription on a canopy arch is accompanied with a figurative representation of the Nativity scene.
Bibliography:	Bréhier (1913) 29 ff; Grabar (1976) vol. 2: 124–125; cat. nos. 152–155; Liveri (1996) 26–34, 178–179, no. 41

Cat. no.:	218
Date:	13 CE
Place:	From Athens, Greece
Canopy:	Arches from a [tomb?] canopy
Inscription:	Ο ΠΡΟΦΗΤΗC COΛOMON; Ο ΠΡΟΦΗΤΗC ΔΑΒΗΔ; Ο ΑΓΙΟC ΙΩ(ΑΝΝΗC) Ο ΠΡ(Ο)ΔΡ(Ο)ΜΟC Prophet Solomon; Prophet David; Hagios John Prodromos
Remarks:	Fragmentary inscription runs on one of the two preserved arches. Because of the dimensions these two arches, they probably belonged to another canopy installation, which is different from the one with the inscriptions with the Christmas hymn. On the arch with inscriptions, names of Old Testament prophets and kings Solomon and David, as well as St. John the Baptist, are inscribed. The names of Solomon, David, and John the Baptist are positioned above their figurative representations in high relief on the intrados of the arch.
Bibliography:	Bréhier (1913) 29 ff; Grabar (1976) vol. 2: 125–126; cat. no. 227; Liveri (1996), 36–39, 179–181, nos. 42, 43

Bibliography

ENCYCLOPEDIAS, DICTIONARIES, AND GENERAL WORKS:

(In alphabetical order under title or author's name; abbreviations and titles used in notes are highlighted in bold)

Bible. *The Holy Bible. Containing the Old and New Testaments.* King James Version. Nashville: Thomas Nelson Pubs., 1984.

Bible. O.T. Psalms. Polyglot. *Bible. O.T. Psalms. Polyglot.* A. Giusiniani, P. P. Porrus, et al. Genoa: Petrus Paulus Porrus, 1516.

Coptic Encyclopedia. *Coptic Encyclopedia.* A. S. Aziz, ed. New York: Macmillan, 1991.

DACL. *Dictionnaire d'archéologie chrétienne et de liturgie.* 15 vols. F. Cabrol and H. Leclercq, eds. Paris: Letouzey et Ané, 1920–1953.

DALA. *Dictionary of Architecture and Landscape Architecture,* 2nd ed. J. S. Curl, ed. Oxford: Oxford University Press, 2006.

DArt. *Dictionary of Art.* 34 vols. J. Turner, ed. New York: Grove's Dictionaries, 1996.

Dictionary of Architecture. *Dictionary of Architecture,* 2nd ed. J. Fleming, H. Honour, N. Pevsner, eds. Woodstock, NY: Overlook Press, 1977.

Dictionary of the Liturgy. *Dictionary of the Liturgy.* J. P. Lang, ed. New York: Catholic Book Pub. Co., 1989.

EAM. *Enciclopedia dell'arte medievale.* 12 vols. A. M. Romanini, ed. Rome: Istituto della Enciclopedia Italiana, 1991–c2002.

Glossary of Theological Terms. *Glossary of Theological Terms. English-Greek/Greek-English.* M. Makrantonaki-Farasa, ed. Thessaloniki: Pournaras P. Pubs., 2000.

Great Greek Encyclopedia. *Μεγάλη Ελληνική Εγκυκλοπαίδεια,* vol. XV, 2nd ed. Athens: Pyrsos, 1960.

Great Lent. *Great Lent.* A. Schmeman, Crestwood: St. Vladimir's Seminary Press, 1969.

Lampe. *A Patristic Greek Lexicon.* 5 vols. G. W. H. Lampe, D.D., ed. Oxford: Oxford University Press, 1964–1968.

Leksikon ikonografije. *Leksikon ikonografije, liturgike i simbolike zapadnog kriščanstva* [Lexicon of iconography, liturgy and symbolism in Western Christianity]. A. Badurina, ed. Zagreb: Institut za povijest umetnosti, 1979.

Lenten Triodion. *The Lenten Triodion.* Mother Mary and Kallistos Ware, trans. London and Boston: Faber and Faber Ltd., 1984.

Lexicon of the Septuagint. *A Greek-English Lexicon of the Septuagint.* J. E. E. Lust and K. Hauspie, eds. Stuttgart: Deutsche Bibelgesellschaft, 1996.

Liddell. *An Intermediate Greek-English Lexicon: Founded upon the Seventh Edition of Liddell and Scott's Greek-English Lexicon.* H. G. Liddell, ed. Oxford: Clarendon Press and New York: Oxford University Press, 1997a [ca. 1889].

Liddell and Scotts. *Greek-English Lexicon.* Liddell and Scott, eds. Oxford: Clarendon Press, 1997b [1889].

Living Bible. *Living Word Bible Collection.* CD. Waconia, Minn., 2002–2004.

LMA. *Lexikon des Mittelalters.* R. Auty et al., eds. München and Zürich: Artemis-Verlag, 1977–1999.

Modern Catholic Encyclopedia. *Modern Catholic Encyclopedia.* M. Glazier and M. K. Hellwig, eds. Collegeville: Liturgical Press, 1994.

New Catholic Encyclopedia. *New Catholic Encyclopedia,* 2nd ed. 15 vols. Catholic University of America, in association with Thomson-Gale. New York: Thomson, Gale, 2003.

New Dictionary of the Liturgy. *New Dictionary of the Liturgy.* G. Podhradsky, ed. London/Dublin/ Melbourne: Geoffrey Chapman, 1967.

ODA. *Oxford Dictionary of Art,* 3rd ed. I. Chilvers, ed. Oxford: Oxford University Press, 2004.

ODB. *Oxford Dictionary of Byzantium.* 3 vols. A. P. Kazhdan, ed. New York and Oxford: Oxford University Press, 1991.

ODE. *Oxford Dictionary of English,* rev. edition. C. Soanes and A. Stevenson, eds. Oxford: Oxford University Press, 2005.

Orthodox Study Bible. *The Orthodox Study Bible.* Nashville: Thomas Nelson, 2008.

Oxford Greek Dictionary. *Oxford Greek-English Learner's Dictionary,* 10th ed. D. N. Stavropoulos, ed. Oxford: Oxford University Press, 1998.

RAC. *Reallexikon für Antike und Christentum.* 21– vols. T. Klauser, ed. Stuttgart: A. Hiersemann, 1950–.

RBK. *Reallexikon zur Byzantinischen Kunst.* 6– vols. K. Wessel, ed. Stuttgart: A. Hiersemann 1963–.

Roman World. *The Roman World. The Oxford History of the Classical World.* J. Boardman, J. Griffin, and O. Murray, eds. Oxford and New York: Oxford University Press, 1988.

Souda lexicon. *Suidae lexicon.* I. Bekker and G. E. Reimer. Berolini: typis et imprensis Georgii Reimeri, 1854.

PRIMARY SOURCES:

(In alphabetical order under author's name or title; when several editions were consulted, these are consolidated by alphabetical listing: a, b, c)

A

Achilles Tatius. Achilles Tatius, *Leucippe and Clitophon.* E. Vilborg, ed. Stockholm: Almqvist och Wiksell, 1995.

Acta et diplomata. *Acta et diplomata Graeca mediiaevi,* vol. III. F. Miklosich and J. Muller, eds. Aalen: Scientia Verlag, 1968 (reprint of the 1865 ed. published in Vienna).

Acta Sanctorum. *Acta Sanctorum.* H. Delehaye, ed. Brussels, 1902 (repr. Wetteren, Belgium: Imprimerie Cultura, 1985).

Aëtius. Aëtius, *Iatricorum libri.* A. Olivieri, *Aëtii Amideni libri medicinales i–iv* [*Corpus medicorum Graecorum* 8.1. Leipzig: Teubner, 1935]: 17–146.

Agatharchides. Agatharchides Geogr., *Fragmenta.* F. Jacoby, FGrH 86. [Leiden: Brill, 1923–1958 (repr. 1954–1969)]: 2A:206–222; 3B:741 addenda.

Agathias. Agathias, *Historiae.* R. Keydell, *Agathiae Myrinaei historiarum libri quinque* [*Corpus Fontium Historiae Byzantinae. Series Berolinensis* 2. Berlin: De Gruyter, 1967]: 3–197.

Agnellus. Agnellus, *XXVI, De Victore.* c. 66 in *SD* (1972) 105.

Allatios. Allacci, L. *The Newer Temples of the Greeks* [*Templis Graecorum recentioribus*]. A. Cutler, trans. University Park: Pennsylvania State University Press, 1969.

Alexiad:

Alexiad-a. *Annae Comnenae Alexias.* D. R. Reinsch and A. Kambylis, eds. *Corpus fontium historiae Byzantinae,* vol. 40. Berlin: Walter de Gruyter GmbH & Co., 2001.

Alexiad-b. *The Alexiad of Anna Comnena.* E. R. A. Sewter, trans. Baltimore: Penguin Books, 1969.

Anastasius (the Librarian). Anastasius (the Librarian), *LIII. Sanctus Symmachus. Anno Christi* 498, Anastasii Imp. 8 Theodor. Regis 5, *PL* 128: 451–471.

Andrew of Crete. Andrew of Crete. *Magnus canon, PG* 97: 877–1386.

Athanasius Theol.:

Athanasius Theol., ***Expositiones in Psalmos.*** *PG* 27: 60–545, 548–589.

Athanasius Theol., ***Letters.*** Athanasius of Alexandria, *Selected Works and Letters,* in: *Nicene and Post-Nicene Fathers, Second Series,* vol. 4. P. Schaff and H. Wace, eds., R. Payne-Smith, trans. Buffalo: Christian Literature Publishing Co., 1892; also online at http://www.newadvent.org/fathers/2806039.htm.

Athenaeus:

Athenaeus-a. Athenaeus Soph. *Deipnosophistae.* G. Kaibel, *Athenaei Naucratitae deipnosophistarum libri xv,* 3 vols. Leipzig: Teubner. Vols. 1–2:1887; 3:1890 (repr. Stuttgart, 1–2:1965; 3:1966): 1:1–491; 2:1–498; 3:1–560.

Athenaeus-b. *Banquet of the Learned of Athenæus,* vol. 1. C. D. Yonge, ed. London: Henry G. Bohn, 1854.

Augustine. St. Augustine, Bishop of Hippo. *The Works of St. Augustine.* New York: Augustinian Heritage Institute, 1997.

B

Basil the Great:

St. Basil the Great, *Historia Mystagogica.* ***H.myst.*** 4 (258.18). F. E. Brightman, E. G. Cuthbert, and F. Atchley, *Notes and Studies: The Historia Mystagogica and Other Greek Commentaries on the Byzantine Liturgy.* London: n.p., 1908.

St. Basil. ***On the Holy Spirit.*** D. Anderson, trans. Crestwood: St. Vladimir's Seminary Press, 1997.

St. Basil. ***Homilia in Psalmum 115.*** *PG* 30: 104–116.

BMFD. *Byzantine Monastic Foundation Documents: A Complete Translation of the Surviving Founders' Typika and Testaments.* 5 vols. J. Thomas and A. Constantinides Hero, eds. Washington, DC: *DORLC,* 2000.

Ath.Rule. *Rule of Athanasios the Athonite for the Lavra Monastery,* in *BMFD* vol. 1 (2000): 205–231.

Kecharitomene. *Empress Irene Doukaina Komnene for the Convent of the Mother of God Kecharitomene in Constantinople,* in *BMFD* vol. 2 (2000): 649–724.

Pantokrator. *Typikon of Emperor John II Komnenos for the Monastery of Christ Pantokrator in Constantinople,* in *BMFD* vol. 2 (2000): 725–781.

Skoteine. *Skoteine [Boreine]: Testament of Maximos for the Monastery of the Mother of God at Skoteine near Philadelphia,* in *BMFD* vol. 3 (2000): 1176–1195.

Studios. *The Rule of the Monastery of St. John Stoudios in Constantinople,* in *BMFD* vol. 1 (2000): 84–119.

Buildings. Procopius. *Buildings,* vol. 7. H. B. Dewing, trans. Cambridge: Harvard University Press, and London: W. Heinemann, 1968–1979.

C

Callixenus. Callixenus Hist., *Fragmenta.* K. Müller, FHG 3. Paris: Didot, 1841–1870: 55–66.

Camblak:

Camblak, ***Žitije Stefana Dečanskog.*** G. Camblak, "Žitije Stefana Dečanskog," in *Književni rad u Srbiji.* Belgrade: Prosveta, 1989: 49–82.

Camblak, ***Služba Stefanu Dečanskom.*** G. Camblak, "Služba Stefanu Dečanskom," in *Srbljak. Službe-kanoni-akatisti.* Belgrade: Prosveta, 1970: 306–349.

Catenae. *Catenae (Novum Testamentum), Catena in Acta.* J. A. Cramer, *Catenae Graecorum Patrum in Novum Testamentum,* vol. 3. Oxford: Oxford University Press, 1838 (repr. Hildesheim: Olms, 1967): 1–424.

Chronicon 1234. *Chronicon ad annum Christi 1234 pertinens* (Dedicatory hymn of 622 recorded in Chronicle of 1234). J. B. Chabot, ed. *Anonymi auctoris Chronicon ad annum Christi 1234 pertinens.* Corpus scriptorium Christianorum Orientalium 82; Scr. Syri 3.15. Paris: Typographeo Reipublicae.

Chronicon Moreae. *Chronicon Moreae* (recensiones H et T). J. Schmitt, *The Chronicle of Morea.* London: Methuen, 1904: 3–597.

Chronicon paschale. *Chronicon paschale.* L. Dindorf, *Chronicon paschale,* vol. 1. [*CSHB.* Bonn: Weber, 1832]: 3–737.

Claudius Iolaus. Claudius Iolaus Hist., *Fragmenta.* K. Müller, FHG 4. Paris: Didot, 1841–1870: 363–364.

Clavijo. Clavijo, *Embassy to Tamerlane.* G. Le Strange, trans. London: Routledge, 1928.

Clement of Alexandria:

Clement of Alexandria, ***Stromata***. L. Früchtel, O. Stählin, and U. Treu, *Clemens Alexandrinus*, vols. 2, 3rd ed., and 3, 2nd ed. [*Die griechischen christlichen Schriftsteller* 52(15), 17. Berlin: Akademie Verlag, 2:1960; 3:1970]: 2:3–518; 3:3–102.

Clement of Alexandria, ***Excerpta ex Theodoto***. F. Sagnard, *Clément d'Alexandrie. Extraits de Théodote*, 2nd ed. [*Sources chrétiennes* 23. Paris: Éditions du Cerf, 1948 (repr. 1970)]: 52–212.

Cod.Just. *Codex Justinianus*. P. Krueger, ed. Hildesheim: Weidmann, 1954.

Codex Theodosianus. *Codex Theodosianus, Theodosiani libri XVI cum constitutionibus Sirmondianis. Pars posterior, Textus cum apparatus*. P. Krueger and T. Mommsen, eds. Berlin: Weidmann, 1990.

Constantinus Manasses. Constantinus Manasses, *Compendium chronicum*. *PG* 127.

Corippus. Flavius Cresconius Corippus, *In laudem Iustini Agusti minoris* (*In praise of the Emperor Justin II*). A. Cameron, trans. London: The Athlone Press, 1976.

Cos. Indicopl. Cosmas Indicopleustes, *Topographia Christiana*. W. Wolska-Conus, *Cosmas Indicopleustès. Topographie chrétienne*, 3 vols. [*SC* 141, 159, 197. Paris: Éditions du Cerf, 1:1968; 2:1970; 3:1973]: 1:255–569: 2:13–373; 3:13–381./*La topographie chrétienne de Cosmas Indicopleustes; théologie et sciences au VIe siècle*. Wolska-Conus, Wanda, ed. Paris: Presses Universitaires de France, 1962.

Cyrillus Alexandrinus:

Cyrillus Alexandrinus, ***Commentarii in Joannem***. P. E. Pusey, *Sancti patris nostri Cyrilli archiepiscopi Alexandrini in D. Joannis evangelium*, 3 vols. Oxford: Clarendon Press, 1872 (repr. 1965): 1:1–728; 2:1– 737; 3:1–171.

Cyrillus Alexandrinus, ***Commentarius in xii prophetas minores***. P. E. Pusey, *Sancti patris nostri Cyrilli archiepiscopi Alexandrini in xii prophetas*, 2 vols. Oxford: Clarendon Press, 1868 (repr. 1965): 1:1–740; 2:1–626.

Cyrillus Alexandrinus, ***De adoratione et cultu in spiritu et veritate***. *PG* 68: 132–1125.

D

De Ceremoniis:

De Ceremoniis-a. *De Ceremoniis Aulae Byzantinae*. *PG* 112.

De Ceremoniis-b. Constantine Porphyrogenitus, *Constantini Porphyrogeniti imperatoris de cerimoniis aulae Byzantinae libri duo Corpus scriptorum historiae Byzantinae*. J. J. Reiske, ed. Bonn: Weber, 1829–1840.

De Ceremoniis-c. Constantinus VII Porphyrogenitus, *De cerimoniis aulae Byzantinae*. A. Vogt, *Le livre des cérémonies*, 2 vols. Paris: Les Belles Lettres, 1:1935; 2:1939 (repr. 1967): 1:1–179; 2:1–187.

De Ceremoniis-d. Constantine Porphyrogenitos, *The Book of Ceremonies*, 2 vols. A. Moffatt and M. Tall, trans. with the Greek edition. Canberra: Australian Association for Byzantine Studies. *Byzantine Australiensia* 18, 2012.

Dig. Akrit. *Digenes Akrites*. J. Mavrogordato, ed. and trans. Oxford: Oxford University Press, 1956.

Diodorus Siculus. Diodorus Siculus Hist., *Bibliotheca historica* (lib. 1–20). K. T. Fischer (post I. Bekker & L. Dindorf) and F. Vogel, *Diodori bibliotheca historica*, 5 vols., 3rd ed. Leipzig: Teubner, 1:1888; 2:1890; 3:1893; 4–5:1906 (repr. Stuttgart, 1964): 1:1–533; 2:1–461; 3:1–497; 4:1–426; 5:1–336.

Dionysius Areopagita:

Dionysius Areopagita, **CH.** [*De caelesti hierachia*]. Dionysius Areopagita, *Corpus Dionysiacum*, 2 vols. B. R. Suchla, G. Heil, and A. M. Ritter, eds. Berlin: De Gruyter, 1990–1991: 2:7–59.

Dionysius Areopagita, **EH-a.** [*De ecclesiastica hierarchia*]. *PG* 3, cols. 369–485.

Dionysius Areopagita, **EH-b.** [*De ecclesiastica hierarchia*]. Dionysius Areopagita, *Corpus Dionysiacum*, 2 vols. B. R. Suchla, G. Heil, and A. M. Ritter, eds. Berlin: De Gruyter, 1990–1991: 2:63–132.

Dionysius Areopagita, **EH-c.** [*De ecclesiastica hierarchia*]. *Dionysius the Pseudo-Areopagite: The Ecclesiastical Hierarchy*. E. T. L. Campbell, trans. Washington, DC: University Press of America, 1981.

Dioscorides Pedanius. Dioscorides Pedanius Med., *De materia medica*. M. Wellmann, Pedanii Dioscuridis, *Anazarbei de materia medica libri quinque*, 3 vols. Berlin: Weidmann, 1:1907; 2:1906; 3:1914 (repr. 1958): 1:1–255, 2:1–339, 3:1–108.

E

Egeria. *Itinerarium Egeriae. Egeria's travels to the Holy Land*. 3rd ed. J. Wilkinson, trans. Warminster, England: Aris & Phillips, 1999 [1981, 1971].

Ennodius. Ennodius, *Carmen*. F. Vogel, *Magnus Felix Ennodius, Opera*. Berlin: Weidmann, 1885.

Epiphanius. Epiphanius of Cyprus, *In laudes S. Mariae deiparae, (dubia)*. *PG* 43.

EtLP. *Etude sur le Liber Pontificalis I*. L. Duchesne, ed. Paris: Ernest Thorin, 1877.

Etymologicum Gudianum. *Etymologicum Gudianum*. F. W. Sturz, *Etymologicum Graecae linguae Gudianum et alia grammaticorum scripta e codicibus manuscriptis nunc primum edita*. Leipzig: Weigel, 1818 (repr. Hildesheim: Olms, 1973); *Etymologicum Graecae Linguae Gudianum*. F. W. Sturz. Cambridge: Cambridge University Press, 2011.

Euripides. Euripides, *Ion*. G. Murray, trans. London and New York: Oxford University Press, 1954.

Eusebius:

Eusebius, ***Demonstratio evangelica.*** Eusebius, *Demonstratio evangelica*. I. A. Heikel, *Eusebius Werke, Band 6: Die Demonstratio evangelica* [*Die griechischen christlichen Schriftsteller* 23. Leipzig: Hinrichs, 1913]: 1–492.

Eusebius, ***Eccl.Hist-a.*** *Historiae Ecclesiasticae*. *PG* 20, 45–906.

Eusebius, ***Eccl.Hist-b.*** Eusebius of Caesarea. *The History of the Church*. G. A. Williamson, trans. New York: Penguin Books, 1965.

Eusebius, ***VC***. Eusebius of Caesarea. *Life of Constantine* [*Vita Constantini*]. A. Cameron and S. G. Hall, intro., trans. and comm. Oxford: Clarendon Press, 1999.

Eustathius. Eustathius, *Commentarii ad Homeri Iliadem*. M. van der Valk, *Eustathii archiepiscopi Thessalonicensis commentarii ad Homeri Iliadem pertinentes*, vols. 1–4. Leiden: Brill, 1:1971; 2:1976; 3:1979; 4:1987: 1:1–802; 2:1–838; 3:1–944; 4:1–991.

Evagrius Scholasticus. Evagrius Scholasticus, *Historia ecclesiastica*. J. Bidez and L. Parmentier, *The ecclesiastical history of Evagrius with the scholia*. London: Methuen, 1898 (repr. 1979): 5–241.

F

Fathers of the Church. *Fathers of the Church*. Washington, DC: The Catholic University of America Press, 1958 (repr. 2010).

Flavius Josephus. *Flavius Josephus, Antiquitates Judaicae*. B. Niese, *Flavii Iosephi opera*, vols. 1–4, Berlin: Weidmann, 1:1887; 2:1885: 3:1892; 4:1890 (repr. 1955): 1:3–362; 2:3–392; 3:3–409; 4:3–320.

Fragmenta Alchemica. *Fragmenta Alchemica*. M. Berthelot and C. É. Ruelle, *Collection des anciens alchimistes grecs*, vol. 2. Paris: Steinheil, 1888 (repr. 1963): 377–379.

G

Galenus Med. Galenus Med., *De alimentorum facultatibus* libri iii. G. Helmreich, *Galeni de alimentorum facultatibus* libri iii [*Corpus medicorum Graecorum* 5.4.2. Leipzig: Teubner, 1923]: 201–386.

Gennadius Scholarius. Gennadius Scholarius, *Grammatica*. M. Jugie, L. Petit, and X. A. Siderides, *Oeuvres complètes de Georges (Gennadios) Scholarios*, vol. 8. Paris: Maison de la bonne presse, 1936: 351–498.

Georgius Cedrenus. Georgius Cedrenus, *Compendium historiarum*. I. Bekker, Georgius Cedrenus Ioannis Scylitzae ope, 2 vols. [CSHB. Bonn: Weber, 1:1838; 2:1839]: 1:3–802; 2:3–638.

Georgius Choeroboscus. Georgius Choeroboscus, *De orthographia*. J. A. Cramer, *Anecdota Graeca e codd. manuscriptis bibliothecarum Oxoniensium*, vol. 2. Oxford: Oxford University Press, 1835 (repr. Amsterdam: Hakkert, 1963): 167–281.

Georgios Pachymeres. Georgios Pachymeres, *Συγγραφικαὶ ἱστορίαι (libri vi de Michaele Palaeologo)*. A. Failler and V. Laurent, *Georges Pachymérès. Relations historiques, 2 vols.* [*Corpus Fontium Historiae Byzantinae. Series Parisiensis* 24.1–2. Paris: Les Belles Lettres, 1984]: 1:3–325; 2:329–667.

Germanos:

Germanos-a. Germanos, *Ecclesiastical History and Mystical Contemplation. Historia mystica ecclesiae catholicae* (e cod. Vat. graec. 790 et cod. Neapolit. graec. 63).

Germanos-b. *St. Germanus of Constantinople on the Divine Liturgy*. P. Meyendorff, ed. Crestwood, NY: St. Vladimir's Seminary Press, 1984.

Gregory Nazianzes. Gregory Nazianzes, *De vita Mosis*. J. Danielou, Grégoire de Nysse. *La vie de Moïse*, 3rd ed. [SC 1 ter. Paris: Éditions du Cerf, 1968]: 44–326.

Gregory Nazianzes, *In sanctum baptisma*. Gregory Nazianzes, *Oratios in sanctum baptisma*. *PG* 36:360–425.

Gregory Palamas, *Capita physica, theologica, moralia et practica* [*Κεφάλαια ἑκατὸν πεντήκοντα φυσικὰ καὶ θεολογικά, ἠθικά τε καὶ πρακτικὰ καὶ καθαρτικὰ τῆς Βαρλααμίτιδος λύμης*]. R. E. Sinkewicz, *Saint Gregory*

Palamas, The One Hundred and Fifty Chapters [*Studies and Texts* 83. Toronto: Pontifical Institute of Medieval Studies, 1988]: 82–256.

H

Hegesander. Hegesander, *Fragmenta.* K. Müller, ed. FHG 4. Paris: Didot, 1841–1870: 412–422.

Herodianus. Aelius Herodianus and Pseudo-Herodianus, *Περὶ ὀρθογραφίας.* A. Lentz, *Grammatici Graeci,* vol. 3.2. Leipzig: Teubner, 1870 (repr. Hildesheim: Olms, 1965): 407–611.

Hesychius. Hesychius Lexicogr., *Lexicon.* K. Latte, *Hesychii Alexandrini lexicon,* vols. 1–2. Copenhagen: Munksgaard, 1:1953; 2:1966: 1:3–492; 2:1–806.

Hosios Ephraim. Ephraem Syrian *Encomium in gloriosos martyres, qui in toto mundo martyrium sunt passi.* Phrantzoles, K. G. *Ὁσίου Ἐφραίμ τοῦ Σύρου ἔργα,* vol. 7. Thessalonica: To Perivoli tis Panagias, 1998: 163–175.

I

Icon and Logos. *Icon and Logos: Sources in Eighth-Century Iconoclasm. An annotated translation of the Sixth Session of the Seventh Ecumenical Council (Nicea, 787), containing the Definition of the Council of Constantinople (754) and its refutation, and the Definition of the Seventh Ecumenical Council.* J. D. Sahas, ed. Toronto, Buffalo, and London: University of Toronto Press, 1986.

Isidorus Glabas. Isidorus Glabas, *Homiliae in sanctum Demetrium.* B. Laourdas, "Ἰσιδώρου ἀρχιεπισκόπου Θεσσαλονίκης ὁμιλίαι εἰς τὰς ἑορτὰς τοῦ ἁγίου Δημητρίου." *Ἑλληνικά* 5 (1954): 19–65.

J

Jerome. Jerome, *Contra Vigilantium. PL* 23: 339–352.

Jerusalem. *Jerusalem: The Holy City in the Eyes of Chronicles, Visitors, Pilgrims, and Prophets from the Days of Abraham to the Beginning of Modern Times.* F. E. Peters, ed. Princeton: Princeton University Press, 1985.

Jerusalem Pilgrims. *Jerusalem Pilgrims before the Crusades.* J. Wilkinson, trans. Warminster: Aris & Phillips Ltd., 2002 [1977].

Jerusalem Routes. P. Geyer, *Itinera Hierosolymitana.* Prague: Tempsky, 1898.

John Malalas:

John Malalas-a. Ioannes Malalas, *Chronographia. PG* 97.

John Malalas-b. Dindorf, L. *Ioannis Malalae chronographia* [*CSHB.* Bonn: Weber, 1831]: 23–496.

John Malalas-c. *The Chronicle of John Malalas.* E. Jeffreys et al. eds., E. and M. Jeffreys, trans. Melbourne: Australian Association for Byzantine Studies; [Sydney, NSW]: Dept. of Modern Greek, University of Sydney, 1986.

John Malalas-d. Thurn, I. *Ioannis Malalae chronographia* (*Corpus Fontium Historiae Byzantinae. Series Berolinensis* 35. Berlin and New York: De Gruyter, 2000): 3–432.

John Chrysostom:

Joannes Chrysostomus, ***De prophetiarum obscuritate.*** *PG* 56:163–192.

Joannes Chrysostomus, ***In Acta apostolorum.*** *PG* 60:13–384.

Joannes Chrysostomus, ***1 Cor. Hom.*** *PG* 61:9–382.

Joannes Chrysostomus, ***In Genesim. Hom.*** *PG* 53:21–385; 54:385–580.

Joannes Chrysostomus, ***De Beato Philogonio*** (*=Contra Anomoeos, homilia 6*). *PG* 48:747–756.

John Damascus:

John Damascus, ***On the Divine Images.*** St. John Damascus. *On the Divine Images. Three Apologies Against Those Who Attack the Divine Images.* D. Anderson, trans. Crestwood: St. Vladimir's Seminary Press, 1980.

John Damascus, ***Orthodox Faith.*** St. John of Damascus. Writings. Orthodox Faith [De Fide Orthodoxa], in *Fathers of the Church. St. John of Damascus. Writings* (Washington, DC: The Catholic University of America Press, 1958, reprint 2010), book 1. [Same as John of Damascus, *An Exposition of the Orthodox Faith,* in: *Nicene and Post-Nicene Fathers, Second Series,* vol. 9. Philip Schaff and Henry Wace, eds. E. W. Watson and L. Pullan, trans. (Buffalo: Christian Literature Publishing Co., 1899); also online at http://www.newadvent.org/fathers/33041.htm].

L

Life and Miracles StDemetrios:

Life and Miracles StDemetrios-a. Joannes I (Archbishop of Thessaloniki), *Miracula sancti Demetrii* (collection I) [Title in Greek: Διήγησις τῶν θαυματουργιῶν τοῦ ἁγίου καὶ πανενδόξου μεγαλομάρτυρος Δημητρίου]. P. Lemerle, *Les plus anciens recueils des miracles de saint Démétrius et la pénétration des Slaves dans les Balkans,* vol. 1. Paris: Centre National de la Recherche Scientifique, 1979: 50–165.

Life and Miracles StDemetrios-b. *Vita et Miracula Sancti Demetri* (collection II). P. Lemerle, *Les plus anciens recueils des miracles de saint Démétrius et la pénétration des Slaves dans les Balkans,* vol. 1. Paris: Centre National de la Recherche Scientifique, 1979: 168–241.

Life and Miracles StDemetrios-c. *Miracles of St. Demetrios; Comentaries.* P. Lamerle, *Les plus anciens recueils des miracles de saint Démétrius* II, Commentaire. Paris: Centre National de la Recherche Scientifique, 1981.

Life StLuke. *The Life and Miracles of Saint Luke of Steiris.* C. L. and W. R. Connor, trans. Brookline: Hellenic College Press, 1994.

Life StTheokiste:

Life StTheokiste-a. Nicetas Magistros, *Vita S. Theoctistae Lesbiae,* Acta Sanctorum Novembris, 4. Brussels: Société des Bollandistes, 1925.

Life StTheokiste-b. Nicetas Magister, *Vita S. Theoctistae Lesbiae,* Acta Sanctorum Nov. IV, 256, in *SD* 104.

Life StTheokiste-c. *Life of St. Theokiste of Lesbos,* in *Holy Women of Byzantium.* A. C. Hero, trans.; A.-M. Talbot, ed. Washington, DC: *DORLC,* 1996: 95–116.

M

Marcus Eremita. Marcus Eremita. *De baptismo.* G.-M. de Durand, Traités I [SC 445. Paris: Éditions du Cerf, 1999]: 296–396.

Maximus Conf.:

Maximus Conf.-a. *PG* 91: 657–718.

Maximus Conf.-b. *The Church, the Liturgy and the Soul of Man: The Mystagogia of St. Maximus the Confessor.* J. Stead, trans. Still River: St. Bede's Publications, 1982: 57–120.

Maximus Conf.-c *Maxime le confesseur, La mystagogie.* M.-L. Charpin-Ploix, ed. Paris: Migne, 2005.

Meletios Conf. St. Meletios the Confessor, *On Prayer.* Mount Athos: n. p., 1991.

Michael Psellus:

Michael Psellus, ***Epistula ad Michaelem Cerularium-a.*** U. Criscuolo, *Michele Psello, Epistola a Michele Cerulario* [*Hellenica et byzantina neapolitana* 15. (repr. Naples: Bibliopolis, 1990)]: 21–31.

Michael Psellus, ***Epistula ad Michaelem Cerularium-b.*** E. V. Maltese, Epistole inedite di Michele Psello I–III, *Studi italiani di filologia classica* 3 (1987–1988): 5: 88–98, 217–223; 6: 119–131.

Michael Psellus, *Fourteen Byzantine Rulers.* ***The Chronographia.*** E. R. A. Sewter, intro. and trans. Baltimore: Penguin, 1966.

Michael Psellus, ***Laudatio in Joannem Crustulam.*** P. Gautier, Eloge inédit du lecteur Jean Kroustoulas par Michel Psellos, *RSBN* 17–19 (1980–1982): 128–145.

Michael Psellus, ***Theologica.*** P. Gautier, *Michaelis Pselli theologica,* vol. 1. Leipzig: Teubner, 1989: 1–447.

Miraculis sancti Eugenii. Joannes VIII Xiphilinus, *De miraculis sancti Eugenii.* J. O. Rosenqvist, *The hagiographic Dossier of St. Eugenios of Trepizond in Codex Athous Dionysiou 154* [*Acta Universitatis Uppsaliensis. Studia Byzantina Uppsaliensia* 5. Uppsala: University of Uppsala, 1996]: 170–202.

N

Nicander. Nicander, *Fragmenta.* A. S. F. Gow and A. F. Scholfield, *Nicander. The poems and poetical fragments.* Cambridge: Cambridge University Press, 1953: 138–166.

Nicephorus of Constantinople. Nicephorus of Constantinople, Patriarch, *Antirrheticus (Refutation)* 2.5 *PG* 100:344.

Nicetas Choniates. Nicetas Choniates, *Chronographia,* J. van Dieten, *Nicetae Choniatae historia,* pars prior [*Corpus Fontium Historiae Byzantinae. Series Berolinensis* 11.1. Berlin: De Gruyter, 1975]: 1–635, 637–655.

Nicetas Epist. Constantinopolitanus. Nicetas Epist. Constantinopolitanus, *Epistulae ad Nicetam Stethatum.* J. Darrouzès, *Nicétas Stéthatos, Opuscules et Lettres* [*SC* 81. Paris: Éditions du Cerf, 1961]: 230–234.

Nicolaus Mesarites:

Nicolaus Mesarites, ***Descriptio ecclesiae SS. Apostolorum.*** G. Downey, Nikolaos Mesarites: Description of the Church of the Holy Apostles at Constantinople. *TAPA* 47 (1957): 897–918.

Nicolaus Mesarites, ***Seditio Joanni Comneni.*** A. Heisenberg, *Nikolaos Mesarites, Die Palastrevolution des Johannes Komnenos* [*Programm des K. Alten Gymnasiums zu Würzburg für das Studienjahr 1906–1907.* Würzburg: Köningliche Universitätsdruckerei von H. Stürzt, 1907].

Notitiae Episcopatuum. *Notitiae Episcopatuum Ecclesiae Constantinopolitanae.* J. Darrouzès, ed. Paris: Institut Français d'Études Byzantines, 1981: 204–421.

Notitia urbis Constantinopolitanae. *Notitia Dignitatum; accedunt Notitia urbis Constantinopolitanae et latercula provinciarum.* O. Seeck, ed. Frankfurt: Minerva, 1962.

O

Oribasius. Oribasius Med., *Collectiones medicae* (lib. 1–16, 24–25, 43–50). J. Raeder, *Oribasii collectionum medicarum reliquiae,* vols. 1–4 [*Corpus medicorum Graecorum* 6.1.1–6.2.2. Leipzig: Teubner, 6.1.1:1928; 6.1.2:1929; 6.2.1:1931; 6.2.2:1933]: 6.1.1:4–27, 30–65, 67–91, 93–109, 111–153, 155–192, 194–245, 247–300; 6.1.2:4–237, 239–297, 298; 6.2.1:4–291; 6.2.2:4–69.

Orphica. Orphica, *Hymni.* W. Quandt, *Orphei hymni,* 3rd ed. Berlin: Weidmann, 1962 (repr. 1973): 1–57.

P

Palestine Pilgrims Text Society/PPTS:

Antoninus. *Of the Holy Places visited by Antoninus Martyr,* in *PPTS* vol. 2 (1897).

Arculfus. *The Pilgrimage of Arculfus,* in *PPTS* vol. 3 (1897).

Daniel. Pilgrimage of the Russian Abbot Daniel in the Holy Land. Circa 1106–1107, in *PPTS* vol. 4 (New York, 1971[1887–1889]).

John of Würzburg. *Description of the Holy Land by John of Würzburg (AD 1160–1170),* in *PPTS* vol. 5 (1980).

Phocas. *The Pilgrimage of Joannes Phocas in the Holy Land (in the year 1185),* in *PPTS* vol. 5 (1896).

Seawulf. *The Pilgrimage of Seawulf,* in *PPTS* vol. 4 (New York, 1971[1887–1889]).

Palestine Pilgrims. *Early Travels in Palestine, Comprising the Narratives of Arculf, Willibald, Bernard, Seawulf, Sigurd, Benjamin of Tudela, Sir John Maundeville, de la Brocquière, and Maundrell.* T. Wright, ed. London: Bohn, 1848.

Papyri magicae. Magica, *Papyri magicae.* A. Henrichs and K. Preisendanz, *Papyri Graecae magicae. Die griechischen Zauberpapyri,* 2nd ed., vols. 1–2. Stuttgart: Teubner, 1:1973; 2:1974: 1:1–62, 66–200; 2:1–208.

Patriarch Severus. Patriarch Severus, *Sermon.* Les Homiliae Cathedrales de Sévère d'Antioche. Homélies VCIX CIII. I. Guidi, ed. Paris: Firmin-Didot, 1929.

Paulos Silentarios:

Paulos Silentarios-a. Paulus Silentarius Poeta, *Descriptio S. Sophiae. PG* 310. 86, cols. 2147–2148. 720ff.

Paulos Silentarios-b. Paulus Silentarius Poeta, *Descriptio S. Sophiae* in *TLG*: Veh, O. *Prokop. Werke,* vol. 5. Munich: Heimeran, 1977: 306–358.

Paulos Silentarios-c. Paulus Silentarius Poeta, *Descriptio S. Sophiae,* in *SD* (1972) 80–96.

Paulos Silentarios-d. M. L. Fobelli and M. Andoloro, *Un tempio per Giustiniano: Santa Sofia di Costantinopoli e la "Descrizione" di Paolo Silenziario.* Rome: Viella, 2005.

Pausanias. Pausanias, *Fragmenta.* K. Müller, *FHG* 4. Paris: Didot, 1841–1870: 467–471.

PG. *Patrologiae græcae.* 161 vols. J.-P. Migne, ed. Paris: Migne, 1857–1887.

Philo:

Philo, ***De vita Mosis.*** L. Cohn, *Philonis Alexandrini opera quae supersunt,* vol. 4. Berlin: Reimer, 1902 (repr. De Gruyter, 1962): 119–268.

Philo, **De Cherubim.** L. Cohn, *Philonis Alexandrini opera quae supersunt,* vol. 1. Berlin: Reimer, 1902 (repr. De Gruyter, 1962): 170–201.

Philo, **Questions in Exodus** (=*Questione in Exodum*). F. Petit, *Quaestiones in Genesim et in Exodum. Fragmenta Graeca* [*Les oeuvres de Philon d'Alexandrie* 33]. Paris: Éditions du Cerf, 1978: 233–278, 281–306.

Philostorgius. Philostorgius, *Historia Ecclesiastica. PG* 65: 480.

Photius:

Photius, ***Epistulae et Amphilochia***. B. Laourdas and L. G. Westerink, *Photii patriarchae Constantinopolitani Epistulae et Amphilochia*, vols. 1–6.2 [*Bibliotheca Scriptorum Graecorum et Romanorum Teubneriana*. Leipzig: Teubner, 1:1983; 2:1984; 3:1985; 4:1986; 5:1986; 6.1:1987; 6.2:1988]: 1:2–197; 2:1–253; 3:4–166; 4:1–190; 5:1–263; 6.1:1–138.

Photius, ***The Homilies of Photius Patriarch of Constantinople-a***. B. Laourdas, *Ἑλληνικά* 12 Παράρτημα. Thessalonica, 1857–1866: 1–186.

Photius, ***The Homilies of Photius Patriarch of Constantinople-b***. English Translation, Introduction and Commentary. C. Mango, ed. Cambridge: Harvard University Press, 1958.

Preisedikt. Diokletians *Preisedikt*. S. Lauffer, ed. Berlin: de Gruyter, 1971.

Pseudo–Codinus:

Pseudo–Codinus, ***Narratio de aedificatione templi Sanctae Sophiae,*** in *Bonn Corpus*. Bonn, 1843.

Pseudo–Codinus, ***Patria-a***. T. Preger, *Patria Constantinopoleos*, Scriptores originum Constantinopolitanarum, Vol. 2. (Leipzig: Teubner, 1907) 55; (repr. 1975): 135–289.

Pseudo–Codinus, ***Patria-b***. *Accounts of Medieval Constantinople. The Patria*. A. Berger. Cambridge, Mass., and London: Harvard University Press, 2013.

Pseudo-Galenus. Pseudo-Galenus Med., *De theriaca ad Pamphilianum*. C. G. Kühn, *Claudii Galeni opera omnia*, vol. 14. Leipzig: Knobloch, 1827 (repr. Hildesheim: Olms, 1965): 295–310.

R

***RussTravelers* (1984)**. *Russian travelers to Constantinople in the fourteenth and fifteenth centuries*. G. P. Majeska. Washington, DC: *DORLC*, 1984.

RussAnon. Russian Anonym. Anonymous description of Constantinople/Tale of the Holy Places, of The City of Constantinople and of the Holy Relics Preserved in Jerusalem and Collected by the Emperor Constantine in the Aforementioned City, in *RussTravelers* (1984): 114–127; 128–154.

Stephen of Novgorod. Stephen of Novgorod. From the "Wanderer of Stephen of Novgorod" in *RussTravelers* (1984): 15–47.

S

Scriptores orig. Const. *Scriptores originum Constantinopolitanarum*, 2 vols. T. Preger, ed. Leipzig: B. G. Teubner, 1901–1907.

SD. *The Art of the Byzantine Empire, 312–1453; Sources and Documents*. C. Mango, ed. Englewood Cliffs: Prentice-Hall, 1972.

Seven Councils. *The Seven Ecumenical Councils of the Undivided Church*, P. Schaff and H. Wace, eds. Oxford: Parker, 1890-1900, book XIV, 356–408; online at: http://www.fordham.edu/halsall/basis/trullo.html. For the bilingual text in Greek and Latin, see: G. D. Mansi, *Sacrorum conciliorum nova et amplissima collecti.*, vol. XI. Paris, Leipzig, 1901–1927, cols. 977–980.

Seven Pillars. *Sedam stubova Premudrosti. Istorija Vaseljenskih Sabora*. [Seven Pillars of Wisdom. The History of Oecumenical Synods]. M. Stanković, trans. Belgrade: Misionarski duhovni centar manastira Hilandara "Trojeručica", 1998.

Simplicius. Simplicius, *In Aristotelis quattuor libros de caelo commentaria*. J. L. Heiberg, *Simplicii in Aristotelis de caelo commentaria* [*Commentaria in Aristotelem Graeca* 7. Berlin: Reimer, 1894]: 1–361, 365–731.

Sophronius. Sophronius, *Historia liturg. 2 PG* 87, 3984.

Soranus. Soranus Med., *Gynaeciorum* libri iv. J. Ilberg, *Sorani Gynaeciorum libri iv, de signis fracturarum, de fasciis, vita Hippocratis secundum Soranum* [*Corpus medicorum Graecorum* 4. Leipzig: Teubner, 1927]: 3–152.

Stephanus Byzantius. Stephanus Byzantius, *Ethnica*. A. Meineke, *Stephan von Byzanz. Ethnika*. Berlin: Reimer, 1849 (repr. 1958): 1–713.

Strabo. Strabo Amasiotes, *Geographica*. A. Meineke, *Strabonis geographica*, 3 vols. Leipzig: Teubner, 1877 (repr. 1969): 1:xiii–xv, 1–396; 2:397–814; 3:815–1173.

Symeon of Thessaloniki. Symeon of Thessaloniki, *De Sacro Templo*. *PG* 155.

Synaxarion CP. *Synaxarium ecclesiae Constantinopolitanae. Propylaeum ad Acta sanctorum, Acta Sanctorum* 62. H. Delehaye, ed. Brussels, 1902 (repr. Wetteren, Belgium: Imprimerie Cultura, 1985).

Synopsis historiarum. *Ioannis Scylitzae Synopsis historiarum*. I. Thurn. Berlin and New York: De Gruyter, 1973: 14 [B. 501–503].

T

Tertullian. Tertullian, *De Baptismo*. E. Evans, *De baptismo liber. Homily on baptism by Tertullian*. London: SPCK, 1964.

Theodore of Cyrrhus. Theodore of Cyrrhus (Cyrus), *Church History*./Theodoretus of Cyrrhus. *Historia Ecclesiastica*. *PG* 82.

Theodore of Studion:

Theodore of Studion, ***Orations.*** Theodore of Studion, *Orations* 9.12. *PG* 99:788.

Theodore of Studion, ***Iambii-a.*** Theodore of Studion, *Iambii*. *PG* 99.

Theodore of Studion, ***Iambii-b.*** P. Speck, *Jamben auf verschiedene Gegenstaende* [*Supplementa Byzantina* 1. Berlin: De Gruyter, 1968]: 109–308.

Theodorus Andidensis. Theodorus Andidensis *PG* 140.

Theodorus II Ducas Lascaris, *Epistulae*. Theodorus II Ducas Lascaris, Epistulae. N. Festa, *Theodori Ducae Lascaris Epistulae CCXVII* [*Pubblicazioni del R. Istituto di studi superiori pratici e di perfezionamento in Firenze. Sezione di filosofia e lettere* 29. Florence: Istituto di studi superiori pratici e di perfezionamento, 1898]: 1–282.

Theoktistos. Theoktistos the Stoudite, *Oratio de translatione reliquiarum sancti Athanasii Constantinopolitani. Faith Healing in Late Byzantium. The Posthumous Miracles of the Patriarch Athanasios I of Constantinople by Theoktistos the Stoudite*. A.-M. Talbot, trans. Brookline: Holy Cross Orthodox, 1983: 44–123.

Theophanes Confessor. Theophanes Confessor, *Chronographia*. C. de Boor, *Theophanis chronographia*, vol. 1. Leipzig: Teubner, 1883 (repr. Hildesheim: Olms, 1963): 3–503.

Thucydides. *Thucydidis historiae*, 2 vols. H. S. Jones and J. E. Powell, eds. Oxford: Clarendon Press, 1:1942 (1st ed. rev.); 2:1942 (2nd ed. rev.) (repr. 1:1970; 2:1967).

***TLG*.** Henricus Stephanos, *Thesaurus Lingua Graecae* 4 (Paris, 1841)/*TLG* online: http://www.tlg.uci.edu/.

***Typicon of Hagia Sophia*.** *Typicon of Hagia Sophia*. J. Mateos, *Le Typicon de la Grande Église*, Tome I: Le cycle des douze mois [*OCA* 165. Rome: Pontificum Institutum Orientalium Studiorum, 1962]: 2–386.

V

***Vita Eliae Junioris*.** G. Rossi Taibbi, *Vita di Sant' Elia il Giovane*. Palermo: Istituto Siciliano di studi bizantini e neoellenici, 1962: 2–122.

***Vita et Miracula Niconis*.** D. F. Sullivan, *The Life of Saint Nikon*. Brookline: Hellenic College Press, 1987: 26–270.

***Vita et Miraculis Sanctae Theclae*.** Basilius Seleuciensis. *De vita et miraculis sanctae Theclae*, libri ii. G. Dagron, *Vie et miracles de sainte Thècle: Texte grec, traduction et commentaire* [*SH* 62. Brussels: Société des Bollandistes, 1978]: 168–412. [See also *The Life and Miracle of Thecla, A Literary Study*. S. F. Johnson. Washington, DC: Center for Hellenic Studies, 2006.]

***Vita Eustratii*.** A. Papadopoulos-Kerameus, *Ἀνάλεκτα Ἱεροσολυμιτικῆς σταχυολογίας*, vol. 4. St. Petersburg: Kirschbaum, 1897 (repr. Brussels: Culture et Civilisation, 1963): 367–400.

***Vita Joannis Eleemosynarii episcopi Alexandrini*.** Cyprus Leontius, *Vita Joannis Eleemosynarii episcopi Alexandrini*. A.-J. Festugière and L. Rydén, Léontios de Néapolis, *Vie de Syméon le Fou et Vie de Jean de Chypre* [Bibliothèque archéologique et historique 95. Paris: Geuthner, 1974]: 343–409.

***Vita Porphyrii episcopi Gazensis*.** Marcus Diaconus Scr. Eccl., *Vita Porphyrii episcopi Gazensis*. H. Gregoire and M.-A. Kugener, *Marc le Diacre. Vie de Porphyre, évêque de Gaza*. Paris: Les Belles Lettres, 1930: 1–79.

***Vita sancti Hypatii*.** Callinicus, *Vita sancti Hypatii*. G. J. M. Bartelink, *Callinicos. Vie d'Hypatios* [*SC* 177. Paris: Éditions du Cerf, 1971]: 62–298.

***Vita sancti Theodori Syceotae*.** Georgius Syceota, *Vita sancti Theodori Syceotae*. A.-J. Festugière, *Vie de Théodore de Sykeôn*, vol. 1 [*SH* 48. Brussels: Société des Bollandistes, 1970]: 1–161.

***Vita sanctorum Davidis, Symeonis et Georgii Mitylenae*.** J. van den Gheyn, "Acta Graeca ss. Davidis, Symeonis et Georgii Mitylenae in insula Lesbo." *AB* 18 (1899): 211–259.

***Vita Simeonis Novi Theologici*.** Nicetas Stethatus, *Vita Simeonis Novi Theologici*. I. Hausherr, *Un grand mystique byzantin. Vie de Syméon le Nouveau Théologien par Nicétas Stéthatos* [Orientalia Christiana 12. Rome: Pontificum Institutum Orientalium Studiorum, 1928]: 1–230.

Vitae et Miracula Sancti Anastasii Persae. B. Flusin, *Saint Anastase le Perse et l'histoire de la Palestine au début du viie siècle*, vol. 1. Paris: Centre National de la Recherche Scientifique, 1992: 41–91.

Vitae Symeonis Stylitae Junioris. P. van den Ven, *La vie ancienne de S. Syméon Stylite le jeune (521–592)* [Subsidia hagiographica 32. Brussels: Société des Bollandistes, 1962]: 1–224.

Vitruvius:

Vitruvius-a. *The Ten Books on Architecture.* M. H. Morgan, trans. New York: Dover Pubs., 1960.

Vitruvius-b. *The Ten Books on Architecture.* I. D. Rowland, trans. with illustrations by T. Howe. New York: Cambridge University Press, 1999.

Z

Zonaras. Ioannes Zonaras, *Epitome historiarum* (lib. 13–18). T. Büttner-Wobst, *Ioannis Zonarae epitomae historiarum libri xviii*, vol. 3 [CSHB. Bonn: Weber, 1897]: 1–768.

SECONDARY SOURCES:

A

Acconci, A. S. (1993). "Giovanni in Argentella presso Palombara Sabina: le testimonianze altomedievali: il ciborio e l'affresco dell'Adorazione della croce." *ArteM* 7/1: 15–41.

Ahrweiler, H. (1975). "The Geography of the Iconoclastic World," in *Iconoclasm*: 21–27.

Aleksova, B., and C. Mango (1971). "Bargala: A Preliminary Report." *DOP* 25: 265–281.

Alexander, P. J. (1953). "The Iconoclastic Council of St. Sophia (815) and Its Definition (*Horos*)." *DOP* 7: 35–66.

Alexopoulos, S. (2015). "When a Column Speaks: The Liturgy of the Christian Parthenon." *DOP* 69: 159–178.

Alföldi, A. (1950). "Zur Geschichte des Throntabernakels." *Nouvelle Clio* 10: 537–566.

Aliprantēs, T. C. (1996). *Hē Hekatontapylianē tēs Parou: 1670 chronia apo to Tama tēs Hagias Helenēs.* Paros: Ekdose Hierou Proskynēmatos Panagias Hekatontapylianēs Parou.

Almpanē, T., ed. (2001). *To Vyzantio se oikoumenē: Vyzantino kai Christianiko Mouseio.* Athēna: Hypourgeio Politismou.

Altripp, M. (1998). *Die* Prothesis *und ihre Bildausstattung in Byzanz unter besonderer Berücksichtigung der Denkmäler Griechenlands.* Frankfurt am Main: Lang.

Anderson, J., and M. Jeffreys (1994). "The Decoration of the Sevastokratorissa's Tent." *Byz* 64: 8–18.

Angar, M. (2008). "Stiftermodelle in Byzanz und bei christlich-orthodoxen Nachbarkulturen," in *Mikroarchitekturen im Mittelalter,* Christine Kratzke, ed. Leipzig: Kratzke Verlag für Kunst- und Kulturgeschichte: 433–453.

Αντωνάρας, Αναστάσιος Χ. [Antonaras, Anastasios Ch.] (2014). "Ορειχάλκινα ευρήματα από το ιερό της βασιλικής κάτω από την Αγία Σοφία Θεσσαλονίκης" [Bronze findings from the apse of the basilica under Saint Sophia, Thessaloniki], Τριακοστο Τέταρτο Συμπόσιο της Χριστιανική Αρχαιολογικής Εταιρείας Athens: 21–22.

Antourakēs, G. V. (1994). *Arhaia martyria kai hristianikoi naoi.* Athens: n. p.

Asgari, N. (1995). "The Proconnesian Production of Architectural Elements in Late Antiquity, Based on Evidence from Marble Quarries," in *Constantinople and Its Hinterland,* C. Mango and G. Dagron, eds. Aldershot: Variorum: 263–288.

Auxentios of Photiki, Bishop. (1999). *The Paschal Fire in Jerusalem: A Study of the Rite of the Holy Fire in the Church of the Holy Sepulchre.* Berkeley: St. John Chrysostom Press.

Auzépy, M.-F., and Grélois, J.-P., eds. (2001). *Byzance retrouvée: érudits et voyageurs français (XVIe–XVIIIe siècles).* Paris: Centre d'études byzantines, néo-helléniques et sud-est européennes: Publications de la Sorbonne.

B

Babić, G. (1987). *Kraljeva crkva u Studenici.* Belgrade: SANU.

Babić, G. (1975). "O živopisanom ukrasu oltarskih pregrada." *ZLU* 11: 3–49.

Babić, G. (1969). *Les chapelles annexes des églises byzantines: fonction liturgique et programmes iconographiques.* Paris: Éditions Klincksieck.

Bacci, M. (2009). "Side Altars and 'Pro Anima' Chapels in the Medieval Mediterranean," in *The Altar and Its Environment, 1150–1400,* J. Kroesen and V. M. Schimdt, eds. Turnhout: Brepols: 11–30.

Bachmann-Medick, D. (2006). "Spatial Turn," in *Cultural Turns. Neuorientierungen in den Kulturwissenschaften,* Doris Bachmann Medick, ed. Reinbek: Rowohlt Taschenbuch Verlag: 284–328.

Badawy, A. (1978). *Coptic Art and Archeology: The Art of the Christian Egyptians from the Late Antique to the Middle Ages.* Cambridge, MA, and London: The MIT Press.

Bagatti, B. P. (1956–1957). "Gli altari paleo-cristiani della Palestina." *Jerusalem* 7: 64–94.

Baha Tanman, M. (2001). "Depictions of the Mausoleum of Seyyid Ahmed El- Rifa'î in Late Derwish Convent Ottoman Art." *EJOS* IV: 1–37.

Βακάρος, Δ. [Bakaros, D.] (2006). "Ὁ πολιοῦχος τῆς Θεσσαλονίκης καί ὑπέρμαχος τῆς οἰκουμένης," in Ἅγιος μεγαλομάρτυς Δημήτριος ὁ Μυροβλύτης. 1700 χρόνια ἀπό τό μαρτύριό του (305–2005). Thessalonike: n.p.: 68–91.

Bakirtzis, C. (2002). "Pilgrimage of Thessalonike: The Tomb of St. Demetrios." *DOP* 56: 175–192.

Bakirtzis, C. (1997). *The Basilica of St. Demetrius,* Archaeological Guides of the Institute for Balkan studies (I.M.X.A.) no. 6. Thessaloniki: Institute for Balkan Studies.

Bakirtzis, C. (1990). "Byzantine Ampullae from Thessaloniki," in *The Blessings of Pilgrimage,* R. Ousterhout, ed. Urbana: University of Illinois Press: 140–149.

Bannister, T. C. (1968). "The Constantinian Basilica of Saint Peter at Rome." *JSAH* 27: 3–32.

Barag, D., and J. Wilkinson (1974). "The Monza-Bobbio Flasks and the Holy Sepulchre." *Levant* 6: 179–187.

Barber, C. (2002). *Figure and Likeness. On the limits of representation in Byzantine Iconoclasm.* Princeton and Oxford: Princeton University Press.

Bardill, J. (2006). "A New Temple for Byzantium: Anicia Juliana, King Solomon, and the Gilded Ceiling of the Church of St. Polyeuktos in Constantinople," in *Social and Political Life in Late Antiquity,* W. Bowden, A. Gutteridge, and C. Machado, eds. Leiden and Boston: Brill: 339–370.

Bardill, J. (1997). "The Palace of Lausus and Nearby Monuments in Constantinople: A Topographical Study." *AJA* 101/1: 67–95.

Barker, M. (2003). *The Great High Priest. The Temple Roots of Christian Theology.* London and New York: T&T Clark.

Barker, M. (1998). "Beyond the Veil of the Temple. The High Priestly Origin of the Apocalypses." *SJT* 51/1: 1–21.

Barnard, L. (1975). "The Theology of Images," in *Iconoclasm*: 7–13.

Barnard, L. W. (1974). *The Graeco-Roman and Oriental Background of the Iconoclastic Controversy.* Leiden: Brill.

Barnea, I. M. (1940). *To palaiohristianikon thysiastērion.* Athens: n.p.

Barry, F. (2007). "Walking on Water: Cosmic Floors in Antiquity and the Middle Ages." *ArtB* 89/4: 627–656.

Barski, V. G. (1774). *θάυματα Μοναστήρια του Άγιου Όρους Άθω, έτσι όπως τα είδε και τα σχεδίασε με ξήλο και πολλή επιμέλεια, ο ευλαβής οδοιπόρος μοναχός Βασιλειός Γρηγόροβιτς Μπάρσκυ όταν περιηγήθηκε την ιερή πολιτεία του Άθω το έτος 1744.* Thessalonikē: Edkosē Hagioreitikē Phōtothēkē-Reprotime, 1998.

Basić, I. (2014). "Ulomci najstarijeg ciborija splitske katedrale. Dopune splitskoj klesarskoj radionici." *Zbornik Dana Cvita Fiskovića V. Majstorske radionice u umjetnickoj baštini Hrvatske.* Zagreb: Odsjek za povjest umetnosti filozofskog fakultet: 21–36.

Bauer, F. A. (2013). *Eine Stadt und ihr Patron. Thessaloniki und der Heilige Demetrios.* Regensburg, Tübingen, Berlin: Schnell und Steiner.

Beliaev, L. A. (1998). "Russian pilgrim art from the 12th to the 15th century—archaeological elements and problems of Romanesque influence." *JBAA* 151: 203–219.

Belting, H. (2001). *Bild-Anthropologie. Entwürfe für eine Bildwissenschaft.* München: Fink.

Belting, H. (1996). *Likeness and Presence. A History of the Image Before the Era of Art.* 2nd ed. Chicago: Chicago University Press.

Belting, H. (1987). *The End of the History of Art?* Chicago: University of Chicago Press.

Belting, H. (1972). "Zur Skulptur aus der Zeit um 1300 Konstantinopel." *MünchJb* 3/23: 63–93.

Benson, J. L. (1959). "Spirally fluted columns in Greece." *Hesperia* 28/4: 253–272. [Originally published as Benson, J. L. (1956). "Spirally fluted columns in Greece." *AJA* 60/4: 385–387.]

Berger, A. (2000). "Streets and Public Spaces in Constantinople." *DOP* 54: 161–172.

Bettini, S. (1974). *Venezia e Bisanzio*. Milano: Electra.

Biddle, M. (1999). *The Tomb of Christ*. Gloucestershire, England: Sutton.

Bikai, P. M. (2002). "The Churches of Byzantine Petra." *NEA* 65/4: 271–276.

Bikai, P. M., and V. Egan (1997). "Archeology in Jordan." *AJA* 101/3: 493–535.

Bingham, J. (1710–1722). *Origines ecclesiasticae; or, the antiquities of the Christian Church*. 10 vols. London: Printed for R. Knaplock.

Blaauw, S. de (2009a). "Altar Imagery in Italy Before the Altarpiece," in *The Altar and Its Environment, 1150–1400*, J. Kroesen and V. M. Schimdt, eds. Turnhout: Brepols: 47–55.

Blaauw, S. de (2009b). "Arnolfo's High Altar Ciboria and Roman Liturgical Traditions," in *Arnolfo's Moment*, Acts of the International Conference, Villa I Tatti, Florence, 26–27 May, D. Friedman, J. Gardner, and M. Haines, eds. Florence: Olschki: 123–140+.

Blauuw, S. de (1994). *Cultus et Décor: Liturgia e architettura nella Roma tardoantica e medievale. Basilica Salvatoris, Sanctae Mariae, Sancti Petri*. 2 vols. M. B. Annis, trans. Vatican City: Biblioteca Apostolica Vaticana.

Bogdanović, D., et al. (1997). *Chilandar*. Belgrade: Monastery of Chilandar.

Bogdanović, J. (2017a). "Medieval Religious Architecture in the Balkans," in *The Cambridge World History of Religious Architecture*, R. Etlin and A.-M. Yasin, eds. Cambridge: Cambridge University Press, in press.

Bogdanović, J. (2017b). "The Phiale as a Spatial Icon in the Byzantine Cultural Sphere," in *The Holy Water in the Hierotopy and Iconography of the Christian World*, A. Lidov, ed. Moscow: Theoria, in press.

Bogdanović, J. (2014a). "The Rhetoric of Architecture in the Byzantine Context: The Case Study of the Holy Sepulchre." *Zograf* 38: 1–21.

Bogdanović, J. (2014b). "The Moveable Canopy. The Performative Space of the Major *Sakkos* of Metropolitan Photios." *Byzantinoslavica* 72/1–2: 247–292.

Bogdanović, J. (2012). "The Architectural Design of the Church of St. George in Budimlja and Medieval Building Practices," in *Djurdjevi Stupovi and the Eparchy of Budimlja*, B. Todić, ed. Berane-Beograd: Bishopric of Budimlje and Nikšić; Serbian Academy of Arts and Sciences: 95–107.

Bogdanović, J. (2011a). "The Performativity of Shrines in a Byzantine Church: The Shrines of St. Demetrios," in *Spatial Icons. Performativity in Byzantium and Medieval Russia*, A. Lidov, ed. Moscow: Indrik: 275–316.

Bogdanović, J. (2011b). "Rethinking the Dionysian Legacy in Medieval Architecture: East and West," in *Dionysius the Areopagite Between Orthodoxy and Heresy*, F. Ivanović, ed. Newcastle upon Tyne: Cambridge Scholars Publishing: 109–134.

Bogdanović, J. (2008a). *Canopies: The Framing of Sacred Space in the Byzantine Ecclesiastical Tradition*. PhD diss., Princeton University.

Bogdanović, J. (2008b). "Late Byzantine Religious Architecture in Constantinople (Υστεροβυζαντινή ναοδομία στην Κωνσταντινούπολη)," in *Encyclopaedia of the Hellenic World, Constantinople*. Online at http://constantinople.ehw.gr/forms/fLemma.aspx?lemmaId=10893. (accessed December 1, 2015).

Bogdanović, J. (2008c). "Tetrapylon (Τετράπυλο)," in *Encyclopaedia of the Hellenic World, Constantinople*. Online at http://constantinople.ehw.gr/Forms/fLemma.aspx?lemmaid=12429&contlang=58. (accessed December 1, 2015).

Bogdanović, J. (2008d). "Sculpture in Constantinople (Γλυπτική στην Κωνσταντινούπολη)," in *Encyclopaedia of the Hellenic World, Constantinople*. Online at http://constantinople.ehw.gr/forms/fLemma.aspx?lemmaId=10941. (accessed December 1, 2015).

Bogdanović, J. (2008e). "Cisterns (Κιστέρνες)," in *Encyclopaedia of the Hellenic World, Constantinople*. Online at http://constantinople.ehw.gr/Forms/fLemma.aspx?lemmaid=12427&contlang=58. (accessed December 1, 2015).

Bogdanović, J. (2002). "The Proclamation of the New Covenant: The Pre-Iconoclastic Altar Ciboria in Rome and Constantinople." *ATHANOR* 18: 7–19.

Bolman, E. (2010). "Painting Heaven: Art and the Liturgy," in *The Canopy of Heaven: The Ciborium in the Church of St. Mamas, Morphou*, Michael Jones and Angela Milward Jones, eds. Cyprus: International Resources Group: 134–162.

Bolman, E. S. (2006). "Veiling Sanctity in Christian Egypt: Visual and Spatial Solutions," in *Thresholds of the Sacred*, S. E. J. Gerstel, ed. Washington, DC: *DORLC*: 73–106.

Bonfioli, M. (1979). *Tre arcate marmoree protobizantine a Lison di Portogruaro*. Roma: De Luca Editore.

Bonnery, A. (1991). "L'Édicule du Saint-Sépulcre de Narbonne. Recherche sur l'iconographie de l'Anastasis." *CSMC* 22: 7–41.

Boura, L. (1983). *The Griffin Through the Ages*. Athens: Midland Bank.

Boura, L. (1982). "Byzantine Lighting Devices." *JÖB* 32/3: 479–491.

Boura, L. (1980). *Ho glyptos diakosmos tou naou tēs Panagias sto monasatēri tou Hosiou Louka*. Athens: Archaiologikē Hetaireia.

Boura, L. (1977–1979). "Architectural Sculptures of the Twelfth and the Early Thirteenth Centuries in Greece." *ΔΧΑΕ* 9: 63–72.

Boura, L. (1975–1976). "Some Observations on the Grand Lavra Phiale at Mount Athos and Its Bronze Strobilion." *ΔΧΑΕ* 7: 85–96.

Bouras, C. (1982). *Nea Moni on Chios: History and Architecture*. Athens: Commercial Bank of Greece.

Bowes, K. (2011). "Christian Worship," in *Transition to Christianity. Art of Late Antiquity, 3rd–7th Century AD*, A. Lazaridou, ed. Athens and New York: The Onassis Foundation: 53–57.

Bowes, K. (2008a). *Private Worship, Public Values and Religious Change in Late Antiquity*. Cambridge and New York: Cambridge University Press.

Bowes, K. (2008b). "Early Christian Archaeology: A State of the Field." *Religion Compass* 2/4: 575–619.

Boyd, S. A. (1992). "A 'Metropolitan' Treasure from a Church in the Provinces: An Introduction of the Sion Treasure," in *EcclSilver*: 5–38.

Bradshaw, P. F. (2002). *The Search for the Origins of Christian Worship: Sources and Methods for the Study of Early Liturgy*, 2nd ed. New York: Oxford University Press.

Branham, J. (1992). "Sacred Space Under Erasure in Ancient Synagogues and Early Churches." *ArtB* 74: 375–394.

Braun, J. (1932). *Das christliche Altargerät in seinem Sein und in seiner Entwicklung*. München: M. Hueber.

Braun, J. (1924). *Der christliche Altar in seiner geschichtlichen Entwicklung*. 2 vols. München: Alte Meister Guenther Koch & Co.

Braun, J., S.J. (1907). *Die liturgische Gewandung im Occident und Orient*. Freiburg im Breisgau.

Bréhier, L. (1913). *Nouvelles recherches sur l'histoire de la sculpture byzantine*, Nouvelles Archives des missions scientifiques et littéraires 21/9. Paris: Imp. Nationale.

Bremmer, J. (1993). "The Vision of Dorotheos," in *Early Christian Poetry. A Collection of Essays*, J. den Boeft and A. Hilhorst, eds. Leiden: Brill: 253–261.

Brenk, B. (1999). "Il ciborio esagonale di San Marco a Venezia," in *L'arte di Bisanzio e l'Italia al tempo dei Paleologi 1261–1453*, A. Iacobini and M. Della Valle, eds. Rome: Argos: 143–155.

Brenk, B. (1980). "The Imperial Heritage of Early Christian Art," in *Age of Spirituality*, K. Weitzmann, ed. New York and Princeton, NJ: Metropolitan Museum of Art and Princeton University Press: 39–52.

Brock, S. (2005). *Spirituality in the Syriac Tradition*. Kttayam, Kerala, India: St. Efrem Ecumenical Research Institute.

Brody, L. R., and G. L. Hoffmann, eds. (2011). *Dura Europos. Crossroads of Antiquity*. Chesnut Hill: McMullen Museum of Art, distributed by Chicago University Press.

Broilo, F. A. (2009). "'Cleanses the Sins with the Water of the Pureflowing Font': Fountains for Ablutions in the Byzantine Constantinopolitan Context." *Rev. Études Sud-Est Europ.* 47/1–4: 5–24.

Brown, P. (1973). "A Dark-Age Crisis: Aspects of the Iconoclastic Controversy." *English Historical Review* 88/346: 1–34.

Brubaker, L., and J. Haldon (2011). *Byzantium in the Iconoclast Era (c. 680–850). A History*. Cambridge: Cambridge University Press.

Brubaker L., and J. Haldon, eds. (2001). *Byzantium in the Iconoclast Era (c. 680–850). The Sources; an Annotated Survey*. Aldershot: Ashgate.

Brubaker, L. (2012). *Inventing Byzantine Iconoclasm*. London: Bristol Classical Press.

Brubaker, L. (1999). *Vision and Meaning in Ninth-Century Byzantium: Image as Exegesis in the Homilies of Gregory of Nazianzus*. Cambridge and New York: Cambridge University Press.

Brumfield, W. C. (2000). "Rospisi 'neba' v dreviannykh khramakh russkogo severa." *SR* 59/3: 694–965.

Bryer, A. (1993). "The Historian's Digenes Akrites," in *Digenes Akrites: New Approaches to Byzantine Heroic Poetry*, R. Beaton and D. Ricks, eds. Brookfield: Variorum: 93–102.

Bryer, A., and J. Herrin, eds. *Iconoclasm. Papers Given at the Ninth Spring Symposium of Byzantine Studies, University of Birmingham, March 1975*. Birmingham: University of Birmingham.

Bucher, F. (1976). "Micro-Architecture as the Idea of Gothic Theory and Style." *Gesta* 15: 71–89.

Bühl, G., ed. (2008). *Dumbarton Oaks. The Collections*. Washington: *DORLC*, distributed by Harvard University Press.

Buis, M. (1976). "Recherches sur les matériaux employés dans les mobiliers d'église sculptés à l'époque carolingienne dans le Sud-Est de la France." *ArchM* 6: 233–245.

Buschhausen, H., et al. (1986). *Byzantinische Mosaiken aus Jordanien*. Wien: Amt der Nö. Landesregierung, Abt. III/2 Kulturabteilung.

Butler, H. C. (1969). *Early Churches in Syria, Fourth to Seventh Centuries*. Amsterdam: Hakkert.

Buzančić, R. (1994). "Rekonstrukcija konfesije ranokršćanske crkve u Postirima na Braču." *PPD* 34: 39–50.

C

Çakmak, A., R. Taylor, and E. Durukal (2009). "The Structural Configuration of the First Dome of Justinian's Hagia Sophia (A.D. 537–558): An Investigation Based on Structural and Literary Analysis." *Soil Dynamics and Earthquake Engineering* 29: 693–698.

Cameron, A. (1981). "Images of Authority: Elites and Icons in Late Sixth Century Byzantium," in *Byzantium and the Classical Tradition. University of Birmingham Thirteenth Spring Symposium of Byzantine Studies 1979*, M. Mullett and R. Scott, eds. Birmingham: University of Birmingham: 205–234.

Čanak-Medić, M., D. Popović, and D. Vojvodić (2014). *Manastir Žiča*. Belgrade: RZZSK.

Čanak-Medić, M. (1998). "Žička Spasova crkva—zamisao svetog Save" ["The Church of the Holy Savior in Žiča—The Conception of St. Sava"], in *Sveti Sava u srpskoj istoriji i tradiciji*. S. Ćirković, ed. Belgrade: SANU: 173–187.

Čanak-Medić, M. (1989). *Arhitektura Nemanjinog doba* [*L'architecture de l'époque de Nemanja*]. 2 vols. Belgrade: *RZZSK*.

Canard, M. (1965). "La destruction de l'église de la Résurrection par le Calife Hākim et l'histoire de la descente du feu sacré." *Byz* 35: 16–43.

Carile, M. C. (2012). *The Vision of the Palace of the Byzantine Emperors as a Heavenly Jerusalem*. Spoleto: Fondazione Centro italiano di studi sull'alo medioevo.

Castagnino Berlinghieri, E. F., and A. Paribeni (2011). "Byzantine Merchant Ships and Marble Trade." *Skyllis* 1: 64–75.

Cecchelli, C., et al., eds. (1959). *The Rabbula Gospels. Facsimile Edition of the Miniatures of The Syriac Manuscript Plut. I, 56 in the Medicaean-Laurentian Library*. Olten and Lausanne: Urs Graf-Verlag, Pubs.

Chatzidakis, N. (1997). *Hosios Loukas*. Athens: Melissa.

Chatzidakis, M. (1969). "A propos de la date et du fondateur de Saint-Luc." *CA* 19: 127–150.

Chevalier, P. (1995). *Ecclesiae Dalmatiae, L'architecture paleochrétienne de la province Romaine de Dalmatie (IVe – VIIe S.)*. Rome-Split: Collection de l'École française de Rome.

Chotzakoglou, C. G. (2011). "Book review: The Canopy of Heaven: the Ciborium in the Church of St. Mamas, -Morphou." *ΚΣ* 75: 469–485.

Cohen, A. S. (2000). *The Uta Codex: Art, Philosophy, and Reform in Eleventh-Century Germany*. University Park: Pennsylvania State University Press.

Colvin, H. (1992). *Architecture and the After-Life*. New Haven and London: Yale University Press, 1991.

Connor, C. (1992). "Hosios Loukas as a Victory Church." *GRBS* 33: 293–308.

Connor, C. L. (1991). *Art and Miracles in Medieval Byzantium: The Crypt at Hosios Loukas and Its Frescoes*. Princeton: Princeton University Press.

Constans, N. P. (2006). "Symeon of Thessalonike and the Theology of the Icon Screen," in *Thresholds of the Sacred*, S. E. J. Gerstel, ed. Washington, DC: *DORLC*: 163–183.

Corbo, V. C. (1981–1982). *Il Santo Sepolcro di Gerusalemme: aspetti archeologici dalle origini al periodo crociato*. 3 vols. Jerusalem: Franciscan Print. Press.

Cormack, R. (1989). *The Byzantine Eye: Studies in Art and Patronage*. London: Variorum Reprints.

Cormack, R. (1986). "The Making of a Patron Saint: The Powers of Art and Ritual in Byzantine Thessaloniki," in *Themes of Unity in Diversity. Acts of the XXVIth International Congress of the History of Art*, I. Lavin, ed. Washington, DC: n.p.: 547–555.

Cormack, R. (1985). *Writing in Gold: Byzantine Society and Its Icons*. London: George Philip.

Cormack, R. (1975a). "The Arts During the Age of Iconoclasm," in *Iconoclasm*: 35–44.

Cormack, R. (1975b). "The Painting after Iconoclasm," in *Iconoclasm*: 147–163.

Cormack, R. S. (1969). "The Mosaic Decoration of St. Demetrios, Thessaloniki: A Reexamination in the Light of the Drawings of W. S. George." *BSA* 64: 17–52.

Corpus della scultura altomedievale (1974). Spoleto: Presso la sede del centro di studi.

Coüasnon, C. (1974). *The Church of the Holy Sepulchre in Jerusalem*. London: Oxford University Press.

Čremošnik, I. (1953). "Izvještaj o iskopinama u Rogčićima kod Blažuja. [Compte rendu sur les fouilles à Rogačići près de Blažuj]." *GZMS* 8: 303–314.

Crook, J. (2000). *The Architectural Setting of the Cult of Saints in the Early Christian West, c. 300–1200*. Oxford: Clarendon Press.

Cross, F. M. (1947). "The Tabernacle: A Study from an Archaeological and Historical Approach." *BA* 10/3: 45–68.

Cruikshank Dood, E. (1973). *Byzantine Silver Treasures*. Bern: Abegg-Stiftung.

Čuburović, Z. (1997). "Djela jedne klesarske radionice u kotorskoj crkvi sv. Mihajla." *Glasnik odeljenja umetnosti CANU* 16: 139–151.

Čubrović, Z. [Чубровић, З.] (2008). "Првобитни циборијум романичке катедрале Св Трипуна у Котору [The Original Ciborium of the Romanesque Church of St Tryphon in Kotor]." *САОПШТЕЊА* 40: 25–42.

Chukova, T. A. (2004). *The Chancel of the Ancient Russian Church: Late 10th to Early 13th Century. The Principal Architectural Elements According to Archeological Data*. St. Petersburg: Slavica Petropolitana.

Ćurčić, S., E. Hadjitryphonos, et al. (2010). *Architecture as Icon*. New Haven: Yale University Press.

Ćurčić, S. (2010). *Architecture in the Balkans. From Diocletian to Süleiman the Magnificent*. New Haven: Yale University Press.

Ćurčić, S. (2006). "Monastic Cells in Medieval Serbian Church Towers. Survival of an Early Byzantine Monastic Concept and Its Meaning," in *Sofia* [Compendium of scholarly articles about Byzantine and Old Russian art in honor of A. I. Komeč]. Moscow: Severnyĭ palomnik: 491–514.

Ćurčić, S. (2004). "Religious Settings of the Late Byzantine Sphere," in *Byzantium: Faith and Power (1261–1557)*, H. C. Evans, ed. New Haven: Yale University Press: 65–94.

Ćurčić, S. (2001a). "Kalenderhane in Istanbul: The Buildings, Their History, Architecture, and Decoration by Cecil L. Striker, Y. Doğan Kuban (book review)." *Speculum* 76/4: 1106–1109.

Ćurčić, S. (2001b). "The Exonarthex of Hilandar; The Question of Its Function and Patronage," in *Osam vekova Hilandara. Istorija, duhovni život, književnost, umetnost i arhitektura*, V. Korać, ed. Belgrade: SANU: 477–488.

Ćurčić, S. (2000). "Proskynetaria Icons, Saints' Tombs, and the Development of the Iconostasis," in *The Iconostasis. Origins-Evolution-Symbolism*, A. Lidov, ed. Moscow: Progress-Tradicija: 134–142.

Ćurčić, S. (1996). "From the Temple of the Sun to the Temple of the Lord: Monotheistic Contribution to Architectural Iconography in Late Antiquity," in *Architectural studies in memory of Richard Krautheimer*, C. L. Striker, ed. Mainz: Zabern: 55–59.

Ćurčić, S. (1995). "Some Uses (and Reuses) of Griffins in Late Byzantine Art," in *ByzELatinW*: 597–601.

Ćurčić, S. (1992)."Design and Structural Innovation in Byzantine Architecture before Hagia Sophia," in *Hagia Sophia from the Age of Justinian to the Present*, R. Mark and A. Çakmak, eds. Cambridge: Cambridge University Press: 16–38.

Ćurčić, S. (1991). "Late Byzantine *Loca Sancta*? Some Questions Regarding the Form and Function of Epitaphioi," in *The Twilight of Byzantium. Aspects and Religious History in the Late Byzantine Empire*. Princeton: Princeton University Press: 251–261.

Ćurčić, S. (1989). "Architecture in the Byzantine sphere of Influence around the Middle of the Fourteenth Century," in *Dečani i vizantijska umetnost sredinom XIV veka*, V. J. Djurić, ed. Belgrade: SANU: 55–68.

Ćurčić, S. (1988). *Gračanica. Arhitektura*. Belgrade: Prosveta. English version 1979.

Ćurčić, S. (1978). "Articulation of Church Façades During the First Half of the Fourteenth Century," in *Vizantijska umetnost početkom XIV veka*, S. Petković, ed. Belgrade: Filozofski fakultet, Odeljenje za istoriju umetnosti: 17–27.

Ćurčić, S. (1977). "Architectural Significance of Subsidiary Chapels in Middle Byzantine Churches." *JSAH* 36: 95–110.

Ćurčić, S. (1971). "The Twin-Domed Narthex in Paleologan Architecture." *ZRVI* 13: 333–344.

Curl, J. S. (1980). *A Celebration of Death. An Introduction to Some of the Buildings, Monuments, and Settings of Funerary Architecture in the Western European Tradition*. New York: Charles Scribner's Sons.

Curta, F. (1998). "Feasting with 'Kings' in an Ancient 'Democracy': Early Medieval Slavic Society of the Early Middle Ages (Sixth to Seventh Century, A.D.)." *Essays in Medieval Studies* 15: 19–34.

Cutler, A. (1987). "Under the Sign of the Deesis: On the Question of Representativeness in Medieval Art and Literature." *DOP* 41: 145–154.

Cutler, A. (1966a). "A Baroque Account of Byzantine Architecture: Leone Allacci's *De temples Graecorum recentioribus*." *JSAH* 25: 79–89.

Cutler, A. (1966b). "Structure and Aesthetic at Hagia Sophia in Constantinople." *JAAC* 25/1: 27–35.

Cvetković, B. (2000). "Freske u zapadnom traveju crkve Sv. Dimitrija u Pećkoj patrijaršiji i kult kralja Milutina." *PrIz* 33 [i.e.34]: 3–9.

D

D'Ambra, E. (1998). *Roman Art*. Cambridge: Cambridge University Press.

DaCosta Kaufmann, T. (1975). "Pyxes and Ciboria," in *Eucharistic Vessels of the Middle Ages*. Cambridge: Busch-Reisinger Museum: 65–71.

Dagron, G. (1996). *Empereur et prêtre: étude sur le "césaropapisme" byzantin*. Paris: Gallimard.

Dahari, U. (1996). "Hurbat Tinshemet, Church of St. Bacchus." *Excavations and Surveys in Israel* 18: 67–68, 102–104.

Dale, T. E. A. (2010a). "Cultural Hybridity in Medieval Venice: Reinventing the East at San Marco after the Fourth Crusade," in *San Marco, Byzantium and the Myths of Venice*, H. Maguire and R. S. Nelson, eds. Washington, DC: *DORLC*: 151–191.

Dale, T. E. A. (2010b). "Sacred Space from Constantinople to Venice," in *The Byzantine World*, P. Stephenson, ed. New York: Routledge: 406–427.

Davies, C. (2011). *Thinking about Architecture. An Introduction to Architectural Theory*. London: Laurence King Publishers.

Davies, J. G. (1957). "Eusebius' Description of the Martyrium at Jerusalem." *AJA* 61/2: 171–173.

Deichmann, F. W. (1976). *Ravenna. Hauptstadt des spätantiken Abendlandes*. Wiesbaden: F. Steiner.

Delbrueck, R. (1929). *Die Consulardiptychen und verwandte Denkmäler*. 2 vols. Berlin: W. de Gruyter.

Delonga, V. (2000). *Hrvati i Karolinzi*. Split: Muzej hrvatskih arheoloških spomenika u Splitu.

Demangel, R., and E. Mamboury (1939). *Le quartier des Manganes et la première region de Constantinople*. Paris: E. de Boccard.

Dēmētrokallis, G. (2002). "Λακωνικοί λημνίσκοι [Le motif des 'lemniscoi' en Laconie]." *LS* 16: 229–248.

Demiriz, Y. (2002). *Interlaced Byzantine Mosaic Pavements*. Istanbul: Yorum Sanat.

Demus, O. (1998). "The Ciborium Mosaics of Parenzo," in *Studies in Byzantium, Venice and the West*, O. Demus and I. Hutter, eds. London: Pindar Press: 239–244.

Demus, O. (1976). *Byzantine Mosaic Decoration: Aspects of Monumental Art in Byzantium*. London: New Rochele.

Déonna, W. (1934). "Mobilier delien: tables antiques d'offrandes avec ecuelles et table d'autel Chrétien." *BCH* 58: 1–90.

Déonna, W. (1917). "Aphrodite à la coquille." *RA*: 312–416.

Deshman, R. (1995). "Antiquity and Empire in the Throne of Charles the Bald," in *ByzELatW*: 131–137.

Devyver, J. M. (1982). *The Skene: A Universal Symbol of the Divine Presence: Perspectives on the Form and Function of a Symbol.* PhD diss., Michigan State University.
Diehl, C. L. (1889). *L'église et les mosaïques du Couvent de Saint-Luc en Phocide.* Paris, n.p.: 1889.
Dietl, A. (1997). "Die Reliquienrekondierung im Apsismosaic von S. Clemente in Rom," in *Pratum Romanum. Richard Krautheimer zum 100. Geburtstag.* R. L. Colella et al., eds. Weisbaden: Reichert: 97–111.
Djorbadze, W. (1984). "Remains of a Byzantine Ambo and Church Furnishings in Họbi." *AA4*: 627–639.
Djurić, V. J., and G. Babić (1997). *Srpska umetnost u srednjem veku.* 2 vols. Belgrade: SKZ.
Djurić, V. J. (1974). *Vizantijske freske u Jugoslaviji.* Belgrade: Jugoslavija.
Dodge, H., and B. Ward-Perkins, eds. (1992). *Marble in Antiquity.* London: British School at Rome.
Dodwell, C. R. (1971). *Painting in Europe 800–1200.* London: Penguin Books.
Downey, G. (1957). "Nikolaos Mesarites: Description of the Church of the Holy Apostles at Constantinople." *TAPA* 47/6: 855–921.
Downey, G. (1948a). "Pappus of Alexandria on Architectural Studies." *Isis* 38/3–4: 197–200.
Downey, G. (1948b). "Byzantine Architects. Their Training and Methods." *Byz* 18: 99–118.
Downey, G. (1946). "On Some Post-Classical Greek Architectural Terms." *TAPA* 77: 22–34.
Downey, G. (1937). "The Architectural Significance of the Use of the Words Stoa and Basilike in Classical Literature." *AJA* 41/2: 194–211.
Downey, R. E. G. (1935). "References to Inscriptions in the Chronicle of Malalas." *TAPA* 66: 55–72.
Downing, C. J. (1998). "Wall Paintings from the Baptistery at Stobi, Macedonia, and Early Depictions of Christ and the Evangelists." *DOP* 52: 259–280.
Drioton, E. (1937). "Art syrien et art copte." *BSAC* 3: 29–40.
Drpić, I. (2012). "The Serres Icon of Saints Theodores." *BZ* 105/2: 645–694.
Du Cange, C. (1937). "Descriptio ecclesiae S. Sophiae Constantinopolitanae," in *CSHB* 44: 118–130.
Du Cange, C. (1688). *Glossarium.* Lyons: Lugduni, apud Anissonios, J. Posuel, & C. Rigaud.
Duranti, J. E. (1591). *De ritibvs ecclesiae catholicae.* 3 vols. Romae: Ex typographia Vaticana.
Duval, N. (2003). "Architecture et liturgie dans la jordanie byzantine," in *Les églises de Jordanie et leurs mosaïques.* Beyrouth: Institut français d'archéologie du Proche-Orient: 35–114.
Duval, N., and A. Lezine (1959). "Necropole Chretienne et Baptistere Southeran a Carthage." *CA* 10: 71–147.
Duval, Y. (1982). *Loca Sanctorum Africae* I. Rome: Ecole française de Rome.
Dvornik, F. (1953). "The Patriarch Photius and Iconoclasm." *DOP* 7: 67–98.

E

Eisler, R. (1966). *Orphisch-Dionysische Mysteriengedanken in der Christlichen Antike,* 2nd ed. Hildsheim: Olms.
Esiner, R. (1991). *Travelers to an Antique Land: The History and Literature of Travel to Greece.* Ann Arbor: University of Michigan Press.
Eliade, M. (1961). *Images and Symbols: Studies in Religious Symbolism.* New York: Sheed & Ward.
Elsner, J. (1988). "Image and Iconoclasm in Byzantium." *ArtHist* 11: 471–491.
Etlin, R. (2015). "A propos du symbolisme de la voûte à nervure et de l'arc-boutant." Unpublished conference paper presented at the symposium, "Épures d'histoire: un processus pragmatique: Perspectives pour l'histoire de l'architecture et le la construction en hommage à Joël Sakarovitch." Lecture presented at Colloque international avec le soutien de l'Académie de l'Architecture, du Centre Alexandre Koyré, du Centre de Théorie et Analyse du Droit, du Centre Jean Pépin et du Laboratoire de médiévistique occidentale de Paris: Paris, October, 13–14, 2015.
Evangelatou, M. (2003). "The Holy Sepulchre and Iconophile Arguments on Relics in the Ninth-Century Byzantine Psalters," in *Eastern Christian Relics,* A. Lidov, ed. Moscow: Progress-Tradicija: 181–204.
Evangelatou, M. (2002). *The Illustration of the Ninth-Century Byzantine Marginal Psalters: Layers of Meaning and Their Sources.* PhD diss., University of London.
Evans, E. P. (1896). *Animal Symbolism in Ecclesiastical Architecture.* New York: Henry Holt.
Eyice, S. (1963). "Two Mosaic Pavements from Bithynia." *DOP* 18: 373–383.

F

Farbridge, M. H. (1970). *Studies in Biblical and Semitic Symbolism.* New York: Ktav Pub. House.
Fekeža, L., and M. Gavrilović (2000). *Od dolaska Slavena do pada bosanskog kraljevstva.* Sarajevo: Ilidža.

Ferguson, E. (2009). *Baptism in the Early Church: History, Theology, and Liturgy in the First Five Centuries.* Grand Rapids: Eerdmans.
Ferguson, G. W. (1959). *Signs and Symbols in Christian Art.* New York: Oxford University Press.
Fink, W. O. (1971). *Das byzantinische Monogramm.* PhD diss., University of Wien.
Flusin, B. (2005). "L'ekphrasis d'un baptistère byzantin." *TM* 15: 163–181.
Fobelli, M. L. (2006). "The Imagery of the Heavenly City in Sixth-Century Byzantium: Marbles and Images 'Not Made by Human Hand'," in *New Jerusalems,* A. Lidov, ed. Moscow: Indrik: 48–53.
Folda, J. (1995). *The Art of the Crusaders in the Holy Land, 1098–1187.* Cambridge and New York: Cambridge University Press.
Forster, G. (2008). *The Contested Public Square: The Crisis of Christianity and Politics.* Downers Grove: IVP Academic.
Fotić, A. (2000). *Sveta Gora i Hilandar u Osmanskom carstvu: XV–XVII vek.* Belgrade: SANU, 2000.
Fotić, A. (1998). "Prilagodjavanje i opstanak: Hilandar u Osmanskom carstvu (XV–XVII vek)," in *Manastir Hilandar,* G. Subotić, ed. Belgrade: SANU: 91–102.
Frantz, A. (1934). "Byzantine Illuminated Ornament: A Study of Chronology." *ArtB* 16: 43–76.
Friedman, R. E. (1980). "The Tabernacle in the Temple." *BA* 43/4: 241–248.
Fundić, L. (2013). "Art and Political Ideology in the State of Epiros During the Reign of Theodore Doukas (r. 1215–1230)." *Byzantine Symmeikta* 23: 217–250.
Fundić, L. (2009). "Byzantine Architectural Members form the Tripoli Archaeological Museum." *ΔXAE* 30: 141–148.

G

Gabelić, S. (1998). *Manastir Lesnovo. Istorija i slikarstvo.* Belgrade: Stubovi kulture.
Galavaris, G. (1969). *The Illustrations of the Liturgical Homilies of Gregory Nazienzus.* Princeton: Princeton University Press.
Gamber, K. (1985). "Ein byzantinisches Prothesis-Bild und der spätmittelalterliche Erbärmde-Christus." *Hermeneia* 1/2–3: 61–71.
Gates, M.-H. (1995). "Archeology in Turkey." *AJA* 99/2: 207–255.
Gates, M.-H. (1984). "Dura-Europos: A Fortress of Syro-Mesopotamian Art." *BA* 47/3: 166–181.
Gatti, S. (1987). "Breve nota storica sul ciborio dell'altare maggiore della Basilica di San Giuseppe a Seregno." *ArteL* 83: 70–71.
Gavrilović, M. (1999). "Dvije predromaničke crkve iz okolice Sarajeva." *Hrvatska misao* 11–12: 111–118.
Gem, R. (2013). "From Constantine to Constans, The Chronology of the Construction of Saint Peter's Basilica," in *Old Saint Peter's, Rome,* R. McKitterick et al., eds. Cambridge: Cambridge University Press: 35–64.
Gero, S. (2000). "What Were the Holy Images of the Iconoclasts?" *OCA* 260: 331–343.
Gero, S. (1974). *Byzantine Iconoclasm During the Reign of Leo III. With Particular Attention to the Oriental Sources.* Louvain: Corpus Scriptorium Christianorum Orientalium.
Gerstel, S. E. J., and J. A. Lauffenburger, eds. (2001). *A Lost Art Rediscovered: The Architectural Ceramics of Byzantium.* Baltimore: Walters Art Museum; University Park: Pennsylvania State University Press.
Gerstel, S. E. J., ed. (2006). *Thresholds of the Sacred.* Washington, DC: *DORLC.*
Gerstel, S. E. J. (1999). *Beholding the Sacred Mysteries. Programs of the Byzantine Sanctuary.* Seattle and London: CAA in assoc. with University of Washington Press.
Gerstel, S. (1996). "Apostolic Embraces in Communion Scenes of Byzantine Macedonia." *CA* 44: 141–148.
Geymonat, L. (2012). "The Syntax of Spolia in Byzantine Thessalonike," in *Approaches to Byzantine Architecture and Its Decoration,* M. Johnson, R. Ousterhout, and A. Papalexandrou, eds. Surrey: Ashgate: 47–65.
Giakalis, A. (1994). *Images of the Divine. The Theology of Icons at the Seventh Ecumenical Council.* Leiden: Brill.
Glass, D. (1980). *Studies on Cosmatesque Pavements.* BAR International Series 82. Oxford: Oxford University Press.
Glass, D. (1969). "Papal Patronage in the Early Twelfth Century: Notes on the Iconography of Cosmatesque Pavements." *JWCI* 32: 386–390.
Goldfus, H. (2006). "St. Euphemia's Church by the Hippodrome of Constantinople Within the Broader Context of 7th-Century History and Architecture." *Ancient West and East* 5/1–2: 178–197.

Goldfus, H., B. Arubas, and K. Bowes. (2000). "New Excavations in the East Church at Halutza (Elusa): Preliminary Report." *Journal of Roman Archaeology* 13: 331–342.

Goldman, B. (1960). "The Development of the Lion-Griffin." *AJA* 64/4: 319–328.

Golitzin, A. (2005). "Temple and Church: Some Reflections on Continuities in Early Syriac Tradition." Paper presented at the Symbols of Church and Kingdom Conference, Princeton University, May 4, 2005.

Gouma-Peterson, T. (1978). "Christ as Ministrant and the Priest as Ministrant of Christ in a Palaeologan Program of 1303." *DOP* 32: 197+199–216.

Grabar, A. (1979–1980). "Essai sur les plus anciennes representations de la 'Resurrection du Christ.'" *Monuments et mémoires de la Fondation Eugène Piot* 62–63: 105–141.

Grabar, A. (1976). *Sculptures byzantines du Moyen Âge*, vol. 2. Paris: A. et J. Picard.

Grabar, A. (1972). *Martyrium*. 2 vols. London: Variorum Reprints.

Grabar, A. (1968). "Le reliquaire byzantin de la cathédrale d'Aix-la-Chapelle." *L'art de la fin de l'Antiquité et du Moyen-Âge* 33/1: 427–433.

Grabar, A. (1958). *Ampoules de Terre Sainte (Monza, Bobbio)*. Paris: C. Klincksieck.

Grabar, A. (1954). "Un nouveau reliquaire de saint Démétrios." *DOP* 8: 305+307–313.

Grabar, A. (1951). "Images Bibliques d'Apamée et fresques de la synagogue de Dura." *CA* 5: 9–14.

Grabar, A. (1950). "Quelques reliquaires de saint Démétrios et le martyrium du saint à Salonique." *DOP* 5: 1+3–28.

Grabar, O. (2005). *Jerusalem*. Aldershot and Burlington: Ashgate/Variorum.

Gray, M. (2001). "The Pilgrimage as Ritual Space," in *Holy Ground: Theoretical Issues Relating to the Landscape and Material Culture of Ritual Space Objects: Papers from a Session Held at the Theoretical Archaeology Group Conference, Cardiff, 1999*, A. T. Smith and A. Brookes, eds. Oxford, Archaeopress: 91–97.

Greene, V. (1992). "Accessories of Holiness: Defining Jewish Sacred Objects." *Journal of the American Institute for Conservation* 31/1: 31–39.

Greenhalgh, M. (2009). *Marble Past, Monumental Present. Building with Antiquities in the Mediaeval Mediterranean*. Leiden and Boston: Brill.

Grelot, G.-J. (1683). *A Late Voyage to Constantinople*. English edition J. Philips. London: Printed by John Playford.

Grossman, P. (1998). "The Pilgrimage Center of Abû Mînâ," in *Pilgrimage and Holy Space in Late Antique Egypt*, D. Frankfurter, ed. Leiden, Brill: 281–302.

Grossman, P. (1989). *Abû Mînâ*. Mainz am Rhein: P. von Zabern.

Grozdanov, C., and L. Hadermann-Misguich (1992). *Kurbinovo*. Skopje: Makedonska knjiga.

Grozdanov, C. (1980). "Iz ikonografije Markovog manastira. Božanska liturgija." *Zograf* 11: 63–84.

Grozdanov, C. (1969). "Prilozi proučavanju Sv. Sofije ohridske u XIV veku." *ZLU* 5: 49–63.

Guérin, M. V. (1875). *Description géographique, historique et archéologique de la Palestine*. Paris: Imprimé par autorisation de l'empereur à l'Impr. impériale.

Guide. (1980). Split: Museum of the Croatian Archaeological Monuments.

Guidobaldi, F. (1999). "I cyboria d'altare a Roma fino al IX secolo." *Mededelingen van het Nederlands Instituut te Rome* 59: 55–69.

Guillou, A. (1995). "Inscriptions Byzantines importées en Italie," in *Epigrafia Medievale Greca e Latina. Ideologia e Funzione*, G. Cavallo and C. Mango, eds. Spoleto: Centro Italiano di studi sull'Alto medioevo: 119–152.

Gutmann, J. (1989). *Sacred Images: Studies in Jewish Art from Antiquity to the Middle Ages*. Northampton: Variorum Reprints.

Gutmann, J. (1984). "Early Synagogue and Jewish Catacomb Art and Its Relation to Christian Art," in *Aufstieg und Niedergang der römischen Welt*, Hildegard Temporini and Wolfgang Haase, eds. II: *Principat*, vol. 21/2. Berlin and New York: Walter de Gruyter: 1313–1342.

Gutmann, J. (1971). "The History of the Ark." *ZAltW* 83: 22–29.

H

Hadjitryphonos, E. (2010). "Presentations and Representations of Architecture in Byzantium: The Thought Behind the Image," in *Architecture as Icon*, S. Ćurčić and E. Hadjitryphonos, eds. New Haven: Yale University Press: 113–154.

Hahn, C., and H. A. Klein, eds. (2015). *Saints and Sacred Matter: The Cult of Relics in Byzantium and Beyond.* Washington, DC: *DORLC*, 2015.

Hahn, C. (1997). "Seeing and Believing: The Construction of Sanctity in Early-Medieval Saints' Shrines." *Speculum* 72/4: 1079–1106.

Haitovsky, D. (1994). "A New Look at a Lost Painting: The Hebrew Inscription in Lorenzo Costa's 'Presentation in the Temple.'" *AH* 15/29: 111–120.

Halkin, F. (1966). "Euphémie de Chalcédoine: Légendes Byzantines." *Speculum* 41/3: 536–538.

Hallensleben, H. (1965). "Zur Annexbauten der Kilise Camii in Istanbul." *Istanbuler Mitteilungen* 15: 208–217.

Harrison, M. (1989). *A Temple for Byzantium. The Discovery and Excavation of Anicia Juliana's Palace-Church in Istanbul.* Austin: University of Texas Press.

Harrison, R. M. (1986). *Excavations at Saraçhane in Istanbul,* vol. 1. Princeton, NJ: Princeton University Press.

Harrison, J. E. (1899). "Delphika.-(A) The Erinyes. (B) The Omphalos." *The Journal of Hellenic Studies* 19: 205–251.

Harvey, S. A. (1990). *Asceticism and Society and Crisis: John of Ephesus and the Lives of the Eastern Saints.* Berkeley: University of California Press.

Harvey, W. (1935). *The Church of the Holy Sepulchre in Jerusalem: Structural Survey, Final Report.* Oxford: Oxford University Press.

Haussherr, R. (1968). "Templum Salomonis und Ecclesia Christi: Zu einem Bildvergleich der Bible moralisée." *ZKunstg* 31/2: 101–121.

Hawkins, E. J. W., M. C. Mundell, and C. Mango (1973). "The Mosaics of the Monastery of Mar Samuel, Mar Simeon, Mar Gabriel near Kartmin with a Note on the Greek Inscription." *DOP* 27: 279–296.

Heath, T. (1965). *A History of Greek Mathematics,* 2nd ed. Oxford: Clarendon.

Hill, S. (1996). *The Early Byzantine Churches of Cilicia and Isauria.* Hampshire: Variorum.

History of the Melkite Patriarchates (Alexandria, Antioch, Jerusalem) from the sixth-century monophysite Schism until the present (1910) (1998–1901). N. Samra, ed., J. Collorafi, trans. Fairfax: Eastern Christian Publications.

Hjort, Ø. (1979). "The Sculpture of Kariye Camii." *DOP* 33: 199–289.

Hoddinott, R. F. (1963). *Early Byzantine Churches in Macedonia and Southern Serbia: A Study of the Origins and the Initial Development of East Christian Art.* London: Macmillan.

Hoddinott, R. F. (1954). "The Tradition of Wood Carving in Macedonia." *BM* 96/618: 278–283.

Hoffmann, A., and G. Wolf, eds. (2012). *Jerusalem as Narrative Space: Erzählraum Jerusalem.* Leiden: Brill.

Hopkins, C. (1979). *The Discovery of Dura-Europos.* New Haven: Yale University Press.

Hoppe, L. J. (1994). *The Synagogues and Churches of Ancient Palestine.* Collegeville: The Liturgical Press.

Hunt, L.-A. (1989). "The al-Mu allaqa Doors Reconstructed: An Early Fourteenth-Century Sanctuary Screen from Old Cairo." *Gesta* 28/1: 61–77.

Hurowitz, V. A. (1995). "The Form and Fate of the Tabernacle: Reflections on a Recent Proposal." *JQR* 86/1–2: 127–151.

Hussey, J. M. (2010). *The Orthodox Church in the Byzantine Empire.* Oxford: Oxford University Press.

I

Ivanišević, V., and S. Stamenković (2013). "Razgradnja fortifikacije Akropolja Caričinog grada (Deconstruction of the Caričin Grad fortifications)." *Leskovački zbornik* 53: 22–31.

Ivanović, F. (2010). *Symbol and Icon: Dionysius the Areopagite and the Iconoclastic Crisis.* Eugene: Pickwick.

Ivison, E. (2008). "Middle Byzantine Sculptors at Work: Evidence from the Lower City Church at Amorium." *La sculpture byzantine, VIIe–XIIe siècles, Suppl. BCH* 49: 487–513.

J

Jakšić, N. (1999–2000). "Predromanički reljefi 9. stoljeća iz Kotora." *PPD* 38: 129–150.

James, L. (2001). *Empresses and Power in Early Byzantium.* London and New York: Leicester University Press.

James, L. (1996). "'Pray Not to Fall into Temptation and Be on Your Guard:' Pagan Statues in Christian Constantinople." *Gesta* 35/1: 12–20.

Janin, R. (1964). *Constantinople byzantine. Développement urbain et répertoire topographique.* Paris: Institut français d'études byzantines.

Janin, R. (1953). *La géographie ecclésiastique de l'Empire byzantin: Première partie, Le siège de Constantinople et le patriarcat œcuménique,* vol. 3. Paris: [Institut français d'études byzantines].

Jensen, R. (2011). *Living Water: Images, Symbols, and Settings of Early Christian Baptism.* Leiden and Boston: Brill.

Jeudy, A. (2004). "Icônes et ciboria: relation entre les ateliers coptes de peinture d'icônes et l'iconographie du mobilier liturgique en bois." *Eastern Christian Art in Its Late Antique and Islamic Contexts* 1: 67–88.

Jewell, H. H., and F. W. Hasluck (1990). *The Church of Our Lady of the Hundred Gates (Panagia Hekatontapyliani) in Paros.* London: Macmillan.

Johnson, M. (2014). *The Roman Imperial Mausoleum in Late Antiquity.* Cambridge: Cambridge University Press.

Johnson, M. (2012). "Architecture of the Empire," in *The Cambridge Companion to the Age of Constantine,* N. Lenski, ed. Cambridge: Cambridge University Press.

Johnson, M. (1986). *Late Antique Imperial Mausolea.* PhD diss., Princeton University.

Josi, E. (1924). "Il Cimitero di Panfilo, I." *RACr* I: 52–211.

Jurković, M. (1995). "Il ciborio di Novigrad, Cittanova d'Istria." *HAM* 1: 141–149.

Jurlaro, R. (1973). "Un Ciborio del Secolo 8 in Bari." *Archivio Storico Pugliese* 26/1–2: 315–324.

K

Kader, I. (1996). *Propylon und Bogentor: Untersuchungen zum Tetrapylon von Latakia und anderen frühkaiserzeitlichen Bogenmonumenten im Nahen Osten.* Mainz: P. von Zabern.

Kalamara, P. (2001). "The Sculptures," in *Monemvasia.* Athens: Epikonia Ltd: 19–39.

Kalavrezou, I. (1997). "Reliquary of Saint Demetrios. Cat. entry 36," in *Glory of Byz*: 77–78.

Kalavrezou, I. (1975). "The Imperial Chamber at Luxor." *DOP* 29: 225–251.

Kalavrezou-Maxeiner, I. (1985). "The Byzantine Knotted Column." *ByzMetabyz* 4: 95–103. [Originally published as Kalavrezou, I. (1978). "The Knotted Column." *BSCA* 4: 31–32.]

Kaldellis, A. (2009). *The Christian Parthenon: Classicism and Pilgrimage in Byzantine Athens.* Cambridge: Cambridge University Press.

Kalopissi-Verti, S. (2006). "The Proskynetaria of the Templon and Narthex: Form, Imagery, Spatial Connections, and Reception," in *Thresholds of the Sacred,* S. E. J. Gerstel, ed. Washington, DC: *DORLC*: 107–134.

Kandić, O. (1998–9). "Fonts for the Blessing of the Waters in Serbian Medieval Churches." *Zograf* 27: 61–78.

Kapitän, G. (1980). "Elementi architettonici per una basilica del relitto navale del VI secolo di Marzamemi (Siracusa)." *CorsiRav* 27: 71–136.

Kapitän, G. (1969). "The Church Wreck off Marzamemi." *Archaeology* 22/2: 122–123.

Karagiorgou, O. (2001). *Urbanism and Economy in Late Antique Thessaly (3rd –7th century A.D.). The Archaeological Evidence.* PhD diss., Oxford University.

Karelin, D. [Карелин, Д.А.] (2014). "ВИЗУАЛИЗАЦИЯ ПОЗДНЕРИМСКОЙ КРЕПОСТИ – 2: Компьютерная реконструкция храма культа римского императора в позднеримской крепости в Луксоре (Египет)." ["Imaging of the Late Roman Castrum – 2: Computer Reconstruction of the Roman Imperial Cult Temple in the Late Roman Fortress at Luxor in Egypt."] *AMIT* 1/26: 6–22.

Karelin, D. [Карелин, Д.А.] (2013). "К вопросу о развитии балдахина (кивория) как архитектурного элемента," ["About the Development of Baldachin (Ciborium) as Architectural Element,"] in *Наука, образование и экспериментальное проектирование/Science, Education and Experimental Design.* Moscow: Московский Архитектурный Институт: 116–117.

Karelin, D. [Карелин, Д.А.] (2012). "Сакральная архитектура римских крепостей в Египте/Sacred Architecture of the Roman Fortresses in Egypt," in *Исследования по истории архитектуры и градостроительства* [Studies in Architecture and Urban History], D. Shvidkovsky, ed. Moscow: DPK Press: 57–82.

Karivieri, A. (2006). "The Ilissos Basilica and the Introduction of Christian iconography in Athens," in *Acta congressus internationalis XIV archaeologiae christianae: Akten des XIV. Internationalen Kongresses für Christliche Archäologie* 62: 895–898.

Kazhdan, A. P., and A. Wharton Epstein. (1985). *Change in Byzantine Culture in the Eleventh and Twelfth Centuries*. Berkeley and Los Angeles: University of California Press.

Kazhdan, A., and H. Maguire (1991). "Hagiographical Texts as Sources on Art." *DOP* 45: 1–22.

Kazhdan, A. (1987). "A Note on the 'Middle Byzantine' Ambo." *Byz* 57/2: 422–426.

Kennedy, G. A. (1999). *Classical Rhetoric and Its Christian and Secular Tradition from Ancient to Modern Times*. Chapel Hill: University of North Carolina Press.

Kennedy, G. A. (1983). *Greek Rhetoric Under Christian Emperors*. Princeton: Princeton University Press.

Kessler, H. L. (1988). "On the State of Medieval Art History." *ArtB* 70/2: 166–187.

Khodakovsky, E. (2015). *Wooden Church Architecture of the Russian North. Regional Schools and Traditions (14th –19th centuries)*. London and New York: Routledge.

Khouri-Sarkis, G. (1962). "Le voile rideau intérieur." *OrSyr* 7: 277–296.

Khouri-Sarkis, G. (1960). "Notes sur l'anaphore syriaque de Saint Jacques." *OrSyr* 5: 363–384.

King, A. (1965). *Eucharistic Reservation in the Western Church*. New York: Sheed and Ward.

Kinney, D. (2005). "Spolia," in *St. Peter's in the Vatican*, W. Tronzo, ed. Cambridge: Cambridge University Press: 16–47.

Kirschbaum, E. (1959). *The Tombs of St. Peter and St. Paul*. J. Murray, trans. New York: St. Martin's Press.

Kirwin, W. C. (1997). *Powers Matchless: The Pontificate of Urban VIII, the Baldachin, and Gian Lorenzo Bernini*. New York: P. Lang.

Kissas, S. (1996). "A Sepulchral Monument in Hagia Sophia, Thessaloniki." *Museum of Byzantine Culture, Thessaloniki* 3: 36–49.

Kitzinger, E. (1954). "The Cult of Images in the Age of Iconoclasm." *DOP* 8: 83–150.

Kitzinger, E. (1951). "Studies on Late Antique and Early Byzantine Floor Mosaics: I. Mosaics at Nikopolis." *DOP* 3: 81+83–122.

Kitzinger, E. (1946). "A Survey of the Early Christian Town of Stobi." *DOP* 3: 81–162.

Klauser, T. (1961). *Das Ciborium in der älteren christlichen Buchmalerei*. Nachrichten der Akademie der Wissenschafen in Göttingen, Philologisch-istorische Klasse 7, Göttingen: Vandenhoeck and Ruprecht.

Klein, H. A. (2006). "Sacred Relics and Imperial Ceremonies at the Great Palace of Constantinople," in *Visualisierungen von Herrschaft*. F. A. Bauer, ed. *Byzas* 5: 79–99.

Klein, H. A. (2004). "Constantin, Helena, and the Cult of the True Cross in Constantinople," in *Byzance et les reliques du Christ*, J. Durand and B. Flusin, eds. Paris: Association des amis du Centre d'histoire et civilisation de Byzance: 31–59.

Kleiner, D. E. E. (1987). *Roman Imperial Funerary Altars with Portraits*. Rome: Giorgio Bretschneider Editore.

Koltsida-Makre, I. (2002). "Μολυβδόβουλλα με απεικόνιση σκηνής από το βίο του αγίου Δημητρίου." ["Lead Seals Representing a Scene from the Life of St. Demetrius."] *ΔΧΑΕ* 23: 149–154.

Komeč, A. I. (1975). "Spaso-Preobraženskii sobor v Chernigove." *DrevIsk*: 9–26.

Kominko, M. (2013). *The World of Kosmas: Illustrated Byzantine Codices of the Christian Topography*. Cambridge: Cambridge University Press.

Kondić, V., and V. Popović (1977). *Caričin Grad*. Belgrade: SANU.

Korać, V. (2001). *Martinići. Ostaci srednjovekovnog grada*. [*Martinići. Les vestiges d'une ville du haut Moyen âge*.] Belgrade: SANU.

Korres, G. N. (1954). *Hē Hekatontapylianē tēs Parou*. Athens: Typogr. A. Mauridē.

Kostof, S. (1989). *Caves of God*, 2nd ed. Oxford: Oxford University Press.

Kotoula, D. (2007). "The Tomb of the Founder-Saint," in *Founders and Re-Founders of Byzantine Monasteries*, Margaret Mullett, ed. Belfast: Belfast Byzantine Texts and Translations 6.3: 210–233.

Kratzke, C., ed. (2008). *Mikroarchitektur im Mittelalter: Ein gattungsübergreifendes Phänomen zwischen Realität und Imagination; Beiträge der gleichnamigen Tagung im Germanischen Nationalmuseum Nürnberg vom 26. bis 29. Oktober 2005*. Leipzig: Kratzke Verlag für Kunst- und Kulturgeschichte.

Krautheimer, R. (with S. Ćurčić) (1986). *Early Christian and Byzantine Architecture*. New Haven and London: Yale University Press.

Krautheimer, R. (1985). *St Peter's and Medieval Rome*. Rome: Unione internazionale degli istituti di archeologia, storia e storia dell'arte in Roma.

Krautheimer, R. (1974). "Again Saints Sergius and Bacchus at Constantinople." *JÖB* 23: 251–253.

Krautheimer, R. (1967). "The Constantinian Basilica." *DOP* 21: 115–140.

Krautheimer, R. (1960). "Mensa-coemeterium-martyrium." *CA* 11: 17–40.

Kreytenberg, G. (2002). "Die Bildhauer von Altarziborium und Grabmal des Kardinals Philippe d'Alencon in Santa Maria in Trastevere in Rom: Giovanni d'Ambrogio, Lorenzo di Giovanni und Piero di Giovanni Tedesco." *ArteM* 1: 91–126.

Krinsky, C. H. (1970). "Representations of the Temple of Jerusalem before 1500." *JWCI* 33: 1–19.

Kroesen, J. (2014). "The Altar and Its Decorations in Medieval Churches. A Functionalist Approach." *Medievalia* 17: 153–183.

Kroesen, J. (2013). "Ciborios y baldaquinos en iglesias medievales. Un panorama europeo." *Codex Aquilarensis* 29: 189–222.

Kroesen, J. A. E. (2009). *Staging Liturgy: The Medieval Altarpiece in the Iberian Peninsula*. Leuven and Walpole: Peeters.

Kroesen, J., and V. M. Schimdt, eds. (2009). *The Altar and Its Environment, 1150–1400*. Turnhout: Brepols.

Kroetch, K. J. (2013). *"And You Will Find the Truth Here": A Neglected Seventh-Century Description of the Holy Sepulchre*. Honors thesis for the Department of Art History, Tufts University.

Krsmanović, B. (2001). *Uspon vojnog plemstva u Vizantiji XI veka*. ["The Rise of Byzantine Military Aristocracy in the 11th Century."] Belgrade: SANU.

Krüger, J. (2000). *Die* Grabeskirche *zu Jerusalem: Geschichte, Gestalt, Bedeutung*. Regensburg: Schnell und Steiner.

Ksingopoulos, A. (1975–1976). "Ἡ τοιχογραφία τοῦ μαρτυρίου τοῦ Ἁγίου Δημητρίουεἰς τοὺς Ἁγίους Ἀποστόλους Θεσσαλονίκης" [La scène du martyre de saint Démétrius dans l'église des Saints-Apétres de Thessalonique]. *ΔΧΑΕ* 8: 531–553.

Kühnel, B., G. Noga-Banai, and H. Vorholt, eds. (2014). *Visual Constructs of Jerusalem*. Turnhout: Brepols.

Kühnel, B. (1987). *From the Earthly to the Heavenly Jerusalem. Representations of the Holy City in Christian Art of the First Millennium*. Rome: Herder.

Kurtz, D. C., and J. Boardman (1971). *Greek Burial Customs*. Ithaca, NY: Cornell University Press.

Kurtz, E. (1907). "Unedierte Texte aus der Zeit des Kaisers Johannes Komnenos." *BZ* 16: 104–107.

L

Laderman, S. (2013). *Images of Cosmology in Jewish and Byzantine Art*, Jewish and Christian Perspectives 25. Leiden: Brill.

Laderman, S. (2003). "Images of the Temple in Jewish Art and Their Parallels in Literary Sources," in *Envisioning the Temple: Scrolls, Stones, and Symbols*, A. Roitman, ed. Jerusalem: The Israel Museum: 97–125.

Lafli, E., and H. Bru (2013). "Inscriptions gréco-romaines d'Anatolie II." *Chronique d'Orient, Dialogues d'histoire ancienne* 39/2: 287–303.

Lavin, I. (1968). *Bernini and the Crossing of Saint Peter's*. New York: CAA and New York University Press.

Leader-Newby, R. E. (2004). *Silver and Society in Late Antiquity. Functions and Meanings of Silver Plate in the Fourth to Seventh Centuries*. Aldershot and Burlington: Ashgate.

Lefebvre, H. (1991). *The Production of Space*. Oxford and Cambridge: Blackwell.

Lehmann, K. (1945). "The Dome of Heaven." *ArtB* 27/1: 1–27.

Liapis, H. (2005). *The Monastery of Hosios Loukas in Boeotia*. Athens: [s.n.].

Liakos, D. (2008). "The Byzantine Opus Sectile Floor in the Katholikon of Iveron Monastery on Mount Athos." *Zograf* 32: 37–44.

Lidov, A. (2015a). "Creating the Sacred Space. Hierotopy as a New Field of Cultural History," in *Spazi e percorsi sacri*, C. Cremonesi and L. Carnevale, eds. Padua: Libreriauniversitaria.it: 61–90.

Lidov, A. [Лидов, А.] (2015b). "Иудео-христианская икона света: от сияющего облака к вращающемуся храму," in *Образ и символ в иудейской, христианской и мусульманской традиции*, Ковельман and Гершович, eds. Moscow: Indrik: 127–152.

Lidov, A. (2014). "The Temple Veil as a Spatial Icon: Revealing an Image-Paradigm of Medieval Iconography and Hierotopy." *IKON* 7: 97–108.

Lidov, A., ed. (2011). *Spatial Icons. Performativity in Byzantium and Medieval Russia*. Moscow: Indrik.

Lidov, A. [Лидов, A.] (2009a). *Иеротопия: пространственные иконы и образы-парадигмы в византийской культуре.* [Hierotopy: Spatial Icons and Image-Paradigms in Byzantine Culture.] Moscow: Theoria.

Lidov, A., ed. (2009b). *Hierotopy: Comparative Studies of Sacred Spaces.* Moscow: Indrik.

Lidov, A. (2007). "The Creator of the Sacred Space as a Phenomenon of Byzantine Culture," in *L'artista a Bisanzio e nel mondo cristiano-orientale,* M. Bacci, ed. Pisa: Edizioni della Normale: 135–176, 366–371.

Lidov, A. (2006a). "The Holy Fire and the Translations of New Jerusalems: Hierotopical and Art-Historical Aspects," in *New Jerusalems,* A. Lidov, ed. Moscow: Indrik: 58–70.

Lidov, A., ed. (2006b). *Hierotopy. Creation of Sacred Spaces in Byzantium and Medieval Russia.* Moscow: Progress-Tradition.

Lidov, A. (2005). "Tserkva Bogomateri Faroskoi. Imperatorskii hram-relikviarii kak Konstantinopolskii Grob Gospodnii." *Viz.Mir* (2005): 1–26.

Lidov, A., ed. (2004). *Hierotopy, Studies in the Making of Sacred Spaces.* Moscow: Radunitsa.

Lidov, A. (2000). *Ikonostas.* Moscow: Progres-Traditsiia.

Lidov, A. (1999). "Heavenly Jerusalem: The Byzantine Approach." *JewArt* 25: 340–353.

Lightfoot, C. S., et al. (1998). "The Amorium Project: The 1996 Excavation Season." *DOP* 52: 323–336.

Lightfoot, C. S., and E. A. Ivison. (1997). "The Amorium Project: The 1995 Excavation Season." *DOP* 51: 291–300.

Liveri, A. (1996). *Die byzantinischen Steinreliefs des 13. und 14. Jahrhunderts im griechischen Raum.* Athens: Hetaireia tōn Philōn tou Laou.

Lobel, D. (1999). "A Dwelling Place for the Shekhinah." *Jewish Quarterly Review* 90/1–2: 103–125.

Love, I. C. (1970). "A Preliminary Report of the Excavations at Knidos, 1969." *AJA* 74/2: 149–155.

Loverance, R. (1990). "Early Byzantine Marble Church Furnishings: Some Examples from the Episcopal Basilica of Kourion in Cyprus," in *Church and People in Byzantium,* R. Morris, ed. Birmingham: Centre for Byzantine, Ottoman and Modern Greek Studies, University of Birmingham: 225–243.

M

Macpherson, J. R. (1892). "The Church of the Resurrection, or of the Holy Sepulchre." *EHR* 7/27: 417–436.

Macrides, R., and P. Magdalino (1988). "The Architecture of Ekphrasis: Construction and Context of Paul the Silentary's Poem on Hagia Sophia." *BMGS* 12: 47–82.

Macridy, T. (1964). "The Monastery of Lips and the Burials of the Palaeologi." *DOP* 18: 253–277.

Magdalino, P. (2015). "Some Lost and Little-Known Byzantine Churches in the Vicinity of Hagia Sophia." Lecture presented at the Symbolic Aspects of Architecture: Late Roman, Byzantine and Ottoman Perspectives international conference, Swedish Research Institute in Istanbul, Turkey, Nov. 2015.

Magdalino, P. (with L. Rodley) (1998). "The Evergetis Fountain in the Early Thirteenth Century: An *Ekphrasis* of the Paintings in the Cupola," in *Work and Worship at the Evergetis,* M. Mullett and A. Kirby, eds. Belfast: Belfast Byzantine Enterprises, School of Greek, Roman and Semitic Studies, the Queen's University of Belfast: 432–447.

Magdalino, P. (1996). *Constantinople médiévale: etudes sur l'évolution des structures urbaines.* Paris: De Boccard.

Magdalino, P. (1991). "Water," in *ODB,* vol. 3, A. Kazhdan et al., ed. New York and Oxford: Oxford University Press: 2191.

Magdalino, P. (1990). "Church, Bath and *Diakonia* in Medieval Constantinople," in *Church and People in Byzantium,* R. Morris, ed. Birmingham: Centre for Byzantine, Ottoman and Modern Greek Studies, University of Birmingham: 165–188.

Magdalino, P. (1987a). "The Literary Perception of Everyday Life in Byzantium: Some General Considerations and the Case of John Apokaukos." *Byzantinoslavica* 48: 28–38.

Magdalino, P. (1987b). "Observations on the Nea Ekklesia of Basil I." *JÖB* 37: 51–64.

Maguire, H. (2006). "The Empress and the Virgin on Display in Sixth-Century Art." Lecture presented at the 21st International Congress of Byzantine Studies, London, August 26, 2006.

Mainstone, R. J. (1988). *Hagia Sophia. Architecture, Structure and Liturgy of Justinian's Great Church.* New York: Thames and Hudson.

Majeska, G. (2002). "Russian Pilgrims in Constantinople." *DOP* 56: 93–108.

Majeska, G. P. (1997). "The Emperor in His Church: Imperial Ritual in the Church of St. Sophia," in *Byzantine Court Culture from 829 to 1204,* H. Maguire, ed. Washington, DC: *DORLC,* distributed by Harvard University Press: 1–11.

Majeska, G. P. (1978). "Notes on the Archeology of St. Sophia at Constantinople: The Green Marble Bands on the Floor." *DOP* 32: 299–308.

Maksimović, J. (1983). *Srpske srednjovekovne minijature.* [Serbian Medieval Illuminated Manuscripts.] Belgrade: SANU.

Maksimović, J. (1977). "Kamen" [Stone], in *Istorija primenjene umetnosti kod srba* [History of the Applied Arts with the Serbs], vol. 1. Belgrade: Muzej primenjene umetnosti: 237–262.

Maksimović, J. (1961). *Kotorski ciborij iz XIV veka i kamena plastika susednih oblasti.* Belgrade: Naučno delo.

Malpas, J. (2015). "Place and Singularity," in *The Intelligence of Place: Topographies and Poetics.* London: Bloomsbury: 65–92.

Malpas, J. (2006). *Heidegger's Topology. Being, Place, World.* Cambridge: Cambridge University Press.

Mamaloukos, S. (2002). "Φιάλες αγιασμού [Phiale Fonts for the Blessing of Water.]" *Η Καθημερινή* (April 14, 2002): 9–10.

Mamaloukos, S. (2001). *Το Καθολικό της Μονής Βατοπεδίου: ιστορία και αρχιτεκτονική.* [The Katholikon of the Monastery Vatopedi: History and Architecture.] PhD diss., University of Athens.

Mango, C. (2000). "The Triumphal Way of Constantinople and the Golden Gate." *DOP* 54: 173–188.

Mango, C. (1999). "The Relics of St. Euphemia and the Synaxarion of Constantinople." *Opora: Studi in onore di Mgr. Paul Canart per il LXX compleanno* 53: 79–87.

Mango, C. (1995). "Sépultures et épitaphes aristocratiques à Byzance," in *Epigrafia Medievale Greca e Latina. Ideologia e Funzione,* G. Cavallo and C. Mango, eds. Spoleto: Centro Italiano di studi sull'Alto medioevo: 99–117.

Mango, C. (1991). "Approaches to Byzantine Architecture." *Muqarnas* 8: 40–44.

Mango, C. (1990). "Constantine's Mausoleum and the Translation of Relics." *BZ* 83/I: 51–61.

Mango, C. (1985a). *Le développement urbain de Constantinople, IVe–VIIe siècles.* Paris: Boccard.

Mango, C. (1985b). *Byzantine Architecture.* New York: Rizzoli.

Mango, C. (1982). "The Life of St. Andrew the Fool Reconsidered." *RSBS* 2: 297–313.

Mango, C. (1979). "On the History of the Templon and the Martyrion of St. Artemios at Constantinople." *Zograf* 10: 40–43.

Mango, C. (1975a). "Historical Introduction," in *Iconoclasm:* 1–6.

Mango, C. (1975b). "The Church of Sts. Sergius and Bacchus Once Again." *BZ* 68: 385–392.

Mango, C. (1972). "The Church of Saints Sergius and Bacchus at Constantinople and the Alleged Tradition of Octagonal Palatine Churches." *JÖB* 21: 189–193.

Mango, C. (1969–1970). "Notes on Byzantine Monuments." *DOP* 23: 369–375.

Mango, C. (1959). *The Brazen House: A Study of the Vestibule of the Imperial Palace of Constantinople.* København: I kommission hos Ejnar Munksgaard.

Mango, C. (1956). "The Date and Significance of the Tenth Homily of Photius." *DOP* 9–10: 123+125–140.

Mango, C., and J. W. Hawkins (1964). "Report on Field Work in Istanbul and Cyprus, 1962–1963." *DOP* 18: 319–340.

Mango, C., and J. Parker (1960). "A Twelfth-Century Description of St. Sophia." *DOP* 14: 233–245.

Mango, C., and I. Ševčenko (1973). "Some Churches and Monasteries on the Southern Shore of the Sea of Marmara." *DOP* 27: 235–277.

Marasović, T. (1988). "Byzantine Component in Dalmatian Architecture from 11th to 13th Century," in *Studenica et l'art Byzantin autour de l'année 1200,* V. Korać, ed. Belgrade: SANU: 455–461.

Marcattili, F. (2011–2012). "Tetrastyla. Ipotesi sull'origine del ciborio d'altare." *RACr* 87–88: 147–174.

Marinis V., and R. Ousterhout (2015). "'Grant Us to Share a Place and Lot with Them.' Relics and the Byzantine Church Building," in *Saints and Sacred Matter: The Cult of Relics in Byzantium and Beyond,* C. Hahn and H. A. Klein, eds. Washington, DC: *DORLC*: 153–172.

Marinis, V. (2015). "The Historia Ekklesiastike Kai Mystike Theoria: A Symbolic Understanding of the Byzantine Church Building." *BZ* 108: 753–770.

Marinis, V. (2014). *Architecture and Ritual in the Churches of Constantinople. Ninth to Fifteenth Centuries.* Cambridge: Cambridge University Press.

Marinković, D. (2011a). "Ciborijumi u manastiru Žiči." ["The Ciboria of Žiča Monastery."] *Zbornik Muzeja primenjene umetnosti* 7: 79–94.

Marinković, D. (2011b). "Циборијум над фијалом у манастиру Студеници." ["The ciborium over the phiale in the Monastery of Studenica."] *Naša prošlost* 12: 99–110.

Marković, M. (2009). *Prvo putovanje Svetog Save u Palestinu i njegov značaj za srpsku srednjovekovnu umetnost* [The First Voyage of St. Sava to Palestine and Its Importance for Serbian Medieval Art]. Belgrade: Institute for Byzantine Studies.

Marta, R. (1985). *Architettura Romana. Tecniche costruttive e forme architettoniche del mondo romano.* Rome: Kappa.

Martinović, J. J. (1995). "Pokušaj rekonstrukcije ciborija kotorske katedrale." *PPD* 35: 345–355.

Mathews, T. F. (1993). *The Clash of Gods: A Reinterpretation of Early Christian Art.* Princeton: Princeton University Press.

Mathews, T. (1976). *The Byzantine Churches of Istanbul: A Photographic Survey.* University Park: Pennsylvania State University Press.

Mathews, T. F. (1974). "Architecture et liturgie dans les premières églises palatiales de Constantinople." *RArt* 24: 22–29.

Mathews, T. F. (1971). *The Early Churches of Constantinople: Architecture and Liturgy.* University Park: Pennsylvania State University Press.

Mathews, T. F. (1962). "An Early Roman Chancel Arrangement and Its Liturgical Uses." *RACr* 38: 73–95.

Mau, A. (1982) [c. 1899]. *Pompeii. Its Life and Art.* Francis W. Kelsey, trans. New Rochelle: Caratzas Brothers.

McClanan, A. (2002). *Representations of Early Byzantine Empresses: Image and Empire.* New York: Palgrave Macmillan.

McClendon, C. B. (2011). "The Articulation of Sacred Space in the Synagogue and Christian Building at Dura Europos," in *Dura Europos: Crossroads of Antiquity,* L. R. Brody and G. L. Hoffmann, eds. Chesnutt Hill: McMullen Museum of Art, distributed by Chicago University Press: 155–167.

McCormick, M. (1986). *Eternal Victory. Triumphal Rulership in Late Antiquity, Byzantium, and the Early West.* Cambridge: Cambridge University Press, 1986.

McVey, K. E. (1983). "The Domed Church as Microcosm: Literary Roots of an Architectural Symbol." *DOP* 37: 91–121.

Meek, H. A. (1995). *The Synagogues.* London: Phaidon Press.

Meek, H. A. (April, 1952). "The Architect and His Profession in Byzantium." *R.I.B.A. Journal*: 216–220.

Megaw, A. H. S. (1976). "Excavations at the Episcopal Basilica of Kourion in Cyprus in 1974 and 1975: A Preliminary Report." *DOP* 30: 345–371.

Megaw, A. H. S. (1974). "Byzantine Architecture and Decoration in Cyprus: Metropolitan or Provincial?" *DOP* 28: 57–85.

Megaw, A. H. S. (1963). "Notes on Recent Work of the Byzantine Institute in Istanbul." *DOP* 17: 333–364.

Melvani, N. (2015). "The Middle Byzantine Sanctuary Barriers of Mount Athos: Templon and Iconostasis," in *ΔΑΣΚΑΛΑ*. Athens: University of Athens: 305–335.

Mentzos, A. (1994). "Τὸ προσκύνημα τοῦ Ἁγίου Δημητρίου Θεσσαλονίκης στὰ βυζαντινὰ χρόνια," in *Ἑταιρεία τῶν Φίλων τοῦ Λαοῦ. Κέντρον Ἐρεύνης Βυζαντίου*, 1. Athens: Banias: 56–67.

Mepisašvili, R., and T. Virsalaže (1982). *Gelati: arkitektura, mozaika, preskebi.* Tbilsi: Gamomcemloba "Xelovneba."

Mepisashvili, R., and V. Tsintsadze (1977). *The Arts of Ancient Georgia.* London: Thames and Hudson.

Metsanē, A. D. (1998). "Apo tēn katagraphē palaiohristianikōn glyptōn stēn Katapolianē: to palaiohristianiko kibōrio," in *Hē Hekatontapylianē kai hē Hristianikē Paros.* Paros: Hieron Proskynema tos Panagias Hekatontapylianēs Parou: 85–95.

Metsanē, A. D. (1996–1997). "To palaiohristianiko kiborio tēs Katapolianēs Parou." ["Le ciborium paléochrétien de l'église de la Vierge Katapoliani à Paros."] *ΔΧΑΕ* 19: 319–334.

Michel, A. (2001). *Les églises d'époque byzantine et umayyade de Jordanie.* Turnhout: Brepols.

Michelson, D. A. (2014). *The Practical Christology of Philoxenos of Mabbug.* Oxford: Oxford University Press.

Mihajlovski, R. (2007). "The Basilica of the Dormition of the Holy Virgin in Velushina." *Journal of the Australian Early Medieval Association* 3: 225–241.

Mihaljević, M. (2012). "Change in Byzantine Architecture: Architects and Builders," in *Approaches to Byzantine Architecture and Its Decoration*, M. Johnson, R. Ousterhout, and A. Papalexandrou, eds. Surrey: Ashgate: 99–119.

Mijović, P. (1989). "Le ciboire d'Ulcinj," in *Studi in memoria di Giuseppe Bovini*. Ravenna: Ed. del Girasole: 403–418.

Mijović, P. (1985). "Ulcinjski ciborijum." *Starinar* 36: 91–104.

Milanović, V. (2004–2005). "O fresci na ulazu u Bogorodičinu crkvu arhiepiskopa Danila II u Peći." ["The Fresco at the Entrance to Danilo II's Church of the Mother of God at Peć."] *Zograf* 30: 141–165.

Miles, G. C. (1964). "Byzantium and the Arabs: Relations in Crete and the Aegean Area." *DOP* 18: 1–32.

Millet, G. (1923). "La coupole primitive de Ste. Sophie." *Revue beige de philologie et d'histoire* 2: 599.

Millet, G. (1910). *Monuments byzantins de Mistra; matériaux pour l'étude de l'architecture et de la peinture en Grèce aux XIVe et XVe siècles*. Paris: E. Leroux.

Millet, G. (1905). "Recherches au Mont-Athos (1) Phiale et simandre à Lavra." *BCH*: 104–141.

Milner, C. (1996). "'Lignum Vitae' or 'Crux Gemmata'? The Cross of Golgotha in the Early Byzantine Period." *BMGS* 20: 77–99.

Milojević, M. (1996). "Forming and Transforming Proto-Byzantine Urban Public Space." *ByzAus* 10: 247–262.

Mirković, L. (1995) [1919]. *Pravoslavna liturgika ili nauka o bogosluženju pravoslavne istočne crkve*. [The Orthodox Liturgy I] Prvi, opći deo. Belgrade: Sveti arhijerejski sinod Srpske pravoslavne crkve.

Mirković, L. (1983). *Pravoslavna liturgika ili nauka o bogosluženju pravoslavne istočne crkve*. [The Orthodox Liturgy II] Drugi deo, posebni deo. Belgrade: Sveti arhijerejski sinod Srpske pravoslavne crkve.

Mirković, L. (1961). *Herotologija: ili Istorijski razvitak i bogosluženje praznika Pravoslavne istočne crkve* [Heortology: Or the Historical Development and Liturgical Service of the Feasts of the Orthodox Eastern Church]. Belgrade: Sveti arhijerejski sinod Srpske pravoslavne crkve.

Moore, B. K. (2017). *The Architecture of the Christian Holy Land: Reception from Late Antiquity Through the Renaissance*. Cambridge: Cambridge University Press, in press.

Morano, M. P. (1980). "Documenti per la storia dei restauri della basilica di S. Cecilia in Trastevere dal Rinascimento agli interventi di Federico Hermanin," in *Roma anno 1300: atti della IV settimana di studi di storia dell'arte medievale dell'Università di Roma*. Rome: L'Erma di Bretschneider: 331–342.

Morganstern, J. (1945). *The Ark the Ephod and the "Tent of Meeting."* Cincinnati: The Hebrew Union College Press.

Morrisson, C. (2002). "The Emperor, the Saint, and the City: Coinage and Money in Thessalonike from the Thirteenth to the Fifteenth Century." *DOP* 56: 173–203.

Moskowitz, A. F. (1998). "Arnolfo, Non-Arnolfo: New (and Some Old) Observations on the Ciborium in San Paolo Fuorile Mura." *Gesta* 37/1: 88–102.

Mouriki, D. (1970). *The Octateuch Miniatures of the Byzantine Manuscripts of Cosmas Indicopleustes*. PhD diss., Princeton University.

Mueller-Jourdan, P. (2005). *Typologie spatio-temporelle de l'ecclesia byzantine: la Mystagogie de Maxime le Confesseur dans la culture philosophique de l'antiquité tardive*. Leiden and Boston: Brill.

Müller-Wiener, W. (1977). *Bildlexikon zur Topographie Istanbuls*. Tübingen: E. Wasmuth.

Mundell-Mango, M. (1992). "The Monetary Value of Silver Revetment and Objects Belonging to Churches, A.D. 300–700," in *EcclSilver*: 123–136.

Mundell Mango, M. (1990). "The Uses of Liturgical Silver 4th–7th Centuries," in *Church and People in Byzantium*, R. Morris, ed. Birmingham: Centre for Byzantine, Ottoman and Modern Greek Studies, University of Birmingham: 245–261.

Mundell, M. (1975). "Monophysite Church Decoration," in *Iconoclasm*: 59–74.

Murray, S. C. (1981). *Rebirth and Afterlife. A Study of the Transmutation of Some Pagan Imagery in Early Christian Funerary Art*, BAR International series 100. Oxford: BAR.

Mylonas, P. (1992). "Nouvelles remarques sur le complexe de Saint-Luc en Phocide." *CA* 40: 115–122.

Mylonas, P. (1990). "*Gavits* arméniens et *Litae* byzantines. Observations nouvelles sur le complexe de Saint-Luc en Phocide." *CA* 38: 99–122.

N

Nelson, R. S. (1997). "The Map of Art History." *ArtB* 79/1: 28–40.

Nenadović, S. (2002). *Ilustrovani rečnik izraza u narodnoj arhitekturi*. Belgrade: Vojna štamparija.

Netzer, N. (1983). "Redating the Consular Ivory of Orestes." *BM* 125/962: 265–271.

Nikolajević, I. (1983). "L'arte bizantina: ricettività e creatività locale," in *Gli Slavi occidentali e meridionali nell'alto medioevo*. Spoleto: Presso la sede del centro: 801–829.

Noeal, W., and D. Weiss, eds. (2002). *The Book of Kings: Art, War, and the Morgan Library's Medieval Picture Bible*. Baltimore: Walters Art Museum, and London: Third Millennium Pub.

Nordenfalk, C. (1988). *Early Medieval Book Illumination*. Geneva: Skira, and New York: Rizzoli.

Nordenfalk, C. (1973). "Outdoors-Indoors: A 2000-Year-Old Space Problem in Western Art." *PAPS* 117/4: 233–258.

Nussbaum, O. (1965). *Der Standort des Liturgen am christlichen Altar vor dem Jahre 1000: Eine archäologische und liturgiegeschichtliche Untersuchung*. 2 vols. Bonn: Hanstein.

O

Oikonomides, N. (1992). "The First Century of the Monastery of Hosios Loukas." *DOP* 46: 245–255.

Oikonomides, N. (1985). "Remarks on the Apse Mosaics of St. Sophia." *DOP* 39: 111–115.

Oikonomides, N. (1980–1981). "St. George of Mangana, Maria Skleraina, and the 'Malyj Sion' of Novgorod." *DOP* 34/35: 239–247.

Olovsdotter, C. (2015). "From Earth to Heaven: Transcendental Concepts of Architecture in Late Roman and Early Byzantine Art (c. 300–700)." Lecture presented at the Symbolic Aspects of Architecture: Late Roman, Byzantine and Ottoman Perspectives international conference, Swedish Research Institute in Istanbul, Turkey, Nov. 2015.

Orlandos, A. K. (1965). "La forme primitive de la cathédrale paléochrétienne de Paros," in *Atti del VIe Congresso Internazionale di Archeologia Cristiana, Ravenna, 23–30 Sett. 1961*. Vatican: Pontificio Istituto di archeologia cristiana: 159–168.

Orlandos, A. (1963). *Η Παρηγορήτσσα της Άρτης*. Athens: Hē en Athēnais Archaiologikē Hetaireia.

Orlandos, A. (1952–1957). *Hē xylostegos palaiochristianikē vasilikē tēs Mesogeiakēs lekanēs*. Athens: Hē en Athēnais Archaiologikē Hetaireia.

Orlandos, A. (1949). "Ἡ μητρόπολις τῶν Σερρῶν κατὰ τὴν ἔκφρασιν τοῦ Πεδιασίμου." *EEBS* 19: 259–271.

Orlandos, A. (1935–1973). *Archeion tōn Vyzantinōn mnēmeiōn tēs Hellados*. Athens: Hestia.

Osborne, J. (1991). "Lost Roman Images of Pope Urban V (1362–1370)." *ZKunstg* 54/1: 20–32.

Ostrogorsky, G. (1969). *History of the Byzantine State*, rev. ed. J. M. Hussey, trans. New Brunswick: Rutgers University Press.

Ousterhout, R. (2010a). "The Architectural Decoration of the Pantokrator Monastery: Evidence Old and New," in *First International Byzantine Studies Symposium Proceedings*. Istanbul: 432–439.

Ousterhout, R. (2010b). "New Temples and New Solomons: The Rhetoric of Byzantine Architecture," in *The Old Testament in Byzantium*, P. Magdalino and R. Nelson, eds. Washington, DC: *DORLC*: 223–253.

Ousterhout, R. (2008). *Master Builders of Byzantium*. Philadelphia: University of Pennsylvania Museum of Archeology and Anthropology.

Ousterhout, R. (2001a). "Architecture, Art and Komennian Ideology at the Pantokrator Monastery," in *Byzantine Constantinople: Monuments, Topography and Everyday Life*, N. Necipoğlu, ed. Leiden, Boston, Köln: Brill: 133–150.

Ousterhout, R. (2001b). "The Architecture of Iconoclasm: Buildings," in *Byzantium in the Iconoclast Era, Byzantium in the Iconoclast Era (c. 680–850): A History*. L. Brubaker and J. Haldon, eds. Aldershot, England, and Burlington: Ashgate: 3–19.

Ousterhout, R., et al. (2000). "Study and Restoration of the Zeyrek Camii in Istanbul: First Report, 1997–1998." *DOP* 54: 265–270.

Ousterhout, R. G. (1998). "The Holy Space. Architecture and Liturgy," in *Heaven on Earth: Art and the Church in Byzantium*, L. Safran, ed. University Park: Pennsylvania State University Press: 81–120.

Ousterhout, R. (1997). "Reliquary of Saint Anastasios the Persian," in *Glory of Byz*: 460–461, cat. no 300.

Ousterhout, R. (1992). "Originality in Byzantine Architecture: The Case of Nea Moni." *JSAH* 51/2: 48–60.

Ousterhout, R. (1990). "The Temple, the Sepulchre, and the *Martyrion* of the Savior." *Gesta* 29/1: 44–53.

Ousterhout, R. (1989). "Rebuilding the Temple: Constantine Monomachus and the Holy Sepulchre." *JSAH* 48: 66–78.

Ousterhout, R. G. (1987). *The Architecture of the Kariye Camii in Istanbul*. Washington, DC: *DORLC*.

Ousterhout, R. G. (1981). "The Church of Santo Stefano: A 'Jerusalem' in Bologna." *Gesta* 20/2: 311–321.

Ovadiah, A., and C. G. de Silva (1984). *Supplementum to the Corpus of the Byzantine Churches in the Holy Land*. Jerusalem: British School of Archaeology. Originally published in *Levant* 13 (1981), 14 (1982), 16 (1984).

Ovidiah, A., and C. G. de Silva (1982). "Supplementum to the Corpus of the Byzantine Churches in the Holy Land (Part II): Updated Material on Churches Discussed in the Corpus." *Levant* 14: 122–170.

Ovadiah, A. (1970). *Corpus of the Byzantine Churches in the Holy Land*. Bonn: Peter Hansten Verlag GMBH.

P

Pace, V. (1992). "Il ciborio di Arnolfo a Santa Cecilia: una nota sul suo stato originario e sulla sua committenza," in *Studi di storia dell'arte sul Medioevo e il Rinascimento nel centenario della nascita di Mario Salmi*. Florence: Polistampa: 389–400.

Pace, V. (1991). "Committenza benedettina a Roma: il caso di San Paolo fuori le mura nel XIII secolo." *ZKunstg* 54/2: 181–189.

Pagoulatos, G. (2009). *Tracing the Bridegroom in Dura: The Bridal Initiation Service of the Dura-Europos Christian Baptistery as Early Evidence of the Use of Images in Christian and Byzantine Worship*. Piscataway: Gorgias Press.

Pajares-Ayuela, P. (2001). *Cosmatesque Ornament. Flat Polychrome Geometric Patterns in Architecture*. New York: Norton and Company.

Pallas, D. I. (1979). "Le ciborium hexagonal de Saint-Démétrios de Thessalonique. Essai d'interprétation." *Zograf* 10: 44–58.

Pallas, D. (1977). *Les monuments paléochrétiens de Grèce découverts de 1959 à 1973*. Città del Vaticano: Pontificio Istituto di archeologia cristiana.

Pallis, G. [Παλλης. Γ.] (2012). "Λίθινες φιάλες και κολυμβήθρες με ανάγλυφο διάκοσμο της μέσης και ύστερης βυζαντινής περιόδου από την Ελλάδα." ["Stone Phiales and Fonts with Relief Decoration of the Middle and Late Byzantine Period from Greece."] *ΔΧΑΕ* 33: 119–130.

Pallis, G. (2006). "New Evidence on the Sculpture Workshop of Samarina (Late Twelfth–Early Thirteenth Century." *ΔΧΑΕ* 27: 91–100.

Pani, E. L. (1976). "Il ciborio della basilica di S. Ippolito all'Isola Sacra," in *Roma e l'Età Età carolingia*. Rome: Multigrafica editrice: 337–344.

Parmenter, D. M. (2006). "The Iconic Book: The Image of the Bible in Early Christian Rituals." *Postscripts* 2.2–3: 160–189.

Patout Burns, J. Jr., and R. Jensen (2014). *Christianity in Roman Africa*. Grand Rapids: William E. Eerdmans Publishing Company.

Papacostas, T., C. Mango, and M. Grünbart (2007). "The History and Architecture of the Monastery of Saint John Chrysostom at Koutavendis, Cyprus." *DOP* 61: 25–156.

Papageorghiou, A. (1998–). "Cyprus. Early Christian and Byzantine Architecture," in *Grove Art Online. Oxford Art Online*: http://www.oxfordartonline.com/subscriber/article/grove/art/T020849pg4. (accessed November 16, 2013).

Papalexandrou, A. (2001). "Text in Context: Eloquent Monuments and the Byzantine Beholder." *Word and Image* 17/3: 259–283.

Papamastorakis, T. (1998). "Ιστορίες και ιστορήσεις βυζαντινών παλληκαριών." ["Tales and Images of Byzantium's Warrior Heroes."] *ΔΧΑΕ* 20: 213–230.

Papamastorakis, T. (1992). "The Representation of Christ as the Great Arch-Priest." *ΔΧΑΕ* 4/12: 67–68.

Parani, M. G. (2005). "Representations of Glass Objects as a Source on Byzantine Glass. How Useful Are They?" *DOP* 59: 147–171.

Parani, M. G. (2003). *Reconstructing the Reality of Images: Byzantine Material Culture and Religious Iconography (11th–15th Centuries)*, The Medieval Mediterranean 41. Leiden and Boston: Brill.

Parrish, D. (2001). "An Early Byzantine Mosaic Workshop Based on Kos: Architectural Context and Pavement Design." *AntTard* 9: 331–349.

Parry, K. (1996). *Depicting the Word. Byzantine Iconophile Thought of the Eighth and Ninth Centuries*. Leiden, New York, and Köln: E.J. Brill.

Paterson-Ševčenko, N. (1991). "Icons in the Liturgy." *DOP* 45: 45–57.

Patrich, J. (1995). *Sabas, Leader of Palestinian Monasticism. A Comparative Study in Eastern Monasticism, Fourth to Seventh Centuries*. Washington, DC: *DORLC*.

Patrich, J. (1993). "The Early Church of the Holy Sepulchre in the Light of Excavations and Restoration," in *Ancient Churches Revealed*, Y. Tsafir, ed. Jerusalem: Israel Exploration Society: 101–117.

Pazaras, T. (1994). "Protasē anaparastasēs tou 'Ambōna tes Palaias Metropolēs stē Veroia," in *Thymiama: stē mnēmē tēs Laskarinas Boura*. Athens: Mouseio Benake: 251–254.

Peirano, D., and E. Garberoglio (2013). "L'attività dell'Unità di ricerca sull'architettura religiosa. Campagna 2012." *Bollettino dell'associazione Iasos di Caria* 19: 11–14.

Peirano, D. (2012). "Il ciborio della basilica dell'acropoli." *Bollettino dell'Associazione Iasos di Caria* 18: 25–33.

Peirano, D. (2012). "Some Observations about the Form and Settings of the Basilica of Bargala." *Macedonian Historical Review* 3: 65–84.

Pejić, S. (2012). "Spolia from the Church of St. Nicholas in Nikoljac." *Zograf* 36: 13–20.

Pelekanidis, S. M. (1974). *The Treasures of Mount Athos: Illuminated Manuscripts, Miniatures-Headpieces-Initial Letters*, vol. I. Athens: Ekdotike Athenon.

Pelikan, J. (2000). *What Has Athens to Do with Jerusalem? Timaeus and Genesis in Counterpoint*, 2nd ed. Ann Arbor: University of Michigan Press.

Pelikan, J. (1974). *The Spirit of Eastern Christendom (600–1700)*, vol. 2 of *The Christian Tradition. A History of the Development of Doctrine*. Chicago and London: The University of Chicago Press.

Peña, I. (1997). *The Christian Art of Byzantine Syria*. [England]: Garnett Publishers.

Pennas, C. (2005). *Byzantine Aigina*. Athens: Pergamos.

Pentcheva, B. V. (2010). *The Sensual Icon: Space, Ritual, and the Senses in Byzantium*. University Park: Pennsylvania State University Press.

Pentcheva, B. V. (2006). *Icons and Power: The Mother of God in Byzantium*. University Park: Pennsylvania State University Press.

Perl, E. D. (2007). *Theophany. The Neoplatonic Philosophy of Dionysius the Areopagite*. Albany: State University of New York Press.

Peschlow, U. (1994). "Der mittelbyzantinische Ambo aus archäologischer Sicht," in *Thymiama: stē mnēmē tēs Laskarinas Boura*. Athens: Mouseio Benake: 255–260.

Petković, V. (1911). *Spasova crkva u Žiči, Arhitektura i živopis*. Belgrade: Sveti Sava.

Petricioli, I. (1995). "Ciborij katedrale hrvatskog biskupa u Ninu." *Peristil* 38: 23–26.

Petricioli, I. (1990). *Od Donata do Radovana. Pregled umjetnosti u Dalmaciji od 9. do 13. stoljeća* [From Donat to Radovan: A Review of Art in Dalmatia from the 9th Through the 13th Centuries]. Split: Književni Krug.

Petricioli, I. (1985). *Katedrala sv. Stošije u Zadru* [Cathedral of St. Anastasia in Zadar]. Zadar: Zadarska Nadbiskupija.

Petricioli, I. (1981). "Ciborij iz zadarske crkve s.v. Tome." ["Le ciborium de l'église Sv. Toma (St-Tomas) de Zadar."] *SHP* 3/11: 163–168.

Petricioli, I. (1960). *Pojava romaničke skulpture u Dalmaciji*. Zagreb: Društvo historičara umjetnosti Hrvatske.

Piccirillo, M. (2006). "The Architecture and Liturgy of the Early Church," in *Cradle of Christianity*, 2nd ed. Jerusalem: Israel Museum: 51–113.

Piccirillo, M. (2005). "A New Church in the Village of Massuh in the Territory of the Diocese of Esbus in Jordan," in *Studium Biblicum Franciscanum*, Jerusalem. Online at http://servus.christusrex.org/www1/ofm/fai/mass00.html. (accessed February, 1 2005).

Piganol, A. (1945). "L' Hemispheiron et l'omphalos des lieux saints." *CA* 1: 7–14.

Pinatsi, C. (2006). "New Observations on the Pavement of the Church of Hagia Sophia in Nicaea." *BZ* 99/1: 119–125.

Ponsich, P. (1993). "Le problème du ciborium d'Oliba, 1040." *CSMC* 24: 21–27.

Popović, V. (2004). "Култ светог Димитрија Солунског у Сирмијуму и Равени" ["The Cult of St. Demetrios of Thessaloniki in Sirmium and Ravenna"], in *Sirmium i na nebu i na zemlji. 1700 godina od stradanja hrišćanskih mučenika*. Sremska Mitrovica: Blago Sirmijuma: 87–98.

Popović, V. (1998). "Kult Svetog Dimitrija Solunskog u Sirmijumu i Raveni." *SANU* 10: 43–57.

Popović, V. (1979). "La signification historique de l'architecture religieuse de Tsaritchin Grad." *CorsiRav* 26: 249–311.

Preradović, D. (2013). "Prenosi relikvija iz Vizantije na Jadran u period između VI i XI veka." ["Translation of Relics from the Byzantine Empire in the Adriatic between the Sixth and Eleventh Centuries."] *Niš i Vizantija* 11: 187–207.

Preradović-Petrović, D. (2002). "Ulcinjski ciborijum; natpis i reljefne predstave." *GPMK* 50: 247–264.

Preradović, D. (2000). *Ulcinjski ciborijum*. Final work for the bachelor degree in Art History, University of Belgrade.

Pringle, D. (2007). *The Churches of the Crusader Kingdom of Jerusalem, A Corpus*, vol. 3 (*The City of Jerusalem*). Cambridge: Cambridge University Press.

Prokopios, G. A. (1981). *Ho kosmologikos symvolismos stēn architektonikē tou Vyzantinou naou*. PhD diss., University of Athens.

R

Radujko, M. (2001). "L' 'Ἀρχιερατικός θρόνος' des évêques de Moravica et la peinture de Saint-Achille à Arilje." *CA* 49: 143–178.

Revel-Neher, E. (1995). "On the Hypothetical Models of the Byzantine Iconography of the Ark of the Covenant," in *ByzELatW*: 405–414.

Rodov, I. (2015). "Hebrew Inscriptions. Visual Arts and Architecture: Christian Art," in *Encyclopedia of the Bible and Its Reception: Halah –Hizquni*, vol. 11, D. C. Allison, Jr., C. Helmer, V. Leppin, C.-L. Seow, H. Spieckermann, B. D. Walfish, and E. J. Ziolkowski, eds. Berlin, Boston: De Gruyter: cols. 631–637.

Rodov, I. (2103). "Script in Christian Art," in *Encyclopedia of Hebrew Language and Linguistics*, vol. 3. Boston: Brill: 642–477.

Rodov, I. (2010). "Tower-like Torah Arks, the Tower of Strength and the Architecture of the Messianic Temple." *JWCI* 73: 65–98.

Ronchaus, L. de (1886). *Au Parthénon*. Paris: Leroux.

Rosenau, H. (1979). *Vision of the Temple. The Image of the Temple of Jerusalem in Judaism and Christianity*. London: Oresco Books.

Roueche, C., and R. R. R. Smith, eds. (1996). *Aphrodisias Papers 3. The Setting and the Quarries, Mythological and Other Sculptural Decoration, Architectural Development, Portico of Tiberius and Tetrapylon. JRA* Suppl. 19. Ann Arbor, Mich.: Dept. of Classical Studies, University of Michigan.

Ruggieri, V., S.J. (1991). *Byzantine Religious Architecture (582–867): Its History and Structural Elements*, OCA 237. Roma: Pontificio Instituto Orienatle.

Rupp, D. W. (1974). "The 'Baldacchino' in Greek Architecture." *AJA* 78/2: 176.

Rush, A. (1941). *Death and Burial in Christian Antiquity*. PhD diss., The Catholic University of America.

Russo, L. (2004). *The Forgotten Revolution: How Science Was Born in 300 BC and Why It Had to Be Reborn*. Berlin and New York: Springer.

Ryndina, A. V. (1996). "Новгородское серебряное дело XIII–XV вв.," in *Dekorativno-prikaldnoe iskusstvo Velikogo Novgoroda: khudozhestvennyĭ metall XI–XV veka*, I. A. Sterligova, ed. Moscow: Nauka: 69–106.

S

Saller, S. J. (1949). *The Town of Nebo (Khirbet el-Mekhayyat). With a Brief Survey of Other Ancient Christian Monuments in Transjordan*. Jerusalem: Franciscan Press.

Saller, S. J. (1941). *The Memorial of Moses on Mount Nebo*. Jerusalem: Franciscan Press.

Sarabianov, V. D. (2005). "Алтарная преграда церкви Спаса на Нередице: типология и иконография," in *The Church of Our Saviour on Neredista: From Byzantium to Russia*. Moscow: Indrik: 83–98.

Sarabianov, V. (2000). "The Sanctuary Barrier of the 12th-Century Churches in Novgorod," in *The Iconostasis. Origins-Evolution-Symbolism*, A. Lidov, ed. Moscow: Progress-Tradicija: 312–359, 730–731.

Saradi-Mendelovici, H. (1990). "Christian Attitudes Toward Pagan Monuments in Late Antiquity and Their Legacy in Later Byzantine Centuries." *DOP* 44: 47–61.
Saunders, W. B. R. (1982). "The Aachen Reliquary of Eustathius Maleinus, 969–970." *DOP* 36: 211–219.
Schibille, N. (2014). *Hagia Sophia and the Byzantine Aesthetic Experience*. Farnham: Ashgate.
Schibille, N. (2009). "The Profession of the Architect in Late Antique Byzantium." *Byz* 79: 360–379.
Schöller, W. (1998). "Beobachtungen an Baldachinen. Ein Beitrag zur gotischen Skulptur in Frankreich." *ZKunstg* 61/2: 190–205.
Schulz, H.-J. (1986). *The Byzantine Liturgy. Symbolic Structure and Faith Expression*. New York: Pueblo Pub. Co.
Schultz, R. W., and S. H. Barnsley (1901). *The Monastery of Saint Luke*. London: Macmillan.
Schwarzer, M. (2001). "The Architecture of Talmud." *JSAH* 60/4: 474–484.
Scott, J. B. (2003). *Architecture for the Shroud: Relic and Ritual in Turin*. Chicago: Chicago University Press.
Sedov, V. V. (2015). "The Omphalos in the Church of Saint Boris and Saint Gleb in Kideksha and Similar Objects in the Interiors of Medieval Russian and Byzantine Churches" ["Седов В. В. "Омфалий церкви Бориса и Глеба в Кидекше и подобные формы в интерьерах древнерусских храмов"], in *Города и веси Средневековой Руси. Археология, история, культура. К 60-летию Н.А. Макарова*. Москва – Вологда: Древности Севера: 349–364.
Sedov, V. (2014). "The Bogoliubovo Ciborium and Its Byzantine Analogies," in *Life-Giving Spring: Water in Hierotopy and Iconography of the Christian World*. Proceedings of the International Symposium [*Живоносный источник. Вода в иеротопии и иконографии христианского мира: Материалы международного симпозиума*], A. Lidov, ed. Moscow and Yaroslav: Filigran: 110–111.
Sekules, V. (2005). "Easter Sepulchre," in *Grove Dictionary of Art Online*. Available at http://www.groveart.com. (accessed February 1, 2005).
Setton, K. M. (1952). "The Emperor Constans II and the Capture of Corinth by the Onogur Bulgars." *Speculum* 27/3: 351–362.
Setton, K. M. (1944). "Athens in the Later Twelfth Century." *Speculum* 19/2: 179–207.
Sharon, I. (1987). "Phoenician and Greek Ashlar Construction Techniques at Tel Dor, Israel." *BASOR* 267: 21–42.
Sheppard, C. D. (1969). "Byzantine Carved Marble Slabs." *ArtB* 51/1: 65–71.
Siggh, M. (1993). *The Sun. Symbol of Power and Life*. New York: Harry N. Abrams.
Sinclair, T. A. (1989). *Eastern Turkey: An Architectural and Archaeological Survey*, vol. 3. London: Pindar Press.
Sinković, I. (2002). "Western Chapels in Middle Byzantine Churches: Meaning and Significance." *Starinar* 52: 79–92.
Sinković, I. (2000). *The Church of St. Panteleimon at Nerezi: Architecture, Programme, Patronage*. Wiesbaden: Ludwig Reichert Verlag.
Skedros, J. C. (1999). *Saint Demetrios of Thessaloniki: Civic Patron and Divine Protector 4th–7th Centuries CE*, Harvard Theological Studies 47. Harrisburg: Oxford Bodleian Canon.
Skoblar, M. (2017). "Patriarchs as Patrons: The Attribution of the Ciboria in Santa Maria Delle Grazie at Grado," in *Imperial Spheres and the Adriatic: Byzantium, the Carolingians and the Treaty of Aachen (812)*, M. Aničić, J. Shepard and T. Vedriš, eds. Abingdon: Ashgate, in press.
Skoblar, M. (2005). "Ranosrednjovjekovni ciborij iz Novalje." ["Early Medieval Ciborium from Novalja."] *RIPU* 29: 7–16.
Small, D. B. (1980). "A Proposal for the Reuse of the Tower of the Winds." *AJA* 84/1: 96–99.
Smith, B. E. (1978). *The Dome: A Study in the History of Ideas*. Princeton: Princeton University Press.
Smith, B. E. (1956). *Architectural Symbolism of Imperial Rome and the Middle Ages*. Princeton: Princeton University Press.
Smith, C. (1987). "Cyriacus of Ancona's Seven Drawings of Hagia Sophia." *ArtB* 69/1: 16–32.
Smith, J. (1990). "Form and Function of the Side Chambers of the Fifth and Sixth-Century Churches in Ravenna." *JSAH* 49: 181–204.
Smith, J. Z. (1987). *To Take Place: Towards Theory in Ritual*. Chicago, University of Chicago Press.
Smith, M. T. (1974). "The Development of the Altar Canopy in Rome." *RACr* 50: 379–414.
Smith, M. T. (1970). "The Lateran Fastigum: A Gift of Constantine the Great." *RACr* 46: 149–175.

Smith, M. T. (1968). *The Ciborium in Christian Architecture at Rome, 300–600. A.D.* PhD diss., New York University.

Smolčić-Makuljević, S. (2000). "Hilandarska katapetazma monahinje Jefimije. Ikonografija i bogoslužbena funkcija" ["Iconostasis Curtain of the Nun Jefimija in Hilandar"], in *Medjunarodni naučni skup Osam vekova Hilandara: istorija, duhovni život, književnost, umetnost i arhitektura: oktobar 1998*. Belgrade: SANU: 693–701.

Snyder, B. (2014). "Mikvah (The Jewish Ritual Bath)," in *The Lexham Bible Dictionary*, J. D. Barry et al., eds. Online at https://www.logos.com/product/36564/lexham-bible-dictionary. (accessed December 30, 2015).

Snyder, G. F. (2003). *Ante Pacem: Archaeological Evidence of Church Before Constantine*. Macon: Mercer University Press.

Sodini, J.-P. (2002). "Marble and Stone Working in Byzantium; Seventh–Fifteenth Centuries," in *The Economic History of Byzantium: From the Seventh Through the Fifteenth Century*, A. E. Laiou, ed. Washington, DC: DOCRL: 129–145.

Sodini, J.-P. (1995). "La sculpture médio-byzantine: le marbre en ersatz et tel qu'en lui-même," in *Constantinople and Its Hinterland*, C. Mango and G. Dagron, eds. Aldershot: Ashgate: 289–311.

Sodini, J.-P. (1989). "La commerce des marbres à l'époque protobyzantine," in *Hommes et richesses dans l'Empire byzantin I (IVe–VIIe siècle)*. Paris: P. Lethielleux: 163–186.

Sodini, J.-P. (1984). "Les dispositifs liturgiques des basiliques paléochrétiennes eu Grèce et dans les Balkans." *CorsiRav* 31: 441–473.

Solovey, M. M. (1970). *The Byzantine Divine Liturgy. History and Commentary*. D. E. Wysochansky, trans. Washington, DC: The Catholic University of America Press.

Sōtēriou, G. A. (1962). Χριστιανική και βυζαντινή αρχαιολογία [*Christianikē kai vyzantinē archaiologia*; Christian and Byzantine Archaeology], vol. 1, 2nd ed. Athens: tou ekdotou I. P. Sōtērakou.

Soteriou, G. A., and M. G. Soteriou. (1952). *Hē Vasilikē tou Hagiou Dēmētriou Thessalonikēs*. Athens: Hēen Athēnais Archaiologikē Hetaireia.

Soteriou, G. A. (1931). *Hai christianikai Thēvai tēs Thessalias kai hai palaiochristianikai vasilikai tēs Hellados*. Athens: Hēen Athēnais Archaiologikē Hetaireia.

Spagnolo, M. (2006). *Bernini: il baldacchino di San Pietro*. Modena: F. C. Panini.

Spartharakis, I. (1974). "The Proskynesis in Byzantine Art." *BABesch* 49: 190–205.

Speck, P. (1966). "Die ENΔYTH." *JÖB* 15: 323–375.

Spieser, J.-M. (2000). "Du Cange and Byzantium," in *Through the Looking Glass. Byzantium Through British Eyes*, R. Cormack and E. Jeffreys, eds. Aldershot: Ashgate: 199–210.

Spieser, J.-M. (1999). "Le développement du templon et les images des Douze Fêtes," in *Les images dans les sociétés médiévales: Pour une histoire comparée*, J.-M. Sansterre and J.-C. Schmitt, eds. Bruxelles; Rome: Institut historique belge de Rome: 131–164.

Spieser, J.-M. (1976). "La christianisation des sanctuaires païens en Grèce," in *Neue Forschungen in griechischen Heiligtümern*, U. Jantzen, ed. Tübingen: Wasmuth: 309–320.

Spon, J. (1679). *Voyage d'Italie, de Dalmatie, de Grèce, et du Levant, fait aux années 1675 & 1676*, 2nd ed. Amsterdam: H. & T. Boom.

St. Clair, A. (1979). "The Visit to the Tomb: Narrative and Liturgy on Three Early Christian Pyxides." *Gesta* 18/1: 127–135.

Stăniloae, D. (1994). *The Experience of God*, vol. 1. Brookline: Holy Cross Orthodox Press.

Stanković, N. (2008). "Nea Ekklesia (Νέα Εκκλησία)," in *Encyclopaedia of the Hellenic World, Constantinople*. Online at http://constantinople.ehw.gr/forms/fLemmaBodyExtended.aspx?lemmaID=12328. (accessed December 15, 2015).

Stead, G. C. (1989). "St. Athanasius on the Psalms." *Vigilae Christianae* 39: 65–78.

Sterligova, I. (2000). "The Precious Decoration of the Russian Sanctuary from the 11th to 13th Century: Evidence of Written Sources," in *The Iconostasis. Origins-Evolution-Symbolism*, A. Lidov, ed. Moscow: Progress-Tradicija: 360–381, 731–732.

Sterligova, I. A. (1996). "Памятники серебряного и золотого дела в Новгороде XI–XII вв," in *Dekorativno-prikaldnoe iskusstvo Velikogo Novgoroda: khudozhestvennyĭ metall XI–XV veka*, I. A. Sterligova, ed. Moscow: Nauka: 46–62.

Sterligova, I. A. (1994). "Jerusalems as Liturgical Vessels in the Old Rus," in *Jerusalem in Russian Culture*, A. Batalov and A. Lidov, eds. New Rochelle: A.D. Caratzas: 46–62.

Stevens, S. T. (2000). "Excavations of an Early Christian Pilgrimage Complex at Bir Ftouha (Carthage)." *DOP* 54: 271–274.

Stevović, I. (1998–1999). "Sveti Andreja u kotorskom natpisu ANDREESCI AD HONOREM SOCIORVMQ MAIOREM+" ["Saint Andrew in the Inscription ANDREESCI AD HONOREM SOCIORVMQ MAIOREM+"]. *Zograf* 27: 23–33.

Stikas, E. (1974–1975). *Ὁ Κτίτωρ τοῦ Καθολικοῦ τῆς Μονῆς Ὁσίου Λουκᾶ*. Athens: Epimeleia tou Grapheiou Dēmosieumatōn tēs Hetaireias.

Stikas, E. (1970). *Τὸ Οἰκοδομικὸν Χρονικὸν τῆς Μονῆς Ὁσίου Λουκᾶ Φωκίδος* [The Architectural History of the Monastery of Hosios Loukas in Phokis]. Athens: Athēnais Archaiologikēs Hetaireias.

Stričević, Dj. (1958–1959). "Djakonikon i protezis u ranohrišćanskim crkvama." *Starinar* 9–10: 59–65.

Striker, C. L., et al. (1997). *Kalenderhane in Istanbul: The Buildings, Their History, Architecture, and Decoration: Final Reports on the Archaeological Exploration and Restoration at Kalenderhane Camii, 1966–1978*. Mainz: Verlag Philipp von Zabern.

Strzygowski, J. (1889). "Die Akropolis in alt-byzantinischer Zeit." *Mittheilungen der k. d. archaeol. Instit., Athen. Abt.* 14: 272–273.

Šuput, M. (1984). "Mramornici u Žiči." ["Marble Workers in Žiča."] *ZLU* 20: 157–160.

T

Taft, R. F., S.J. (2006). "The Decline of Communion in Byzantium and the Distancing of the Congregation from the Liturgical Action: Cause, Effect, or Neither?" in *Thresholds of the Sacred*, S. E. J. Gerstel, ed. Washington, DC: *DORLC*: 27–52.

Taft, R. F., S.J. (1992). *The Byzantine Rite. A Short History*. Collegeville, MN.: Liturgical Press.

Taft, R., S.J. (1980–1981). "The Liturgy of the Great Church: An Initial Synthesis of Structure and Interpretation on the Eve of Iconoclasm." *DOP* 34–35: 45–75.

Taft, R. (1975). *The Great Entrance. A History of the Transfer of Gifts and other Pre-anaphoral Rites of the Liturgy of St. John Chrysostom*, OCA 220. Rome: Pontificio Instituto Orientale.

Talbot, A.-M. (2001). "Byzantine Pilgrimage to the Holy Land from the Eighth to the Fifteenth Centuries," in *The Sabaite Heritage in the Orthodox Church from the Fifth Century to the Present*, J. Patrich, ed. Leuven: Uitgeverij Peeters en Departement Oosterse Studies: 97–110.

Talbot, A.-M. (1999). "Epigrams in Context: Metrical Inscriptions on Art and Architecture of the Palaiologan Era." *DOP* 53: 75–90.

Talbot, A.-M. (1993). "The Restoration of Constantinople under Michael VIII." *DOP* 47: 243–261.

Tarasov, O. (2011). *Framing Russian Art: From Early Icons to Malevich*. London: Reaktion Books.

Tarasov, O. (2002). *Icon and Devotion*. London: Reaktion Books.

Terry, A. (1988). "The Sculpture at the Cathedral of Eufrasius in Poreč." *DOP* 42: 12–64.

Teteriatnikov, N. (1998a). "Devotional Crosses in the Columns and Walls of Hagia Sophia." *Byz* 68/2: 419–445.

Teteriatnikov, N. (1998b). "Liturgical Furnishing: Entrance Areas/Church," in *Grove Art Online. Oxford Art Online*. At http://www.oxfordartonline.com/subscriber/article/grove/art/T017565pg4. (accessed November 9, 2013).

Teteriatnikov, N. (1996). *The Liturgical Planning of Byzantine Churches in Cappadocia*, OCA 252. Rome: Pontificio Instituto Orientale.

Thelen, H. (1967). *Zur Entstehungsgeschichte der Hochaltar-Architektur von St. Peter in Rom*. Berlin: Gebr. Mann.

Theocharidou, K. (1994). *Hē architektonikē tou Naou tēs Hagias Sophias stēn Thessalonikē: apo tēn hidrysē tou mechri sēmera*. Athēna: Ekdosē tou Tameiou Archaiologikōn Porōn kai Apallotriōseōn.

Theocharidou, K. (1988). *The Architecture of Hagia Sophia, Thessaloniki, from Its Erection up to the Turkish Conquest*, BAR International Series 399. Oxford: BAR, 1988.

Theocharis, M. (1978). "Ψηφιδωτὴ τοῦ ἁγίου Δημητρίου καὶ ἡ ἀνεύρεσις τῶν λειψάνων τοῦ ἁγίου εις Ἰταλίαν" [Une icone en mosaïque de saint Déméterius et la découverte des reliqie du saint en Italie], in *Proceedings of the Academy in Athens* 53. Athens: Academy of Athens, 508–536.

Theotoka, N. (1941–1952). "Περὶ τῶν κιβωρίων τῶν ναῶν τοῦ ἁγίου Δημητρίου Θεσσαλονίκης καὶ Κωνσταντινουπόλεως." *Μακεδονικά* 2: 395–413.

Thiel, A. (2005). *Die Johanneskirche in Ephesos*. Weisbaden: Reichert Verlag.

Thiel, W. (2002). "Tetrakionia. Überlegungen zu einem Denkmaltypus tetrarchischer Zeit im Osten des Römischen Reiches." *AnTard* 10: 299–326.

Thomas, J., et al. (2012). "Font," in *The Grove Encyclopedia of Medieval Art and Architecture*, vol. 2. C. Hourihane, ed. Oxford: Oxford University Press: 542–547.

Thomas, T. K. (2000). *Late Antique Egyptian Funerary Sculpture. Images for This World and the Next.* Princeton: Princeton University Press.

Timmermann, A. (2013). "Micro-architecture," in *Grove Art Online. Oxford Art Online*. At http://www.oxfordartonline.com/subscriber/article/grove/art/T2216986. (accessed November 16, 2013).

Timmermann, A. (2009). *Real Presence: Sacrament Houses and the Body of Christ, c. 1270–1600.* Turnhout: Brepols.

Todić, B. (1988). *Gračanica. Slikarstvo*. Belgrade: Prosveta and Priština: Jedinstvo.

Todić, B., and M. Čanak-Medić (2005). *Manastir Dečani* (Monastery Dečani). Belgrade: Muzej u Prištini.

Todt, K.-P. (2001). "Religion und griechisch-orthodoxes Patriarchat von Antiocheia in Mittelbyzantinisher Zeit (969–1084)." *BZ* 94: 239–269.

Tournefort, J. P. de (1717). *Relation d'un voyage du Levant*. Lyon: Anisson et Posuel.

Toynbee, J. M. C. (1996). *Death and Burial in the Roman World*, 2nd ed. Ithaca: Cornell University Press.

Toynbee, J. M. C., and J. Ward Perkins (1956). *The Shrine of St. Peter and the Vatican Excavations.* London: Longmans.

Trilling, J. (1995). "Medieval Interlace Ornament: The Making of a Cross-Cultural Idiom." *ArsM* 9/2: 59–86.

Trkulja, J. (2011). "Divine Revelation Performed: Symbolic and Spatial Aspects in the Decoration of Byzantine Churches," in *Spatial Icons: Performativity in Byzantium and Medieval Russia*, A. Lidov, ed. Moscow: Indrik: 213–246.

Trkulja, J. (2004). *Aesthetics and Symbolism of Late Byzantine Church Façades, 1204–1453*. PhD diss., Princeton University.

Tronzo, W. (1987). "Setting and Structure in Two Roman Wall Decorations of the Early Middle Ages." *DOP* 41: 477–492.

Tsaferis, V. (1985). "An Early Christian Church Complex at Magen." *BASOR* 258: 1–15.

Tsamakda, V. (2002). *The Illustrated Chronicle of Ionnes Skylitzes in Madrid*. Leiden: Brill.

U

Ulbert, T., et al. (1986). *Resafa II: Die Basilika des Heiligen Kreuzes in Resafa-Sergiupolis*. Mainz am Rhein: von Zabern.

Underwood, P. (1950). "The Fountain of Life in Manuscripts of the Gospels." *DOP* 5: 43–138.

Underwood, P. A., and E. J. W. Hawkins (1961). "The Mosaics of Hagia Sophia at Istanbul. The Portrait of the Emperor Alexander." *DOP* 15: 187–218.

Ouspenski, L. (1987). "Icon and Art," in *Christian Spirituality. Origins to the Twelfth Century*, McGinn, B., and J. Meyendorff, eds. New York: Crossroad: 382–394.

V

Valverde, J. F., and J. R. Fernández-Oxea (1987). *Baldaquinos gallegos: catalogación arqueológica y artistica de Galicia del Museo de Pontevedra*. La Coruña: Fundación Pedro Barrié de la Maza.

Vanderheyde, C. (2005). "Le ciborium de l'Église de la Dormition de la Vierge à Kalambaka (Thessalie)." *TM* 15: 427–442.

Vasić, M. (1922). *Arhitektura i skulptura u Dalmaciji*. Belgrade: Izdavačka knjižarnica Gece Kona.

Veikou, M. (2012). *Byzantine Epirus: A Topography of Transformation. Settlements of the Seventh–Twelfth Centuries in Southern Epirus and Aetoloacarnania, Greece*. Leiden: Brill.

Vežić, P., and M. Lončar. (2009). *Hoc Tigmen. Ciboriji ranoga srednjeg vijeka na tlu Istre i Dalmacije*. Zadar: Sveučilište u Zadru.

Vežić, P. (2002). "Krstionica i ciborij u Puli i Novigradu," in *Novigrad - Cittanova, 599–1999*, J. Ziherl et al. eds. Novigrad: Pučko otvoreno učilište = Cittanova: Università popolare aperta: 75–87.

Vežić, P. (2001–2002). "Ciboriji ranoga srednjeg vijeka u Kotoru." ["Ciboria of the Early Middle Ages in Kotor."] *PPD* 39: 91–122.

Vežić, P. (1997). "Bazilika Sv. Ivana Krstitelja (Sv. Nedeljica) u Zadru." *RIPU* 23 (1999): 7–16.

Vežić, P. (1997). "I cibori a pianta esagonaler isalenti all'alto medioevo in Istria e in Dalmazia." *HAM* 3: 101–116.

Vikan, G. (1982). *Byzantine Pilgrimage Art.* Washington, DC: *DORLC.*

Vincent, H., and F. M. Abel (1926). *Jérusalem: Recherches d'archéologie et d'historie,* vol. 2, *Jérusalem nouvelle.* Paris: J. Gabalda.

Vio, O. (1999). *The Basilica of St. Mark in Venice.* New York: Scala/Riverside.

Vitto, F. (1995). "The Interior Decoration of Palestinian Churches and Synagogues," in *Bosphorus: Essays in Honour of Cyril Mango,* S. Efthymiadis et al., eds. Amsterdam: Adolf M. Hakkert: 283–300.

Vogué, C. de (1860). *Les Églises de la Terre Sainte.* Paris: Librairie de Victor Didron.

Voronin, N. N. (1961). *Zodchestvo severo-vostochnoĭ Rusi XII–XV vekov.* 2 vols. Moscow: Izd. Akademii nauk SSSR.

Voyatzis, S. (with V. Sythiakakis-Kritsimallis) (2011). "Redating the Basilica of Dormition, Kalambaka, Thessaly." *JÖB* 61: 195–227.

Voyatzis, S. (2009). "The Sculpted Decoration of the Andromonastiro in Messenia." *ΔXAE* 30: 129–140.

Voyatzis, S. (2006). "The Sculptural Decoration in the Church of the Metamorphosis at Alepospita, Lamia." *ΔXAE* 27: 101–114.

Voyatzis, S., and V. Sythiakaki (2008). "The Byzantine Church of Ayios Nikolaos at Exarchos, Phthiotida." *ΔXAE* 29: 207–220.

W

Walter, C. (2003). *The Warrior Saints in Byzantine Art and Tradition.* Aldershot and Burlington: Ashgate.

Walter, C. (1993). "New Look at the Byzantine Sanctuary Barrier." *Revue des études byzantines* 51: 203–228.

Walter, C. (1982). *Art and Ritual of the Byzantine Church.* London: Variorium.

Walter, C. (1974). "La place des évêques dans le décor des absides byzantines." *RArt* 24: 81–89.

Walters, C. C. (1974). *Monastic Archeology in Egypt,* Modern Egyptology Series. Westminster: Aris & Philips.

Ward-Perkins, J. B. (1994a). "The Shrine of St. Peter and Its Twelve Spiral Columns," in *Studies in Roman and Early Christian Architecture,* J. B. Ward-Perkins, ed. London: Pindar: 469–489. [Originally published as Ward Perkins, J. B. (1952). "The Shrine of St. Peter and Its Twelve Spiral Columns." *JRS* 42/1–2: 21–33.]

Ward-Perkins, J. B. (1994b). "Memoria, Martyr's Tomb and Martyr's Church." *Studies in Roman and Early Christian Architecture.* London: Pindar Press: 495–526. [Originally published as Ward-Perkins, J. B. (1993). "Memoria, Martyr's Tomb and Church," in *Art, Archeology, and Architecture of Early Christianity,* P. C. Finney, ed. *Studies in Early Christianity.* New York: Garland: 386–403.]

Ward-Perkins, J. B. (1981). *Roman Imperial Architecture.* Harmondsworth and New York: Penguin Books.

Ward-Perkins, J. B. (1954). "Constantine and the Origins of the Christian Basilica." *PBSR* 22: 81.

Ward-Perkins, J. B. (1949). "The Shrine of St. Menas in the Maryût." *PBSR* 17: 26–71.

Warland, R. (1993). "Frühbyzantinische Vorlage und mittelalterliche Adaptation: die Szenenfolge zur Kindheitsgeschichte Christi auf einer des Ciboriumssaulen von San Marco in Venedig." *ZKunstg* 56/2: 173–182.

Weber, M. (1990). *Baldachine und Statuenschreine.* Roma: G. Bretschneider Editore.

Weigel, T. (2000). *Le colonne del ciborio dell'altare maggiore di San Marco a Venezia: nuovi argomenti a favore di una datazione in epoca protobizantina.* Venezia: Centro tedesco di studi veneziani.

Weigel, T. (1997). *Die Reliefsäulen des Hauptaltarciboriums von San Marco in Venedig.* Münster: Rhema.

Weiss, D. H. (1995). "Architectural Symbolism and the Decoration of the Ste.-Chapelle." *ArtB* 77/2: 308–320.

Weitzmann, K., and H. L. Kessler (1990). *The Frescoes of the Dura Synagogue and Christian Art,* DOS 28. Washington, DC: *DORLC.*

Wharton, A. J. (1995). *Refiguring the Post Classical City: Dura Europos, Jerash, Jerusalem, and Ravenna.* Cambridge, Cambridge University Press.

Wharton, A. J. (1992). "The Baptistery of the Holy Sepulcher in Jerusalem and the Politics of Sacred Landscape." *DOP* 46: 313–325.

Wharton, A. J. (1988). *Art of Empire. Painting and Architecture of the Byzantine Periphery. A Comparative Study of Four Provinces*. University Park and London: Pennsylvania State University Press.

Wharton Epstein, A. (1975). "The 'Iconoclast' Churches of Cappadocia," in *Iconoclasm*: 103–111.

Whitby, M. (2006). "The St. Polyeuktos Epigram (AP 1.10): A Literary Perspective," in *Greek Literature in Late Antiquity: Dynamism, Didacticism, Classicism*. Aldershot and Burlington: Ashgate: 159–188.

White, A. W. (2015). *Performing Orthodox Ritual in Byzantium*. Cambridge: Cambridge University Press.

Wieland, F. (1912). *Altar und Altargrab der christlichen Kirchen im 4. Jahrhundert*. Leipzig: J.C. Hirnrichs'sche Buchhandlung.

Wilken, R. L. (1988). "Byzantine Palestine: A Christian Holy Land." *BA* 52/4: 214–217, 233–237.

Wilkinson, J. (1993). "Constantinian Churches in Palestine," in *Ancient Churches Revealed*, Y. Tsafrir, ed. Jerusalem: Israel Exploration Society: 23–27.

Wilkinson, J. (1979). "Jewish Influences on the Early Christian Rite of Jerusalem." *Le Muséon* XCII: 347–359.

Wilkinson, J. (1974). "The Tomb of Christ. An Outline of Its Structural History." *Levant* 6: 83–97.

Willis, R. (1845). *The Architectural History of Canterbury Cathedral*. London: Logman.

Woodfin, W. (2012). *The Embodied Icon. Liturgical Vestments and Sacramental Power in Byzantium*. Oxford: Oxford University Press.

Woodfin, W. (2004). "Liturgical Textiles," in *Byzantium: Faith and Power (1261–1557)*, H. C. Evans, ed. New Haven: Yale University Press: 295–299.

Woods, D. (2000). "Thessalonica's Patron: Saint Demetrius or Emeterius?" *Harvard Theological Review* 93: 221–234.

Woudstra, M. H. (1965). *The Ark of Covenant from Conquest to Kingship*, International Library of Philosophy and Theology. Philadelphia: [Presbyterian and Reformed Pub. Co.].

Wybrew, H. (1989). *The Orthodox Liturgy. The Development of the Eucharistic Liturgy in the Byzantine Rite*. London: SPCK.

X

Xydis, S. G. (1947). "The Chancel Barrier, Solea, and Ambo of Hagia Sophia." *ArtB* 29/1: 1–24.

Y

Yannopoulos, P. (1994). "La Grèce dans la vie de S. Élie le Jeune et dans celle de S. Élie le Spéléote." *Byz* 64: 193–221.

Yasin, A.-M. (2015). "Sacred Installations: The Material Conditions of Relic Collections in Late Antique Churches," in *Saints and Sacred Matter: The Cult of Relics in Byzantium and Beyond*, C. Hahn and H. A. Klein, eds. Washington, DC: *DORLC*: 133–151.

Z

Zambrano, A. J. G. (1984). *El baldaquino de la Catedral de Puebla*. Mérida, Venezuela: Ediciones La Imprenta.

Zchomelidse, N. (2010). "The Aura of the Numinous and Its Reproduction." *Memoirs of the American Academy in Rome* 55: 221–262.

Zikos, N. (1989). *Early Christian and Byzantine Amphipolis*. Athens: Har. I. Papadopoulos S. A.

Index

Note: Photographs, illustrations and drawings are indicated by an italic page number. Information from the endnotes are indicated by an italic "*n*" and note number.